The Hospitaller Knights of Saint John, 1523–1565

The Hospitaller Knights of Saint John, 1523–1565

Gordon Ellyson Abercrombie

Pen & Sword
MILITARY

First published in Great Britain in 2024 by
Pen & Sword Military
An imprint of Pen & Sword Books Limited
Yorkshire – Philadelphia

ISBN 978 1 39903 932 1

A CIP catalogue record for this book is available from the British Library

Typeset by Mac Style
Printed in the UK by CPI Group (UK) Ltd, Croydon, CR0 4YY.

MIX
Paper | Supporting responsible forestry
FSC® C013604

Pen & Sword Books Limited incorporates the imprints of After the Battle, Atlas, Archaeology, Aviation, Discovery, Family History, Fiction, History, Maritime, Military, Military Classics, Politics, Select, Transport, True Crime, Air World, Frontline Publishing, Leo Cooper, Remember When, Seaforth Publishing, The Praetorian Press, Wharncliffe Local History, Wharncliffe Transport, Wharncliffe True Crime and White Owl.

For a complete list of Pen & Sword titles please contact

PEN & SWORD BOOKS LIMITED
47 Church Street, Barnsley, South Yorkshire, S70 2AS, England
E-mail: enquiries@pen-and-sword.co.uk
Website: www.pen-and-sword.co.uk
or
PEN AND SWORD BOOKS
1950 Lawrence Rd, Havertown, PA 19083, USA
E-mail: Uspen-and-sword@casematepublishers.com
website: www.penandswordbooks.com

Contents

Introduction

This Volume II of the *Hospitaller Knights of Saint John* succeeds Volume I relating the Order's history at Rhodes during the years 1306 through 1522, and precedes Volumes III and IV covering the years 1566–1688 still in manuscript form. The author came to the writing of the manuscript with an unflagging interest in history and decades of residence and travel in the Near East. A former naval officer and sailing yacht owner, he also brought to the undertaking a deep respect for seamen of the age of sail. As importantly, he brought tens of thousands of sea miles to the undertaking, including thousands of miles of solo sailing, leaving him with a profound awareness of weather at sea and its impact on maritime history. He in addition brought hundreds of personal explorations of Mediterranean arenas of history including that remarkable redoubt called Malta, not to overlook multiple inspections of most other Hospitaller facilities in the Eastern Mediterranean. He is deeply indebted to the Hospital's official historian Giacomo Bosio, who has already written an unsurpassable *Istoria della Sacra Religione et Illustria Militia di San Giovanni Gierosolimitano.* And Bosio did it without the worldwide library available today. The manuscript's working title *Mostly Bosio* appropriately recognizes this principal source of its content. The author is also deeply indebted to Bosio's 1671 successor Bartolomeo dal Pozzo, a Hospitaller who participated in some of the history he describes, an history as detailed as that of his predecessor.

For many readers and students of history, however, the Renaissance Italian of Giacomo Bosio and Bartolomeo dal Pozzo is a difficult read, as it was for this author. It is this author's hope that he has nevertheless transcribed some of the wealth of Bosio and Dal Pozzo content to his four volumes and complemented it with truths revealed in the nearly 400 years of scholarship since Bosio's death in 1627. These complementary truths are the work of scores of learned historians too numerous to name here but who are named in endnotes to the text and in its bibliography. One standing out among others, however, is linguist and historian Kenneth M. Setton, whose four-volume *The Papacy and the Levant 1204–1571* and *Venice, Austria, and the Turks in the Seventeenth Century* are must-reading for anyone with an interest in the Hospitaller Knights of Saint John, or with an interest in the Levant, or simply with an interest in history.

This volume's opening chapters deal with Hospitaller relocation from Rhodes to Malta during the years following the Order's heart-rending loss of Rhodes to Ottoman Sultan Suleiman. This loss was also that of 4,000 non-belligerent Christians choosing to abandon their homes and livelihoods and to accompany the Order in its search for a new home, an odyssey including interim homes at Viterbo and Corneto, Italy, which ended in 1327 when forced by peste (plague) further north to Nice, then a part of Savoy. Volume II further deals with the first thirty-five years of Hospitaller residence at Malta including operations from there along the coast of North Africa, with major sieges of Tripoli, Tunis, and Algiers, with penetrating exposés of corsair admirals such as Barbarossa and Dragut, and with giants of Christian history such as Andrea Doria. Finally, this volume deals with the Ottoman Empire's 1565 attempt to eradicate the Order with that year's Great Siege of Malta.

While initial chapters focus on Philippe Villiers de l'Isle-Adam, 44th Grand Master of the Hospitaller Knights of Saint John and a giant among individuals making history, this history also brings to light the contributions of properly identified lieutenants as well as of properly identified allies and opponents. Succeeding chapters deal similarly with the individuals making history, but not at the expense of history itself. The author hopes the reader finds this volume as instructive and interesting as did he, and will find two succeeding volumes covering the years 1565 to 1687 equally so. This Volume II is believed to be the only continuous history since Bosio of the Hospitallers during the period 1523 through 1565, and is certainly the only such history in English.

Chapter I

Phillipe de Villiers de l'Isle-Adam 1523–27

Following dinner in the evening of 1 January 1523, Philippe Villiers de l'Isle-Adam mounted his horse and with heavy heart unaccompanied by staff or attendant rode to the Sultan's pavilion south of Rhodes Town to take his leave of the Grand Turk and to thank him for provisioning the evacuation flotilla. Suleiman wished the Grand Master a quick and safe voyage and, in addition, provided the Grand Master with a written safe-conduct over his own tughra. Six days earlier the Sultan is said to have remarked to one of his staff, 'It is not without regret that I drive this brave old man from his home.' And so began a seven-year Odyssey in which the Hospitaller Knights of Saint John and 4,000 fleeing Rhodians searched for a new home, first pausing at Candia (Crete) and then at Messina, only to be driven from the latter by peste (plague). They then paused at the port for Rome, where at the Holy City the Grand Master was celebrated, not as a losing general but as the saviour of Christendom. Settling at the walled Papal city of Viterbo, an infirmary or hospital was the first order of business, soon receiving casualties from combat at sea with Barbarossa and his lieutenants. By June 1527, however, peste (plague) had made its way to Viterbo, and the Order plus Rhodian entourage were forced to a higher elevation closer to the sea at Corneto. Dying of plague at Corneto was Grand Hospitaller Pierre de Gouriault while overseeing transfer of the infirmary from Viterbo, and a further relocation was soon under consideration.

There is no report of the number of surviving Hospitallers departing from Rhodes other than an unsourced figure of 170. Neither is there a count of surviving soldiers evacuating Rhodes. Nor is there a count of Hospitallers left behind, though there is a figure of 1,800 slain between Hospitallers, hired soldiers, militia, and other defenders. Bosio also cites a figure of about 4,000 departing inhabitants of Rhodes, mostly Latin Christians unwilling to submit to Turkish rule, most of those remaining Orthodox Christians with a longer history and deeper roots on the island. This number is exclusive of several hundred Latins departing other islands of the Rhodian archipelago, most of them Latin residents of Lango (modern Kos). All departing were embarked aboard about fifty ships including the great carrack *Santa Maria* commanded by William Weston, as well as the three war galleys carrying the Grand Master and most surviving knights. The majority of those departing Rhodes made first landfall six days later at Sitia, Candia, before proceeding to Candia City, now Heraklion, capital of the island. There they were joined by Hospitallers and others coming from the Rhodian Archipelago and the Castle of Saint Peter and there they were welcomed by Venetian authorities.[1]

It was an evacuation not without problems. Idled for six months in Rhodes Harbour, underwater hulls of the evacuation flotilla were worm and sea-growth infested. Hull planking had separated and bilge pumps had to be operated continuously. Some vessels such as Guillot de Castellane-Régusse's *Barciotto de la Religion* were barely afloat and had to be beached on arrival at Candia to avoid going under.[2]

At Candia numerous assignments were made by the Grand Master and Council. Doctor Thomas Guichard of Rhodes was appointed Vice Chancellor, a lay post. Bernardino d'Airasca, Admiral, and Gregorio Morgut, Prior of Navarre, were appointed interim Treasurers in place of Emery de Combault who had been advanced to Bailiff of the Morea. Antoine de Jaminy of Cases-de-Pène, who had assumed the dignity of Prior of Toulouse in Rhodes succeeding the deceased Gabriel de l'Estaing de Pomérols, was himself succeeded by Didier de Sainte-Jalle. He in turn renounced the dignity of Bailiff of Manosque to which Raymond Ricard (the Younger) succeeded. Tristan de Sales advanced to Grand Commander.[3] Juan de Homedes became Draper with concurrence of Juanito Ferrer, senior Aragonese knight. Juan de Gotor advanced to Bailiff of Caspe succeeding Francisco de Montserrat who died in mid-life during the Siege. William Weston of England succeeded to the dignity of Turcopolier, his predecessor John Bouch killed repelling a 17 September assault on the posts of England and Spain. João de Menezes was appointed Prior of Crato but Gonçalo Pimentel, in possession, refused to relinquish more than the title and remained acting prior. Diego dell Aguila of Castile succeeded the executed André d'Amaral as Chancellor. As Admiral, Airasca was assigned command of the galley *Santa Caterina*, capitana of three galleys, his padrone or number two Matteo Provana. *San Giovanni* was commanded by Prior of Saint-Gilles Pregeant de Bidoux with Fernando de Mata as padrone in spite of a challenge by Marshal Antoine de Claveson not on the basis of longevity or Convent seniority, but on the basis of competence. Claveson lost. The third galley, *Santa Maria*, was under command of l'Isle-Adam himself with Robert d'Aube de Roquemartine as padrone. William Weston commanded the Great Ship or Carrack of Rhodes, also called *Santa Maria*. Francisco de Benítez of Aragon commanded the great galleon *San Buonaventura*, while Juan Maringo Farfan of Castile commanded the barque called *La Perla*. Commander of Montpellier François de la Tour skippered Bidoux's personal galleon, and Giovan Battista Shiattesi of Rome commanded the small galleon called *Il Siciliano*.[4]

Bailiff of the Morea Emery (Merry) de Combault, a knight of considerable valour at arms and an individual of belles lettres, was dispatched in February to the courts of Rome and Paris for the purpose of relating recent Hospitaller developments as well as to make known the Order's dire financial circumstances and homelessness. Luis de Andujar was similarly dispatched to the Imperial court of Emperor Charles V. It was following Andujar's detailed account of the Siege the Emperor reportedly exclaimed, 'Nothing in the world has ever been so well lost as Rhodes.' Admiral Bernardino d'Airasca, Grand Commander Tristan de Sales, and Prior of Navarre Gregorio Morgut were deputised to make European commanderies aware of the Order's need for 12,000 gold ducats each year in addition to normal responsions, the additional support to fund homelessness of both Convent and Rhodian followers.[5]

In March the evacuation flotilla was at Frasquia 10 miles west of Heraklion. There a dispute developed between the two langues of Spain concerning the vacant dignity of Bailiff of Negroponte. Cristóbal Sarnace, as Procurator to Commander Alvaro Pinto, as well as Procurators Martín Pimental and Paz Correa each considered themselves most deserving. So, too, did Ramón Marquet and Gaspar Glior. Ramón Marquet was appointed Bailiff of Negroponte entitled to wear the Grand Cross.[6]

Early in April the Rhodian flotilla of ten oared and numerous sailing ships, all carrying the Convent and an ever-increasing number of non-combatants fleeing the Rhodian Archipelago, departed Frasquia bound for Suda Bay at the western end of Candia. From Suda Bay they proceeded by way of Cerrigotto (modern Antikythera) to Cerigo (modern Kythera) where the larger sailing ships under command of William Weston caught a favourable wind and proceeded directly to Messina. At Cerigo Catalan Commander Miguel de Arenys of Aragon succumbed to a wound received during the Siege and was interred on the island. Remaining vessels climbed the Morean and Greek mainland coasts to Corfu, where they jumped off for Gallipoli di Apulia on the inside heel of the Italian boot. There they paused to treat sick and wounded. At Gallipoli l'Isle-Adam wrote to Pope Adrian VI seeking a new home for the Order of Jerusalem, while debarking the seriously ill and injured before continuing on to Messina where the rump-flotilla arrived on the last day of April. Amid a celebratory welcome more sick and wounded found a place at the infirmary of the Hospitaller Priory of Messina.[7]

At Messina a general inquiry was convened in June 1523 into the failure of ambassadors including Claude d'Ancienville to obtain succour for the besieged at Rhodes. To l'Isle-Adam's intense relief the inquiry brought forth no indictments. He had no wish to find fault among his Hospitallers. The reasons in Ancienville's case were instructive of the others and went beyond the inability or unwillingness of Francis I and Henry VIII to divert crown resources to succour Rhodes. The Priory of England and the several priories of France did respond. England assembled a well-supplied relief force of Hospitallers and hired soldiers, and chartered a large broad-beamed, square-rigged urca, which set out in August under command of Bailiff of Eagle Thomas Newport. This ship encountered a southerly in the Bay of Biscay, was dismasted, and was blown all the way back to the shoals of Cornwall with the loss of everyone on board. In France Hospitaller Jean d'Iseran of Auvergne chartered two large merchantmen from Genovese condottiero Andrea Doria, *La Doria* and *La Ferrare*, as well as the large barque *La Trimouille* plus three smaller merchantmen from Marseille, aboard which were embarked almost 300 Hospitallers together with 800 hand-picked soldiers, all provided with everything necessary to supply themselves and resupply the garrison at Rhodes. This was all financed by the Order's Common Treasury in France with advances from the Bank of Saint George at Genoa. Cruel fortune, however, assaulted the ships at sea, only three reaching Messina. *La Ferrare* went to the bottom in a storm. *La Doria* was forced to halt at Sardinia, made totally unseaworthy by storm damage. The barque *La*

Trimouille flying the flag of France was seized in Neapolitan waters by Viceroy Don Juan de Cardona as compensation for a similar Spanish-flag barque seized by the French including Hospitaller Bernardin d'Ornesan in 1521. Those on board the French barque including Ancienville and Iseran were permitted to hire transportation to Messina and join the three smaller ships reaching that port on their own. Depleted ranks of French reaching Messina were then necessarily forced to wait for Spanish and Italian company. Many Spanish Hospitallers and soldiers under command of Hospitaller Antonio de San Martín failed to arrive in consequence of storm and North African corsairs, San Martín losing his life in the attempt. Italian Hospitallers, meanwhile, were set back by the death of Prior of Pisa Luca di Tornabuoni who controlled the purse strings. By September-end, when a relief force had been assembled, wind and weather turned against it and the relief force never left Messina.[8]

At Messina Gabriele Tadino di Martinengo, mastermind of the defence of Rhodes, was appointed Prior of Pisa succeeding the deceased Tornabuoni. The Bailiwick of Eagle, formerly that of Newport, was conferred on Thomas Sheffield of South Cave, Yorkshire. Succeeding Sheffield as Seneschal was future Grand Master Pierino del Ponte. Raymond de Rogier, Captain of the Post of Auvergne during the Siege, was appointed Bailiff of Lureil (Lyon). Because the Order's Treasury had no funds to pay ongoing or past due expenses, Draper Juan de Homedes arranged for knights and serving brothers to contribute funds with which to compensate hired soldiers as much as two years of back pay, and otherwise organised payment in kind such as clothing and military hardware from stores aboard the relief fleet that never sailed. At this point the Grand Master began to license return to priories and commanderies of those so wishing. A considerable number departed in company with Prior of León Don Diego de Toledo, who had license to represent the Grand Master at the Court of Spain. Others authorised to depart included Marshal Antoine de Claveson, Prior of Toulouse Didier de Sainte-Jalle, Bailiff of Manosque Raymond Ricard the Younger, and Bailiff of Mallorca Jaume Gilberto, each a Knight of the Grand Cross. Meanwhile, plague had appeared at Messina and quickly spread to several Hospitaller vessels. Tommasso Sanmartino of Turin, Jerome Grimault of Monaco, and Marcantonio Avogadro of Vercelli succumbed. The Grand Master necessarily ordered a sudden exit from Messina, the galleon belonging to Pregeant de Bidoux becoming the Rhodean flotilla's hospital ship. Departing on 22 June l'Isle-Adam, then embarked aboard the Great Carrack, took the flotilla to the Gulf of Baia north of the Gulf of Naples, and arrived on 7 July 1523. That evening Gregorio de Morgut, Prior of Navarre, also succumbed to the plague.

The flotilla was self-quarantined at Baia for twenty-five days. It was 2 August before the Rhodians again got under way, large ships to Porto Ercole in Tuscany, oared vessels to Civitavecchia, a seaport on the Tyrrhenian located 80km west-north-west of Rome. With plague still evident on board, it was not until 23 August that the Grand Master and oared vessels arrived at Civitavecchia. Waiting that same day to greet his heroic subordinate in Rome was ailing Dutch Pope Adrian VI, who would reach the end of his life in little more than three weeks.[9]

Before departing Civitavecchia for Rome, l'Isle-Adam ordered Siege historian and Lieutenant Grand Hospitaller Jacques de Bourbon, assisted by Chaplain Jean Potier, Head Nurse, to establish an infirmary ashore and during his absence to transfer the sick and wounded from ship to shore. Care and support rotations were to be redistributed among all knights, priests, and serving brothers at Civitavecchia. Also before departing he commended for valour four more senior of the hired soldiers at the Siege: John Zambara of Scotland, Nicolo di Costi of Vercelli, Antonio di Montenegro of Vicenza, and Francesco Latese of Corsica.[10] Accompanying the Grand Master to Rome was Greek Metropolitan of Rhodes Klemes, or Clemens, as well as heir apparent Euphemios. Latin Archbishop of Rhodes and new Prior of the Church Leonardo Balestrini also accompanied the Grand Master. These three were prominent among those who prevailed upon the Grand Master to accept Suleiman's surrender terms. Also in company were all members of the Sacred Council and most other senior Hospitallers. En route these were greeted by Hospitaller Prior of Rome Pietro Salviati, Prior of Capua Giuliano Ridolfi, Prior of Castile Don Diego de Toledo, and a number of commanders and other knights resident at Rome. Among still others greeting the Grand Master was his nephew Anne de Montmorency, Marshal of France, at Rome on a diplomatic mission.

Reaching Rome, the Grand Master was greeted by patriarchs, archbishops, and bishops, the Governor of Rome and the Auditor of the Camera among other prelates of the Court and *all* of the cardinals.

Crossing the Pont Sant'Angelo to the Palace of Saint Peter, he was saluted by mortars and artillery. Finally he was welcomed in the Sala of Saint Peter by an ailing Pope Adrian VI and the College of Cardinals as the Great Champion of Christ and Defender of the Catholic Faith. Because of his failing health the Pope soon retired and died three days later. A Conclave of Cardinals was convened on 1 October. Eight weeks later, on 26 November, Cardinal Giulio di Giuliano de' Medici, himself a Hospitaller, was proclaimed Pope Clement VII. It was not until 18 December 1523 that Vice Chancellor Thomas Guichard, an eloquent doctor of law and medicine who lived through the Siege, speaking for the Grand Master, laid out his 'Oratio' (twenty-three pages available in Latin from Google) before the new Pope in Consistory. He began by referring to the twelfth tyrant of the Ottoman family and that family's insatiable greed and callous disregard for human life. He went on, paraphrasing Kenneth Setton, to describe the Siege, fifteen bitter engagements in five months, the ghastly pounding of cannon, Christian losses, shortage of munitions, the slaughter of Turks, heroism, hardships, and surrender on honourable terms, his oration bringing tears to a number of cardinals. He further described the island so lost as the last best refuge for Christians in the Levant and as a hospital for all. Before closing, he praised the promise of Clement's Papacy and then asked of the new Pope confirmation of the Order's extant privileges and an injunction warning greedy princes against seizure of the Order's commanderies and priories in Europe. Most princes heeded the injunction; Henry VIII of England did not.[11]

In October 1523 Gabriele Tadino di Martinengo was appropriately appointed Bailiff of Santo Stefano in succession of the deceased Carlo Gesualdo of Naples, appropriately because both were heroes of the Great Siege of Rhodes, Gesualdo at the beleaguered Italian Post. Gesualdo, it should be noted, had also been a hero at the 1480 Siege of Rhodes when as Commander of Larino forty-two years earlier he had supervisory authority at the same post.

Having accordingly renounced the Priory of Pisa, on 8 October Martinengo, Prior of Castile Toledo, and Antonio Bosio were dispatched as special ambassadors to Emperor Charles V in his capacity of King of Spain to discuss availability of Malta as future home of the Order of Jerusalem. The three ambassadors travelled by means of galley from Civitavecchia to Porto Ercole. There they transferred to the large galleon

San Buonaventura commanded by Hospitaller Francisco de Benítez of Aragon, the galleon accompanied by the barciotta or small galleon *Il Siciliano* commanded by Giovan Battista Schiattese. At about the same time the Great Carrack *Santa Maria*, commanded by Pedro de Cardenas of Castile, conveyed by way of Villefranche four ambassadeurs extraordinaire to the courts of England and France to apprise those courts of the Siege of Rhodes and subsequent developments. William Weston was dispatched to the court of England in company with a second, unnamed, English knight, likely Nicholas Roberts, who had met the Sultan. Prior of Saint-Gilles Pregeant de Bidoux and Antoine de Grolée de Passim were dispatched to the court of France. At Villefranche a new Great Carrack, *Santa Anna* built at Nice, was delivered, and her captain, Pons d'Urrè of the Langue of Provence, appointed. Urrè and the other captains were ordered over winter months to ready their ships for sea in the spring. Similar orders concerning the galleys were transmitted by l'Isle-Adam's Master of the House Troilo Castagnole to Admiral Bernardino d'Airasca at Civitavecchia. It was the Grand Master's hope to then take possession of Malta.[12]

In January 1524 l'Isle-Adam prevailed upon new Pope Clement VII, Hospitaller Giulio di Giuliano de' Medici, to grant to the Order of Jerusalem the walled Papal city of Viterbo as its temporary residence. Most non-Hospitaller Rodiots including the Rhodes Militia followed the Convent to its new home. Viterbo was not on the sea but was proximate to both the galley port at Civitavecchia (40km) and the warship port at Porto Ercole (60km). It also had its own citadel or castle. An Hospitaller for more than a quarter century, Jacques Mitte de Chevrières of the Langue of France was taken to the new infirmary with peste, but sanitation and distancing measures were not enough. Meanwhile, Antonio Bosio had been discussing with the Emperor a permanent home at Malta. Bosio would also soon engage in discussions with the Grand Master concerning recapture of Rhodes. At Viterbo, Konrad von Schwalbach, absent from the Convent during the Great Siege and wrongly feared dead, was reconfirmed as Grand Bailiff of Germany.[13]

On 13 February 1524 l'Isle-Adam dispatched Chancellor Diego Nunnez dell'Aguila and Prior of Toulouse Didier de Sainte-Jalle to Civitavecchia because Admiral Bernardino d'Airasca and Lieutenant Grand Commander Guillot de Castellane Régusse had taken delivery of the sacred relics shipped from Rhodes, including the Image of the Madonna of Filermo and all of the Order's gold and silver vessels all packed in thirty-six large cases. These were conveyed to Viterbo and stored in the Church of San Faustino. Not able to rejoice in safe delivery of the relics was Archbishop of Rhodes and Prior of the Church Leonardo Balestrini, who was bed-ridden at Rome and soon died of his affliction. He was succeeded as Prior of the Church by Chaplain Miguel Font of the Langue of Aragon.[14]

To prevent Hospitallers from becoming indolent and to carry on the Order's campaign against infidels, a well-provided squadron of the Order's vessels was constituted under command of Sinforian de la Roche-Aymon de Saint-Messan of the Langue of Auvergne embarked aboard the *Germa of the Religion*. Aboard smaller vessels accompanying the germa, the crews and embarked soldiery were largely Rhodian or from other nearby islands of the former Hospitaller dominion. Also embarked were two Commissioners of Care and Charity, Diego de Torres and Luis Lull, responsible for distributing cargoes of grain and other provisions among former vassals in the eastern Aegean. Another part of the squadron's mission was to collect information concerning feasibility of the Order's return to its former home.

Meanwhile, ambassadors sent to petition Emperor Charles V concerning possession of Malta reached him in December at Pamplona preparing to cross the Pyrenees to confront Francis I, Charles V in alliance with Henry VIII of England and France's own Charles III, Duke of Bourbon. In discussions with the Emperor and Don Fadrique Álvarez de Toledo, 2nd Duke of Alba, Malta and Gozo were presented as a package with Tripoli on the coast of Africa. There were additional considerations such as the need to disband the military force then at Victoria or Rabat, capital city of the island of Gozo, but these two islands and Tripoli were available in perpetual fief of the Emperor and his successors in the Kingdom of Sicily. There were a number of ancillary conditions, however, designed with intent of having the Order become an arm of the Empire and limiting its independence. Antonio Bosio returned in April to obtain the Grand Master's instructions concerning these matters while Martinengo and Toledo carried on discussions. Grand Master and Council found Tripoli impossible of defence, but it was the ancillary conditions that threatened to be deal-breakers. Draper Juan de Homedes and Chancellor Diego

Nunnez dell'Aguila were dispatched to Rome to so inform Pope Clement VII. Fluent in Greek, Antonio Bosio immediately volunteered to return to Rhodes to ascertain whether its recapture was feasible.[15]

In May Ottoman Ahmed Pasha of 1522 Siege fame succeeded Suleiman's brother-in-law Mustafa Pasha, also of Siege fame, as Governor of Egypt. Said to be discontented by Suleiman's selection of boyhood companion Ibrahim Pasha as Ottoman Grand Vizier, Ahmed Pasha one year later gathered a Mamluk army and rebelled, anointing himself Sultan of Egypt. Hoping for support from the west, Ahmed dispatched two loyal janissaries together with a Greek called Zoppo (Pegleg) to seek assistance from both Grand Master and Pope, such assistance causing Suleiman to divide his forces. Sensing an opportunity to return to Rhodes, the Grand Master dispatched the corsair galliot of Jean de Bressols to both return the janissaries to Syria and to assess the extant situation. Antonio Bosio, travelling incognito, was also embarked. Because Zoppo was no longer present to require transportation back, it is reasonable to assume the transportation coming was his vessel, and that this Zoppo was the Greek corsair of Candia using the nom de guerre of Acsac Reis. Called Zoppo since the loss of a lower leg, Acsac had for twenty years been a companion of Dragut operating out of Alexandria. He was destined to become yet more renowned.[16]

Eight knights representing each of the eight langues were appointed to inspect and assess the feasibility of relocating the Order of Jerusalem from Viterbo to Malta, Gozo, and Tripoli. They were Nicholas Hussey for England, Jean de Castellan de Roquemartine for Provence, Jean du Bois de Favières for Auvergne, Jacques de Chevrières for France, Gaspar Glior for Aragon, Paolo Simeoni for Italy, Georg Schilling for Germany, and Diego de Torres for Castile. When returned from their mission several months later, they had mixed reviews concerning the isolated vulnerability of Tripoli in a Muslim world together with positive assessments of the port of Malta.[17]

At about this same time Barbarossa lieutenant Sinan of Smyrna, often called *il Giudèo*, assailed the Tyrrhenian coast of Italy with a dozen or more galliots and fustas. Bernardino d'Airasca was meanwhile at Civitavecchia with three galleys of the Order, his capitana *Santa Caterina*, the others *Santa Maria* commanded by Claude Gruel as padrone and *San Giovanni* commanded by Fernando de Mata as padrone. The annual caravan of knights was embarked. Notable by his absence was Siege veteran and Preceptor of Carbrooke and Halston George Aylmer. An Hospitaller until the 1558 Coronation of Elizabeth I, Aylmer failed to see combat after 1522's Great Siege while suffering from what is today termed PTSD or Post Traumatic Stress Disorder. The squadron in June 1524 joined two Papal galleys commanded by Marchese della Gorgona and Papal Galley Squadron Commander Paolo Vettori hoping to fall upon isolated Sinan detachments. Flying the gold and white Papal battle standard, Vettori commanded. At the island of Giannutri two idle corsair galliots were surprised and put to the chase. Following a long pursuit, the lagging Sinan galliot turned on Mata's *San Giovanni* out ahead of the others. The contest was fierce and bloody, with the leading corsair eventually assailed by the other two Hospitallers. Both corsairs were captured by Hospitallers on the strength of numbers as well as on clean and waxed underwater hulls. Commanding all five Christian galleys, Paolo Vettori was the Christian victor, but neither he nor his galleys were fast enough to reach the scene of combat. Two hundred Christians were liberated from corsair oars while 300 captured Turks and Moors were shared with Papal galleys. The five Hospitaller and Church galleys returned to Civitavecchia with captures under tow. At Civitavecchia Hospitaller dead and wounded were sent to the new hospital at Viterbo. Among the dead was Jacques Bruneau de La Rabatelière of Pays de la Loire in western France. Among the severely wounded were Luigi Broglia and Gabriele Simeoni, who fortunately mended after touch-and-go convalescences.[18]

Gabriele Simeoni's roots are omitted in history texts and he is frequently confused with Paolo Simeoni. He was received into the Order of Jerusalem in 1505 by way of the Diocese of Chieri not more than two years after reception of Paolo, whose reception also went unrecorded but who was a native of the same Chieri in Italy's Piedmont. They were not the same person as Gabriele's hospitalisation while Paolo was surveying Malta and Tripoli makes clear. Each having a biblical name, though, added to the logic of concluding they were both second sons of Paolo's parents, Alessandro Simeoni and Caterina di Romagnano.[19]

Meanwhile, tension between langues had developed by virtue of Bernardino d'Airasca's continuance as Captain of Galleys, the tension not a matter of Airasca's competence but rather the length of his command, which some considered to have commenced in January 1523 when in fact l'Isle-Adam commanded from January to August of that year. A change of command was scheduled for August two months thence.[20]

In July 1524 Prior of Saint-Gilles Pregeant de Bidoux was dispatched back to France with ample authority to collect past-due responsions and replace anyone culpable from the Order's Common Treasury in that country; he found the treasury bereft of funds, necessitating use of 2,000 silver marks deposited by an earlier Prior of England for use by an English knight in an emergency.[21] Draper Juan de Homedes succeeded Bernardino d'Airasca as Captain of Galleys in August but did not serve because his reputation exceedingly aggravated the Langue of Italy. Fernando de Mata, as senior padrone commanding *San Giovanni*, served. *Santa Caterina* and *Santa Maria* were respectively assigned to Paolo Simeoni and to Claude d'Ancienville. Bailiff of Eagle Thomas Sheffield died at Viterbo and was succeeded by Preceptor of Mount Saint John Alban Pole.[22] A pension of 10 ducats each per month was awarded to Giorgio di Conversalo and Benedetto Scaramosa. Engineers and valorous soldiers, both had come to Rhodes in company with Gabriel Tadino di Martinengo at the outset of the 1522 hostilities.[23]

In mid-October 1524 Francis, King of France, launched the latest failed French invasion of Italy, crossing the Alps with up to 40,000 troops and capturing Milan, then besieging Pavia. An Hospitaller on his staff, Emery de Veaux of the Langue of Provence, was dispatched to Rome to render the King's obeisance to Pope Clement.[24]

The Order's Small Galleon of the Religion *Il Siciliano* commanded by Battista Schiatesse, in the waters of Trapani western Sicily carrying a cargo of foodstuffs, was informed that eight Turkish galliots had seized a Christian caravel nearby. With a company of Spanish soldiers furnished by Hospitaller Castellan of Trapani Gaspar Sanguesa, *Il Siciliano* and a Genovese ship together headed toward the island of Favignana a bit further west. Between Favignana and Saline (Isola Grande) they came upon the corsairs, but in larger numbers. It was the squadron of Sinan of Smyrna, sixteen galliots and Sinan's larger galley capitana plus the captured caravel. In no time the Genovese ship was also captured by the Barbarossa lieutenant. *Il Siciliano* had no cannon, but did have arquebusiers and crossbowmen plus embarked Spanish pikemen. These were able to repel would-be boarders in an engagement that persisted for the remainder of the day, thinning both corsair and galleon crews. Both sides disengaged under cover of darkness, the corsairs for reasons of time and shortage of square-rigged sailing skill abandoning both captures. The three sailing ships pointed back to Trapani. Among the gravely wounded were Hospitallers Giovan Battista Pescatori and the same Luigi Broglia who was earlier wounded in combat with the same Sinan of Smyrna.[25]

Hospitaller Prior of Barletta Fabrizio Pignatello died at Naples in November 1524 and was succeeded by Gabriel Tadino de Martinengo, Martinengo renouncing the Bailiwick of Santo Stefano to which Francesco de Caymi succeeded. Commander of Ivrea Luigi dal Pozzo succeeded to the Priory of Pisa vacated earlier by Martinengo. Pietro Bembo, scholar, poet, paramour of Lucrezia Borgia, official historian of Venice, composer, and linguist with a variety of other talents, retired as a Knight Hospitaller. He would in four years be elevated to the Roman Catholic Cardinalate. Grand Master l'Isle-Adam honoured his Seneschal Pierino del Ponte for his successful 1522 defence of the island of Lango with a Grand Cross, also appointing him Bailiff of Lango.[25]

Early in the 1525 Jubilee Year, the ninth such Jubilee Year in Roman Catholic history forgiving the repentant their sins, the Grand Master's overriding concern as it had been for the past twenty-four months was preservation of the Order of Jerusalem and location of a permanent home. He announced that Hospitaller collections would be devoted to those goals. The aforementioned Jean de Bressols and his galliot returned from their Care and Charity mission to the Levant bringing with them a letter-report to the Grand Master from Antonio Bosio concerning prospects for a Hospitaller return to Rhodes. Among other things Bosio reported it would be necessary to arm the Christian population prior to any assault on the island. As for the rebel Sultan of Egypt, his insurrection had been crushed by new Grand Vizier Ibrahim Pasha, and no assistance could be expected from that direction. Meanwhile, the Italian Wars pitting France against Spain continued to rage, inhibiting assistance from either direction.[25]

As senior squadron padrone, Fernando de Mata had been seen at sea flying the admiral's pennant which Italian Hospitallers believed was the exclusive prerogative of the Admiral, who was always Italian. When the Hospitaller Council refused to censure Mata, the Italians took the matter to the Pope. The Pope ruled there should be two flags, one for the Admiral when embarked and another for the Captain of Galleys whether appointed or acting, as customary in navies today. Mata, Paolo Simeoni, and Claude d'Ancienville remained padrones of individual galleys. Pursuant to the Pope's Brief on the matter requiring a Captain of Galleys who serves, Jean de Rivière, Commander of Bellechassagne, was so appointed, succeeding Juan de Homedes.[26]

At about this time the Priory of Rome was vacated by the death of Pietro Salviati. The Grand Master and Council, at the suggestion of Pope Clement VII (Giulio di Giuliano de' Medici), appointed as successor Bernardo Salviati, son of the Pope's cousin Lucrezia Maria Romola de' Medici." He would remain Prior of Rome for forty-three years. Also dying at about this time was Prior of Catalonia Antonio de San Martín (Anton de San Martí in Catalan). He was succeeded by Bailiff of Mallorca Jaume Gilberto, who was in turn succeeded as Bailiff by Catalan Juan Ferrer (Joan Ferrer). Chancellor Diego dell'Aguila advanced to Bailiff of Bóveda and was succeeded as Chancellor by Commander of Leza Don Alvaro Pinto. The Priory of Lombardia, too, became vacant with the death of incumbent Costanzo d'Operti. He was succeeded by Admiral Bernardino d'Airasca, while Filippo Provana advanced to Admiral, vacating the Priory of Messina to which Don Hugo de Moncada succeeded, the latter Admiral of the Holy Roman Empire and Commander of the Imperial Fleet. Moncada was at the time departing Genoa with an Imperial squadron of eighteen galleys having 3,000 infantry embarked intending to seize Varazze near Savona, where he put his infantry ashore. Abandoned by his galleys because of a lee shore, he was confronted by Michele Antonio, Marchese di Saluzzo, commanding French infantry, defeated, and captured.[27]

King Francis diverted a part of his invasion force under John Stewart, Duke of Albany and grandson of King James II of Scotland, to seize Naples, frightening the people of Viterbo on the French route south. Meanwhile the final battle of the French failure took place outside the city walls of Pavia on 24 February, resulting in loss of the majority of the French army. Captives included Francis himself as well as the Grand Master's nephew Anne de Montmorency (the latter ransomed for 10,000 French crowns, the former not so fortunate). Albany's section of the army passed clear of Viterbo but suffered numerous desertions and returned to France without having reached Naples.[28]

Antonio Bosio returned from Rhodes having departed Civitavecchia twelve months earlier. He reported that with the Sultan on campaign in Hungary it would be possible to retake not only Rhodes but Lango and the Castle of Saint Peter, as well. He found, however, the Grand Master unwilling to consider the matter with the current state of Franco-Spanish relations ensuring an absence of external support. In addition, such an undertaking would require the full force of the Order while the two carracks of the Religion, *Santa Anna* and *Santa Maria* were, respectively, laid up and out of service, and would take too long to make ready for sea. Further, the Barciotto of the Religion also called *San Giovanni* had recently gone down fully laden in the waters of Trapani.

Pursuant to a request from Queen Mother Louise of Savoy, Regent during the captivity of King Francis, the Galley Squadron under Jean de Rivière in June 1525 departed Civitavecchia with Grand Master l'Isle-Adam embarked bound for France by way of La Spezia. In France the Grand Master expected to rendezvous with Marguerite of Navarre, Duchess of Alençon and sister of King Francis, and to convey her to Barcelona. Captain of the Papal Squadron, Paolo Vettori, sailed in company with another three galleys escorting Papal legate Cardinal Giovanni Salviati to Spain. Vettori, flying the flag of the Church, was in nominal command. Reaching Spanish ministers, reports of galley numbers and direction excited suspicion of an Hospitaller plot to liberate Francis. Hospitaller priories, bailiwicks, commanderies, and other assets in the Kingdoms of Spain and Naples were sequestered. At Viterbo there was consequent tension between langues concerned. Magistral Lieutenant Bernardino d'Airasca and Council dispatched Commander of Tortosa Gaspar Glior to Naples, where a ransomed Don Hugo de Moncada was acting Viceroy in the absence of Charles de Lannoy (French of Spanish Flanders). Moncada was informed the Grand Master was en route to France in service to the Religion and not in service to either France or Spain. The acting Viceroy replied the sequestrations were by order of the Emperor himself. Antonio Bosio was accordingly dispatched by brigantine to locate the Grand Master and apprise him of developments. Alternatively he was to seek an end to sequestrations. Bosio took with him a favourable Papal Brief. In the meanwhile the Grand Master and Hospitaller galleys had reached Marseille and were awaiting rendezvous instructions. That is where Bosio found them. Learning of the sequestrations, l'Isle-Adam dispatched Commander of Trinquetaille Robert d'Aube de Roquemartine to Viterbo to assure the Convent he had matters in hand. Bosio was ordered back to Rhodes. L'Isle-Adam was resolved to himself meet with Emperor and King to not only have sequestrations lifted but to plead for aid in reconstituting the Order at a home of its own. Unbeknownst to the Grand Master, Emperor Charles V was loath to meet with Marguerite of Navarre, with whom it had been proposed he wed, for fear of succumbing to her charm and weakening his proposed terms for release of Francis.[29]

In July 1525 Hospitaller Francisco José García Jofre de Loaísa of the Langue of Castile commanding seven Spanish-flag vessels set sail from La Coruña, Spain, bound for the western Pacific around Cape Horn. Seeking the Spice Islands or Moluccas, his was the first such exploratory expedition beyond South America since that of Fernando Magellan six years earlier. His expedition would be the first to sight Cape Horn and would discover the Marshall Islands along the way. Only one of the seven vessels reached the Spice Islands, however, Garcia de Loaisa's galleon *San Lesmes* disappearing in 1526 in the vicinity of Polynesia's Tuamotu Islands.[30]

At Viterbo a fear took hold that the Grand Master was about to retire to France. On 22 August 1525 a letter was addressed to l'Isle-Adam from the Sacred Council at Viterbo requesting his urgent return to the city. The Order had been forewarned by letter of the Emperor's expectation that Signorino della Gattinara would succeed to the Priory of Messina when next vacated. Hospitaller Gattinara was a nephew of Mercurino Arborio, Grand Chancellor of Charles V. Given the Order's impoverished circumstances, it would be necessary to comply with the request.

Also at Viterbo several cases of peste or plague had been discovered. The Convent, which led a relatively sanitised existence, was stunned and bewildered. Hospitallers Francesco di Ventimiglia, Procurator for the Langue of Italy, together with Laurent Palon of Auvergne and Scipione Parente of Capua, were deputised to coordinate with the Governor of Viterbo acquisition of necessary medical supplies. Before the disease could be contained, Bailiff of Lyons Raymond de Rogier of Savoy, who commanded the Post of Auvergne during the 1522 Siege, succumbed. He was succeeded as Bailiff of Lyons by Jean de Laure and as a Conventual

Conservator or Common Treasury Auditor by Pierre d'Artogue, Lieutenant Grand Hospitaller of the Langue of France.

Rafaello de Sartori and Nicolo Allegretto, non-Hospitaller agents of the Order in the Levant, returned from Constantinople with information concerning Sultan Suleiman's preparations for another campaign in Hungary.[31] These campaigns had never permitted a second Ottoman initiative.

Summoned to a rendezvous at Aigues-Mortes west of Marseille, the Galley Squadron with l'Isle-Adam still embarked and the Papal squadron still in company reached the destination in mid-August, but for two weeks were prevented from continuing on to Spain by foul weather. Finally, the Duchess and Hospitaller galleys, Cardinal Salviati and the Papal galleys, departed Aigues-Mortes at the outset of September and proceeded to Barcelona by way of Palamos. From Barcelona the Duchess and her suite, which included the Grand Master's ransomed nephew and Marshal of France Anne de Montmorency, the Cardinal and his suite, and the Grand Master, were escorted to Madrid by the same Hospitaller Don Hugo de Moncada petitioned during the summer by Bernardino d'Airasca. When Moncada apologised for his poor command of French, the Duchess responded in fluent Castilian. Marguerite of Navarre was fluent not only in Castilian but in Latin, Greek, and most modern European languages. While still at Barcelona the Grand Master had encountered the Emperor's ambassador, Hospitaller Pedro Fernandez de Heredia, enroute to Viterbo. Heredia gave the Grand Master a copy of the Empire's position paper concerning Malta and continued on his way. Then or sometime later Jean de Rivière was given leave to depart, as the Duchess of Alençon intended returning to France by road upon the mid-winter expiration of her safe-conduct, while the Grand Master was uncertain of his plans.[32]

The Galley Squadron under Rivière departed Barcelona and returned in company with the Papal Galley Squadron by way of Porto Levanto (modern Porto Venere near La Spezia) where it was discovered and requisitioned by Charles III, Duke of Bourbon (1490–1527, wealthiest man in Europe before Francis expropriated his estates). One of Charles V's victorious generals in the Franco-Spanish war just ended, Bourbon was in need of an escort back to Barcelona. During the Squadron's second return from Barcelona Fernando de Mata, padrone of *San Giovanni*, fell ill and died of his malady.

Arriving in Madrid on 19 September 1525, the Grand Master soon obtained from Emperor Charles V a lifting of the sequestrations. Both the Duchess of Alençon and the Grand Master found Francis gravely ill, so grave that last sacraments were administered on 22 September, but he was earlier able to receive both his 'beloved sister' and his 'father'. Over the two months following the sacraments his health improved while the clock ran on his sister's safe-conduct (visa). She was at the same time unable to reach an agreement with the Emperor on terms for the King's release, and in fact was rarely accorded an audience. At an audience on 4 October the most significant difference had to do with Burgundy. The Duchess proposed a marriage between Francis and the Emperor's sister Eleanor, Queen of Portugal, with Burgundy her dowry, or alternatively, that suzerainty of Burgundy be determined by a jury of French peers. Charles was determined that Burgundy be returned to his military commander, the Duke of Bourbon. That difference remained when the Duchess was forced by terms of her safe-conduct to leave Madrid at the end of November.[33]

Jean de Rivière made his report to Bernardino d'Airasca and the Council of the galley excursion early in December 1525. Juanito de Vilatorta (Jan de Vilatorta in Catalan) of the Langue of Aragon was then appointed successor padrone of *San Giovanni*.[34] Marguerite of Navarre reached Salses on the Franco-Spanish border on 22 December one week before her safe-conduct expired. An agreement between Charles V and Francis was reached during her flight from the country, leading to January's Treaty of Madrid pursuant to which the French King renounced his claims in Italy, Flanders, and Artois, surrendered Burgundy to the Emperor, agreed to send two of his sons to be hostages at the Spanish court, and to restore to Charles III, Duke of Bourbon, the territories seized from him. According to Hospitaller historian Giacomo Bosio, the remaining differences between King and Emperor were put to the Grand Master for resolution.[35]

The Grand Master discussed with the Emperor considerations of any return to Rhodes, and made much of a letter received from new Metropolitan of Rhodes Euphemios citing the inhumane tyranny of Turkish overlords; Euphemios was Antonio Bosio's host when secretly at the island. He also disclosed correspondence with the Aga of Janissaries at Rhodes promising to abandon the three towers securing the port of Rhodes on any siege of the city by returning Hospitallers. In that vein the Grand Master was hopeful of lasting peace between the Empire and France, he told the Emperor, without which recovery of Rhodes could not even be considered. The Grand Master, of course, also discussed with the Emperor considerations of any cession of Malta to the Order. Tripoli was indefensible in his opinion, particularly by a small Convent. A Christian outpost on the coast of Libya, however, was essential in the Emperor's view to maintain a friendly Hafsid Kingdom of Tunis as a barrier to Ottoman expansion.[39]

In January 1526 Prior of Catalonia Jaume Gilberto died of unreported cause and was succeeded by Bailiff of Negroponte Ramón Marquet. Francisco de Castillo succeeded to the Bailiwick of Negroponte.[36] Kheir-ed-Din Barbarossa, successor to his deceased brother Aruj and Ottoman Sancakbey or Governor of Algiers, proceeded by galley from Djerba to Constantinople during the Winter of 1525–26. He was accompanied by lieutenant Turgut Reis, also known as Dragut, for discussions with Sultan Suleiman and Grand Vizier Ibrahim, all but Suleiman Greek by birth. Some biographers believe Suleiman himself to have been more than half Greek with his mother Hafsa from Greek Pontus or Trabzon and his father Selim bringing to the union a measure of additional Greek blood. In any event Suleiman was fluent in Greek, the language of Ottoman diplomacy, while the others were fluent in Turkish. This was the first meeting of the four and a principal subject of discussion was the evacuation of Moors from Spain in the context of Spanish King Charles I's November 1525 declaration that resident Moors must convert or depart. The four agreed the only practical way to depart was aboard Barbarossa hulls. Seventy thousand Moors of Aragon would make their departure on thirty-six oared Barbarossa hulls beginning in August 1529, 10,000 in each of seven evacuations from Valencia.[37]

News came to the Grand Master at the Imperial Court from Portugal of the death of Count of Tarouca and nominal Prior of Crato João de Meneses; his widow had taken the Habit, calling herself Conte Priore. John III, King of Portugal, however, had bestowed the same priory on his brother, Infante Dom Luis. The local chapter of Hospitallers represented by Prior in possession Gonçalo Pimentel was opposed to both claimants.

King John, moved by conscience, asked Pimentel for an accord. To the surprise of the local chapter, the accord provided that Infante Dom Luis was to be styled Administrator of the Priory, and not as Prior, and that the Crown would do all in its power to recover and remit 15,000 Portuguese silver *cruzados* in past due responsions.[38]

l'Isle-Adam departed the Imperial Court for France full of plans for the recovery of Rhodes fostered by influential courtiers Don Fernando Álvarez de Toledo y Pimentel, 3rd Duke of Alba, and by the aforementioned Mercurino Arborio, Grand Chancellor. His intention was to gather a large sum of money from priories and commanderies in France to fund purchase of equipment and supplies necessary for a besieging force as well as to pay for hired soldiery. In France he dispatched Commander of Trinquetaille Robert d'Aube de Roquemartine to Viterbo to apprise Bernardino d'Airasca and the Council of his actions and purpose as well as of developments with the Priory of Crato. In his letter to Airasca and Council he also proposed a levy on Hospitaller assets. Perhaps in part reflecting the Grand Master's nine-month absence from the Convent, Airasca and Council responded suggesting these matters were matters for a Chapter General gathering of Hospitallers. Airasca and Council also redirected the Commander of Trinquetaille to Rome for the purpose of petitioning Pope Clement VII concerning the Grand Master's plans. Francis, meanwhile, was released from captivity and escorted to the border, where on 18 March he was exchanged for two of his children: eldest son Francis III, barely eight years of age, and future King Henry II, a year younger. Four days later, with Papal forgiveness, Francis renounced the Treaty of Madrid as coerced and therefore invalid. Unbeknownst to the Grand Master, during the captivity of Francis, his mother Regent Queen Louise had petitioned Sultan Suleiman for assistance and the Sultan had responded with a letter received by Charles V in February warning of unpleasant consequences should Francis not be released forthwith. Thus the encouragement the Grand Master received from prominent courtiers, and thus increasingly less likely any assistance from France. Without assistance from both sources the recapture of Rhodes would be impossible.[39]

In the continued absence of the Grand Master, Airasca and the Council in April 1526 appointed Prior of Pisa Lodovico dal Pozzo as Captain of the Galleys for one year succeeding Jean de Rivière.[44] During the same period Prior of Capua Giuliano Ridolfi founded at Penne in the Abruzzo a hilltop Convent of Nuns of the Order of Saint John of Jerusalem. The dignity of Bailiff of the Morea was vacated by death of Emery Combault, a Knight of the Grand Cross who commanded the Grand Master's personal guard at the Siege of Rhodes and who thus was engaged at every critical point during the Siege. Combault was succeeded by Treasurer Michel d'Argillemont, who was himself succeeded as Treasurer by Commander of Sterpigny Jacques de Saint-Maurice. Returning to Viterbo was Gaspar Glior who, commanding the Galleon of the Religion *San Buonaventura* with a company of Hospitallers embarked, in Turkish waters over the winter sent several Turkish ships to the bottom while enslaving their crews and passengers. Among the latter were thirty who would bring large ransoms. For that purpose Rhodiot Markos Kantakouzenos was dispatched to Constantinople to treat for the amounts. Passing through Viterbo at the time was Hospitaller Don Pedro Fernandez d'Heredia, sent by the Emperor to the Pope to plead for His Holiness's assistance in maintaining the peace just negotiated between France and the Holy Roman Empire and already refuted.[40]

Charles V and his bride Isabella of Portugal wed on 11 March 1526, at the Palace of Alcázar in Seville, and departed immediately on honeymoon at Granada. Isabella brought to the marriage a huge dowry of 900,000 Portuguese cruzados, significantly bolstering Spanish finances. Begun as a political union, the marriage proved during the honeymoon to be a love match that would produce six children and endure until Isabella's death on 1 May 1539.

Don Pedro Fernandez de Heredia departed Rome with no encouragement from Pope Clement VII, the latter already fostering a League of Cognac composed of the Papal States, France, Venice, Milan, and Florence opposed to a Holy Roman Empire presence in Italy. Paolo Vettori, long-time General of Papal Galleys, who died in March was succeeded by seagoing condottiero Andrea Doria, who for 30,000 Venetian ducats leased to the Church his six galleys, two of which belonged to his cousin Antonio. Doria himself was recognised with an annual retainer of 16,000 additional ducats. Stipulated in his contract was that he take under management two Papal galleys and two brigantines. He immediately recruited 200 arquebusiers in Piedmont for the Papal squadron. On 22 May at Cognac in Angouleme the treaty of the League of Cognac was signed by representatives of each member state. In June the Grand Master scheduled a Chapter General at Viterbo to convene on the first Sunday of July 1527.[41]

With three galleys, the capitana *Santa Caterina* commanded by Paolo Simeoni, the others *Santa Maria* commanded by Claude d'Ancienville and *San Giovanni* commanded by Juanito de Vilatorta, Dal Pozzo in June 1526 sortied from Civitavecchia in company with the eight-galley and three-fusta Papal squadron of Andrea Doria to counter Kheir-ed-Din Barbarossa who had been raiding the Tuscan coast with sixteen galliots, fustas, and brigantines. Barbarossa was surprised by Doria in the waters of Piombino, 40 nautical miles north of Porto Ercole where the Order's square-rigged ships were harboured. Following a fierce engagement during which Doria lost a galley, Barbarossa was compelled to flee, leaving in the hands of his enemies fifteen of his smaller ships and their crews. Captive renegades were hanged. More than a thousand Barbarossa crewmen were enslaved and confined in the prisons at the port of Civitavecchia. An equal number of Christians were freed from the oars. Barbarossa saved himself with difficulty; his galliot, pursued a long while by Simeoni's *Santa Caterina*, escaped only during the dark of night. While reaching safety at Djidjelli (Jijel, Algeria), Barbarossa would never forget his pursuer.[42]

Given impoverishment of the Order's Treasury, Dal Pozzo in July and August re-equipped the galleys at his own expense and strengthened the crews with prisoners sentenced to the oars at Parma. The convicts were assigned to him by Cardinal Alessandro Farnese who in 1534 would become Pope under the name of Paul III.[43]

Empire forces commanded by Hugo Moncada (here termed by Bosio Lieutenant to Viceroy of Naples Charles de Lannoy) and Cardinal Pompeo Colonna together with condottieri Vespaziano and Ascanio Colonna commanding 3,000 infantry and 800 cavalry, entered the city of Rome in September. The Senate and people failed to rally to the defence of Pope Clement VII, who sought safety within Castle Saint Angelo. The Vatican and Saint Peter's Basilica were sacked. The Pope met with Moncada, who extracted a number of concessions including Andrea Doria's withdrawal from Genoa. Pompeo Colonna was furious the Pope had not been arrested. Following withdrawal of Imperial forces

Pope Clement reneged on his concessions and deprived Moncada of his Hospitaller Habit.[44]

Lodovico dal Pozzo had orders not to put into Ligurian ports while patrolling, nor those of the French. To preserve the Order's neutrality he must only put into Villefranche or Nice, both controlled by Duke of Savoy Charles III. Prior to departure he was summoned to Rome by Pope Clement VII, and while there the Pope ordered him to embark the Grand Master's agent Raffaello de Sartori, who was en route to Hungary where 20-year-old King Louis II's army had been destroyed in an open-field battle at Mohacs in August, the King succumbing to battle wounds. Much of Hungary had then become a province of Suleiman's Ottoman Empire, and most of the rest was absorbed by Charles V's Holy Roman Empire.

The three-galley squadron departed Civitavecchia in October bound for Villefranche in the Nicoise to embark Grand Master l'Isle-Adam for transport back to Civitavecchia. Shortly after departure two brigantines arrived at Civitavecchia one after the other, the first that of Hospitaller Juan de Parades of the Langue of Aragon transporting Rhodiots Crosolora Gratiani, Manolis Coschigniati, and Franculli Zacuri. The second brigantine belonging to non-Hospitaller Benedetto Ruggiero transported three more Rhodiots. All six had come to plead for no further delay in the recapture of Rhodes and to explain the danger to collaborators. They were assured two new galleys were nearing construction completion and that sailing ships were almost ready. The Grand Master anticipated proceeding with recapture following the March Chapter General. He either believed the level of hostilities between adversaries in the War of the League of Cognac would permit one or the other side to provide him assistance, or he intended to effect the recapture without outside assistance, or his heart was taken with Rhodes, as any who have seen it today much as l'Isle-Adam left it in January 1523 will readily understand. Antonio Bosio returned to Rhodes aboard the Parades brigantine to help pave the return home.[45]

Charles V in December returned to Madrid from his honeymoon at Grenada realising he would have to again win all he had won before. Six months earlier he had expected in 1527 he would be crowned Emperor at Rome, after which he would proceed to Germany and deal with the Lutherans. Thereafter he would be free to confront the Turks.[46]

Early in the new year knights of the Priory of France obtained a Brief from Pope Clement shrinking the authority of Prior Pierre de Cluis to award commanderies and mandating the system customary among other langues in which commanderies are retained until death or retirement. Meanwhile, winter's exceptional cold had brought an end to the incidence of plague at Viterbo. The Grand Master was transported to Civitavecchia, bringing with him a large number of bailiffs and commanders coming for the approaching Chapter General, then to convene in March rather than July. Much to the relief of the Convent, the Grand Master arrived safely at Civitavecchia on 21 January 1527, nineteen months after his departure in June 1525.[47]

At the second Council meeting following his return the Grand Master appointed Prior of Saint-Gilles Pregeant de Bidoux and Prior of Barletta Gabriel Tadino de Martinengo his lieutenants for the recapture of Rhodes. At Rome he used his familiarity with the Emperor and the loss of Hungary to argue the necessity for an accommodation between Church and Empire. He observed that a mixed force of 11,000 Empire allies under the Duke of Burgundy had made rendezvous at Piacenza little more than 300 miles to the north with 12,000 Lutheran landsknechts under Georg von Frundsberg, who had promised to hang the Pope with a golden rope, and that the Papal States were inadequately defended. It was to no avail. Pope Clement refused to listen to reason.[48]

While Isabella of Portugal brought to the Empire a substantial dowry, it was hardly enough to pay past due amounts and certainly not enough to pay the troops of Bourbon and Frundsberg. Like most armies of the day, this one lived off the land it passed through, and off the people along its path. It was horrid and in some cases worse by virtue of Lutheran hatred for Roman Catholics. On 16 March Clement caved in and signed a humiliating truce with the Empire's resident representative. But the truce was too late. At about the same time Frundsberg suffered a stroke and was lost to the campaign, his unpaid landsknechts becoming even more undisciplined. The tsunami of people from the north claimed everything in its path. At Viterbo the Chapter General convened in the citadel on 17 March. Cardinal Egidio (Antonini) of Viterbo gave a benediction and read a Papal Brief extolling the virtues of the Order of Jerusalem. Tommaso Bosio, brother of Antonio Bosio and both uncles of historian Giacomo Bosio, succeeded Thomas Guichard as Vice Chancellor. Simone Bonnano of Palermo and the Langue of Italy was dispatched to Messina to make advance arrangements to provision the Order's armada when it passed through the Strait of Messina en route to Rhodes. Orders were issued to captains of the carracks *Santa Anna* and *Santa Maria*, respectively Pons d'Urrè of Provence and Luis de Turienzo of Castile, to make their ships ready for sea. The two langues of Spain, Aragon and Castile, wished to accept the Emperor's conditioned offer of Malta, Gozo, and Tripoli, the conditions converting the Order of Jerusalem into an extension of the Empire. The other six langues wished to turn the matter of Rhodes versus Malta over to a decision of the Sixteen *Capitolanti* or Legislators, two for each of the eight langues. Cardinal Egidio recessed the Chapter General by order of the Pope to be reconvened at Rome.[49]

In April Prior of Capua Giuliano Ridolfi died in mid-life. Emanuele d'Airasca, a knight for thirty-eight years who had long aspired to the dignity, remained a candidate. The other candidate was Leon Strozzi, 12-year-old son of Clarice d'Medici and nephew of Pope Clement VII. An individual of whom much was expected, Strozzi would in 1553 become the Order's first General of the Galleys. In the interim he would command the galleys of France. Strozzi, not Emanuele d'Airasca, was appointed Prior of Capua.[50]

As the Grand Master and Bernardino d'Airasca readied for the reconvened Chapter General at Rome, Bailiff of Negroponte Francisco de Castillo was appointed Airasca's Lieutenant to remain in Viterbo during the latter's absence. Almost coincidentally plague reappeared in the city, particularly among the lay staff of Vice Chancellor Tommaso Bosio. All Hospitallers at Viterbo were quarantined within the Convent while the disease raged without. Reconvening of the Chapter General was postponed. At Rome Pope Clement had pared his defences to the bone to pay an instalment on the ransom he expected to save him from the tsunami of people. Giovanni de Medici's Bande Nere had been dismissed and the Swiss Guard cut back. Only the condottiero Renzo di Ceri (Lorenzo dell'Anguillara of Ceri, near Rome) and 950 hired soldiers stood between the Pope and Bourbon's 35,000. Toward the end of April Bourbon's line of march brought him to Viterbo, but told by the Grand Master's messengers the Knights of Jerusalem were prepared to resist until the last man, many of whom were subjects of the Empire, Bourbon sent back an expression of his fondness for the Order and bypassed the city.

Watching the Imperial force through a window, Metropolitan Klemes of Rhodes, who had fled the island with the Hospitallers, was killed by an arquebus round. The Grand Master's nephew, Louis de Tinteville, took a brigantine full of munitions acquired for the retaking of Rhodes from Civitavecchia to Ostia and up the Tiber to supply Castle Saint Angelo.[51]

Empire forces commanded by Imperial Generals Charles III Duke of Bourbon, Charles de Lannoy, and Bourbon's successor and Prince of Orange Philibert de Chalon, joined by condottieri Ascanio, Pompeo, and Vespaziano Colonna, as well as by other opportunists, reached Rome on 6 May and brutally and sacrilegiously sacked the city. Bourbon was one of a handful of Empire soldiers to fall during the eight-day orgy, while more than 6,000 Romans were victims of the butchery and more than one million ducats in valuables were looted. And then there would be ransoms for the ransomable. Clement VII and Renzo di Ceri retired into Castle Saint Angelo, where they were besieged until surrendering on 6 June. Ceri and his remaining 400 soldiers were permitted to pass through enemy lines and take ship from Civitavecchia for France. The Pope agreed to a ransom of 400,000 ducats he did not have and remained imprisoned for six months before buying off his guards and escaping in disguise. He took shelter first at Orvieto and then at Viterbo and would not return to Rome until October 1528. Lost as a part of this sacrilegious tragedy were the last remaining copies of Hospitaller archives covering the Order's history up to 1522.[52]

At Viterbo the Grand Master, not wishing to delay in spite of developments at Rome, issued orders to have the two carracks at Villefranche proceed to Palermo in Sicily to load fresh provisions Simone Bonnino had arranged earlier. The rest of the Hospitaller armada was on stand-by. The Chapter General interrupted in March reconvened at Viterbo on 18 May, and following a recapitulation of the Order's circumstances the Sixteen Capitolanti were elected, as follows: Prior of Toulouse Didier de Tholon Sainte-Jalle and Lieutenant Grand Commander Guillot de Castellane Régusse for Provence, Marshal Antoine de Claveson and Didier de Chevrier for Auvergne, Bailiff of the Morea Michel d'Argillemont and Conventual Conservator Pierre d'Artogue for France, Draper Juan de Homedes and Prior of Catalonia Ramón Marquet for Aragon, Lieutenant to the Grand Master Bernardino d'Airasca and Bailiff of Lango and Seneschal to the Grand Master

Pierino del Ponte for Italy, Turcopolier William Weston and Preceptor of Quenington Thomas Rawson for England, Lieutenant Grand Bailiff Georg Schilling, who was the only German resident at the Convent, and Catalan Luis Lull for Germany, and Bailiff of Boveda Diego dell Aguila and Portuguese Gaspar de Silva for Castile. The Sixteen gathered for two weeks discussing the pros and cons of Malta and Rhodes but in the end the two Spanish langues refused to accept anything but Malta. The decision of the Sixteen was to accept Malta and Gozo with total sovereignty, that is, without Tripoli and without becoming an arm of the Holy Roman or Spanish Empires. To this end ambassadors were to be sent to the Imperial Court to represent the Order's position and the Chapter General adjourned on 7 June 1527.[53]

One day following the Chapter General l'Isle-Adam and the Council determined for reasons of famine and plague to relocate the Convent and its Rhodean followers from Viterbo to Corneto (modern Tarquinia). Corneto was also a walled city situated on an elevation 130m above the sea, normally breathing fresh sea air. It was also closer to both Porto Ercole and Civitavecchia where the Order's vessels were homeported. Bailiff of Naples Battista Carafa was dispatched to inform the Pope in Castle Saint Angelo (accessible from the Tiber) of the Chapter General, of the relocation to Corneto, and of pressure from the Spanish langues and the agreement to accept Malta as the Order's future home. Carafa was also to inform Spanish commanders at Rome of the Convent's relocation. The departure from Viterbo took place on 15 June to no little regret of the citizenry, and by the following evening the Convent and its entourage were within the walls of Corneto. The carracks *Santa Anna* and *Santa Maria*, though, had been recalled from Palermo and there was already consideration of further flight. Dying of plague at Corneto was Grand Hospitaller Pierre de Gouriault while overseeing transfer of the infirmary from Viterbo. He was succeeded by Michel d'Argillemont, who vacated the Bailiwick of the Morea, which was conferred upon Jacques de Sainte-Maure. The latter renounced the dignity of Treasurer to which Commander of Moulins Joachim de Saint-Simon was assigned.[54]

At about the same time news was received of the death of Grand Prior of England Thomas Docwra, who so narrowly lost the election in which l'Isle-Adam succeeded to the dignity of Grand Master. By Bull of Grand Master l'Isle-Adam issued at Corneto, Italy, on 27 June 1527 Turcopolier

William Weston was appointed in Docwra's stead and was himself succeeded by Prior of Ireland John Rawson who in turn was succeeded by Preceptor of Dalby and Rothley John Babington. All three were present at Corneto and all three were given permission to proceed to England to effect the changes. Prior of Toulouse Didier de Sainte-Jalle and Bailiff of Lyon Jean de Laurè were permitted to return to their duties in France. The latter's vessel was seized en route to France by several Turkish galliots, and he was enslaved. Not much later an Hospitaller brigantine carrying a tapestry of the Conventual Church of Saint John to Nice was also captured. Corsair Jean de Bressols was sent to the slave market at Trapani, where he employed an agent able to proceed to North Africa and buy back Laurè and a part of the tapestry.

In June 1527 the Grand Master dispatched three ambassadors to Madrid: Prior of Catalonia Ramón Marquet of the Langue of Aragon, Commander Antonio Melo of the Langue of Castile, and Antoine de Grolée of the Langue of Auvergne, he who had negotiated the terms of Hospitaller surrender, or he who had accepted the terms of Hospitaller surrender from Sultan Suleiman. All three were ordered to report to Hospitaller Prior of Castile Don Diego de Toledo upon reaching Madrid, and with Toledo to acquaint the Emperor with recent developments, most pertinently the Chapter General's decision to accept the Emperor's offer of Malta and Gozo, if free and clear, in return for which the Order of Jerusalem would each year convene a Mass of Thanksgiving. Marquet and Grolée were further ordered, should the Emperor agree, to proceed to the Court of France and obtain the approval of King Francis. Melo was to obtain the same approval from the King of Portugal. He was to obtain as well the King's permission to have Infante Dom Luis, Administrator of the Priory of Crato, transfer governance of the Priory to aging Prior of Portugal Gonzalo Pimental.[55]

In July plague contamination spread at both Viterbo and Corneto, with a concomitant increase in the incidence of sickness and death. The Grand Master determined to embark the Convent and its Rhodean followers aboard the carracks, ships, and galleys, and together seek cleaner air. All vessels of the Religion were summoned. In the midst of this apocalyptic nightmare came news that Henry VIII, King of England, had seized the Priory of England and all of its assets including the estate of Thomas Docwra, and that new Prior William Weston, who together with John

Rawson and John Babington had only recently departed the Convent, were all three at the English presidio of Calais without authority to enter the country. A mentally and physically exhausted Grand Master dispatched Prior of Saint-Gilles Pregeant de Bidoux and Commander Jacques de Bourbon with a plea to Henry VIII for restoration, written in Latin, en route to seek an endorsement from Francis.[56] In August uninfected Hospitallers and followers were embarked aboard ships of the armada, leaving four Hospitallers to care for the sick at the Order's medical facility at Corneto. These courageous four were Juan Pertusa de Sarnes of the Langue of Aragon, Charles Carlé du Boulay of the Langue of France, Álvaro Romero of Castile, and Domingo de San Juan of Aragon. The Grand Master and the Armada of the Religion passed the month of August and much of September at Porto Santo Stefano near Porto Ercole in Tuscany seeking clean air to avoid the plague. There the Grand Master determined to take the entire armada north to Villefranche in the territory of Savoy, which was neutral in the war involving all around it. When all evidence of the disease had been purged, Commander Ercole di None of Turin was dispatched as ambassador to Charles III, Duke of Savoy, seeking permission for the Armada to harbour at Villefranche and for the Order to settle at nearby Nice. Charles de Lannoy, Commander of Imperial forces in Italy, on 23 September 1527 succumbed to the plague at Naples.[57] He was but 40 years of age.

Chapter II

Phillipe de Villiers de l'Isle-Adam 1527–30

The Order's Armada arrived at Villefranche on 8 October 1527, and was welcomed to Savoy in large part because it would provide a deterrent to Barbary corsairs infesting local coast. The Grand Master and staff were quartered in the Castle of Nice, while remaining Hospitallers and Rhodian followers were provided lesser accommodation, but accommodation indeed. Pursuant to Ercole di None's agreement with Duke Charles, Honoré de Tourettes of the Langue of Provence and a native of Savoy, was appointed to administer justice to transgressing Hospitallers and Rhodians alike. Savoy not only promised a haven from plague, but a respit during which plans for the return to Rhodes could be re-evaluated, two new and improved galleys could be commissioned, and the Order's status in England could be addressed.

Upon receipt of a report Bailiff of Caspe Geronimo de Cañel had passed away, Draper Juan de Homedes was appointed his successor and was himself succeeded by Janot Torres. Similarly, Francisco de Castellot was advanced to the dignity of Bailiff of Mallorca upon the death of incumbent and senior Aragonese knight Juanito (Jan) Ferrer. Castellot renounced the Bailiwick of Negroponte to which Sancho Mudarra succeeded. At about the same time Bailiff of Boveda Diego Nunnez dell'Aguila died and was succeeded by Inigo Lope de Ayala of Spain's Basque Country.[1]

Not much later came news that Odet de Foix, Vicomte de Lautrec, was leading a strong French force into Italy to rescue Pope Clement VII from imprisonment in Castle Saint Angelo. Lautrec was said to be a dear friend of l'Isle-Adam stemming from years the latter spent at the French Court prior to election as Grand Master. A letter was immediately dispatched on 22 October by hand of Seneschal Pierino del Ponte to Lautrec seeking return of artillery left at Siena by the Duke of Bourbon in his haste to reach Rome, artillery earlier requisitioned from the carracks *Santa Anna* and *Santa Maria*. Del Ponte's letter was well received by Lautrec, who ordered release of the requisitioned artillery then in the possession of his subordinate Boniface IV Palaeologus, Marchese of Montferrat. The artillery was placed in the care of resident Hospitaller Benvenuto Sangiorgio, who had earlier written a history of Montferrat entitled *Cronica del Monferrato.*[2]

On order of the Grand Master at Nice rooms in the Castle of Nice were set aside for the Order's infirmary and for the auberges of the various langues. By 14 November the entire Convent was located within the city walls of Nice. Toward the end of the month came news of the death of Marshal Antoine de Claveson. He was succeeded by Siege veteran Gabriel du Chief. Pregeant de Bidoux and Jacques de Bourbon returned to Nice from England and reported they had been unable to make any progress in restoring normalcy at the Priory of England. The Grand Master in Council decided to go to England himself. Magistral Lieutenant Bernardino d'Airasca was to resume command of the Convent in the Grand Master's absence. Expecting to soon take delivery of two new galleys under construction at Villefranche, all five were ordered to be ready for sea in May. The Order's Receiver-General Jean de Boniface was directed to assume responsibility for the Order's Treasury. Pons de Laurenzin of Lyons was appointed Prior of the Church, succeeding the deceased Miguel Font. Hugo de Moncada was appointed Viceroy of Naples by Emperor Charles V, succeeding the deceased Charles de Lannoy. Moncada reached yet another agreement with imprisoned Pope Clement VII, this one freedom now against promise to pay. The Pope immediately took to his horse and fled Rome for Orvieto.[3]

In December 1527 Antonio Bosio returned again from Rhodes, this time to report that understandings with Rhodiots and others to do with recapture of the island had been abandoned because of continued delays in acting upon such understandings and continuing fear of discovery.[4] The Grand Master, patently refusing any such end to his dream, departed Nice on the second day of 1528 with the galleys of the Religion, debarking at Antibes in the company of Prior of Saint-Gilles Pregeant de Bidoux and Bailiff of Caspe Juan de Homedes as well as a good number of other commanders and knights. Among these others was the same Antonio Bosio, who as the Convent's most able diplomat was dispatched directly to England to obtain an invitation for the Grand Master to visit. In the meanwhile the Grand Master would be courting the Court of France.[4]

Bosio returned in February 1528 with letter invitations in Latin from Henry VIII and from Thomas Wolsey, Cardinal Archbishop of York and Lord Chancellor of England, both dated 25 February 1528. That from the King was signed 'Your Good Friend, Henry'. At the Court of France, l'Isle-Adam was heartened by the letters. He was also heartened at having obtained from Francis a commitment for a good number of convicted felons to man the oars of the Order's galleys, including two new galleys. For their service the felons could earn an abbreviated sentence. Bidoux was left to see to transport for the felons to Marseille and thence to Nice. Commander of Bacconet Pierre Cartier and Commander of Villedieu Antoine Philippe de Perdicque were authorised to obtain timbers in the La Selve district of the Pyrenees for use by their commanderies of northern France in effecting structural repairs.[5]

Grand Master l'Isle-Adam reached England early in March 1528. Before entering the City of London he proceeded to the Preceptory of Saint John (now St John's Gate, the entry to the former preceptory). There he was welcomed by Prior of England William Weston, by Turcopolier John Rawson, by Prior of Ireland John Babington, and by Bailiff of Eagle Alban Pole, the four English knights of the Grand Cross, prior to appearing before an assembly of all English and Scottish knights present. Knowing that Henry VIII had sequestered the rich estate of former Prior Thomas Docwra and had levied a 4,000 pound annual tax on new Prior William Weston, he intended an appropriate petition to the King and sought council of those present. Later, at the court of Henry VIII he was received admiringly by ministers, barons, and lords of the realm, a legend of their time, and was royally received by the King himself. Lodged in Greenwich Palace, the royal residence, he spent considerable time in private conversation with the King, who had an abiding interest in details of the Siege of Rhodes. He also had an interest in the island's recovery and for that purpose promised 20,000 scudos while remaining content with a fall-back plan of making Malta the Order's home. In the end the King restored the Docwra estate to the Order, repealed the tax on the new Grand Master, and confirmed all of the Order's pre-existing privileges within his Kingdom. In return he asked only that Turcopolier John Rawson might resume his former duties as Prior of Ireland, where he had proved invaluable to the King. This was of course agreed, and the dignities of Rawson and Babington were therefore exchanged with the Preceptory of Dinsmore also going from Rawson to Babington. With that the Grand Master requested leave to return to his Convent, to the profound regret of both King Henry VIII and Queen Catherine of Aragon.[6]

During the Grand Master's absence in England Draper Janot Torres died at Nice of unreported cause. He was succeeded by Commander of Tortosa Gaspar Glior, who a bit earlier had returned from Sicily with a large barque carrying a cargo of much-needed grain. This in spite of deadly famine sweeping Italy in consequence of war and plague. Perversely, famine now decimated armies. Henry V, Duke of Brunswick-Lüneburg and Imperial General, unable to feed his 7,000 Germans in Lombardia, was abandoned. His troops went home without him. Odet de Foix, Vicomte de Lautrec, hoping to seize Naples for the French and swap it for the French Dauphin and his younger brother, hostages to the bad faith of their father, instead encountered another horseman of the Apocalypse, the pale horse, Plague.[7] Hospitaller corsair Bernardin d'Ornesan, hero of the French siege of Mitilini in 1501, a mainstay of 1512 galley operations in La Manche combatting the English, and a notable presence in many other operations, passed away in his palace at Marseille. First Baron of Baux (Les Baux-de-Provence) since 1513, the entirety of his substantial estate including the galleon *La Brava* and all of her artillery was bequeathed to the Order of Jerusalem.

The city of Naples had since the first week of April 1528 been under siege by France in one of the latter's many attempts to re-establish the French Kingdom of Naples. The city's external water supply had been interrupted and wells were running dry. Hospitaller and Viceroy of the Spanish Kingdom of Naples Hugo de Moncada was increasingly desperate. He was besieged ashore by Odet de Foix, Viscount Lautrec, and the French Army of Italy, which had already subjugated Genoa and Milan, like Naples parts of Charles V's Holy Roman Empire. At sea it was seagoing condottiero Andrea Doria's 'nephew' Filippino Doria under contract to France with a mixed flotilla of eight galleys, four galleons, and five fustas. Moncada and his naval commander Fabrizio Giustiniani had six galleys, two fustas, and three brigantines (the latter small fustas, both without cannon) at Posillipo near Ischia in the north-west corner of the Gulf of Naples.[8]

Moncada and Giustiniani, Giustiniani like the Dorias a native of Genoa, concluded their best chance was at sea, but they would need to level the field by catching Doria without his heavily armed galleons. As combat at sea without heavily armed warships continued to be a matter of boarding and numbers of boarders, arrangements were made to embark 700 infantry commanded by Marchese del Vasto Alfonso d'Avalos as well as 200 Germans, both accustomed to combat in close quarters. Doria, made aware of these additional combatants, borrowed 300 arquebusiers from Lautrec. Moncada and Giustiniani sailed from Posillipo in full view of Doria directly across the Gulf of Naples toward Capri, left the Amalfi Peninsula's Cape Minerva to port, and proceeded east toward Salerno. Filippino Doria was not reluctant to take advantage of the perceived opportunity; his record in significant part one of enhancing the record of distant cousin Andrea.

The Imperial squadron was returning from Salerno when each unit on 28 April 1528 sighted the other a bit west of Salerno's Capo d'Orso. Filippino Doria had Nicolò Lomellini well to seaward with three galleys and placed his remaining five galleys and five lightly armed fustas opposite the centre of the six galley and five fusta/brigantine Imperial formation. As anticipated by Giustiniani, Doria's four galleons were meanwhile becalmed under the perennially windless Amalfi Peninsula well astern. Opposing units appeared relatively equal. In any event, the Imperial flotilla had nowhere to run even should it wish. The two flagships engaged and in succession so too did the remainder of the central cast. Lomellini, however, was no longer well to seaward but rather closing at speed with bow cannons targeting exposed port beams, which collapsed. The Imperial squadron was totally destroyed. Gravely wounded, Giustiniani was captured with other Imperial captains including Alfonso d'Avalos, Ascanio Colonna, and Ferrante Sanseverino. One thousand Imperial infantry died, as did Moncada himself. Half as many Franco-Genovese were lost. The death of 50-year-old Hugo de Moncada, a Catalan of Chiva, Valencia, 4th son of Pedro Moncada, Lord of Aitona (Catalonia), and of Beatrice de Cardona, former *French* soldier, Governor of Spanish Calabria (1506), *Spanish* Admiral and General, Viceroy of Sicily (1509–17), Admiral of Naples (1517), Viceroy of Naples (1527–28), Knight of Jerusalem, Langue of Aragon, Bailiff of Santa Eufemia (1509–28), and Prior of Messina (1527–28) marked the last of a warrior destined to lose every military contest in which he commanded. His death seemed even more tragic for reason of his impotence.[9]

Following a compensation dispute with French King Francis, Andrea Doria in June 1528 switched sides upon expiration of his contract, leveraging Filippino's victory in the Battle of Capo d'Orso in negotiation of a new contract with Charles V by throwing in return of Filippino's captives. Andrea Doria would outlive his celebrated lieutenant, who would never again be given the opportunity to make the pages of history.[10] Brizio Giustiniani would recover from his wounds and live another seven years, during which time he would become father-in-law to yet another Doria, Antonio, increasingly a rival of self-absorbed Andrea. Odet de Foix would soon come down with plague and die in August. Hugo de Moncada was interred in the Church of San Andrea at Amalfi, as fitting a resting place as any other between Catalonia and Rhodes. In accordance with the Emperor's wish, Moncada was succeeded as Viceroy of Naples by Prince of Orange Philibert de Chalon and as Hospitaller Prior of Messina by Signorino della Gattinara, nephew of Grand Chancellor Mercurino Arborio and former Ambassador to the Holy See for the Order of Saints Maurizio and Lazarus. Naples itself would remain Spanish until the coming of Bonaparte.[11]

Prior of Saint-Gilles Pregeant de Bidoux reached Nice with felon-oarsmen donated by King Francis embarked aboard *San Giovanni* commanded by Juanito de Vilatorta. Upon his arrival he accelerated completion of *San Iacomo* and *San Filippo* under construction at nearby Villefranche. The new galleys were soon launched; in assigning oarsmen he apportioned veterans from the three older galleys among all five galleys and filled the balance with felons and new hires from the coast of Genoa.[12]

On 10 July 1528 Magistral Lieutenant Bernardino d'Airasca and Council appointed Commander of Blodès Claude Gimel as interim Captain of Galleys for the purpose of returning the Grand Master to the Convent. The annual caravan of knights nominated by individual langues was embarked. So, too, was Bidoux. Before embarking the Grand Master at Marseille, Gimel was to take the squadron to Corneto and embark Cardinal Lorenzo Campeggio for transport to Marseille. Campeggio, Cardinal Protector of England, was en route to England as one half of a joint commission with Cardinal Thomas Wolsey to decide whether

Henry VIII's marriage to Catherine of Aragon might be annulled. He was also to do what he could to bring about peace between France and England on the one hand and the Holy Roman Empire on the other. News of this latter mission was expected to bring cheer to the Grand Master as he continued to dream of a return to Rhodes. Meanwhile, with famine in France approaching the severity of that in Italy, Luis de Turienzo, Commander of Salamanca in Castile, was ordered to take the old carrack *Santa Maria* to Spanish Oran and to return with a cargo of foodstuffs. At Sicily, Teodoro Saluzzo, commanding the new carrack *Santa Anna* in relief of Pons d'Urrè, was ordered to do the same thing. Diplomat Antonio Bosio, carrying a Papal Brief in support of the recovery of Rhodes, was dispatched to the Emperor's court seeking Empire support for the undertaking.[13] Andrea Doria left the service of France and entered the service of the Empire and obtained supreme command of the Imperial Armada.[14]

With Prior of Saint-Gilles Pregeant de Bidoux embarked as company for Cardinal Campeggio, the squadron of five galleys reached Marseille and put the Cardinal safely ashore. There news was received that the Grand Master, at Lyon for an assembly of senior prelates of the Kingdom of France, had fallen gravely ill and would be unable to make the rendezvous. While returning to Nice the squadron espied a lone Turkish corsair galliot lurking among the Pomègues islands just outside of Marseille. Following a long chase, she was overhauled and taken, to the great satisfaction of the embarked caravan. In accordance with past Hospitaller practice, the galliot's captain and officers were hanged from a spar as a lesson to other infidel corsairs, particularly to renegades. Ninety-five Turks and Moors were sent to Hospitaller oars while 150 Christians were liberated from infidel oars. During conquest of the galliot, however, Pregeant de Bidoux, there only to honour Cardinal Campeggio, was mortally wounded. He succumbed to his wound soon after return to Nice, to the universal grief of all those who knew him and to many who had only known of him. Sixty years of age and most renowned as French Admiral John Perry for galley prosecution in the English Channel of war with England, Pregeant de Bidoux even in occasional defeat emerged from every contest a winner.[15]

With approval of the entire Langue of Provence, according to Bosio, particularly of veteran knights thus by-passed, Bidoux's Priory of Saint-

Gilles, senior dignity short of Grand Master in the entire Order of Jerusalem, was conferred on Jacques de Manas, until that day never appearing in Bosio's *History*, not known to be a veteran of the Great Siege of Rhodes, and never before having earned a Grand Cross through advancement. This mysterious elevation may have had to do with another Manas assignment as Commander of Salier, 4km from Saint-Gilles. Or it may have been that Manas's advancement opportunities had been side-tracked by Bidoux's sudden 1514 positioning at the top of Provence's advancement ladder. Perhaps only a little less confounding, Manas would not again be mentioned in Bosio's *History* until his 1535 death and succession as Prior of Saint-Gilles. Meanwhile, the Bailiwick of Lango also vacated by the death of Pregeant de Bidoux, with attendant Grand Cross, was conferred on Jacques de Bourbon, diarist of the Great Siege of Rhodes. Prior of Champagne Jacques d'Aimer died at about the same time and was succeeded by Jacques de Sainte-Maure, who was in turn succeeded as Bailiff of the Morea by Joachim de Saint-Simon. The latter was in turn succeeded as Treasurer by Jean d'Aubin de Malicorne. Antonio Bosio, diplomat-for-the-ages, returned from discussions with Charles V not with a promise of support for the reconquest of Rhodes, but rather with a modified offer for cession of Malta, Gozo, and Tripoli, which suggested Hospitaller reservations might soon be overcome.[16]

The Grand Master returned from his convalescence at Lyon to the Convent at Nice on 12 December 1528. Pope Clement VII, meanwhile, preached Crusade against infidels and asked all parties to prepare over the winter and to be ready in May 1529. Given the Pope's activism and intermediary activities between the Order of Jerusalem and the Emperor, 20-year-old Prior of Rome Bernardo Salviati, Pope Clement's nephew by his sister, was appointed the Order's Procurator-General at Rome and Resident Ambassador to the Holy See.[17]

The Pope intended contributing two of his own five galleys to a May expedition secretly dedicated to the recovery of Rhodes, and requested the Grand Master gather all responsions due from priories and commanderies. For this reason the Grand Master dispatched Georg Schilling to the Priory of Germany and Luis de Andújar to the Priory of Castile, both priories usually tardy in their payment of responsions. Schilling and Andújar carried with them a Papal Brief to the Emperor, expected to be in one or the other country, outlining a superficial plan for the Order to be at sea the entire month of May investigating Malta, and a secret plan for the recovery of Rhodes. The Brief contemplated a safe-conduct from Andrea Doria for all Papal and Hospitaller vessels at sea during the summer plus uninhibited use of the ports of Sardinia, Sicily, and Naples. Others carried summonses to remote corners of the Hospitaller world seeking not just responsions but Hospitallers, as well.[18]

The Pope addressed a secret letter to Metropolitan Euphemios of Rhodes dated 14 April to be delivered by Antonio Bosio in person informing the Metropolitan of plans to retake the island in the summer. Bosio carried a separate public plan as well. The Grand Master considered the secret plan difficult of accomplishment, relocating the Hospital and its followers not 100 or 200 miles up or down a coast but almost half the length of the Mediterranean. Secrecy, too, was a problem. And resentment of Spanish langues suspicious of the overt plan. And the trial and tribulation for 4,000 noncombatant refugees. And feeding so many mouths on the move. One week short of eight months to come the other way six years earlier, and once there doing that which took Suleiman six months. But he could not forget what had once been.[19]

Kheir-ed-Din Barbarossa, Ottoman Sancakbey or Governor of Algiers, compelled surrender of the Penon de Algiers following a fifteen-day bombardment in May 1529. Built by Pedro de Navarro in 1510 on an islet in a roadstead loosely termed the city's harbour, the Penon had for those nineteen years prevented commercial shipping from approaching any nearer than one mile from the city. The commanding officer, Martín de Vargas, was among fifty-three survivors of the 200-man garrison, all wounded. Two weeks after the fall of the Penon, nine Spanish carracks appeared carrying troops and munitions to succour the garrison. The squadron, commanded by Jorge Ruiz de Alarçon, attempted to return to Spain but was promptly assailed by Barbarossa's Algiers Guard. These captured the entire convoy. There were 2,700 prisoners who would increase the number of those employed in the Algiers public works construction programme. Taken with the convoy was a large quantity of munitions, cannon, and provender. Barbarossa sent to Sultan Suleiman as a personal gift several cannon and the most handsome prisoners.[20]

Martin de Vargas was in August accused of organising a revolt on the part of 7,000 Christian oarsmen and other captives confined in the city's baths and was executed. These same captives were utilised for the two succeeding years to construct a seawall of more than 200m joining the islet to the mainland so that Algiers would for the first time in history be provided with a somewhat secure harbour.[21]

Prior of France Pierre de Cluis had long since been commended for bravery during the 1480 Ottoman Siege of Rhodes. He had also long since reached his senility. Nevertheless refusing to retire, the Priory remained in his unstable hands. Following a series of complaints concerning his conduct, Grand Master and Council in May 1529 appointed Bailiff of Lango Jacques de Bourbon his administrative assistant. Bourbon did his duty with a deference the Prior could appreciate even in his senility.[22]

Some agitation arose within the Sacred Council when the Commandery of l'Aumusse became available within the Priory of Auvergne. Prior of the Church Pons Laurenzin demanded the Commandery by virtue of the Church's prioral seniority. Emery de Mesnil de Maupas, to whom the commandery had preliminarily been assigned, was forced by the Council to step aside. Prior of Catalonia Ramón Marquet, a 1522 last-minute Ambassadeur Extraordinaire to the Ottoman Porte in Constantinople, died in June 1529 of unreported cause and was succeeded by Francisco de Castillo, who in turn was succeeded as Bailiff of Mallorca by Miguel Ferrer.[23]

The dignity of Bailiff of the Morea was vacated by the death of Joachim de Saint-Simon, who was succeeded by Jean d'Aubin de Malicorne. Aubin in turn was succeeded as Treasurer by Jerome d'Humières. Because Prior of Saint-Gilles Jacques de Manas had leapfrogged Grand Commander Tristan de Sales, the latter was assigned a pension of 600 gold scudos per year, Sales renouncing the dignity of Grand Commander to which Raymond Ricard the Younger succeeded. He renounced in turn the Bailiwick of Manosque to which Jean de Boniface succeeded. The Grand Master, meanwhile, readied the Hospitaller Armada for sea. The two carracks had returned from Oran full of foodstuffs and munitions. The Galleon of the Religion had arrived from Cartagena full of Spanish Hospitallers. The ship belonging to Giovan Antonio Bonaldi had arrived from Marseille with French Hospitallers, while many more French had come in by land. Many French, hearing of the overt plan to proceed to Malta objected, citing a French position at the last Chapter General. These feared the Pope was making them subjects of the Emperor, but nevertheless obeyed their commanders. At the last minute the Pope himself bowed out, claiming each of his six galleys was allocated to the transport of Cardinals moving here and there.[24]

On 18 June 1529 four of the Order's five galleys departed Nice under the command of Marshal Gabriel du Chief with orders to take course for the Freo Channel between Malta and Gozo by way of Corsica, Sardinia, and Trapani, Sicily, alert for infidel activity of which the full armada should be aware.

Early in July Andrea Doria's armada bound from Barcelona to Genoa with Emperor Charles V embarked passed Nice. Hospitaller Juan de Bozmediano of León, the Order's resident ambassador at the Imperial Court, was put ashore to meet with the Grand Master. The Emperor wished to confirm Hospitaller possession of all of its priories and commanderies in the Kingdom of Naples, some of which had been despoiled by encamped armies. Bozmediano also reported that the Governor of Brindisi had been directed to release a valuable prize taken by a brigantine of the Religion commanded by non-Hospitaller Benedetto Ruggiero, confiscated by port authorities in contravention of the Emperor's safe-conduct. Meanwhile, the Order's armada was ready for sea: the carracks *Santa Anna* and *Santa Maria*, the ship *Marieta di Rodi*, Bonaldi's own ship, three well-armed cargo ships furnished with additional artillery and all other things necessary hired at Villefranche, the galley *San Filippo* commanded by Archambault de Luynes, and two brigantines, one commanded by Hospitaller Geronimo Pegulla and the other by non-Hospitaller Bernardo Scotto of Genoa. Seven hundred hired Gascons were embarked, while ten troops of Italian soldiery were waiting at Augusta. The people of Rhodes at Nice, too, soldiers, seamen, and Hospitallers of the Convent. Altogether about 4,000 combatants and an equal number of non-combatants. The armada sailed from Nice on 17 July 1529 and from Villefranche one day later.[25]

Hindered by little wind and then by adverse wind, the Hospitaller armada did not reach Trapani on the western end of Sicily until 10 August. At Trapani the armada found the four galleys sent on ahead in mid-June. These had failed to proceed further for fear of much-larger corsair squadrons infesting the coast of Sicily. For this reason the Grand Master altered the armada's destination from Freo, a corsair watering hole, to the main port at Malta called Grand Harbour, which was reached on 26 August. Without debarking, the Grand Master dispatched one of the two brigantines to take station at Cape Passero, the south-eastern extremity of Sicily, to look out for Antonio Bosio returning from Rhodes. Within a few days, Bosio was intercepted and brought to Malta. He had nothing good to report. All prior arrangements had been disrupted. Not because parties to the arrangements had betrayed those arrangements but because the corsair Zoppo, who had transported emissaries of Egypt's Ahmed Pasha to Rome in 1524, had become suspicious of Hospitaller interest. The enemy's Rhodes Guard had been reinforced and sympathetic janissaries removed. Suspects had been hunted down, tortured, and killed, most of them innocent. Only with great difficulty and at considerable peril was Bosio even able to reach and then to leave the City of Rhodes. Having heard Bosio's report in Council, Grand Master and Council with great sadness and disappointment abandoned all hope of returning to Rhodes and would so inform Pope Clement VII and Emperor Charles V by letter. These letters refer to Bosio as a knight, thus necessarily knighted at Malta.[26]

The Hospitaller armada did not depart Malta until 13 September 1529, thus leaving ample opportunity for Hospitaller decision makers to explore their future home. From Malta the armada headed north to Augusta 100 nautical miles distant, arriving on the 15th. The Hospitallers were looking for a winter home for themselves and for their followers, and it is from Augusta that letters were addressed to Pope and Emperor and at Augusta that Italian soldiery were paid off. The Grand Master's nephew Louis de Tinteville and, again, Antonio Bosio were dispatched to the Courts of England and France with similar messages. Prior to his departure Bosio broached to the Grand Master yet another possible home, this one the fortress town of Modon (modern Methoni) at the south-west corner of the Morea (Peloponnese). To Bosio, Modone (Italian) or Modon (Venetian Italian) represented a stepping stone on the way back to Rhodes. Formerly Venetian and then Ottoman, Bosio had Greek acquaintances willing to help in its recapture. According to Bosio, the galleys and a single grippo for transport and support would be sufficient to wrest Modon from the Ottomans. While the Grand Master's interest was tweaked, for the time being he was settled on Malta; anything else would be unfair to the refugees in his train.[27]

At a Council meeting convened on board the grand carrack *Santa Anna* Hugo de Copons was appointed Draper succeeding the deceased Gaspar

Glior. Learning the Emperor was again at Genoa to finally be crowned by the Pope at Bologna, the aforementioned ambassadors Louis de Tinteville and Antonio Bosio were redirected to represent the Convent at the Coronation in the company of Prior of Rome Bernardo Salviati. They were to also communicate to the Pope the Convent's interest in Modon. Reflecting the absence of adequate winter accommodation at Augusta, the armada on 7 October moved 7 miles south to Syracuse, where everyone but oarsmen and skeleton crews was put ashore and assigned housing with the infirmary settled in the municipal palace. At the request of the Emperor in the person of Viceroy of Sicily Ettore Pignatelli e Caraffa, 1st Duke of Monteleone, the galleys were to join an Imperial Armada searching for Sinan of Smyrna, then terrorising the coast of Sicily with a large number of fustas. For this undertaking Hugo de Copons was appointed Captain of Galleys. The Order had five galleys, three brought from Rhodes, *Santa Maria* then the capitana, *Santa Caterina*, and *San Giovanni*, plus the new galleys *San Iacomo* and *San Filippo*. The squadron under Copons' command departed Syracuse on 27 October 1529 bound for Messina, where it would receive its instructions. From Messina, though, the squadron was not ordered to join a hunt for Sinan but rather to proceed to Palermo and there embark the person and household of Cardinal Enrique de Cardona y Enríquez and with the Galley Squadron of Sicily to transport all of them to Naples. From Naples the Hospitaller squadron's five galleys alone were to proceed north to Monte Argentario and the island of Giannutri in Tuscany before returning to Syracuse, that is, in winter weather the squadron was to log 125 nautical miles from Syracuse to Palermo, another 150nm from Palermo to Naples, yet 200nm more to Monte Argentario, plus an additional 350nm to return to Syracuse by way of Giannutri. That was a total of 825 nautical miles. During the galley squadron's excursion it caught no sight of the Kheir-ed-Din Barbarossa lieutenant, who with his smaller fustas had sensibly returned to Djerba for the winter months.

Barbarossa lieutenant Aydin Caramano that autumn of 1529, however, prowled the western Mediterranean with eleven oared galliots, fustas and brigantines. Having captured three merchant vessels, this Coptic Christian native of Smyrna was informed that at Oliva, a small port on the coast of Valencia, many Moriscos forced to abjure their faith in favour of Christianity, vassals of the Conde (Count) de Oliva, were ready to pay large sums to escape Spain. Off Oliva, Aydin embarked at night 200 Morisco families and sailed in the direction of Formentera. Eight Spanish galleys returning from transporting Emperor Charles V to his February 1530 coronation at Bologna soon appeared off Oliva where they were made aware of developments. Under command of Rodrigo Portundo, General of Spanish Galleys, these turned in pursuit toward the Balearic Islands. Aware of the pursuit, Aydin anchored his refugee-laden merchantmen at Isla de Espalmador just north of Formentera and prepared to fight. Eager to earn a 10,000 ducat reward for the return of the Moriscos, the Spanish admiral found himself too far ahead of the rest of his squadron. The corsairs pounced; galliots of Hassan Çelebi and Suleiman Reis invested Portundo's capitana, the first upon a flank, the second at his prow. Portundo was killed and his galley overrun. Aydin, meanwhile, had the better of Juan Biscaglino's galley, while Spanish corsair Mateo Sanchez fell to Saba Reis. The galley of son Domingo Portundo succumbed, the son a captive. In all, seven of eight Spanish galleys were captured, one escaping, with those captured towed to Algiers. Almost a thousand Spaniards were taken captive and more than fifteen hundred Muslim oarsmen were liberated. The Spanish admiral's Standard was sent to the Sultan in Constantinople together with his son. With this victory Aydin earned the appellation *Caza Diablo* or *Cacciadiavoli* or Hunting Devil.[28]

The Hospitaller Order had a need to remove the 700 hired Gascons from its payroll, and so in late autumn 1529 loaded the Gascons aboard the Galleon of the Religion commanded by Giovan Battista Schiattese for transport to Marseille. While en route the galleon encountered two large infidel galliots, which pretended to be merchantmen without artillery. Fooling no one, on approach the galliots were greeted by a tempest of arquebus rounds, which left them totally harmless, much to the distress of 700 Gascons eager for hand-to-hand combat. The engagement was not entirely successful, however, as Schiattesi had hoped to capture the enemy vessels, but the oar-powered Turks turned tail upwind and could not be caught by a sailing vessel.[29]

Meeting in January 1530 with Pope Clement VII concerning matters he had been charged with as ambassador, Antonio Bosio was appointed the Pope's secretary for confidential matters. With another stroke of the pen Bosio was also appointed Bailiff of Santo Stefano entitled to wear the

Grand Cross, in both cases succeeding the deceased Francesco di Caymi. The Pope then penned a letter of explanation to the Grand Master and Council. It was unlikely, however, that anyone at the Convent would object other than the Grand Master, who was thus deprived of an extension to his right arm.

At about this time the Grand Master received letters from Nicholas, Count of Salm, and from Philip of the Palatinate of the Rhine and Prince-Bishop of Freising, the former the principal Imperial commander at the successful defence of Suleiman's Siege of Vienna in the autumn of 1529, and the latter brother of Louis V, Count Palatine of the Rhine. These letters extolled contributions to the successful defence by German Hospitallers, including Prior of Germany Johann von Hattstein, Prior of Bohemia Johann III von Rosenberg, and many others. Among the latter was Wolfgang Hoder, who sortied through siege lines with a small group to destroy enemy artillery but with great loss of life. In doing so he stumbled upon a mining operation likely to bring down a section of the city's wall. Because of this discovery listening devices like those developed at Rhodes by Martinengo were put in place and the enemy mines countermined.[30]

The Squadron's five galleys under Hugo de Copons returned to Syracuse in February 1530. Copons reported to the Council that during the Hospitaller squadron's return it proceeded between the Aeolian islands of Vulcano and Lipari north of Sicily, where it first captured the galliot of Kara Saime Reis. From captives Copons learned a second galliot, that of Kara Mustafa, was sailing in company with the first. He also obtained the recognition signal used between the two galliots, manned the captured galliot with a complement of knights and soldiers, and with it surprised and captured the galliot of Kara Mustafa. A few less than three hundred Christian slaves were liberated, many of them captured with Bailiff of Lyon Jean de Laurè while en route to France in the summer of 1527, others captured not much later on board a brigantine of the Order carrying a tapestry of the Conventual Church of Saint John to Nice. Held for ransom, Laurè and a part of the tapestry had soon been recovered. Not so those who had been enslaved. The two corsair captains were not instantly hanged by their captors because they had not behaved cruelly upon capture of the Order's brigantine; neither were they sent to the oars with the other 160 Turks and Moors captured in the twin actions. Because the two corsair captains were natural Turks and not renegades, they were held for ransom or exchange. Upon the Squadron's February return to Syracuse there had been near disbelief and rejoicing among numerous reunited families.

Soon the Squadron's five galleys under Copons again proceeded to Messina and towed in the absence of wind to Syracuse an English vessel, aboard which Preceptor of Beverley and Temple Bruer John Sutton had escorted from London nineteeen pieces of large beautifully wrought bronze artillery and 1,023 iron cannon balls donated to Grand Master Philippe de l'Isle-Adam by King Henry VIII. These cannon would be mounted at Tripoli following transfer of sovereignty later in the year.[31]

In March 1530 Emperor Charles V as King Charles I of Spain and Sicily granted the Order of Jerusalem the islands of Malta and Gozo plus the North African port of Tripoli 'in perpetual, noble, full and free enfeoffment', binding the Order only to annual payment to Charles or his successors as King of Sicily of a hawk or a falcon on All Saints Day. Importantly, the grant clearly released the Order from any form of military service other than pursuit of the Order's mission. The document containing the grant was signed by the Emperor at Castelfranco Veneto near Treviso while en route to Germany and was placed in the care of Antonio Bosio who so importantly contributed to its birth. Near Bologna, while speeding to the Grand Master at Syracuse, Bosio's carriage suddenly overturned and he was hit on the head. To the deep sorrow of Pope Clement VII, of Emperor Charles V, of King Francis, and even of King Henry VIII, of the entire Convent, but especially of Grand Master Philippe Villiers de l'Isle-Adam, Antonio Bosio regained consciousness only long enough to request that Yannis Maria Stratigopolos of Rhodes be received into the Order of Jerusalem as a knight. Only 35 years of age, he then died almost immediately. With his passing went a bit of the heart of the Order of Jerusalem. In extraordinary recognition of his accomplishments, Antonio Bosio was interred at the Vatican.[32]

Over the six months since arrival at Syracuse the Hospitaller infirmary housed in the municipal palace had found on its doorstep at night sixty new-born infants abandoned by single mothers. With some of its remaining heart the Order had then employed the same mothers to nurture their own babies. When departing Syracuse for its new home at Malta the Order would bestow on these single mothers a dowry sufficient to provide for their future. Overseeing this programme were Commanders Dom Diogo d'Almeida the Younger of Almeida, Portugal, and Niccolò Pazzi of Florence.[33]

In April 1530 the Order's acceptance of the Emperor's grant was dispatched in the hands of Yannis Maria Stratigopolos. Not yet a Hospitaller, he was diplomatic successor to Antonio Bosio and would soon be received into the Order as 'le chevalier Grec'. Stratigopolos departed Syracuse with the Galley Squadron commanded by Hugo de Copons exiting on patrol. Also departing Syracuse was the newer carrack *Santa Anna* commanded by Emery des Reaulx delivered at Nice in 1523 and not the carrack *Santa Maria* captured from Egyptians in 1507. Bound for Barcelona and Marseille to return foodstuffs and munitions acquired for the aborted siege of Rhodes no longer needed, *Santa Anna* was a huge vessel of six decks, three masts, three sails on the mainmast, and fifty bronze cannon; a floating fortress. Embarked were Juan de Homedes, Bailiff of Caspe, and Konrad von Schwalbach, Grand Bailiff of Germany, to audit assets of the Religion at those destinations. *Santa Anna* was then ordered to Genoa to encumber certain amounts deposited in Genoa's Bank of Saint George. Reaulx was ordered during his return to Syracuse to embark Hospitaller Don Juan of Aragon in all honour and comfort. An illegitimate son of the influential Alfonso, Duke of Luna, Don Juan years earlier had been appointed Castellan of Amposta at Zaragosa by his Hospitaller and Castellan (1506–12) grandfather of the same name. Commanders and knights of the Castellania, however, rebelled against the appointment and elected the aforesaid Juan de Homedes, who declined the position. Since that time appointment of Castellans appears to have been a prerogative of Zaragosan nobility of which the earlier Don Juan of Aragon and Alfonso, Duke of Luna, had been the most prominent. At the Convent Grand Master and Council appointed Muzio Costanzo of the Langue of Italy to succeed Antonio Bosio as Bailiff of Santo Stefano.[34]

Hugo de Copons and the Galley Squadron scoured mainland Italian coasts of Calabria and Basilicata (which adjoins Calabria on both coasts) into Campania on the Tyrrhenian side. At Cape Palinuro in southern Campania a fast corsair galley-sottile was sighted that had been pillaging coastal communities. She was pursued from early morning until Vespers, when she was overhauled and invested by *San Filippo*, the fastest galley in the squadron commanded by Pietro Vasco of Turin. The enemy galley was taken, but only after an obstinate defence. Following the arrival of Copons and the other four galleys, corsair skipper Memi Reis, an Albanian renegade and lieutenant of Kheir-ed-Din Barbarossa, was hanged from a capitana spar. Seventy-five native Turks were enslaved while, in accordance with Hospitaller practice to not pardon corsairs who had abjured Christianity, twenty-five more renegades were executed. In addition to about 200 Christians liberated from corsair oars were several merchants of Salerno only recently captured. The squadron returned to Syracuse on 23 May with the captured galley in tow. Yannis Maria Stratigopolos embarked, returning from his mission to Pope Clement VII in Rome having delivered the Order's acceptance of the Emperor's grant of Malta, Gozo, and Tripoli. The following day Bailiff of Manosque Jean de Boniface was dispatched with Copons and the squadron to Messina and the Viceregal Court of Ettore Pignatelli, where the two ambassadors made arrangements to speed the transfer of sovereignty. This took place with all due formality on 29 May 1530 at the Royal Palace of the City of Messina.[34]

The two aforementioned ambassadors together with representatives of the Viceroy of Sicily proceeded to Malta aboard both the galley capitana *San Giovanni* and *San Filippo* where a second transfer of sovereignty was effected in the presence of representatives of residents of Malta, Gozo, and Tripoli, as well as representatives of the University of Malta. Hospitaller Aurelio Bottigella of Pavia was appointed interim Governor and Captain at Arms of Malta, while Hospitaller Augustino di Ventimiglia of Palermo was appointed Bottigella's lieutenant. Flemish Hospitaller Pierre Pitoys of the Langue of France was appointed Castellan of Castle Saint Angelo with a squad of soldiers at his command. Similarly, Commander of Aliaga Gaspar de Sanguesa of the Priory of Navarre was appointed the Order's first Governor of Tripoli with Commander of Ansemil Bernardino Machado of the Langue of Castile his lieutenant and Commander of Turin Paolo Simeoni a senior advisor. These were supported by the galleys *San Iacomo* and *Santa Caterina* with caravans of knights embarked as well as by the Galleonetto of the Religion *Il Siciliano* full of foodstuffs and munitions. One of the caravan knights was William Weston's nephew Thomas Dingley who in 1539 would, without trial, be condemned by

Parliament of treason for opposition to Royal church policy and beheaded in the Tower of London.[35] He is a martyr of the Roman Catholic Church.

Remaining galleys of the squadron returned to Syracuse in mid-July 1530. Shortly thereafter the Grand Master's nephew Louis de Tinteville, Standard Bearer at the Great Siege of Rhodes, was dispatched as ambassador to Kings Francis of France and Henry VIII of England to inform those monarchs of developments and of Hospitaller needs such as artillery and associated munitions to properly fortify Castle Saint Angelo at Malta. Luis de Andujar was similarly dispatched to King John III of Portugal and to various princes of Spain. The old Carrack of the Religion *Santa Maria* at that time commanded by Catalan Joan de Vilatorta was dispatched to various destinations for the acquisition of timber, iron, and mortar for construction or rehabilitation of living quarters and other structures at Malta. Employment of stone masons, carpenters, and blacksmiths was the responsibility of Portuguese Hospitaller Engineer and Superintendent of Construction Serving Brother Diogo Peres de Malveira. He was to be assisted by Rhodean Nicolo Flevari. Simone Bonanno, the Order's Receiver at Licata, was charged with acquisition of grain and other foodstuffs as well as of additional mortar. He had at his disposition the Small Galleon *Il Siciliano* as well as a number of lesser vessels. To apprise Emperor Charles V of the state of disrepair of the various presidios and to seek confirmation of duty-free grain shipments, Commander Don Luis de Lara of a Castilian family prominent throughout Spain and in the New World was dispatched to the Emperor in Germany.[36]

In Germany the Emperor had convened the Diet of Augsburg in June 1530 to address Lutheran matters and to gather support for the Emperor's brother Ferdinand, King of Bohemia and Hungary threatened by Ottoman Sultan Suleiman. The Diet was the beginning of reconciliation between Catholics and Protestants that would conclude with the Peace of Augsburg in 1555 formally recognising Protestantism as a legitimate religion of the Empire. Lara, however, failed to confirm with the Emperor annual duty-free shipments of 6,000 salme of grain, about 1,000 ordinary tons, necessary for subsistence of the people of Malta and Gozo.[37]

Improvement of fortifications and facilities at Tripoli was estimated to cost 25,000 Rhodian gold scudos equivalent to florins or Venetian ducats. Prior of Pisa Lodovico dal Pozzo, future Grand Master Pierino del Ponte, Commander of Trinquetaille Robert de Rocquemartine, and Commander of Genoa Francesco Salvago were deputised to identify financing. Many other initiatives were also undertaken to ready Malta, Gozo, and Tripoli for arrival of the Convent. In August 1530 there were two very unfortunate developments. On the 23rd of the month Hospitaller vessels laden with supplies incident to relocation of the Convent, together with escorting galleys, were assailed by a violent storm in the vicinity of Licata, Sicily. The galley *San Iacomo*, commanded by Battista della Rovere, was forced onto the rocks near Forgia di Santa Croce (modern Spiaggia Baia Rio Forgia). All of the oarsmen and some of the crew were lost. Of equipment only the artillery was recovered. Escorted vessels and the other four galleys miraculously survived. The second untoward development had to do with succession to the Sicilian Bailiwick of Santa Eufemia recently assigned to future Grand Master Pierino del Ponte rather than to Fabrizio Pignatello, grand-nephew of Viceroy of Sicily Ettore Pignatello. While forewarned by Simone Bonanno, the Order's Receiver in Sicily, of the Viceroy's wishes in the matter, Grand Master and Council failed to heed the warning and selected Del Ponte as the stronger candidate. This decision would have short and long-term repercussions. The first developed almost immediately. Viceroy Pignatello attempted to levy duty on a shipment of grain to Malta, and the Order refused to pay, threatening to back out of its agreement to assume sovereignty of the islands. Similarly, Hospitaller currency was refused in a coincident transaction, the Viceroy claiming only Empire currency was good within the Empire, the last untrue. These two matters in the Grand Master's view were deal-breakers.[38]

On 9 October 1530 the Grand Master addressed letters to both Pope and Emperor renouncing the Order's acceptance of the Imperial grant. (These letters were written on parchment in Latin, lingua franca among European states excepting the Ottoman Empire where the lingua franca was Greek.) Almost immediately Yannis Maria Stratigopolos was dispatched to the Venetian island of Zante aboard the fusta of Rhodiot Leonardo Miriti to rendezvous with Rhodiot Stefi Marchetto. Together they proceeded in disguise to Modon, where both met former Bosio collaborators who assured Stratigopolos they were prepared to open the gates to Hospitallers. Only the intercession of Pope Clement in the person of Bernardo Salviati, the Order's ambassador to Rome, interrupted planning for a night assault on Modon. Salviati convinced the Emperor of the reasonableness of the Grand Master's position. Residents of barren Malta should have the same privileges as before the change of sovereignty, including the right to 6,000 salme of duty-free grain each year. Salviati further observed that all sovereign entities had the right to coin their own currencies, a right enjoyed by the Hospitallers for hundreds of years. And, he added, the Hospitaller Priory of Germany was already using Hospitaller coinage in the Empire. The Emperor agreed. Salviati thus resolved duty and currency matters in favour of the Order. He as well obtained a revised grant incorporating these two new provisions.

Chapter III

Phillipe de Villiers de l'Isle-Adam 1530–34

On 20 October 1530 the old carrack *Santa Maria* at Malta, with provisions and munitions, was lying in the harbour between the peninsula of Birgu and the adjacent peninsula later called Senglea. She had three anchors ahead and four warps ashore in what is today called a Mediterranean moor, her stern to Birgu. All of a sudden she was hit by a not-unexpected torrential storm blowing from the northwest almost directly into the harbour. Tossing in disturbed harbour waters she pulled her anchors. The strain on her warps then began to force the ship broadside to the shore. Those lines were cut and dragging her anchors, she grounded twice before finally grounding stern-to the beach at the inner end of the harbour. A frantic search of the underwater hull revealed no more than bilge and rain water. She appeared to have survived. Refloated later on an easterly wind which filled her sails, her underwater hull was indeed undamaged. It was a good piece of work by her skipper Juan de Vilatorta. During the same storm four Maltese fustas in the same port had been swamped and went to the bottom. The carrack's survival was taken by the Grand Master to be a sign from God and he ordered Licata Receiver Simone Bonanno to present a falcon to the Viceroy on All Saints Day, 1 November, as required by the grant ceding the islands and Tripoli. He also ordered embarkation of Convent and Rhodian followers not for Modon but for Malta.[1]

During the final Council meeting at Syracuse, Ercole di None of Turin was appointed Admiral in succession of the deceased Emanuele d'Airasca of Turin. (The two preceding admirals had also been natives of Turin.) Sacred relics were loaded aboard the galley *Santa Croce* while the Grand Master, Council, and Knights of the Grand Cross reached Malta on 26 October on board the new carrack. They were escorted by *Santa Croce,* commanded by Bault de Luynes, and *San Giovanni,* commanded by Philippe Girault du Broc. Sailing in company was the galliot commanded by Filippo Mazza of Messina, likely one of those captured by the galleys in January. So, too, sailing in company was the Galley Squadron's brigantine. Catching a moderate north-westerly wind in the Malta Channel they covered the 90 nautical miles to Malta in a full day, arriving two hours after daybreak. At Malta l'Isle-Adam took possession of his new fief. At this date the island was nothing but an arid rock with the Castle of St. Angelo for its only protection, and a few houses called the Bourg (Birgu) grouped at the landward end of the Castle now called Fort St. Angelo. In the castle itself one gun and two falconets were the port's only defence. The capital of the island, established by Greeks in 1404 BC and re-named Notabile by King Alphonso the Magnanimous of Aragon twenty-eight centuries later, lay in the centre of the island surrounded by feeble fortifications. Several small villages were scattered here and there over the island. The magnificence of Grand Harbour was the island's only redeeming feature.

Disaffection soon rose among the Convent given the uninviting appearance of their surroundings. But l'Isle-Adam, although not averse to removing his Order to a location more favourable than Malta, soon perceived the advantages the island could offer if properly fortified. Having assumed sovereignty over the islands of Malta and Gozo, he fixed his temporary residence in the Castle and established the Convent of the Order in the Bourg, which was in a very short time enclosed by a line of entrenchments for protection of the new Hospital and of the Convent itself. The Grand Master next turned to fortifying the capital of the island (Notabile, the name later changed to Mdina), where he made his solemn entry on 13 November.[2] Accordingly the old fortifications were restored and the city strongly garrisoned. The island of Gozo was entrusted to the care of a Governor, and its defence confided to a company of hired infantry.[3]

Having completed his tour in command of the galley squadron, Hugo de Copons was at Papal suggestion succeeded as Captain of Galleys by 22-year-old Papal nephew and Prior of Rome Bernardo Salviati (and temporarily in the absence of Salviati by Admiral Ercole di None). Copons requested of the Council time to take a cure for an unspecified indisposition, a request duly granted. Meanwhile, None was ordered to immediately take the squadron to Messina and Palermo for winter upkeep. Understanding, however, that Naples was free of plague, he circumnavigated Sicily and proceeded to that city, all the while alert for Barbarossa or Sinan of Smyrna and their large armadas.[4]

The Spanish langues of Aragon and Castile which heretofore had shared a single auberge found themselves too numerous for Malta quarters and split into two auberges, one for Aragon, Catalonia, and Navarre, the other for Castile, León, and Portugal. These auberges provided both living and dining spaces. Many knights took up private living quarters, though few dined anywhere but at the auberge. Meanwhile, at Tripoli Governor Gaspar Sanguesa was having trouble with Moors from Tagiora (modern Tajura) 9 miles to the east. On the west almost at Tripoli's gates were the Moors of Zanzor (modern Zanzur) with whom the Hospitallers had reached an accommodation involving payment of an insignificant amount of tribute, resulting in active buying and selling between the parties. Not so the Moors of Tagiora, who were demanding much larger tribute and who were a constant presence among the sand dunes to the east kidnapping careless minions of the Sheik of Zanzor. And worse. Jean d'Arlè, a young knight of the Langue of France, was the first Hospitaller fatality at Tripoli, punctured by a poisoned assegai spear. Having relocated with the Convent to Malta, Commander of Bellechassagne and former Captain of Galleys Jean de Rivière became the first Hospitaller fatality at Malta, dying before his time at year-end presumably a victim of disease.[4]

On 5 January 1531 Francesco Nibbia returned to Malta from Rome with advice Pope Clement VII, embracing Hospitaller fortunes more strongly than ever had dispatched Prior of Rome Bernardo Salviati to Aquisgrana (modern Aachen) in Flanders, where the Emperor had retired following the Diet of Augsburg. Salviati was to represent the Order as Ambassador at the coronation of the Emperor's brother Ferdinand as King of the Romans. As King of the Romans, Ferdinand became the Empire's heir apparent. Nibbia also brought with him to Malta a Papal Brief dated 1 October 1530 by which the Order and its agents might treat with Moors of Africa without risk of excommunication. Arriving with the brigantine transporting Nibbia to Malta was news of the death of Aymar (or Adhèmar) du Puy (the Younger), Prior of Auvergne since the 1517 death of Jean Dadeù. Marshal Gabriel du Chief was appointed his successor, while Commander Jean de Château-Arnauld succeeded to the dignity of Marshal. News was also received of the death in August of Bailiff of Eagle Alban Pole. Turcopolier John Babington was appointed his successor, while Clement West succeeded to the dignity of Turcopolier. Not long afterward the newer carrack *Santa Anna* returned to Malta from Genoa and Marseille with a large amount of needed coin as well as a cargo of fabrics and clothing. Also on board were many French commanders and other knights, some who had come to see the Convent's new home and others who had come for caravan service. With them was Bailiff of the Morea and Siege veteran Jean d'Aubin de Malicorne.[5]

News was received of the death of Draper Hugo de Copons at an unreported venue of unreported cause. A Catalan, Hugo de Copons had been the senior knight of Aragon without rank mustering in May 1522 for the Great Siege of Rhodes. When asking for a break in service in 1530 he must have suspected his end was near and likely returned to his roots at Copons, Catalonia, 85km north-west of Barcelona. He was succeeded as Draper by Fernando Diaz. Diaz soon retired to the Monastery of San Geronimo, however, and was succeeded as Draper by Bautista de Vilaragut (Baptista de Vilagut in Catalan). Likewise dying of unreported cause was Bailiff of Boveda Inigo Lope de Ayala, who with Copons were justice-administering wardens during the Siege of Rhodes, assignments reflecting their advancing ages. Francisco de Sarria of Galicia was appointed Ayala's successor. Late in the month the Grand Master was informed from Tripoli of the death early in the month of Muley Muhammad, King of the Hafsid Berber Kingdom of Tunis and an ally of Emperor Charles V. It is said the King was poisoned by a concubine, Leleti Gesia, mother of heir apparent Muley Hassan. Muley Hassan immediately had twenty-two of his twenty-three half-brothers blinded, and dispatched a eunuch confidant, Gioan Rabti, as Berber Governor of Tripoli including Tagiora.[6]

Ercole di None, Admiral and acting Captain of Galleys, in April returned to Malta from Naples with the three galleys wintering there, *Santa Croce* commanded by None himself, *San Filippo* commanded by Bault de Luynes, and *San Giovanni* commanded by Philippe Girault du Broc. They entered port with a galliot in tow, one of two sailing in company captured by the combined Squadrons of Malta and Sicily near the Aeolian island of Salina. About three hundred Christians had been freed from the oars of these galliots and set at liberty in Sicily while natural Turks captured were sent to the oars of those galleys needing them. Officers and renegades were hanged. Arriving with the galleys was

Hospitaller Don Juan of Aragon, son of Alfonso Duke of Luna, with a ratified accord between knights and brothers of Aragon on the one hand and Bailiff of Caspe Juan de Homedes on the other acknowledging the Order's right to appoint Castellans of Amposta at Zaragosa. With this accomplishment Homedes requested and received permission to return to Spain, and for that purpose boarded the new carrack *Santa Anna* bound for Toulon under command of Emery des Reaulx. This would be Reaulx's final carrack command. At Toulon he would be succeeded in command of *Santa Anna* by François de Toucheboeuf of the Langue of Provence. The old 1,500 metric ton carrack *Santa Maria* was meanwhile converted into a floating storeship.[7]

Prior of Rome Bernardo Salviati embarked aboard one of six Andrea Doria galleys bound to North Africa from Civitavecchia. Off the Neapolitan coast a Turkish fusta was overhauled and captured. In mid-April he debarked at Malta and took command of the Order's galley squadron, succeeding Ercole di None. With him he brought a letter from the Emperor datelined Brussels 9 March 1531 directing Viceroy of Sicily Ettore Pignatello to provide all the grain and other foodstuffs required by the people of Malta and Gozo without impediment or duty. Arriving on the same Doria galley was Yannis Maria Stratigopolos returning from another inspection of Modon with assurance that gate and other arrangements were on track. At Malta Salviati received instructions from a Grand Master still nourishing a dream of returning to Rhodes to do those things necessary for the conquest of Modon; the Order had no interest in a hit and run assault. Dispatched to Messina, Stratigopolos informed Viceroy Pignatello of the Order's secret plan for Modon. While doing so and for purposes of the plan he asked for and received loan of an unarmed galley called *Aquila* laid-up at Messina. Francesco Nibbia of Novara was assigned to get *Aquila* ready for sea and was appointed her skipper.[7]

In command with his lieutenant and brother-in-law Sinan of twenty-five oared vessels, thirteen of which were large galliots and the others fustas out of Djerba and other North African ports, Kheir-ed-Din Barbarossa surprised between the Sicilian island of Favignana and its neighbour Levanzo the newer Carrack of the Religion *Santa Anna* bound from Toulon and Marseille to Malta under fore, main, and topsails. Commanded by François de Toucheboeuf de Clermont, the Carrack of the Religion readied for action, hoisted her colours, and fired a broadside damaging some of the nearer corsairs before laying and entering an island cove, where she was able to cover the entrance with a withering fire. Retiring, Barbarossa here termed the 'King of Algiers' and sailing under Ottoman colours, chose to head for the Calabrian and Apulian coasts of mainland Italy. At the northern end of the Strait of Messina the sometime corsairs pillaged and put to flame a ship bound from Naples to Malta, cargo of salted beef and other provisions for the Order, in this way evening the score.[7]

Not long after this Bishop of Malta Balthasar Waltkrik passed away, and pursuant to terms of the Grant of Malta and Gozo the Order nominated three successors for submission to Emperor and Pope. These were Prior of the Church Pons Laurenzin of Lyon, Vice Chancellor of the Religion Tommasso Bosio, and Sacristan of the Conventual Church of the Langue of Aragon Domenico Cubelles, each a Hospitaller.[8]

On the feast day of Saint Paul, 29 June 1531, while Grand Master l'Isle-Adam and his staff living in Castle Saint Angelo were at Notabile for several days for associated festivities, enslaved Turks and Moors held captive within the castle took possession of it. Among these captives were Kara Saime and Kara Mustafa, reis taken captive by the galley squadron eighteen months earlier. Their lives had been spared by Hugo de Copons because of their not-unkind treatment of Christian captives. In possession of Castle Saint Angelo, these considered or attempted an escape by means of a carrack skiff to the brigantine of Bernardo Scotto at anchor in the port. If attempted, the escape was foiled because the escapees returned to the castle where they then planned to send a skiff directly to Djerba, meanwhile maintaining possession of the well-stocked and well-armed castle until help came from Djerba or from the Sultan. This second skiff was spotted by Pierre de Beaulac Trébons and intercepted by a launch full of arquebusiers commanded by Pierre de Noë. The escapees within the castle lost hope and surrendered on 29 July. Kara Mustafa, Kara Saime, and ten others considered ringleaders were hanged.[9]

By letter of Pope Clement dated 29 August 1531 Tommasso Bosio was appointed Bishop of Malta. In the letter the Pope made it clear the deciding factor in awarding the Bishopric was the esteem in which Emperor and Pope held Tommasso's deceased brother Antonio Bosio.[10]

Grand Master l'Isle-Adam had adopted the concept of Modon (modern Methoni) as a stepping stone to the Levant and to a possible return to Rhodes, Modon and nearby Coron, both lost by Venice to the Ottomans in 1500. Captain of Galleys Bernardo Salviati was appointed captain-general for Modon's conquest, with Bailiff of Manosque Jean de Boniface under him in command of the squadron when Salviati was ashore. Salviati's capitana or flagship was *Santa Croce*, which he commanded himself. Galcerán Tamarite of Huesca commanded *Santa Maria la Vittoriosa*, Gonzalo Gomez de Cervantes of Castile commanded *San Giovanni*, Francesco Nibbia of Novara commanded *Aquila*, Giacomo Grimaldi of Monaco commanded one of his own galleys, while the other was commanded by Hospitaller Baptiste du Broc of Provence. Jean de Boniface was embarked aboard the Grimaldi capitana, as was Giovanni Battista Schiattese, who had commanded the Galleon of the Religion *San Buonaventura* when unsuccessfully beset by two corsair galliots in the Autumn of 1529. In addition to the galleys there were two grippos or small cargo carriers owned and commanded by Maltese residents Luigi Abel and Cola Scarpello. Both were piloted by Yannis Scandali of the Venetian island of Zante and were bound for Zante to load cargo consigned to collaborators at Modon. Between them, they had 300 arquebusiers embarked. With these arquebusiers and the 300 hired soldiers aboard the galleys, there were about 200 Hospitallers including caravan knights. Finally, there were two brigantines, one commanded by Malta resident Sabastiano Cuculemi and the other by Bernardo Scotto of Genoa. Yannis Maria Stratigopolos was embarked as an advisor and go-between with Greek supporters at Zante and Modon.[11]

Grand Master l'Isle-Adam was well aware of fine points of the plan and personally instructed Salviati, even as to details such as the route to Modon. Salviati was to avoid being sighted along the Morean coast and to swing wide of the Strofadi Islands south of Zante. But it was the strategic purpose he stressed in his conversations with Salviati. L'Isle-Adam had yet to abandon his dream of returning to Rhodes, a garden of Eden when compared to the desert island of Malta. Modon was to be taken if at all possible, not raided, and when taken, it was to be garrisoned and Salviati himself was to remain as Governor with the additional title of Lieutenant to the Grand Master. Twenty-three years of age, Salviati had proved himself adept at leveraging his uncle the

Pope's influence, but he was untried in combat. The Modon flotilla sailed from Malta on 17 August 1531 bound initially for Zante. There the grippos were left to take on cargo and the galleys and brigantines took course to pass wide of the Strofadi Islands before turning toward the island of Sapientza south of Modon. Arriving at night on 31 August, Stratigopolos had the eight oared vessels take shelter in a cove on the west side of the island 3 miles south and out of sight of Modon. Modon was a walled city situated on a peninsula with a four-bastion gate or castle at the landward end leading to a draw-bridge over a moat turning the peninsula into an island. There was a second gate at the head of a mole at the seaward end of the city. At the other end of the mole was a tower fortress. A frigate arrived at Sapientza with several Greeks of Zante who had reached agreement with some in Modon to support the Maltese. These were joined by Schiatessi, Grimaldi, and Du Broc disguised as Venetian merchants who together proceeded to the beach end of the city and entered through the castle gate with Turkish-speaking Greeks doing the talking. Meanwhile, one of the grippos arrived at the mole with a cargo of wine, samples of which were generously offered to janissaries of the guard stationed at the mole tower. These became inebriated. The second grippo came alongside the mole on signal and a contingent of knights and soldiers debarked from both grippos, did in the inebriated janissaries, occupied the tower fortress, and signalled for the galleys and brigantines at Sapientza.

The arrival of these was itself signal for disguised merchants and local collaborators to open the sea gate. Modon was seized, the Ottoman garrison taking refuge in the castle-gate. Hired soldiers, however, rather than secure the city immediately abandoned themselves to looting and kidnapping if not burning and molesting. Meanwhile help for the Ottoman garrison had been summoned and appeared by evening of the second day. On appearance of the relief force, Salviati withdrew and took with him 800 kidnap victims, mostly women and children as the men had retired into the castle-gate. While the Grandmaster was deeply disappointed at this near-fatal blow to his dream of returning to Rhodes, most of the captives turned out to be Greek Orthodox Christians who declined transportation back to Zante and from there further transport to Modon. Rather, they found homes locally and would, in 1534, elect to be baptized as Latin Christians. Another, a young Greco-Turkish girl baptized as Lucrezia, would later relocate from Malta to Messina and there catch the eye of seagoing condottiero Vincenzo Cicala. They would wed and have two sons. In 1561 younger son Scipione would be captured with his father at sea by renegade-Italian Uluç Ali. In 1571 Uluç Ali would be appointed Kapudan Pasha or Commander-in-Chief of the Ottoman Armada. Scipione, then known as Cigalazade Yusuf Sinan, twenty years later would himself be twice appointed Kapudan Pasha. In between he would briefly serve as Grand Vizier, the highest appointed office in the Ottoman Empire. In 1598 he would, under a flag of truce, take 40 Ottoman galleys into the anchorage at Messina. Lucrezia, local Cicala family, and friends would for two days be entertained aboard the Ottoman capitana. Lucrezia would not only be re-united with her son Scipione but would also be introduced to a grandson.

Salviati left behind at Modon a number of dead including a single Hospitaller, Hernando *della* Torre of Castile, who took an arquebus round in the head. Wounded evacuated during the withdrawal included Hospitallers Antonio de Ledesma of Salamanca, François de Monchy de Briand and Frédéric d'Élancourt, both of the Langue of France, Pantaleone Coradengo of Turin, Martín de Medrano of Navarre, and Galcerán de Torres of Catalonia. The commended included Hospitaller Commander Jean d'Humieres of the Langue of France, a veteran of the Great Siege of Rhodes, Vincenzo Polidori of the Commandery of Orvieto, and Don Antonio Herrera of Seville, who guarded the mole tower.[13]

Coincident with the 1531 expedition to Modon, Prior of Castile Don Diego de Toledo made known his wish that upon his death the Priory devolve in two parts upon two of his Hospitaller nephews. Don Bernardino de Toledo, legitimate and natural son of Don Garcia de Toledo of the House of Alva was to be appointed Prior of Castile. Don Antonio de Toledo, legitimate and natural son of Don Diego Enriquez de Guzman and Countess of Alva Donna Leonoro de Toledo, was to be appointed Prior of León. Certain bailiwicks and commanderies also were to devolve on the Priory of León, including the Bailiwick of Lora. At about the same time the Commandery of Boncourt was vacated by the death of Frédéric (Ferry) de Conty, twenty-two years the incumbent. Using his magisterial prerogative l'Isle-Adam appointed his nephew Jacques de Wignacourt d'Aurigny as Conty's successor. Upon the death from natural causes of Bailiff of Lyon Jean de Laurè while en route to Malta, the Grand Master appointed Emery de Chevrier de Pody his successor as Bailiff of Saint-Georges pursuant to a geographic name change approved at the last Chapter General. To the universal distress of the Convent, Prior of Lombardia and Lieutenant to the Grand Master Bernardino d'Airasca also came to the end of his life in 1531. He was succeeded as Prior of Lombardia by Admiral Ercole di None, who renounced the dignity of Admiral, to which Bailiff of Santo Stefano Muzio Costanza succeeded.[12]

Upon the flotilla's return to Malta on 24 September, l'Isle Adam learned with deep disappointment and heavy sadness of Salviati's failure to take and hold Modon. His dream of returning to Rhodes suffered an almost terminal blow. Following Salviati's report he sifted through his mind how things might have gone differently and came up with too many answers. He nevertheless commended Salviati for his effort, put Greek participants on salary, some of whom had since Modon been classified as criminals by Venice, and received Yannis Maria Stratigopolos into the Order of Jerusalem as a knight of grace in the Langue of Italy, assigned the commanderies of Teano and Pontecorvo.[12]

Salviati, for his part, immediately readied to proceed to Tripoli with his four galleys including *Aquila* plus the two of Grimaldi to support Hospitaller Governor of Tripoli Gaspar de Sanguesa against attacks by Barbarossa. Within the Kingdom of Tunis, Muley Raschid, a rebel half-brother of King Muley Hassan (Hafsid King Muhammad V r1526-43), had rebelled and allied himself with Barbarossa. Barbarossa wrested Tagiora (modern Tajura, 8nm east of Tripoli) from the Sheik of Tagiora and from the dominion of Muley Hassan, ally of Charles V and of the Hospitaller Order in their fight against the corsairs of Algiers. At Tagiora Barbarossa installed a garrison of Turks and Moors, the latter commanded by Muley Rashid, all commanded by Barbarossa's 'disciple Cairadino'.

Cairadino's origins and background are never identified by Bosio or other sources; he was simply Cairadino, soon known as the King of Tagiora. In addition to the garrison, Barbarossa left at Tagiora a crewed galliot and several brigantines within the city fosse, which was a canal to the sea. Thus a nuisance to the Order's outpost at Tripoli was replaced with a threat.[14] Cairadino followed subjugation of Tagiora with an unsuccessful assault on Tripoli, repulsed by the garrison of Governor Sanguesa at considerable cost of Turkish and Moorish dead.[13]

Salviati sailed from Malta on 6 October 1531 with the same six galleys and all of the embarked soldiers hired for the siege of Modon other than the loot laden, first heading for the Freo Channel between Malta and Gozo where fresh water might more easily be loaded aboard shallow-draft vessels at the island of Comino. During the night of 8 October the squadron was hit by a violent storm, forcing *Aquila* up onto rocks of neighbouring Cominotto which holed her underwater hull. She was almost immediately twisted off the rocks by shifting gusts of wind and soon sank in shallow water. Notwithstanding the quick reactions of skipper Francesco Nibbia, not all embarked personnel could be saved. Seventeen hired soldiers and chained oarsmen were lost. The other five galleys came within a hair of similar disasters. When trouble arises it usually travels in pairs. At the main port of Malta one day earlier munitions stored aboard the old carrack *Santa Maria* ignited and the ship went to the bottom. On board were quartered those kidnapped from Modon, mostly women and children. Miraculously, all survived. As for *Aquila*, all of the bow artillery and sails as well as much of the planking were recovered and transported by barque with survivors to the port of Malta. So, too, the artillery and other useful items on board *Santa Maria* were recovered. Departing Freo on 10 October, Salviati's five remaining galleys reached Tripoli on the third evening out having had no sight of Barbarossa. Briefed by Gaspar de Sanguesa concerning developments at Tagiora as reported by Berber agents, Salviati and the squadron departed Tripoli that same night ahead of news of their arrival and descended upon Tagiora at dawn the following day before labourers arrived at the unfinished defensive works. Barbarossa's galliot was assailed, her skeleton crew overcome, and about 150 Christians released from the benches. Galliot, two brigantines, and several smaller craft were incinerated. Absent any confrontation with Cairadino or his minions, the squadron returned to Tripoli where, pursuant to instructions from Malta, the Grimaldi galleys were dismissed.[14]

From Tripoli a Tripolitan Moor on the Order's payroll was transported by Grimaldi to La Goletta, the fortress guarding Tunis 12 miles distant around a lagoon. The Moor was to represent the Order's interest in friendly relations and combined operations against the corsairs of North Africa.

The emissary was well received by Muley Hassan and dispatched back to Tripoli with the King's own emissary to discuss a campaign against Cairadino. Muley Hassan needed siege artillery and gunners, Sanguesa promised assistance. Pursuant to a summons from the Grand Master, Sanguesa then returned to Malta with the three galleys of Bernardo Salviati, leaving his lieutenant Bernardino Machado in command at Tripoli. From Malta the Grand Master dispatched Sanguesa to the Emperor in Germany with complaints of further harassment by ministers of Sicily inhibiting shipments of grain and other foodstuffs as well as with a report of developments at Tripoli, which the Grand Master continued to believe indefensible. Cairadino, undeterred by his twin setbacks, had meanwhile purchased from Sinan at nearby Djerba a replacement galliot and had been provided over winter months the corsair's Turks and Azaps (irregular light infantry) to strengthen the defence of Tagiora while the construction of defences was accelerated. With the Sinan galliot and a brigantine, Cairadino seized at Seccagne (islands of Kerkenna, west of Tripoli) two Maltese brigantines that had come out from Tripoli. Paolo Simeoni, an observer aboard one of the brigantines, was among the captives. Cairadino thereby earned enough credit to be acclaimed by Moors as King of Tagiora and to accrue tribute that might otherwise have gone to the King of Tunis.[15]

Simeoni was known by Cairadino to have very nearly captured Barbarossa following a long pursuit in June 1526. The King of Tagiora was quick to reject Tripoli's first of many ransom offers and to notify mentor Barbarossa of his capture. Among Caradino's new minions were the Sheiks of Zanzor, Almaia (modern Almaya), Almansor (Almanzor), Langir, Tegibin, Alascian, Ladabus, Zegua, and even the Sheik of old Tripoli.

It was the expectation of Pope Clement VII and Ferdinand, King of the Romans, that Lutheran Hospitaller Joachim von Münsterberg, son of Duke Charles I of Münsterberg-Oels and lieutenant to the Prior, would succeed the ailing Prior of Bohemia Johann III von Rosenberg, an expectation to which Grand Master and Council subscribed and which took place in February 1532.

Also early in 1532, Muley Hassan (King of Tunis Muhammad V), considering Tagiora still a part of his Kingdom, resolved to besiege Cairadino's redoubt with intent to raze the new fortress and evict the corsairs. Cairadino at this point had been joined by numerous Tunisian rebels, and his fortress was well supplied with munitions and provisions. He was also about to receive reinforcements from Barbarossa at Algiers. Muley Hassan, for his part, had enlisted services from the seagoing condottiero Vincenzo Cicala and his galleon. Cicala immediately solicited cannon and gunners from Tripoli. Acting Tripoli Governor Bernardino Machado, however, did not believe it prudent to diminish Tripoli's own defences in spite of an earlier promise by Governor Gaspar de Sanguesa. Machado did, however, authorise Hospitaller Luigi Broglia commanding the small galleon or Galleonetto of the Religion *Il Siciliano* on assignment at Tripoli to transport Muley Hassan's emissaries to Malta in order to make their case before the Grand Master. Meanwhile, Machado suggested the artillery aboard Cicala's own galleon lying at Porto Farina (modern Ghar al Milh) in the Gulf of Tunis might be more quickly made available.

At Malta l'Isle-Adam weighed the inadequacies of Malta's own defences against the promise made by Sanguesa and determined to send Hospitaller Aurelio Bottigella to the assistance of Muley Hassan with instructions to coordinate with both Machado and with his Captain of Cavalry Martín de Barrosa. In addition to the small galleon, Bottigella had two grippos and a brigantine carrying sixty knights, a strong force of hired infantry, a load of munitions and foodstuffs, plus a quantity of artillery sufficient to reinforce Tripoli and provide assistance to Muley Hassan. Arriving at Tripoli, Bottigella opened negotiations with the King of Tunis, to whom he consigned a battery of six large cannon against assignment of certain hostages as guarantee. With the artillery Muley Hassan laid siege to Tagiora at the end of January 1532, encircling the forces of Cairadino not only within Tagiora but at the new tower overlooking the port and at the fortress of Zegua between Tripoli and Tagiora. At Malta, meanwhile, the Grand Master was slowly improving the defences of Castle Saint Angelo and the Borgo or Birgu as well as those of Notabile, realising that in the event of a serious siege at present the Convent would of necessity have to withdraw to Sicily, which would mean the beginning of the end of the Order of Jerusalem.[15]

At Tripoli Bottigella was informed by Hospitaller Francesco Terno da Crema that Cairadino was receiving reinforcements from Sinan of Smyrna at Djerba and from other corsair redoubts and was putting up a stubborn defence against Muley Hassan's besieging force. This in spite of a cadre of first-class gunners manning the six pieces of artillery provided which had opened a breach in the city walls. Assault after assault, however, was turned back by a 'valorous'[16] defence. Neither was success possible at the tower fortress overlooking the port because Barbarossa had sent fifteen large galliots from Algiers, which lay at anchor in the harbour, and Barbarossa was said to be preparing an even larger rescue force should one be needed. In mid-March the Grand Master ordered Commander Garcia Cortèz and the same Terno da Crema to Sicily to brief the Viceroy on the stalemate that, in their view, might be broken only by a combined flotilla of all Maltese and Sicilian galleys plus the two of Giacomo Grimaldi and the galleon of Vincenzo Cicala. For this undertaking the Order expected to have a fourth galley then under construction at Messina. She was to be christened *San Filippo* and to be commanded by Costantino Provana of Turin. Viceroy Pignatello gave the order to put the proposal in motion. Bosio furnished no credentials for Terno da Crema but he was received into the Order of Jerusalem, Langue of Italy, through the Diocese of Crema in 1526. Given a novitiate and some or all of four caravans, he may have been assigned to Tripoli with Gaspar de Sanguesa in June 1530, long enough ago to have cultivated sources of information. He would in the future prove himself equally resourceful as a sea commander.[16]

The plan and the motion came to naught. Barbarossa assembled sixty vessels at Modon, which he led toward Djerba, entering the Gulf of Gabes through the Sfax Channel and putting his own force of Arabs ashore under the command of Muley Rashid. Rashid cut his brother's line of communication with Tunis at Gabes 320km to Muley Hassan's rear and rolled up the King's rearguard at frightening speed, forcing Muley Hassan to lift the siege of Tagiora. There was no way home by land or sea. Muley Hassan survived, but we are not told how; fighting his way through the passage at Gabes or abandoning his army for the safety of Tripoli. Aurelio Bottigella obtained the only success in this disappointing affair, seizing the small fort at Zegua with a company of Hospitaller cavalry; Zegua so close to Tripoli as to offer little warning of the enemy's approach. The price, however, included the life of Hospitaller Josseran d'Isnard, completing his final caravan before becoming eligible for a commandery.[17]

At end-May 1532 the corsair galliot of Hospitaller Robert de Valergues of the Langue of Provence returned from the Levant with a wealth of plunder and with forty Turkish captives. Valergues reported the Turkish Armada had sailed from Constantinople and exited the Strait of Gallipoli. A galley was dispatched to Sicily, where Hospitaller Commander Miguel Peralta of Navarre hired a large company of soldiers to be assigned to the presidio of Castle Saint Angelo. Attending the Diet of Ratisbon (Regensburg), Emperor Charles V dispatched a letter by hand of Gaspar de Sanguesa to Viceroy of Sicily Ettore Pignatello warning of a Turkish Armada approaching Sicilian waters. Pignatello invited Malta to gather necessary provisions at a Sicilian port of its choosing. There then arrived uncertain advice that the Turkish Armada had proceeded only as far as Mitilini. To ascertain exactly what the Turkish Armada was doing the Grand Master dispatched two fustas to the Levant, one commanded by Hospitaller Pietro Vasco of Turin and the second by Giraldo della Mota of the Langue of Castile. If finding the armada outside of the Dardanelles, one fusta was to return with the location and the other was to follow the force at a safe distance. The galley *Santa Croce* was sped across the Gulf of Lyon to Barcelona under command of Santiago de Vilatorta, Commander of Mas-Deù in Barcelona, to take delivery of all coin in the local Treasury from Custodian Francisco Ferrer and to return to Malta forthwith.[18]

In the context of the Emperor's warning, the Ottoman Armada might be expected in Sicilian waters, as well as in the context of Malta's indefensibility two years on, Grand Master l'Isle-Adam and designated members of the Council including Admiral Muzio Costanza, Prior of Auvergne Gabriel du Chief, and Lieutenant Draper Garcia Cortez, embarked aboard the carrack *Santa Anna* recently returned from the west. Together with the other three galleys of the squadron aboard which the Order's Holy Relics had been loaded, they stood ready in the harbour for a sudden departure to Sicily should the enemy appear on the horizon. In that event 300 knights and a large number of soldiers divided between Castle Saint Angelo and Notabile would remain under the command of Marshal Jean de Château-Arnauld. But on 29 July, understanding that a powerful armada had reached Modon threatening Malta, came certain news from the two fustas dispatched earlier, returning one after the other, that with the Sultan on campaign in Hungary the armada had no intention of leaving Greece unless summoned to do so. Grand Master, Council, and Holy Relics were immediately put ashore.[19]

A few days later the Grand Master received a letter from Commander Gaspar Sanguesa containing a full and complete accounting of the Turkish Armada, which Sanguesa obtained from Count Leonardo Nugarola of Vicenza, one of the ambassadors of Ferdinand, King of the Romans, sent to negotiate an accord with Sultan Suleiman, an accord that would be reached in 1533. In the meanwhile an Imperial Armada began to assemble at Messina commanded by Prince of Melfi Andrea Doria consisting of forty galleys and numerous support vessels for the purpose of confronting the Turkish Armada. These were joined on 6 August by a Papal Squadron of six galleys commanded by the Prince's cousin Antonio Doria. Meanwhile, emissaries of the Imperial commander reached Malta with requests from both Emperor Charles V and Pope Clement VII that the galleys of Malta as well as the carrack *Santa Anna* also join the Imperial Armada. Salviati's mini-squadron consisted of *San Filippo* commanded by Costantino Provana as capitana in the absence of *Santa Croce*, *Santa Maria de la Vittoria* called *Il Gallo* commanded by Gabriel de Serris of the Langue of France, and *San Giovanni Battista* under Gonzalo de Cervantes. The carrack *Santa Anna* continued under command of François de Toucheboeuf. All embarked knights and soldiers but for crews were under the command of Prior of Auvergne Gabriel du Chief assisted by Lieutenant Draper Garcia Cortez as sergeant-major. An additional 100 knights and 120 soldiers were embarked aboard the carrack, bringing the total of embarked Hospital combatants aboard the carrack to 500. Fifty additional knights were embarked aboard each galley. The carrack and galleys departed Malta on 4 August 1532, replenished at Syracuse, and joined the Imperial Armada on 7 August. During the month *Santa Croce* returned from Barcelona, delivered the currency received from Custodian Francisco Ferrer, embarked a caravan of fifty knights, and joined the Imperial Armada still at Messina. Meanwhile, Turkish corsair Seganta Reis, as pilot, accompanied the Captain of Gallipoli Ahmad Pasha to Preveza with thirteen galleys and six fustas, presumably to join the Omer Ali cited below.[20]

Doria's Imperial Armada – comprised of forty-three galleys, thirty-five large ships, fustas and other vessels for a total of 100 sails – departed Messina on 28 August 1532. According to Spanish sources of the forty-three galleys, seventeen were those of Doria, thirteen were Papal, four of Sicily, three of Naples, and two of Monaco in addition to four of Malta. Of the thirty-five large ships, there were fifteen galleons and two carracks, that of Malta and *Grimalda* of Genoa. The armada sailed along the Calabrese coast toward the Ionian Sea, at Doria's right the Papal flagship and at his left that of Malta. At Cape Rizzuto he altered course to Santa Maria di Leuca, where he pointed toward the Greek coast. Antonio Doria was then placed in the vanguard with twelve Papal and private galleys, Andrea Doria himself was positioned in the centre, and Bernardo Salviati brought up the rear with the four Maltese galleys. Ottoman Admiral Omer Ali, with eighty Turkish galleys in poor readiness, was believed to be ahead in the Gulf of Arta (or Gulf of Preveza). In between was the Strait of Otranto patrolled by a Venetian Armada commanded by Vincenzo Capello and by Girolamo da Canal, sixty galleys strong. But Venice was not at war with the Ottoman Empire, and so after imparting information her commanders went their own way. Omer Ali's Turkish ships had meanwhile fled south to Coron east of Modon on the Christian armada's approach. Six of Antonio Doria's Imperial vanguard together with *Santa Maria de la Vittoria*, called *Il Gallo* and the fastest galley in the fleet, were detached to investigate. Not finding the enemy at Coron, these galleys turned Cape Maleo at the south-east corner of the Morea and reached Napoli di Romania (Nauplia) without sighting the enemy armada. They learned, however, that much of the enemy armada was infested with bubonic plague, and so reversed course to rejoin Andrea Doria.[21]

Doria had meanwhile paused at Venetian Zante on 6 September, thereafter towing his sailing ships in light air he neared Coron on 16 September, 17 sea miles the far side of Modon. One day later he opened fire against the triangular walled city on a peninsula rising above the city's port. The great castle visible today overlooking the port surrendered in a few days after guns from the two carracks and a number of warships had dismantled defensive works; a second castle higher up at the inland corner of the walls, called Molineo, held out. Girolamo Tuttavilla, Count of Sarno, and Hospitaller Don Geronimo de Mendoza, respectively commanding Italian and Spanish infantry each with a battery of seven pieces of light siege artillery and a large number of men, assailed the castle from the shore.

These assaults were repulsed and the assailants withdrawn given the degree of resistance and a significant number of casualties. In the early hours of the night came information from an infiltrator, Theodoros Hayapostolitis, that the following morning a corps of 500 Turkish cavalry, spahis from Mistra, would arrive to attack the Imperial camp from the side. Tuttavilla put his sappers to work building a trap to be covered with branches, foliage, and earth. The Ottoman cavalry was lured to the trap, ended up in the pit, and suffered heavy losses; 300 spahis of the janissary corps were killed. In the end the remaining spahis surrendered on honourable terms. Doria then opened a second front on 21 September, this time on the south side of the peninsula. He sent in the 500 Hospitallers and soldiers commanded by Gabriel du Chief assisted by Garcia Cortez as sergeant-major. Forced to first scramble up a steep incline carrying scaling ladders, the Hospitallers were eventually able to surmount the walls near the corner without a fortress and, planting the Order's standard, seized control of wall boulevards, forcing Molineo to yield on 22 September.

There were many dead on both sides, including more than 300 Italian and Spanish infantry. Two Hospitallers lost their lives, Galician Nicolás San Xes of the Langue of Castile and Pierre Galéan des Issards of the Langue of Provence. Many others were wounded. Of two great guns found in Molineo Castle, one was given by Doria to Tuttavilla and the other to Salviati. Aware Coron was untenable, smaller cannon would be transported as trophies to the Church of the Madonna that Andrea Doria was building at Genoa with other plunder from his raids. On 25 September surviving Turks were permitted to march out of Coron without their arms but with their families. Provided with provisions and munitions for twelve months, Don Geronimo de Mendoza was left as governor of the fortress with a garrison of 2,500 Spanish and a number of Bourgognese, but with a severely diminished arsenal.[22]

In council with his commanders Andrea Doria advocated widespread hit-and-run raids in the Morea designed to reach the ears of Sultan Suleiman in Hungary, thus prompting the Sultan's withdrawal from Hungary to turn his attention to matters closer to home. Beyond hit-and-run Doria proposed conquest of the City of Patras, a seaport controlling access to the Gulf of Corinth. Following a morale-boosting speech to the new garrison at Coron in which Doria promised a rapid response should it come under threat, the Imperial Armada moved from Coron to Zonchio, ignoring Modon 10 nautical miles to the south. Nearby areas including Navarin were put to the sack. Salviati, meanwhile, proceeded with his four galleys and four Papal galleys into the Aegean in a further search for Omer Ali's Turkish Armada, this a part of the promise made to the garrison at Coron. They would have no fear from this direction; the Turkish Armada had already returned to Constantinople.

Toucheboeuf's carrack *Santa Anna* remained with Doria, who moved from Zonchio to Patras. At mid-month Patras was assailed, its defenders almost immediately retiring into the Byzantine fortress high on a hill 800m from the sea. Tuttavilla was put ashore with infantry and artillery, the latter soon opening breaches in city walls. Two days later his infantry penetrated into Patras through these breaches and took more than 2,000 non-combatants prisoner. On 17 October 1532 defenders of the fortress surrendered on terms, and for that reason Doria forbade the sack. Learning that two soldiers had snatched jewels from a local woman, both were hanged.

Leaving a garrison at Patras under nephew Erasmo Doria, Andrea Doria headed for Lepanto on the north shore of the Gulf of Corinth and by means of Toucheboeuf's carrack was soon in possession of one of the two castles controlling the harbour entrance. Tuttavilla assailed the other castle from the shore, while Doria bombarded it from the sea. Relief attempting to succour the castle was repulsed and defending janissaries, having lost hope, elected eternity rather than surrender. They went up with their powder magazine. Rescuing several pieces of Turkish artillery, Doria then had Lepanto razed.

Salviati had meanwhile returned from a raid as far as the Dardanelles, putting raiding parties ashore at mainland Cape Saint Demetrius near Scio (Chios) and enslaving a large number of Turks. He later seized a vessel headed for Modon with a cargo of wheat and took her in tow. Rejoining Doria at Lepanto, he informed the Prince of Omer Ali's winter quarters at Constantinople. From Lepanto Doria ravaged the coast of Sicyon on the south shore of the Gulf and then ravaged Corinth itself before taking the armada for a final visit to Coron.

From Coron the armada took course toward its various home ports for the winter. It is not clear how long the Spanish maintained control of Patras; Erasmos Doria, left as Governor, was back in the company of Andrea within six months. Coron would be abandoned in April 1534 as untenable. Andrea Doria's signal achievement this year and next would be to induce Sultan Suleiman in March 1534 to appoint Kheir-ed-Din Barbarossa as his Kapudan Pasha or Commander-in-Chief of the Ottoman Armada. Salviati and the four galleys of the squadron returned to Malta from Coron in company with Toucheboeuf's carrack *Santa Anna* on 8 January 1533.[24]

In Germany, meanwhile, Prior of Barletta and hero of the defence of Rhodes Gabriel Tadino di Martinengo had been attached to the Imperial Army as General of Artillery. He had a staff of ten other Hospitallers. Also attached to the Imperial Army had been Prior of Germany Johann von Hattstein, Prior of Bohemia Johann III von Rosenberg, and Joachim von Münsterberg and about fifty others from the Priories of Germany and Bohemia. But truth be told, 1532 in Europe had been a year of armies on the march never encountering the enemy. It was to have been Suleiman's second attempt to take Vienna. While unpersuaded by Doria's distractions, Suleiman detoured to take the small and insignificant fortress at Guns (modern Koszeg) in Hungary and failed, or failed long enough to eliminate any chance to take Vienna before the rains came.[23]

Grand Master l'Isle-Adam's second Chapter General convened at Malta on Sunday, 9 February 1533. Prior of the Church Pons Laurenzin recited the Mass of the Holy Spirit in the Church of San Lorenzo before those gathered, following which the Convent in procession proceeded to the new Great Hall of Castle Saint Angelo. There the Grand Master delivered a prudent, serious, and concise rationale for the Order's existence followed by a summary of matters bearing on the Convent's near future. There was then a period of ceremony accompanied by a presentation of colours, that is, the Order's Standard raised in the hands of noble Rhodian and non-Hospitaller Benedetto Ruggieri, Standard Bearer of the Religion by virtue of his contribution to the defence of Rhodes and as a leader of the large Rhodian community settled on the islands of Malta and Gozo. Also participating in the ceremony were Knights of the Grand Cross Marshal Jean de Château-Arnauld, Draper Bautista de Vilaragut, and Admiral Muzio Costanzo. Present as well was Lieutenant Governor of Tripoli Bernardino Machado, new Governor Aurelio Bottigella at Tripoli in succession of Gaspar Sanguesa on assignment with the Emperor in Germany. Machado was there as senior knight of the Langue of Castile as well as representing Tripoli.

On the third day of the Chapter General the Sixteen *Capitolanti* or Legislators were elected, two per langue. These would deliberate on matters of Convent administration and direction not resolved by the Chapter itself. Representing Provence were Grand Commander Raymond Ricard and Bailiff of Manosque Jean de Boniface, representing Auvergne were Prior of Auvergne Gabriel du Chief and Commander of Sainte-Anne Antoine de Grolée, representing France were Grand Hospitaller Michel d'Argillemont and Lieutenant Treasurer Jacques de Pelloquin, representing Aragon were Commander of Ascó Garcia Cortèz and Commander of Mas-Deù Santiago de Vilatorta, representing Italy were Admiral Muzio Costanzo and Prior of Rome Bernardo Salviati, representing England were Turcopolier Clement West and Preceptor of Baddesley and Mayne Roger Boydell, representing Germany Commander of Dorlisheim Georg Schilling and Wilhelm Hahn, and representing Castile Lieutenant Chancellor Don Pedro de Robles and Dom Diogo d'Almeida the Younger.[25]

Because the Priors of England and Ireland were absent, as was the Bailiff of Eagle, Chaplain of the Langue of Provence Gérald Romer and Serving Brothers Santiago Mondragón of the Langue of Castile, and Heinrich Pipa of the Langue of Germany were by vote of the Sixteen, Clement West and Roger Boydell dissenting, appointed Procurators for the Langue of England. Clement West protested angrily, asserting these positions should be filled by Englishmen, of whom there were sixteen others presently at the Convent, and that the named appointees would be influenced on procurator matters by their own Langues to the detriment of the Langue of England. The Sixteen responded, West and Boydell again dissenting, that because the Langue of England had not named its own procurators, the appointments must stand pursuant to the rules. Clement West became violently angry and insultingly abusive of the three appointees and at the decision, a decision that may have reflected widespread disapproval of the failure of Prior of England William Weston, Prior of Ireland John Rawson, and Bailiff of Eagle John Babington to heed the summons to the Chapter General, and it may have reflected widespread disapproval of West himself. Their honour impugned, the three appointees demanded justice. Given an opportunity to apologise, West not only refused but made the situation worse. He was consequently deprived of the dignity of Turcopolier, to which Boydell was appointed, and was deprived of his Habit, as well.[25]

More mundane matters coming before the Chapter General included the Religion's debt to its own Grand Master of more than 100,000 gold scudos incurred in part by expenses of the earlier Chapter General at Viterbo, and in part by amounts paid Genoa's Bank of Saint George on behalf of the Religion. There was also recognition of the Convent's need for six fully equipped galleys in order to protect the islands of Malta and Gozo from corsair incursions and to carry out its mission. Finally there was a mid-year levy on all commanderies to support construction of a proper home for the Convent. The Chapter General adjourned on the last day of February. During the Chapter General Don Pedro Fernandez de Heredia fled the Convent for Spain to take possession of the Commandery of Alfambra, usurping the dignity of Prior of Alfambra even though Alfambra was but a commandery, this apparently as a reward for soliciting the Emperor's gift of Malta, Gozo, and Tripoli. He was stripped of his Habit and the commandery was returned to Francisco de Benedettes.[25]

A concordat negotiated between Clement VII and Charles V at Bologna on 25 February 1533 provided that the Pope should maintain three galleys and the Emperor eleven, which should be ready at all times to defend eastern Europe and Italy. Under the concordat the Pope was to seek aid from other princes and to try to prevail upon the Hospitallers to defend Coron and other places that Andrea Doria had occupied in the name of the Emperor, and which the Emperor was prepared to turn over to the Hospitallers for the good of the Christian commonwealth. The commonwealth thus spared was comprised of the Empire, Papal States, Milan, Genoa, Ferrara, Siena, and Lucca.[26]

In mid-March the island was involved in a bloody brawl dividing most of the Convent in two camps. The inception was a duel between a French knight, a nephew of the Commander of Servières in Provence, and a secular Florentine in the suite or household of Prior of Rome Bernardo Salviati. Even though duelling was forbidden at Malta, the Florentine killed the French knight. A wealthy individual, Salviati did not reside at the Auberge of Italy but rather at his own quarters in Birgu large enough to house an extant suite of sixty. The Florentine was on the street in the company of other members of Salviati's household, both secular and of the

Habit, when assaulted and wounded by the uncle, relatives, and friends of the dead knight. A general melee ensued in which the Italians came off the worse with several wounded, bringing Salviati and his bodyguards to the scene. The tumult was quelled with imprisonment of ten of his men, who were chained on board his capitana. The French gathered in secret conclave at the house of Antoine de Varigues de Bleville, Commander of Orleans, while Salviati made ready to sail. On 25 March, Feast Day of the Annunciation, however, the conspirators suddenly boarded the capitana and murdered four of the chained captives in cold blood while maltreating the others. There followed renewed fighting between the French and Italian knights, the latter supported by the Spanish. Never before in the history of the Order had there been such discord and death. Tension was only eased by deployment of the armed Castle Guard commanded by Bailiff of Manosque Jean de Boniface. Eased but not extinguished. It would be some time before the matter became history. During the foregoing Turcopolier Roger Boydell developed a fever on 25 March, the Day of the Annunciation, and soon succumbed to his illness. He was succeeded by John Rawson the Younger, son of Prior of Ireland John Rawson.[27]

On the first day of April 1533 at Constantinople Jerome of Zara, King Ferdinand's emissary to the Ottoman Porte responsible for negotiating a peaceful accord between Christian West and Ottoman East, was summoned by Grand Vizier Ibrahim Pasha. Ibrahim, born Greek and a boyhood friend of Suleiman, showed Jerome, much to his chagrin, two letters from Coron either intercepted or provided to Ibrahim by Venetian Ambassador Pietro Zen. These letters dated 15 February and 12 March disclosed separate Spanish raids from Coron on nearby Kalamata, on Mistra (ancient Sparta), and on a village near Zonchio. There had also been at least four senseless fusta raids on Turkish hamlets. These raids took place in spite of letters from Jerome to Coron seeking a cessation of all hostilities.

Back at Malta Bailiff of Manosque Jean de Boniface was in April appointed Magistral Lieutenant, succeeding Bernardino d'Airasca who had passed away in October 1531. The brigantine of the Galley Squadron, which had delivered to Naples a record of Chapter General proceedings and there embarked several knights en route to Malta, encountered in the Gulf of Policastro south of Capri a much larger Turkish fusta with fifty combatants embarked and took her. Twenty-five of the Turks were killed during the engagement and the other twenty-five taken captive. Forty Christian slaves were liberated. Brigantine and larger prize reached Malta on 20 April. One of the knights embarking at Naples was Giovan Battista Nibbia, brother of Francesco Nibbia, who was skippering *Aquila* when it was lost in the Freo Channel. Nibbia had been sent by Emperor Charles V and Pope Clement VII to urge the Religion to proceed to the defence of the city of Coron, and to that effect carried a Papal Brief addressed to the Grandmaster datelined Bologna, 3 March 1533. Having studied the Papal Brief and considered the matter, Grand Master and Council concluded that (1) given its location Coron would be continually under siege by Ottomans on every side; (2) that the Ottomans on every side were of infinite number; (3) that Coron did not have a port secure from enemy fire at which to succour defenders; (4) that it was far distant from any source of succour; (5) from experience, Venetians who were the nearest Christians could not be relied upon to even provide port services to any relief force; and (6) the garrison left at Coron by Andrea Doria had been a continual irritant to the Ottoman Empire and a continual burden to the vice-regencies of Naples and Sicily. Coron's circumstances were even worse than those of Tripoli, which were intolerable. There was no recognition that Modon, ignored by Doria, was much more defensible and did have a secure port. Nor was there mention in the Papal Brief conveyed by Giovan Battista Nibbia of the February concordat between Emperor and Pope, all of which had been made known to the Sultan by Venice. Only the Hospitallers were in the dark. By letter dated 24 April the Grand Master replied diplomatically that it would not be possible for the Order of Jerusalem to take responsibility for Coron. Meanwhile, an unofficial truce between East and West was being observed everywhere but at Coron, where Hospitaller Don Geronimo de Mendoza's orders were to guard the town and make war on the Turks, a recipe for disaster.

Prior of Pisa and former Galley Squadron Commander Luigi dal Pozzo died of unreported cause at Pisa. Aurelio Bottigella, commanding at Tripoli as senior knight of the Langue of Italy, demanded the dignity and returned to Malta to make his case. He was successful and was appointed new Prior of Pisa. He was succeeded as Governor of Tripoli by Catalan Commander of Ascó Garcia Cortèz, who proceeded immediately to Tripoli aboard the Small Galleon *Il Siciliano* escorted by two brigantines.

Cortèz had orders for the purpose of display to make a sortie in strength and to return to Malta the wounded and exhausted for replacement. He was to maintain the strength of the garrison other than knights and chaplains at 200 soldiers and gunners. Cortèz also had special orders to not loan any artillery to the forces of Muley Hassan.

Soon after the departure of Cortèz there arrived at Malta two corsair fustas belonging to Gérald de la Motte of Provence and to Salvo Burlò of Malta, which sailing in company had taken an extraordinarily rich Turkish vessel, yielding as well a large number of captives. On board one of the fustas were both Castrofilaca Vestiariti, son-in-law of Metropolitan of Rhodes Euphemios, and Nikolaos Kantakouzeno who reported that following the Hospitaller sack of Modon in 1531 some Rhodians friendly with the Order had paid the price, including Metropolitan Euphemios and non-Hospitaller Gérard d'Aubigny, who for many years was complicit in Antonio Bosio's plans for the recapture of Rhodes. All Aubignys, it should be noted, were Stuarts, and one of those in France usually commanded the French King's Scots Guards. Seven others were or would become Hospitallers. The Grand Master bestowed on those affected the relief he was able. Elsewhere, Prior of Rome Bernardo Salviati proceeded to Civitavecchia with the four galleys of the Religion and from there continued on to Rome, where he met with his uncle Pope Clement. The Pope had Salviati recount his experience at Coron and sought his opinion. Salviati told him Coron could be held successfully only with the strength of the Empire; that it was beyond the capability of the Order of Jerusalem.[28]

During the meeting a letter arrived from Don Geronimo de Mendoza at Coron addressed to Viceroy of Naples Don Pedro de Toledo reporting that Coron expected to soon be besieged by both land and sea, further reporting, however, that provisions were adequate and the affection of the Greek populace genuine. He asked only for the Imperial Armada, and with it promised certain victory. This letter was forwarded rapidly to the Emperor, who ordered Andrea Doria to make ready and, as well, ordered Alvaro de Bazan the Elder, Marqués del Viso, Admiral of Castile, and Captain-General of Spain's Mediterranean Galley Fleet, to ready twelve galleys then in Spain. The Emperor also requested the participation of Papal and Hospitaller galleys. Pope Clement placed nephew Salviati in command of Papal galleys, succeeding Antonio Doria, while Salviati continued in command of the galleys of Malta. [28]

Andrea Doria sent his nephew Erasmo from Alicante to Civitavecchia with fourteen galleys, while Salviati readied four galleys of Malta and three galleys leased by the Church. Of the four galleys of Malta, *Santa Croce* the capitana was commanded by Salviati himself with future Grand Master Pietro del Monte his padrone, *San Filippo* was commanded by Costanzo Provana, *San Giovanni Battista* was commanded by Gonzalo de Cervantes, and *Santa Maria de la Vittoria* was commanded by Pierre de Beaulac Trébons of the Langue of Provence. Doria himself proceeded from Alicante to Naples by galleon.[29]

Bernardo Salviati and Erasmo Doria with twenty-one galleys rendezvoused with Andrea Doria at Naples. The latter lost precious time there putting down a mutiny caused by overdue payment of wages to a Spanish tercio to be embarked for the relief of Coron. Once the mutiny was quelled he proceeded to Messina to prepare his armada for coordinated combat. More days were lost awaiting the arrival from the Barbary Coast of twelve Spanish galleys commanded by the aforementioned Alvaro de Bazan the Elder. Doria would in the end proceed without Bazan to relieve the siege of Coron.[29]

Before the Armada's departure from Messina Doria in July sent his adopted nephew Cristoforo Pallavicini to Coron commanding a fast galley for reconnaissance of opposing forces. Having first reconnoitered the enemy fleet, Pallavicini broke through enemy encirclement and entered the port with his ship and 10,000 scudos, also bringing comfort and cheer. With the information sought he then rejoined Doria at Messina. There he reported Ottoman Admiral Lutfi Bey no longer had his entire force, having released Moro of Alexandria with his squadron as well as all western corsairs.[29]

Andrea Doria departed Messina on 2 August 1533. Salviati was at the right of the formation with seven Papal and Maltese galleys; Antonio Doria was to the left with six galleys of Naples and Sicily; Andrea Doria was in the centre with fourteen galleys and was followed by another thirty ships including four carracks and three galleons carrying the support train and 3,000 infantry, mostly Spanish. Doria met at Zante with officers of the Venetian fleet, by whom he was informed Lutfi Bey had been rejoined by Moro of Alexandria and other western corsairs, bringing his strength to sixty galleys and twenty others between fustas and brigantines. Reaching the island of Sapientza, Doria obtained the same advice from local Greeks. He again sent Pallavicini to reconnoitre and to alert the defenders at Coron that relief was coming. Pallavicini soon ascertained that the enemy was in fact more numerous than one month earlier and that he would not be able to penetrate the encirclement as before. From a proximate cove he determined Coron was suffering a furious siege from all sides.

The next day Doria determined to go ahead with relief of Coron, even though outnumbered by the enemy. He put all of his ships under sail bound for Coron around Cape Gallo, sending two large galleons out in advance, one his own and the other belonging to the corsair Guglielmo Bellomo. These two castles in the sea mounting heavy artillery appeared to psychologically damage the enemy. Doria's galleys, meanwhile, followed the ships with bow-chasers threatening any enemy moving against the sailing ships. At this point two Spanish troop carriers became entangled by the bowsprit and drifted behind the Christian formation. These attracted the attention of Moro of Alexandria. Some of those aboard one of the ships, not accustomed to combat at sea, took to the lifeboats. The second of the two, commanded by Captain Ermosiglia, put up a stout defence from the sterncastle until shore batteries at Coron drove the enemy away. The siege of Coron was lifted; defenders, encircled on the land side by entrenched Ottomans, immediately benefitted from debarked troops, who scattered the enemy. Coron was resupplied with provisions and munitions. Don Geronimo Mendoza was succeeded in command by Rodrigo Machicao. Lutfi Bey, who had been expressly warned by the Sultan himself not to risk his Armada, withdrew to Modon. Withdrawing himself from Coron the following day, Doria offered battle between Modon and Sapientza, but Lutfi refused to come out from under the protection of shore batteries. Thereafter touching only Corfu, Doria returned to Messina, where he was finally joined by Alvaro de Bazan and the galleys of Spain.[30]

Salviati escorted Pope Clement VII and sixteen cardinals to Florence. Still in the company of Pope Clement and several of the cardinals, he sailed from Livorno to Marseille by way of Finale Ligure and Villefranche in the territory of Nice. At mid-month he reached Marseille, where he assisted at the wedding of his 14-year-old cousin Caterina dei Medici to 14-year-old Henri, duc d'Orleans, future King Henry IV of France.

At the month end, Sinan's galliots and fustas, ten in number, were located at the island of Comino in the Freo Channel between Malta and Gozo, where they were taking on fresh water. Two grippos appeared aboard which were 23 knights, returning to Malta from the siege of Coron. These had been left by Salviati at Messina to make room on galleys bound for Marseille and had embarked aboard the unarmed grippos at Syracuse. The first of the ships, commanded by Ceylo Xucreb of Malta, was captured. Embarked knights were made captive but would soon be ransomed at Djerba by Hospitaller Pedro Fernandez de Felizes, assigned to the garrison at Hospitaller Tripoli. The second grippo, appearing some distance astern of the first, was able to grab a fair wind, crowd on canvas, and return to Sicily. With reports of his success, Sinan held Malta and Gozo in a semblance of siege because at the time none of the Maltese galleys or other warships were in local waters, and none were expected to soon return. During this interregnum no friendly vessels dared come near Malta. Chevalier Pierre de Noé of the Langue of Provence, commanding the Arsenal or Shipyard, however, had a French galleon in the yard which had come in from the Levant in need of repair. Noé accelerated repair, increased the armament, embarked 300 combatants in addition to crew, each armed with arquebus or musket, and moved at night to Saline, a cove on the Malta side of the Freo Channel. When Sinan's ten galliots and fustas next appeared, Noé's galleon also appeared with cannons blazing. The galliots decided to lift the siege, taking with them a large number of dead and wounded as well as considerable ship damage.[31]

Irritated by the ability of corsairs to come and go as they pleased at Malta in the absence of the Galley Squadron, Grand Master l'Isle-Adam conceived of a series of towers or bastions around both Malta and Gozo and at Comino. Construction on the first such bastion, to be named Fort Saint Elmo, commenced on the point of land opposite Castle Saint Angelo where the city of Valletta now stands. Also in December, those women and children kidnapped from Coron by Bernardo Salviati so wishing were baptised Latin Christians in the nearby Chapel of Saint Elmo.[32]

Reports reached Malta early in 1534 of the death of Jacques de Sainte-Maure, Prior of Champagne since 1528 and veteran of the Great Siege of Rhodes. Jean d'Aubin de Malicorne was appointed his successor, Aubin necessarily renouncing the dignity of Bailiff of the Morea to which Jacques de Bourbon, diarist of the Great Siege, was appointed. Jacques de Pelloquin was appointed Treasurer in succession of Bourbon. Also in January there was a rebellion of the Langue of Castile against an impost levied by the February 1533 Chapter General to raise funds for constructing defensive works at Malta. The Grand Master was both outraged and disheartened. A tribunal was established investigating eleven knights of the Priory, those found complicit to be defrocked. Those under investigation promised an appeal to the next Chapter General. Santiago de Vilatorta, Commander of Mas-Deù, one of the sixteen *Capitolanti* who levied the impost, proceeded to Castile to reason with the rebels. En route he fell ill and died of his illness. Francesco Nibbia was dispatched to Castile to take up Vilatorta's assignment. Before reasoning with the rebels, however, Nibbia made it known that short of a complete retreat on the part of the rebels, he would put the matter before Emperor Charles V, who was also King of Spain. There was a complete retreat.[32]

Having accompanied Pope Clement VII to Marseille, the galleys of the Religion on 11 February returned to Malta by way of Civitavecchia. Embarked was Hospitaller John Sutton, Receiver in England, dispatched to Malta by Grand Prior William Weston with a letter from Duke of Norfolk Thomas Howard. Datelined Greenwich, 6 November 1533, the letter professed affection for the Order, for Grand Master l'Isle-Adam, and prayed that Clement West be both liberated from incarceration and reinstated as a Knight of Jerusalem with his former dignity of Turcopolier. Norfolk's letter also asserted that many in England considered West's punishment unjust. Sutton also brought an earlier letter from Weston reporting West's written communications with King Henry VIII and his Royal Council in which West stated he had been imprisoned only for professing loyalty to the Crown.

Norfolk warned in his letter of the possibility of permanent damage to the Order's status in England absent a pardon for West, whether deserved or not deserved. This matter weighed heavily on the Grand Master, as had the rebellion in Castile and the fighting between French langues and that of Italy with murder an outcome. He could foresee loss of the Langue of England. Doctor of jurisprudence Ramón Benitez of the Langue of Aragon together with Lieutenant Turcopolier Edward

Bellingham, Draper Don Bautista de Vilaragut, and Aurelio Bottigella, were appointed to a committee of investigation into whether West impugned the honour of the Grand Master. Later in the year West would be reinstated irrespective of the committee's findings.[33]

The carrack *Santa Anna* meanwhile remained at Marseille for continuing celebration of the marriage of future King Henry II to Catherine de Medici. *Santa Anna* was so large, though, she could not actually enter the port of Marseille but must anchor among the Pomeguès Islands 3 miles distant where she was visited by the Royal Galley bearing King, Queen, princes, and princesses.

Having completed his term as Captain of Galleys, Bernardo Salviati was reassigned in February 1534, re-assuming his duties as the Order's Procurator-General and Resident Ambassador at Rome. He was succeeded as Captain of Galleys by Great Siege veteran and Prior of Pisa Aurelio Bottigella. Aware that *Santa Maria de la Vittoria* commanded by Pierre de Beaulac Trébons was the slowest of the four under oars, Bottigella received permission to haul her out of the water and to reassign her oarsmen to the remaining three galleys, concerning which new assignments were made. Luigi Broglia of Chieri succeeded Pietro del Monte in command of the capitana *Santa Croce*, Parisot de la Valette of the Langue of Provence succeeded Gonzalo de Cervantes in command of *San Giovanni Battista*, and Catalan Francisco Giron succeeded Costanzo Provana in command of *San Filippo*. The squadron brigantine, reinforced with young men from *Santa Maria de la Vittoria*, was commanded by Castilian Juan de Tobía, an experienced corsair.[34]

At Constantinople Ottoman Sultan Suleiman in March appointed Kheir-ed-Din Barbarossa as kapudan-i derya or Kapudan Pasha with supreme command of the Armada, the Arsenal, the Golden Horn, islands of the Aegean, and more. Greater Algiers was created a beylerbeylik encompassing thirteen sanjaks on the shores and islands of the Mediterranean, and Barbarossa was appointed beylerbey or Viceroy.[35]

The Committee of Investigation interrogated persons with first-hand knowledge of Clement West's outbursts at the Chapter General convened in February a year earlier, and a record of Committee findings was sent back to the Duke of Norfolk.[36]

Aurelio Bottigella readied his three remaining galleys for sea, and in late April 1534 moved to the North African coast with intentions of punishing Sinan and other corsairs of Djerba. At Seccagne, not far from the island of Djerba, he encountered a galleon of Alexandria bound from Thessaloniki with a cargo of wheat, iron, lead, and cotton. There were 150 combatants on board, some Turks and some Moors. Following a protracted exchange of gunfire, Parisot de la Valette boarded from the left and Giron from the poop. The galleon was captured, though not without numerous Hospitaller wounded and dead. Among the latter were Catalans Lorenzo de San Pedro and Bartolomé de Torrero of Aragon, Luigi Lonati of the Lombard and Paulo Correa of Portugal, while André Guiremant of Provence was left with a mangled arm. Few of the galleon's crew remained alive. From these few Bottigella learned of other galleons in the area. Re-manning the galleon and offloading his wounded, he sent her in company with the squadron brigantine to Malta, where she arrived safely on 27 May. In the days to follow the squadron took possession, this time with ease, of two less well-armed galleons, one commanded by Chagi Iosuf (Yusuf) and one by Mansur Reis. A prize-crewed Portuguese-flag caravel sailing in company with the second galleon was also recovered. Its vessel and cargo of olive oil would bring a particularly handsome price.[37]

Bottigella returned to Malta on 1 June with the three rich prizes in tow, one to each galley. He did not share in the plunder but rather obtained permission from the Council to distribute his share to those most valorous in combat. These were: Gilbert de Serpens and Antoine de Villars of Auvergne, Gaspare di Beinasco and Fabio Bobba of the Piedmont, and Juan de Villalbos and Luis Tallavera of Spain. Also rewarded were the three non-Hospitaller pilots of the three galleys, Paolo d'Aula, Tomeo Cascia, and Antonio Baldichino. North African coastal waters were notoriously shallow, and pilots who knew the passages through the shallows were invaluable.[38]

Prior of Champagne a mere six months, Jean d'Aubin de Malicorne died in July of an unreported cause and was succeeded by Michel d'Argillemont. The latter was succeeded in turn as Grand Hospitaller by Jacques de Bourbon, who was succeeded as Bailiff of the Morea by Jacques de Pelloquin. The latter was succeeded as Treasurer by Antoine d'Harville de Villenes.[38]

Lope de Ordas, earlier dispatched by brigantine to ascertain Barbarossa's movements, returned with advice that on 1 August Barbarossa transited the Strait of Messina northbound with eighty-two galleys, laying waste to Reggio Calabria while doing so. Subsequently San Lucido, Cetraro, Capri, Naples, Procida, and Gaeta suffered the same fate.[39]

Aware Malta's defences were inadequate to repulse Barbarossa's Ottoman Armada, l'Isle-Adam at mid-month came down with a burning fever, and on 16 August was transferred to the higher altitude and fresher air of Rabat where he died on the 21st of August 1534. He was accorded the pomp and ceremony due a legend of his time, a legend who had made of defeat a victory, a legend who had given new life to a corpus near extinction. Philippe Villiers de l'Isle-Adam was interred in the chapel of Castle Saint Angelo whence thirty-three years later his sarcophagus would be transferred to the Conventual Church of Saint John erected in 1567 in the city opposite Castle Saint Angelo called Valletta. His initial epitaph in 1534 indicated that the Grand Master lived more than seventy years. His later epitaph on transfer to the Conventual Church states that he lived for seventy-five years and was Grand Master for thirteen years and eight months. His estate when assessed amounted to more than 100,000 scudos and was left in its entirety to the Order of Jerusalem.[40]

Chapter IV

Piero del Ponte 1534–35

Bailiff of Manosque Jean de Boniface, as Lieutenant to the Grand Master, on 26 August 1534 convened a General Assembly of all knights, serving brothers, and chaplains at Malta eligible to vote numbering in the order of 400 for the purpose of electing a new Grand Master. The authority of Boniface to do so was challenged unsuccessfully by Marshal Jean de Château-Arnauld as pre-eminent Conventual Bailiff in the Grand Commander's absence. It would seem an unwarranted affront to those aware that Jean de Boniface and the deceased l'Isle-Adam had been two of five invited to attend to the last rites for Pierre d'Aubusson in 1503. Even so, all present retired by langue, and voting in camera selected an initial elector as follows: Lieutenant Grand Commander Guyot de Panât for Provence; Bailiff of Lango Antoine de Grolée de Passim for Auvergne; Claude-Jacques d'Aspremont for France; Bautista de Vilaragut for Aragon; Costanzo Provana for Italy; Preceptor of Mount Saint Joseph Richard Brooke for England; Grand Bailiff Georg Schilling von Cannstatt for Germany; and Antonio de Viveiro for Castile. These eight from assembled Hospitallers appointed Bailiff of the Morea Jacques Pelloquin as non-voting President of the Election, Commander of Monsones Gabriel de Servières of the Langue of Provence as Knight on the Election, Gabriel Puchuert of Aragon as Chaplain of the Election, and Serving Brother Diogo Perez of Portugal as Sergeant-at-Arms of the Election. The eight initial electors then retired, leaving as electors only Gabriel de Servières, Gabriel Puchuert, and Diogo Perez. These three then selected a fourth from the Assembly, and the four selected a fifth, and the five a sixth until there were Sixteen Electors at two per langue. The additional thirteen so appointed in order of appointment were: Humbert de Montmorel of Auvergne, Pierre Pitoys of France, Giorgio Vagnone of Italy, Lieutenant Turcopolier Henry Pole of England, Rudolf z Rudnica of Germany, Guyot de Marcillac of Provence, Humbert de Murinais of Auvergne, Jean Audibert de l'Aubuge of France, Juan Ferrer of Aragon, Costanzo Provana of Italy, Richard Brooke of England, Christoph van Rassenghien of Germany, and Gonzalo Cervantes of Castile. These Sixteen Electors on the same day of 26 August in solemn conclave elected Piero del Ponte of Asti 45th Grand Master of the Order of Saint John of Jerusalem. In the new Grand Master's absence from the Convent as Bailiff of Santa Eufemia the electors reappointed Bailiff of Manosque Jean de Boniface as his Lieutenant with full power to govern the Convent in his absence or incapacity. Vice Chancellor Tommaso Bosio was at about this time appointed by the Church Bishop of Malta, and he was nominated to take the election news to the Grand Master.[1]

Piero or Pierino del Ponte was born on 26 August 1462 at Asti in northern Italy's Piedmont, a younger son of Antonio Giovanni del Ponte, Lord of Castellero and Lombriasco, and Luisa di San Martino di Agliè. The newborn's destiny pre-determined, he was on the same date received into the Order of Jerusalem, Langue of Italy, Diocese of Turin, where he later completed his novitiate. He is presumed to have entered into the study of theology and law at the University of Turin and for that reason alone missed the 1480 Ottoman Siege of Rhodes. He first appears in Bosio's History in 1501 as Commander of Pancalieri in Turin and as Receiver-General for the Langue of Italy. Enjoying the complete confidence of Grand Master l'Isle-Adam, Piero del Ponte was in 1523 appointed Seneschal by the Grand Master, serving as such until the latter's death eleven years later. In 1524 he was appointed Bailiff of Lango (Kos) and assigned one of the Grand Master's discretionary Grand Crosses for his defence of that island during the Great Siege of Rhodes.

Leaving death and destruction in the 1534 wake of his Ottoman Armada, Kheir-ed-Din Barbarossa proceeded north from the Strait of Messina past Capri and Naples, reaching a sheltered anchorage between Naples and Rome proximate to inland Fondi. He was seeking to repay the Sultan's confidence by kidnapping Giulia Gonzaga for the Sultan's seraglio. Descended from one of Italy's more prestigious families, celebrated by painters and poets, a lady of royal blood, Giulia Gonzaga was said to have been the most beautiful woman in Italy. Barbarossa failed in his attempt only because this fair maiden escaped in her night clothes on a barebacked stallion, alerted by a loyal retainer in the middle of the night. Fondi paid the price, turned upside down for four days in the Kapudan's frantic search. Weeks later Barbarossa would subdue

Bizerta and Tunis in less time than his failed search for Julia Gonzaga, thus adding Tunisia to the Ottoman realm. As host to fleeing Christians, Hospitaller Tripoli would be caught in an Ottoman vice. Malta itself was only 200 nautical miles from the Gulf of Tunis with little in between. Gonzalo Cervantes was appointed Captain of 100 Reserves and detailed to the City of Notabile. Giacomo Lengueglia of Albenga was dispatched on a brigantine to gather further information.[2]

Barbarossa resupplied his Ottoman Armada with water from the Tiber, put to fire nearby forests, came down into the lower Tyrrhenian, ignored the island of Ponza, navigated between Sicily and Sardinia, and at the end of August beached at Bizerta immediately outside the Gulf of Tunis. Tunisia had suffered the damages of twenty-something Muley Hassan (Hafsid Muhammad V r1526–44), who, upon the death of his father blinded all but one of his brothers. Neither had he been popular with his citizens. Sultan Suleiman had put at Barbarossa's disposition numerous janissaries, 800,000 Venetian ducats, and a fleet of eighty-two galleys. Barbarossa had in his retinue Muley Rashid, the only brother to escape blinding. To Barbarossa Rashid offered Bizerta in exchange for his support. The former corsair intended, however, seizure of the entire realm in the name of his Sultan. He began with Bizerta and a day later entered the port of Tunis, where he debarked two contingents, one of which was led by his lieutenant (kaya) Mourad Aga, and the other by Ali of Malaga commanding 1,000 janissaries. His galleys bombarded La Goletta, the fortress 12 miles from the city by way of the north shore of the inner harbour or lagoon. Abandoned, the fortifications would soon be improved with new and more balanced bastions. Muley Hassan fled. Barbarossa broke into his capital city by a side gate opposite the lagoon and seized the city fortress. The city of Tunis was reduced in a single day, and he was applauded by a nervous populace; local residents, however, fruitlessly awaited arrival of Muley Rashid with his forces, but Rashid had been sent in chains to Constantinople. For this reason some in the city rose in revolt and recalled Muley Hassan; the latter presenting himself at the head of a Berber tribe. A sortie by Barbarossa's militia, making a move from two city gates, beat off the desert tribesmen. The tribal chieftain was killed and the ex-king retreated to Constantine in north-eastern Algeria. Inland Kairouan (Al Qayrawan) 100km to the south was subdued. In the blink of an eye Tunisia was Ottoman and Mourad was appointed governor.

Between late October and November 1534, however, Barbarossa was confronted with two janissary revolts. On the first occasion he felt compelled to meet their demand, withdrawing funds from his personal reserve. The second time, however, the janissaries were thwarted by his militia captained by loyal lieutenants. Two hundred janissaries died in combat while others rebelling were hanged from the walls. Order in the city was thus restored and Tunis appeared a proper capital. At Madrid and Vienna, however, there was alarm. The Ottomans were to be kept east of Hospitaller Tripoli, not within striking distance of southern Spain.[3]

One month and four days after the death of l'Isle-Adam, Pope Clement VII died on 25 September 1534 following a protracted stomach illness having lived fifty-six years, eleven of them as Pope. He was in October succeeded as Pontiff by Alessandro Farnese as Pope Paul III. The new Pope announced his accession the next day with a letter to the Grand Master commending Hospitaller bearer and nephew of Cardinal Santa Cruz, Pedro Ponce de León, to the Grand Master's attention. Received in 1520 but never present at Rhodes or during the Order's vagabond years, Ponce de León was one of the Castilians who rebelled in January, so disheartening Grand Master l'Isle-Adam. He was also a cousin twice removed of Juan Ponce de León, *conquistador* and first governor of Puerto Rico, on whose fame he traded.[4]

In late October 1534 Aurelio Bottigella was dispatched with the galley squadron to the Gulf of Santa Eufemia in Calabria to embark and transport the new Grand Master to Messina and thence to Malta. He was accompanied by both the Grand Carrack *Santa Anna* still commanded by François de Toucheboeuf and by the *Grand Galleon of Alexandria* captured by Bottigella in April, re-equipped with many pieces of large artillery and placed under the command of Lope de Ordas of Castile. Received in 1518, a native of A Coruña on the Galician coast, Ordas had never been far from the sea and had earlier completed numerous brigantine missions on behalf of the Order. Bottigella was all the while aware of the threat of Barbarossa or one or another of his many lieutenants. The flotilla, however, returned safely to Malta on 10 November, the Grand Master, having rendered homage at Messina to interim Viceroy Simone Ventimiglia, Marchese di Geraci. Luigi Broglia, who in 1524 combat with corsairs of Sinan of Smyrna had been gravely wounded, was dispatched as ambassador to new Pope Paul III and other princes of Italy to announce the election of Del Ponte as Grand Master and his safe arrival at Malta. Martínho Barroso of Portugal and the Langue of Castile was similarly dispatched to the Emperor, the King of Portugal, and to the grandees of Spain, while Charles de la Barre of the Langue of France was dispatched to French King Francis.[5]

With Tripoli squeezed between Cairadino, King of Tagiora, and Barbarossa, Ottoman Beylerbey of Tunisia and Algeria, a force for the succour of Tripoli was organized at Malta. *Santa Maria de la Vittoria* commanded by Pierre de Beaulac Trébons, hauled out in February to provide additional crew for the remaining three galleys, was relaunched. Called *Il Gallo*, she was the fastest of the galleys under sail and slowest under oars. And her launch ignited a dispute between Trébons, her skipper when hauled, and Parisot de la Valette commanding *San Giovanni Battista*, which was to be hauled in *Il Gallo*'s place. Who was to command *Il Gallo*, Trébons or Valette? The Council decided in favour of Valette. Grand Bailiff Georg Schilling von Cannstatt was appointed Captain of Succour, commanding a good caravan of knights and many hired soldiers. His orders were to bring the garrison at Tripoli to a state of readiness comparable to that of Rhodes immediately prior to the Great Siege, of which he was a veteran.[6]

In consideration of the letter from Duke of Norfolk Thomas Howard datelined Greenwich, 6 November 1533 (see above), Clement West was in January 1535 freed from incarceration and reinstated as a Knight of Jerusalem with his former dignity of Turcopolier, succeeding John Rawson the Younger. Rawson succeeded the deceased John Babington as Bailiff of Eagle.[7]

Also in January, the squadron was about to depart for Tripoli when reports came of several Turkish galliots lurking off the coast of Sicily impeding the resupply of Malta. Grand Master and Council decided to dispatch the Galley Squadron to Sicily and to embark Schilling's relief force aboard the *Grand Galleon of Alexandria* commanded by Lope de Ordas and aboard the small galleon *Il Siciliano* then commanded by non-Hospitaller Ianulli Nicolò. The three galleys were redirected to Sicily and were engaged in patrolling the south coast of the island and in escorting shiploads of provisions from Sicily to Malta when at Cape Passero they came upon a large well-armed galliot of twenty-three banks. While the weather was intemperate, the three galleys gave chase in a disturbed sea under a gathering storm. Bottigella pressed on so much canvas his masts threatened to snap. So, too, did Valette with *Il Gallo*, the fastest galley in the squadron, and it was *Il Gallo* that drove her beak into the galliot's hull. The ship swamped in the disturbed sea and went to the bottom. Only seventeen of her crew were rescued, and none of her chained oarsmen, but two accompanying brigantines were seized, from one of which Bottigella learned the galliot was the largest in the Tagiora fleet. The three galleys and two captured brigantines returned to Malta on 29 January, where someone may have wondered whether it was worth the death of so many chained innocents.[7]

Several days after the squadron's return a caravel appeared in bad weather outside of Grand Harbour within sight of Castle Saint Angelo. With no reason to believe anything amiss, the castle signalled permission to enter port. Watched from afar, however, it became clear she was attempting to avoid the island, not to enter port, from which it was surmised she must be an enemy vessel. With three of the four galleys hauled for the winter, the capitana alone ready, it did not appear a single galley was strong enough in foul weather to tow the ship into port. Fortunately at that moment *Grand Galleon* commanded by Lope de Ordas heaved into sight returning from Tripoli and was able to attach a line to the caravel and tow her into Grand Harbour. She turned out to be a ship of Ragusa captured by galliots of Tagiora with a Turkish prize crew of only eighteen unequal to the task. The crew was eventually sent on to Tagiora and the ship returned to Ragusa. A number of Christian slaves were liberated.[8]

A new galley was launched in mid-April 1535, *Santa Caterina*, built in the Arsenal at Malta and commanded by Claude-Jacques d'Aspremont of Sorcy, a part of the Langue of France 60km north-east of Reims. Described as the fourth galley, she replaced *San Giovanni Battista*. On her launch, construction of yet another galley was commenced in the same ways or skids. Her name was to be *Santa Petronilla*.[9]

Twenty-year-old Prior of Capua Leone Strozzi embarked at Sicily aboard one of the Order's galleys and was conveyed to Malta, where on 23 May he was received into the Order of Jerusalem, Langue of Italy, Diocese of Florence by Grand Master Pierino del Ponte. Appointed Prior of Capua eleven years earlier by his uncle Pope Clement VII, he had then been granted an annual pension of 700 ducats on the income of the Royal Monastery of San Zoilo in Palencia, Spain. Renaissance educated at the University of Padua, Strozzi spoke Greek and Latin in addition to French and Italian. He had studied military science and would prove himself expert in the subject. The Langue of Italy was summoned to make him a part of the Auberge.[9]

Arriving on board the same galley was Hospitaller Diego de Briseño, Pilier and Capo of the Langue of Castile. He bore a letter from Emperor to Grand Master summoning the Order to gather at Cagliari, Sardinia, for the reconquest of La Goletta and the City of Tunis lost to Barbarossa one year earlier. Briseño bore a second letter from the Pope supporting the call to arms. The Church itself would provide twelve galleys armed and equipped at Genoa and Civitavecchia and commanded by Gentile Virginio Orsini, Lord of Monterano and inspired leader who would remain Papal Galley Commander until his death in 1548. Orsini would be seconded by Paolo Giustinian of Venice, an individual who thirteen years earlier had provided extraordinary support of the Order at the Great Siege of Rhodes despite Venice's neutrality. While France would not participate, the Pope wrote, twenty French galleys from Marseille would defend the Christian coast, particularly Rome's Lazio coast. There was a third letter from Prince Andrea Doria advising that the Armada would be comprised of units from Spain, Portugal, the Church, Naples, Sicily, Genoa, and elsewhere excluding Venice. Doria himself was to be General of the Sea while Alfonso d'Avalos, VI Marchese of Pescara and II of Vasto, was to be General of Infantry. Five thousand Italian infantry were to be commanded by Count of Sarno Girolamo Tuttavilla, Marchese of Finale Federico del Carretto, and Agostino Spinola, eight companies each. Maximilian von Herberstein of Styria was to command 8,000 Germans embarked in eight of thirty ships commanded by Antonio Doria. Viceroy of Naples Don Pedro de Toledo was to contribute fourteen galleys, four of which were to be armed and equipped at the expense of the Prince of Salerno, the Prince of Bisignano, the Marqués de la Val Siciliana Hernando de Alarcón (five years later to become the first non-Native American to set foot in Alta California), and Don Federico de Toledo, son of the Viceroy. The same princes were to provide a new Royal galley of thirty banks, four oars to a bank, the oarsmen uniformed, with a richly appointed poop. The Royal galley was to be accompanied by sixteen

Spanish galleys and three galleons of Barcelona to embark the Emperor and the flower of Spanish nobility, including *conquistador* Hernán Cortés. The Infante Don Luis of Portugal, the Emperor's brother-in-law as brother of the Empress, was to bring twenty-five Portuguese caravels and a large galleon carrying 2,000 soldiers of the standing army plus a large quantity of artillery. Captain Mendoza, son of the Count of Tendiglia called El Monteggio, was to bring 8,000 Spanish infantry and 700 light cavalry. From Flanders there were seventy large sailing ships. Finally, there was the Armada of Spain coming from Port Mahon in Menorca.

Soon after the arrival of the three letters on 21 May 1535, the Marqués del Vasto reached Trapani at the western end of Sicily en route to Cagliari with thirty-seven galleys and sixty sailing ships. And there was the newly appointed Viceroy of Sicily Don Ferrante de Gonzaga in succession of Simone Ventimiglia, who died suddenly, still assembling the galleys and ships of Sicily. The Grand Master immediately ordered preparation of the Order's contribution to the Armada: Bottigella's four galleys, himself commanding the capitana *Santa Croce*, Parisot de la Valette commanding *Santa Maria de la Vittoria*, Francisco Giron commanding *San Filippo*, and Claude-Jacques d'Aspremont commanding *Santa Caterina*, each with fifty additional knights embarked. Toucheboeuf's Grand Carrack *Santa Anna* with seventy extra knights and a regiment of hired infantry, knights and soldiers commanded by Bailiff of Lango Antoine de Grolée. The large *Grand Galleon of Alexandria* had to be held in reserve to succour Tripoli, while the garrison at Malta and Gozo would be cut to 100 knights and a handful of infantry.[9]

The Hospitaller contingent departed Malta the final day of May 1535. Touching Trapani days later, the Hospitallers were forced by contrary wind to leave Toucheboeuf's *Santa Anna* to proceed alone to rendezvous with the Imperial Armada at anchor off Cagliari. According to Kenneth Setton,[10] the Imperial Armada at Cagliari eventually consisted of seventy-four galleys, thirty galliots, fustas, and brigantines, as well as some 300 transports and other vessels, including Portuguese galleons and caravels but excluding Toucheboeuf's *Santa Anna*, as Charles himself twice reported the figures. In his war council the Emperor paid particular heed not only to Doria and Del Vasto but also to experienced warriors Aurelio Bottigella and Gentile Virginio Orsini commanding six Papal galleys,[11] not the twelve promised. The Emperor was also introduced to Muley Hassan's ambassador Xeriffe accompanying Bottigella by way of Tripoli. Descended from Moors of Granada, Xeriffe spoke fluent Castillian Spanish and was promising assistance from his king. The Armada sailed for Tunis on Sunday, 13 June. The Royal galley had on her left Bottigella's Hospitaller capitana, on her right in the place of honour was Orsini's capitana flying the colours of Pope Paul III, to her rear was the capitana of the Republic of Genoa. The Armada caught a fair north wind (Mistral) and on the second morning reached Porto Farina at the north-western corner of the Gulf of Tunis, 140nm south of Cagliari. Not pausing, the Armada continued another 25nm to Cape Carthage, which was reached the same evening 5 miles short of La Goletta.[12]

Sighted by Toucheboeuf's *Santa Anna* from Cimbalo (Zembra) Island off the north-eastern entrance to the Gulf of Tunis, a rendezvous was effected at Cape Carthage. On Thursday and Friday, 17 and 18 June, 15,000 Spanish, Italians, and Germans plus siege artillery were put ashore between Cape Carthage and La Goletta. Most of the warships soon proceeded to the outer harbour of Tunis facing La Goletta, the fortress defending the inner harbour or lagoon accessible only by a passage 300 yards in length and 100ft in width cutting a narrow neck of land enclosing the inner harbour. It was another 6 miles across a lagoon or 12 miles by the north shore to the walled city of Tunis governed by Mourat Aga (Murat of Ragusa), appointed to his position ten months earlier. Of heavy stone construction, La Goletta was rectangular in shape with its long sides parallel to the passage and with a bastion at each corner. The keep or castle or tower was in the centre. The bastions, ramparts, and tower contained more than three hundred pieces of artillery. There was an additional outer wall on the north or land side crossing most of the isthmus and connected to the ring wall. In addition to the aforementioned artillery, La Goletta was defended by Barbarossa lieutenant and brother-in-law the eye-patched Sinan of Smyrna with a garrison of 5,000 Turks and additional Moors. Sinan's own lieutenants included Aydin Caramano, a Coptic Christian called *Terror del Diablo* by the Spanish since his overwhelming 1529 defeat of Spanish Admiral Rodrigo Portundo; Giaffer Reis, the Aga of Janissaries and long-time confidant of Barbarossa; the other brother-in-law Salih Reis, a Greek from the plains of Troy, he and Sinan wed to Barbarossa's two Greek sisters; and Tabach Reis, a Greek of Laodicea (Latakia, Syria).[13]

Cannonading of La Goletta commenced upon the Armada's arrival on 20 June and continued until seizure of the fortress on 14 July. Meanwhile, the 15,000 Imperial infantry had advanced from Cape Carthage pulling their artillery by hand in the absence of draft animals. These cannon emplaced opposite the land wall and, according to Merriman, opposite the west wall facing Tunis were also firing continuously. Barbarossa's lieutenant and Governor Mourat Aga, who was said to command upward of 30,000 Arabs and Moors, continually harassed besiegers from ambush among olive groves, his ambushes often coinciding with sorties on the part of Sinan and the others. Shortage of water was a major problem for the Christians, the few water sources also controlled by Mourat; wine was accordingly consumed in quantity by the thirsty. A famous painting by Flemish contemporary (born 1535) Frans Hogenberg depicts Armada galleys six to a line. Firing their bow chasers and retiring to reload, these come in successive waves. Behind them are the Royal Galley with the Emperor's Eagle at the stern and next to the Royal Galley Toucheboeuf's *Santa Anna* with Hospitaller colours at the truck. Also depicted are the Genovese carrack *Grimaldi* and the Portuguese galleon *São João Baptista*, said to mount 366 bronze cannon and making it the most powerful ship in the world, also known as *Botafogo*.

After nearly a month of bombardment by sea and by land and of harassment from olive groves, with the Emperor himself frequently mounted in defence of sorties or in trenches snaking toward La Goletta urging his sappers forward, after a month in which two Hospitaller galleys among others were disabled, and after a month of debilitating thirst, a part of the central keep or tower fell, brought down by *Santa Anna*'s large cannon.[14] That day had coincidentally been scheduled for the assault, and the tower's fall proved an encouragement. Spanish infantry under Álvaro de Bazán, Marqués del Viso, assailed north walls. Hospitallers and hired infantry under Bailiff of Lango Antoine de Grolée came ashore in small boats and assailed south walls. Scaling ladder erected, Savoyard Hospitaller and Flag Bearer Guillaume Coppier was among the first on the ramparts, where the Order's standard was planted; Hospitaller Luigi Peletta of Asti was killed at his side. Sinan of Smyrna led three unsuccessful counterattacks; in the end the Turks and Moors were driven out for good.[13]

Captured at La Goletta in their entirety were 340 pieces of artillery, large quantities of gunpowder, projectiles, arrows, arquebuses, and muskets; also captured in the inner harbour was a corsair fleet consisting of forty-two galleys, among which were Barbarossa's capitana and the former capitana of Rodrigo Portundo, forty-four galliots, fustas, and brigantines, as well as twenty-seven other ships of all kinds. Days after the fall of La Goletta, soldiers debarked at Carthage were forced to again pull in the absence of draft animals six heavy and six medium cannon through 12 miles of sand along the north shore while opposed by Barbarossa himself. At the forefront were two battalions of 4,000 infantry, one led by the Marqués del Vasto and one by Prince of Salerno Ferrante da San Severino. Arquebusiers were placed on the flanks and the cannon were followed by the rearguard. Barbarossa was driven back to Tunis, where his Arabs and Moors made one last stand at the major water source outside of the city, unsuccessfully, before retiring into the city. That night 7,000 Christian slaves led by Hospitaller Paolo Simeoni burst from the citadel baths, raided the Arsenal, and, joined by the army at the gates, put the defenders to flight.

Tunis was captured on 21 July but 'merciless' plundering continued for three more days, with soldiers and ex-slaves competing for the spoils. Women, including elderly women and girls, were raped, tortured, and murdered. The men were killed or maimed or both. The perpetrators were revealed as mindless savages. The massacre of the local population left an estimated 30,000 dead, but Barbarossa with Sinan, Salih, and most others of his trusted lieutenants as well as 7,000 Turks and 2,000 Moors eventually reached Bona (Annaba), where fourteen galleys had been concentrated in advance of the Christian assault. Just in case siege defence went badly. Perhaps left behind was Barbarossa's long-time confidant and Aga of Janissaries Giaffer Reis. According to Bosio,[14] Giaffer was cut down by arquebus fire at La Goletta. If so, Barbarossa had another Giaffer by 1543, this one Sancakbey of Gallipoli, including the fleet janissary school in that city, just senior enough to have been the Giaffer at Tunis. The presidio of La Goletta was entrusted to Spaniard Bernardino de Mendoza with a strong garrison and twelve captured galleys, while Tunis itself was left to the vultures and Muley Hassan. The Emperor and the flower of Spanish nobility set sail for Sicily with the Imperial Armada less Doria plus ninety-nine rearmed Ottoman vessels manned by 7,000 liberated Christians with newly enslaved Tunisians at the oars.[13]

Charles V left Tunis and assigned Muley Hassan with an encampment of friendly Arabs the task of pursuing Barbarossa by land. Informed by Arab telegraph that Aydin Catch-the-Devil and others in flight, burning from the heat of the sun, had died by over-ingestion of water from the Medjerda River, these hastened in pursuit. The distance to Bona as the crow flies, however, was 220km over unfriendly territory. Andrea Doria himself was assigned the task of taking Barbarossa at sea. The Genovese admiral, fueling speculation, first refused Bottigella's insistence on going and then sent his inexperienced cousin Adam Centurione, a banker at Genoa, with a squadron of eighteen galleys to entrap and destroy the Ottoman admiral at Bona.

The squadron included two Hospitaller galleys, Francisco Giron's *Cornuto* (a Barbarossa galley replacing the battle-scarred *San Filippo*) and Jacques d'Aspremont's *Catarinetta* (a diminutive for *Santa Caterina*). Centurione returned to Goletta with a report that he found Barbarossa already at sea with a large number of galleys packed with janissaries and other Turks, and because his own galleys were undermanned with some assigned soldiers still at the sack of Tunis, he had decided, without consulting Giron and Aspremont, prudence was the better part of valour. Giron and Aspremont were and remained incensed. The speculation fueled was that Doria and Barbarossa had an understanding that should one be done in, there would be no need for the other. Better late than early, Doria proceeded to Bona, confirmed Barbarossa had departed, and with great ferocity stormed the city and its castle. The former was put to the sack, after which a Spanish garrison was installed in the latter under Don Alvaro Gomez Zagal. In the end Doria returned to Sicily with thirty-eight galleys, including four Maltese. He put in to the island of Favignana at the western end of Sicily and then proceeded to Messina, where, on hearing his report, Charles V was livid. As noted, those surviving Barbarossa's forced march indeed reached Bona and, with 7,000 Turks squeezed on fourteen galleys and galliots, had taken course for Algiers. At Algiers they were joined by thirteen additional galleys, relieving loads on the first fourteen, and all twenty-seven took course for Spain's Balearic Islands, where the news of Barbarossa's death had far outpaced the fact. All over southern Europe the news had provoked manifestations of popular exultation, processions, and Te Deums of thanksgiving, especially in Spain and especially at Menorca. At Menorca's Port Mahon the manifestations were in full swing when twenty-seven galleys and galliots flying the flag of Spain returned from the Tunis Expedition. One was even hanging a Barbarossa effigy. The Ottoman Admiral left Port Mahon with the entire population enslaved, most of them embarked aboard a Portuguese caravel seized in the port decorated for the festivities. Still at Messina with Doria when the news arrived, the Emperor became apoplectic. By then Barbarossa was devastating the Tyrrhenian coast of Italy not too far to the north.

Toucheboeuf's *Santa Anna* meanwhile reached Malta on 23 August. With the Imperial Armada en route to Sicily, one of the Spanish galleons had sprung a leak and was close to foundering off Mazara at the western end of the island. Among *Santa Anna*'s crew was a Master Shipfitter by the name of Marangoni, who was transferred by skiff to the foundering vessel. Not only a Master Shipfitter, Marangoni was a practised underwater diver who was able to locate the leak and repair it. The Malta galleys returned home in early November.[15]

Grand Bailiff Georg Schilling had meanwhile remained a visitor and Captain of Reserves at Tripoli, aiding Governor Garcia Cortèz in the latter's frequent encounters with King of Tagiora Cairadino's minions. An uneasy stalemate persisted when in October 1535 Cortèz completed his term as Governor and, by order of Grand Master and Council, was succeeded by Schilling. A bit later there was a major hiccup at Malta occasioned by a Proclamation from Pope Paul III. Defrocked Don Pedro Fernandez d'Heredia, who had illegally (shades of his forebear Juan Fernandez d'Heredia) seized the Commandery of Alfambra in February 1533, usurping the dignity of Prior of Alfambra even though Alfambra was but a commandery, and ousting incumbent Commander Francisco de Benedettes before himself being ousted, was by order of Pope Paul III to be reinstated with the dignity of Prior of Alfambra, Benedettes to be reassigned. While there was consternation at Malta at the Pope's usurpation of local authority and anger at the wrong done, especially among the Langue of Aragon, a Papal Proclamation is rarely if ever overturned. History does not tell the history student the nature of Fernandez d'Heredia's influence, but suggests it was as Charles V's Ambassador to the Holy See. This development and the political need to acquiesce is believed to have pushed an ailing Grand Master over the edge. He asked that Bailiff of the Morea and Magistral Lieutenant Jacques Pelloquin be appointed his lieutenant and vicar to temporarily govern the Convent during his incapacity, and nominated Prior of Toulouse Didier de Sainte-Jalle as his successor.[16]

Piero del Ponte passed away on 18 November 1535. Seventy-three years of age, he was initially interred in the Chapel of Our Lady of Victories within Castle Saint Angelo at Birgu. Eventually his remains were reinterred in the crypt of St John's Co-Cathedral at Valletta.[17]

Chapter V

Didier de Tholon de Sainte-Jalle 1535–36

Grand Master Pierino del Ponte passed away on 18 November 1535 and with all due ceremony was interred in the Chapel of Our Lady of Victories within Castle Saint Angelo. Immediately following interment a General Assembly of knights, serving brothers, and chaplains eligible to vote, about 300 in number, was convened in the Great Hall of the Castle by Bailiff of the Morea and Lieutenant to the Grand Master Jacques de Pelloquin. By statutory procedure an initial elector was chosen by each langue. These were Commander of Durban Bertrand de Rousset for Provence, Bailiff of Lango Antoine de Grolée for Auvergne, Commander of Fieffes Roland de Rouy for France, Commander of Alfambra Francisco de Benedettes for Aragon, Prior of Capua Leone Strozzi for Italy, Turcopolier Clement West for England, Polish-born Hungarian Rudolf z Rudnica for Germany, and Chancellor Jacobo de Briceño for Castile. These eight appointed Clement West non-voting President of Elections while the remaining seven selected from among those assembled Nicolas de Paci d'Aubigny of Provence as Knight of Elections, Gabriel Puguert of Aragon as Chaplain of Elections, and Serving Brother João Ayres of Portugal as Sergeant-at-Arms of Elections.[1]

These three electors, called the Triumvirate, had the responsibility of selecting a fourth elector from among those assembled, and the four a fifth, and the five a sixth and so on until there were Sixteen Electors at two per langue. The thirteen additional electors were Commander of Dole Imbert de Moriniers for Auvergne, Commander of Villedieu Philippe de Carleau for France, Commander of Parma Francesco Romagnano for Italy, Preceptor of Temple Bruer Giles Russell for England, Rudolf z Rudnica for Germany, Commander of Granier Jean de Gléon for Provence, Commander of Chambéry Gaspard de Vallier for Auvergne, Commander of Chalon Calixte de la Barre for France, Commander of Barbens and Lieutenant Draper Gaspar Ferrer for Aragon, Giorgio Vagnone of Turin for Italy, Preceptor of Mount Saint Joseph Richard

Brooke for England, Commander of Salamanca Gonzalo Cervantes for Castile, and, there being no other eligible Germans at the Convent, Chaplain Thomas Tinel of France for Germany. These Sixteen Electors in solemn conclave on 22 November 1535 elected Prior of Toulouse Didier de Tholon de Sainte-Jalle forty-sixth Grand Master of the Order of Jerusalem. There is no report of other candidates considered.[1]

Didier de Tholon de Sainte-Jalle was born in about 1470, thought to be a second son of Antoine de Tholon de Sainte-Jalle, co-Seigneur of Sainte-Jalle, 170km north of Marseille. Early in life he was received into the Order of Jerusalem, Langue of Provence, probably by way of the Diocese of Avignon, where he appears to have been placed on a fast track, attending university for the study of law and the classics. By 1503 he was already absentee Commander of the former Templar Commandery of Joucas in eastern Provence and of Homps in southern Provence, and that year was selected an honorary pall bearer at Rhodes, attending last rites for Cardinal-Grand Master Pierre d'Aubusson, the junior of four pall bearers so honoured.[2]

In July 1522, with Rhodes Town under siege by sea and land, Sainte-Jalle, as Bailiff of Manosque, guided a sailing vessel laden with artillery and attendant gunners among and between besieging oared galleys and without a scratch into the commercial harbour. He was immediately assigned as co-commander of artillery, a command shared with Prior of Saint-Gilles Pregeant de Bidoux. Three months later he was placed in command of the beleaguered Post of Aragon where he, Prior of France Pierre de Cluis, and Grand Master l'Isle-Adam bedded down each night. In November he presided over the trial of Portuguese Chancellor Andrea d'Amaral, a trial in which Amaral was found guilty of conspiring with the enemy and executed. A survivor marching out of Rhodes on the evening of 1 January 1523, Sainte-Jalle was within months appointed Prior of Toulouse.

With election of Sainte-Jalle as Grand Master, the dignity of Prior of Toulouse was conveyed to Raymond de Ricard, who vacated the dignity of Grand Commander to which Guyot de Panât, Commander of Argentens, was appointed. Grand Prior of France Pierre de Cluis died and was succeeded by Jacques de Bourbon, Bourbon vacating the dignity of Grand Hospitaller to which Jacques de Pelloquin was appointed, while Pierre de Nesdez succeeded Pelloquin as Bailiff of the Morea and

Philippe de Carleau succeeded Nesdez as Treasurer. Importantly, Grand Hospitaller Jacques de Pelloquin was reaffirmed as Lieutenant to the Grand Master with Magistral power to act in the Grand Master's absence or incapacity. News of these developments was conveyed to the princes of Europe by the former skipper of *Santa Maria de la Vittoria* Pierre de Beaulac-Trébons.[3]

The dignity of Prior of Lombardia fell vacant upon the November 1535 death of incumbent Ercole di None. None was succeeded by Admiral Muzio Costanzo, who in turn was succeeded by Lieutenant Admiral Filippo Pilli of Florence, all three veterans of the Great Siege of Rhodes. Prior to his elevation Costanzo had appointed William Tyrell of the Langue of England to succeed Lope de Ordas in command of *Grand Galleon of Alexandria*, at the time renamed *Grand Galleon* or *Galleon of the Religion*. The Council annulled this appointment as the prerogative of the new Admiral. Pilli reappointed Tyrell to the same position, and the Council appointed Tyrell Lieutenant Admiral, a dignity of the Langue of Italy. In April, however, Costanzo renounced the dignity of Prior of Lombardy in view of the Franco-Spanish War ongoing in the Piedmont, and reassumed the dignity of Admiral, with Pilli reassuming the office of Lieutenant Admiral. Paolo Simeoni was appointed Prior of Lombardia in Costanzo's stead. And because Aurelio Bottigella would soon reach the end of his term as Captain of Galleys, on 20 December Prior of Capua Leone Strozzi was less than unanimously elected his successor. Turcopolier Clement West quite rightly observed that at 21 years of age and with no galley experience whatsoever, Strozzi was less than qualified. It was his insolence in describing his own qualifications, though, which earned West few admirers. Appointed with Strozzi were Costanzo d'Operti, who succeeded Bottigella in command of the capitana, Tristan de Melo succeeding Parisot de la Valette in command of *Santa Maria de la Vittoria*, Gaspard de Vallier succeeding Claude-Jacques d'Aspremont in command of *Santa Caterina*, and Pierre de Noé succeeding to command of *Santa Croce*. Most of these appointments would take place nine months later in September 1536.[1]

Primarily reflecting the Emperor's exasperated interest in purging the North African coast of corsairs, particularly his interest in eliminating Algiers as a threat to nearby Spain, Francois de Toucheboeuf was ordered to forego a previously planned careening of the Great Carrack *Santa*

Anna at Villefranche and instead to spruce and refit afloat and from Villefranche proceed to embark new Grand Master Didier de Sainte-Jalle and return to Malta. At about this time the brigantine assigned to Tripoli reached Malta to report Barbarossa, with twenty-six oared vessels in good order, was headed in the direction of Constantinople for the purpose of reporting to the Sultan on the loss of Tunis and to expedite construction of new galleys and support vessels. Because the Convent at Malta was in only modest readiness to resist any Ottoman assault, Lieutenant to the Grand Master Jacques de Pelloquin and Council in December 1535 issued a general call to all priories and commanderies summoning resident Hospitallers to Malta.[4]

Barbarossa arrived at Constantinople accompanied by Piali Bey, Sinan, Tabach, Salih, Memi Reis, Kara Mustafa, Murat of Puglia, and others. He never again returned to Algiers.[5] Expecting censure for the loss of Tunis, he was on arrival instead formally appointed Kapudan Pasha succeeding Kemankesh Ahmed, Kapudan then ranked second in the government behind Grand Vizier Pargali Ibrahim Pasha.[5]

Early in 1536 Captain of Galleys Aurelio Bottigella took the squadron consisting of the same galleys under the same commanders from Malta to Messina pursuant to a request to relocate the Viceregal household of Don Ferrante Gonzaga from Messina to Palermo. This and similar requests reflected outlaw control of Sicilian roads where roads existed. In Milan, meanwhile, 14-year-old Christina of Denmark, widow of deceased Duke Francesco II Sforza and niece of Emperor Charles V, ceded the Duchy of Milan to the Emperor's son Philip, angering French King Francis. At Rome new Cardinal Priest Girolamo Ghinucci, former titular Bishop of Worcester, England, and current Administrator of Malta, petitioned Pope Paul III to rescind Pope Clement VII's August 1531 Bull appointing Tommasso Bosio Bishop of Malta so that he might be advanced from Cardinal Priest of San Clemente, a minor basilica, to Cardinal Bishop of Malta. Unfortunately for Cardinal Ghinucci, the Emperor himself was instrumental in Bosio's appointment, and no one, not even the Pope, was going to override the Emperor.[6]

Hospitaller Jean de la Foret of the Langue of Auvergne, a veteran of 1522's Great Siege of Rhodes and French Ambassador to the Ottoman Porte, obtained agreement in February 1536 to Capitulations that remained the foundation of Franco–Ottoman relations into the nineteenth century.[7] A codicil to this agreement provided for a Franco–Ottoman assault on Italy in 1537.

Grand Vizier Ibrahim Pasha, originally an Orthodox Christian from Parga kidnapped as a child and delivered to Prince Suleiman's court at Manisa, was murdered on 15 March 1536 in the Topkapi Palace at the behest of Suleiman's wife Roxelana, or Hurrem Sultan, so that her son-in-law Rustem might succeed to the grand vizierate. This development, rumours of war, and reports of heavy shipbuilding activity at Constantinople were of increasing concern to the interim government of Malta. Grand Hospitaller and Lieutenant to the Grand Master Jacques Pelloquin, assisted by Marshal Jean de Château-Arnauld, also wrestled with more mundane problems such as cash flow, concerning which former Tripoli Governor Garcia Cortèz had been appointed Procurator of the Treasury. There was also an unusual degree of bickering among Hospitallers, fed in large part by an unhappy Clement West, senior holder of the Grand Cross, who believed he, not Pelloquin, should be running things in the Grand Master's absence.[8]

French King Francis, believing Milan as well as Asti and Genoa his by right of birth but having learned nothing from recent history, sent an army of 24,000 foot and 3,000 cavalry under Philippe de Chabot, seigneur de Brion, into Savoy and the Piedmont, occupying Savoy's Turin on 3 April 1536. The Duchy of Savoy for all intents and purposes ceased to exist for the next quarter century. Pro-French elements in Asti rose up and overthrew their Imperial government and garrison. For a week. Chabot's expeditionary force turned on Genoa with 10,000 Italian allies, but an expected uprising within the city failed to materialise and the expeditionary force returned to France with Savoy its only gain. Milan was never threatened. During these months three French Priors came to the end of their lives. Jacques de Manas, Prior of Saint-Gilles since 1528, was succeeded by Grand Commander Guyot de Panât, who was succeeded by Pierre de Grasse. Charles des Ursins, Prior of Aquitaine for sixteen years, was succeeded by Jacques Pelloquin, who would remain Prior for twenty-three years. Pelloquin was succeeded as Grand Hospitaller by Philippe de Carleau, who was succeeded as Treasurer by absentee Jean de la Roche-Andry. Prior of Champagne Michel d'Argillemont, who lost an eye at the Great Siege, also passed away. He was succeeded by Bailiff of the Morea Pierre de Nesdez, who was himself succeeded by

Robert d'Aché, an Hospitaller for thirty-four years and also a veteran of the Great Siege. Finally, Battista Schiatessi was succeeded as Governor of Gozo by Salvador de Sin of Huesca and the Langue of Aragon.[9]

With continuing rumour concerning the activity or lack thereof on the part of Barbarossa, Francesco Nibbia was dispatched by brigantine to the Levant to get at the truth. Soon afterward Aurelio Bottigella's squadron returned to Malta on 25 May with four galleys towing two galliots belonging to Kara Mustafa (of Foca) and to Morat Reis (Murat of Puglia) captured, respectively, at the Sicilian island of Favignana and at the nearby island of Filicudi. Bottigella had with him eighty-two Turkish survivors excluding the owners who were not embarked. A Christian merchantman with a cargo of wine, captured earlier by the two galliots, was recovered. From these captives Bottigella understood all Barbary corsairs, after accompanying Barbarossa to Constantinople, would be returning with many other Levantine corsairs to depredate Christian coasts. For this reason the squadron immediately departed Malta to patrol the coast of Sicily.

In the late Spring of 1536 a renegade corsair raiding Calabria's Gulf of Squillace ahead of Barbarossa's return from Constantinople, by name simply Giaffer Reis or Djafer Reis and himself Calabrian by birth, kidnapped among others a 17-year-old native of Licastella by the name of Luca Galeni. Described as both a fisherman and a Dominican novitiate, Galeni would be sent to his kidnapper's oars, advance to boatswain, wed Giaffer's daughter, and become a renegade corsair in his own right. Commanding an Algerian galliot squadron under the nom de guerre of Kiliç Ali, he would in 1570 overwhelm the Hospitaller Galley Squadron, and in 1571 would be renamed Kilic Ali (Ali the Sword) and appointed by Ottoman Sultan Selim II Kapudan Pasha or Commander of the Ottoman Armada.

On the final day of May 1536 Juan de Sangorrin returned from Spain by way of Rome. He had been dispatched by the Langue of Aragon to the Court of Emperor Charles V to seek redress for Pope Paul's Bull of the previous October. The Bull had mandated that defrocked Don Pedro Fernandez d'Heredia, who had illegally seized the Commandery of Alfambra in February 1533, usurping the dignity of Prior of Alfambra even though Alfambra was but a commandery, and ousting incumbent Commander Francisco de Benedettes, be reinstated with the dignity of

Prior of Alfambra, Benedettes to be reassigned. Sangorrin had in hand a new Brief of Pope Paul reversing the Bull and absolving Benedettes and others involved of any wrongdoing. Once again the Emperor proved more powerful than the Pope.[10]

Early in June came news of the passing of Prior of Saint-Gilles Guyot de Panât after less than two months in office. The Priory was assigned to Prior of Toulouse Raymond Ricard, while Pierre de Grasse succeeded to the dignity of Prior of Toulouse and was succeeded himself as Grand Commander by Giraud de Massas. Still patrolling Sicilian waters, Bottigella off Messina surprised and captured one of the more astute and practised Barbary corsairs and his swift (sottile) galley of twenty-three banks. Called Memi Liparoto, he was said to be a Turk and not a renegade. Promised his life and the lives of his officers in return for information, Liparoto revealed the rendezvous of another corsair sailing in company at the island of Filicudi. At Filicudi Bottigella sent two of his galleys around in one direction and the other two galleys and brigantine around in the other direction. The corsair, called Quel Velli of Palatia (ancient Miletus), was captured by Parisot de la Valetta commanding *Santa Maria de la Vittoria*. Quel Velli was also believed to be Turkish. The squadron returned to Malta with the captured galliots in tow.[10]

Sinan of Smyrna was ordered to Suez by Sultan Suleiman to take command of the Red Sea Fleet; Dragut succeeded Sinan as Governor of Djerba. Francesco Nibbia returned from the Levant with news that Barbarossa had exited the Dardanelles with forty galleys, twenty galliots, and a multitude of fustas all in good order and carrying scaling ladders, pickaxes, and trenching tools, with observers opining there was to be an assault on Tripoli. The Council sent the same brigantine back to the Levant, this time with Pedro de Felizes embarked with orders to keep an eye open for Barbarossa. Antonio de Viveiro of Galicia, Captain of Reserves for Tripoli, was ordered to Tripoli with a good number of knights and soldiers. Bottigella's squadron took them there, towing a Maltese vessel full of provisions, munitions, and items necessary for strengthening fortifications. Bottigella returned to Malta, where on order of Jacques de Pelloquin and the Council, and in spite of his protest, Liparoto and his officers were hanged as renegades at Rinella to the seaward of Birgu. Again despite his remonstrations, several knights were punished for taking part in the looting of Liparoto's galley, full of silks and other stolen merchandise.[11]

Galleys and cargo ship departed Malta on 8 August 1536. En route the squadron surprised the germa of Ardor Reis, which was bound from Djerba to Alexandria with a cargo of olive oil. The value of the plunder amounted to 80,000 ducats; 109 persons were captured, mostly Moors with a handful of Turks. From the captives Bottigella learned several Barbary fustas had earlier captured a Maltese frigate from which Nicolas de Rossignac, a Knight of Malta of the Langue of France, was taken prisoner and later in Djerba beaten on the stomach with a club until dead. In revenge, any Djerba corsairs caught by Bottigella in the future would be hanged. This practice begot the execution of Hospitallers held captive by corsairs, and would little by little lead to the elimination of the practice of hanging captives.[11]

Succeeding the deceased Aydin Catch-the-Devil,[12] Scander Reis was under way off the coast of Tripoli in August 1536 with five corsair galliots bound from Tagiora to Djerba. Of his five galliots, three would be found reinforced with additional crew and oarsmen, the complement for a new galliot awaiting delivery at Djerba. When sighted from Tripoli just before evening Vespers, two slower galliots were lagging well behind the others. Normally a corsair unit bound from Tagiora to Djerba would pass Tripoli over the horizon, and Bottigella considered the current circumstance a sign of disdain on the part of the squadron commander, believed to be an Ottoman Greek like Barbarossa himself. Because Tripoli was an isolated Christian outpost in a hostile Muslim world, Bottigella believed it imperative there be a demonstration of strength. He convened a council of his commanders, including pilots as the route to Djerba bordered shallows, and including caravan commanders as hand-to-hand fighting was anticipated. His four galleys exited Tripoli at sunset and on a fresh wind went in pursuit. He commanded the capitana *Santa Croce*, Parisot de la Valette commanded *Santa Maria de la Vittoria* called *Il Gallo*, fastest of the four under sail, Francisco Giron commanded *Cornuto*, and Claude-Jacques d'Aspremont commanded *Santa Caterina*.[12]

Because the enemy had its sails furled, by dawn the next morning the two laggard galliots were only 2 miles ahead. The larger of the two, which was not much smaller than a Hospitaller galley, turned her beam to the pursuers and took to the high seas, leaving the other inshore, the latter seeking safety among shallows. Bottigella signalled Valette to take the first and Giron to take the galliot remaining inshore. The latter was moving slowly toward the shore, grounding and sliding off again and again, her bow chasers of no use against Giron's *Cornuto*, which was meanwhile opening holes in the enemy stern with her own bow chasers. The enemy settled ever lower in the water and in a deeper patch went to the bottom, taking her chained Christian oarsmen and some armoured Turks with her.

A third galliot a bit further ahead and still headed toward Djerba had been assigned to Aspremont's *Catarinetta*. The enemy still had her sails furled, presumably to have clear decks and more manoeuvrability, and was soon overhauled. She suddenly reversed course to save herself as *Catarinetta*'s sails would become a hindrance should she do the same thing. This manoeuvre was partly successful and, seeing it, Bottigella brought his capitana into action, coming in astern of the galliot and plunging the capitana's bow spur and boarding ramp into the enemy. The ensuing contest swung back and forth, with the more numerous Turks behind scimitars and shields frequently having the upper hand, but eventually concluded in a bloody victory for the Hospitallers. Among notable contributions to the victory were those of Hospitallers Francisco Burghès, the senior and oldest knight on board the capitana, and Battista Bellomo of Syracuse commanding embarked soldiers. While Bosio[13] reports numerous wounded, he makes no mention of the dead other than mortally wounded Damián La Raya of the Langue of Castile who will die later. Nor does Bosio make it clear what became of this galliot after its looting, but presumably she went to the bottom, 'traboccata', when the capitana disengaged and the hole in her underwater hull proved decisive. It would seem certain that Christian oarsmen, about 200 in number, were liberated before disengagement.

Valette's *Il Gallo* had lost sight of the other three Hospitaller galleys while pursuing the galliot that turned toward open sea. This larger galliot turned out to be Scander's capitana rather than one of the two laggards it was thought to have been. Also on board was the sixth captain for the galliot waiting at Djerba as well as more than 130 veteran Azaps, each an experienced soldier. In the absence of wind both galley and galliot had stowed their sails. During the pursuit, which had been a long arc to the west, *Il Gallo*'s bow cannon had done some damage, while the fleeing galliot had been unable to bring her guns to bear. The pursuit ended with galley spur in galliot stern and the two coupled together in a second bloody melee.

Valette soon took two crossbow bolts in the shoulder occasioning a great loss of blood. Command was turned over to the senior knight on board, the Portuguese Cristóvão da Cunha. Da Cunha felt a need to get proper medical attention for Valette but before doing so put a handful of men on the spur under the galliot's poop while *Il Gallo*'s arquebusiers were decimating Azaps gathered above. This handful of men were believed by the enemy to be readying the spur for disengagement by creating a larger hole in the galliot's stern. But at great cost these brave men were in fact ensuring the galliot remained afloat when the two detached and that the lives of 200 Christian oarsmen would be spared.

The two coupled vessels were at that point within sight of Zuara (modern Zuwara) and those suspicious among the enemy, including a wounded Scander and the sixth reis, began to jump ship in hope of swimming to shore. Two on the spur, Hospitaller Antonio Godinez of Castile and non-Hospitaller Giorgio Carpaccio, had been killed when with a lurch the two ships pulled apart. The galliot did not sink, and there were insufficient defenders remaining to fight the ship. These yielded. Christian oarsmen were liberated and taken aboard Bottigella's capitana just arriving. Renegade former Christians were hanged. Captured Turks were sent to the oars. There was an insufficient number of defenders remaining on board to fight the ship.

Scander did not make it to Zuara but some did. Among the survivors was wounded caravan knight David Gonson of Deptford, Kent. He would live another five years before being condemned to death for denying the authority of King Henry VIII in spiritual matters. The squadron returned to Tripoli, where it was greeted by the brigantine of Geronimo Vela newly arrived from Malta with orders for the Expeditionary Force to stand down. Barbarossa was not destined to assail Tripoli this year. In fact, he had already returned to Constantinople after putting fire and sword to the coasts of Naples and Calabria. Coincident with Vela's arrival at Tripoli was that of Lope de Ordas, yet to be succeeded by William Tyrell in command of the *Grand Galleon of Alexandria*, as well as arrival of the corsair galliot of non-Hospitaller Cicco of Palermo flying the Order's standard, both returning from successful raids in the Levant.[12]

Given the large number of troops and ships at their disposal, Aurelio Bottigella, Governor Georg Schilling, and Captain of the Expeditionary Force Antonio de Viveiro jointly decided to put an end to Cairadeno, King of Tagiora. Still harbouring intent to wrest Tripoli from the Hospitallers, Cairadino had in August laid unsuccessful siege to the city and fortress, taking only the Tower of Alcaide which shields or threatens the city depending on the garrison. A first step was recapture of the tower from its small garrison of Tagiorans. Bottigella, at the head of a company of musketeers, arquebusiers, and sappers, took this task on himself, recapturing the tower after blasting with large mines. All but two of the garrison of twenty were victims of mine blast. Of Hospitallers, François de Gaillard of Savoy and the Langue of Provence was killed. In the meanwhile Georg Schilling, who controlled a corps of native cavalry led by knights of the Tripoli garrison, cut off Muslim reinforcements coming from Tagiora. Squeezed between the troops of Bottigella and the cavalry of Schilling, the Africans sought safety in flight and were chased back to Tagiora, leaving behind numerous dead.[12] Cairadeno was among the mortally wounded and soon succumbed to his wounds. The King, without forebears and without successors, was dead.[14]

Tagiora temporarily fell to the Hospitallers, Cairadino's fortress was destroyed, fortifications of the town were razed, and three galliots were seized with the release of approximately 600 more Christian oarsmen. Son of Sicily's Nicolas Peralta Count of Caltabellotta, Hospitaller Luc Peralta of the Langue of Aragon did not survive Tagiora's denouement. Following the successful conclusion of operations, Bottigella returned to Malta with 200 Turkish captives, plunder valued at 80,000 Rhodian *scudos*, and three galliots. He was received with great honour, and went in procession to the Church of San Lorenzo, where he sang a solemn Te Deum laudamus. The conquered flags were placed in the chapel of Our Lady of Filermo. Bottigella also filed a report with numerous recommendations for improving the defence of Tripoli.[15]

Grand Master Didier de Sainte-Jalle passed away on 26 September 1536 at Montpellier, France, ten months after his election without having taken office at Malta. He was thought to have been no older than 66 years of age and died of unreported cause. With most Hospitallers located in France present, he was interred in the Church of the former Templar Commandery at Montpellier.[14]

Chapter VI

Juan de Homedes y Coscon 1536–40

News of Didier de Sainte-Jalle's death reached Malta on 18 October 1536, and a General Assembly of 370 knights, chaplains, and serving brothers eligible to vote was convened on 20 October for the purpose of electing a new Grand Master. The Sixteen final electors were Nicolas de Paci d'Aubigny and Chaplain Gerald Romieu for Provence, Commander of La Racherie Jean l'Evêsque de La Cassière and Bailiff of Lango Antoine de Grolée de Passim for Auvergne, Lieutenant Treasurer Pierre Audebert de l'Aubuge and Commander of Senlis Jacques d'Aspremont for the Langue of France, Juan Onofre Monsuar de Aragona and Garcia Cortez for Aragon, Commander of Racconigi Costantino Provana and Great Siege veteran Giorgio Vagnone of the Piedmont for Italy, Preceptor of Temple Bruer Giles Russell and Preceptor of Mount Saint Joseph Richard Brooke for England, Polish-Hungarian Rudolf z Rudnica and Lieutenant Grand Bailiff Philipp Schilling for Germany, and Commander of Salamanca Gonzalo Cervantes and Jacobo de Briseño for Castile. These Sixteen on 21 October elected Bailiff of Caspe Juan de Homedes y Coscon forty-seventh Grand Master of the Order of Jerusalem. Others considered by the Sixteen Electors included Lieutenant to the Grand Master Jacques de Pelloquin, Prior of Pisa Aurelio Bottigella, Bailiff of Lango Antoine de Grolée, and Bailiff of Naples Giovan Battista Carafa. Prior of Aquitaine Jacques de Pelloquin was confirmed as Lieutenant to the new Grand Master.[1]

Like his inspiration Juan Fernández de Heredia, Catalan Juan de Homedes y Coscon was a native of Zaragoza and an irregular presence at the Convent with little reception among his peers. At the time of his election he was 63 years of age and wore a patch over one eye lost at the Siege of Rhodes, a loss some say caused his immediate and permanent retirement from the Post of Aragon when others losing an eye, such as Gabriele Tadino di Martinengo, soon returned to their posts. Like his inspiration, Juan de Homedes was characterised by abiding self-interest as well as a similar pursuit of wealth and the power bringing wealth. As Prior of Caspe he had not been present for the three most recent General Assemblies, including that at which he was elected. When appointed Captain of Galleys in 1524 he had been forced to stand down because Italian knights refused to serve under his command. His candidacy emerged only from the two Spanish langues and was opposed by four better-qualified candidates. His election remains a mystery best explained by a perceived need to end a seventy-year interregnum since Pedro Ramón Zacosta, the last previous Spanish Grand Master. Or, alternatively, as a quid pro quo for sixteen years of the Spanish Emperor's solicitude.

Before ceding command of the galleys, Aurelio Bottigella obtained permission to hunt down Barbary corsairs newly arrived on the coast of Sicily. Departing Malta on the first day of Carnival, the squadron almost immediately encountered off Cape Passero the galliot of Veli Reis, a name that in Turkish can be construed as meaning God's Captain. No fool, Veli Reis immediately drove his galliot up on a Sicilian beach and ran for it. Almost 150 liberated Christian oarsmen were pleased to take the galliot to Malta supervised by a small prize crew. From Cape Passero at the south-eastern extremity of Sicily Bottigella made a clockwise circumnavigation of the island without encountering any company Veli might have had. Reaching Messina at the north-east corner of Sicily, he was hailed by Navarrese Hospitaller Hernando de Aoiz dispatched from Caspe by Grand Master Homedes demanding either the galleys or the Great Carrack be sent to Spain to bring he and his staff to Malta as in all of Spain no convenient transportation was available. Aware the Great Carrack should soon be returning from overhaul at Villefranche in the former Duchy of Savoy, having no galleys of his own, and having no love for the new Grand Master, Aurelio Bottigella escorted Aoiz to Malta to address his request to Magistral Lieutenant Jacques Pelloquin.[2]

Jacques Pelloquin was perpetually striving to make ends meet at a cash-strapped Convent that would not be ready to repel an Ottoman siege until summer 1565, and then only with extraordinary sacrifice. He knew Sultan Suleiman, having returned in 1536 from a successful conquest of greater Baghdad (modern Iraq), had been personally involved at the Golden Horn Arsenal and elsewhere in readying an inordinately large Ottoman Armada at Constantinople. It was assumed this armada would deploy in 1537 under command of Kheir-ed-Din Barbarossa. One of the

Armada's several possible destinations was Malta. Pelloquin could ill afford to part with either the galley squadron or the carrack *Santa Anna*. With Council concurrence he dispatched the same Hernando de Aoiz to Villefranche with orders for François de Toucheboeuf to accelerate completion of the carrack's winter overhaul and then to proceed directly to Barcelona or to nearby Saloù to embark the Grand Master and coterie for transport to Malta. Aoiz had on arrival at Malta brought ill tidings of the death of Prior of Catalonia Francisco de Castillo (Francesc de Castelló in Catalan), Bernardino d'Airasca's deputy during the turbulent times at Viterbo, Airasca then Magistral Lieutenant to Grand Master l'Isle-Adam. Pelloquin and Council appointed Bailiff of Mallorca Miguel Ferrer his successor, Francisco Ferrer succeeding brother Miguel at Mallorca. At about this time the Bailiwick of Venosa, not known to have had an incumbent since Consalvo Vela in 1480, was awarded together with Habit and Grand Cross by the Church to new Hospitaller Alfonso Garlone of Naples, a relative of the Counts of Alife. In a linked development, Hospitaller Cardinal Antonio di Sanseverino renounced the titular see of Santa Maria in Trastevere at Rome, which dignity was assigned with permission of the Langue of Italy to Grand Master Homedes. Cardinal Sanseverino remained a Convent benefactor.[2]

In 1528, with Spanish Naples besieged on land by French forces of Odet de Foix, Viscount of Lautrec, and at sea by Filipino Doria in service to his 'uncle' and maritime condottiero Andrea Doria then contracted to France, Hospitaller Andrea Pignatello of Naples had been executed with excessive severity by then Viceroy of Naples Don Pedro Álvarez de Toledo. History does not reveal why Pignatello was executed but does record that his brother, condottiero Troilo Pignatello, then in service to Spanish Naples, in consequence took service with the Ottoman Empire. At Constantinople he is said to have impressed the Sultan himself with his knowledge of and ingenuity with siege engines. Troilo Pignatello was also said by historian Giacomo Bosio to have convinced Sultan Suleiman to undertake an assault on the Viceregency of Spanish Naples. Suleiman in February 1536 agreed to such an assault in a codicil to Capitulations agreed with the Kingdom of France. Whether his influence was significant or not, Troilo Pignatello would be with Ottoman forces gathered at Valona in July 1537 commanding a militia of hundreds of disaffected Europeans enlisted in Ottoman service. That militia was awaiting transport to Apulia, a part of the Viceregency of Naples.[3]

At the end of April 1537 Barbarossa sailed from Constantinople with 170 galleys, seventy galliots and fustas and eighty other vessels to assail the Italian coast. Suleiman at about the same time set out for Valona with a powerful army said to number 200,000 veterans of Hungarian campaigns. In the same month there appeared at the court of Ferrante Gonzaga, Viceroy of Sicily, a Spanish gentleman by the name of Alonso de Alarcón who for five years had been a prisoner of Barbarossa. Alarcón informed Gonzaga that Barbarossa wished to switch sides. Barbarossa was said to have taken the murder of Ibrahim Pasha thirteen months earlier as cause for personal alarm, and in addition had an unhappy relationship with Third Vizier and future Grand Vizier Lutfi Pasha commanding embarked ground forces. Gonzaga communicated this information to Viceroy of Naples Pedro Álvarez de Toledo and to others including Andrea Doria before sending Alarcón by swift brigantine to Barcelona to deliver his message to the Emperor himself.[4]

On 8 July 1537 the Ottoman Armada in its entirety appeared in the Corfu Channel between Corfu and the mainland en route to Valona (Vlorë) 50 nautical miles to the north. Six days later Suleiman's army, with French Ambassador to the Porte Jean de la Forêt in company, arrived and encamped in and around Valona. Barbarossa had among his auxiliary vessels a large number of palandarias able to transport Suleiman's ground force including cavalry and artillery the 45 nautical miles from Valona to Otranto. All of Italy was terrorised. While there had been signs of Franco–Ottoman cooperation for twelve or more months, even explicit warnings from Venice, the build-up of Ottoman marine and ground forces over the winter and spring had been assumed to be for another purpose, or Venice's problem, not for an unholy alliance with the French threatening Spanish Naples. Andrea Doria was thus able on awakening to gather but a modest defensive force and had at mid-month assembled eighteen Imperial galleys at Messina including his own and those of cousin Antonio Doria leased to the Empire. He had in addition seven galleys of Naples, three of Sicily, and six others of the Church commanded by Gentile Virginio Orsini, the same Virginio Orsini who with Hospital commanders had refused to permit those under their command during the 1535 siege of Tunis to participate in the unholy sack of that city that had resulted in the death of so many innocent thousands.

Arriving at Messina as Doria's armada assembled was the brigantine of Hospitaller Francesco Terno da Crema en route to the Levant, sent by Pelloquin and the Council to ascertain the whereabouts of Barbarossa's armada. Doria sent Terno da Crema back to Malta with a letter to Pelloquin accompanied by a Papal Brief summoning both galleys and carrack to the fleet gathering. Doria, aware the carrack was scheduled to transport the Grand Master from Spain, but very much desirous of having Malta's floating fortress in his armada, had earlier chartered two ships of Sicilian Ragusa as substitute transport for the Grand Master. These were then en route to Malta. Christianity was in great peril, Doria wrote to Pelloquin. The latter took the correspondence received to heart and by messenger ordered the carrack *Santa Anna* under Toucheboeuf to abort the rendezvous with Grand Master Homedes and to proceed directly to Messina to await further instructions from Imperial commander Andrea Doria.

Leone Strozzi was ordered to ready his galleys for sea, and when ready to take the galleys to Messina. Strozzi would sail aboard the new Maltese capitana *Santa Petronilla* commanded by Costanzo d'Operti the Younger, who would in the coming month lose his life in combat, *Santa Petronilla* replacing Francisco Giron's *Cornuto*. The capitana would be accompanied by the galleys *Santa Maria de la Vittoria*, commanded by Tristan de Melo, succeeding Parisot de la Valette; *Santa Caterina*, commanded by Gaspard de Vallier, succeeding Claude-Jacques d'Aspremont; and *Santa Croce*, commanded by former Arsenal commander Pierre de Noé. Prior of Lombardia Paolo Simeoni, who led the prisoner break-out during the Siege of Tunis, would command the embarked caravan of knights.[5]

Unwilling to wait for the Maltese, Doria departed Messina on 25 July 1537 and reached Cape Bianca in the vicinity of Parga, Greece, on 30 July, where he was 80 nautical miles south of Valona. In fairness, Doria did not have sufficient force to challenge Barbarossa; he could only hope to nab stragglers and supply ships, and when the time came nip at the edges of any movement across the Strait of Otranto. On the final day of the month he in fact intercepted fourteen small cargo ships, cargoes of munitions, arms, and foodstuffs bound from Alexandria to resupply Ottoman forces at Valona. Captured crew were sent to the oars while ships and cargo were destroyed. Perhaps unbeknownst to Doria, however, Barbarossa had already put troops ashore in Italy. Two days prior to Doria's departure from Messina the Ottoman admiral had landed 10,000 mounted Ottoman spahis outside of Otranto under command of Lutfi Pasha, Beylerbey of Roumelia. The spahis had moved south along the coast and at the month's end were occupying the area around the coastal town of Castro. The experience had not been pleasant for those in their path.[5]

Five days into August Doria galleys intercepted two enemy galleys and a galliot transporting Yunus Bey from Suleiman's camp at Valona to Venetian naval headquarters at Corfu. An Ottoman emissary well-known to the Senate at Venice, Yunus Bey had come to register a complaint with Girolamo da Pesaro, Venetian Provveditore or Governor of Corfu. The Venetian galley *Zaralina* had taken threatening action in the presence of Turkish forces. Venice was on edge but not yet engaged in hostilities, and those involved were censured by the Venetian Senate while an apology was transmitted through Giacomo da Canale, Venice's representative in the Ottoman camp at Valona. In a later incident the Venetian galley squadron of Alessandro Contarini fired on two galleys transporting the Sancakbey of Gallipoli, sending both galleys to the bottom though rescuing the Sancakbey. Contarini was recalled but too late to prevent war. Lutfi Pasha had meanwhile taken his spahis across much of the Italian heel to Ugento, once a Roman port on the Gulf of Taranto. That is where Lutfi received Suleiman's recall, re-embarking on 11 August. Suleiman had concluded French King Francis had no intention of living up to his agreement to invade northern Italy, at least not then. It was perhaps no coincidence that Hospitaller Jean de la Forêt, architect of the Capitulations, fell ill at Valona and died during the return to Constantinople.[6]

Departing Malta on 15 August, and with further instructions from Andrea Doria departing Syracuse two days later, the four galleys of the Malta Squadron caught sight of Doria's armada between the islands of Othoni, Mathraki, and Ereikoussa north-west of Corfu. Following a day-long pursuit rendezvous was effected at Cape Ayios Maria (modern Kassiopi) on the north-east corner of Corfu, where there was no sign of Toucheboeuf's carrack *Santa Anna*. Having proceeded down the narrow north–south channel between Corfu and the mainland in pairs, Leone

Strozzi was placed in command of twelve galleys in the right wing of the cruising formation. Antonio Doria commanded another twelve galleys in the left wing, while Andrea Doria was in the centre with fourteen galleys. Just before dawn on 23 August 1537 between mainland Parga and Riglia (Riza) opposite the island of Anti-Paxos, Doria's entire fleet came within sight of what turned out to be twelve well-armed Turkish galleys full of janissaries and spahis bound for Valona under command of Ali Çelebi (Bosio's Ali Zelif, 'a prosperous and highly regarded commander') and almost immediately invested one another.

Galley war is war of numbers – galley numbers and especially embarked personnel numbers – and Doria liked these numbers. Çelebi presumably realised too late in the poor light of dawn what he was up against. The mainland on his right was, after all, Turkish, and the islands on his left belonged to Venice, an ally of thirty-odd years. In spite of disproportionate numbers, however, Strozzi's capitana found herself invested by two of the twelve enemy, one of the two by the prow and the second partially alongside. It might be that the Order's distinctive pomegranate-coloured sails with black Maltese Cross were an attraction. In great peril and at the cost of much blood as well as the life of skipper Operti, victory was finally obtained by means of medium cannon carried on each side of the midships mezzanine deck. Depressed, a tricky operation with muzzle-loaded cannon orchestrated by Strozzi, one of these holed the alongside enemy at the waterline and she sank in minutes, while the other filled with small shot mowed down embarked janissaries and spahis on board the enemy investing by the prow, in spite of lion-like fury on their part and on the part of all other Ottomans present. At the last these soldiers of God threw their scimitars over the side so that no infidel might get his hands on a sword of God.[7]

It might be noted these janissaries and spahis were all Christian-born, conscripted as children, and educated at one or another janissary college. They were *yeñiçeri* in Turkish, meaning new soldiers, and a part of the first standing army in Europe, ready 365 days a year. This second galley full of *yeñiçeri*, the enemy capitana according to René-Aubert *Vertot*, was said also by him to have been taken without a single survivor. These twelve Ottoman galleys held out for three long hours against thirty-eight Christian galleys. Of the few janissaries to survive, most were badly wounded. Many Christians were also among the dead and wounded.

Antonio Doria was among the gravely wounded. Of the Hospitaller dead, other than skipper Operti, historian Giacomo Bosio was able to identify only Lope Barba of the Langue of Castile, but there were many more. Of the eleven Ottoman galleys remaining afloat, the Maltese received the one taken by Strozzi's capitana, while the other ten were divided among Empire, Church, Neapolitan, and Sicilian participants. Following combat Doria took his armada with captures to Lakka, a large deserted bay at the north end of the island of Paxos, where repairs were made to the wounded and to the galleys. Knowing that Barbarossa was or would be looking for him, and that the numbers no longer weighed in his favour, Doria next headed for Messina, where he found the Malta carrack together with other warships in attendance.[7]

At about the time Doria departed Paxos for Messina, 26 August 1537, Kheir-ed-Din Barbarossa put 25,000 men and thirty cannon ashore less than 3 miles north of the huge Venetian fortress at Corfu, one island north of Paxos. He was much too busy to come looking for Doria. Seven days earlier Suleiman had folded camp at Valona and was marching overland toward Butrinto with the balance of his army, including a proper siege train. Butrinto was a stone's throw across the Corfu Channel. Meanwhile, Corfu Town was plundered and razed and siege was laid to the formidable Venetian fortress, which had a garrison of 2,000 hired soldiers abetted by 2,000 more Corfiot militia. It was fully supplied with munitions and foodstuffs, and was nearly impregnable. Also meanwhile the first of the Ottoman's French allies appeared in the person of Bertrand d'Ornesan, Baron of Saint-Blancard, Vice-Admiral of Provence, and Marquis of the Iles d'Or. Saint-Blancard had a flotilla of French corsair vessels consisting of thirteen galleys and three smaller oared vessels carrying 530 soldiers of fortune. His orders were to persuade the Sultan to turn back against Apulia and Spanish Naples. While feted handsomely by Barbarossa, Saint-Blancard's persuasion was futile and he was of no assistance in the Siege of Corfu.[8]

Early in September unseasonable rain began to fall on Corfu, turning the island's roads and other surfaces into quagmires and bringing misery to those without adequate shelter, including Barbarossa's besiegers, now numbering far more than the original 25,000, and to their thousands of Corfiot hostages, many of whom had been refused entry to the fortress as hungry mouths useless to its defence. On 11 September 1537 the Venetian

Senate appealed to Pope Paul III, specifically requesting that Papal and Rhodian fleets come to the Republic's assistance. Two days later the Senate addressed a letter directly to Andrea Doria at Messina requesting Imperial succour and a fleet rendezvous at Brindisi. Doria, however, was already at sea. His armada, then said to approach 100 vessels of all types including Toucheboeuf's *Santa Anna* and Strozzi's four galleys, had departed Messina on 11 September bound for Corfu. It appeared that on departure Doria had anecdotal knowledge of Barbarossa's activities. The Venetian armada that had fortuitously quitted Corfu prior to Barbarossa's arrival had since been ordered to await reinforcement at Brindisi, a former Venetian port 40 nautical miles north of Otranto. It is not clear whether Doria was in possession of this information, but his failure to rendezvous at Brindisi was later attributed to his visceral (Genovese) dislike of Venetians developed over 2,000 years of cut-throat mercantile competition. Reaching the north end of Corfu on 17 September, Doria intercepted an empty Barbarossa supply ship returning to Djerba from which he obtained current information. The Great Siege of Corfu had been lifted on 15 September. With Ottoman soldiery suffering from the rain and widespread dysentery, with five Barbarossa galleys at the bottom of the Corfu Channel, and especially with the arrival of the siege-wizened Suleiman, the order had been given to withdraw. Barbarossa and his armada had disappeared to the south, while Suleiman and his army had taken the road to Adrianople. Doria immediately sent his source of information to the bottom and returned to Messina.[9]

Even as the Venetian Senate wrestled with overtures to the Ottoman Porte concerning a resumption of the peace, on 19 September 1537 Venice's Ambassador to Rome Marc' Antonio Contarini agreed,[10] subject to Senate approval, on the terms of a pact between the Church, the Empire, and Venice therein termed the Holy League. While Corfu may have been saved for Venice, it was inadequate solace for what happened next. One by one Malvasia (Monemvasia) and Nauplion were assailed by the Ottomans, Venice's last remaining outposts in the Morea. Then followed the islands of Aegina and Skiros in the western Aegean, Paros and Ios in the central Aegean, and Astipalaia and Patmos in the eastern Aegean.

At Naxos, Giovanni Crispo, Venetian Duke of the Aegean, for lack of means of defence, was obliged to recognise and pay tribute to the Sultan.

With Crispo's submission the Aegean became an Ottoman sea. Anxious to avoid winter weather, Andrea Doria, upon return to Messina, on 21 September licensed individual components of the armada to proceed of their own volition. François de Toucheboeuf took *Santa Anna* back to Malta. Leone Strozzi's four galleys were also intent on returning to Malta when upon turning Faro Light they caught sight of an unidentified brigantine on the opposite shore of Sant'Eufemia (Bagnara Calabra). The brigantine was a corsair and was captured without opposition. Interrogated, the captain revealed the presence of two large corsair galliots and an accompanying fusta. The numbers were good. Strozzi took his four galleys to Stromboli and posted lookouts well up the eastern side with a good view of the passage between Calabria and the Aeolian Islands, of which Stromboli is one. The three corsairs were sighted southbound for Sant'Eufemia and were pursued for many miles. Commanded by Tacchà Reis, the smaller fusta was overhauled at sea, again without opposition. The two quite large galliots beached themselves, the crews taking to the hills. Altogether including the brigantine 400 Christians were freed from the oars. Because the two galliots were captured on the shores of the Kingdom (Viceregency) of Naples, however, possession had to be settled in a summary legal proceeding at Naples, which required intercession by the Emperor in the person of Doria before the galliots were awarded to the Maltese. The squadron with the two galliots and fusta in tow, the brigantine abandoned, reached Malta on 8 October with eighty-three captive Turks removed from the fusta and brigantine.[11]

One of the captured galliots would be refitted by Francesco Terno da Crema for corsair operations, and would meet with great success. Upon the news Strozzi's father Filippo was among Republicans captured on 2 August 1537 at Montemurlo by forces of the Medici Duke of Florence, Strozzi in October sailed by brigantine from Malta to Naples, where he sought in vain to save his father from retribution. His brother Pietro and others in his family had meanwhile fled to France and had obtained the protection of Catherine de Medici, wife of future King Henry II. Not obtaining the assistance he expected from Emperor Charles V, Leone Strozzi passed with his brother Pietro into the service of the King of France. He was succeeded as Captain of Galleys by Prior of Lombardia Paolo Simeoni. For the second time Prior of Pisa Aurelio Bottigella was appointed Governor of Tripoli, this time succeeding Grand Bailiff of

Germany Georg Schilling von Cannstatt. The exchange of governors was facilitated by the *Galleon of Alexandria* commanded by England's William Tyrell of Heron Hall, Essex.[11]

Prior of France and Great Siege diarist Jacques de Bourbon passed away at the Priory in September and was there interred. He was succeeded by Grand Hospitaller Philippe de Carleau who was in turn succeeded by Bailiff of the Morea Robert d'Aché. Aché was succeeded by Treasurer Jean de la Roche-Andry who was in turn succeeded by Commander of Senlis Balthazard d'Aspremont.[12]

The two Ragusan cargo vessels chartered for Malta by Andrea Doria in July had earlier been placed under the command of Chancellor Jacobo de Briseño and assigned an honour guard of fifty knights to accompany Grand Master Juan de Homedes from Tarragona to Malta. The honour guard consisting of knights of each langue included Enrique Peralta of the Langue of Aragon; Gonzalo Cervantes of Castile, who would become Master of the Grand Master's House; Jacques d'Aspremont de Nantheuil of the Langue of France; and Lamberto Doria of the Langue of Italy. Arriving Menorca in late October, the chartered vessel carrying the Grand Master went aground at Port Mahon with only enough damage to further delay the return to Malta. A full month was passed at Port Mahon and another at Trapani, where Hospitaller Gaspar de Sanguessa remained Castellan. Finally the Grand Master and entourage entered the Channel of Freo between Malta and Gozo on Monday 21 January, where the four galleys under Paolo Simeoni were dispatched to welcome and tow the Grand Master's two sailing vessels into the Port of Malta.[12]

Holy League articles and understandings were formally approved by all participants at Rome on 24 February 1538. Pursuant to the agreement the Empire would fund three sixths of all costs, Venice two sixths, and the Church one sixth. The Church would arm and equip thirty-six galleys in addition to the four galleys to be provided by Malta, the thirty-six galley hulls to be provided by Venice. The Emperor would provide eighty galleys, as would Venice. The Emperor would also provide the sailing vessels necessary to support the Holy League Armada, including troop, munitions, and provisions carriers. Prince Andrea Doria, General of the Empire, was to be General of the Holy League Armada. Marco Grimani, Patriarch of Aquileia and nephew of former Venetian Doge Antonio Grimani, was to command Church galleys with Venetian Paolo

Giustiniani as Lieutenant. Vincenzo Capello, Venetian Captain-General, was to command Venetian units. Viceroy of Sicily Ferrante Gonzaga was to command League ground forces.[13]

There was widespread unhappiness with and rebellion in greater Tunis (Tunisia) against the rule of Muley Hassan (Hafsid King Muhammad V) threatening the Order's outpost at Tripoli within his realm. Also within Muley Hassan's realm was nearby Tagiora, which following the September 1535 death of Cairadeno and destruction of the city's fortifications by Georg Schilling and Aurelio Bottigella had been reoccupied by minions of Barbarossa. These since January had been led by Mourad Aga, briefly Governor of Tunis in 1534–35. Otherwise known as Murat of Ragusa, he was a renegade Christian educated at the elite Enderun Kolej within Constantinople's Topkapi Palace. Formerly Barbarossa's *kaya*, a Turkish word meaning rock or principal lieutenant, he would earn a lasting place in Hospitaller history. So far he had only begun to refortify Tagiora.[12]

Muley Hassan dispatched to Malta Afranio Camogli, a captain of his Christian Guard, to discuss corsair infractions including those of Mourad Aga as well as other unrest and to seek Hospitaller assistance. The Grand Master was also requested to seek further assistance from Don Ferrante Gonzaga, Viceroy of Sicily. Muley Hassan was willing to pay 200 ducats per month plus reimburse the cost of foodstuffs and munitions for each galley sent to his assistance. When the galleys next proceeded to Sicily for provisions, Captain of Galleys Paolo Simeoni was directed to transport Camogli to Sicily in furtherance of Muley Hassan's wishes. The Viceroy determined to dispatch ten galleys of Sicily and four of Malta to Muley Hassan's assistance, all fourteen under command of Giovanni d'Aragona Tagliavia, Marchese di Terranuova and Admiral of Sicily.

In April the fourteen galleys made rendezvous at Trapani on the western end of Sicily with four sailing vessels carrying 2,000 Spanish soldiers commanded by Regimental Commander Diego de Castilla and by Alvaro de Sande, later Marqués de Piobera. The entire Expeditionary Force was under the command of Terranuova. He was accompanied aboard his galley capitana by Muley Hassan's emissary Camogli, who directed the Expedition toward the city of Susa (Sousse) then under siege by Muley Hassan. Eighty miles south of Cape Bon on the Gulf of Hammamet, Hospitaller pilots warned Simeoni the anchorage was safe only in fair weather. Garrisoned by a force of Turks, Moors, and corsair renegades, Susa had loose command ties to Algiers where Barbarossa's adopted son and lieutenant Hassan of Sardinia was Governor. Susa's presidio was walled with a tower or ribat still standing today. Put ashore with eight pieces of galley artillery, the ground force encamped in a small cove to the north of the city protected from presidio artillery fire but able to take the presidio under fire. There they were joined by Muley Hassan, and a bombardment of presidio walls was initiated. A good breach had begun to open when a former Christian appeared in the camp purporting to wish a return to the Church of his birth. This renegade convinced Terranuova over the objection of Muley Hassan to relocate and alter the direction of his artillery fire in order to breach a different line of wall, which proved more robust than the first section assailed. A small gap had nevertheless been opened when artillery munitions ran short. An assault on the part of 130 caravan knights of Malta and 400 Spanish soldiers was attempted. Immediately caught in enemy fire from proximate wall bastions, the assailants failed to penetrate into the city and withdrew with huge losses, among whom were Diego de Castilla commanding the soldiers and Tristan de Melo commanding *Santa Maria de la Vittoria*.[13]

A second assault was essayed by the Hospitaller Galatian de Sese at the head of thirty knights and other soldiers. Sese was the first assailant into the city, cutting down an enemy captain with his sword as he passed through the breach. The enemy then retreated into the tower, which turned out to be unassailable without artillery but from which a withering arquebus fire was laid. Among the severely wounded were Hospitallers Don Bernardo de Guimeran and Antonio Maldonado. To the great disgust of Muley Hassan, withdrawal was ordered when a frigate appeared sent by the Viceroy summoning Terranuova and his Expeditionary Force back to Sicily for a forthcoming Holy League fleet assembly. Ordered to first put into Messina and then into Palermo seeking further instructions concerning a fleet gathering that would not take place until August, the Expeditionary Force was intercepted off Sciacca, Sicily, by Yannis Maria Stratigopolos, le Chevalier Grec, with a letter from Grand Master Juan de Homedes directing the Maltese galleys with Terranuova's permission to proceed first to Palermo to transfer the wounded, of which there were many, to the care of the Order's Receiver in that city, after which they were to proceed to Civitavecchia by way of Naples for the purpose of transporting Pope Paul III to Nice. At Naples, though, Simeoni learned the Pope had departed Rome for Nice by land on 23 March, prior even to the Susa Expedition. Receiving confirmation at Sicily that his assignment had been cancelled, he took his four galleys full of Sicilian foodstuffs back to Malta at the end of April.[11]

The Truce of Nice was signed on 18 June 1538 by Charles I for Spain and Francis I for France in the presence of Pope Paul III, ending the Italian War of 1536–38 and leaving Savoyard Turin in French hands but affecting no other significant change in the map of Italy. Overall, Spain increased its control over Italy simply by extending the term of her dominion, solidifying the end of Italian independence. The Truce did not relieve all tension between the Spanish and French, but it did interrupt ties between France and the Ottoman Empire, the latter terminating the credentials of French Ambassador Antonio Rincon and forcing him to leave Constantinople. The Truce, moreover, freed up Spanish forces to confront Ottomans in the Mediterranean, the Pope's objective in bringing about the Truce.[14]

In July 1538 ten French galleys bound from Constantinople to France put into Malta but did not clear pratique and were quarantined. These were the escort for evicted French Ambassador Antonio Rincon. Written communications from Rincon, though, led the Grand Master to suspect the Ottoman Armada would be up to its usual tricks. He sent Lope de Ordas by brigantine to ascertain whether the tricks would be played on southern Italy or along the Barbary Coast or along the coast of the Morea, where Argos and Nauplion remained thorns in the Ottoman corpus. Soon after the departure of Ordas two galleys of the Principality of Monaco arrived at Malta west bound. These would transport Bailiff of Naples Giovan Battista Carafa to Italy to take up residence at Rome as the Order's Procurator-General and Ambassador in Residence to the Holy See, replacing Bernardo Salviati, who had become entangled with cousins Piero and Leone Strozzi in the War of Florence. Tommasso Bosio, who by reason of the claim of Cardinal Girolamo Ghinucci had been unable to take up the Bishopric of Malta, then was formally recognised as and invested with the mantle of Bishop of Malta. He took as assistant Hospitaller Chaplain Guillermo Ramón Beneyt of Valencia, a Doctor of Theology. The galleys of the Religion had returned to Malta in April 1538 with instructions to rendezvous with Andrea Doria's Holy League Armada in August, and at the time busied themselves making ready, among other things selecting forty-five knights per galley as caravan. Paolo Simeoni was to command Hospitaller forces both afloat and ashore. Commander of Tortosa Bernardo Salban succeeded the fallen Tristan de Melo in command of *Santa Maria de la Vittoria*. The squadron and embarked caravan departed Malta for Messina at July end, taking Lope Ordas and his brigantine with them. Ordas had failed to catch sight of Barbarossa, then at the far end of Candia (Crete).[13]

Neither did the Malta galleys immediately catch sight of Andrea Doria at Messina. Doria had been at Aigues-Mortes with the Emperor and had left there for Genoa as recently as 16 July. A month later with nineteen Empire galleys, some of which were his own, he was at Naples collecting that Viceregency's ten-galley squadron under command of García Álvarez de Toledo, son of the Viceroy. These reached Messina on 23 August, where waited four galleys of Malta; two galleys of the Pope commanded by Gentile Virginio Orsini that would normally sail in company with those of Malta; ten leased galleys of Sicily under command of Viceroy Ferrante Gonzaga, including two each the property of Vincenzo Cicala and Giovanni Tagliavia, Marchese di Terranuova; as well as six galleys commanded by Antonio Doria which had departed Genoa in company with Andrea Doria bound directly to Messina. There were also twenty-five sailing vessels including a galleon that was the personal property of Antonio Doria. These vessels (others with provisions would follow later) carrying 16,000 soldiers plus fifty-one galleys, representing the Empire contribution to the Holy League Armada, departed Messina together on 1 September bound for Corfu. The galleys arrived on 7 September and rendezvoused with Venice's Vincenzo Capello and the Church's Marco Grimani, who had both been waiting at Corfu since June. Capello had arrived early in June with fifty-five galleys and Grimani had reached Corfu with twenty-seven galleys on 16 June. There was a sense among early arrivals that surely Andrea Doria in the intervening months might have been better employed than as the Emperor's escort. Saving the people of ravaged Candia, for example. Both Capello and Grimani had wished to get going at once, but Ferrante Gonzaga, commanding the ground forces, had forbidden their use from his viceregal palace at Palermo.[15]

From his arrival at Corfu Andrea Doria busied himself doing nothing. He had 134 galleys mounting 750 bow cannon, a third again as many as his opponent. He had 16,000 embarked soldiers, 'the flower of Spanish and Italian soldiery'.[16] He was aware of Barbarossa's depredations in the Venetian Aegean and along the Venetian coast of Candia, and for eighteen days he did nothing. War, if for anyone, is a young man's profession; Andrea Doria was 72 years of age and comfortable in his circumstances. A famous prince with a palace. With most of his fleet resting in the protected waters of Gomenizza (Igoumenitza), a mainland port opposite Corfu, he convened several command conferences. During these conferences he and Gonzaga proposed various raids having little or nothing to do with the menace represented by Barbarossa, until the astounded gaze of other commanders present weighed on their self-esteem or until came news of Barbarossa's arrival. Barbarossa had meanwhile taken Grimani's hint and parked his own Armada within the Gulf of Preveza (Ambracian Gulf), a Turkish lake with an entrance so narrow ship traffic must move in single file in one direction. Carefully. Barbarossa did not need to know history, did not need to know that 1,570 years earlier Octavian had taken the same position when Preveza was known as Actium. While the advantages of a Turkish lake were obvious, both Barbarossa and Doria also knew that Antony's position was a lee shore where a sailing vessel and even an oared vessel could be blown up on the beach should the prevailing wind strengthen sufficiently. Barbarossa and Doria both knew one additional thing: when a besieging armada decided to call it a day and present its cannon-less sterns to the besieged, the besieged coming in pursuit had all of its bow cannon bearing. And that's what happened.[15]

Doria's Armada departed Corfu on 25 September and reached Preveza 45 nautical miles to the south that same evening. En route Doria had Simeoni's Maltese capitana on his left, on his right in the place of honour Gentile Virginio Orsini's Papal galley. With him in the centre was Ferrante Gonzaga aboard the capitana of Sicily. In the vanguard were four fast galleys under the command of his cousin and adopted son Giannettino Doria. In the rear were Papal and Venetian galleys of Marco Grimani and Vincenzo Capello. Many miles astern, labouring in light air, were seventy-two troop carriers and warships under the command of his cousin, Antonio Doria. The warships included Antonio Doria's own galleon and a second of Venice commanded by Alessandro Bondumier. From the Gulf of Preveza six Turkish galleys emerged the next morning bound for Ottoman Santa Maura (modern Lefkas), the first island to the south; Giannettino Doria cut their path and obliged them to retire; another six exited and these were confronted by the four Maltese of Paolo Simeoni and two Church of Virginio Orsini. There was again a withdrawal. Kheir-ed-Din was secure within the Gulf of Preveza while Andrea Doria's superior force was without, preventing exit. Kheir-ed-Din's commanders included Sinan, Salih Reis, Tabach Reis, and Dragut. They had at their command 114 galleys and galliots without counting three dozen ships. That same day, 26 September, Ferrante Gonzaga proposed seizing the Turkish fortress with a ground assault that he would command, after which a sailing vessel could be sunk in the narrow channel to the sea, thus temporarily blockading Barbarossa in a Turkish lake. How long the League garrison might survive at the edge of a Turkish lake was not clear to other commanders. The next day, 27 September, the wind stilled, a sailor's alarm and often the calm before the storm. (Barometers were not to be invented for another 150 years and would not be commonly available at sea for even longer). Doria in fear of adverse weather and a lee shore abandoned his position on the morning of 27 September, little more than 36 hours after arrival. His orders were for the Armada to take course for Porto Suessola (modern Vasiliki), a safe anchorage in prevailing north wind at the foot of Santa Maura. Twenty galleys and ten galliots under the command of Dragut soon exited the Gulf, followed shortly by the rest of the Ottoman galley fleet with Barbarossa in the centre and Tabach Reis in the place of honour to his right. Salih Reis was to his left while Sinan, on leave from the Ottoman Red Sea Armada, was left behind to secure the anchorage. All others went in pursuit of Doria withdrawing to the south, the latter's galleys far in advance of his wind-idled sailing ships.

The principal action occurred off the west coast of Santa Maura, where the Ottomans had the better of the League, capturing two Venetian galleys (which, according to *Merriman III-330*, were the two Venetian galleys recovered with the 1540 capture of Dragut). Also lost were one Papal galley and five Spanish vessels. Doria's force was not able to boast of the capture or sinking of a single Ottoman vessel, though a certain number of Salih Reis galleys were damaged and obliged to retire by gunfire of the becalmed *Galeone di Venezia*, flagship of the Venetian fleet commanded by Alessandro Bondumier, sometimes called Condalmiero. Antonio Doria's galleon was similarly engaged by the galleys of Tabach Reis, but with less ferocity and less consequence. At nightfall Holy

League galleys, continuing their withdrawal to the south, all of a sudden reversed course on a rising south wind known to sailors as a scirocco, in that part of the world a warning of a violent north wind perhaps to follow. Holy League vessels including suddenly mobile sailing vessels now raced to weather shelter at Corfu and Gomenizza. Barbarossa returned to anchorage, secure in his Turkish lake, but some of his captains remained outside of the Gulf in the hope of spoils. It was during the return to Corfu that there were exchanges of gunfire between passing League galleys and waiting Ottomans. Malta's *Santa Maria de la Vittoria*, commanded by Bernardo Salban, took four cannon rounds, one hitting the poop and mortally wounding Hospitaller Alvaro Fernandez d'Almeida of Portugal while killing Diego de Ulloa of Castile and several others.[16] Another cannon ball took the life of Master of Oarsmen Gaspare Sommaripa of *Santa Caterina*. *Galeone di Venezia*, absent fore and main masts and given up for lost, reached Corfu two days later propelled only by the lateen-rigged mizzen mast and wind on the stern. Neither Barbarossa's capitana nor Doria's capitana engaged in combat.[17]

Following his modest victory, Barbarossa immodestly sent his natural son Hassan (not to be confused with his adopted son Hassan of Sardinia) accompanied by two sea captains to Janbol, Bulgaria, where the Sultan was encamped. On the occasion Janbol was illuminated for a *kutlama* or grand celebration. Suleiman raised Kheir-ed-Din's wages by 100,000 silver akçe per year. Doria was meanwhile accused of conniving with Barbarossa, both united by a desire to avoid fighting at sea, especially absent overwhelming numbers. This long-running suspicion is accredited on this occasion by a report that when the Holy League Armada had been at anchor off Preveza, a corsair galliot exited the Gulf at night and covertly came alongside Doria's capitana to deliver a message from the Ottoman commander.[18] Bosio has the temerity to suggest that had it not been for the presence aboard the Ottoman capitana of Munuc (phonetically, Munuch) Aga of the Sultan's household, Barbarossa would not have exited at all. In the game of numbers, Doria had the advantage. On the other hand and pertinently, less than seven weeks later on 11 November a single storm would drive thirty-eight of Barbarossa's galleys on to the coast near Valona, where they would be broken up by the raging sea. This is an interesting juxtaposition with Doria's earlier withdrawal from Preveza in concern for the weather, costing him eight vessels, not thirty-eight. On the other hand and apropos of collusion between Barbarossa and Doria, Zimmerman Giovio, a contemporary historian, wrote that while the League Armada lay off Castelnuovo (Herceg Novi, Montenegro) that month having completed the successful reconquest of that fortified city, Doria was informed that Barbarossa's fleet had been scattered by storm and was vulnerable to attack, but did nothing. From Jerome Maurand in *Itinéraire de Jérome Maurand d'Antibes à Constantinople*, pp.xxiv–xxxi, concerning the collusion of Doria and Barbarossa, in the letter of Gianmatteo Bembo, Venetian provveditore of Kotor, to his famous relative Pietro Bembo of 23 November 1539, the former had questioned a Spanish slave who had escaped from Barbarossa's galley, who asserted 'that one crow does not strike out another's eyes. Barbarossa, once Doria had been defeated, would no longer be valuable to Suleiman, and likewise should Barbarossa be defeated, Doria would no longer enjoy his high repute with the Emperor; it was in the interest of both of them that the war should continue; they quite understood each other, and saw to the progress of their own affairs …' In spite of its prominent place in Ottoman history, *Preveza was no Lepanto.*

When the weather improved Barbarossa took his Ottoman Armada to Lakka Bay, Paxos, where he was only 12 miles from the near end of Corfu. Doria was again at Gomenizza smarting under criticism of his decisions at Preveza. Venice's Vincenzo Capello, wishing to end the campaign with something of value to report to his Senate, proposed a siege of Ottoman-held Castelnuovo at the mouth of the Gulf of Kotor near Ragusa (Dubrovnik), 200 nautical miles north of Gomenizza. Ignoring Ragusa, Venice considered the Adriatic Sea a 'Venetian Gulf', assigning its naval units to a Captain-of-the-Gulf and to a Captain-of-the-Sea. Venice also maintained two garrisons within the Gulf of Kotor at Risan and Kotor City. The Ottoman presence at the mouth of the Gulf of Kotor inhibited ready Venetian access to both Risan and Kotor City and had done so during times of war since the Ottoman seizure of Castelnuovo from Stjepan Vukic Kosaca in 1482. Barbarossa had meanwhile returned to the safety of the Gulf of Preveza by 7 October, encouraging some particularly ashamed Holy League captains to agitate for an additional assault on Ottoman Durazzo (Durres, Albania), also within the 'Venetian Gulf' and situated on the route to Castelnuovo. This latter undertaking was dismissed by Capello, describing Durazzo as a port too well defended to be considered. Judging that with cruel winter not far away Barbarossa would be reluctant to put more distance between his Armada and Constantinople, Andrea Doria agreed to the conquest of Castelnuovo.[20]

Paolo Simeoni and the four Malta galleys were assigned by Doria to a station at Suasino (Sazan) Island off the port of Valona (Vlorë) on the Strait of Otranto. His orders were to maintain lookout for a northbound Barbarossa. Two additional galleys, one Empire and one Venetian, were left at Corfu for the same purpose. Castelnuovo was easily subdued on 27 October 1538. Viceroy of Sicily Ferrante Gonzaga, commanding an overwhelming number of debarked Spanish and Italian soldiery, with artillery, met little resistance. Two thousand Infidels were captured alive. Vincenzo Capello asserted that because Castelnuovo was within the 'Venetian Gulf', articles of the Holy League agreement dictated that the captured city receive a Venetian garrison. Doria, who had less than no love for Venetians, disagreed. More than two weeks were consumed in assigning 4,000 mostly Spanish soldiers to a garrison under the command of Spaniard Francisco de Sarmiento. Those assigned not Spanish were Italians from the Spanish Vice Regency of Naples. None were Venetian as the Holy League Agreement directed. The Spanish tercio was comprised of companies of veteran soldiers from other tercios, while the smaller Italian contribution of 500 would in the following year obtain a place in Italian folklore. Support ships were still offloading munitions and provisions when the two galleys left at Corfu and the four Maltese of Simeoni arrived on or about 9 November with news that Barbarossa had entered the Adriatic and appeared intent on disrupting operations at Castelnuovo. One day later a mountain storm began to develop and within hours an icy north wind, north-east at Kotor, was blowing. Called a Bora wind, Doria knew it could and often did blow in excess of hurricane strength. It was a wind that caused seamen to go weak in the knees and to pray fervently. While a downwind run to Italy was remotely possible, Doria chose to ride out the storm in the relative safety of the Gulf of Kotor. Seeking to beach safely on 11 November at the aforementioned island of Suasino, thirty-eight of Barbarossa's galleys were broken up by the raging sea, after which the survivors were slaughtered by Albanians and the flotsam looted. Still at Castelnuovo, when informed Barbarossa's fleet had been scattered by storm and was vulnerable to attack, Doria ordered a departure, sending the sailing ships to Messina and the galleys to Brindisi. At Brindisi the galleys of Sicily and Malta were released to go their own way.[21] These reached Messina at mid-December to find the sailing ships already arrived with embarked and unpaid soldiers on the verge of mutiny. During the stand-off Ferrante Gonzaga fired on the mutinous. A rampage ensued in which unpaid soldiers ravaged every undefended village and town in Sicily before returning to their place of assembly. The unpaid were paid. Ferrante Gonzaga remained Viceroy of Sicily. The ravaged were not compensated.

Upon return of the galleys to Malta the Grand Galleon of the Religion, or *Grand Galleon of Alexandria* commanded by William Tyrell, sailed to Marseille conveying Prior of Aquitaine and Lieutenant to the Grand Master Jacques de Pelloquin with full authority as Inspector General to correct all deficiencies he might find among priories in the Kingdom of France, especially deficiencies in submission of responsions.[22]

At the outset of 1539 Prior of the Church Pons de Laurenzin died, and was succeeded by Chaplain Domenico Cubelles of Aragon, countryman and favourite of the Grand Master. Also passing away was Bailiff of Lyon (Bailiff of Saint-Georges) Didier de Chevrier (Emery de Chevrier de Pody). This dignity was conferred upon Antoine de Grolée de Passim, who renounced the Bailiwick of Lango, to which Commander of Latronquière Foulques de Caritat succeeded. The Castellany of Amposta was vacated by the death of Don Juan de Aragona, bastard son of Juan II de Ribagorza. Don Bautista de Vilaragut succeeded to the position, renouncing the dignity of Draper, to which Geronimo Coscon was appointed. A Chapter General, long postponed by the deaths of two grand masters, was scheduled for 2 March, with Hospitaller Bishop of Malta and Vice Chancellor Tommasso Bosio scheduled to preside. Because of strong north winds, however, the four galleys under Paolo Simeoni were unable to reach Sicily where Bosio awaited transportation.

The second Chapter General at Malta was consequently convened on 2 March with Regent Chancellor Guillermo Ramón Beneyt of Valencia presiding. Following formalities, Grand Master Homedes summarised the Order's present circumstances and needs, and then the Chapter General proceeded to the election of voting representatives. The Sixteen *Capitolari* or legislators elected by the eight langues were Grand Commander Giraud de Massas and Bailiff of Lango Foulques de Caritat representing

Provence, Marshal Jean de Château-Arnauld and Bailiff of Lyon Antoine de Grolée representing Auvergne, Grand Hospitaller Robert d'Aché and Treasurer Jacques d'Aspremont de Nantheuil for France, Bailiff of Caspe Garcia Cortèz and Bernardo Marquet for Aragon, Lamberto Doria and Don Girolamo Carafa for Italy, Lieutenant Turcopolier Giles Russell and David Gonson for England (Gonson would be beatified by Pope Pius XI on 14 December 1929), Grand Bailiff Georg Schilling and Wilhelm Bombast for Germany, and Lieutenant Chancellor Consalvo Monroy and Henrique Pereira for Castile. Marshal Château-Arnauld fell ill during the proceedings and was replaced by Commander Umbert de Mouriès. Participating in the deliberations of the Sixteen were Master of the Grand Master's House and Seneschal Gonzalo Cervantes, Regent Chancellor Guillermo Ramón Beneyt, and noble Rhodiot Giovanni di Montolivet representing the transplanted Rhodean population.

The Sixteen, in consideration of the recent actions of Turcopolier Clement West, found him in contempt of the Grand Master, placed him under house arrest for three months and, given that this was West's second offence, deprived him of the dignity of Turcopolier and deprived him of the attendant Grand Cross. More importantly, and given the Ottoman naval threat, the Chapter General levied an impost equivalent to two thirds of ordinary annual responsions on all priories, bailiwicks, and commanderies for three full years. A new wall was to be constructed around the Colacchio housing the living quarters of the eight auberges. A new Arsenal for ship construction was approved replacing the old one. The Langue of Aragon received approval to re-entitle the dignity of Draper to Grand Conservator. Serving Brothers were granted the right to wear an eight-pointed cross on their vestments one quarter smaller than a knight's small cross. Finally, the four galleys of the squadron were ordered to the Barbary Coast. The Chapter General adjourned on 21 March 1539.[22]

Paolo Simeoni continued in command of the galleys. His ships re-equipped, Pietro Vasco commanded the capitana *San Giovanni Battista*, Bernardo Salban commanded *Santa Petronilla*, Lope de Ordas commanded *Santa Croce* in succession of Pierre de Noé, and Gaspard de Vallier continued in command of *Santa Caterina*. On 26 March the squadron departed Malta to patrol the coast of the Maghreb or coastal shallows west of Tripoli, where they seized a fusta belonging to Dragut's squadron with thirty-seven Turks on board. From these Simeoni they learned that Dragut, under orders of Barbarossa, was then at Valona, Albania, and that Dragut was accompanied by Corsetto Reis, who long had Sinan lieutenant called 'The Corsican'. Between the two of them they commanded thirty or more galliots and fustas, intercepting supplies to the Spanish garrison at Castelnuovo. In spite of a truce between the Ottomans and Venice, Dragut and The Corsican had cornered five Venetian galleys commanded by Luigi Gritti, of which two were sent to the bottom and the others captured. With this fresh information Simeoni resolved to return to Malta but first paused at Tripoli to similarly advise Governor Aurelio Bottigella. Simeoni found the garrison at Tripoli each day skirmishing with Turks and Moors of Mourad Aga at Tagiora.[23]

The four galleys reached Malta on 15 June 1539 to find a summons from the Emperor forwarded by Viceroy of Sicily Ferrante Gonzaga and Prince Andrea Doria demanding participation of the Malta galleys in a mission of the Imperial Armada to succour Castelnuovo, to give Dragut his marching orders, and to prevent a rendezvous with Barbarossa. Simeoni was to continue in command of the galleys and was to embark reinforced caravans of knights under the command of Grand Commander Giraud de Massas, a knight of prudence and valour. Both prepared for an early departure and did leave on 19 June bound for Messina. Embarked with them was Castellan of Amposta Don Bautista de Vilaragut, headed ultimately to Naples. Days after departure of the galleys there appeared off the mouth of the Port of Malta a vessel that gave every sign of attempting to avoid the port. Two brigantines and the barque of the Great Carrack *Santa Anna* were dispatched to determine what was what. The ship was a small cargo carrier with a single mast and three sails bound for the Barbary Coast. She had been hi-jacked at Sicily by the crew of a larger shipwreck, the crew in service to the Maltese renegade Ganga Rossa. The brigantines escorted her into port and slapped the crew into prison. The Malta Squadron had meanwhile reached Messina and made rendezvous with Doria's Imperial Armada.[24]

The Imperial Armada consisting of forty-nine galleys departed Messina on 7 July, leaving sailing ships behind in order to make better time. Doria reached Otranto 215 nautical miles and four days later, only to learn to his apparent displeasure Barbarossa had, one day earlier, passed through the Strait of Otranto, where he had been joined by Dragut and other corsairs.

His Ottoman Armada estimated at 150 vessels, mostly galleys and galliots, was pointed toward the Gulf of Kotor and Castelnuovo. Because both Doria and Barbarossa insisted on having information about each other, Doria took a reinforced squadron of galleys north from Otranto toward Brindisi 40 miles distant, while at the same time Bernardo Salban's *Santa Petronilla* and Lope de Ordas's *Santa Croce* were posted back to Taranto for the acquisition of fresh provisions. In the waters of Brindisi seven Turkish galliots were sighted moving fast under both sail and oar. Sent by Barbarossa expressly to ascertain Imperial Armada whereabouts, the speed and elegance of the galliots oozed confidence in an ability to find the enemy and return with number, speed, and direction. One of them approached to investigate the only visible galley, and Gaspard de Vallier's *Santa Caterina*, first to sight the enemy, was quick to pounce. His officers wished to board but Vallier ordered a broadside of arquebus and crossbow fire while passing close aboard, causing many dead and wounded and the oars to be abandoned. She was left for Doria's capitana coming up astern while Vallier set his sights on the largest of the enemy galliots not far ahead. This one was invested by the poop without much loss to his own crew, and taken. Paolo Simeoni's *San Giovanni Battista*, meanwhile, with soldiers and seamen aiding the oarsmen, and with both sails full, closed on a third galliot, which appeared the fastest of the enemy. In galley pursuit, only the pursuer is able to bring cannon to bear, and Simeoni's cannon were doing considerable damage as the gap between the two closed, slowing the enemy by bringing down the antenna (spar) supporting the only sail. She was soon overwhelmed. Meanwhile, Doria had taken the first galliot and hoisted the Hospitaller standard of Saint John to indicate his capture belonged to Vallier. From the three captures 500 Turks and Moors would be made captive and the same number of Christians would be freed from the oars. From the captives Doria would confirm the bad news received at Otranto. And four galliots returning to Barbarossa had news of Doria's meagre presence. On 13 July Barbarossa initiated his siege of Castelnuovo. By the time of capitulation on 7 August 3,700 of the 4,000 garrisoning Castelnuovo would be dead, including commander Francisco de Sarmiento. It was little comfort that Barbarossa would suffer 8,000 dead in Castelnuovo's conquest. In the event, it was already abundantly clear to Andrea Doria he did not have a sufficiently large force at his disposal to confront Barbarossa. Some would soon be asking why.[24]

The eventual outcome at Castlenuovo not yet clear, Doria retired with his forty-nine galleys to Crotone on the forefoot of the Italian boot and summoned from Malta the Order's Great Carrack *Santa Anna*, then laid up and not ready for sea. Doria still intended to succour Castelnuovo, or so it appeared. The summons was transported by the brigantine of the Malta Squadron and did not reach Malta until 5 August. Because the lives of thousands of Spaniards were at stake, the Order hurriedly readied *Santa Anna* for sea. While *Santa Anna* was readied, Commander Lamberto Doria was dispatched to Sicily by means of the same brigantine to coordinate with Viceroy Ferrante Gonzaga the gathering of stores and soldiers beyond 100 Hospitaller knights to be embarked. Off Faro di Messina, however, Lamberto Doria encountered the Imperial Armada of Andrea Doria returning from Crotone to Messina and learned Castelnuovo had surrendered on 7 August.

At about the time Lamberto Doria returned to Malta with the distressing news of Castelnuovo's loss, Bishop of Malta and Vice Chancellor Tommasso Bosio, the second of two Bosio brothers contributing so much to Order and Church, passed to a better life. Bosio had served as Bishop of Malta a mere six months but his concern for the people of Rhodes and Malta as mendicant to the sick, wounded, and hopeless over decades would not soon be forgotten. His death, like that of so many others, was ascribed to peste. He was interred in the Cathedral Church of Saint Paul, the first Hospitaller Chaplain to serve as Bishop of Malta, in a service presided over by Grand Master Juan de Homedes. Pursuant to the terms of Malta's cession, three candidates were nominated as successor Bishop, the names of whom were submitted to Viceroy Ferrante Gonzaga. These were Hospitaller Chaplains Domenico Cubelles of Zaragoza, Lieutenant Vice Chancellor Guillermo Raimundo Beneyt of Valencia, and Jérôme Romey of Dauphiné in southeastern France, all three Doctors of Divinity.[25]

The Order's Sacred Council published the decision reached by the Chapter General in March to strip Turcopolier Clement West of his habit, dignity and honours as well as to confine him for three months. Nicholas Lambert, as Procurator for the Langue of England, was summoned to put the decision into effect. Attorney Lambert asserted that neither Henry

VIII nor Pope Paul III would be pleased with this decision, and did so in insulting manner. He was confined with Clement West. Giles Russell was on 10 November 1539 appointed successor Turcopolier.[25]

From Castelnuovo's Gulf of Kotor, Barbarossa had in September headed for Apulia, that part of Italy's Adriatic coast running from above Gargano to the heel of the Italian boot, next proceeding to southern Calabria, the rest of the boot's sole, in both of which he terrorised the countryside behind the beach. He took particular aim at the cities of Gallipoli di Apulia and Taranto and the countryside in between. There was concern in Malta that he would swoop down to the African coast in support of his Kaya Mourad Aga and the Ottoman garrison at Tagiora 10 miles east of Hospitaller Tripoli. The large *Galleon di Alexandria* commanded by William Tyrell was loaded with provisions and munitions as well as a support battalion of knights and soldiers under Commander of Alcolea Fernando de Bracamonte, the new Governor in succession of Aurelio Bottigella. Also embarked were Captain of Cavalry Alonso Cerdan and Treasurer Francisco de Ribadeneira, the latter in relief of Francesco Ajazza of Vercelli. In addition, Lamberto Doria and Pedro Felizes were embarked as commissioners to account for every individual at Tripoli and to return to Malta all those no longer of fighting age. But it was not Tagiora that Barbarossa had in mind but rather Constantinople by way of Corfu. He headed for that Venetian island and was saluted by the fortress with a salvo of artillery, the same fortress he besieged two years earlier. Because Venice and the Ottoman Empire were technically still at war, Barbarossa offered to mediate peace between Venice and the Porte. A treaty or 'Capitulation' would be signed between Venice and the Ottoman Empire on 2 October 1540 but Venice had already ceased to participate in Holy League undertakings.[26]

Shortly after returning from Messina, the Malta Galley Squadron redeployed to France and Spain to collect responsions from Receivers Pierre de Beaulac-Trebons and Onofre de Monsuar. Embarked was Antoine de Grolée on an ambassadorial mission to both French King Francis and Emperor Charles V meeting at Paris in December. Grolée was to explain the perilous circumstances of Tripoli.[27]

Upon the February 1540 expiration of Simeoni's term as Captain of Galleys, Admiral Muzio Costanzo was nominated as his replacement. Non-Italian langues objected as this assignment for an Italian succeeding an Italian interrupted the rotation of squadron command among the langues. Simeoni was therefore succeeded in command of the galleys by Spanish Commander of Tortosa Bernardo Salban as Regent and not as Captain, Salban receiving the assignment as senior captain among officers of the squadron. Salban also continued in command of *Santa Petronilla*, Lope de Ordas commanded *Santa Croce*, Pons de Balaguer de Savignac commanded *Santa Caterina*, and Antonio Turchetto of Turin, who was second in command of the former capitana *San Giovanni Battista*, was appointed to command of that galley. William Tyrell was succeeded in command of the *Great Galleon di Alexandria* by Pedro Felizes of Valencia. Felizes took his galleon to Sciacca in south-western Sicily, where he loaded a cargo of grain for delivery to Tripoli. Because Venice had placed a limit of one cargo of grain per vessel, Sicily had done so, as well. Felizes therefore returned to Sciacca for a second load with a second galleon. Marshal Jean de Château-Arnauld, who was too indisposed to serve at the Chapter General eleven months earlier, died at the Malta infirmary of an undiagnosed and debilitating disease. He was succeeded by Commander Emery des Reaulx, the same Emery des Reaulx in 1521 commanding the Order's carrack *Santa Maria*, formerly *Mogarbina*.[28]

The Dissolution of the Monasteries, sometimes referred to as the Suppression of the Monasteries, was the set of administrative and legal processes between 1536 and 1541 by which Henry VIII disbanded Catholic monasteries, priories, convents and friaries in England, Wales and Ireland, appropriated their income, disposed of their assets, and reassigned or dismissed their former members and functions. Although the policy was originally envisaged as increasing the regular income of the Crown, profitable monastic property was sold off to fund Henry's military campaigns in the 1540s. He was given the authority to do this in England and Wales by the Act of Supremacy, passed by Parliament in 1534, which made him Supreme Head of the Church in England, thus separating England from Papal authority, and by the First Suppression Act (1536) and the Second Suppression Act (1539). Authorities specialising in that era argue that the dissolution of the monasteries in the late 1530s was one of the most revolutionary events in English history. There were nearly 900 religious houses in England, around 260 for monks, 300 for regular canons, 142 nunneries and 183 friaries; some 12,000 people in total, 4,000 monks, 3,000 canons, 3,000 friars and 2,000 nuns ... one adult man in fifty was in religious orders.[29]

Even before the remonstrances of the Grand Master and Council had reached England, by Statute 32 Henry of the VIII. ch. 24 (April 1540), the Venerable Tongue of England was dissolved and its property incorporated with that of the Crown. The habit of the Order and any of its distinctive badges were forbidden to be worn within the Realm. A pension was granted to such of the knights as had not yet fallen altogether under the Sovereign's disgrace, on condition, however, that they reside within the King's dominions. Grand Prior Weston was granted an annual pension of £1,000 sterling, John Rawson, Prior of Ireland, and Clement West, former Turcopolier, received pensions of £500 each, John Sutton £200, Giles Russell and Edward Bellingham £100 each, Thomas Pemberton £80; Edward Brown £50, Edmund Hussey, Ambrose Cave and Richard Brooke, 100 Scottish merks each; Thomas Coppledike £50, Cuthbert Leighton £60, Henry Pole and John Rawson the Younger 200 marks each, and William Tyrell £30, all of them preceptors, knights, or serving brothers. An allowance of £10 a head was made to the following nine knights: Oswald Massinbert, James Hussey, Thomas Thornehill, Nicolas Upton, Philip Babington, Henry Gerard, Donston Newdegate, Nicolas Lambert, and David Gonson.[30]

Chapter VII

Juan de Homedes y Coscon 1540–41

Dragut with seven galliots, accompanied by Albanian renegade Memi Reis with two galleys, ravaged the Tuscan island of Capraia, destroying the fortress tower guarding the port and carrying off the entire population of 700 men, women, and children plus everything else of value. These nine-oared vessels loaded to the gunnels next proceeded around the top of Corsica and down the island's west coast to its sheltered Gulf of Girolata, where on 15 June 1540 all nine vessels beached. Cook fires were burning on the beach when six Christian galleys under the command of Giorgio Doria, lieutenant to Giannettino Doria, appeared at the mouth of the Gulf, were seen by the beached corsairs, reversed course, and moved out of sight. Dragut launched his seven galliots, went in pursuit and was ambushed by nineteen Genovese and Church galleys under command of the senior Doria. Dragut's capitana went to the bottom, but he was captured attempting escape in a skiff. Two other Christian galleys under command of Gentile Virginio Orsini bottled Memi Reis inside the Gulf. Seven hundred captives and 1,300 Christian oarsmen were liberated. A similar number of corsairs were sent to the oars of six captured galliots and two galleys.

Two months earlier the Order's Galley Squadron had been sent from Malta to Messina at the request of Emperor Charles V himself to participate in a coordinated search for Dragut. Following the squadron's departure Dragut, with two galleys and thirteen galliots, had suddenly descended on Malta's Gozo, putting raiders ashore who penetrated into the interior of the island, enslaving fifty ill-fated residents.

A Christian galley slave escaping from Dragut's capitana appeared at the main port of Malta to report that Dragut had been sent by Barbarossa for the express purpose of capturing or destroying the squadron's four galleys, and to use every artifice to obtain revenge for the loss of Barbarossa's three galliots off Brindisi the past July. On his own account

Dragut sought retribution for the loss of his brigantine to the same galleys off Tripoli exactly one year earlier. The Grand Master sent this information by frigate to Messina, where Empire galleys were assembling. The frigate (a small brigantine with or without deck or mast) was owned and commanded by non-Hospitaller Carquisan of Biscay, who himself had been a slave of Dragut, escaping at Lepanto. The Emperor, moved by the lamentations of coastal residents of Spain, Sardinia, and Italy, had taken time from his endeavours to reconcile Catholic and Lutheran differences in Germany and Flanders to forcefully order Andrea Doria, reluctant to confront Barbarossa, to capture Dragut.[1]

At Messina Andrea Doria divided the assembled galleys into a number of squadrons assigned different locales. Nephew Erasmo Doria was assigned ten galleys and ordered to patrol the Balearic Islands and the mainland coast of Spain. Adopted son Giannettino Doria was assigned twenty-one galleys and ordered to patrol the coasts of Sardinia and Corsica, assisted by the Church's Gentile Virginio Orsini with seven of the twenty-one galleys. Don Federico de Toledo, son of the Viceroy of Naples, was ordered to patrol the Neapolitan coast with the eleven-galley Squadron of Naples. Nephew Cristoforo Pallavicini Doria was assigned eleven galleys and ordered to patrol between Trapani at the western end of Sicily and the islands of Favignana and Marettimo to the west of Sicily, the preferred waypoint of corsairs moving north or south between greater Tunis and the coast of Italy.

The four Maltese galleys were a part of the latter squadron, which as soon as reaching station captured a Turkish galliot of eighteen banks. Among the crew was a Turk by the name of Aci (phonetic Aji), who at one time laboured in the Order's Magistral Palace at Malta as a tailor. Aci understood Dragut had been seen passing the island of Pantelleria well to the south of Trapani, which coming from Gozo would suggest Dragut was headed for Sardinia or Corsica. Pallavicini headed in the same direction. Not yet clear of Sicily, Pallavicini's squadron encountered the six-galley Squadron of Sicily returning from a resupply mission to the Spanish garrison at La Goletta outside of Tunis. Commanded by Catalan Don Berenguer d'Oms de Requesens, he also had news from Pantellaria; Dragut had passed headed north one day prior to Requesens, taking a Sicilian sailing barque in passing from which he might have learned of the Christian squadrons. Thus, the thinking then went, he might have chosen an alternative direction.

Pursuant to instructions from Andrea Doria, Pallavicini absorbed the Naples squadron into his own. That evening cannon fire was heard in the direction of Cape Bon at the north-east corner of Greater Tunis, and Pallavicini decided to investigate. At dawn the following morning six galliots were sighted launching from the beach at Calibia (Kelibia) on the eastern side of Cape Bon. Galliots are lighter and generally faster than galleys, and the six galliots running south toward the shallow waters of the Gulf of Gabès began to open more distance between themselves and Pallavicini's Genovese galleys. Hospitaller galleys that were frequently hauled and waxed, though, closed the distance. Eventually Antonio Turchetto's *San Giovanni Battista*, newest and fastest of the four, overhauled the laggard galliot and boarded. She was taken. A Dragut galliot of eighteen banks that had participated in the raid on Gozo, some of her crew confirmed the advice originally received from the former tailor at Malta. Dragut was headed for Capraia, a small Tuscan island opposite the top of Corsica. A cannon signal alerted Requesens off Calibia, who returned to Sicily from where a heads-up was dispatched by frigate to Gianettino Doria patrolling Corsica.[1]

Prior of England William Weston died of a broken heart on 7 May 1540, the same day the Act of Dissolution came into force under which King Henry VIII disbanded monasteries, priories, convents, and friaries in England, Wales and Ireland, appropriating their income, disposing of their assets, and providing for their former members and functions. He had been given the authority to do this in England and Wales by the Act of Supremacy, passed by Parliament in 1534, which made him Supreme Head of the Church in England, thus divorcing England from Papal authority. For refusing to deny the Pope's supremacy, two English Hospitallers had been executed. One of these was Thomas Dingley, William Weston's nephew. Dingley was executed with Adrian Fortescue in July of 1539. The third would be David Gonson, executed in July 1541. Both Fortescue and Gonson would be beatified.[2]

Memi Reis, born Vicenzo da Cattaro at Kotor in modern Montenegro, had fled into the forest with crews at Gentile Virginio Orsini's mid-June approach, but turned himself in to local authorities two weeks later. Both he and Dragut were sent to Genovese oars, where Dragut would remain until ransomed by Barbarossa in 1544. Memi Reis would pull an oar even longer but would be back in corsair ranks by 1550. As for the two galleys, one was the Venetian *Moceniga* and the other the single Church galley lost at Preveza.[3]

The Grand Master was more than pleased by the capture of Dragut, feeling it put paid to the considerable damage he had done to the island of Gozo. Homedes was also pleased later to welcome home the fifty Gozitans abducted in April, liberated with others at Girolata. Following return of Cristoforo Pallavicini's combined squadrons from Cape Bon and Calibia the seventeen galleys, including the four Hospitallers, had scoured the Sicilian coast without incident. News of Dragut's capture had, after all, not yet been received and neither was he the only corsair living off the toil of innocent people. Moving on from Sicily to Calabria, welcome news of the capture was received and the seven Palavicino galleys took their leave to rejoin other Genovese galleys celebrating the success. The remaining Malta and Sicily squadrons encountered off Capo dell'Arme 5 miles south of Reggio Calabria the twenty-one-bank galliot of the aforementioned Ganga Rossa, renegade of Malta. With a single galliot, ten galleys did not make Ganga Rossa's day; he did not contest his final minutes of freedom. At about that time Requesens' six hired galleys were augmented by three 'house' galleys, which were the property of the Viceregency. These brought orders from Viceroy Ferrante Gonzaga for all thirteen galleys to return to Africa in support of Muley Hassan.[4]

Proceeding by way of Malta, the thirteen galleys were reinforced with all things necessary and departed for Africa on 7 August 1540. Entering the Gulf of Hammamet, a large southbound cargo ship was sighted and pursued. She was overtaken off the island of Cherchene (Chergui of the Kerkennahs) in Tunisia's Gulf of Gabès and easily seized by the Malta capitana. Salban placed a prize crew on board commanded by his lieutenant Catalan Juan Martin d'Argençola rather than ransacking the vessel. Vincenzo Cicala, however, boarded the vessel with his hired soldiers, who were ordered to sort the cargo into thirteen equal parts, four belonging to the Religion. Argençola, with all due courtesy, agreed the cargo was common property of the thirteen galleys but observed the cargo was worth more undivided and its division better done after sale. He also observed that the hired soldiers could be better employed than dividing cargo into thirteen equal portions. When Cicala ordered his soldiers to resume, Argençola firmly observed that he must insist on complying with his orders and that Cicala's conduct was becoming a matter of honour, about which he drew up his prize crew and signalled the Malta capitana to take the prize under tow. The dispute nevertheless continued and ended only when Requesens and Salban ordered Cicala and his soldiers back to their galleys or their galleys would be sent to the bottom. This head-to-head would have nasty consequences, only the first of which was that Cicala threatened to kill Argençola and departed with his two galleys, abandoning the expedition.[5]

The eleven remaining galleys with the cargo ship in tow retraced their own wake north to Monastir in the Gulf of Hammamet, which was one of the locales in rebellion against the rule of Muley Hassan. At Monastir they found three Turkish galleys in the small port with their sail antennas stowed and decked out in bunting as if for a fiesta. The city was surrounded by a wall so low as to be of little hindrance. The higher-walled fortress was known to be equipped with small-bore cannon only, and the whole was considered an easy capture for nine galleys and embarked soldiery. Preparations were under way when an oared frigate approached at speed with a summons from Viceroy Don Ferrante Gonzaga for all nine galleys to join the Imperial Armada assembling at Trapani with forty-three other galleys and twenty sailing ships under command of Andrea Doria. On order of Emperor Charles V, the Armada was to go to the assistance of Muley Hassan (Hafsid Muhammad V) by driving out and exterminating all corsairs within his realm. Gonzaga, as Commander of Ground Forces, would fly his flag from the Requesens capitana. This cleansing of the Kingdom of Tunis was to be a tandem endeavour followed by an assault on and levelling of Ottoman Algiers, thus freeing coastal Christians in the western Mediterranean of constant fear.[5]

The Imperial Armada sailed from Trapani at mid-September and made landfall at the same Calibia (Kelibia) on the eastern side of Cape Bon from which six Dragut galliots emerged in May, one taken by the Hospital's *San Giovanni Battista*. On arrival the two Princes Doria and Gonzaga initiated discussions with local rebels, who defended their rebellion by reciting the misery of Moors living under a Berber tyrant, by whom they were subjected to extortion and execution. But these astute and crafty individuals averted surrender of their fortress by opening up, and by promising loyalty to the Kingdom, knowing this large Armada had arrived not to subdue little Calibia but rather to seize Susa, Monastir, and Sfax. The two Princes departed wiser as well as satisfied, but promising to return, and took their overwhelming Armada to Monastir, only recently abandoned on the verge of reduction by the Viceroy's own naval commander Berenguer de Requesens. Viceroy Gonzaga's troops were put ashore and were immediately taken under fire by bands of Turks and Moors sortieing from the city in spite of covering fire from the galleys. These skirmishes soon ended, however, and the Christians were able to enter the city through an open gate, only to find the enemy absconded with wives and children through another gate. Monastir had been conquered and was thus eligible for the sack, following which a garrison was posted and the sailing ships were left in the port, a port with good anchor holding secure from all winds but a severe northerly. Sworn to poverty, Hospitallers were not known to participate in sacks, the province of inadequately or unpaid soldiery. The galleys covered a march to Susa (Sousse) 10 miles to the north, where Monastir fugitives had fled. Susa had a port able to accommodate fifty galleys inside, as today, both inner and outer harbours secure from all winds. Susa had, in addition, higher and stronger city walls as well as a stout inner fortress. But Susa also succumbed in short order, defenders fleeing. The galleys proceeded next to Maometta (Hammamet) 30 miles up the coast, outside of which Muley Hassan's army was encamped, an army larger in appearance than substance that had yet to subdue the city. While the army included 15,000 cavalry, it also included 2,000 dromedaries and entire families of Moors with children and possessions sprawled over the same area required by 50,000 Christian cavalry. It did not appear an army easily moved. Several volleys of galley bow cannon, however, produced open gates and the city yielded to Muley Hassan. The King then followed the galleys south, marching overland with several squadrons of cavalry while Christian garrisons at Monastir and Susa were replaced by Moors.

Ninety miles south of Monastir was the rebel-held city of Sfax on the Sfax Channel running between the mainland and the Kerkennah islands. Because of shallows left and right, galleys were able to transit the Channel no more than two abreast. Using shallow-draft frigates and skiffs, 6,000 Christian knights and soldiers with artillery were put ashore under command of the Viceroy, at their head embarked knights and soldiers of the Malta Squadron commanded ashore as afloat by Bernardo Salban. These were supplemented by cavalry units under command of Muley Hassan. Heavily populated and strongly fortified with 20,000 men under arms including professional soldiers in the pay of the Ottoman Sultan, Sfax defenders had the advantage.[5]

Motivated by the promise of spoils from a rich city, besiegers, in spite of the numbers, forced the defenders into discussions late in October, which unexpectedly resulted in the city's acceptance of a royal garrison, much to the disgust of those motivated by spoils. Andrea Doria also obtained 30,000 Venetian gold zecchins (replacing ducats at the same gold content) from the city in payment for his time. Early in November Christian forces began to re-embark. At the request of Muley Hassan, a Christian garrison of 2,500 Spanish infantry with artillery was posted back to Monastir under command of Alvaro de Sande. During the coming winter Sande would lead several expeditions against the Khalifa of Kairouan (Al Qayrawan), a day's march into the interior. The Khalifa had been leading a religious crusade against Muley Hassan. The latter did not rule a happy kingdom.[6]

It was the season of sudden storms at sea and a time for sensible seamen to be at home. The sailing vessels were detached to go their own way, sailing as close to the wind as possible. The galleys rowed up the coast, returning to Calibia as promised. The clever sheiks, however, knowing the season and having watched the sailing ships depart, had themselves departed, vowing to never swear allegiance to Muley Hassan. They were then at Mehedia (modern Mahdia, ancient Aphrodisium, Bosio's Citta d'Africa), safe for the moment. Doria had their fortress destroyed and returned to Trapani, where individual units were licensed to go their own way: the Prince continuing on to Genoa, the Malta Squadron accompanying the Viceroy to Palermo and then proceeding to Messina to load provisions for Malta.

Messina was the home of Vincenzo Cicala, and his two galleys were in port. Putting a Hospitaller party ashore to arrange for purchase and delivery of provisions, a second party was put ashore from the Cicala galleys under command of Vincenzo's nephew Filippo, lieutenant on one of the galleys. This second party fell upon the first. In the melee Filippo Cicala was wounded. So, too, was Catalan Hospitaller Joan de Montornès, the latter mortally so. Montornès was a close friend of Catalan Juan Martin d'Argençola, skipper of the prize in dispute and Lieutenant aboard Salban's capitana. Upon Montornès' death Argençola prepared the capitana's bow cannon to fire on Cicala's galleys, prevented from doing so only upon the sudden return of Salban from lodging a complaint with Cicala-friendly city authorities. Realising sensitivities were raw and close to the breaking point, Salban took the squadron from Messina to Syracuse, where provisions were ordered and received.[2]

Upon return to Malta, Bernardo Salban considered it in the best interest of the Convent that the subterfuge of a Regent serving in place of Captain of Galleys Muzio Costanzo be ended. He was also exhausted, and had completed thirty months of galley command, first of *Santa Maria de la Vittoria* and subsequently of *Santa Petronilla*. He was in addition suffering from several minor ailments and asked permission of Grand Master and Council to be allowed to retire to his own house in the Borgo. His request granted, he was succeeded in March 1441 by Grand Bailiff Georg Schilling as Captain of Galleys and as skipper of *Santa Petronilla* by Louis du Pont of the Langue of Provence. The following October he took passage to Marseille aboard *Galleon of Alexandria* commanded by Pedro de Felizes, presumably seeking to set out to his home and commandery in Catalonia. Sadly, his name never again appears in the pages of history.[7]

Grand Master Juan de Homedes and Council appointed Georg Schilling Captain of Galleys over objections of the Langue of Italy, represented by Lieutenant Admiral Giovan Battista Schiatesse, who sought to reserve to the (Italian) Admiral the right to make such appointments. Assuming command, Schilling took the four galleys to Syracuse for provisions, returning with renowned Cartographer and Military Engineer Antonio Ferramolino of Bergamo, dispatched on request of the Grand Master to Emperor Charles V to design a plan for Castle Saint Angelo and the surrounding Borgo. The plan was to include city walls and accommodations in time of siege for citizens living outside of the Borgo. It was also to include a deep water fosse between castle and Borgo able to accommodate galleys.

At about this time, July 1540, news was received of the death a month earlier in France of Prior of Saint-Gilles Raymond Ricard, who at age 57 won his Grand Cross on the walls at the Great Siege of Rhodes. He was

90 years of age. Grand Commander and Lieutenant to the Grand Master Giraud de Massas was appointed his successor, while Bailiff of Lango Foulques de Caritat succeeded to Grand Commander. The Bailiwick of Negroponte was vacated by the death of Alvaro de Pinto, with Grand Conservator (Draper) Gerónimo Coscon succeeding to the dignity. In a few months' time Juan Pertusa de Sarnes would be appointed Grand Conservator. Hospitaller chaplain Domenico Cubelles was appointed Bishop of Malta, the Bishopric vacant since the 1539 death of Tommasso Bosio, uncle of the historian. Antonio Corogna succeeded Cubelles as Prior of the Church. Robert d'Aché succeeded the deceased Pierre de Nesdez as Prior of Champagne, renouncing the dignity of Grand Hospitaller to which Jean de la Roche-Andry succeeded. He in turn renounced the dignity of Bailiff of the Morea, to which Balthazard d'Aspremont succeeded. Claude d'Ancienville was appointed to succeed Aspremont as Treasurer.[7]

While the Diet of Ratisbon (Regensburg) concluded unhappily on 22 May 1541 with no restoration of unity between Catholics and Lutherans, Emperor Charles V remained at that city until 29 June in a futile endeavour to salvage some cohesion among German states. On 29 June, however, he believed he must turn his attention to the threat to western Mediterranean coasts represented by the Ottoman Empire's corsair state at Algiers. Prior to departure he ordered mobilisation of large numbers of ships and soldiers in Spain and additionally ordered Andrea Doria, his fleet commander, to make ready. He wrote as well to the Viceroys of Naples and Sicily and to the Grand Master at Malta for the same purpose. He returned to Italy along the Adige River from the Tyrol and then overland, halting at Lucca in Tuscany for a meeting with Pope Paul III. The Emperor intended to personally lead the assault on Algiers.[7]

Georg Schilling made his second voyage with the squadron in July, taking the four galleys to Sicily, where it transported Viceroy Ferrante Gonzaga from Syracuse to Messina. In escorting several vessels from Sicily to Calabria, cargoes of timber for galley construction, the Squadron of Naples commanded by Don Garcia de Toledo was encountered. Because the coasts of Calabria were infested by corsairs, and because flame and smoke was evidence of their depredations, a decision was reached to patrol in company. The two squadrons together took the galliot of Talaisman

Reis off Capo dell'Armi, Reggio Calabria. This Talaisman had the same name as a deceased veteran of Suleiman's Great Siege of Rhodes, and may have been the latter's son.[7]

The squadron again sailed from Malta on 26 August with four galleys: the capitana *San Giovanni Battista*, commanded by Schilling himself; *Santa Caterina* or *Catarinetta*, commanded by Pons de Balaguer de Savignac; *Santa Croce* called *La Bastarda*, commanded by Francisco d'Azevedo; and *Santa Petronilla*, commanded by 1522 siege veteran Louis du Pont. The four galleys were accompanied by a frigate of eight banks in lieu of a larger and deeper-draft brigantine. Embarked were 150 knights commanded by Juan de Barrientos, Commander of Ciudad Rodrigo in western Spain. Schilling's assignment was to proceed initially to Livorno and from there to convey Pope Paul III to Ostia at the mouth of the Tiber. Fierce headwinds, however, forced the squadron to remain under Sicily's Cape Passero and to take shelter at Porto Palo, which is no more than a cove with meagre shelter 35 nautical miles south of Syracuse. Sometime after anchoring at Porto Palo, wind and disturbed waters of the cove caused *Santa Caterina*'s anchors to pull and she was blown into *Santa Croce*, damaging both galleys, further causing *Santa Croce* to pull her anchors and run up against the shore, where the surge of the sea put her in danger of breaking up. In retrospect, fortune smiled as the damage could have been more serious or irreparable.[8]

Instead *Santa Croce* was careened at Syracuse and repairs were made to both galleys within a few days. Following repairs the squadron again took course for Livorno. Early in the morning of 4 September three Barbary galliots were sighted beached on the volcanic islet of Vulcanello in the Aeolian littoral. It is an area in which corsairs were in the habit of waiting for north–south prey bound to or from the Strait of Messina. Two of the galliots were taken before becoming aware of the squadron, many in the crews fleeing from camps on the beach. The third galliot was able to put to sea pursued by *Santa Caterina* and *Santa Croce*. Following a long pursuit, she ran up on a mainland beach where infantry and cavalry were waiting. The crew was seized, Christian oarsmen liberated, and a prize crew placed on board. Earlier kidnap victims of this and the other two galliots were also liberated. Meanwhile, a party of knights and soldiers put ashore on Vulcanello rounded up those corsairs who had fled on foot. One of the beached galliots was commanded by a renegade Sicilian calling himself Mustafa Reis; he was hanged. Mufsa Reis, commanding the second beached galliot, a natural Turk, was spared. The galliot beached on the mainland was commanded by Kara Memi, also a natural Turk. He was spared. Arriving in Naples with the three galliots in tow, the Maltese were received with enthusiasm. The Order's Receiver at Naples took possession of both galliots and prisoners, and the squadron continued on its way. Six more corsair galliots were encountered off Monte Circello (where Odysseus encountered the siren Circe and remained her guest for twelve months). Schilling found safety under the guns of the fortress on the island of Ponza 20 miles to the south. From Ponza the frigate was dispatched to Livorno in advance to warn of the presence of enemy ships, and the squadron followed.[9]

The squadron was assigned to transport to Rome Pope Paul III, who had been meeting at Lucca with Emperor Charles V. Schilling and twelve senior knights embarked aboard two frigates to proceed up the Arno to Pisa. From there they headed overland to Lucca to pay homage to both Pope and Emperor. At Lucca the Hospitallers were apprised of a setback in Hungary, where Suleiman had come to the defence of Queen Isabella besieged by the Emperor's brother Ferdinand, Suleiman entering Buda earlier that same month of September 1541. The Hospitallers also learned of the unconscionable July assassination of the French Ambassador to the Porte Antonio de Rincon by Alfonso d'Ávalos, Marqués del Vasto and the Emperor's ground force commander at the Siege of Tunis. Finally they learned of preparations by French King Francis for another Italian War. And thus the added importance of diverting the attention of those two allies, the Unholy Alliance of Suleiman and Francis, from the conquest of Algiers. Departing Lucca on 20 September, Pope Paul travelled overland to Rome by way of Bologna and Perugia, not reaching his destination until 31 October. The Emperor, meanwhile, had departed Lucca on 18 September for the port of La Spezia, where he had assembled a large part of the expedition's sailing vessels as well as ground forces including the hired Italian infantry of Camillo Colonna and Agostino Spinola and 6,000 German landsknechts commanded by Jörg von Regensberg and Baron von Seifnech. From La Spezia the sailing units had a storm-tossed passage to Menorca, where they would await other contingents of the Expeditionary Force. The Emperor himself embarked aboard the Royal

Quinquereme, one of thirty-five galleys commanded by Andrea Doria assembling just to the south of La Spezia at Viareggio. Foul weather, however, delayed galley departure. The Malta Squadron, according to Bosio, was nevertheless assigned an unspecified Papal mission that took it first to Civitavecchia and then to Ostia. It was only then Schilling began to ready for the expedition to Algiers, taking his Squadron to Genoa, where he acquired canvas, ropes, and other items needed before proceeding to a galley rendezvous at Bonifacio, Corsica.[10]

Following more than one false start aborted by weather, Andrea Doria in October sailed from Viareggio to Bonifacio, where his galley armada was joined by the four galleys of Malta under Georg Schilling. Schilling had 150 embarked knights and additional soldiery, and was accompanied by Hospitaller Nicholas de Villegagnon as an observer. Villegagnon would pen a report of events that today is a primary source for historians and students of history studying the Siege of Algiers. This French presence in the invasion force, not Villegagnon himself, makes it patently clear should there have been any doubt that the invasion force was awaited at Algiers.

From Bonifacio the galley fleet was blown south along the west coast of Sardinia before a break in the weather enabled passage to Mahon on the island of Menorca, which was reached at mid-October. At the island 5,000 Italian infantry had gathered with the aforementioned 6,000 Germans and another 6,000 Spaniards, without counting a large number of adventurers that included Hernán Cortés, conqueror of Mexico.[11]

The armada at Mahon had been joined by Prince of Salerno Ferrante de San Severino on 1 October, shortly afterward by the Viceroy of Sicily Ferrante Gonzaga with seven galleys and twenty-eight support ships. Upon arrival of Emperor and galleys the small roadstead hosted four galleys of Malta, four of Sicily under the orders of Berenguer de Requesens, six of Antonio Doria, five of Naples under the command of Garcia de Toledo, two from Lord of Monaco Honouré I, two of Vincenzo Cicala, two of the Marchese di Terranuova, four from the Vatican and fifty others from Genoa. Bernardino de Mendoza and Fernando Álvarez de Toledo, Duke of Alba, with the Spanish contingent would proceed separately to Algiers. The Mahon Armada sailed at mid-month in good weather. Pursuant to the consolidated maritime ceremonial, the Papal flagship of Gentile Virginio Orsini placed itself to the right of the royal quinquereme in which Andrea Doria was also embarked. To the left was placed *San Giovanni Battista*, capitana of Malta, and to the rear was the flagship of Genoa.

Doria had initially opposed the expedition, but was insufficiently persuasive to overcome the wishes of the Emperor who, for his part, believed war with France in the coming year inevitable and wished to have done with Algiers.[12] Doria's forecasts were not long in being proved correct. Arriving 19 and 20 October at Algiers where rendezvous was effected with the Spanish contingent on 21 October, a storm for three days prevented all communication with the shore. The force at the Emperor's disposal consisted of sixty-five galleys, 450 other ships, 12,000 sailors, 24,000 troops, and an untold number of galley oarsmen, while Barbarossa's adopted son Hassan Aga was believed to have not more than 1,500 Turks and 5,000 to 6,000 Andalusian Moors.[13] Debarkation was ordered on 23 October. Schilling left senior captain Louis du Pont of *Santa Petronilla* in command of the squadron and led 500 embarked personnel ashore, including adventurers; Pons de Balaguer de Savignac was Schilling's lieutenant and flag-bearer.[14]

The landing 6 miles south-east of the city was perilous and difficult for the major part of the soldiery, who had to enter water up to the neck. Numerous troops of Bedouin cavalry harassed the landing and the 24 October march on the city with close sorties, during which the Bedouin smothered the Imperial column with arquebus fire, with arrows, and with barbed lances. Imperial ground forces managed, nonetheless, to secure the beach below and the heights above the city, from which a violent bombardment of the walls commenced. The Emperor was confident.

A new storm came up, however, one that surprised the assailants who in their haste had not attended to supplies. In a howling gale the camp became a mud swamp. All night Imperial soldiers remained in the open, whipped by icy wind. They were, moreover, famished, exhausted, and demoralised. They were also incapable of using their arquebuses because their powder was wet. Moors, some of them Moriscoes expelled from Spain in 1529 by this same Emperor, carried out a sortie from the city on the morning of 25 October against Italians who broke and ran; the situation was salvaged by a small detachment of Hospitaller Knights and by the Italian rearguard commanded by Camillo Colonna and Agostino

Spinola. The Hospitaller detachment included observer Nicholas de Villegagnon, who was wounded in the arm by the lance of a mounted Turk. The Turk turned to finish the job, but Villegagnon, of considerable strength and stature, rose from the muck into which he had fallen and, grabbing the Turk by the arm, wrested him from his horse and stabbed him to death. By this example, others were encouraged to check the rout and eventually drove the assailants back within the walls.[15] It is in this endeavour that, Bosio[16] asserts, every Hospitaller present was killed or wounded, Pons de Balaguer de Savignac mortally so, and it was apparently the drawbridge to the city gate that was called the Bridge of Fursi that, because of their losses, would be called 'Tomb of the Knights'. Among the dead were Diego de Contreras of Castile, who for a long while survived with a musket ball in his head; Lope Alvarez de Vilate of Navarre who made it over the bridge before his leg was severed by an artillery round; Juan de Pennas; Ernan Alvarez Osorio of Salamanca; Guido Rossi of Naples, one of the first to die at the gate, killed by a large stone block that dropped from ramparts and hit him in the head; Pierre de Reffray and Jean de Babute of the Langue of France; Briand de Sauzet of Auvergne; Charles de Guival of Provence; Jehan Pinart of France; Louis de Navarin of Provence; Guillaume le Piccart of France; Giuseppe della Casa of Italy; Jean Fretart de Lolebron of France; and many others, most of them young caravan knights.

Meanwhile, the storm's onshore winds forced 140 or more sailing ships to pull their anchors and to be blown onto the rocks or overturned on the beach. The enemy stood in ambush on the beach to capture, kill, and strip those able to reach the shore and to prey on all that was possible from the beached ships. Galleys held to the sea with difficulty, with oars supporting anchors; when the storm diminished Doria led the galleys and remaining ships into the bay east of Cape Matifou. On 26 October the Emperor ordered a withdrawal. Artillery and baggage train, rendered unserviceable, were abandoned in place; horses were slaughtered and the meat distributed to troops. The wounded and sick were placed at the head of the column; in the rearguard the Spanish and Maltese were posted, including a wounded Schilling; the cavalry was at the tail end. Furious clashes took place everywhere. The wounded who fell and could not be rescued were murdered by Bedouins where they fell; the rearguard was engaged in continuous fighting with a white-robed army. Three days later the Imperial force reached the Cape, where a council of war was convened. Cortés and some others were in favour of renewing the siege; Doria's alternative view prevailed, and on 1 November exhausted troops began to re-embark. Ships escaping the storm were so crowded horses had to be thrown in the sea to make room for men; 1,400 Turkish oarsmen were set free for the same reason.[17]

The fleet departed early in November just in time to be scattered by a new storm. Many ships were wrecked on the Algerian coast, including eleven of the twenty galleys that Doria had at his disposition, and their crews were taken prisoner. The rest of the Armada fighting the sea repaired to Bougie (Bejaia), where it remained storm-bound for three weeks. From Bougie the squadrons of Sicily and Malta were licensed by the Emperor to proceed east along the coast of Africa and in the event reached Porto Farina on the east coast of Tunisia. There they received succour from Muley Hassan and on a favourable wind reached Trapani in Sicily, the Maltese continuing on to Messina and thence to Malta. Remaining Spanish contingents of the Armada under command of Doria proceeded west from Bougie and reached Cartagena in southern Spain. When in the end the Armada found refuge in Spanish ports, no fewer than 300 captains and 8,000 soldiers (12,000 by Merriman estimate, up to 17,000 according to others) had been captured or killed by injury or drowning. *There were so many prisoners in the bagnos of Algiers that the price of a Christian slave became equal to that of an onion.* Among the dead were Hospitallers Diego de Contreras of Castile; Lope Alvarez of Navarre; 1522 Siege veteran Jean de Panas of Provence; Hernando Alvarez Osorio of Salamanca; Guido di Rossi of Naples; Pierre des Essarts and Jean de Babute, both of the Langue of France; Louis de Brandon de Sauset received five months earlier into the Langue of Auvergne; Antoine de Villars, also of Auvergne; Charles de Guibal of Provence; Antoine de Vaudrey Saint-Phalle, nephew of Prior of France (in-waiting) Claude d'Ancienville; Chaplain Jean Pinard of the Diocese of Mans; Louis de Novarin of Provence; Novitiate Guillaume le Picard d'Artilly of Paris; Giuseppe della Casa of Florence and Pisa; Jean Fretart dit Lotebon of the Priory of France, who by his attendance to the wounded earned the appellation 'Child of God'; Benedictine Chaplain Honouré Colat; and flag-bearer Alfonso Sedeño of Aragon.[18]

To repay the 75-year-old Doria for damages, the Emperor made a gift of thirteen galleys at anchor in Barcelona and granted an annual commission of 3,000 ducats to be paid from taxes of the Kingdom of Naples; Doria would also be appointed Protonotary (First Secretary) of the same Kingdom. At the end of the month Doria left Mallorca to return to Genoa.[19]

Chapter VIII

Juan de Homedes y Coscon 1541–46

Georg Schilling's squadron returned to Malta from the ill-fated Siege of Algiers on 8 December 1541 with all four galleys but without Pons de Balaguer de Savignac, captain of *Santa Caterina*, plus a host of other knights, adventurers, and infantry. Pennants from three Barbary galliots taken off the islet of Ciarelli in September were trailed in the sea by the galleys. During the squadron's absence Malta had been infested with corsairs, particularly in the Freo Channel between Malta and Gozo with its ready access to drinking water. Lamberto Doria had made a valiant effort at clearing the Channel with use of non-Hospitaller Bernardo Scotto's private galliot, the brigantine used as a ferry between the two islands, and the tender for the laid-up carrack *Santa Anna*, but two corsair galliots remained regular visitors. A Christian slave escaping from one of these reported that Parisot de la Valette was months earlier embarked aboard a well-armed galliot he had purchased from a Genovese captain by the name of Garibaldo. Patrolling near Seccagne (the shallows around the Kerkennah islands) late in the day, he was surprised by two galliots no smaller than his own under the command of Acsac Reis (Zoppo) of Candia and Kara Mustafa of Eski Foça (Phocaea in Greek). All three combatants fought with considerable valour, and there was significant loss of life among the enemy when calamity struck and Valette's galliot was overrun. Wounded, he was taken captive to Djerba and condemned to the oars with his officers and crew. He was to remain in slavery for little more than a year until exchanged near the Xercia gate to Tripoli for the Turk Ibrahim Casdagli, whom Schilling had taken captive from one of the Ciarelli galliots, the exchange pursuant to an agreement brokered by Luigi Braccio di Ferro (Luigi Iron Arm), a man of considerable skill and valour greatly respected by Turks and Moors. Casdagli was the father of Kus Ali Abdul Rahman, the latter among those with Zoppo and Kara Mustafa capturing Valette. Braccio di Ferro was one of the mounted arquebusiers brought to Tripoli to aid in the city's defence. The fate of

Valette's officers and crew is unknown, as is his rationale for sailing in enemy waters without company.[1]

During the final four months of the year, and much to the surprise of Grand Master and Council, the number of knights and serving brothers received into the Order of Jerusalem had far exceeded expectations, so much so that the Order's finances were under pressure over and above the extraordinary norm and there was a frantic search for ways to cut costs. All priories and commanderies were consequently ordered not to receive additional applicants for a period of three years. This general prohibition did not apply to the Langue of England for reason of the langue's preservation given Henry VIII's Act of Dissolution.[2]

Entering the new year of 1542, the Grand Master appeared to be aging faster than his 69 years, and there were serious and troubling concerns about his mental and physical state and ability to grasp the larger issues confronting the Order. Ongoing improvement of fortifications at Malta not only drained the Treasury but required constant supervision, particularly construction of a cavalier (elevated fortification within a larger fortification with a clear field of fire) within Castle Saint Angelo, later called Fortress Saint Angelo. Planning for a new fortress on the Peninsula opposite Castle Saint Angelo, called Fort Saint Elmo, had also been initiated, both cavalier and Elmo recommendations of Military Engineer Antonio Ferramolino dispatched to Malta by the Emperor a year earlier. There was escalating pressure on Tripoli from Barbarossa's former *kaya* Mourad Aga, Sheik of Tagiora. There were rumours of war between the Empire and France bringing division and tension to the Convent. Such a war had inevitable consequences for Italian Hospitallers, as well, as Italy was the likely battlefield. With Suleiman's conquest of Buda, the Ottomans were a step closer to Germany, a Germany already riven by Catholic–Lutheran differences leading to expropriation of Hospitaller priories and commanderies in Lutheran states. At sea there were reports Suleiman returned from Buda to Constantinople in November specifically to oversee a naval build-up in support of the Unholy Alliance with France, with consequent heightened danger to Malta. And then, of course, there was Henry VIII.[2]

Calling into Malta at the end of January 1542 were three French galleys bound from Constantinople to Marseille conveying Antoine Escalin des Aimars. Called Captain Polin, he was successor to the assassinated Antonio Rincon as French Ambassador to the Porte, returning to Paris for conversations with the King. At Malta mostly for drinking water, news was conveyed of the Ottoman threat in Hungary and, more pertinently, in the western Mediterranean, where conversation suggested Barbarossa would in time move against the Emperor with an overwhelming armada.

Among administrative matters, Cristóbal Solis Farfan was appointed to the vacant position of Chancellor, succeeding both long-ailing Jacobo de Briseño and Regent Chancellor Guillermo Raimundo Beneyt. Emery des Reaulx was appointed Prior of Auvergne, succeeding the deceased Gabriel du Chief. He vacated the dignity of Marshal, to which Commander Jean des Roches was appointed. A bit later Commander Gaspard de Vallier of the Langue of Auvergne and Gonzalo Guiral of Castile were dispatched to Rome as Procurators for their respective langues to rebut new arguments the Langue of Italy had brought before the Holy See concerning the Admiral's right to appoint galley squadron commanders.[3]

Escalin des Aimars reached Paris on 8 March 1542, conveying to King Francis assurances of Ottoman assistance in the event of war between France and the Empire of Charles V.

Francis declared war on 12 July 1542, naming various injuries as cause, among them Rincon's murder, which he declared an injury so great, so detestable, and so strange to those who bear the title and quality of prince that it could not in any way be forgiven, suffered, or endured. The French immediately launched a two-front offensive against Charles. In the north, the Duke of Orléans attacked Luxembourg, briefly capturing the city; in the south, a larger army under Claude d'Annebault and Francis's eldest son, the Dauphin Henry, unsuccessfully besieged the city of Perpignan in northern Spain. Francis himself was meanwhile at La Rochelle dealing with popular discontent over a proposed increase in duties on imported salt, an increase to help pay the cost of war.

Georg Schilling and the four galleys of the squadron were off Pozzalo, Sicily, in August when advice was received from Torre Cabrera Fortress of Turkish fustas operating near Cape Passero 15 miles to the east. Heading in that direction, a brigantine was sighted ahead that ran for the beach, where the crew was seen to flee ashore. *Santa Caterina*, commanded by Juan de Barrientos in succession of the deceased Pons de Balaguer de

Savignac, closest of the galleys, put a party of knights and soldiers ashore that successfully corralled the fleeing crew.

The brigantine skipper, hoping to save himself, revealed the presence in local waters of a corsair galliot of twenty banks. Schilling ordered the squadron standing off the beach to take up the search without embarking the search party, which remained with the beached brigantine. Thus lightened, *Santa Caterina* was well ahead of the others when the corsair galliot was sighted. The latter took to the open sea in flight and it was well into the night when, thanks to a wind shift, she was overhauled by the pursuing *Santa Caterina* and boarded over the spur buried in her quarter. There was a protracted engagement in which the corsairs were heartened by a galley slave's shout that the Christian galley was undermanned. Thus encouraged, the corsairs attempted to board the Hospitaller galley but were repulsed. In the end the Hospitallers prevailed. Of a complement of eighty Turks and Moors, most arquebusiers and crossbowmen, only forty-four remained alive, almost all wounded including Yunus Reis of Modon, the galliot's captain. Many Hospitallers were also wounded, severely so the Catalan Adrià Maimon and the Castilian lieutenant to Barrientos, Godofredo de Loaysa, who defended the rambade above the bow cannon where the corsairs attempted to board. The first lost an eye and the second a hand. Ninety-five Christians were freed from the oars of both brigantine and galliot, while seventy-four crew were enslaved. Both ships were towed into Malta on 21 August. Yunus, a natural Turk, was not executed but indeed offered his own ransom of 1,000 Venetian sequins (*zecchinos* or Venetian gold ducats). The offer was refused and he was enslaved. He became the house servant of Pietro Giustiniani, a young knight received into the Order as a minor. Giustiniani, however, left Yunus in relative freedom. Yunus took advantage of the situation, stole a sailing boat, and in the company of other similarly treated slaves reached the African coast, where he resumed the life of a corsair.[3]

Barbarossa's adopted son Hassan Aga or Hassan of Sardinia (as distinguished from natural son Hassan) was appointed Beylerbey or Viceroy of greater Algiers by Sultan Suleiman in recognition of his stout defence of the city during the Emperor's October 1541 assault. Mourad Aga, Barbarossa's former *kaya*, was similarly appointed Sanjakbey or Governor of Tagiora on Barbarossa's recommendation. Both thus became pashas. In early autumn Mourad returned to Tagiora with his commission from the Sultan, though he had been at Tagiora off and on since January 1538 without such a commission. He was described as an individual held in great esteem by his superiors as well as by those he commanded, and was also described as an individual of valour and good judgment. Dispatched by Barbarossa, he arrived with two large and well-armed galliots as well as with 300 janissaries on the Sultan's payroll. His assignment was to take the city and fortress of Tripoli.[4]

Among his initiatives, Mourad established a siege perimeter 3 miles from Tripoli preventing Hospitaller contact with allies or potential allies among the native population. Not so restricted, Mourad, with favours and honours, was able to seduce numerous local tribes. Concerned by the perimeter, Grand Master and Council gathered a relief force of knights and soldiers, which Grand Bailiff Schilling's squadron ferried to Tripoli. From Tripoli Schilling proceeded to a meeting at Messina with Viceroy Ferrante Gonzaga to plead for several companies of Spanish infantry from the tercio assigned to Sicily. Schilling also sought assistance and materials, including building stone and mortar, with which to repair Tripoli's ancient walls. While these requests were pending Gonzaga dispatched to Malta Hospitaller Iacomo Bardellone of the Vice-regal staff. Bardellone conveyed to Grand Master and Council the Viceroy's wish that when ailing Prior of Barletta Gabriele Tadino di Martinengo, hero of the Great Siege of Rhodes, should die, the bailiwick be settled upon the Viceroy's son Don Vicenzo Gonzaga, then two-and-a-half years of age. (In a unique perquisite, designated Italian bailiffs were addressed and referred to as priors.) Given a worsening of the matters weighing on the Grand Master in January, and Tripoli's urgent need for Viceregal support, Grand Master and Council had no choice but to agree to propose the matter at the next Chapter General.[5]

Accompanied by Hospitaller Diego de Chavez, apparently to warrant the decision of Grand Master and Council, Schilling and squadron returned to Messina in November, where the Grand Bailiff pursued Viceregal provision of the necessities required by Tripoli as well as reported the decision. The Viceroy was well satisfied with the 'negotiations', and agreed to provide everything requested excepting the companies of Spanish infantry. The Viceregency itself had given up infantry to Imperial forces fighting on two fronts, Flanders and northern Spain.[6]

Pursuant to a prior understanding with the Grand Master, Schilling hired in Sicily at Convent expense sixty veteran Italian soldiers (condottieri). These were embarked aboard the galleys and transported to Malta, which the squadron reached at the turn of the year. At Malta these new additions were augmented by yet another squadron of knights and soldiers garrisoned at Malta accompanied by several pieces of artillery, and the lot were embarked aboard the small galleon or Galleonetto of the Religion and transported to the relief of besieged Tripoli. Sailing in company were two large bulk carriers with cargoes of munitions, provisions, and wood for reinforcing Tripoli's fortifications, the three sailing ships escorted by the four galleys. Off Djerba the galleys were forced by weather to seek shelter, while the Galleonetto and cargo carriers continued safely to Tripoli. During the bad weather *Santa Caterina* suffered damage to her mast and antenna, forcing the squadron to return to Messina, where new spars were readily available. The damaged galley repaired, the squadron escorted Hospitaller Prior of Messina Signorino Gattinara to Malta.[6]

It was not until 6 April 1543 that the squadron again departed for Tripoli. Scouring the coast of Tunisia two weeks out, a bit south of Djerba near modern Porto Palo, Schilling gave up his search for coastal traffic and took course for Tripoli. That evening on the high seas two ships were sighted and were overtaken three hours after nightfall. The prey were high-freeboard galleons with lots of artillery firing continuously all night and doing no damage whatsoever. Schilling decided to wait for morning. At first light on 21 April galley bow cannon holed every single galleon sail, not neat round holes but tattering tears, rendering both ships nearly immobile, sailing on the hull. The capitana and *Santa Caterina* took one of them, *Santa Croce* and *Santa Maria de la Vittoria* the other, the enemy capitana. All four galleys avoided the lateral quadrants in which galleon broadside cannon may be brought to bear, and instead remained astern of the prey pummeling the stern castles. In this position twelve galley bow cannon were pummelling each galleon while two stern cannon of each galleon were divided between two adversaries. Even so, a well-placed galleon cannon ball destroyed the rambade or boarding platform on *Santa Maria de la Vittoria*, killing five soldiers, three oarsmen, and mortally wounding François de la Liere of the Langue of France, Lieutenant to Louis du Pont.

It was not long, however, before galleon stern cannon were silenced and before the galleys closed to arquebus and crossbow range. Then came boarding by the quarter and hand-to-hand combat with pikes and swords. Then it was over, the dead and dying littering the decks. One of the galleons was in service to Sinan of Smyrna, then resident at Suez, and the other was commanded by Mansur Reis, student and protégé of Sinan. Both had come from the mouth of the Nile and Alexandria to Djerba, where Sinan formerly governed, laden with rice, indigo, linens, and other merchandise, and were bound to Lepanto when surrendering, expecting to return to Djerba with proper Lepanto timbers for galliot construction. Each galleon had 160 soldiers embarked between Turks and Moors, not more than thirty of whom remained alive at the end of combat. The victory was costly for Hospitallers, as well, with more than three hundred wounded and nine Hospitallers dead in addition to the dying François de la Liere: Jacques le Brau of the Priory of Aquitaine, Lazaro Rossi of Florence, Claude de Chalùs of Provence, Guillaume de Séelles de L'Estanville of France, Verot d'Argençola of Catalonia, Luis Moix of Mallorca, Barthelemy Clavet de Montfort[7] of Savoy and the Langue of Auvergne, Pélronet de Polastron of Provence, and Serving Brother Trejo of Castile. Arnaud de Gameville-Montpopon of Provence[8] was nearly dead. Thirty soldiers, several seamen, and many oarsmen were also killed. One of the galleons was too damaged to continue beyond Tripoli, but the other, loaded with the best of both cargoes, was sent on to Malta under command of Afonso Correa of Portugal.[6]

Bound for Gallipoli in the Propontis or Sea of Marmara, Barbarossa departed Constantinople on that same 21 April 1543 with seventy galleys, forty galliots, and 100 large ships on which were embarked 14,000 Turks. The forty corsair galliots were commanded by his lieutenant Nizzam. Barbarossa was accompanied by Escalin des Aimars, later Baron de La Garde, French ambassador to the Ottoman Empire since 1541. After taking on cordage and other marine supplies, the Armada departed Gallipoli in mid-May[9] bound for Modon at the foot of the Morea. Following a fast downwind passage and pause to load drinking water, at the end of May Barbarossa's Armada was again under way, this time taking course for southern Italy.[10]

Commanding the Galleon of the Religion, Francesco Terno da Crema in May transported from Marseille to Malta a large number of dignitaries intent at the forthcoming Chapter General on lifting administration of the Order's Treasury from the hands of Grand Master Juan de Homedes. These dignitaries included Grand Commander Foulques de Caritat, Prior of France Philippe de Carleau, Commander and future Grand Master Claude de la Sengle, then the Order's Receiver in France, and many others. Knowing their intent, they were coldly received by the Grand Master.[11]

At Tripoli the galleys were active on day patrols, and in May seized two multipurpose saicas as well as a large square-rigged schierazzo, aboard which they found Corsa Reis, brother of Cairadeno the former Barbarossa protégé and Sheik of Tagiora. Before returning to Malta the Grand Bailiff surveyed anew the shallows off Tripoli, and for this purpose borrowed two shallow-draft frigates. During his survey he saw so many fishing craft from Djerba he reached the conclusion that during any siege of Tripoli by the Ottoman Armada, these same fishermen would be used as Ottoman pilots. The fishermen would also be used to reprovision the armada during any prolonged siege. The Hospitaller's Tripoli outpost was indeed doomed. In the meantime he learned from fishermen the Ottoman Armada had departed Constantinople on the aforementioned 21 April. They had this information from a large cargo carrier then moored in the Djerba Channel dispatched by Barbarossa with all the items corsairs might need.

Both ship and Djerba shore were lightly guarded when Schilling arrived with his Hospitallers, and all fled in skiffs to the mainland. On board, hidden under tarps and cordage, the Hospitallers found a large siege machine and several siege cannon. The cannon were removed and all else set aflame, burning the ship to the waterline. Also removed from the ship was a captive Greek helmsman from Candia by the name of Manolis. He revealed that the prior evening two ships departed Djerba bound for the Levant with cargoes of olive oil and black slaves. Knowing that in light air the two ships had made little progress, Schilling went in pursuit, overhauling them the next morning, one a captured Portuguese caravel and the other a large germa, square-rigged as was the caravel. Again, the crews fled in skiffs; only the black slaves remained. These greeted the newcomers with tambourines and songs, and the two ships were taken in tow to Malta, where they arrived on 18 June. Information gleaned from the brother of Cairadino and from a renegade fleeing Tagiora called Christos of Negroponte had earlier been sent by frigate to Malta, where the Grand Master had become convinced the threat to Tripoli or to Malta or to both of Barbarossa's Armada was very real. Hospitaller Don Diego de Guzmán, brother of Enrique Enriquez de Guzmán, 4th count of Alba de Liste, was on 24 May dispatched to the Emperor seeking assurance of assistance should need come to pass. He found the Emperor at Busseto en route to Germany, who before leaving Italy issued orders to Andrea Doria to keep the Imperial Armada ready to proceed to the aid of Tripoli or Malta if and when threatened.

Following the Franco–Ottoman alliance Barbarossa had been ordered to Marseille for combined operations with the French Navy. Deemed a threat to Reggio Calabria as he transited the Strait of Messina northbound in June, Governor of Reggio Diego Gaetani had fired a single artillery round, killing three Turkish sailors. Enraged, the Ottoman admiral took Reggio under cannon fire, put 12,000 men ashore, and overwhelmed the city. The fortress was sacked and his janissaries captured seventy Spanish soldiers; Captain Polin interceded in favour of Governor Gaetani. Among the Ottoman captives was the daughter of the same Gaetani, of the name Flavia and 18 years of age. Enamoured of her, Barbarossa took her as his bride, notwithstanding the difference in age (he was 65) and, as a wedding gift, freed her parents and spared the city from a murderous sack. He days later, however, put to fire and sword the coast of Neapolitan Campania, and on 29 June appeared at the mouth of the Tiber, from which it could be said that he threatened Rome. His Armada at the Tiber consisted of 120 galleys and galliots, thirty-five sailing ships, and four large transports. Polin wrote to Cardinal Legate Rodolfo Pio, acting Governor of Rome, that Barbarossa had orders from the Sultan to not molest Papal territory. Ignoring Rome, the former corsair departed the same night for Civitavecchia.[12] During his time in southern Italy Barbarossa's corsairs nevertheless pillaged the provinces of Apulia and Basilicata adjacent to Papal territory; hundreds of slaves were taken to the fleet as well as provisions and plunder from raids along the coast and nearby hinterland.[13]

Days after Barbarossa's passage up the Strait of Messina in June Hospitaller Don Diego de Guzmán hired at Messina 200 soldiers through the offices of Costantino Doria de Marchesi of Rhodes. These were immediately escorted to Malta aboard the Galleonetto. Guzmán then returned to Messina, where he hired additional soldiers and these were embarked aboard the crewed Venetian barque *Contarina* chartered by the Order's Receiver at Messina. The ship was otherwise loaded with timber, hardware, and other provisions of war. She would remain in the Order's employ for the foreseeable future.[13] On 19 June the brigantine commanded by Gonzalo dell'Aguila returned to Malta from a search for Barbarossa and confirmed that the Ottoman Armada in the number of 108 large galleys, twenty-five galliots, and four large ships had earlier transited the Strait of Messina northbound. On his next survey Aguila was pursued and captured near Trapani by one of Barbarossa's galliot scavengers; he was later offered for ransom, however, and the ransom was paid.[10]

While Muley Hassan was in Italy seeking assistance from Emperor Charles V to put down rebellion among his minions, Muley Hassan's son Ahmad (Hafsid Ahmad III), by some called Amida and by others called Muley Hameda, seized his throne at Tunis. Viceroy of Naples Pedro Álvarez de Toledo provided Muley Hassan an escort of 2,000 infantry, mostly Florentines, under command of Captain Giovan Battista Lofredi, who together returned to La Goletta, the Spanish fortress commanding the Bay of Tunis. Proceeding from La Goletta to Tunis by the north shore, the Italians were assailed by Ahmad at the head of a large body of loyal Tunisians and Lofredi was killed. Muley Hassan was arrested in the presence of confused Italian soldiery, was blinded as he had blinded his many brothers, was turned over to one of his blinded brothers, and was soon killed. Ahmad immediately declared for the Holy Roman Empire.[14]

Passing through the waters of northern Italy in advance of Barbarossa's armada, his lieutenant Nizzam rampaged along the coast of Tuscany with mounted raiding parties. During one of these rampages he assailed the Collecchio castle at Cala di Forno, 30km north of Porto Ercole, where the Order's warships had been home-ported sixteen years earlier. Ill defended, the only reported plunder was Margherita di Nanni Marsili, 16-year-old daughter of Lord of Collecchio Nanni Marsili. Said to be a red-headed beauty, Margherita was sent back to Constantinople and absorbed into Suleiman's seraglio. There she disappeared from the pages of history, if not from speculative accounts of the Sultan's seraglio.

Barbarossa's Ottoman Armada reached Île Saint-Honourat off Cannes on 5 July expecting to be greeted by elements of the French Navy, but, 'as usual, Francis had done none of the things he had promised to do'. Polin was given two weeks to put things right, and Barbarossa continued on to Toulon, arriving on 10 July. On 21 July 1543 he was accorded full honours at Marseille[15] by François de Bourbon-Vendome, comte d'Enghien and Général des galères de France; the pennant of the French general, the standard of Notre-Dame, was lowered and in its place was hoisted a green swallow-tailed pennant displaying a pair of the Prophet's scimitars in white appearing as chart dividers beneath an Arabic inscription also in white, the dividers squared by four white symbols and centred over a six-pointed star, signifying the Ottoman commander was senior officer afloat. All who had not fled the French city admired the luxury and wealth of the Turkish admiral, who was accompanied ashore by two pashas and twelve other dignitaries clothed in cloaks of gold, and at the rear followed by a crowd of officials, secretaries, and interpreters.

At about this time the barque constructed at Bilbao in 1540 was retired. She was replaced by the arrival at Malta of a large new three-masted square and lateen-rigged round ship of 650 gross tons carrying capacity. Built in Flanders, she had both stern and fore castles and was equipped with broadside cannon in between. On her maiden voyage she had paused in Portugal and Spain to embark Hospitallers coming to the September Chapter General at Malta. Commanded by Francisco Giron, former skipper of the galley *San Filippo*, she had encountered in the Piombino Channel between Tuscany and the island of Elba the entire Ottoman Armada and was assailed by a large squadron of Turkish galleys. In what has to have been a remarkable feat of seamanship and gunnery, the Turkish squadron had been dissuaded from continuing the attack, while the prevailing north-west wind was strong enough to enable a rapid escape to the south. Called the *Barcia of the Religion*, she reached Malta on 3 August. The large number of Latin Hospitallers arriving lifted the spirits of Juan de Homedes given the coming confrontation with French knights wishing to relieve him of the Order's purse strings.[16]

In August Barbarossa assisted the French in a badly planned and unsuccessful siege of Nice, a possession of Charles III's Duchy of Savoy. The Ottoman commander anchored his armada at nearby Villefranche while the French under Enghien anchored in the port of Nice on 10 August. Following nine days of un-coordinated French and Ottoman siege and three of assault, the city came to terms on 22 August. Attacks on the citadel, however, were repulsed by the courageous defence of Hospitaller Paolo Simeoni, a Piemontese in service to his country. Enghien, commander of French galleys, promised to spare citizens of Nice from the sack; he found obstinate opposition on the part of Turks, however, who demanded the sack. Polin himself was in danger of being killed as he struggled to curb the allies and to appease an angry Barbarossa; he narrowly averted being chained to the bench for allegedly deceiving the Ottomans. While a sack entailing rape, fire, and sword was avoided, Nice was thoroughly pillaged.[17]

Prior of Messina Signorino della Gattinara was appointed Captain of Galleys on 20 August 1543 for a period of two years, succeeding Georg Schilling but pending, however, a decision at Rome concerning pre-eminence of the Italian Admiral in the appointment of squadron commanders. The Grand Master also appointed his Master of the House Gonzalo Cervantes as master of ceremonies at the change of command, but Giorgio Adorno, senior knight of the Langue of Italy and Lieutenant Admiral, showed up and insisted on presiding in the name of the absent Admiral. At this point Homedes put his foot down, asserting he was senior knight not merely of his langue but of the entire Convent, and he would make such appointments, no one else. Gattinara took the squadron to Sicily for supplies and in the middle of the Malta Channel encountered a Portuguese caravel full of Turks. Laden with grain, she had been seized from her rightful owners off the Barbary Coast. Recaptured, she was sent under prize crew to Malta.[18] On 8 September French and Ottoman forces withdrew from Nice while Polin 'made every effort' to convince Barbarossa to keep his armada in France over the winter,[15] promising French aid in a 1544 attempt to recover Tunis from Spain.[19] Anchoring his armada at the island of Sainte-Marguerite in the vicinity of Cannes, Barbarossa put to sea with a squadron of nine galleys and headed for San Remo in Genovese Liguria, just east of Nice.

One thousand Turkish soldiers were put ashore at first light and they assailed San Remo for eight hours. Confronted by armed inhabitants behind city walls, the Ottomans were beaten off with losses heavy enough to burn in Barbarossa's memory. Barbarossa returned to the Armada at Sainte-Marguerite along the coast of Savoy, devastating Monaco and adjacent La Turbie en route. At the same time Nizzam's corsairs came ashore at Genovese Vallecrosia and nearby Vallebona, seizing 300 persons at inland Gorbio. The following day, in an analogous action, corsairs descended with twenty-two galliots on the shores of Genovese Bordighera and Ospedaletti. Proceeding inland, they pillaged and burned Seborga. An Imperial force under Alfonso d'Avalos (assassin of Polin's predecessor Antonio Rincon) meanwhile approached Nice to succour a city no longer under siege. He was accompanied at sea by Andrea Doria. The corsairs chose to retire, falling back toward Antibes, while Doria put in to Villefranche immediately east of Nice. A sudden south-west libeccio wind penned the Imperial Armada in the anchorage, a deep coastal recess secure in any other wind. Penned, Doria lost four galleys against the shore and was for several days vulnerable to an attack by some or all of Barbarossa's 14,000 embarked soldiers, an attack that never materialised. Polin pointed out to Barbarossa his opportunity to once and for all destroy Doria and the Imperial Armada with attendant plunder, but Barbarossa was content to send Salih Reis and Salih's lieutenant Cussaim Çelebi with twenty-five galleys to raid the coast and islands of Spain and then to winter at Algiers securing plunder to date.[20] Barbarossa's commanders were said to be astounded.[15] There were whispers of an understanding between Barbarossa and Andrea Doria. Again. The Ottoman Armada, 200 vessels carrying 30,000 combatants plus oarsmen, weighed anchor at Sainte-Marguerite and proceeded to winter anchorage at Toulon, where all but heads of household had been evacuated from the city.

On Sunday, 23 September 1543 (Gregorian calendar) the third Chapter General at Malta and the second of Grand Master Juan de Homedes was convened. Following ritual ceremonials, Chaplain Mateo Castillo, a gifted theologian, opened proceedings with a sermon in Spanish concerning the lawful responsibilities of superiors in the administration of justice and similar responsibilities of the members to accept duly elected authority. On Monday the Sixteen *Capitolari* or legislators were elected, two to each langue. They would tackle issues not settled by unanimous or near-unanimous acclaim. These were Foulques de Caritat and Bernard Castinette for Provence, Jean Thomassin and Guillaume Coppier for Auvergne, Prior of France Philippe de Carleau and Prior of Champagne Robert d'Aché for France, Bailiff of Negroponte Geronimo Coscon and Bailiff of Caspe Garcia Cortez for Aragon, Prior of Pisa Aurelio Bottigella and Giorgio Adorno for Italy, Turcopolier Giles Russell and Preceptor of Yeaveley and Barrow Oswald Massinbert for England, Grand Bailiff Georg Schilling and Wilhelm Bombast von Hohenheim for Germany, and Cristobal Solis de Farfan and Henrique Pereira for Castile. Joining the deliberations of the Sixteen were Master of the Grand Master's House Gonzalo de Cervantes of Castile, Regent Chancellor Martín Rojas de Portalrubio of Aragon, and noble Rhodiot Giovanni di Montolivet as Treasury Secretary. Tribunal or public discussions of the Sixteen dealt with the tricky matter of administration of the Common Treasury, then entirely in the hands of the Grand Master; tricky because criticism was necessarily predicated either on mistrust or mismanagement. In this instance it was apparently both and more, an issue of absolute monarch and private piggy bank, with enrichment of relatives a notable cause of angst. Grand Master Homedes agreed without admitting culpability to refund the common accounts at the rate of 12,000 gold Maltese scudos per year until the next Chapter General then scheduled for the first Sunday of October 1546. A monitoring commission was established for an annual audit of accounts. Future Grand Master Claude de la Sengle was appointed Conventual Conservator or auditor. On other matters a term of one year was established for galley captains. A special impost was levied on the Langue of Italy amounting to a 3 per cent surcharge on normal responsions to pay for litigation at Rome concerning the Admiral's authority. Thirteen-year-old Prior of Venice Ranuccio Farnese, nephew of Pope Paul III, was appointed Procurator General and Resident Ambassador to the Holy See in succession of Giovan Battista Carafa. The dignity of Bailiff of Negroponte was to continue to be shared between the langues of Aragon and Castile rather than to be claimed by one or the other.[21]

During the Chapter General two galleys and a galliot of the Pope commanded by Captain Bartolomeo Peretti di Talamone arrived at Malta with two Papal Briefs for the Grand Master. One of these ordered the galleys, galleon, barcia, and all other armed maritime forces of the

Religion to unite with the Papal Armada to oppose Barbarossa. The Council politely declined. The Order had a well-established right to neutrality during Franco–Spanish wars, and one third of the French flotilla united with the Ottoman Armada was commanded by Prior of Capua Leone Strozzi. There was moreover always the possibility of an Ottoman or corsair assault on Malta, Gozo, Tripoli, or all three in the spring, and for that reason hired soldiers and the Venetian barque *Contarina* were continued on the payroll over the winter.[17]

Shortly after the Chapter General Grand Commander Foulques de Caritat, Prior of Pisa Aurellio Bottigella, and Lieutenant Grand Conservator Juan Miguel de Castellar were appointed Procurators of the Common Treasury in another check to earlier imbalance.[20] Conventual Conservator or auditor Claude de la Sengle and the three Procurators attended over the winter of 1543–44 to funding the ongoing expense of hires, of improvements to fortifications, and of completion of a new galley capitana to be called *Santa Maddalena* in succession of *Santa Petronilla*. Pierre de Gozon Mélac was appointed captain in succession of Louis du Pont. The new *Barque of the Religion* was sent to Messina to have her underwater hull sheeted in bronze, as was the laid-up carrack *Santa Anna*. Grand Bailiff Georg Schilling, a former Governor of Tripoli, was dispatched to the Emperor in Germany to seek solutions for Tripoli's shortcomings. According to Bosio, Homedes, relieved of the burden of the Common Treasury, immersed himself in spiritual matters. And while fortification of Malta continued under the supervision of Imperial Engineer Ferramolino, Homedes took more interest in construction of a new Church of Saint John and in construction of a new infirmary. At the end of 1543 Turcopolier Giles Russell died, the last remaining English veteran of the Great Siege of Rhodes at the Convent. Upon his death it was decreed by Grand Master and Council there would be no further appointment to the dignity of Turcopolier until the Roman Catholic religion was re-established in England; coastal defence duties of the Turcopolier were reassigned to the Grand Master's Seneschal Gonzalo de Cervantes.[22]

The term of Ernando de Bracamonte as Governor of Tripoli expiring, Chancellor Cristóbal de Solis Farfan of Asturias and the Langue of Castile, a knight of good judgment and considerable valour, was appointed his successor. Commander Charles d'Urre de Tessières was appointed

Treasurer at Tripoli, succeeding Francisco de Ribadeneira. Departing Malta on 23 March 1544 aboard the *Galleonetto of the Religion*, Farfan and Tessières had with them a squadron of knights to supplement the existing garrison, while the Galleonetto was laden with provisions and munitions. They were charged with forming a commission to process disgruntled soldiers unhappy with their remote and isolated existence and to return them to Malta to face a summary court.[22]

On 11 April 1544 at a place called Ceresole in the Piedmont almost due north of Nice and some miles east of Turin, France's Army of Italy clashed with the Empire's Army of Italy. The first was commanded by 24-year-old François de Bourbon-Vendome, comte d'Enghien and Général des galères de France, who eight months earlier had been an admiral parked in front of Nice. The second was commanded by Alfonso d'Avalos, who eight months earlier had sped to the relief of Nice after Enghien's withdrawal; Avalos best remembered for the assassination of an unarmed French diplomat. Said to be a French victory, the clash had no tactical or strategic significance other than its cost in men, one of every four of the 30,000 participants, and its cost in coin to pay hired soldiery that left both cupboards bare. It was the bare cupboards that had a significance leading to September's Peace of Crépy.[22]

At about the same time a portion of the Ottoman Armada wintering at Toulon was unsuccessfully besieging San Remo for a second time. These same galleys and galliots then appeared off Genoa, where Ottoman commander Kheir-ed-Din Barbarossa demanded drinking water and provisions for his crews. Some of Andrea Doria's own galleys were in the harbour but unprepared for combat, the remainder of his galleys at La Spezia in the same condition. Water and provisions were supplied while Doria and Barbarossa met at the former's Fassolo Palace. During their conversations Doria agreed to give up the corsair Turgut, called Dragut, captured four years earlier, in exchange for a face-saving ransom of 3,000 gold ducats, funds extorted from Toulon hosts. Within days Dragut had been provided with a single galliot and licensed as General of Western Corsairs. He found Acsac Reis, called Zoppo among Barbarossa's corsairs, friends of forty years, and many others willing to sail under his command. It would be a command initially predicated on revenge.[23]

Barbarossa was en route from winter in France to Constantinople and had paused to ravage the island of Elba opposite the coast of Piombino. While there he liberated from Jacopo V Appiano, Prince of Piombino, 'a captive dear to Barbarossa, the son of old companion at arms'[24] Sinan of Smyrna and his own nephew by his sister wed to Sinan, captured nine years earlier at the Spanish Siege of Tunis. The Appianos complied only under duress as Sinan's son was companion to young Jacopo VI.[25] The Ottomans later anchored near the mouth of the Bruna River in Tuscany to put to the sack the villages of Castiglione della Pescaia and Le Rocchette, the seizure of which was said to have cost the lives of 1,800 Turks. The Ottoman admiral next surprised and seized Talamone near Orbetello. Many young men were enslaved and sent to reinforce galley oarsmen. At Talamone Barbarossa was on a personal vendetta; he removed from its tomb the cadaver of Bartolomeo Peretti di Talamone, recently deceased of kidney stones, burned it in the city's piazza, and scattered the ashes over public places. One year earlier Peretti, at the head of two Papal galleys and a galliot, had raided the Aegean island of Mitilini on which Barbarossa had been born. There Paretti had torched Barbarossa's family home, killing those within. This was at least part of the explanation for the continuing anger and rage reported by Captain Polin.

Barbarossa next appeared at Montiano on the Tuscan coast prior to occupying Porto Ercole and the island of Giglio; the first locality surrendered and yielded thirty hostages against a promise to spare the port and city. The hostages were put in chains, the castle and environs were put to the sack, and the city was torched. Not one single house remained after three days of burning. At about this time Leone Strozzi warned the Grand Master by messenger of Barbarossa's approach and of the possibility the Ottoman admiral might soon proceed against Malta or Tripoli. The messenger was Strozzi's staff officer Hospitaller Giuliano da Fermo, who reached Malta on 23 June 1544. Strozzi also broached the subject of a prisoner swap when he reached Constantinople, and the brother of Cairadeno came up for immediate consideration as Mourad Aga of Tagiora had thrice offered a ransom. Meanwhile, on the island of Giglio 632 people were kidnapped and all of the prominent were decapitated, among whom were the mayor, the notary, and the parish priest. Barbarossa continued with his raiding, intending to burn at Civitavecchia the Papal galleys Bartolomeo di Talamone had used in his raid; Leone Strozzi dissuaded him from the attempt, reminding Barbarossa of the Sultan's injunction against destruction of Papal property. Several of his galleys entered the Sardinian port of Oristano and seized a ship. They put it to flame near Capo San Marco. Barbarossa's nephew, made a slave nine years earlier, was later in the year sent from Constantinople to Egypt with a splendid accompaniment of courtiers and servants. Perhaps apocryphally, Sinan, in residence at Suez, was so astounded when the boy appeared before him, in perfect health and of genteel Renaissance education and manner, that he was taken by a sudden stroke and died in his son's arms. Apocryphally or not, this was Sinan's final appearance in history.[25]

At Malta several steps were taken to prepare for the worst. Giovan Battista Schiatessi, with a healthy squadron of knights, was dispatched to the City of Notabile, renamed Mdina, the island's fortified capital city. Parisot de la Valette of Provence, Juan de Barrientos of Castile, and Francesco Beccuti of Italy were appointed wardens for the three sectors of Birgu. Additional artillery, gunners, and soldiers were sent to Gozo with orders for the fortress commander to prepare to receive the population. And the Galleonetto on 1 July was returned to Tripoli with additional munitions and provisions. This Galleonetto was the galleon captured by the galley squadron in April a year earlier and returned to Malta with a prize crew commanded by Alonso Correa of Portugal. It was a Galleonetto or small galleon only in comparison to the *Galleon of the Religion*. Since arrival at Malta she had been repaired and refitted at Malta's Arsenal, and Balthazar de Colans de Baume of the south shore of Lake Geneva had been appointed her captain. On reaching the coast of Africa six days later in light air she came in too close to Tagiora 10 miles east of Tripoli. Mourad Aga put 150 Turkish arquebusiers aboard a galliot of twenty-three banks and sent it against the Galleonetto with an escort of two smaller craft. Colans underestimated the danger, did not take proper defensive measures, and his ship was boarded and overwhelmed. Survivors surrendered and were enslaved while their ship was towed into Tagiora. The galley squadron later came to the rescue but because of enemy cannon fire could not get close enough to Tagiora to even send the Galleonetto to the bottom. There is little information concerning who or how many of the Galleonetto's crew were killed and how many were captured, but among the dead was Luis Henrique, son of Admiral of Castile Alfonso Henrique, while Colans de Baume would spend the rest of his life in slavery.[26]

In his rage at the mean-spirited destruction of his family home and the killing of those within, Barbarossa burst upon Ischia, fief of Alfonso d'Avalos. Descending at night, he reduced to slavery 1,500 of the population and torched the town of Forio. He sacked the island of Procida between Ischia and mainland Pozzuoli, and threatened Pozzuoli itself; Viceroy of Naples Pedro Álvarez de Toledo raced to the defence of the city from Naples with 1,000 armed men, persuading Barbarossa to retire to his galleys. Giannettino Doria was in the environs with thirty Imperial galleys; Barbarossa gave chase and forced Doria to retire to the south toward Messina, where he withdrew into the port. Wind prevented an assault on Salerno and Barbarossa was found instead off Capo Palinuro, 40 miles to the south-east. There he assailed Catona, Fiumara di Muro, and Calanna, where he burned crops, took 1,000 captives, and killed 200 others. He continued his incursion along the Calabrian coast (Policastro) and in the regions of Reggio Calabria and Cariati, appearing next at Lipari, an Aeolian Island north of Sicily, where the inhabitants refused to yield.

The Ottomans planted forty pieces of artillery around Lipari's Cathedral of San Bartolomeo and bombarded the town for fifteen days. Barbarossa was offered a ransom of 15,000 ducats; he countered with a demand for 30,000 plus consignment of 200 young men and 200 young women. Mayor Giacomo Camagna exhorted the citizenry to accept the terms at discretion; he was contemptuously ignored by them. For this reason Camagna approached the Turks and offered to hand over Lipari against a promise to spare his life and possessions, his family, and sixty friends. The city was put to the sack, torched, and destroyed; 2,000 men and women discovered in a well-hidden refuge were gathered to be sold as slaves. In the cathedral janissaries found a number of aged men and women; these were stripped of their clothing and *butchered* alive. This outrage occurred at the altar, holy images were shredded, and a statue of Christ was defiled before being pulled to the floor and destroyed. The Ottomans then found themselves without gun powder and with holds full of slaves, many of whom died each day from a lack of sustenance. The number of captives taken during the return along the Italian coast has been estimated at 15–20,000. Passing Faro di Messina on 18 July, the Ottoman admiral reached Constantinople on 10 August with 7,000 Christians at the oars; most of the others had been thrown into the sea as cadavers.[27]

Upon Barbarossa's departure for Constantinople, Dragut had been entrusted with the command of all corsair vessels in the western Mediterranean. He flew, however, neither Ottoman colours nor the colours of an African state, but rather his own red and white flag with blue crescent.[28] Soon he was called by Christians *The Drawn Sword of Islam* or *The Avenging Sword of Islam.* Informed by fast frigate from Tripoli of the Galleonetto's loss on 7 July, Gattinara's galley squadron was ordered to Tagiora to recover or sink the captured vessel. Departing on 11 July, his other captains were Pierre de Gozon Mélac, Luis Dormans, and Jean Thomassin. A caravan of knights and soldiers was embarked under Bailiff of Santa Eufemia Don Fabrizio Pignatello, newly returned from Sicily to succour the Convent with a band of gentlemen adventurers and soldiers. Pignatello was posted as Captain of Reserves at Tripoli. Gattinara proceeded against Tagiora as ordered but was unable to get within artillery range of the Galleonetto because of heavier cannon fire from Tagiora's harbour tower. Suffering from such fire, which among other things carried away the head of Don Luis Enriquez de Segovia, he fell back to Tripoli. With news of the end of the threat to Tripoli posed by the Ottoman Armada of Barbarossa, retiring to Constantinople in mid-July, Gattinara returned to Malta with an ill Pignatello. During the return the squadron seized a well-armed[30] grippo (a large square-rigged, flat-bottomed merchantman preferred for shallow-water destinations) bound from Alexandria to Djerba carrying a variety of merchandise with a value compensating for the loss of the Galleonetto, though not for loss of her complement.[29]

Bailiff of Santa Eufemia Don Fabrizio Pignatello, who had commanded embarked soldiery during the galley squadron's unsuccessful attempt to retrieve the Galleonetto, succumbed to his illness at Malta. His estate, four fifths of which was left to the Order, also endowed a new hospital at Naples for pilgrims and foreigners. He would be succeeded in command of embarked soldiery by Don Federico de Urrea of the Langue of Castile. Dying in mid-life at the Convent was Marshal Jean des Roches. Roches was succeeded in August by Commander Imbert de la Morinière. Passing away in France was Prior of Toulouse Pierre de Grasse. His priory was conferred on Grand Commander Foulques de Caritat, who was succeeded as Grand Commander by Pons d'Urre. Also dying at Malta was Grand Conservator (Draper) Juan Sarnes de Pertusa. He was succeeded by long-time Castellan of Trapani Gáspár de Sanguessa. Dying in France was Great Siege veteran and Bailiff of Lyons Antoine de Grolée; he was succeeded by Commander of Charlieu Antoine de Châlus.

Don Alonso di Cardona, Count of Chiusa and President of Sicily, acting as Viceroy during the absence in Germany of Don Ferrante Gonzaga, requested the galley squadron's assistance in transferring the viceregal court and militia posted at Faro di Messina back to Palermo given the departure of Barbarossa. The squadron accordingly departed Malta on 16 August for that purpose. On arrival at Messina, however, squadron commander Signorino della Gattinara was informed that a Turkish galliot had abducted, that same day, the Captain of Palermo from his villa outside the capital. The squadron went in pursuit and a galliot thought to be the galliot was sighted at the island of Vulcano, north of Sicily. Following a further pursuit the corsair was overtaken and captured. On board were several Christian renegades, who realised they would be hanged, including the badly wounded galliot commander Kara Mufsa. Another of these renegades killed with an arquebus round Simone Bonanno, the Order's Receiver at Palermo. An Hospitaller since the 1503 Magistracy of Pierre d'Aubusson, Bonanno had embarked at Messina seeking transport to Malta in order to render an accounting for expenses. His killer was hanged from the galliot's antenna with Kara Mufsa and the other renegades. Twenty-seven Turks were enslaved and more than a hundred young Christians were freed from the oars. If seized at all, the Captain of Palermo had been seized by another galliot. This one would be towed to Malta in September.[31]

Kara Mufsa's galliot was a part of Dragut's new squadron, and the remainder of the squadron was in Sicilian waters. Aware of his loss, Dragut took the others, ten galleys and galliots, to the Malta Channel between Sicily and Gozo, where he would be in position both to intercept the Malta Squadron on its return to Malta and also to raid the south coast of Sicily. He waited in vain, however, as the Malta Squadron relocated the viceregal court and militia. Dragut then decided to swoop down on Gozo. But in the event Governor of Gozo Juan Ximenes forced Dragut's corsairs to re-embark with a cavalry charge.

Left behind, however, was Dragut's dead brother. This would become no small matter. Shortly after being repulsed, Dragut's squadron intercepted a large square-rigged cargo vessel flying the flag of Malta. Bound from Sicily to Malta, she carried a cargo of grain needed at Malta but desperately needed in North Africa, where victims of famine were dying of hunger. This unfortunate development occurred, according to Bosio, because the Grand Master did not have the foresight to dispatch a warning by fast frigate of Dragut's presence, one of a number of Grand Master failings of late. Two squadron galleys were sent in precipitate pursuit, reinforced but without skiffs or artillery primers. These were forced to return immediately because the cargo carrier, called a grippo, was too closely guarded by corsair galleys.[31]

French Galley Commander Leone Strozzi returned to Toulon on 2 October 1544 with Antoine Escalin des Aimars, who had been succeeded as Ambassador to the Porte by his deputy Gabriel de Luetz d'Aramón. d'Aramón would, together with Special Ambassador Jean de Monluc and Imperial Ambassador Gerard Veltwyck, beginning in August negotiate a one-year truce between the Ottoman and Hapsburg Empires effective from 24 October 1545, which would in part account for the subsequent inactivity of Empire and Ottoman forces.[32]

The Procurators of the Treasury made an error in accounting for the amount of grain in storage at Tripoli, and the presumed excess was sold to the allied and grain-short government of Tunis. Soon the Procurators became aware of their error and the galley squadron was ordered to sea at the end of September to escort two grippos with cargoes of grain to Tripoli, thus running down Malta stocks. Later, scouring 100 nautical miles to the east of Tripoli off Cape Misurata (Misrata), the galleys encountered and took a Moorish galleonetto and its cargo of wheat, which was conveyed to Malta, bringing a happy end to the year. During the same month news was received of the Peace of Crépy between France and Empire signed on 18 September 1544, bringing an end to the unsuccessful intrusions of Francis I on the Italian peninsula, and making the end of year even happier at Malta.[33]

Dragut established himself at the walled city of Mehedia on Tunisia's east coast between Monastir and Sfax from where he raged at failure of the Hospital to return his brother's cadaver, all the while threatening to return to Gozo to level the island's fortress. Beyond his anger and sorrow he busied himself both with increasing the size of his corsair flotilla and with plans for raiding excursions during the coming sailing season. At Tagiora, at least nominally falling within Dragut's dominion, Dragut demanded use of Mourad's two galliots. During Mourad's absence a custodian of slaves called Mottigero of Algiers made contact with Governor of Tripoli Cristobal Solis de Farfan seeking a large sum of money, in return for which he would murder three Turkish companions and deliver fifty Christian slaves to Tripoli subject to an escort of Hospitaller cavalry. The ransom was effected and both Christians and Mottigero were embarked aboard the galley *San Giovanni Battista* commanded by Francesco Beccuti and delivered to Malta where Mottigero was baptised as Salvador (Saviour) of Algiers and thus forgiven his sins. Informed by Salvador that Dragut's target was Gozo, Grand Master Homedes reinforced the garrison on that island. While all of this was taking place, Captain of Galleys Gattinara was in Sicily with the other three galleys seeking to hire a company of veteran soldiers. Gattinara was also soliciting the services of the galleys of Sicily and Naples for the purpose of seeking out Dragut in Africa before he launched his depredations. For the same reason the Grand Master had written to Andrea Doria and to Pope Paul III.[34]

Flying his command pennant from the 165ft, twenty-five-bank, galley *Le Chevalier*, Hospitaller Leone Strozzi took twenty-two French galleys from Toulon to the English Channel in the spring of 1545. During the months to follow Strozzi's galleys would participate in July's Battle of the Solent and in the two-month French siege of English-held Boulogne-sur-Mer, which ended on 18 September. It was during the French invasion of the Solent that Henry VIII's flagship *Mary Rose* went to the bottom, taking upward of 400 lost souls with her, some say with her lower gun ports open to the sea, others say holed by a French galley cannon ball. Strozzi would within two years be appointed a General of the Armada of France.[34]

Gathering at Malta were three galleys of the Pope, four of Sicily, two of Marchese di Terranuova Giovanni Tagliavia, three of maritime condottiero Vincenzo Cicala, and two of the Lord of Monaco, together with the four galleys of Malta for a total of eighteen well-armed fighting ships. Andrea Doria was absent suffering from gout and it was not clear who was in command. Because a bit earlier five Infidel galliots run out of the Freo Channel by the *Barque of the Religion* and by *San Giovanni* had last been seen on course for Sicily, the eighteen allied galleys departed Malta on 18 June and took the same course. Seen later at Trapani, the five galliots sped into the night headed toward the Tyrrhenian and were lost. The allied flotilla, rather than pursue the fleeing galliots, took course for Africa, where it searched unpopulated places as well as Cape Bon, Tunis, and the Galite Islands north-west of the Gulf of Tunis without result. For this reason, a lack of results, Gattinara was licensed to return to Malta, which was reached on 16 July.[34]

Unbeknownst to allied galleys, but which might have been presumed from the heading of the five fleeing galliots, Dragut was somewhere to the north. He was in fact again devastating the Tuscan island of Capraia last devastated in June 1540 just before his capture and enslavement by Gianettino Doria. This time he got away with it. From Capraia he assailed the Italian Riviera with fifteen galleys and galliots. There the corsairs put fire and sword to Monterosso and Corniglia near La Spezia, after which they were repulsed at Manarola, the inhabitants of which had joined with others and were together too many behind walls. The corsairs were later more successful at Rapallo, Pegli, and Levanto before parking in the Gulf of La Spezia to ransom those just kidnapped. At Tripoli, meanwhile, several Moorish hostages held against payment of tribute by the Sheik of Almaia had escaped. An attempt to seize new hostages from Almaia had failed with the Sheik swearing allegiance to Tagiora, thereby threatening tribute from Xercia, Rabta, old Tripoli, and Zegua. Governor Farfan advised Malta that an immediate response was required. By decree of the Council, Prior of Messina Gattinara was ordered to Tripoli with the four galleys, with the germa of Rhodiot Sidero Metaxi, and with the grippo of Maltese Francesco Scarpello. The galley caravans were reinforced with additional knights and soldiers. These forces were to be combined with those of Tripoli and the fortress of Almaia was to be razed. Additionally, the two galliots of Mourad Aga were to be destroyed. By these measures it was believed the supremacy of Tripoli in its alien world would be restored.[34]

The four galleys were put in good order, Gattinara commanding the capitana *Santa Maria Madelena*, Francesco Beccuti commanding *San Giovanni Battista*, Pascal du Broc commanding *Santa Petronilla*, and Geronimo de Guete commanding *Santa Caterina* called *La Catarinetta*. The two sailing vessels were taken in tow in the absence of wind and all departed Malta at the end of July. Embarked were the flower of the Order resident at the Convent as well as the flower of Rhodiot and Maltese youth embarked as gentlemen adventurers, not to mention hired soldiery. These entered the Port of Tripoli at night without salutes or fanfare, ready for business. The plan of attack developed by Gattinara and the Governor included taking captive all of the Moors of Almaia. The strike force assembled at the presidio early in August, Hospitaller Bernardino Lombardo commanding mounted arquebusiers, the Sheik of Almanzor commanding loyal Moorish cavalry, the latter numbering 200 armed with light assegai spears. Proceeding by sea were the four galleys, two brigantines and a frigate assigned to Tripoli, plus the galliot of Hospitaller Cristobal de Frigiliana of Andalusia. These proceeded along the coast and put their caravans and adventurers ashore 3 miles from the Castle of Almaia, 110 knights and 800 infantry. Gattinara himself commanded the shore parties pike in hand while the galleys were left under command of Geronimo de Guete. Suddenly a member of the strike force began to thoughtlessly beat his tambourine in step with the advancing caravan, and the Moorish garrison of Almaia was alerted. Most fled successfully, including the Sheik; 425 persons including the feeble were snared. The castle was plundered and then destroyed, but the attempt to destroy Mourad's two galliots failed. Two thirds of the plunder was assigned to the participants, one third to the Common Treasury. This failure to consider recovering more of the cost of the bungled operation cost Gattinara and two of his three captains their jobs upon their return to Malta on 10 August.[35]

Upon Muzio Costanzo's renunciation of the dignity of Prior of Lombardia in April 1537 in consequence of the Franco–Spanish War ongoing in the Piedmont, Grand Master and Council had appointed Paolo Simeoni, with an unblemished record of extraordinary service, his deserving successor. Pope Paul III eight years later, however, similarly appointed his undeserving 23-year-old grandson Carlo Sforza, and following unsuccessful pleas to the Holy See, Simeoni was forced to step down and was assigned the dignity of Admiral. Sforza, by Papal fiat, also became heir apparent as Captain of Galleys, but because he had not yet been received into the Order of Jerusalem and had not yet even appeared at Malta, senior knight of the Langue of Castile and 1522 Siege veteran Fernando de Bracamonte was on 18 August 1545 appointed

Captain of Galleys, also commanding the redesignated capitana *San Giovanni Battista*. Francesco Terno da Crema, meanwhile, commanded *Santa Maria Madelena*, Robert de Valsergues of Provence commanded *Santa Petronilla*, and Geronimo de Guete remained in command of *Santa Caterina*. In deference to the fiat, a letter was sent to the Holy Father observing that Bracamonte's appointment was for one year only and that it would be appropriate should his grandson take up residence at Malta during that period to become acquainted with the Order's customs and statutes. Perhaps sensing trouble, the Sheik of Almaia had meanwhile sent new hostages and gifts to the Governor of Tripoli and had asked for forgiveness.

In September 1545 there arrived at Malta a gentleman of the household of French King Francis seeking seniority with consent of the Langue of France in respect of the Priory of Champagne for 11-year-old Hospitaller François de Lorraine de Guise without prejudice to Grand Hospitaller Jean de la Roche-Andry and to Treasurer Léon de Montalembert, next in line for that dignity. Natural and legitimate son of Claude de Lorraine, 1st Duke of Guise, and of Antoinette de Bourbon, Francis of Lorraine's eldest sister Mary of Guise was Queen Mother and Regent for Mary, Queen of Scots. The seniority requested was unanimously approved but Lorraine would in 1549 alternatively be appointed Grand Prior of France at the request of King Henry II. Notwithstanding peace between the Empire and France, Prior of Capua and Florentine rebel in service to France Leone Strozzi remained deprived of the fruits of the priory and of his commandery of San Giacomo di Campo Corbellini at Florence, the income stream of which had been attached by Cosimo d'Medici. Spanish Grand Master Juan de Homedes had little sympathy for Strozzi, who was left to appoint personal intermediaries with the Emperor and King of France. At Rome Cardinal Francisco Mendoza de Bobadilla and Alessandro Cardinal Farnese, another grandson of Pope Paul III, ruled against the Langue of Italy's petition asserting the right of the Admiral to appoint galley squadron commanders. Towards the end of October news was received of the death of Bailiff of Manosque Jean de Boniface, a senior commander at the Great Siege of Rhodes and a man of deep religious conviction. He left a healthy estate to his fraternity. Grand Commander Pons d'Urre succeeded to the bailiwick and was himself succeeded as Grand Commander by Commander Robert d'Aube de Roquemartine. Roquemartine was licensed to wear the Grand Cross outside of the Convent, in spite of the statute that prohibited a Conventual Bailiff such as the Grand Commander from doing so, this in recognition of his service, which included late arrival at the Great Siege of Rhodes; late only because he had been assigned to the defence of the Castle of Saint Peter at Petronium.[36]

Under the direction of Pope Paul III, the Council of Trent was convened on 13 December 1545 at Trento, Italy, by Cardinal Giovanni Maria Ciocchi del Monte (future Pope Julius III), by Cardinal Marcello Cervini degli Spannochi (future Pope Marcellus II), and by Cardinal Reginald Pole, last Roman Catholic Archbishop of Canterbury. The Council would meet in twenty-five sessions through December 1563. The first session marked the beginning of Counter Reformation confronting Protestant Reformation. Three Hospitallers attended the first session as observers: Bailiff of Santa Eufemia Don Federico de Urria, Conventual Conservator and Lieutenant Grand Hospitaller Claude de la Sengle, and Commander Francesco Ajazza of Vercelli.[33]

At Malta during the year a magnificent new port facility was completed below Birgu adjacent to the Arsenal able to accommodate visiting ships and the Order's vessels either alongside or stern to the mole. Above the new port facility were new quarters for the Common Treasury. There was also a new device for laundering sails under the supervision of Pietro della Calibia, a Tunisian Moor converted to Christianity. For the Grand Master's pleasure a wild animal park and garden had been created on the island of Saint Michael on the other side of the port. There was unhappiness among the Order's vassals working Hospital estates in Cyprus, which was resolved when Aurelio Bottigella sped to the island and met with Hospitaller Grand Commander of Cyprus Alvise Cornaro of Venice. They agreed to an increase in compensation of these vassals, called 'Parichi' meaning tenant farmers, to two gold ducats per person per annum plus one third of production.[37]

Early in January 1546 a member of the staff of Don Ferrante Gonzaga appeared at Malta to notify Grand Master and Council that the Viceroy had been reassigned from Sicily to Milan, where he would succeed Alfonso d'Ávalos, Marqués del Vasto, as Commander of Empire Forces in Northern Italy. He would be succeeded as Viceroy of Sicily in the interim by Ambrogio Santapace Branciforte, Marchese of Licodia, until

Juan de Vega y Enríquez, 6th Lord of Grajal, became available in 1547. While assuring Grand Master and Council that Gonzaga would remain a patron of the Order of Jerusalem, Gonzaga's emissary also reminded both of the earlier agreement to make his son, Don Vicenzo Gonzaga, then 6 years of age, the next Prior of Barletta. At about this time news was received of the death in France of Prior of Saint-Gilles Giraud de Massas. He was succeeded by Grand Commander Robert d'Aube de Roquemartine, who was himself succeeded as Grand Commander by Antoine de Barras. Arising at this time was a difference between Grand Master and Procurators for the Langue of Provence. When the Commandery at Marseille became vacant it was assigned to Bailiff of Manosque Pons d'Urre, who renounced the Commandery at La Cavalerie. Homedes immediately assigned this latter commandery to Pierre de Beaulac Trébons, a veteran of the Great Siege of Rhodes. The Procurators protested to the Council that the Grand Master had such a right of assignment only upon death of an incumbent. The Council sided with the Grand Master.[37]

Extortion and dissension at Tripoli were brought to the attention of Grand Master and Council by Pierre de Chabaud-Tourettes, Commander of Corte Serre, and by Niccolo Orsini di Rivalta. These unpleasant circumstances resulted from the appointment by Governor Christobal Solis de Farfan of a tyrannical deputy, Giannis of Saloniki. The Council thereupon appointed Commander of Le Bastit Jean Parisot de la Valette to succeed Farfan; Valette a knight of integrity, prudence, and valour. He had in the past been convicted of "juvenile excesses" (an armed assault on an unarmed Maltese involving a local woman) and confined for several months at Gozo, following which he served two years as further punishment at Tripoli. While at Tripoli he earned the respect of Christians, Tripolitans, and Moors. He was an ideal replacement for Farfan. Diego de Chaves was assigned as his Treasurer, succeeding Charles d'Urre de Tessières. The four-galley squadron of Fernando Bracamonte conveyed both to Tripoli, departing Malta on 17 April 1546. Bracamonte proceeded by way of the shallows (Seccagne) of eastern Tunisia expecting to be able to intercept enemy traffic confined to narrow sea lanes, but was forced to abandon the effort on 5 May having given up all hope of success. Approaching Tripoli, however, he encountered a large, high-pooped, lateen-rigged, and well-armed caravel that had attempted to enter Tripoli by error of the pilot. Realising the error, she was then attempting to reach Tagiora 10 miles to the east, but the galleys quickly took position astern and shredded her sails. There followed boarding by the quarters and protracted combat with more than one hundred would-be corsairs hoping to join Dragut. Bound from the Levent to Mehedia, 190 nautical miles to the north-west, when taken no more than thirty-three of the would-be corsairs remained alive. Also dead were several Christians. Many more were wounded. Among these was Francesco Terno da Crema, captain of *Santa Maria Maddelena*, who succumbed upon the May 1546 arrival at Tripoli. His enterprise and inspiration would be mourned. The caravel was commanded by Abdela (Abdullah) Reis, who reported that several years earlier Mehedia had rebelled against the Kingdom of Tunis and that since then Dragut had seized the city and that he and many corsair followers had made the city their headquarters.[38]

The caravel was towed into Tripoli, where the wounded received immediate attention and where Giovanni Francesco Langosco della Motta of Vercelli was promoted from Lieutenant to Captain of *Santa Maria Maddelena*. During the days to follow Valette took possession of city and fortress and in the name of the Religion received oaths of obedience and homage not only from officers and soldiers but from Moorish subjects and confederates, including a march-past by and inspection of infantry and cavalry. Individuals with equipment in good order were complimented, those with equipment not in good order were punished. City and fortress were purged of idle individuals and replacements ordered. And Valette did not neglect to file reports of Tripoli's weaknesses and vulnerabilities. Availing himself of the presence of galleys guarding the port, he one night sent his mounted arquebusiers to raid under the city walls of Tagiora with a disposition suggesting an even larger force. While the defenders scurried to counter this new threat he sent by two frigates a number of cannon gunners and a handful of brave Moorish Azaps, who sped into the fosse or canal protected by the harbour tower and with artificial fire torched the same galliot that had overwhelmed the Galleonetto of the Religion in July 1544. Francesco Marziglia, commanding the mounted arquebusiers, seeing the flames, gave the order to retire. Some of his soldiers retired with plunder and captives from homes outside of the city walls, and Mourad Aga came in pursuit with a large body of horse intent on recovering the captives and taking revenge. Fresh and faster Mourad overtook the retiring Hospitallers, slowed by captives; these were recovered. In the ensuing skirmish the Hospitallers gave a good account of themselves, but Marziglia's horse was shot out from under him. He was captured and sent to the dungeon of Tagiora, a dungeon that had already seen the death of two brave Hospitallers, Castillian Esteban de Argote[39] (*Martyrologe I–15*) and Jacques Gobieù of Aquitaine. The universally respected and admired Francesco Marziglia would be ransomed only with a contribution from every knight and soldier at Tripoli.[38]

News of the caravel's capture spread rapidly from Tagiora to Dragut at Mehedia, where three large galleys and fifteen galliots exited Mandraki (the galley port) and took an easterly course. Calculating that the four galleys of the Religion would slowly tow the caravel from Tripoli to Malta, he headed for the Freo Channel between Gozo and Malta, 155 miles a bit north of east of the galleys and tow, where his numbers and manoeuvrability would give him an overwhelming advantage. The enemy at the very least would be forced to abandon its prey. Reaching the Freo Channel on 27 May, he chose not to idle but to move against the people of Gozo, who would be gathering crops. Putting a secure guard around his ships, he sent a strong raiding party ashore. Alerted at the Castle of Gozo, a signal was sounded and all but five Gozitans retired into the Castle. Undeterred, Dragut put artillery ashore, his new objective destruction of the Castle. Of a sudden, though, he had for an unknown reason a change of heart, perhaps sighting the nearby Imperial galley squadron of Antonio Doria, perhaps a tribute to the soul of his dead brother. In the event he withdrew and re-embarked, departing Freo on 29 May bound for the north. In the Malta Channel between Gozo and Sicily his squadron seized a large square-rigged merchantman and its cargo of Malvasia wine, bound from Crete to Spain. Antonio Doria's Imperial Squadron meanwhile put into the port of Malta on 31 May and, informed, immediately went in pursuit, taking station at Sicily's Cape Passero on the south-east corner of Sicily. Dragut was then at the island of Favignana, however, 4 nautical miles beyond the north-west corner.[40]

Kheir-ed-Din Barbarossa came to the end of his time on 4 July 1546 at Constantinople. The youngest of four brothers born Khizr to an Ottoman janissary named Yakup believed native to the Aegean island of Mitilini (Lesbos) and to a Greek woman by the name of Katerina also native to Mitilini, he died of fever at Constantinople in his sixty-eighth year. The only brother not to die in combat, he was a master of the odds who rarely engaged in battle at sea and made his name preying on the defenceless. He was entombed near the Bosphorus at Besiktas in the north of Constantinople, in a mausoleum designed by renowned Ottoman architect Sinan.[41]

Chapter IX

Juan de Homedes y Coscon 1546–51

Throughout July 1546 Dragut terrorised the Italian Riviera west of Genoa, burning, looting, and kidnapping women, children, and men worthy of ransom. Moving to Toulon in August, while ransoms were demanded he remained a man possessed, if not over his brother's fate then in consequence of his four years at Genovese oars and the scars on his back. Mourad Aga, in the interim until he obtained a second galliot, combined with Zoppo and other corsairs of Djerba to resume harassing Tripoli, even entering the port at night in hope of destroying vessels sheltered there. Port artillery, however, soon made such ventures counterproductive. Governor of Tripoli Valette also responded by inviting the friendly Sheik of Almanzor, the Sheik of Xercia, and other Moorish and Arab captains, enemies of the Turks, to bring pressure on Ottoman Tagiora. Mourad responded in turn by sending an emissary to Constantinople with gifts to solicit from the Sultan a force strong enough to seize Tripoli from its Hospitaller garrison. Valette similarly asked for galley assistance from Malta. François Moniornal de Montbrison of Auvergne was appointed captain of *Santa Maria Maddalena*, succeeding interim commander Giovanni Francesco Langosco, who again became lieutenant, and Galley Squadron Commander Fernando de Bracamonte sped immediately to Tripoli with orders to take his instructions from Valette. Arriving at night, two galleys were posted 25–30 miles off Tagiora while the remaining two were similarly posted off Xar (Ain Zara), leaving the squadron brigantine within sight of Tagiora. The following morning Mourad's galliot exited the port and feinted toward Tripoli but could not be lured to the waiting galleys, instead returning to the safety of Tagiora. There were additional attempts to lure the enemy galliot into a trap, but all failed. At Malta former Governor of Tripoli and Chancellor Cristobal Solis de Farfan had been exonerated of charges of extortion by a board of inquiry. He was assigned the Bailiwick of Boveda, which became available upon the death of incumbent Don Pedro de Cardenas.

Commander Hernando Soler advanced to the dignity of Chancellor thus vacated. Meanwhile, a Papal Brief was delivered to the Grand Master by hand of Hospitaller Giovan Antonio Pescatore of Pope Paul III's Papal staff insisting on the immediate assumption of squadron command by the Pope's 22-year-old grandson Carlo Sforza at Civitavecchia, the military port for Rome. Fernando Bracamonte accordingly resigned his position and was replaced by Regent of Galleys Gaspar Ferrer, pilier or senior knight of the Langue of Aragon.[1]

The galleys departed for Civitavecchia on 13 August 1546 under command of Regent Ferrer. Off the island of Vulcano north of Sicily a small galliot of seventeen banks was captured; otherwise the trip was uneventful. From Civitavecchia Ferrer proceeded by horse to Rome, where he professed the Order's obedience at the foot of Pope Paul III. The chartered Venetian barque *Contarina* meanwhile returned to Malta from Venice laden with a heavy chain ordered for the purpose of enclosing the galley port between the peninsula of Birgu and the adjacent peninsula of Saint Michael. Returning to Malta from France at about the same time was the bronze-sheathed *Barque of the Religion* commanded by Lieutenant Grand Commander Pierre de Gozon-Mélac. Embarked was Prior of Auvergne Emery des Reaulx returning to the Convent. A veteran of the Great Siege of Rhodes, a knight of considerable prudence, much experience, and grand reputation, Reaulx was appointed Lieutenant General to Grand Master and Council in governing the Convent. During this period report was received of the death in Germany of Grand Prior of Germany, Prince of the Empire, and veteran of the 1480 Great Siege of Rhodes Johann (Hansen) von Hattstein, who lived ninety-nine years, thirty-four of them as Grand Prior. Georg Schilling von Cannstatt was appointed his successor and was himself succeeded as Grand Bailiff of Germany by cousin Philipp Schilling. The dignity of Prior of France was vacated by the death of Philippe de Carleau, a veteran of the 1522 Great Siege of Rhodes. Carleau was not succeeded by Grand Hospitaller Jean de la Roche-Andry by virtue of the latter's continued absence from the Convent, but was rather succeeded by Bailiff of the Morea Claude d'Ancienville. Ancienville was in turn succeeded by Conventual Conservator Claude de la Sengle.[2]

The four galleys of the Religion returned to Malta at the outset of November 1546 having located Papal grandson Carlo Sforza at Naples, where he succeeded Regent Ferrer in command of the galleys. In recognition of Sforza's youth and inexperience, future Grand Master Pietro del Monte was appointed Sforza's lieutenant, counsellor, and guide. The squadron departed almost immediately to Messina to take delivery of two new galley hulls ordered by the Spanish garrison of La Goletta outside of Tunis but which were no longer required. These were transferred to the account of the Hospital and would replace the existing *Santa Caterina* and *Santa Maria de la Vittoria* called *Il Gallo*.[3]

At Naples in January 1547 the citizenry rebelled against Viceroy Don Pedro de Toledo over his plan to introduce the Spanish Inquisition. At London King Henry VIII died, leaving the Kingdom to 9-year-old son Edward VI and regents. At Genoa Dragut's captor Giannettino Doria was killed during the Fieschi Conspiracy against the power of Andrea Doria, and as the adopted and only son of Andrea Doria, his descendant Gian Andrea Doria would inherit the titles granted the Genovese Admiral. At Malta the Sheik of Almanzor was invited to address the Council concerning his assessment of the situation at Tripoli. At Messina, Pietro del Monte, as Lieutenant to the Squadron Commander, supervised outfitting of the two new galleys, and hired 200 infantry for transport to Tripoli. Pope Paul III's grandson Carlo Sforza was dispatched to Paul III to beg for Papal assistance at Tripoli. It was Tripoli or Tagiora; only one would survive. At Mehedia, Bosio's *Citta d'Africa*, Dragut had increased his squadron from eighteen to twenty-three galleys and galliots. In Spain Bailiff of Caspe Garcia Cortez reached the end of his life. Grand Master and Council appointed Bailiff of Negroponte Geronimo Coscon his successor, while Pedro Nunnez de Herrera succeeded to Bailiff of Negroponte. Prior of Barletta Muzio Costanzo also died. On 25 February Grand Master and Council conferred the Priory on Admiral and former Prior of Lombardia Paolo Simeoni, who accordingly renounced the dignity of Admiral, to which Giorgio Adorno succeeded. Lo and behold, Pope Paul III had immediately assigned the vacant Priory to his 16-year-old Hospitaller nephew Ranuccio Farnese, who was already Prior of Venice. Both ports on the Adriatic, there were 760km in between. Meanwhile, seven-year-old Don Vincenzo Gonzaga was also a claimant. The Langue of Italy, in total disgust, was left to simply designate Paulo Simeoni as Senior Knight of the Langue, senior to all Priors and Bailiffs. The Pope kindly removed his nephew from contention by promoting him to the

Cardinalate, and Gonzaga became Prior of Barletta. He would remain Prior of Barletta for forty-four years. There was so much going on at Malta that Lieutenant General Emery des Reaulx had to assume a lion's share of the authority normally reserved to Grand Master and Council. French King Francis died on 31 March in his fifty-third year, leaving an unhappy legacy. He was succeeded by 28-year-old second son Henry II.[3]

In the absence at Rome of Carlo Sforza, Pietro del Monte was ordered with the galleys from Messina to Naples, where new Viceroy of Sicily Juan de Vega required transportation to Palermo. And protection. At Naples Del Monte's four galleys joined sixteen others belonging to the vice-regencies of Naples and Sicily to defend against the threat of Dragut. Meanwhile, the company of 200 condottieri hired by Del Monte in the winter was embarked aboard the *Germa of the Religion* for transport to Malta.[4]

Under command of Del Monte the four galleys returned to Malta on 26 May from Palermo. Sforza separately returned to Malta from Rome, where he had been seeking Papal assistance in countering the Ottoman threat to Tripoli, but his grandfather had so far left him with prayers, not assistance, likely because the expense of 12,000 hired Italian infantry and 500 cavalry sent to the assistance of Charles V combatting Lutheran heresy in Germany had strained Papal coffers.[5]

At Malta Captain of Galleys Carlo Sforza became involved in a ferocious brawl among knights of the Order over the killing of a soldier in the plaza of the port; the soldier a member of Sforza's household, the killers soldiers in the service of Francisco de Ribadeneira, first officer aboard *San Giovanni Battista* readying to depart for Tripoli. Shades of an almost identical brawl involving Captain of Galleys Bernardo Salviati in March 1533, this one between men of the Church was just as shameful. One of the Sforza family treacherously killed Ribadeneira with a well-placed musket ball. Ribadeneira's Castilians sought revenge in turn. On 6 June Sforza was attacked from ambush in the plaza of Birgu and wounded; he was saved by the intervention of other Italian knights, among whom was Admiral Giorgio Adorno, permitting Sforza to flee to the port, where with a great leap he was able to reach the poop of a skiff that took him quickly to his capitana. Ashore, meanwhile, the knights fought on by nationality, soon dividing the galley squadron along similar lines, Sforza's capitana *Santa Petronilla* and Louis de Vallée-

Passy's *Santa Maria Maddelena* on one side and Juan de Sangorrin's *Santa Caterina* and Afonso de Solis's *San Giovanni Battista* on the other. Pierre de Gozon-Mélac defused the confrontation, placing his barque between contesting galleys with a furious Grand Master Juan de Homedes and staff embarked. Sforza assailant Don Pedro de Chaves was soon deprived of his Habit. Relieved as Captain of Galleys, Sforza on 16 June for his own safety went by small ship to Gaeta and from there reached Rome. While returning to Spain by way of Florence, the defrocked Chaves was killed at Ponte-Centino, a Papal check-point entering or leaving Papal territory, in an ambush ordered by Carlo Sforza. Philippe de Bolyers of Guyenne was condemned by a jury of his peers to a weighted sack (the condemned and a cannon ball were stitched inside a canvas sack, rowed several miles to sea and dropped overboard) for treacherously killing during the brawl a sleeping Michel le Bel de la Tour of Provence. Others were imprisoned on the island of Gozo.[4]

A five-year truce between the Ottoman Empire on the one hand and the Holy Roman Empire together with the Church, France, and Venice on the other was signed on 19 June 1547. Pursuant to the Treaty, Ferdinand, King of Bohemia and Hungary, was to pay the Ottomans 30,000 gold ducats per year in tribute for that part of Hungary under Ferdinand's rule.[6]

Prior of Auvergne Emery des Reaulx was appointed galley commander for one year in Sforza's stead. There ensued a good deal of planning to relieve Parisot de la Valette's Tripoli from the threat of Mourad Aga, particularly upon receipt of a letter from Valette suggesting Mourad and Dragut were ready to combine forces and together besiege Tripoli. Coincident with receipt of Valette's letter, a member of the Viceroy's staff arrived in Malta from Sicily with an urgent summons to Palermo, and it was to Palermo the squadron proceeded. There Reaulx made Viceroy Juan de Vega known of Tripoli's peril, and there the Viceroy made known his immense displeasure with the outrageous developments at Malta, even so committing for duty at Tripoli four companies of Spanish and Italian infantry, a part of the tercio of Sicily at Messina. No sooner were the soldiers embarked, though, than alarming letters were received from Naples praying for succour of Viceroy Pedro Álvarez de Toledo, besieged within the vice-regal palace by both nobles and citizens violently opposed to the introduction at Naples of the Spanish Inquisition, the letters begging for a relief force. Juan de Vega immediately ordered the Malta galleys to Naples, and Reaulx complied but with a written objection that intervention in a national rebellion ran counter to the Order's mission. The largest city in the Holy Roman Empire, Naples was 180 nautical miles and two days north of Messina. On reaching Naples there was nothing but hostility toward the new arrivals and no plausible chance of peacefully or otherwise overcoming much of the population and bringing succour to the Viceroy. While at Naples, Reaulx fell ill and was bedridden when the squadron departed with its four companies of infantry and took course for Malta. Unbeknownst to Reaulx and the squadron, while they were assessing the possibilities at Naples, Dragut, with twenty-three galleys and galliots, had chosen, given the fame of Parisot de la Valette and news that the *Germa of the Religion* had reached Tripoli with substantial reinforcements, to temporarily shelve the agreement he had with Mourad Aga to go to the aid of Tagiora, but rather to assail Malta itself.

Sailing east from Mehedia, before daybreak on 21 July Dragut put corsairs ashore in a cove of Marsa Scirocco (Marsaxlokk), a sheltered bay on Malta's south coast. Unobserved by sentries at Marsa Scirocco, his men, guided by a renegade familiar with the terrain, soon reached the Parish of Santa Caterina near the modern airport. Parish sentries fled for the safety of Birgu without warning the local residents of the corsair presence, not even igniting the box of gun powder that was the normal danger signal. Three hundred persons were seized, their homes pillaged. Alerted by the fleeing sentries, however, there soon arrived from Birgu a company of knights and troops mounted and foot, compelling the corsairs to withdraw. In the haste of their withdrawal more than half of their captives were abandoned. Also leaving a number of dead behind, Dragut's flotilla of beached galleys and galliots hastily withdrew with their remaining victims during the afternoon of its morning arrival. On departure a sail was sighted and pursued. Soon overhauled by Dragut's fast galliots, the sail was that of a corsair galley the property of Vincenzo Cicala of Messina commanded by his eldest son Giulio. She was bound under sail from the Requesens-family island of Pantelleria to Messina with a furnace for baking biscuit fabricated at Porto Solimano, Pantelleria's only town. When overhauled and captured the Cicala galley's guns were neither manned nor loaded and her oarsmen were resting. Giulio Cicala was enslaved and would remain so until exchanged in 1551 for Hisar

Reis, Dragut's nephew by his sister. Dragut soon passed northbound off Malta's Grand Harbour with Cicala's ship in tow. The Grand Master, realising Tripoli could not be Dragut's destination, dispatched a fast frigate to so notify Valette. He dispatched a second fast frigate to alert the island of Sicily. At the salt island of Saline near Saint Paul's Bay, 6 miles up the coast from the port of Malta, Dragut seized the Maltese vessel of Braito Xaquato bound from Licata, Sicily, to Grand Harbour with a cargo of foodstuffs. Dispatched with a prize crew to Mehedia, this ship and her crew were recaptured en route by the *Germa of the Religion*.[7]

En route to Malta one month after assuming Squadron command, Emery des Reaux succumbed to his affliction. Prior of Auvergne and Lieutenant to the Grand Master as well as Galley Squadron Commander at his death, he was among the early commanders of the original 100-gun Great Carrack *Santa Maria*, a veteran of the Great Siege of Rhodes, and an ambassador to kings and popes on numerous occasions. He was also a sensitive and caring individual wearing armour, one of a rare breed. He was succeeded as Prior of Auvergne by Marshal Imbert de la Morinière, while Commander Pierre du Mont succeeded to the dignity of Marshal. Reaulx was succeeded as Captain of Galleys by Admiral Giorgio Adorno.

In August Grand Master and Council appointed Oswald Massinbert of Sutton, Lincolnshire, Prior of Ireland, succeeding the deceased John Rawson, on condition he not be entitled to the Grand Cross until, if ever, the priories, monasteries, and other religious properties in Ireland expropriated by the deceased King Henry VIII be returned to the Order of Jerusalem. The Regency Council, governing for young King Edward VI, however, had no intention of restoring Roman Catholic properties to either Church or Order of Jerusalem.[7]

Admiral and Squadron Commander Giorgio Adorno struck a blow at Dragut that went some way in mitigating the sense of shame stemming from the corsair's sack of the Parish of Santa Caterina. On 13 September, alerted by the Sheik of Almanzor, the squadron captured at sea the germa of Ali Fuat with many Turks embarked sent by Dragut for service with Mourad Aga. She was carrying a cargo of valuable barracan, or camel's hair material, the wares of unrelated merchants and was towed safely to Malta.[8]

The absence of war between France and Spain, as well as inactivity on the part of the Ottoman Armada, suggested a breathing spell. Grand

Master and Council scheduled a Chapter General at Malta to convene on Sunday, 6 May 1548. For this purpose a summons was sent to Grand Commander Antoine de Barras, as Grand Commander and also pilier of the Langue of Provence at the Convent but currently Depositor General in the Kingdom of France. Also summoned were Prior of Saint-Gilles Robert d'Aube de Roquemartine, Treasurer Léon de Montalembert, and many others. Sent to Barcelona for the purpose of transporting Spanish Hospitallers back to Malta for the Chapter General was the *Barque of the Religion*, commanded by Pierre de Gozon-Mélac. Having acquired considerable renown at sea and ashore in war with England, Prior of Capua Leone Strozzi was appointed a General of the Armada of France. He would be dispatched with twenty-two galleys in 1548 to remove Mary, Queen of Scots from Scotland to France, where she would be betrothed to Dauphin Francis rather than to King Edward VI of England. The year about to end would also be remembered for the death in January of Hospitaller Cardinal Pietro Bembo, scholar, linguist, poet, official historian of Venice, and lover of Lucrezia Borgia. A Knight of the Small Cross not a warrior, he should have been a Knight of the Grand Cross not a warrior.[9]

Grand Bailiff of Germany Philipp Schilling von Canstatt died early in 1548 at Malta. He was succeeded by Commander Wilhelm Bombast von Hohenheim. Not long afterward Grand Commander Antoine de Barras died of old age, also at Malta. He was succeeded by Commander Philippe du Broc. Gaspard de Vallier was appointed Bailiff of Lango, a dignity renounced by Prior of Toulouse Foulques de Caritat. Also early in the year the *Barque of the Religion* returned from Barcelona with Spanish knights attending the May Chapter General. Because Captain of Galleys Giorgio Adorno was Admiral and Pilier of the Langue of Italy and should attend the Chapter General, and because he was also a Procurator of the Treasury and must attend the Chapter General, Commander of Flanders and senior captain Louis de Vallée-Passy was appointed Regent of Galleys.[10]

Bound for the African coast, the squadron under command of Vallée-Passy departed Malta on 6 May 1548, the same day as the Chapter General convened. The fourth Chapter General at Malta convened in the great salon of Castle Saint Angelo with all due solemnity and ceremony. As at the previous Chapter General, Chaplain Mateo Castillo opened proceedings with a sermon, this time concerning the charitable, hospitable, and obedient duties of a Hospitaller. There was general satisfaction among attendees that administration of the Treasury had been removed from the Grand Master at the previous Chapter General, negating a concern that might have been. The Sixteen *Capitolari* or legislators elected by the eight langues were: Grand Commander Philippe du Broc and Prior of Saint-Gilles Robert d'Aube de Roquemartine for Provence; Gilbert de la Gillière and Charles de Chalùs for Auvergne; Bailiff of the Morea Claude de la Sengle and Guillaume de Montalembert for France; Grand Conservator (Draper) Gaspar de Sanguessa and Don Garcia Glior, Procurator for the commanderies of the Castellania of Amposta for Aragon; Admiral Giorgio Adorno and Battista Agliata of Palermo for Italy; Lieutenant Turcopolier Nicholas Upton and Knight of Grace (not born in England) Antoine de Guèvre for England; Grand Bailiff Wilhelm Bombast von Hohenheim and Adam von Schwalbach for Germany; and Bailiff of Negroponte Pedro Nunnez d'Herrera and Sebastião de Fana of Portugal for Castile. Remaining Procurators of the Treasury were Prior of Auvergne Imbert de la Morinière, Lieutenant Chancellor Fernando de Bracamonte, and Commander of Golfech Jean de Macanan of the Langue of Provence. The Sixteen congregated in the house of Miguel de Homedes, nephew and Master of the Grand Master's House, and did not conclude their deliberations until the final day of May. Ordinary responsions of commanderies, bailiwicks, and priories were to remain unchanged. A 12,000 scudo special impost to fund Treasury operations was approved. Administration of the Treasury was to remain in the hands of the Grand Commander, the aforementioned Procurators of the Treasury, and Conventual Conservator Giorgio Vagnone of the Piedmont. Bailiff of the Morea Claude de la Sengle and Preceptor Antoine de Guèvre of the Langue of England were respectively appointed Ambassador and Lieutenant Ambassador to the Holy See, the latter fluent in Latin. Commander of Flanders Louis de Vallée-Passy and Commander Pedro de Felizes were similarly appointed Ambassadors to the Imperial Court, while Prior of Saint-Gilles Roquemartine was appointed Ambassador to the French Court, all to plead for and obtain secular labourers such as debtors needed for the local workforce. The bronze-sheathed *Barque of the Religion* commanded by Pierre de Gozon-Mélac, too expensive to operate and too large to enter the Port of Tripoli, was in 1548 retired to be replaced by two galleonettos each of 100 tons carrying capacity. The interrupted tour of Giorgio Adorno as Captain of Galleys was extended by one year, and he was to be succeeded by Claude de la Sengle in December 1549 for a two-year assignment. With the death of Rhodiot Benedetto Ruggieri, thenceforth standard bearers were to be Hospitallers.[10]

An expedition was in May entrusted by French King Henry II to André de Montalembert d'Essé to remove Mary Queen of Scots at age 6 from sequestration at Dumbarton and to bring her to France. The necessary naval force was commanded by General of the Armada and Hospitaller Leone Strozzi and Vice Admiral Charles de Moy, Sieur de la Meilleraye. An embarked force of 5,440 left Brest on 20 May. Hospitaller Nicolas Durand de Villegagnon, 'a person of exceptional dignity to whom one commits matters of importance', commanded the four royal galleys. Removal of the young queen was his responsibility. He was assisted by Hospitaller Michel de Seurre de Lumigny, later Resident Ambassador to the Court of Saint James and still later Prior of Champagne.[9]

As the Chapter General broke up, news was received eighteen Turkish vessels had been sighted south of Capo delle Arme, Calabria. Soon a second report was received that the same eighteen had been sighted off Cape Passero, Sicily. On 14 June twelve of them, galleys and galliots, appeared in the Freo Channel between Malta and Gozo to take on water at Gozo. An escaped Christian slave from one of these warships made his way to Gozo Governor Diego del Rio, who sent him on to Malta. These vessels were escorting Barbarossa's brother-in-law Salih Reis (Bosio's Sala Rais) from Constantinople to Algiers. Deputy Beylerbey or Lieutenant Viceroy to Hassan, son of Barbarossa, Salih Reis was returning to his post. The other six vessels had been sent ahead under Cussaim Çelebi with orders to locate Dragut for the purpose of joining or coordinating forces before continuing on to Algiers. The reinforced squadron was carrying a large complement of janissaries and veteran soldiers. Concerned for the safety of the Malta Squadron, two fast frigates were sped to the Barbary Coast, one to Tripoli and the other to the shallows near Djerba. The squadron, meanwhile, had put ashore at Tripoli Catalan Hospitaller Damià de Rajadel as Captain of Cavalry. Rajadel had already seized the Tower of Rapta, part of greater Tagiora. From Tripoli the squadron proceeded to Secca di Palo (modern Porto Palo) south of Djerba where two vessels the property of Yunes of Djerba had been seized, one of which was a local shuttle with a cargo of indigo, dates, and barracan, and the other of which was a shallow-draft schirazzo with a cargo of foodstuffs sent on to Tripoli. The squadron then returned safely to Malta, where *Santa Caterina* under Juan de Sangorrin almost immediately readied to sail for Marseille conveying Louis de Vallée-Passy and Prior of Saint-Gilles Roquemartine on their ambassadorial missions.[11]

On 23 June 1548 French troops debarked at Leith 4km north of Edinburgh. Strozzi took possession of Edinburgh. Villegagnon set out to simulate a return to France, evaded English Admiral Edward Clinton, skirted the Shetlands and reached Dumbarton on Clyde on the west coast of Scotland on 28 July. One day later 7-year-old Mary, Queen of Scots embarked aboard the galley *Reale* with four other Marys to confuse the enemy in case of capture and was transported to France. In April 1558 she would wed the Dauphin Francis, later King Francis II.

With adjournment of the Chapter General Vallée-Passy was succeeded in command of the galleys by Giorgio Adorno. The galley *Santa Caterina* commanded by Juan de Sangorrin of Aragon,[12] lightest and fastest in the squadron, transported to Marseille ambassadors and others with assignments on the mainland. Prior of Saint-Gilles Roccamartine proceeded to the court of new French King Henry II seeking and obtaining reaffirmation of the Order's privileges in the Kingdom while pursuing the matter of secular labour. Vallée-Passy trans-shipped to Barcelona for a similar purpose. At the same time Commander of Chantereine Pierre de la Fontaine and a number of other senior knights embarked transporting responsions to the Common Treasury from priories and commanderies in France in the amount of 70,000 gold ducats.[10]

In August Dragut, with twelve galleys, prowled the waters of Castellammare di Stabia in the Gulf of Naples. Corsairs were put ashore, who kidnapped eighty persons of both sexes and of every age but were forced to retire by resistance and the loss of twenty men. The corsair chief next headed to the island of Procida also in the Gulf, from where he solicited ransoms for the abducted. Days later, he surprised and captured at Cape Miseno between Procida and Pozzuoli a Spanish galley carrying troops and coin.

At about the same time Malta's *Santa Caterina* commanded by Juan de Sangorrin bound from Marseille to Malta paused in the Strait of

Bonifacio to give chase to a frigate of Sardinia mistaken for a corsair fusta. Later *Santa Caterina* was caught in a storm but put safely into Monte Circeo, 100km south-south-east of Rome. At sea almost continuously for four months, Sangorrin was eager to get home and on 30 August resumed the voyage. He did not pause at Gaeta, preferring to continue on to Naples. He turned into the channel between Procida and the mainland only to find himself enveloped by Dragut's galliots. Dragut, however, was still located in the shallows near the island of Procida, then with twenty galleys and galliots. Sighting the Maltese galley when she was well north of Ischia, he surprised her as she approached the passage between Procida and Capo Miseno to head for Naples. *Santa Caterina* immediately altered course for the shore at Cuma (ancient Cumae), her crew hoping to beach and flee. As she approached the shore, though, her Muslim oarsmen rebelled and the galley was taken intact with most of the wealth on board: 70,000 gold ducats collected in France and destined for the expense of reinforcing the defence of Tripoli. Only twenty-five to thirty knights survived, most remaining on the poop deck when the ship was seized. Among these were Louis and Hugues du Sart de Thury, who were received into the Langue of France less than two years earlier. Louis would soon be ransomed. His brother would not. Another among the dead was a French knight by the name of Camus who dared to resist; he lost his head to a scimitar.[13]

Others attempting to swim for the shore were with few exceptions slain. Charles d'Urre de Tessières was one of the exceptions, Jean de la Tour of Picardie and the Langue of France as well as Spanish Bailiff of Santa Eufemia Don Federico de Urrias were not. Another exception was Commander of Chantereine Pierre de la Fontaine, who with other senior knights and some of the gold gambled that the corsairs would not be able to get to everyone in the sea. Dragut was not inhumane and did not enjoy killing. In fact, he needed ransom money to build ships and their home port, and the dead brought no ransoms. Over a period of six months during which Hospitaller Augusto Espannol proceeded between Djerba and Malta in a frigate to obtain agreement to payment of 300 gold scudos per knight, and during which Hospitaller Don Carlo de Espés died in captivity, the exchange of knights for gold was effected from two corsair galliots with safe-conducts, one to Malta and the other to Tripoli. Juan de Sangorrin was exchanged not for gold but for Dragut disciple Golfa Reis, a captive at Rhodes.[14]

Despite a sense of carelessness concerning Juan de Sangorrin's return from France, but reflecting an otherwise commendable history as a knight, he was absolved by the Council of misconduct and was not censured over the loss of galley and lives. At about this time Bailiff of Naples (San Giovanni a Mare di Napoli) Giovan Battista Carafa the Younger died and was succeeded by Admiral Giorgio Adorno, who was in turn succeeded as Admiral by Francesco Romagnano of Turin, a veteran of the Great Siege of Rhodes. Claude de la Sengle, heir apparent as Captain of Galleys, located in the Arsenal at Messina a half-finished galley abandoned by her owner. Given the condition of the Common Treasury exacerbated by the loss of 70,000 gold scudos, Sengle acquired the galley and commissioned her completion at his own expense. She would be called *San Claudio*. Gaspard de Vallier succeeded to the dignity of Marshal upon the death of Pierre du Mont, renouncing the Bailiwick of Lango, which temporarily remained vacant.[15]

By Bull of Grand Master Homedes dated 5 November 1548 Nicholas Upton of Northolme, Devon, was appointed Turcopolier, succeeding the deceased Giles Russell. Francis of Lorraine was appointed to the dignity of Grand Prior of France upon the death of incumbent Claude d'Ancienville, succeeding at age 14 'in the same wave of favour that brought his family the dukedom of Guise' (Sire's *Knights of Malta*). That is, at the request of French King Henry II. The Priory of Champagne also became vacant upon the death of Robert d'Aché and, the langue's senior knight waiving his right, Treasurer Léon de Montalembert was appointed to this dignity. Commander Jean de Neuchèze was appointed successor Treasurer.[16]

Early in the new year Jean de la Roche-Andry was deprived of the dignity of Grand Hospitaller and Conventual Bailiff for his continued absence from the Convent and was succeeded by Conventual Conservator Claude de la Sengle, Roche-Andry appointed to Sengle's former dignity of Bailiff of the Morea. Grand Conservator (Draper) and long-time Castellan of Trapani Gaspar de Sanguessa died and left most of his considerable estate at Trapani to the Common Treasury. Francisco Martinez de Casseda was dispatched to Trapani to take possession of the assets, while Commander Miguel de Torreglia was appointed successor Grand Conservator. The three-galley squadron wintered at Messina, where Giorgio Adorno and Captain-designate Catalan Don Bernardo de Guimeran were able to supervise the completion and outfitting of *San Claudio*. *Santa Maria Maddelena* commanded by François de Gozon-Mélac transported the two ambassadors Sengle and Guèvre from Ostia to Malta to alert the Grand Master and Council to two indictments to be handed down in February in the Vatican's law chambers. The first of these was a charge brought by Mallorcan Mateu Zaforteza Tagamanente in the amount of more than 100,000 scudos for unpaid relief missions to the Castle of Saint Peter at Petronium in 1475 pursuant to an accord between then Prior of Lombardia Giorgio Piozzasco and Juan Tagamanente. This matter had been settled in 1479 by Bull of Pope Sixtus IV, suggesting a new twist to the matter not in the Order's favour. The second indictment stemmed from a claim in the same amount concerning a Genovese carrack bound from Alexandria to Scio (Chios) that in April 1522 diverted to Rhodes and four months later was sent to the bottom of Rhodes Harbour by an errant Ottoman cannon ball. The owner-captain who did the diverting, Domenico Fornari, was assigned to the walls of the Post of Aragon with his entire crew and met his death on 10 October from a Turkish scimitar. Grand Master and Council responded by dispatching Hospitaller Vice-Chancellor Martín Rojas de Portalrubio, Doctor of Law Francesco Mego, noble Rhodiot Gentile di Montolivet, and Notary Vicenzo Bonaventura to Messina to examine the testimony and evidence.[16] Because there is no further mention of these potential charges, they presumably died a faulted death.

Infidel Corsairs were already at sea in April of 1549. Corsair galliots and fustas passed singly by the ports of Palermo and Messina with evident intent to lure lone Hospitaller or Sicilian galleys out in pursuit. Adorno wisely sought the company of the Squadron of Sicily. Following a number of fruitless pursuits, the fusta of Mohammad Reis of Monastir was trapped at the island of Favignana. Monastir is 25 nautical miles north of Dragut's Mehedia, and Mohammad revealed Dragut was in 1549 expected to again raid the Genovese Riviera. Adorno took his leave of the Sicilian squadron and returned to Messina, where *San Claudio* was ready for sea. The squadron took on board foodstuffs and other supplies for Malta and Gozo and readied to depart.[17]

Passing away at Malta in May was Wilhelm Bombast von Hohenheim, Grand Bailiff and Pilier of the Langue of Germany. By common consent appointment of his replacement was delayed as there was no quorum of qualified German Hospitallers present at Malta. A few months later he was succeeded by his brother, Commander Georg Bombast.[17]

The four galleys of Giorgio Adorno's squadron departed Messina on 8 May 1549 at first light with the south-flowing current. Later in the morning at the foot of the Strait a galley-sottile was sighted hugging the south shore of Calabria, apparently waiting for the current to reverse. Believing her to be a corsair, Adorno ordered pursuit. Light and fast (sottile), the corsair headed east then north-east along Calabria's south coast 27 nautical miles and four hours before finally beaching at Bianco. Concerned at the possibility of ambush, Adorno sent in the squadron frigate under command of Giacomo Raschieri of Chieri with a company of arquebusiers. The corsairs, eighty in number commanded by Agiali Reis of Anatolia, yielded not so much to Raschieri as to the four war galleys standing offshore. A little fewer than 200 Christians were freed from the oars. Because the galley had been taken without combat and without damage, Adorno recovered plunder and vessel for the Common Treasury in compensation for the loss of *Santa Caterina*; that is, in compensation for the galley, not for the 70,000 gold ducats she carried. Putting into Syracuse with his prize, Adorno found Prior of Lombardia Carlo Sforza with three galleys of his grandfather Pope Paul III flying Church colours. Their meeting was one of soulmates, Adorno having saved Sforza's life during the internecine strife at Malta in June two years before. Sforza, however, still harboured resentment toward Grand Master Juan de Homedes for his dismissal as squadron commander, but remaining an Hospitaller, had been ordered to Malta by the Pope to render his obedience. The eight galleys proceeded together and reached Malta on 21 May. Having complied with his uncle's orders, Sforza continued on to the Barbary Coast, where he was later reported to have had a successful cruise, returning to Civitavecchia to a grand reception. It is worth noting again that his predecessor Gentile Virginio Orsini, Papal Squadron Commander for fourteen years until August 1548, prohibited plundering and enslavement.[17]

Chancellor Pedro Núñez de Herrera was in June 1549 appointed Governor of Tripoli, succeeding Parisot de la Valette. He took with him a company of fifty knights. Valette, with departing staff and garrison, embarked aboard the galleys and left Tripoli in late July. En route to Malta Adorno seized a square-rigged germa similar to a round ship in the Malta Channel between Malta and Africa. Commanded by Caidan Reis with a crew of thirty-two Turks and Moors, she was transporting 109 black slaves from Djerba to Lepanto and other ports in the Levant, laden as well with a variety of Barbary merchandise. She was towed into Grand Harbour on 4 August 1549. Hospitaller Diego del Rio, commanding a frigate at La Goletta to recover items due to Malta, while there suffered the loss of fellow Hospitallers Sancho Rodriquez de Lugones of Asturias and Antonio Osorio of Astorga to an unprovoked assault by local Moors. Subsequently dispatched to the Levant to observe Ottoman fleet activity, Del Rio found the enemy confining its movements to the Aegean consistent with peace between major Mediterranean powers, thus permitting Suleiman to concentrate on Persia.

Prior of Saint-Gilles Robert d'Aube de Roquemartine died in France, another of a declining number of Great Siege veterans. He was succeeded by Grand Commander Philippe du Broc, who was in turn succeeded as Grand Commander by Antoine de Jaminy de Pène. Grand Master and Council appointed and dispatched to the French Court Commander Gilbert de Serpens of Auvergne as successor resident ambassador to France. He would remain ambassador to France for seventeen years. Don Antonio de Toledo was appointed ambassador to the Imperial Court in Flanders.[18]

In September Dragut's squadron was sighted in the waters of Trapani, Sicily, and the four galleys of Malta were summoned to join the Squadron of Sicily in search of the predator. The island, however, was circumnavigated by the combined squadrons with no further sighting. At Messina Claude de la Sengle was embarked returning to Malta as successor Captain of Galleys. England's Antoine de Guèvre remained at Rome as the Order's acting Resident Ambassador to the Holy See.[19]

Pope Paul III died at Rome on 10 November 1549. The Conclave of Cardinals sat until 7 February 1550 before Cardinal Giovanni Maria Ciocchi del Monte, cousin of future Grand Master Pietro del Monte, was elected in secret consistory as Pope Julius III. Antoine de Guèvre would in 1553 compose a Latin Oratory acclaiming the Papacy of Julius III.[20] Claude de la Sengle in December succeeded Giorgio Adorno as Captain of Galleys pursuant to a decision reached at the May 1548 Chapter General. That same month he took the galleys to winter at Messina.[19]

Upon reports of the new Pope's election, Grand Master and Council dispatched Luigi Barbiano as Ambassador Extraordinary to render the Order's obedience, while Pietro del Monte was appointed Castellan of Castle Saint Angelo, the Vatican redoubt connected by covered passage to Saint Peter's Basilica. Fifty knights rotated into Tripoli and fifty rotated out in a partial garrison change mandated by the Chapter General. Giacomo Raschieri was appointed Master of the Auberge housing knights at Tripoli. Jean de Neuchèze was appointed Captain of Reserves with authority to command and discipline knights. He was conveyed to Tripoli by Claude de la Sengle with two galleys, leaving the other two at Messina.[19]

From Germany Emperor Charles V ordered that North African corsairs be extirpated, particularly Dragut, and assigned the task to 83-year-old Andrea Doria. Sengle departed Malta for Messina and Palermo with two galleys, the capitana *San Claudio*, which he commanded himself, and *San Giovanni Battista* called *La Cornuta*, commanded by Catalan Don Bernardo de Guimeran. The other two galleys, *Santa Maria Maddelena* called *Il Gallo*, commanded by François de Gozon-Mélac, and *Santa Barbara*, commanded by Guillaume Coppier, were retrieved at Messina and the squadron proceeded to rendezvous with Andrea Doria's Imperial Armada at Palermo. The four galleys carried 140 knights and 260 other combatants, all 400 under the command of Guimeran. All allied ground forces including Hospitallers would come under the command of Don Garcia Alvarez de Toledo, son of Don Pedro Alvarez de Toledo, Viceroy of Naples, and of Juan de Vega, Viceroy of Sicily.[21]

Exclusive of the Galley Squadron of Spain and other galleys gathered for the same purpose under Don Bernardino de Mendoza to patrol the Balearics, Doria had fifty-four galleys under his command, four of Malta, twenty of his own, three galleys of the Duke of Florence commanded by Giordano Orsini with 1,000 embarked infantry under the command of Chiappino Vitelli, three of the Pope commanded by Carlo Sforza, and twenty-four between the squadrons of Naples and Sicily respectively commanded by Don Garcia de Toledo and Berenguer de Requesens. These latter two squadrons included galleys provided by the Grimaldis of Monaco, Vincenzo Cicala, the Marchese di Terranuova, the Prince of

Salerno, and others. Upon reaching Cape Bon at the north-east corner of modern Tunisia the armada was forced by a sudden storm to shelter for two days in the large lagoon at Porto Farina (Ghar al Milh) within the Gulf of Tunis, thus losing the advantage of surprise. Then proceeding directly to Dragut headquarters at Mehedia, the empty galley port told Doria they had missed their prey. From Mehedia Doria searched south to Djerba, the large corsair anchorage at the foot of the Gulf of Gabes, again without success. Dragut, with his own armada of twenty-seven oared vessels, was at the moment 500 nautical miles to the west approaching Cabo de Gata, Spain, with intent to raid Cartagena. Doria turned back the way he had come and on 20 May 1550 appeared off Monastir, a small and poorly defended port 20 miles north of Mehedia. Embarked troops were put ashore, Georges de Dyo, senior knight of the Langue of Auvergne, carrying the Order's Standard. The city of mixed Turkish, Christian, and Moorish populations was besieged from the sea, pummelled mercilessly by galley bow chasers for eight days. A Grimaldi galley went to the bottom when one of its cannon exploded, too hot for the next powder and shot, killing a large number on the gun platform as well as causing terminal leaks in its underwater caulking. On 28 May the city walls were breached, Hospitallers and a Spanish tercio of Naples penetrating into the city. Moorish defenders abandoned by Dragut's fleeing Turks were taken, as well as the fortress where 300-odd monks had sought safety. At least seventy Christians lost their lives, with a larger number wounded. Among the latter were Louis Doria of the Langue of Provence, severely burned by artificial fire, Alonso de Escobar of Castile, and Giovan Antonio delle Cause of Messina. Recently knighted Aimar de Ferrières-Sauvebeuf of Provence was killed. Eighteen hundred inhabitants were enslaved, a Christian depredation making Dragut look like a petty thief.[22]

Don Garcia de Toledo did not care to submit to orders of the Viceroy of Sicily and threatened to walk away with the galleys of Naples to search for Dragut alone. Unbeknownst to Toledo, Dragut was far to the north raiding Corsica and Sardinia. To appease Toledo, Doria sent him with twenty-four galleys including *Santa Maria Maddelena* and *San Giovanni Battista* back to Naples for reinforcements and supplies. Surrender of Susa and of a safe anchorage nearby were meanwhile obtained, and Doria decided to take Dragut's strongly fortified homeport. His armada appeared off Mehedia at dawn on 26 June, some galleys assigned to look for points of debarkation. One of these, Guimeran's *San Giovanni Battista*, suffered cannon-fire damage doing so. Mehedia (ancient Aphrodisium, Bosio's Citta d'Africa, Morgan's Africa), where Dragut had made his residence, would not be a Monastir, falling in eight days. Hisar Reis, nephew of Dragut by Dragut's sister, was governor. Caid Ali, who withdrew from Monastir, was his lieutenant. 'This great city, lying some leagues east of Tunis, was built on a slip of land which advanced into the sea. Its fortifications were regular, the walls of an extraordinary height, thickness, and solidity, strengthened with many good towers and bulwarks, and the artillery numerous and in good order. On an eminence within and commanding the city stood a large fortress which served it for a citadel. The harbour was capacious and secure; besides which there was a smaller and very commodious port for gallies (sic) whose entrance was defended by a strong chain. The sea washed the city walls, and indeed surrounded it only but for the narrow neck of land joining it to the continent.'[21]

The siege was protracted in part because of caution by besieging ground forces and in part because of hostility between ground force commanders. Doria, too, was accused of taking little interest in siege operations, standing aside to avoid squabbles between ground-force commanders. Progress was also slow because the city was well defended by 1,750 Turks and Moors, arquebusiers, crossbowmen, cannoneers, cavalry, and others in addition to a population largely loyal to Dragut. Aiding the Christians were the King of inland Kairouan, whose realm reached the sea at Mehedia as well as other Moorish enemies of Dragut. The besiegers were divided into two units, one under Garcia de Toledo and the other under Juan de Vega which included Hospitallers under Guimeran. At this point, 15 July, Dragut was in the Freo Channel between Malta and Gozo with three galleys and nine galliots where he learned of the siege. He took on water at Gozo and headed for Mehedia, the Grand Master meanwhile having alerted Doria by fast frigate. Putting ashore near Sfax, Dragut marched to relief of Mehedia but was turned away after several skirmishes with Vega's ground force in which Hospitallers Jean de Roman de Belz and Jean de Lescout de Lissy lost their lives, both of the Langue of France. Also leaving a number of his best fighters behind, the newly appointed

Sancakbey or Ottoman Governor of Santa Maura retired to his twelve vessels and then to Djerba.[23]

Following seventy-six days of bombardment (comparable to the 1480 Ottoman Siege of Rhodes) from the sea, city walls were breached between 8 and 12 September 1550. Bernardo de Guimeran led the Hospitaller final assault supported by Astor Baglioni, a Perugian adventurer, while Guillaume Coppier backed up Standard Bearer Georges de Dyo.[24] Debarked ground forces were commanded by galley number-twos Christophe le Bouleur de Montgaudry (the younger) of *San Claudio*, Juanito de Torreglias of *San Giovanni Battista*, Antoine de Ver of *Santa Barbara*, and Hector Pellegrin la Rocca of François de Gozon-Mélac's *Santa Maria Maddelena*; Gozon-Mélac unhappy believing that as senior captain he, not Guimeran, should be leading the assault. Christian forces poured into the city, in Bosio's III-277 words, 'making great carnage' of resident Muslims. Those seeking safety in the largest mosque were by the sword slaughtered within. Women with babes in arms rushed into the sea seeking death by drowning to avoid the sword or enslavement. Mehedia capitulated on 20 September, with most of the Turkish garrison dead including Dragut lieutenant Cait Ali. The Maltese went home with thirty-six dead and many wounded, the former including non-Hospitaller Engineer Antonio Ferramolino; Louis Romei of Auvergne, Chaplain aboard *Santa Barbara*; Guillaume de Thorodes; Claude d'Azaville; Georges Maistre de la Papinière and Charles de Montreüil of the Langue of France; Aimar de Ferrières-Sauvebeuf and 18-year-old novice Joachim de Romieu of Provence; Claude de Maretes d'Aspremont and François de Choisy, both of Auvergne; Pompeo Abenante of Cosenza[25] and Fabbio Bobba of Casale, both Italian knights; Wilhelm Blos von Diesendorf of Germany; and Antonio de Vaca;[26] Hernando Ramirez de Vargas; Vasco Chemudo; Juan de Montalvo; Antonio Ozores; and Don Luis de Atiensa of Guadalajara;[27] all six of the Langue of Castile. Also dead was flag-bearer Georges de Dyo of Auvergne, so senior that his name does not appear on any list of Hospitaller receptions. Of defenders Nephew Hisar and his staff were captured attempting to flee from the harbour in a barque, Hisar recognised by Vincenzo Cicala and to eventually be exchanged for Cicala's son Giulio captured by Dragut in 1547. Seven thousand others were enslaved, but the object of the entire undertaking, Dragut himself, had avoided capture or death. Juan de Vega having seen to the rebuilding of walls, rearming, and garrisoning of the city, Doria's entire armada departed for Trapani on 22 September, releasing the galleys of the Religion en route to arrive in Malta on 25 September. There they found the island short of almost everything, and without clearing pratique but after disembarking the wounded and infirm, the squadron again sailed on 26 September for Sicily to load necessities for Malta.[28]

Finding no spare grain at Sicily, the squadron was forced to lurk around Faro di Messina at the north end of the Strait in hope of intercepting a grain carrier. Rewarded, they seized a small grain carrier, aboard which a prize crew was placed under command of Catalan Jorge de Sant Joan, which sailed her to Malta, reaching the island on 11 November 1550 to find cruel famine raging. Children and some adults were dying. Famine was truly relieved only when the squadron hi-jacked three grain carriers of Apulia in Apulian waters bound from the Levant and towed them to Malta arriving 10 December. Departing Malta at the same time was Juan de Sangorrin, bound for the Levant with the Galleonetto of the Religion looking for additional supplies. The Galleonetto soon intercepted a caravel in service to Dragut carrying a variety of foodstuffs and munitions bound from Alexandria to Djerba with many Turks and Moors embarked. The engagement persisted over thirty hours, costing the lives of many on both sides among whom was Hospitaller Lucas de Cáseda of Navarre. On completion of combat the caravel was towed into Malta. This capture helped to ease the sting of Dragut's capture of the same Juan de Sangorrin's *Santa Caterina* in August 1548.[29]

Reaching a natural end to his accomplished life in 1550 was Prior of Pisa Aurelio Bottigella. In the annals of Hospitaller history there are few who approached him in command ability and peer esteem. Seventy years of age, he was interred at Pisa in the Church of San Tommaso, and was succeeded as Prior of Pisa by Admiral Francesco Romagnano, who was in turn succeeded as Admiral by Commander Ardicino Goritio Barba of Turin. Within weeks Bailiff of Venosa Alfonso Carlone also died and was succeeded by Barba. Barba was succeeded as Admiral by Filippo Pilli of Florence.[30]

In January 1551 Dragut speeded his Kaya or principal lieutenant to Constantinople with gifts and a written plea to Sultan Suleiman for assistance in opposing Doria's Imperial Armada, which in its conquest of Mehedia, Monastir, and Susa, together with a continued Christian presence at La Goletta, Tripoli, Bougie, and Oran, were seven too many Christian outposts in the Ottoman Empire. Mourad Aga, likewise suspicious of the Hospitallers at Tripoli, sent his own gifts to the Porte, writing in the same vein as did Dragut and additionally reporting on a movement within the Convent to transfer the Order's home from Malta to Tripoli. Suleiman wrote to Emperor Charles V and demanded return of Mehedia, illegally seized during a period of peace between empires.[30] On 7 February the Venetian Senate voted to warn the colonial governments of Cyprus, Candia, Zante, and Corfu of the large armada that Suleiman was reported to be preparing for an expedition in the spring.[31] The aforementioned Jorge de Sant Joan was assigned an armed frigate and dispatched to Messina, Gallipoli di Apulia, Santa Maria di Leuca, Corfu, and Zante seeking news of the Ottoman Armada.

Hospitaller Baron Ludwig von Bolwiler was assigned as Deputy Ambassador in Residence to the Imperial Court in support of Resident Ambassador Don Antonio de Toledo. Hospitaller Alonso de Contreras the Elder was appointed Captain-General of the Imperial Armada of the Danube. Bolwiler and Contreras, while in Greater Germany, were to coordinate with Prior of Bohemia Johannes von Württemberg.

Hospitaller Alonso Rodriquez de Lourenzá of Castile was dispatched to Sicily to discuss with Viceroy Juan de Vega problems in feeding the large populations of Malta, Gozo, and Tripoli. While relocation to Sicily of some portion of these populations was postulated in the way of persuasion, the intent was to obtain an increased allotment from the Girgenti (Agrigento) 'Granary of Rome'. Such an increase could be obtained but at the cost of appointing Vega's young son Suero de Vega to a commandery of grace with accompanying Grand Cross. This proposition was received with irritation and disgust by Grand Master and Council.

Because Pietro del Monte could not act as both Castellan of Sant'Angelo and Resident Ambassador to the Holy See, Grand Hospitaller Claude de la Sengle was appointed on 12 February to succeed Prior of Venice Ranuccio Farnese as Ambassador, Farnese elevated to the Cardinalate in 1545 by his grandfather Pope Paul III. Sengle would also assume the duties of Procurator General at Rome. He accordingly took the squadron to Naples, where he was succeeded in command by senior captain François Piedefer as Regent to complete Sengle's two-year term. Piedefer also assumed command of *San Claudio*. Battista Bellomo had earlier been appointed to command of *San Michele Arcangelo*, newly constructed at Malta, and Pedro Fernandez de Felizes had been appointed to command of *Santa Maria Maddelena*, succeeding François de Gozon-Mélac. Bernardo de Guimeran remained in command of *San Giovanni Battista*, while Guillaume Cossier's *Santa Barbara* had been hauled for refit. The four captains accompanied Sengle overland from Naples to Rome, where they were most graciously received in consistory of the Cardinals in the company of Antoine de Guèvre. Guèvre recited his own eloquent oration in Latin rendering the Order's obedience and specifically that of Juan de Homedes, Pietro del Monte, and Claude de la Sengle.[31]

Dragut had in January 1551 been appointed Sancakbey or Governor of Santa Maura by Sultan Suleiman. His status thus became that of a senior member of government; he was no longer a corsair but rather an admiral and a pasha. The five-year truce signed on 19 June 1547 between the Ottoman Empire on the one hand and the Holy Roman Empire together with the Church, France, and Venice on the other had seventeen months to run. Meanwhile, fifty additional galleys assigned to Lepanto and Preveza had fallen under Dragut's direct command.[32]

Likely unaware of Dragut's elevated status, the Emperor early in the new year renewed his call for Doria to take Dragut dead or alive. Doria was aware Dragut could be found at Djerba, and that when Dragut exited from behind the island, only one galley at a time might navigate the narrow Cantera Channel to the sea. Should Dragut attempt to wait him out in the security of Djerba, Doria had a plan to enlist the assistance of Sheik Sala, Lord of Djerba, and together destroy Dragut's squadron in place, liberating captive Christian oarsmen. Early in April he put to sea with twenty-seven well-equipped galleys. Dragut meanwhile still had some of his galleys and galliots beached on the shore surrounding the lagoon, tallowing underwater hulls. Doria soon appeared off the narrow passage leading into the lagoon and bottled the corsairs in the thin strip of channel that lies between the coast and the island of Djerba. The channel was practicable from one end only, because at the other end a field of rocks and shallows formed an isthmus on or near the surface of the sea. Hospitaller Juan Vasquez de Coronado, in service to Doria, was dispatched to Naples with letters for Viceroy Don Pedro de Toledo, for Vega, and for Grand Master Juan de Homedes of the Knights of

Malta seeking all possible assistance for the battle to ensue when Dragut attempted to exit. The Hospitaller Galley Squadron returned to Malta from Naples on 17 April just as Doria's courier arrived. It was the Order's position, however, that the galleys could not be made ready for combat until the end of April.

Just prior to the squadron's departure on 1 May a messenger arrived at the Borgo from the two families living at Casal Chibir with a report that seventeen sails had been spotted several miles offshore appearing to be those of corsairs, as galliots have only a single mast and sail. By reason of number these were presumed to be Dragut's flotilla. At about the same time Doria sent a frigate into the Cantera Channel, which found it empty. Dragut had disappeared. With the assistance of ally Sheik Sala, Lord of Djerba, the corsairs had created an exit at the far end of Cantera Channel, dug at night and in a hurry. Mortified, Doria sailed immediately for Genoa, from where he proceeded to Barcelona with his twenty-seven galleys to embark Maximilian of Austria, son of future Holy Roman Emperor Ferdinand I. Dragut, still at war, headed for the southern coast of Italy in search of prey.[33]

The Turks were assembling men and munitions at a rate that worried the Holy See.[34] At Malta it was believed the Armada's objective had to be Malta, Gozo, or Tripoli because of the Hospitaller role in seizing Dragut's Mehedia, if not in the ensuing sack. Defensive measures were adopted. Grand Master and Council appointed Commanders Antonio Pescatore of Novara, Pierre de Gozon-Mélac of Provence, and Afonso de Solis of Castile as Sector Wardens for the walled city of Birgu with authority to order all things necessary for the sector's defence. Marshal Gaspard de Vallier de Chambéry was appointed Governor of Tripoli, succeeding Chancellor Pedro Nunnez de Herrera. Treasurer Jean de Neuchèze was assigned to Tripoli as Deputy Governor, to whom Vallier delegated wide-ranging authority. Commander Pedro de Herrera (not Pedro Nunnez de Herrera) was appointed local Treasurer. Grand Bailiff of Germany Georg Bombast von Hohenheim accompanied the new Governor as Inspector-General to ascertain military shortcomings at the Presidio. Vallier assumed command of the four galleys, flying his flag from Bernardo de Guimeran's *San Giovanni Battista*. Georg Bombast would command the squadron during its return to Malta. François de Piedefer did not make the journey; on the squadron's return he would again assume command not as Regent but as Captain of Galleys. Galley Captains Pedro de Felizes of *Santa Maria Maddelena* and Battista Bellomo of *San Michele Arcangelo* were assigned additional duties at Tripoli to sit in judgment over any differences or dissension between the former Governor and new Deputy Governor Neuchèze with orders to return to Malta one or the other. The squadron departed on 5 May and prowled the entire coast of North Africa between Cape Bon and Cape Misurata, capturing only a few Turks, the latter believing the Ottoman Armada's objective was Malta or Tripoli. The squadron reached Tripoli on 23 May, several days after the arrival of a galleonetto dispatched from Malta conveying munitions, foodstuffs, and fifty soldiers under command of Simão de Souza, who would become Captain of Cavalry. The returning Pedro Nunnez de Herrera succeeded to the dignity of Bailiff of Boveda on the death of incumbent Christobal de Solis Farfan, and was in turn succeeded as Chancellor by Lope Fernandez de Paz. Fernandez vacated the Bailiwick of Negroponte, to which Commander Don Dimas de Requesens succeeded. At the same time Catalan Commander Onofre de Monsuar succeeded to the dignity of Bailiff of Mallorca upon the death of Francisco Ferrer. Dragut, meanwhile, had in May been devastating the southern coasts of Calabria and Apulia (the entire sole of the Italian boot), so much so that the Viceroys of Naples and Sicily had united their squadrons under command of the absent Andrea Doria's cousin Antonio Doria, and were requesting the four galleys of Malta join them in pursuit of their elusive foe.[35]

Arriving at Malta early in June was Hospitaller Scipione Strozzi commanding a well-armed galley, the property of his father Pietro Strozzi. Soon to become a Marshal of France, Pietro was the elder brother of Prior of Capua Leone Strozzi. The younger Strozzi's lieutenant was Hospitaller Paolo del Rosso, like Strozzi of Florence, a man of letters who had translated the Order's statutes from Latin to Tuscan. The two of them had already concluded a successful year of corsair raids in the Levant and now wished to obtain a patent or letter of marque from Malta or to enter the Order's service flying the flag of Malta. Strozzi brought with him a letter from his uncle, then an Admiral of France, informing the Grand Master that the Ottoman Armada had not been invited to any French port, and therefore could not be expected to take course for France. While the French langues accepted the advice as well intended, the Langue of Italy and Turcopolier Nicholas Upton questioned the letter's veracity.

Grand Bailiff Georg Bombast returned to Malta with the squadron on 10 June. He reported that there were a large number of non-combatants at Tripoli who must be fed from reserve food stocks during any siege, most of whom were elderly, women, and children who should be relocated to Malta and Gozo. He also reported that the garrison was short of the requisite number of knights and soldiers. Pursuant to aforementioned vice-regal requests, Antonio Doria and Don Berenguer d'Oms de Requesens, with subordinate command of the Sicilian squadron, arrived at Malta on 18 June with fourteen galleys. Two of these were the property of Honouré Grimaldi, Lord of Monaco, and one of which was the property of Captain Domenico Varino, delivering the written specifics from the two viceroys. On 23 May, though, an Ottoman fleet said to have exceeded one hundred vessels in number had exited the Golden Horn, and the Hospitaller Council was at odds over preparation for a suspected Ottoman assault on Malta or Tripoli or participation in Doria's undertaking, now an excursion to North Africa to resupply and reinforce Mehedia taken from Dragut in September 1550. By ballot, however, it was decided to proceed with Doria, and on 20 June François Piedefer, as Captain of Galleys, was issued his instructions, Piedefer commanding *San Claudio*, Battista Bellomo commanding *San Michele Arcangelo*, Pedro Fernandez de Felizes commanding *Santa Maria Maddelena*, and Don Bernardo de Guimeran commanding *San Giovanni Battista*. The three squadrons departed the next day, first sailing to Sicily to load foodstuffs and infantry. There Juan de Vega warned of the proximate arrival of the Ottoman Armada under command of Sinan Pasha, not Sinan of Smyrna but Sinan, brother of Grand Vizier Rustem Pasha, both born Latin Christians in Venetian Dalmatia. The Viceroy, however, firmly believed the Armada to be en route to a rendezvous with the French Fleet at Toulon or Marseille, and that the ultimate purpose was recovery of Mehedia. Antonio Doria had accordingly been ordered to the support of Mehedia. Following his own instructions, Piedefer nevertheless decided to return to Malta. In late June the Ottoman Armada consisting of ninety-three galleys, thirty galliots, and twenty transports reached Preveza adjacent to Dragut's new sancak at Santa Maura. Dragut's flotilla became the Armada's vanguard. Venice believed its outposts in the Adriatic were the

Armada's objective.[36] Andrea Doria appeared oblivious. At Malta it was still believed the Armada's objective was Malta, Gozo, or Tripoli.[37]

Ten days later the heavily laden four-galley squadron returned to Malta having been escorted from Sicily to Malta by Antonio Doria and his fifteen galleys (one added in Sicily). Doria then proceeded through the Freo Channel between Gozo and Malta before continuing due west to the North African coast. Sailing at night west of Malta, the fifteen galleys were caught in the early stages of a storm. Requesens counselled returning to Gozo; Doria asserted his wish they remain on course. The sea gradually swelled and in the dark of an overcast night with wave tops appearing as islands, eight galleys were shipwrecked on the rocks of Lampedusa midway between Malta and Mehedia with great loss of life.[38] During June one year later most of the lost artillery would be recovered by the galleys of Malta with the assistance of Maltese divers, but there would be no recovery for families of the deceased.

Returning to Malta with the squadron were a number of knights smelling trouble. One of these was Nicholas de Villegagnon, a student of rhetoric, the classics and languages, fluent in ancient and modern Greek, Latin, Italian, and Spanish, a friend and contemporary of John Calvin, both having studied law at the University of Orleans, and a Hospitaller for twenty years. He was also a veteran of 1541's abysmal Siege of Algiers who had penned what is today the leading historical reference concerning the Siege, and he was an essential component of the French team in 1548 who successfully removed Mary, Queen of Scots from sequestration at Dumbarton to France. He arrived with a coterie of French knights and several companies of Calabrian soldiery, but was given a cold shoulder by Juan de Homedes because of his prominent position at Henry II's French Court.

At about this time Catalan Jorge de Sant Joan and his armed frigate returned from a reconnaissance mission initiated in February. The Ottoman Armada commanded by Sinanüddin Yusuf or Sinan Pasha assisted by former Barbarossa lieutenants Salih Reis and Dragut, 'the two most expert men of the sea',[39] was sighted at the foot of the Strait of Messina on 14 July headed south. There could be little doubt that Malta, Gozo, and/or Tripoli was the Armada's destination. On 16 July came news by way of Hospitaller Antonio Gotto, who arrived by fast barque from Syracuse: Augusta, Sicily, had been plundered and torched one day earlier when Juan de Vega was unable to return Dragut's Mehedia to the Ottomans without first consulting the Court at Madrid. War had then and there been declared in the name of the Sultan by Sinan Pasha. Given the Alliance between France and the Ottoman Empire, this declaration of war may be considered the outset of the Italian War of 1551–59 between France and the Ottomans on the one hand and the Holy Roman Empire of Charles V on the other. On 18 July 1551 a galleon commanded by Serving Brother Girolamo Pegulo reached Malta from Licata and Girgenti (Agrigento) with desperately needed food supplies. That same evening the Ottoman Armada was sighted from Malta in the number of 145 sails approaching on a moderate east wind. Of these, 105 were galleys, two were mahons, one was a galleon, and the remainder were galliots and support vessels. The Grand Master quickly convened a meeting of the Council where Turcopolier Nicholas Upton was appointed Captain-General of the island's 400 Maltese cavalry accompanied by an additional thirty well-mounted knights. Don Bernardo de Guimeran was appointed to command of an infantry force composed of 100 knights and 300 arquebusiers.

That same evening advance elements of the Ottoman Armada entered Marsa Muscietto on the north side of the Sciberras Peninsula that forms the north shore of Grand Harbour. Ottoman reconnaissance parties of janissaries were put ashore on both sides of Marsa Muscietto and skirmishes with Hospitaller cavalry and infantry followed immediately. Guimeran's infantry even took Sinan's Royal Galley under arquebus fire and forced her withdrawal. Nevertheless, both Dragut and Sinan came ashore. From the Peninsula they had a clear view of Castle Saint Angelo and the walled city of Birgu. Counselled by Corsa Reis, brother of deceased King of Tagiora Cairadeno and a former captive at Malta, Dragut is reported to have concluded that both Saint Angelo and Birgu could be taken but not with the ground force presently embarked. The two admirals turned their attention to Notabile, formerly and currently Mdina, in the centre of the island. Notabile was governed by Bailiff of Naples Giorgio Adorno, and on news of arrival of the Ottoman Armada he had solicited the assistance of Nicholas de Villegagnon. Villegagnon and the six knights with whom he had arrived at Malta responded. At Mdina he so deployed Hospitallers and inhabitants that the Ottomans soon abandoned their assault. The principal street of the walled city of Mdina, Triq il Villegaignon, still bears his name.[40]

While the foregoing was transpiring, the Master Gunner aboard Scipione Strozzi's galley was laying punishing fire from his bow cannon on Turkish parties exposing themselves on the Sciberras Peninsula. Of Hospitallers there were no combat fatalities but Turcopolier Nicholas Upton, too long exposed to the elements while wearing breastplate and helmet, died of sunstroke. As the Ottoman Armada withdrew from Marsa Muscietto to the north along the coast of Malta, cavalry and infantry forces followed and were present when the Armada reached Saint Paul's Bay, where an enemy force intent on seizing Notabile was put ashore. Harassed by sniper fire, this force plundered and burned as it made its way inland but was stopped in its tracks at the approaches to Notabile. While the role of Villegagnon was paramount, there were others who were notable in the city's defence. These included Paolo Chiesa of the Lombard, senior knight present at Notabile and Lieutenant to Governor Giorgio Adorno. He was a vital cog in overall defence. Scipione Strozzi was another, bringing with him a part of his galley crew. Non-Hospitaller Girolamo d'Allerona, a citizen of Notabile who had hired a company of soldiers commanded by non-Hospitaller Captain Varga. Geronimo Sagra of Valencia, responsible for the Greek section of the city wall, laid a withering cannon fire on the valley approach used by the enemy. Gomez Perez de Patiño was responsible for the wall nearest the Magistral Palace. Aleramo Conti della Lengueglia was responsible for defence of one of the two monasteries. Raffaello Salvago of Genoa commanded the local cavalry, while others confronted the enemy during its approach and later from within the walled city. There were extraordinary contributions, as well, from Villegagnon's coterie of French knights: Olivier d'Aulx of Aquitaine, Nicolas de Feuquerolles-Cantelou of the Langue of France, Joachim Poussard de l'Hommelière of Aquitaine, Jean de Gaillardbois-Marconville of the Langue of France, Louis de Belloy of the Langue of France, and Pierre des Boves of Champagne, all of whom ensured Villegagnon's orders were carried out properly. Through their joint effort the siege of Notabile was lifted during the night of 21–22 July after a mere two days. In the process the Ottomans left behind 300 dead and captured against no Christian fatalities. The Ottomans also dropped into the sea of Saint Paul's Bay a huge siege cannon and a large number of 60lb iron cannon balls, all of which, cannon and shot, would be recovered for the future defence of Mdina.[41]

The Ottoman Armada clawed its way the 5 miles from Saint Paul's Bay to Gozo, towing sailing vessels in the absence of wind. There on 22 July 1551 its ground force was again put ashore. At about the same time, Dragut galliots on patrol seized two Maltese vessels, the first bound from Licata, Sicily, to Malta with a cargo of foodstuffs and with news of the arrival or imminent arrival at Messina of Andrea Doria's Imperial Armada seeking to locate the Ottoman Armada. A copy of this news was delivered to the frigate of Catalan Jorge de Sant Joan, who successfully carried it to Malta. The second vessel seized was a small sailing barque dispatched at the earlier request of Gozo Governor Galatian de Sessé carrying a badly needed cargo of gunpowder as well as a number of cannoneers. Why this second supply had not been sent during the weeks of suspicion of Ottoman intent, rather than during the Ottoman presence, was an issue that would come back to haunt the Grand Master. In the event, the Ottomans knew the citadel or walled town of Rabat was short of munitions. They also knew that more than 5,000 Gozitans would seek shelter within 270m of weak walls without flanks or terrepleins, of whom a mere 700 would be combatants including militia. On the other hand, because Sinan's business was the conquest of Tripoli and not of Rabat, Dragut's conquest needed to be completed quickly or the attempt would be abandoned, as was the siege of Notabile. This, too, would haunt the Grand Master. *But for a few days more.* Siege cannon began firing on Friday, 24 July. Two days later there was a breach in the wall. But for the effectiveness of a lone English cannoneer, it would be over. But he was soon dead. That same day it was over. The citadel and the refugees within surrendered unconditionally. More than 5,000 Gozitans were carried into slavery aboard ships of the Ottoman Armada, which departed Gozo on the final day of July bound for Tripoli. Forty-five fortunate individuals survived to tell the tale. It would be 150 years before the population of Gozo again equalled that of 1551. No comparable number of years is available concerning Mehedia and its 7,000 enslaved by Christians a bare ten months earlier.[42]

Chapter X

Juan de Homedes y Coscon 1551–53

The Grand Master dispatched Bernardo de Guimeran in a fast frigate on the tail of the Ottoman Armada with orders to warn Tripoli if at all possible. It was not possible and Guimeran was pursued all the way back to Malta. Appearing at Malta shortly thereafter were two French galleys and a galliot escorting Gabriel de Luetz, Baron d'Aramón and French Ambassador to the Porte. He was under order of French King Henry II to make known to Sinan Pasha the specious argument that the Order of Malta and its possessions had not been identified as enemies in the Franco–Ottoman alliance against the Habsburgs, and d'Aramón followed the Ottomans to Tripoli for the purpose of making his case. Meanwhile, an investigation into the loss at Gozo was initiated with the appointment of three Commissioners: Commanders Francesco Nibbia of Novara, Francisco Faria of Portugal, and Jean de Condé de Vendières of the Langue of France. This Commission eventually exonerated the enslaved Galatian de Sessé of culpability, acknowledging the weak garrison, Rabat's aged walls, insufficiency of munitions, and other factors that indirectly raised questions about the competency of the Grand Master. Hospitallers Francisco Maldonado and Melchor d'Eguaras, the only other surviving knights at Gozo, were similarly absolved. Both would be liberated from slavery in 1556. Sessé would die in slavery. Two other Hospitaller commanders inadequately identified by Bosio, an Italian and a Portuguese, lost their lives during the siege.[1]

On 5 August 1551 a letter was received from Marshal de Vallier stating that the Ottoman Armada had put troops ashore on the beaches of Zuara, 60 miles west of Tripoli. That same date, the enemy armada appeared 2 miles off Tripoli. While the armada remained in position off Tripoli, Sinan Pasha proceeded to Tagiora, where he was royally received by Mourad Aga. From Tagiora a mounted herald carrying a white flag proceeded to Tripoli, where he planted outside of the city walls a stick bearing a letter. The letter recounted the Sultan's distress at violations of the truce between empires and demanded over Sinan's signature that in return for liberty Tripoli be vacated by a single-file exodus of all Christians bearing nothing but clothing worn. Vallier replied after consultation with his own lieutenants that only the Grand Master and Council at Malta could authorise a withdrawal from Tripoli, and short of that Tripoli would be defended to the last man standing. The reply was attached to the same stick, collected by the same herald, and returned to Sinan Pasha.

The enemy armada almost immediately began debarking a ground force with siege artillery. A second letter from Vallier was received at Malta on 8 August recounting the foregoing. The letter also prayed for a storm to disperse the Ottomans to distant ports. The Grand Master's thoughts turned not to what might be done to succour Tripoli, or even to what might have been done earlier, but to the possibility that Malta would be next to feel the Sultan's wrath. He considered evacuation to Sicily of non-combatants, but failed to act. He penned a letter to Emperor Charles V in Germany, conveyed by Don Francisco de Zanoguera, complaining of damages already done to Malta and Gozo and about to be done to Tripoli, and pled for succour. He also wrote in the same vein to the Viceroys of Sicily and Naples, and to Andrea Doria. These letters were conveyed by Captain of Galleys François de Piedefer who departed Malta on 12 August, the four galleys towing for lack of wind the Grand Master's own galleon and other vessels bound for Licata to load grain. From Licata, Piedefer was to proceed to Syracuse and Messina in order to press Viceroy Juan de Vega on the Emperor's responsibility to Tripoli and to warn of the Ottoman Armada's potential descent on Malta. Reflecting this latter concern, Commander Alonso de Lorenzana of Castile was soon dispatched to Sicily for the purpose of hiring two companies of Italian infantry from other than Calabria, each company comprised of 300 infantry.[2]

During the foregoing hand-wringing the Ottomans had put their ground force ashore to the east of Tripoli and its natural harbour, circumvented the harbour, and on 8 August begun to build artillery emplacements for their siege cannon opposite the south face of the Presidio fortress, itself in the south-east corner of the walled city. Tripoli's strongly constructed harbour fortress was thus ignored, while walls constructed to deter mounted Arab cavalry could be taken under fire from a direction in which most of the city's forty bronze cannon could not be brought to bear. Having made landfall at Tagiora and not at Tripoli, French Ambassador d'ARamón was redirected to the Armada, where with cannon salutes from both parties he made his way to the Royal flagship for discussions with Sinan Pasha concerning the fate of Tripoli that would prove fruitless. Marshal de Vallier, curious about the saluting, sent out at night a mounted party of his 200 loyal Moors of Xercia, which fell upon enemy trenches and returned with two captured janissaries who disclosed arrival of the French ambassador. Discussions continued a second day between Pasha and Ambassador but proved equally fruitless. Sinan refused to lift the Siege of Tripoli. During the next three days, 9, 10, and 11 August, thirty-six pieces of large siege cannon were hauled by enslaved Christian oarsmen to their new emplacements, thirty pointed at the Presidio, six on higher ground to fire over the walls of the Presidio.[3] All of this was accomplished under fire from resolute defenders, an Hospitaller gunner taking off the left arm of Kambil Bey[3] commanding Ottoman artillery, who came close to losing his life. Other defenders, not-so-resolute Calabrese infantry, began to abandon their posts. Confronting these rebels, Hospitaller Francesco Valperga of Turin[4] was gravely wounded by one of them. Meanwhile, emplaced batteries, each of six Ottoman cannon, commenced firing at both walls of the Presidio and at adjacent city walls. While battering of these walls continued there was also an assault on the sea wall by 4,000 Ottomans with scaling ladders brought ashore in skiffs and similar small boats. The assault was not successful. Serving Brother Jacques des Roches of the Langue of Auvergne commanding the harbour fortress would later be knighted for valour for his part in defence of the sea walls.[5]

Also during this period Simão de Sousa of Portugal and the Langue of Castile commanding Moorish cavalry sortied with thirty-four handpicked horsemen through the Gate of Saint George. These fell upon Turks separated from the besieging force, one taken alive. During the sortie scaling ladders were noticed, and the following night Sousa exited with sixty foot, returning with two isolated ladders of many more behind enemy trenches. The Ottomans were readying to scale the walls. Orders had been issued, according to the most recent captive, to take no

Christian alive other than Marshal de Vallier. Soon a breach in the city wall adjacent to the Presidio was opened more than 20ft in width. Within the walls those Calabrese soldiers yet to rebel threw down their arms and refused to fight. These were 200 of the 360 soldiers expected to defend the walls, not the 200 mounted Moorish allies. Vallier consulted with Lieutenant Governor Guillaume Coppier, Cavalry Commander Simão de Sousa, Treasurer Don Pedro de Herrera, and others of his lieutenants, and after two fruitless pleas to the rebels, decided to treat with the enemy.

On 13 August Serving Brother Pierre de Favars of the Langue of Auvergne climbed onto the wall with a white flag and asked for talks. A ceasefire was agreed while Commander Juan Antonio Fuster of Mallorca and a Spanish representative of the soldiers named Guevara were sent as ambassadors to the enemy camp. They asked Sinan Pasha for the terms accorded by Sultan Suleiman to survivors of the Siege of Rhodes; to wit, unmolested exit to waiting ships with side-arms of the entire garrison with the exception of allied Moors, who were to have unmolested passage to the territory of the King of Tunis with their mounts. After protracted haggling with Sinan Pasha himself, who initially demanded reimbursement of the expense of the Armada's deployment from Constantinople, then agreed to the release of only 300 defenders, and after an interruption with renewed hostilities on the part of the Ottomans, these terms were accepted absent side-arms, but limited to 300, a number coinciding with the capacity of the three French vessels present. These terms were warranted by Ottoman lieutenants Dragut, Salih Reis, and Mourad Aga. Hostages were exchanged, an unidentified Turk said to be close to Sinan on the part of besiegers, and Marshal de Vallier, on the part of the besieged, escorted to Sinan's Pavilion by Marc-Antoine Clavet de Montfort of Auvergne.

During the night of 13 August the 200 allied Moors led by Sheik Ben Alchi of Almanzor attempted a mounted escape through the Gate of Saint George. Fifty of them did not make it. One hundred mutinous Calabrians were selected to remain at Tripoli and would be enslaved with 500 non-combatant residents of the city. The balance of 300 including 30 Hospitallers, 100 Calabrians, and 170 others mostly Sicilian soldiers with a handful of Christian non-combatants exited Tripoli on the morning of 14 August. The gunner Juan de Chabas[6] who severed the arm of Kambil Bey, however, was singled out, mutilated, and executed in violation of capitulation terms. The rest were remanded to the custody of Ambassador d'ARamón, without whom the same outcome would be doubtful, and embarked aboard his two French galleys and single galliot, which would return them to Malta. With the victory Sinan Pasha, Mourad, and Dragut took part in a fiesta organised at the Governor's summer house outside the walls organised by Ambassador d'ARamón. There Dragut learned Mourad had by the Sultan been appointed Governor of Tripoli and of Tagiora. Grand Vizier Rustem Pasha had separately made Tripoli a fief of his brother Sinan Pasha. On this advice Dragut, 'enraged, hoisted his personal red, white, and blue colours, and sailed away'.[7]

Four days later, during the evening of 18 August, the French ships departed Tripoli bound for Malta. Sixty miles out of Tripoli, however, a strong north wind forced them to return whence they had come. It was not until Sunday, 23 August that Malta was reached late at night. From the harbour mouth ARamón sent a lieutenant in by skiff to announce their presence. And the loss of Tripoli. According to *Bosio III-315*, Grand Master Juan de Homedes was initially stunned speechless by the news and could not respond to the lieutenant, but then contemptuously refused to lower the chain to the galley port between Birgu and Saint Michael until the morning when he had assembled the Council and decided how to respond. Parisot de la Valette, however, took an oared frigate full of bread, wine, fresh water, and other provisions to the anchored vessels and removed Marshal de Vallier, knights, and other refugees to the shore, where they passed the night in Birgu. The port was opened the following morning, but the French ambassador was received by Parisot de la Valette and other French knights rather than by the Grand Master. His galliot under command of Hospitaller Michel de Seurre de Lumigny was dispatched to France to report to King Henry II what had transpired, and on 26 August ARamón resumed his voyage to Constantinople.

Grand Master and Council meanwhile refused to hear from or even to confront Marshal de Vallier. There was also a public outcry at the loss of so many Rhodiots and Maltese among non-combatant residents of Tripoli enslaved; tinkers, tailors, cobblers, and municipal workers. Jacques de Roches, permitted by Sinan to exit the Presidio with honours, argued that absent deceit or treachery it would have been impossible to lose Tripoli. All the while Vallier and most other refugee knights were incarcerated without a hearing as debate raged. Finally, the same

Committee of Investigation that had inquired into the Gozo tragedy was appointed to look into this one: Commanders Francesco Nibbia of Novara, Francisco Faria of Portugal, and Jean de Condé de Vendières of the Langue of France. Christoph von Octum of the Langue of Germany was appointed an alternate, while non-Hospitaller Agostino Combo, Maltese Doctor of Law, was to provide legal advice. Vallier and all others under investigation were incarcerated so none might speak with another. While the investigation was moving ahead François de Piedefer and the four galleys were recalled from Sicily, as was Alonso de Lorenzana of Castile, dispatched to Sicily for the purpose of hiring two companies of Italian infantry. Don Bernardo de Guimeran, similarly dispatched to Sicily to hire two companies of Spanish infantry, was likewise recalled, all because of the presumed threat to Malta represented by the Ottoman Armada.[8]

Guimeran and Laurenzin reached Malta early in September with one company of 300 good Spanish and Italian soldiers sprinkled with French hired by Guimeran. A partial company of 200 infantry arrived soon thereafter aboard a small Neapolitan ship. These infantry were hired at Rome by Hospitaller Julián de Aguero of Aragon for and at the expense of the municipal authorities of Notabile and the University of Malta. Bailiff of Naples and Governor of Notabile Giorgio Adorno remedied at great personal risk the inadequate flow of drinking water to Notabile by reopening an ancient Roman underground aqueduct transporting water derived from sweating rock, perhaps the purest of all drinking water. As a sector warden, Parisot de la Valette relocated tenants living in Birgu homes close to Castle Saint Angelo and levelled the vacated houses to provide defenders with a clear field of fire. Giovan Francesco Langosto de Conti della Motta of Vercelli was dispatched to Lombardia to acquire large numbers of corselets, pikes, arquebuses, helmets, and other armament. Giustiniano Giustiniani of a leading Venetian family and thirty years an Hospitaller was honoured with the title of Lieutenant to the Grand Master and permitted to wear the Grand Cross only to signify the esteem in which he was held.

On 24 September 1551 the frigate of Stefano Sifugno was sent to the North African coast to ascertain the whereabouts of the Ottoman Armada and returned with eight Turkish and Moorish captives taken near Tagiora. Sifugno also returned with certain news that the Ottoman

Armada had departed for home by way of Sapienza and Modon in the Morea.[9]

Leone Strozzi, having resigned from French service, arrived at Malta on 3 October. He did not initially enter the main port for fear his departure from French service would not be believed, but instead anchored at Marsa Muscietto. Juan de Homedes and the Order's Council dispatched Hospitaller Francisco Martinez de Casseda Navarro to Juan de Vega, Viceroy of Sicily, seeking approval for Strozzi's return to service with the Religion. Not wishing to remain idle in the interim, Strozzi, with three galleys including that of his nephew Scipione Strozzi, spent the final months of the year in the Levant raiding Turks. Not resupplied with provisions and munitions at Malta or elsewhere, he was forced to plunder not only Turkish vessels but also those belonging to Christian merchants. In company with Dominico Gondi of Florence he seized two ships in the waters of Venetian Candia (Crete), *Narancera* and another commanded by Simone Belloca.

The Spanish had meanwhile detained a galley owned by Hospitaller Ardouin de Castillon de Beynes, which departed Marseille in company with Strozzi under licensed command of Pierre de Beaulac Trébons, a veteran of the Great Siege of Rhodes. Eventually released, she brought with her many knights responding to a summons stemming from the earlier Ottoman threat.[10]

The Committee of Investigation into the loss of Tripoli completed its work early in November. Having studied the sworn testimony of eighty witnesses over two months, the Committee concluded the loss was not attributable to deceit or treachery but rather to insufficient courage. The Committee recommended that Marshal Gaspard de Vallier, whose duty it was to not abandon Tripoli without authority of Grand Master and Council, be stripped of his Habit and remanded to trial by secular authorities as responsible for the enslavement of 600 persons. Commander Juan Antonio Fuster of Mallorca was found to have exceeded his authority by treating with the enemy, and the Committee similarly recommended he be stripped of his Habit and remanded to trial by secular authorities on the same charge. Captain of Cavalry Simão de Souza and Treasurer Don Pedro de Herrera were found guilty of failing to resist the actions of Vallier and Fuster, and the Committee recommended they be stripped of their Habit. The Committee concluded they had insufficient testimony to reach a conclusion respecting Lieutenant Governor Guillaume Cossier, Marc-Antoine Clavet de Montfort, Marc de la Goutte of Auvergne, Fernando Nietto of Castile, and Serving Brother Pierre de Favars. Judgements respecting these individuals were referred to higher authority, and all would be declared innocent and released from confinement on 8 April 1552. A hastily convened General Assembly of Hospitallers present at Malta endorsed the Committee's recommendations on 4 November. Vallier, Fuster, Souza, and Herrera were stripped of their Habit, and all of the aforementioned individuals were returned to custody. Vallier and Fuster would be found guilty in secular court, Fuster would be condemned to death. Vallier would be saved from the same fate only by the informed legal defence of Nicholas de Villegagnon, arguing 'la place a été perdue par la négligence et l'avarice de ceux qui auraient du la fortifier' ('the place was lost by the avarice and greed of those responsible for its fortification').

Vallier was instead to be confined for life. He would appeal against the court's decision to Papal authority in 1553 but it was upheld. In consideration of his long suffering he would be released from custody during the Magistracy of Jean Parisot de la Valette, reappointed Bailiff of Lango, and his Habit and Grand Cross restored. At the outset he was succeeded as Marshal by Pierre des Roches.[11] Friends and family of the enslaved must have wondered why those in authority had not accepted Ottoman terms at the outset: in return for liberty that Tripoli be vacated by a single-file exodus of all Christians bearing nothing but clothing worn.

By letter dated 17 November 1551 to King Henry II of France, Grand Master Juan de Homedes absolved Gabriel de Luetz, Baron d'Aramón , of any complicity in the loss of Tripoli. This letter was placed in the care of the King's emissary Monsieur du Belloy, who then returned to France in the company of Nicholas de Villegagnon and his coterie of six Hospitaller knights aboard a ship of Marseille. Belloy was meanwhile sought by Viceroy of Sicily Juan de Vega as a spy. The ship was seized in Corsican waters by Imperial galleys lying in wait and escorted to Genoa. At Genoa Villegagnon was not kindly received in the belief the French were responsible for loss of Tripoli. He penned a letter in Latin to Emperor Charles V citing the letter of Grand Master Homedes absolving the French of complicity in the loss of Tripoli. He, his coterie, and Belloy were all eventually released on warrant of Grand Master Homedes.[12]

Towards the end of the year another emissary arrived from the French Court. It was his business to ensure a place in Hospitaller ranks for the new-born son of French King Henry II and his mistress Janet Stewart, Lady Fleming, an illegitimate daughter of King James IV of Scotland then governess to her half-niece, Mary Queen of Scots. At an appropriate time the new-born son, Henri de Valois, was to be appointed Hospitaller Grand Prior of France. Meanwhile, the vacant dignity of Bailiff of Caspe was conferred on Commander Juan Miguel de Castellar of the Langue of Aragon. Grand Commander Antoine de Jaminy died, and Claude de Gruel-Laborel was appointed his successor.[13]

The four galleys of the squadron wintered at Palermo and Messina, where they were readily available to run foodstuffs to Malta. Also in Sicily was Leone Strozzi at Syracuse with his three galleys and a captured Turkish sailing ship. Upon arrival at Syracuse he had been greeted by Don Ernando de Vega, son of the Viceroy, as befitted a former Admiral of France. Vega was able to confirm the Viceroy approved Strozzi's return to the Convent, and on 3 January Strozzi did return to Malta. At a meeting of the Council on 8 January 1552 Strozzi was appointed to lead a Board of Survey to ascertain necessary improvements to the island's defences. Other members of the Board were Grand Bailiff Georg von Bombast, Lieutenant Marshal Louis de Lastic, and Captain Pedro Pardo, Spanish Engineer, arrived only two days earlier at the behest of Viceroy Juan de Vega. Recognising the optimum plan for improvement of defences included construction of an entirely new city on the Sciberras Peninsula (modern Valletta) beyond the present means of the Order, the Board turned its attention to more practical improvements. Among these was construction of the planned fortress at the tip of the Sciberras Peninsula to be called Fort Saint Elmo, which would not only assist in control of Grand Harbour but would be the Order's only control over the anchorage at Marsa Muscietto on the north side of the peninsula. The Board's second recommendation was the construction of another new fortress on the island/peninsula of Saint Michael forming the western side of the galley port. A fortress on Saint Michael would not only protect the exposed side of the galley port but would protect the same side of Birgu and Castle Saint Angelo. Grand Master Homedes laid the cornerstone of Fort Saint Elmo on 14 January 1552 with the entire Convent present. Construction ran in three shifts preceding each of the three meals, overseen by Strozzi, Bombast, and Lastic in that order. The cornerstone for Fort Saint Michael would similarly be laid on 8 May, while further improvement of the defences of Birgu was also undertaken. All of this weighed on the Common Treasury, and the Convent responded with individual contributions from many Hospitallers. Emissaries seeking financial support were also dispatched to mainland commanderies. Charles d'Urre de Tessières was dispatched to France for that purpose, Girolamo Avogadro to Italy, Don Francisco de Zanoguera to Spain, and Cristóvão de Cernache to Portugal. Don Bernardo de Guimeran was dispatched to the Emperor in Germany. Each of these emissaries departed Malta in February 1552.[13]

Jacques des Roches of Auvergne was appointed Fort Saint Michael's first Captain in recognition of his performance at Tripoli, and upon the fort's completion he would be appointed Governor. At this point the three Hospitaller members of the Board of Survey were lodging within the three construction zones: Bombast at Birgu, Strozzi at Elmo, and Lastic at Fort Saint Michael, where an external terreplein was under construction. The oarsmen of Strozzi's three galleys were hired as construction labourers at a cost to the Common Treasury of 500 gold scudos per month. The galley squadron was recalled from Sicily for the same purpose. Planning was set in motion to hire a responsible number of Italian soldiers to garrison the two new forts in the spring as well as for the purchase of necessary artillery. François Piedefer, having completed Claude de la Sengle's term as Captain of Galleys, was succeeded as Regent by senior captain Battista Bellomo, who retained command of *San Michele Arcangelo*. Bernardino Scaglia succeeded Piedefer in command of *San Claudio*. The four galleys were then sent to Lampedusa as escort for four Maltese grippos, there to take on cargoes of timber and wood faggots for construction at Malta.[14]

By 18 March Fort Saint Elmo had taken on enough substance that Leone Strozzi was elected its first Governor. Grand Bailiff Georg Bombast assigned the idle caravan of knights to barracks at Birgu, and to the table of Nicolas de Blanchelayne of Auvergne, where they were fed at Common Treasury expense, all for the purpose of accelerating construction at Birgu. When the galleys returned from Lampedusa on the first of April, their salutes were returned by Fort Saint Elmo.[15]

April arrived with rumours of Ottoman Armada activity. Grand Master and Council dispatched Jerónimo da Cunha of Portugal by fast frigate to the Levant for facts to be obtained from the Order's agents in that part of the world. Don Pedro de Aldovera of Castile was appointed Captain of Arms and Governor of Notabile, succeeding Giorgio Adorno. At the request of Notabile's municipal government and of the University of Malta, Julián de Agüero of Aragon was for a second time sent to Naples and Rome to hire 500 infantry for the Presidio of that city. Engineer Captain Pedro Pardo was also dispatched to Notabile to ascertain defensive shortcomings. Hospitaller Don Fernando de Alarcón, Governor of Milazzo, Sicily, and son of Spanish explorer Hernando de Alarcón, said to be the first non-Native to navigate the Colorado River and to set eyes on California, was dispatched to Viceroy of Sicily Don Juan de Vega to discuss the apportionment of grain stocks. Alarcón was also to purchase artillery and to hire the gunners needed to fire the artillery. Commander Luis de Rengifo of Castile was sent to Sicily to hire capable soldiers and returned with a company of 500 infantry, while Giovan Antonio Bisballe of Messina and Bernardino d'Abenante of Cosenza each returned with a company of 300 infantry. Two knights from each langue were deputised to blanket the island and to enrol every male capable of bearing arms between the ages of 18 and 70, and to arm those who had no arms. For each company so enrolled two professional soldiers were to be assigned. Finally, 3,000 noncombatants were to be evacuated to Syracuse. For this purpose several grippos and the galley squadron were assigned, Battista Bellomo commanding. These departed Malta on 20 April 1552, the grippos under tow in the absence of wind. Early the following morning before daybreak, the convoy having traversed the Malta Channel and nearing Sicily, a large flame was sighted in the direction of Cape Passero accompanied by the sound of artillery fire. A council of war was convened. Because oarsmen were exhausted from towing heavily laden grippos for almost twenty-four hours, and because the galleys were charged with the safe transport of non-combatants, galleys and grippos took shelter under the Tower (fortress) of Pozzallo, 13 miles west of Cape Passero, the grippos anchoring and the galleys beaching. A body of horsemen passing by let it be known that a large number of Ottomans had trapped a lone merchantman at Cape Passero. Crews, passengers, and oarsmen repaired to the Tower carrying portable items of value including sails and small artillery and set up to defend the fortified ravelin some distance from the Tower.[15]

At break of day Bellomo discovered eleven Turkish galleys and a brigantine had struggled all night against a single sailing vessel still burning. The galleys and grippos were likewise sighted by the Turks. Hospitaller Mateo Cano, an Aragonese Chaplain captive aboard one of the Turkish vessels, escaped in the confusion and walked to Pozzalo. The sailing vessel was a Maltese ship bound from Naples to Malta on order of Antonio Pignone, the Order's Receiver in Naples, with a cargo of saltpetre, salted meats, and other provisions. She was done for. The galleys and grippos were also in great peril. The enemy was Salih Reis, a Greek from the plain of Troy and brother-in-law of the deceased Barbarossa brothers, en route to assume the position of Ottoman Beylerbey or Viceroy of Algiers. For reasons of his own, the new viceroy ignored the eight Maltese vessels and took to the sea. The grippos reached Syracuse and the galleys returned safely to Malta, where they remained into June.[15]

Early in June 1552 Jerónimo da Cunha and his fast frigate returned from the Levant with agent advice. The Ottoman Armada was headed for the Adriatic to storm the shores of the Kingdom of Naples, which border that sea. On 20 June Cunha was again sent out to verify his advice, bound for Otranto and Corfu, this time aboard the frigate of non-Hospitaller Cola Aniello. He had orders that should the Ottoman Armada be found in the Gulf of Venice (the Adriatic) he was to put to the nearest shore and send a courier with the news. Should the Armada put artillery ashore to besiege some city in Apulia, Cunha was to return to Malta, where the burdensome expense of unneeded hired soldiery could immediately be relieved. Or, of course, should the Armada be bound for Malta or for North Africa, he was to return immediately to Malta.[16]

Again under command of Sinan Pasha, the Ottoman Armada consisting of 120 vessels, mostly galleys, in fact on 6 July 1552 turned northbound into the Strait of Messina. With this confirmation of the ruptured peace between Ottoman ally France and the Holy Roman Empire came cries from Reggio Calabria to Cape Vaticano spreading north for a popular revolt against the formerly French Kingdom of Naples, where attempts by unpopular Spanish Viceroy Don Pedro Álvarez de Toledo to introduce the Spanish Inquisition had already brought Neapolitans into the streets in protest. On these developments Hospitaller Don Fernando de Alarcón, Governor of Milazzo, dispatched a frigate under command of Genovese Captain Fantone, who brought the news to Malta on 9 July.

Jerónimo da Cunha, who had been tailing the Armada, brought news on 30 July of the separate sacking of many locales in Neapolitan Calabria and Terra di Lavoro north of Calabria, particularly at Scalia, Policastro Bussentino, and Pisciotta, each successively nearer Naples itself. These depredations were the work not of Sinan and the Ottoman Armada but of Dragut in command of his squadron of Djerba corsairs accompanied by Salih Reis with his own eleven galleys and brigantine. The two units had rendezvoused off the Gulf of Naples on or about 10 July. Cunha brought with him a somewhat dated letter from Hospitaller Ambassador to the Holy See Claude de la Sengle with 'certain' news that the Ottoman Armada was en route to a rendezvous with the French Fleet at Piombino in Tuscany. The French Fleet, according to Sengle, was commanded by rebel Prince of Salerno Ferrante di Sanseverino, who following a series of clashes with Don Pedro de Toledo in opposition to the institution of Holy Inquisition tribunals in the Kingdom of Naples, had fled the country for France.

The Ottomans, however, expected the rendezvous to take place off Naples as that Kingdom was the subject of joint planning, but none took place at either location. The Ottomans probed north as far as Ponza, while the French had yet to depart France. Returning to the Gulf of Naples, Dragut despoiled Massa Lubrense and Sorrento, enslaving masses of the local population. Nevertheless comfortable at Malta, especially with seven galleys including the three of Leone Strozzi, Grand Master and Council donated the laid-up and altered galley *Santa Barbara* to Boschetto Gardens, Malta's only wooded area cultivated since arrival of the Order in 1530. In addition to the remaining seven galleys the Order had at its disposition the Sicilian-flag galliot of Hospitaller Battista Agliata, a fusta the property of Paolo Micciolo, a brigantine belonging to Rosso of Piombino, plus nine other oared vessels. So many shallow-draft vessels, in fact, Grand Master and Council began to consider an assault on Mourad Aga's Zuara between Tripoli and Djerba.[17]

At the outset of August 1552 the Ottoman Armada was unsuccessfully besieging the Kingdom of Naples' Gaeta, 20 nautical miles east of Cape Circe, and successfully laying waste to the countryside all around while abducting ill-fated inhabitants. Andrea Doria, then 86 years of age, had meanwhile moved south from Genoa with forty Imperial galleys and 3,000 embarked German infantry for the purpose of relieving Naples, which was beset by its own citizens within and by the Ottomans without. At Ostia at the mouth of the Tiber he was informed that the Ottoman Armada was divided between mainland Monte Circeo and the island of Ponza; he recklessly decided to sail between the two. Sighted by the enemy, he was assailed on 4 August from right and left by overwhelming numbers. Doria abandoned his vanguard of seven galleys, which was captured by Dragut, and turned back with his main body to relative safety at Ostia. There were 700 hired Germans embarked aboard the seven captured galleys, including their commanding officer, a nephew of Cristoforo Madruzzo, Cardinal of Trent. With this victory, Sinan Pasha, notwithstanding opposition by Dragut, abandoned Neapolitan waters for the Levant in as much as he had not yet been joined by the French Fleet, and planned coordinated operations had missed essential milestones. Dragut, even so and undismayed, continued his raids, pausing at Reggio to demand ransoms of 12,000 scudos for the German commander plus 20 scudos for each of the 700 other Germans plus return of his nephew Hisar Reis captured two years earlier at Mehedia.[18]

Seemingly oblivious of the Ottoman Armada's new direction, a decision had been reached at Malta to undertake an assault on Mourad Aga's Zuara for the ignoble purposes of employing idle soldiery and to acquire slave labour for construction at Malta. There is no report of discussion or objection to this radical deviation from past practice. It is one practice to send enemy combatants to the oars and quite another to enslave non-combatants. Battista Bellomo was temporarily replaced as Regent of the Galleys by Parisot de la Valette, and the squadron readied to proceed in company with Leone Strozzi. The Order's standard was hoisted aboard Strozzi's private capitana. Strozzi's *La Porsiada* was commanded by Hospitaller Francisco Martinez de Casseda, while his *Sainte-Barbara* was commanded by his Hospitaller nephew Scipione Strozzi. Of the Order's galleys, *San Michele Arcangelo* was commanded by Bellomo, *San Claudio* was commanded by Valette, *San Giovanni Battista* by Miguel de Aldovera, and *Santa Maria Maddelena* by Pedro Fernandez de Felizes.

The assault flotilla sailed from Marsa Muscietto with these and a dozen smaller ships on 6 August 1552, 300 knights[19] and 900 hired soldiers embarked. Strozzi took the flotilla first to Gozo, and from there grabbed an Imbat or north wind, which carried him in two days to the African coast. There the same wind prevented him from debarking for six days. Some must have wondered whether their landing force would be welcomed, but trusted in the wisdom of their leaders. During the night of 13–14 August, however, Strozzi put ashore 15 miles from Zuara 1,200 men divided into three units. The first, commanded by Bernardo de Guimeran, consisted of 300 hand-picked arquebusiers, the more experienced of the hired soldiery, preceded by hand-picked knights including galley first-officers commanded by Strozzi's nephew Scipione, who would all be lost. The second unit consisted of the corps of Hospitallers commanded by Hospitaller Captain-General Parisot de la Valette assisted by Charles d'Urre de Tessieres with future grand masters Jean l'Evesque de la Cassière and Hugues Loubenx de Verdalle carrying the Order's standards. The third unit consisted of mercenary infantry hired in Italy commanded by three Hospitallers: Luis Rengifo of Castile, Giovan Antonio Bisballe of Messina, and Marzio d'Abenante of Cocenza. Every soldier had been guaranteed two scudos blood money for each slave delivered to Malta. These were guided in their approach to Zuara by several Zuari Moors, slaves at Malta who for this had been promised freedom. Leone Strozzi, too, was in the van.

Encamped Arabs were spotted during the approach to Zuara but were ignored. The Maltese ground force surprised the local population at dawn on 14 August; 1,500 were made captive before or just after waking. It was only during the plundering that a Moor known by Valette when Governor of Tripoli came forward and made it known that the encamped Arabs seen earlier were those of Lord of Tripoli Mourad Aga, 3,600 Arab horsemen, mostly mounted arquebusiers plus another 2,000 Tunisian tribesmen from Nefta (modern Naftah), all en route to Djerba to force obeisance of the local sheik. Valette ordered a recall, but too late. Some knights and others failed to hear the trumpet and tambours. Others, rather than withdraw, continued to plunder the homes of the city and were surprised by troops of Mourad, who entered Zuara as easily as had Strozzi's force.

Most Malta captives were abandoned during the chaos that ensued. Leone Strozzi positioned himself with a rear guard to permit troops to re-embark. His nephew Scipione was killed in the clash, the son of brother Piero. Leone Strozzi himself was wounded by an arquebus round in the thigh and had to be carried to a skiff by Juanito Torreglias of Mallorca. The enemy in the end had by far the best of it: 101 Hospitallers were left on the field or succumbed to their wounds during or after the return to

Malta. Twenty-two were from the Langue of Provence, fourteen from Auvergne, twenty-three from France, sixteen from Italy, fifteen from Aragon, two from Germany, and nine from Castile, all as listed by name at *Bosio III-331*. Mortality among soldiers approximated 200 dead with another sixty wounded. Only a dozen of the wounded could be evacuated, and some of these died in the days to follow. A larger number of the badly wounded were captured and enslaved, both soldiers twenty to thirty in number and knights; the latter including Juan de Bracamonte, François de Moreton de Chabrillan, Miguel Marziglia, and Charles de Grasse Briancon, who would later be ransomed. The latter's brother Jerome was among the dead, both received five years earlier. Many others survived but were maimed for life. Enemy losses were estimated at 900, many of them victims of cannon fire from the galleys, which had also moved toward Zuara during the night. Strozzi returned to the island of Lampedusa in a violent storm causing the loss of a frigate and the drowning of her entire crew. This spur-of-the-moment and ill-planned undertaking may have been the greatest disaster in Hospitaller history, certainly greater than the loss of Tripoli a year earlier if not the precedent loss of 5,000 Gozitans, and by some measures greater even than 1522's noble loss of Rhodes. The only blessing attending this unholy disaster was that both Sinan Pasha and Dragut were as ignorant of it as its planners.[20]

The flotilla reached Malta on 21 August, where Strozzi took convalescent leave of his command. His own three galleys continued to the Levant under command of Martinez de Casseda and new captains Domenico Gondi and Valentino da Piombino, a pilot and corsair called Il Rosso, where they engaged and sank a galleon that was the property of Grand Vizier Rustem Pasha, Suleiman's son-in-law. Six other Turkish vessels were also taken and dispatched to Malta with cargoes of sugar, silk, linen, rice, and olive oil, not to mention a good deal of coin. None of it even began to cover the Order's losses at Zuara.[21]

The French Fleet under Prince of Salerno Ferrante di Sanseverino composed of thirty galleys caught up with the Ottoman Armada on 30 August at Santa Maura south of Corfu, where there was a season-ending exchange of formalities.[21] With return of the Ottoman Armada to Constantinople, Hospitaller contracts for hired soldiery were terminated. Surviving commanders, bailiffs, and priors who had rallied to the defence of Malta earlier in the year were licensed to return to their respective domains, and all, soldiers and knights, on 7 September 1552 embarked aboard the four galleys of the Religion for transport to Messina and transshipment to ultimate destinations. The galleys were again under the command of Regent Battista Bellomo. During the Council meeting that authorised these post-Zuara releases, Leone Strozzi was selected the next Captain of Galleys to succeed Regent Bellomo, pending authorisation of the Emperor. Hospitaller Paolo Rossi of Florence was dispatched to the Emperor's Court in Germany for the purpose of both having the Priory of Capua restored to Strozzi but also to obtain authorisation for his appointment as Captain of Galleys in the spring. Rossi returned with satisfaction of both requests. With the reassignment of Strozzi, Grand Bailiff Georg Bombast von Hohenheim selected Commander Giovan Antonio Pescatore of Novara as Captain of Fort Saint Elmo. Elmo was additionally assigned a garrison of thirty knights, forty soldiers, and six cannoneers replaced every four months.

During this same month Prior of Catalonia Miguel Ferrer passed away in Spain. Grand Conservator Gaspar Ferrer was appointed his successor, while Commander Pedro de Montserrat of Valencia succeeded to the dignity of Grand Conservator. The changing tides of war between Empire and France, waged primarily in the Low Countries, occasionally resulted in occupation of commanderies by one side in the other's territory. Pedro de Felizes was dispatched to the Emperor to plead for recognition of the Hospital as a neutral. Having obtained the Emperor's acquiescence, Felizes was dispatched to the Court of French King Henry II, where he obtained a similar undertaking.[21]

Two thousand unpaid Spanish soldiers garrisoning Mehedia mutinied against new Governor Sancho de Leyva. This was the prelude to several requests from the Emperor that the Knights of Malta assume responsibility for this isolated Imperial outpost seized from Dragut in September 1550. Imperial intermediaries unsuccessfully attempted to repair the breach, failing largely because of Leyva's pompous attitude and the low esteem in which he was held by the garrison. A soldier-ambassador was even elected to put the garrison's grievances before Grand Master Juan de Homedes in February, including the ill state of preparedness for a return of Dragut.[22] By 27 February the Venetian Senate had been informed by the Republic's ambassador at Constantinople that the Sultan did not intend to send the Ottoman Armada to the west in 1553, only Dragut with forty to fifty galleys. By separate report of the French ambassador at Constantinople, French King Henry II was advised that Dragut would depart Constantinople on 1 June with twenty galleys. Meanwhile, the thirty French galleys under Sanseverino had returned to Marseille in October, but in apparent royal chagrin at missing scheduled 1552 combined operations with the Ottomans, some had almost immediately been reordered to winter quarters at Chios not far south of the Dardanelles, where such a failure was unlikely to be repeated in 1553. The Grand Master was sufficiently concerned about the threat to Mehedia to send his own emissary, Don Pedro de Mendoza of Castile, to discuss the matter with Viceroy of Sicily Don Juan de Vega. Wishing to relieve the plight of fellow Spaniards but not wishing to become officially involved in Imperial matters, Homedes asked Leone Strozzi to take his three private galleys to Mehedia accompanying the private Maltese vessel of Domenico Balio, the latter with a cargo of biscuit, wine, grain, and other foodstuffs.[23]

Still searching for firm political footing of his own, Leone Strozzi, no longer welcome at the place of his birth in Florence, no longer welcome in France by Queen Catherine de Medici of Florence, and regarded with suspicion by many of his fellow knights, suddenly conceived of establishing his own fiefdom at Mehedia. A man of great strength and high ambition, if faulted judgement, the conception rested comfortably on his shoulders. He conceived not only of an impregnable military redoubt but of a centre of commerce on the North African coast to fund it. And the Emperor would be grateful. He planned in addition on currying the favour of both French King Henry II and Ottoman Sultan Suleiman while remaining neutral during their wars. He accepted the Grand Master's charge with alacrity.[24]

Strozzi took his three galleys and food-carrier to Mehedia, where he became even more enamoured with his conception of converting this proud and ancient city into a capital of North Africa. His enthusiasm was even imparted to the rebellious garrison. Before his return to Malta he proceeded to the shallows of the low-lying Kerkennah Islands in modern Tunisia's Gulf of Gabes, where he captured a small square-rigged cargo ship commanded by Yusuf al Arabi, carrying a cargo of linen, flax, cotton, and cotton wool, with many Turks and Moors embarked. He sank another similar ship and returned to Malta with 205 captives, consigning by agreement half to the Common Treasury in the person of

Conventual Conservator Giorgio Vagnone of Lombardia, a veteran of the Great Siege of Rhodes. His enthusiasm for Mehedia was infectious, and soon enveloped Viceroy Juan de Vega, effectively postponing Strozzi's chances of acquiring the ancient port.[25]

While Sinan remained Kapudan Pasha the Venetian Senate had been informed that the Ottomans would not send out a large fleet in 1553, rather forty to fifty galleys under Dragut.[26] The corsair-admiral in fact exited the Dardanelles in early June[27] with sixty galleys and galliots, where he was joined by Ferrante Sanseverino, rebel Prince of Salerno, coming up from winter quarters at Chios with twenty additional galleys. Later in the month, at Lepanto in the Gulf of Corinth, they were joined by Antoine Escalin des Aimars, former French Ambassador to the Ottoman Porte and at the time General of French Galleys, with sixteen additional galleys, bringing the French total to thirty-six oared vessels.[28] At Lepanto Aimars succeeded Sanseverino in command of the French contingent. Proceeding north from Lepanto, the combined galley armada jumped off across the Strait of Otranto from Venetian Corfu. Expecting and aware of these developments, the Grand Master and Council at Malta readied to defend the island in the event of an assault. Future Grand Master Jean l'Evêsque de la Cassière of the Langue of Auvergne was appointed to command of the island's mounted militia; Lieutenant Turcopolier Oswald Massinbert was appointed Cassière's lieutenant. Commander of Rubiales Luis Rengifo of Castile was appointed Captain-at-Arms for the city of Notabile with a strong force of knights, soldiers, arms, and munitions. Commander Niccolo Orsino Rivalta of Turin was similarly appointed Captain-at-Arms for the Castle of Gozo. Prior of Capua Leone Strozzi assumed command of the seven galleys on the first day of June, the four belonging to the Order and his three leased to the Order. Because he commanded seven captains, and because there were galliots in the service of the Order commanded by captains, Leone Strozzi was appointed General of Galleys rather than Captain of Galleys, the first such appointment in Hospitaller history. Strozzi flew his flag from the capitana *San Claudio*; Battista Bellomo moved from command of *San Michele Arcangelo* to command of the capitana; Jean de Condé de Vendières of the Langue of France succeeded Pedro de Felizes in command of *Santa Maria Maddelena*, while Adam von Schwalbach of Germany succeeded Bellomo in command of *San Michele Arcangelo*. Miguel de Aldovera of

Aragon remained in command of *San Giovanni Battista*. Strozzi's three leased galleys continued to be commanded by Hospitaller Martinez de Casseda and non-Hospitallers Domenico Gondi and Valentino da Piombino called Il Rosso. The expanded squadron made two trips to Sicily for provisions without incident.[25]

Ignoring French pleas to make haste toward the northern Tyrrhenian, Dragut put ashore early in July 1553, first at Crotone and then at Roccella Ionica, 60 nautical miles to the south-west, both on the sole of the Italian boot, destroying everything but the latter's castle. Hungry for prey, he found it, and for good measure put harvest and buildings to the torch, while male captives were sent to the oars. Speeding across the foot of the Strait of Messina, Dragut fell on the Sicilian city of Augusta which was also sacked, the French standing impatiently offshore. Then, beginning on 11 July, Dragut crews sacked Licata on the south coast of Sicily for eight consecutive days, including Limpiados Castle, completely destroying the town. Prior to departure with[29] 700 male inhabitants chained and collected in Ottoman holds, a party of hundreds of raiders made its way inland toward Modica where, however, forty Turks fell in an ambush by 200 Spanish cavalry and 2,000 infantry under Modica Governor Don Guillen de Belvis, and hundreds were captured including a handful of French. The remainder hastily departed Licata with newly joined corsair lieutenants Kara Mustafa and Acsac Reis, the former to become Ottoman Sancakbey of Mitilini in 1560 and the latter, known as Zoppo for his peg leg, a Dragut compatriot since 1504. From them Dragut learned of the rebellion against Sancho de Leyva at Mehedia. Moving across the underbelly of Sicily, Dragut sacked Sciacca while taking on water from its river, after which he diverted toward his 'City of Africa' and home of the six years immediately following his release from Genovese captivity, reaching the island of Pantelleria, where only the strong objections of Escalin des Aimars, Baron de la Garde, and of Ferrante di Sanseverino prevented him from proceeding further. Pantelleria, though, felt Dragut's wrath. He destroyed the church and every standing structure, getting the island's historical archives among other items while carting away its citizenry. These, one thousand of them according to Bosio,[26] were dispatched from Pantelleria to the slave market at Porto Farina, Tunisia.[27] The combined armada then turned towards western Sicily and took course toward Sorrento but failed to reach its destination. Slammed by a north-easterly for several days, and perhaps mindful of Sanseverino protestations that Sorrento was full of pro-French partisans, the armada on 29 July beached at the Sardinian port of Murta Maria, 200 nautical miles west of Sorrento, probably much to the satisfaction of French allies. Their ultimate interest was the conquest of Corsica, a mere 30 miles distant.

At Malta Prior of the Church Antonio Corogna died, and on 12 July Graciano Gálvez, Chaplain of the Langue of Aragon, was appointed his successor. Also dying was Chaplain Commander Claude de Saint-Blaise de Brugny of the Diocese of Soissons of the Langue of France, apparently still in his thirties, after many years attending patients in the Order's infirmary. Arriving at Malta on 14 July were two French galleys and a frigate under command of Bernard d'Ornesan, Baron de Saint-Blancard (son of Bertrand d'Ornesan, deceased Baron de Saint-Blancard), sent by the aforementioned Antoine des Escalins des Aimars, Baron de la Garde, to notify the Grand Master the galley armada commanded by Dragut would be returning to Constantinople in September by way of the Malta Channel with no intention of harming Malta or Gozo. There must, however, be no manifestation of hostility from the Maltese. On the day of Saint-Blancard's arrival several barques also arrived from Sicily with news of Dragut's savagery at Licata and with news that Viceroy Juan de Vega had reprovisioned and reinforced Mehedia with a company of fresh soldiers. Two days later, on 19 July, a Ragusan argosy safely reached Malta having been fortunate to flee Pantelleria on a favourable wind on sight of the Franco–Ottoman armada's approach. The galliot, the personal property of Hospitaller Giovan Luigi Carracciola of Naples, returned to Malta on 23 August from a corsair expedition to the Levant, where Carracciola had been killed during the conquest of a square-rigged Turkish merchantman. The galliot reverted to the Common Treasury, while the spoils funded her rearmament. Bernardino Scaglia was assigned to her command.[30]

Fifteen-year-old King Edward VI died at Greenwich Palace on 6 July of tuberculosis, and a few days later was succeeded as monarch by half-sister Mary I, daughter of Henry VIII and Catherine of Aragon, who restored the legitimacy of Roman Catholicism in England and Ireland, restoring as well the legitimacy of the Order of Jerusalem in England and Ireland.[31]

From Murta Maria, Sardinia, the Franco–Ottoman Armada moved toward Porto Ercole on the Tuscan mainland east of the island of Giglio, failing because of wind to beach on the coast. Alternatively proceeding toward the island of Elba, the armada put into Porto Longone (Porto Azzurro) on 7 August, the fleet's very appearance coming up from Montecristo to the south panicking all but infants. Panic was no defence and the population retired into Fort Giogo at the top of the island. Dragut's corsairs burned and looted almost everything else including Marciana Marina and Capoliveri among other island towns. Kara Mustafa had meanwhile beset Pianosa, 15 miles to the south-west, and put it to fire and sword, making slaves of about two hundred persons.[29] An assault by Dragut on Elba's Cosmopoli (Portoferraio), however, was repulsed with heavy loss. Because of time constraints, the combined fleet on 9 August again attempted to beach at Porto Ercole, this time successfully. Porto Ercole was controlled by French ally Siena, and Aimars had induced a reluctant Dragut into an expedition against Genovese Corsica, Dragut reluctant only because he knew from experience that the spoils would be slim. In mid-August at Siennese Maremma, 15 miles south-east of Porto Ercole, the fleet embarked aboard its galleys for transport to Corsica the French militia of Marshal Paul de la Barthe de Thermes. Also embarking were Corsican rebels Sampiero Corso and Giordano degli Orsini, a Corsican general in the service of France. The city of Bastia on the east side of Cape Corse, 100 nautical miles distant from Maremma, was first to be punished. Bombarded from the sea by the combined armada, Bastia opened its port to besiegers on 24 August. Escalin des Aimars appeared off Saint-Florent on the other side of Cape Corse two days later on 26 August. This small fishing port was immediately occupied by the troops of Giordano Orsini. Bonifacio, at the opposite end of Corsica, came to terms on 15 September following a ruse in which a Genovese emissary was captured. Sent to inform defenders that help was on the way, in fear of his life he told them no help was available. The garrison of 1,200 Genovese surrendered under honourable terms on 15 September, marched out of the presidio under arms and with flags flying, and were told they were free to return to Genoa. However, Dragut violated the agreed terms and assailed and enslaved the Genovese and their families. Those few resisting were killed. Dragut demanded 30,000 scudos from the French in compensation for munitions expended in the siege, for gifts he would make to the families of lost galley officers, and for release to French custody of the 1,200 Genovese families. Thermes and Aimars issued a letter of credit payable at Constantinople within five months. With occupation of Bonifacio, Dragut left Corsica.[32]

At Malta 80-year-old Grand Master Juan de Homedes y Coscon fell terminally ill late in August and delegated to Lieutenant Claude de Gruel-Laborel of the Langue of Provence his power of attorney.[30] Juan de Homedes died at Malta on 6 September 1553 and was interred in the Church of San Lorenzo at Birgu. He left an unhappy legacy beginning even before his Magistracy and continuing with his election not on merit but on the need for a Spanish Grand Master. His legacy continued with both self-enrichment and that of his immediate family. It ended with catastrophic losses at Gozo and Tripoli in 1551 and at Zuara in 1552. Having been confirmed by the Council as Magistral Lieutenant, Claude de Gruel-Laborel convened a General Assembly at Malta on 11 September to elect Homedes' successor.[33]

Chapter XI

Claude de la Sengle 1553–55

Claude de la Sengle was unanimously elected forty-eighth Grand Master in spite of a strong challenge from Leone Strozzi and a prolonged twenty-three hour debate by the sixteen electors. He would prove to be the right choice.

Having been confirmed by the Council of State as Magistral Lieutenant, Grand Commander Claude de Gruel-Laborel, on 11 September convened a General Assembly of eligible voters present at Malta, about 400 knights, chaplains, and serving brothers, to elect a successor to deceased Grand Master Juan de Homedes y Coscon. These Hospitallers gathered in the Great Room of Castle Saint Angelo and divided into eight langues for the purpose of selecting eight initial electors. They were: Commander of La Bastit Parisot de la Valette for Provence, Prior of Auvergne Imbert de la Morinière, Lieutenant Grand Hospitaller François de Piédefer for France, Prior of the Church Graciano Gálvez for Aragon, Prior of Capua Leone Strozzi for Italy, Lieutenant Turcopolier Oswald Massinbert for England, Lieutenant Grand Bailiff Adam von Schwalbach for Germany, and Cristóvão da Cunha for Castile. These eight selected from the Assembly Admiral Filippo Pilli as non-voting President of Elections, and then before retiring also selected from the Assembly the Triumvirate of Elections, who were Alonso de Solis of Castile as Knight of Elections, Antoine Cressin of Auvergne as Chaplain of Elections, and Serving Brother Victor Ricardeau of France as Servant-at-Arms of Elections. These three selected a fourth from the Assembly, who was Commander Francesco Nibbia of Italy. The four then selected a fifth and the five a sixth and so on until there were Sixteen Electors at two per langue. The additional electors were: 5th Commander of Golfech and Monsones Pierre de Gozon-Mélac of Provence, 6th Pedro de Junient of Aragon, 7th Oswald Massinbert of England, 8th Adam von Schwalbach of Germany, 9th Parisot de la Valette of Provence, 10th Jean l'Evésque de la Cassière of Auvergne, 11th Jean d'Aulnis de l'Île-Bouchard of France, 12th Conventual Conservator and Governor of Fort Saint Elmo Giorgio Vagnone of Italy, 13th Catalan Jorge de San Juan (Jordi de Sant Joan in Catalan) of Aragon, 14th Diego Montero of Castile, 15th because there were no eligible English Hospitallers at Malta other than Massinbert, Georg Sebut von Schönborn of Germany, and 16th Cristóvão da Cunha of Castile. These sixteen in solemn conclave sensed the Convent believed election of Prior of Capua Leone Strozzi a foregone conclusion. They were also aware of promises made contingent on election. It became clear after twenty-three hours of conclave, however, that Commanders Valette, Nibbia, Gozon-Mélac, and Junient could not be persuaded to vote for Strozzi, and that the only unanimously endorsed candidate was Claude de la Sengle, who was accordingly elected forty-eighth Grand Master of the Order of Jerusalem.[1]

A son of lesser noble Laurent de la Sangle (sic) and Marie de Hangest of Beauvais in Picardy, 75km north of Paris, when elected Claude de la Sengle Montchavel was 59 years of age and a veteran of the Great Siege of Rhodes, during which he is believed to have served on Collachium walls at the head of the galley port as well as at Fort Saint Nicholas on the east wall of the galley port. Ten years later he was appointed Commander of Saint-Étienne-de-Renneville in Normandy, an assignment continued until his election as Grand Master. In 1543 he was nominated by his peers and appointed by the Sacred Council (State Council) as Conventual Conservator responsible for auditing the Common Treasury, a Common Treasury that theretofore had been the exclusive preserve of Grand Master Juan de Homedes. Attending the Conventual Conservator's inspection report was the Grand Master's warrant to reimburse the Common Treasury at the rate of 12,000 Maltese scudos per annum until the books balanced. As Bailiff of the Morea resident at the Convent, Sengle was in 1546 awarded the Order's Grand Cross. He served as Grand Hospitaller responsible for the Order's renowned infirmary from 1549 to 1553, as Captain of the Galley Squadron, in 1550 and as Ambassador to the Holy See from 1551 to 1553, the latter assignment the Order's most critical diplomatic post.

Upon Sengle's election, Claude de Gruel was appointed Magistral Lieutenant during Sengle's absence at Rome, while Lieutenant Grand Hospitaller François de Piédefer replaced Sengle as Grand Hospitaller.

News was received at about this time of the death in France of Prior of Toulouse Foulques de Caritat. Caritat was succeeded by the same Claude de Gruel, who in turn was succeeded as Grand Commander by Pierre de Beaulac-Trébons. On the same day came news that elements of Dragut's Galley Armada absent the French contingent had raided the Aeolian Island of Lipari north of Sicily as well as the smaller island of Saline di Trapani off western Sicily, and Gruel began to think seriously about the new Grand Master's safety travelling from Rome to Malta. One day later, on 13 September, the frigate of Cola Aniello was dispatched to Ostia at the mouth of the Tiber carrying Christophe le Bouleur de Montgaudry bound for Catona in Calabria, thence to Rome, as well as Pedro de Mendoza and Rafaello Salvago bound for Ostia, thence to Rome, each in secrecy of Sengle's election.

Gruel also addressed security at Malta. Parisot de la Valette of Provence, Antoine de Choiseul Rimaucourt of France, Antonio Bologna of Palermo, and Melchor de Montserrat of Aragon were each assigned a coastal zone of Malta to patrol for sight of Ottoman sails. Commanders Jean l'Evesque de la Cassière and Jorge de Sant Joan were assigned as Commissioners or Inspectors-General to ensure readiness of fortifications at Birgu, Saint Michael, and Saint Elmo. Bouleur de Montgaudry, for many years personal lieutenant to the new Grand Master, meanwhile by fast horse from Catona reached Rome during the night of 25–26 September but was prevented from waking Sengle in his bed chamber. The following morning Montgaudry broke the news to Sengle in the presence of Hospitaller Secretary Antoine de Guèvre of England and of agent of the Religion Gianotto Bosio (older brother of historian Giacomo Bosio). Two days later, with the arrival of Mendoza and Salvago, emissaries were dispatched notifying heads of state of Homedes' passing and Sengle's accession. Mendoza proceeded to Flanders seeking Holy Roman Emperor Charles V, Salvago to the princes of Italy, and Montgaudry to the French Court of King Henry II.[2]

With Kara Mustafa in company, and with his ships crammed with plunder, Dragut brazenly transited the Strait of Messina southbound on 1 October. Berenguer de Requesens, with six Sicilian galleys, could not intervene.[2] On 14 October six galleys of the Malta/Strozzi squadrons departed Malta under Strozzi to collect the new Grand Master and return him to Malta. An escort of two knights from each langue was embarked. Forced to return to Malta by adverse season-changing weather, the squadrons again departed on 21 October with an altered escort, paused at Messina, and then proceeded to Terracina, 60km south-east of Rome on the coast between Cape Circe and Gaeta. There Grand Master Claude de la Sengle embarked on 7 December and reached Messina on 12 December to court and be courted by Viceroy Juan de Vega and others. While at Messina he was offered the City of Africa, Mehedia, lock, stock, and barrel at no cost, the offer coming from a member of the Emperor's official family, Dom Fernão da Cunha, a poet when not on official business. Sengle graciously offered to discuss cession with the Council, knowing as a former Council member, however, there would be no Council interest in defending yet another isolated outpost along the long arm of the Islamic Caliphate. Sengle and the six galleys departed Messina on 22 December. Because of a strong south wind, the galleys were eventually forced into Malta's Saint Paul's Bay, where on the first day of the new year Sengle disembarked and made his way to Notabile. The following day, though, the galleys were able to proceed and did so to Grand Harbour, arriving with all the pomp and circumstance normally attending the first appearance of a new Grand Master.[3]

The Grand Master's arrival at Malta was followed in short order by arrival of the Emperor's Ambassador Fernão da Cunha, who in shorter order was courteously received by the Council of State to attend to the ambassador's presentation concerning the Emperor's wish that the Knights of Malta assume responsibility for the City of Africa, also known as Mehedia. Among other persuasions the ambassador reminded the Council of the Emperor's steadfast support over the years since the loss of Rhodes. He made further mention of common knowledge that many in the Convent had advocated relocation from Malta to Tripoli, and that Mehedia was infinitely more defensible than Tripoli. Finally, the Emperor offered an annual subsidy of 72,000 gold scudos to be paid by the Kingdom of Sicily. Several members of the Council received the proposal favourably, foremost among them the Prior of Capua Leone Strozzi.[4]

Before any vote, though, the Council resolved to first send a fact-finding Commission to Mehedia, the Commission to be composed of one senior knight from each langue, as follows: Parisot de la Valette of Provence, Jean l'Evesque de la Cassière of Auvergne, Jean de Condé de Vendières of

France, Pedro des Felizes of Aragon, Giovan Antonio Pescatore of Italy, Oswald Massinbert of England, Adam von Schwalbach of Germany, and Alonso de Solis of Castile. These eight departed Malta on 15 January embarked aboard the four galleys of the Religion plus one belonging to Strozzi, all commanded by Strozzi, and took course a bit south of west 175 nautical miles to Mehedia. While at Mehedia, Pescatore died suddenly, and poison was soon suspected. A 37-year-old native of Novara in the Piedmont, Pescatore did not have a position within the Order to which might be ascribed a slight or worse, nor was he otherwise known to have an enemy. Out of nowhere there was nevertheless born a whispered suspicion that Giovan Antonio Pescatore was poisoned by a Strozzi minion, Biagio Pesce. Returned to Malta on 22 January, the Commission's detailed analysis of Mehedia took a back seat to rumour. During the weeks to follow, the alleged perpetrator, Pesce, was murdered, as were recently the received brothers Aleramo and Bernardone Parpaglia and Conventual Conservator Giorgio Vagnone, all three of the latter, like Pescatore, natives of the Piedmont. The genesis of the killing was said to be unhappiness that Strozzi was not elected Grand Master, but of the dead, only Vagnone was an elector. In the history of the Order of Jerusalem this was at least the third blood feud, all three exclusively Italian.[5]

On 30 January 1554 the Council rejected the Emperor's proposal, primarily because the Order had insufficient resources to defend the City of Africa and because the City did not have a secure deep-water port. Commander of La Figuera Alonso de Solis of Castile and Commander of Jales and Avignon Charles d'Urre de Tessières of Provence were appointed ambassadors extraordinary to convey a letter from the Grand Master to the Emperor explaining the Council's decision.[5]

Georg Bombast von Hohenheim was elevated to Grand Prior of Germany and Prince of the Empire upon the February death of Prince Georg Schilling von Canstatt. Bombast, having accordingly renounced the dignity of Grand Bailiff, was succeeded in that position by Adam von Schwalbach, Captain of the galley *San Michele Arcangelo*.[6]

Ambassadors Solis and Tessières departed Malta on 18 March bound for Aachen in Flanders, where the Emperor was in residence. Solis had further orders to proceed to the Court of England at Greenwich for the purpose of informing Queen Mary of the demise of Juan de Homedes and the accession of Claude de la Sengle. Solis was also to apprise himself of the status of the Order's Chapter in England, particularly concerning the recovery of chapter properties. Imperial Ambassador to Malta Dom Fernão da Cunha left the island on 4 May, his mission to transfer responsibility for Mehedia from Empire to Order of Malta a failure. His report of this failure to Viceroy of Sicily Juan de Vega intensified friction between Sicily and Malta, the first the second's grain lifeline. In Council Grand Master Sengle began to unwind his predecessor's Magistral awards to family and friends, including the Commandery at Marrugio near Taranto, Italy, the Commandery at Polizzi Generosa near Palermo, the Seneca Commandery in Cordoba, and the Commandery at Aliaga in Aragon, at all of which collections were reported to be so meagre there could be no remittance to Malta. His sins so egregious, Commander of Aliaga Don Pedro de Herrera was stripped of his Habit. Given the aforementioned death of Giovan Antonio Pescatore, a veteran of the Great Siege of Rhodes, he was succeeded as Governor of Fort Saint Elmo by Commander of Vera Cruz Cristóvão da Cunha. At Faenza, 30 miles south-east of Bologna, Hospitaller Sabba da Castiglione, Commander of that city and of its magnificent new cathedral, died on 16 March. An Hospitaller since 1505 and Commander of Faenza since 1514, Castiglione of Milan had dedicated his entire life to the most saintly pursuits. At Faenza this included construction of the Cathedral, establishment of an extensive library, construction and staffing of a school for the poor, and publication of his own work entitled *Ricordi*, an advocacy for arms and letters and a guide for Christian soldiers republished twenty-five times between 1546 and 1613. Seventy-four years of age, he was interred within the Cathedral of his conception.[7]

On 3 April 1554 the Venetian Ambassador to the Ottoman Porte advised the Senate that Dragut was scheduled to sail for the Adriatic on 15 May with fifty-five galleys. In the meanwhile reports streamed into Malta of so many corsair depredations in Sicily that General of the Galleys Leone Strozzi was licensed to strip one galley of six and with the men and armaments so stripped to reinforce the other five galleys. The remaining five galleys departed Malta in pursuit of corsairs, taking with them Commander Niccolò Orsino di Rivalta of Turin as the Order's Deputy Procurator-General in Sicily. His predecessor, Alonso Madrigal of the Langue of Castile, stood accused of self-enrichment and was deprived of his Habit and referred to the secular justice system.[8]

While Strozzi was at Palermo a courier arrived with a letter from his brother Pietro announcing the latter's appointment as the French King's Lieutenant for Italy, and Pietro's wish that Leone Strozzi take charge of his naval arm. At the time Pietro commanded French forces ashore in the Republic of Siena under threat by Cosimo I d'Medici of Florence, the same Cosimo I d'Medici who drove both brothers into exile and who was responsible for father Filippo's death. It was Leone Strozzi's blood feud.[9]

While Viceroy Juan de Vega unsuccessfully attempted to prevent Leone Strozzi's departure from Palermo, and thus prevent him from going to the support of the Emperor's French enemies in northern Italy, Strozzi was able to return to Malta, to resign his commission, and to depart with his three proprietary galleys, one of them *Leona* new off the ways at Malta replacing the older of the three with which he had arrived. She was commanded by Giovanni Moretto (also known as Jean Moret) of Villefranche, a name that recurs in this history. Strozzi was even able to depart with a large number of young Hospitallers eager to serve under such a famous sea commander. Within a few days of his July arrival in northern Italy, however, Strozzi was killed by a sniper while unsuccessfully assailing the Imperial fortress at Scarlino, Tuscany. He left a legacy of unsuccessfully assailing fortresses from Boulogne to Guernsey to Zuara to Scarlino as well as suspicion in all of the courts of Europe.[10]

Meanwhile, the same Bernard d'Ornesan, Baron de Saint-Blancard, who had appeared at Malta with three French galleys ten months earlier, was dispatched to Constantinople seeking both help in the War of Siena and in defending France's tenuous hold on the coasts of Corsica. Finding Sultan Suleiman at Aleppo combatting the Safavid Shah Tahmasp, Blancard nevertheless emerged from the Bosphorus in company with fifty 'hired' Turkish galleys under command of Dragut Pasha.[10]

At Malta Grand Master and Council in May 1554 appointed Parisot de la Valette General of the Galleys. He flew his flag aboard *San Michele Arcangelo*, which was the best galley in the squadron. The new capitana *Santa Maria della Vittoria* was assigned to Etienne d'Arsac of the Priory of Toulouse. Philipp Flach von Schwarzenberg was appointed to command *San Claudio*, finishing the term of Adam von Schwalbach, who had commanded *San Michele Arcangelo* prior to his elevation to Grand Bailiff.

The other two galleys, *San Giovanni Battista* and *Santa Maria Maddelena*, were respectively assigned to Don Pedro González de Mendoza and to Antoine de Thésan-Vénàsque,. The squadron was immediately dispatched to Sicily to procure foodstuffs for the Maltese islands, much to the disgust of Juan de Vega, Viceroy of Sicily, who had taken Mehedia from Dragut in 1550 only to find Valette had recommended against retaining the city. Vega's greater disgust, however, had to do with the threat of Dragut and his fifty galleys and Malta's professed neutrality in the War between France and Dragut on the one hand and Spain on the other. The galley squadron of Sicily under Berenguer de Requesens was alone too small to take to the sea.[11]

Among other assignments at Malta, Francisco Martinez de Casseda, former captain of the Strozzi capitana, was appointed Captain-at-Arms and Governor of Notabile. Tragically, he would die at Notabile in the still heat of August. Sengle's new fortress construction engineer Nicolò Bellavanti had recommended development of a walled town on the seaward end of the island of St Michael, which would prove essential to Malta's defence in 1565. The new town would replace the wild animal park initiated by Juan de Homedes, called the Homedes Garden, and would be named Senglea in the Grand Master's honour. Construction also began on a cavalier higher than and within the star-shaped walls of Fort Saint Elmo as well as of a fifth star-point or spur pointing toward the open sea.[11]

Early in July 1554 Prince Philip of Austria, 27-year-old son of Emperor Charles V, was betrothed to 38-year-old Queen Mary I of England. Philip, newly crowned as King of Naples for the occasion, embarked at La Coruña, Spain, on the Bay of Biscay aboard one of an Armada of Spanish sailing vessels which reached Southampton five days later. Another five days later, on 25 July, Queen Mary I of England and Ireland wed the future King Philip II of Spain at Winchester Cathedral. As Philip spoke no English, they conversed in a mixture of Spanish, French, and Latin. Accompanying Philip to England and present at the wedding were Spanish Hospitallers Don Antonio de Toledo, Grand Conservator Pedro de Montserrat, and Pedro Fernandez de Felizes della Nucia. Separately present representing the Grand Master was Alonso de Solis of Castile. Following the wedding Felizes, a veteran of the Great Siege of Rhodes, remained in England as Imperial Ambassador and conducted the negotiations leading to the Restoration of the Order of Saint John in England. In the deed of Philip and Mary restoring the Order dated 2 April 1557, Felizes was confirmed as Bailiff of the Bailiwick of Eagle, a dignity normally entitled to wear the Grand Cross.[12]

The Priory of Capua, vacant with the death of Leone Strozzi, was in August 1554 awarded to Admiral Filippo Pilli, like Strozzi, of Florence. Pilli would be succeeded as Admiral in April 1555 by Commander Francesco Cataneo of Novara. Paolo della Chiesa of Turin returned to Malta from scouting the Ottoman Armada with news that Dragut had no more than fifty oared vessels and earlier in the month had been on the Adriatic coast of Apulia.

That same month of August 1554, Andrea Doria, then 88 years of age, reached Messina from Genoa commanding sixty Imperial galleys, presumably including the six galleys of Sicily and perhaps ten of Naples. At Naples, Cardinal Pedro Pacheco de Villena had one year earlier succeeded the despised Fernando Álvarez de Toledo as Viceroy. From Messina, Doria addressed a letter to the Grand Master seeking support of Hospitaller galleys in a plan to pounce on Dragut's armada, support denied because Dragut was allied with France in a war with Spain, concerning which Malta was neutral. Doria persisted, suggesting that should French vessels be in company with Dragut, then he would understand the need for a Maltese withdrawal. On that basis Parisot de la Valette was licensed by Grand Master and Council to rendezvous with Doria, and a few days later Valette found the Imperial Armada off Gallipoli di Apulia on the inside of the Italian heel, where he was royally received. Twenty-nine years younger than Doria, Valette was nevertheless a veteran of the Great Siege of Rhodes and of most everything since. Doria received him as an equal, and at Valette's request released French Hospitallers captive aboard his ships. Dragut, for his part, savaged the city of Vieste on the slopes of Mount Gargano, 110 nautical miles up the Adriatic from Brindisi and a good 170 miles from Gallipoli, carrying away 3,000 hapless citizens of the wasted city. Dragut's excursion into the Adriatic is said to have been a diversion, distracting Imperial forces from the conquest of Siena. And it had distracted Andrea Doria. The sea off Siena had become a French sea in Doria's absence, but controlling no Tuscan port, the French had been unable to put additional troops and supplies ashore. On 2 August 1554 Leone Strozzi's brother Pietro and a force of 15,000 were routed at the Battle of Marciano by Imperial and Florentine troops commanded by Gian Giacomo Medici and Niccolò Madruzzo, the same Madruzzo commanding 700 Germans captured by Dragut in August 1552 and ransomed for 12,000 scudos. On news of the apparent success of his diversion, Dragut, his fifty galleys, and his 3,000 captives returned to Constantinople with a fruitless pause in the Corfu Channel to waylay merchant traffic.[13]

Learning from a passing Ragusan ship of Dragut's return to Constantinople, Doria with Valette in company returned to Messina, arriving at the end of August 1554. Because of the hostility of Viceroy Juan de Vega, Valette did not enter port but took his leave of Doria and set off in a search for Barbary corsairs parked among islands off the coast of Sicily. It was only at Messina that news of the defeat of Pietro Strozzi was received. And of Strozzi's escape, even though severely wounded, leaving behind 4,000 dead and 4,000 captured. Having turned the Aeolian Islands without discovering any enemy, Valette returned by way of Messina to discover the Imperial Armada disbanded with individual squadrons returned to their home ports. With no little disgust at returning home empty-handed, the four-galley squadron fortuitously captured a lone corsair fusta near Cape Passero on 12 September. While the numbers were small – a handful of Christians liberated from the oars and twenty-two Turks sent to the oars – the Barbary captain was Abda Racman Casdagli (Kust Ali), Valette's principal tormentor when he was himself at the oars of a corsair galliot. Abda Racman was also the son of Ibrahim Casdagli, a Malta captive swapped for Valette in October 1542. The fusta was towed to Malta.[14]

During the return to Malta liberated Christians had told of other corsairs operating near Licata on Sicily's south coast. The four galleys soon returned to Sicily in search of Licata waters but without success. They loaded foodstuffs and again returned to Malta. During this month of September Commander Louis de Lastic succeeded the deceased Pierre des Roches as Marshal. The latter had himself succeeded the disgraced Gaspard de Vallier as Marshal following loss of Tripoli in August 1551. Des Roches was subsequently captured by corsairs of Algiers while en route to Malta from France and taken to that city until the accord between France and the Ottoman Empire. While being returned to freedom in 1554 he died at sea near the Sicilian island of Favignana.[14]

Having equipped a galley with the financial backing of the Catalan merchant family Caçador, one-eyed Hospitaller Adrián de Maimón took her into the Levant, where in September 1554 he encountered a large galliot with 120 Turks embarked including two captains. The galliot was en route to man and equip another vessel. The engagement was perilous and bloody as Maimon's galley had fewer combatants. To bring the engagement to an end the Turks rallied around the galley masts. Maimón's courageous combatants, however, finally repelled the Turkish boarders, but Maimón and his lieutenant Juan Antonio Fuster remained gravely wounded. Maimón's men even so pursued the Turks, forcing some to jump into the sea. Nevertheless, they were unable to overcome the remainder and so set the galliot on fire before withdrawing. Maimón returned victorious to Malta but his backers did not wish to better arm the galley, forcing Maimón to resign his command. He was succeeded by the Catalan soldier Jaime Losada, who unfortunately soon lost her to two fustas of Uluç Ali. Formerly a Dominican novice by the name of Luca Galeni, the latter was in those days a small-time pirate who would rise on merit to become Kapudan Pasha or Commander-in-Chief of the Ottoman Armada in 1572.[15]

Claude de la Sengle was meanwhile applying himself to governance of the Order of Jerusalem with affection and prudence. In addition to the Council he was aided in his endeavours by a coterie of five loyal knights: Charles de Hangest du Mesnil Saint-Georges of the Langue of France as Seneschal, Christophe le Bouleur de Montgaudry the Younger of the Langue of France as Maître de la Maison, Pierre de Gioù of the Langue of Auvergne as his Horseman, Charles d'Urre de Tessières of the Langue of Provence as Receiver, and Antoine Guèvre le Vigneron of the Langue of England as Secretary. In October Bernard d'Ornesan, Baron de Saint-Blancard, with his three galleys en route from Constantinople to Marseille, paused at Malta and Saint-Blancard briefed Grand Master, coterie, and Council on the outlook for the coming year. It appeared there would be no combined offensive in 1555; the Ottomans would assail targets of opportunity.[14]

Commander Bernardo de Guimeran was dispatched to Spain with orders to collect from Receivers in Catalonia, Navarre, Aragon, Castile, and Portugal all of the funds available and to return with them by fast galley to the Convent for an accelerated programme of defensive preparation. Guimeran took with him a summons for all Hospitallers able to travel to attend a Chapter General to convene at Malta in the spring and to remain through the period during which Malta might be assailed. Finally, Guimeran was ordered to put down a mini-rebellion of knights refusing to accept Pedro de Aldovera as Receiver at the Castellany of Amposta. Guimeran did so and Aldovera remained Receiver.[14]

At Sicily Viceroy Juan de Vega increasingly evidenced his contempt for all things Maltese, the first and foremost consequence delays and outright cancellations of essential food shipments. Initiative after initiative of Procurator (an attorney also a corsair) Niccolò Orsino di Rivalta was frustrated. So too were the undertakings of emissaries Gil de Andrade of the Langue of Castile and Alonso de Escobar of León. Fully loaded grain carriers of Maltese owners Michele Rosso and Paolo d'Aula were sunk in place at Sicilian wharves in November. All of this occurred at a time of extreme shortages at Malta, some going without for as long as fifteen days at a stretch. Eight days before Christmas yet a third emissary was sent to plead Malta's case before the Viceroy, this one Don Luis de Lara, Commander of Bamba, who diplomatically made it clear that Spanish subjects at Malta were dying of starvation, and that the Empire was in danger of losing its first line of defence at Malta. A shipload of grain was found and sold to Lara at an exorbitant price. As the year ended, there was no change in the attitude of the Viceroy. And the Emperor was at war in Flanders.[14]

During 1555 the great scarcity of flour began to be overcome by a new technology, mule-driven mills able to produce much more flour in the same period of time required by windmills, without the vagaries of wind but with the vagaries of mules. As for the grain itself, the Order was constrained to intercept grain carriers at sea, force them into Maltese ports, and if Christian carriers, pay them a fair price. On 29 March Pope Julius III died, ending a Papacy noted not merely by the usual nepotism but also by his relationship with an adopted nephew. He was succeeded for three weeks by Marcellus II, and on 23 May by Giovanni Pietro Carafa as Pope Paul IV. During this period of change at Rome numbers of commandery and priory-based Hospitallers began to arrive at Malta for the Chapter General then scheduled for Sunday, 21 April, the first of Claude de la Sengle's Magistracy and the fifth to be convened since 1530 settlement at Malta. Also arriving was news of the imminent departure from Constantinople of the Ottoman Armada said to number sixty galleys and forty smaller craft under command of Croatian Piali Pasha, in succession of Croatian Sinan Pasha. Piali, like Sinan, was to be accompanied by Dragut Pasha. Also like Sinan, Piali was a protégé of Croatian Grand Vizier Rustem Pasha, but unlike Sinan had also been a protégé of the deceased Kheir-ed-Din Barbarossa, at the time of Barbarossa favour said to be an amateur marine cartologist.[16]

On Sunday, 21 April 1555 the Convent gathered in the great hall of Castle Saint Angelo where, as at the previous Chapter General in May 1548, Chaplain Mateo Castillo opened proceedings with a sermon. The Chapter General opened, however, without General of the Galleys Parisot de la Valette and all of the Hospitallers who would be departing with him on 25 April for a raid along the Barbary Coast. Hospitaller Domenico Cubelles was the first Bishop of Malta to participate in a Chapter General; he and not Lieutenant to the Grand Master Claude de Gruel-Laborel led the ceremonial entrance. Gruel, though, as Prior of Toulouse followed shortly with all other Knights of the Grand Cross. Behind Cubelles came Prior of the Church Graciano Gálvez, who presented to the waiting Grand Master the roll of Hospitallers attending. Then came Lieutenant Marshal Guillaume Coppier carrying the Order's Standard, also presented to the Grand Master. Then came Knights of the Grand Cross, then all other knights, then chaplains and serving brothers. Separating into eight langues, Sixteen *Capitolanti* or legislators were selected, two per langue as follows: for Provence Lieutenant Grand Commander Pierre de Gozon-Mélac and Commander Charles d'Urre de Tessieres; for Auvergne Bailiff of Lyon Jean Thomassin and Pilier Guillaume Coppier; for France Grand Hospitaller François de Piédefer and Seneschal Charles de Hangest du Mesnil Saint-Georges; for Aragon Grand Conservator Pedro de Montserrat and Commander Pedro de Iunient; for Italy Prior of Messina Signorino della Gattinara and Bailiff of Naples Giorgio Adorno; for England Lieutenant Turcopolier Antoine Guèvre le Vigneron and, there being no other member of the langue eligible to vote at Malta, Martín de Duero of Castile (John James Sandilands of Scotland had been received a year earlier but was not yet eligible to vote); for Germany Grand Bailiff Adam von Schwalbach and, there being no other member of the langue at Malta, Diego Montero of

Castile; and for Castile Lieutenant Chancellor Don Luis de Lara and Cristóvão da Cunha.[16]

These Sixteen adjourned to the Private Residence at Birgu of Christophe le Bouleur de Montgaudry the Younger, who had recently been granted by Magistral Grace the Commandery at Saint-Étienne-de-Renneville. At Montgaudry's residence they were joined by Vice Chancellor Martín Rojas de Portalrubio to opine on financial matters and by Antoine Cressin the Burgundian Chaplain and Scribe for the Common Treasury, and there they considered policy proposals and disputes requiring resolution as well as Common Treasury finances and other matters brought before the Chapter General. One of the more notable actions of the Sixteen was to delegate to the Grand Master authority to sell or encumber to Hospitallers housing constructed in the new walled city on Saint Michael's island/peninsula to be called Senglea. The Grand Master was also authorised to approve disposition of the one fifth share of a Hospitaller estate to a third party subject to further approval of Grand Bailiff Adam von Schwalbach as senior member of the Sixteen. Sengle was as well authorised to maintain and fund six war galleys in addition to the Great Galleon and several other vessels. While given the power to appoint captains of galleys and ships, he accepted only the power to nominate such individuals, reserving appointments to the Council of State. Through these and other decisions the Grand Master was given authority to govern the Convent until the next Chapter General.

Finally, because of his familiarity with the Vatican Library, because of his fluency in Latin, Greek, Italian, French, Spanish, and English, because of his unparalleled popularity among and respect of fellow brethren, and because of his demonstrated skills at composition, Lieutenant Turcopolier Antoine Guèvre of the Langue of England was appointed to write a history of the Order of Jerusalem.[16]

The aforementioned history was never completed because in December of the following year Guèvre died of exhaustion. Neither was any of this history located by successor historian Giacomo Bosio. What was located, as attested on unnumbered page 5 of the introduction to Bosio's Volume I, is Guèvre's reduction to one manuscript of all things pertinent to the Order of Jerusalem, which Guèvre found in the Vatican Library during his years as one of the Order's emissaries to the Holy See. That manuscript, Bosio wrote, is the foundation of his *History*. Also found is an earlier history of the Ottoman Empire written in Guèvre's native French. This history has been translated into Latin and published in Germany under the title *Aulai Turcicae, Ottomannicīq; Imperij Descriptio.*[18]

Departing from the Freo Channel between Gozo and Malta early in the morning of 25 April 1555, Valette's five galleys plus the frigate of Cola Aniello reached Lampedusa, 90 nautical miles west-south-west in twenty-four hours. Standing offshore, a reconnaissance party was put ashore to ascertain whether corsairs were present. Three large Turkish galliots were discovered, as large as Maltese galleys, beached in the main port on the south side of the island. While the shore party returned to the galleys, Cola Aniello, incredulously and in contravention of Valette's orders, took his fast frigate across the harbour mouth, where he separately discovered the galliot presence. One of his crew lofted a useless arrow at the enemy while Cola Aniello signalled loudly for the galleys. Enemy oarsmen were well rested, however, while galley oarsmen were exhausted from rowing all night. The galliots easily got away. Because Cola Aniello was widely admired, there was little more than angry censure.[17]

Disappointed as well as angry, the squadron continued from Lampedusa to the coast of Africa, where a Venetian sailing ship was halted and searched for contraband. Moors and Turks discovered on board were removed. Off Zuara a large garbo was seized bound from Djerba to Egypt, her skipper Salem Reis of the Berber tribe of Macares (modern Libya), her cargo barracan or camel-hair cloth; sixty Moors were taken captive, many of them pilgrims en route to Mecca. The captured vessel, commanded by Malta pilot Cayla, was sailed back to the Freo Channel in company with the galleys, where she grounded in shallows near the island of Comito (modern Kemmuna). It took a lot of pushing and pulling and a full set of sails to get her off. While getting the garbo off her sand bank, captive Moors rose in rebellion. Without arquebus or even bow and arrow but with assegai spears, they took after the prize crew. Catalan Rodrigo Ortiz took an assegai in the mouth, wrenched it out and threw it at the nearest Moor. During a second assault by the Moors a match was put to the magazine. Prize crew and Moors went over the side; most were rescued by galley skiffs. Taken from a passing Christian vessel that same day, 30 April, were two Turks, five Moors, and several pieces of iron artillery bound for Tripoli. On the first of May a sudden Borrasca hit with very high winds. Philipp Flach's *San Claudio* suffered rigging and other damage, and the squadron returned to Birgu for repairs.[17]

With the 21 April Chapter General still in session, four of the five galleys again departed Malta on 22 May 1555, again bound for North Africa. Two days later the Sixteen *Capitolanti* imposed a property tax on all of the wealth of the Order to yield 30,000 gold scudos per year over and above normal responsions, to continue until the next Chapter General. In one more final act, the Chapter General conferred the Bailiwick of Lango and its attendant Grand Cross on General of the Galleys Parisot de la Valette and adjourned that same day. Also at Malta, Grand Master and Council appointed Grand Conservator Pedro de Montserrat Ambassador to the Court of Emperor Charles V in Flanders as well as to that of his son King Philip of England and Ireland at Greenwich.[19]

On 9 June 1555 Valette's four galleys returned to Malta towing three Infidel merchant ships with cargoes of foodstuffs. Two of these were taken off Cape Misurata (Misrata), 95 nautical miles south-east of Tagiora, both under command of Metin Karadeniz Reis. The third was a galleon taken following strong resistance within sight of Malta. She was commanded by Recep Galipoglu, who fell in the fighting. A third capture at Cape Misurata and fourth overall was a caramussal, which was sailed to Malta but got a ceremonial tow entering Grand Harbour. With a cargo of general merchandise and commanded by Memmi Reis of Galata (Karaköy), she was bound from Alexandria to points west. With these captures Malta's food stocks were adequate for the winter no matter the angst of Viceroy Juan de Vega. In addition, more than 250 labourers were added to the workforce, while many pieces of both bronze and iron artillery were added to defensive armaments.[19]

Not many days later Genovese corsair captain Bendinello Sauli, with two of his three galleys, reached Malta with two Infidel prizes, one with a cargo of rice and the other with a cargo of wheat, which when purchased by the Maltese brought food stocks to a level of abundance. Sauli reappears in this history in service to Naples or Sicily or both. With peace between Ottoman and Persian Empires, and with reports of a very large Armada assembling at Constantinople, Hospitaller Gil de Andrade of Castile was dispatched aboard the frigate of Cola Aniello to the Corfu Channel in search of activity or news. Bernard d'Ornesan, Baron de Saint-Blancard, in what was becoming an annual routine, arrived at Malta with five French galleys en route to rendezvous with the Ottoman Armada. His orders were to accompany the Ottomans to a further rendezvous with French galley forces. He assured the Grand Master that Malta had nothing to fear as the 'hired' Ottoman Armada would in 1555 be in service to King Henry II of France along the coasts of Corsica and Tuscany at Siena.[20]

Since the August 1554 defeat of Pietro Strozzi at Marciano, the Republic of Siena, the only republic in Italy other than Venice, had been dying a slow death, its remaining French and Sienese garrison commanded by Blaise de Montluc within the walls of the capital city surrounded by Florentine troops of Gian Giacomo de Medici, aided at sea by the Imperial Armada of Andrea Doria. The garrison had been starved to death and the cats and rats had all been eaten. Apparently unbeknownst to Saint-Blancard, Siena had fallen on 21 April 1555 following nine months of siege. Montluc had survived to tell the heart-wrenching tale of children sacrificed and mothers killed at the walls in his *Commentaires de Messire Blaise de Montluc* (Bordeaux, 1592, free online). Perhaps also unbeknownst to Saint-Blancard, the Ottoman Armada of seventy or so galleys had departed Constantinople on 18 May under command of Piali Pasha but with Dragut Pasha at the ripe age of 70 giving advice. Following Saint-Blancard's visit, Grand Master and Council decided not to waste funds on hired soldiery but rather to fund accelerated construction of fortifications. Catalan Jorge de Sant Joan and François de Salviati were appointed Commissioners to oversee the work, the latter a bright young engineer of Sengle's Langue of France and an Italian expatriate related to Queen Catherine de Medici.[21]

Early in the month of July Hospitaller Gil de Andrade and his fast frigate returned to Malta with a report that he had sighted the Ottoman Armada off Cape Santa Maria de Leuca (heel of the Italian boot) bound for the Strait of Messina with eighty galleys and twenty smaller oared vessels. On this advice Don Pedro de Mendoza, commanding the galley *San Michele Arcangelo*, was dispatched on 15 July to Barcelona by way of Mallorca to embark and return to Malta Don Bernardo de Guimeran. Guimeran had in October been dispatched to Spain with orders to collect from Receivers in Spain and Portugal all of the funds available and to return with them by fast galley to the Convent for an accelerated programme of defensive preparation. Guimeran had in his possession

60,000 scudos in gold pieces-of-eight. Mendoza was accompanied by Gil de Andrade aboard the fast frigate of Cola Aniello, and went with the blessing of all of the Convent, most of whom too well remembered loss of the galley *Santa Caterina* to Dragut while transporting 70,000 gold ducats from France in November 1548.[20]

During July new and streamlined statutes for regulation of the Convent were introduced. The product of Grand Conservator Pedro de Montserrat, Lieutenant Turcopolier Antoine de Guèvre, and Vice Chancellor Martín Rojas de Portalrubio, this was the first revision of the Order's statutes since that of Pierre d'Aubusson's Vice Chancellor Guillaume Caoursin in November 1482.[20]

Saint-Blancard and his galleys, on reaching Corfu, discovered that the Ottoman Armada had come and gone. It did not appear that Saint-Blancard would be able to overtake the Ottomans before their northbound transit of the Strait of Messina, in which event the five French galleys would have to circumnavigate Sicily far offshore to avoid capture. Having transited the Strait of Messina, the Ottomans early in July 1555 raided San Lucido and Paola on Calabria's Tyrrhenian coast, removing as many local citizens as could be sent to the oars or held for ransom. One week later they conducted similar raids at Populonia and Piombino in Tuscany, the latter on 12 July a disastrous encounter with an Imperial German garrison during which 700 janissaries were left on the field. Two weeks later, on 25 July, twenty-three tardy French galleys under command of rebel Prince of Salerno Ferrante di Sanseverino rendezvoused with the Ottomans off Elba. Piali exchanged courtesies; Dragut, never one to be kept waiting, seethed.[22]

Grand Conservator Pedro de Montserrat departed Malta on his ambassadorial mission to the Emperor and the new King Philip of England, amended to include rendering the Order's obedience to new Pope Paul IV, as well. Viceroy of Sicily Juan de Vega forbade the Order's galleys to enter Sicilian ports, and Montserrat in August brought this to the Emperor's attention as well. Later in the month at the Court of England Montserrat encountered Don Antonio de Toledo, Hospitaller councillor to King Philip, and Oswald Massinbert, who with the Grand Master's license had returned to England to obtain the Priory of Ireland, but recovery of Hospitaller assets scattered so widely to so many interests, often resold, was proving a legal morass.[23]

At Greenwich the Priory of England was conferred on Hospitaller Richard Shelley, while the Preceptory of Templecombe was conferred on his brother James Shelley. Hospitaller Oliver Starkey, about whom more will be written in this history, was preliminarily awarded the Preceptory at Quenyngton. Returning to Malta by way of the Imperial Court in Flanders, Montserrat obtained a letter from Emperor Charles V to Juan de Vega ordering and commanding that the people of Malta and Gozo be fed with Sicilian grain and that other relations with Malta immediately be restored to the status quo ante. With Siena under Imperial control the Franco–Ottoman Galley Armada withdrew to Corsica, where first Genoa's Calvi and then Genoa's Bastia were besieged from sea and shore, both unsuccessfully, the former costing another 300 janissary dead, the latter siege lifted on 23 August. And so concluded the 1555 chapter of the Franco–Ottoman Entente, four weeks, three strikes, and out. The Ottoman Armada took a direct course for home.[23]

The galley *San Michele Arcangelo* returned to Malta on 23 September, having safely transported Don Bernardo de Guimeran and his 60,000 scudos in gold pieces-of-eight, but without Cola Aniello and the crew of his frigate. Following *San Michele*'s initial departure from Malta on 15 July, she had been forced to return by four corsair galliots from Porto Farina in the Gulf of Tunis. Sailing again on 23 July, she and the frigate had made it to Mallorca in five days and five nights for rendezvous with Guimeran, thence proceeding to Barcelona. Three nights and two days out of Barcelona returning to Malta, 12 miles to windward of Sicily's Favignana Island, galley and frigate encountered five galliots of Uluç Ali, also known as Occhiali. Cut loose from tow, Aniello lured the galliots in one direction, while galley and gold proceeded in another. Aniello was captured but soon ransomed absent the frigate. Galley and gold proceeded by way of Sicily's north coast to safety at Palermo. When the coast was clear, galley and gold proceeded east along the north coast of Sicily and transited the Strait of Messina southbound, then taking course for Malta. Some miles south of Cape Passero, in the Malta Channel between Sicily and Malta, a half-moon formation of Ottoman galliots, the vanguard of Dragut's corsairs followed by Piali's Ottoman Armada returning from Corsica, was spotted to the west eastbound. Galley and gold reversed course and beat a hasty retreat to presumed safety in Sicily's port of Syracuse. The Ottoman vanguard, however, beached in the Gulf of Vendicari just south of Syracuse, waiting for the main body. Soon both vanguard and main body took course for the south coast of the Italian boot, passing Syracuse and firing into the port in the process. Mendoza recklessly brought *San Michele Arcangelo* to the harbour mouth and with the Syracuse fortress returned Ottoman fire. Fortunately, neither Piali nor Dragut could be bothered. As Kapudan, Pasha Piali for a decade and a half displayed none of the tendency of corsairs to live off the land. As for Dragut, he had sacked Syracuse in the past and appeared to have no further interest.[24]

In Italy the Bailiwick of Santo Stefano became vacant upon the October death of incumbent Camillo Muscetola of Naples; he was succeeded by Admiral Francesco Cateneo, who was himself succeeded as Admiral by Commander and future Grand Master Pietro del Monte. Reaching the end of his life while in France was Prior of Toulouse and Magistral Lieutenant to the Grand Master Claude de Gruel-Laborel. He was succeeded as Prior of Toulouse by Grand Commander Pierre de Beaulac-Trébons, who was himself succeeded as Grand Commander by Parisot de la Valette. Valette renounced the dignity of Bailiff of Lango, which was conferred upon Commander of Chantereine Pierre de la Fontaine. It was a period in the life of Malta and the life of the Order of Jerusalem when progress was being made on all fronts. There was even enough money in the Common Treasury to fund construction of the fifth and sixth galleys mandated by April's Chapter General.[24]

The four existing galleys of the squadron and two belonging to the Genovese corsair Bendinello Sauli were in Malta harbour ready for a provisioning run to Messina, moored in Dockyard Creek sterns with twin quarter-warps to Birgu's mole, bows roped to mooring buoys out in front. Parisot de la Valette was in his quarters ashore, as were most other officers. A furious storm, a typhoon composed of south-west, west, and north winds, bore down on the island during the night of 23–24 October 1555 and for seven hours struck ships in the harbour; several smaller vessels sank, others were driven ashore, galliots and brigantines were shattered. With north winds broad on their starboard side, unable to swing on their buoys with lines ashore, the six galleys were turned keel up. Most of the oarsmen and skeleton crews drowned, others were crushed between vessels. As galley squadron commander, Valette rushed to the scene; when the howling of the wind subsided a tapping on the hulls was answered from within the new galley *Santa Fede*, and a ship's mascot, a monkey, emerged having exited through a submerged stern hatch. The Gascon knight Mathurin d'Aux de Lescout, called Romegas, Lieutenant to skipper Antoine de Thésan-Vénàsque, and several others followed. All had passed the long hours clinging to galley frames with water to their chins, and had reached the extreme limit of their strength. Of the four Malta galleys, three, the capitana *Santa Maria della Vittoria*, *Santa Fede*, and *San Michele Arcangelo*, were recovered. *San Claudio*, however, was damaged beyond repair. Both of Sauli's two galleys were also recovered.[25]

Two knights died, Sicilian Francesco Crisafi, Lieutenant to Pietro Vasco of the Piedmont commanding *San Claudio*, and Catalan Rodrigo Ortiz, Lieutenant to Luis Cortit, skipper of *San Michele Arcangelo*. Cortit had succeeded Pedro de Mendoza one day earlier, and brought Ortiz to the assignment. Six hundred individuals were dead in the sea, most of them Muslim oarsmen chained to Hospitaller benches, the balance crew and paid oarsmen without quarters ashore. The hands of Romegas shook for the rest of his life. Valette was nonetheless so impressed with the strength of character exhibited that he made Romegas his protégé and, later, commander of one, sometimes more, of Valette's own corsair vessels. It was in this latter capacity that Romegas developed his reputation. There is no report of a Board of Inquiry even though the gathering storm was predictable.[25]

Chapter XII

Claude de la Sengle 1555–57

Exactly one month after the storm disaster at Malta, on 23 November 1555, the galley squadron departed for winter overhaul at Messina, the three surviving galleys propelled by sparse rowing crews of petty criminals, or *buonovoglie*. A fourth galley had been ordered from the shipyard at Messina while a search for oarsmen had been initiated by Lieutenant Turcopolier Antoine de Guèvre, who continued to serve the Grand Master as Secretary, addressing pleas for assistance to various princes and legates seeking petty criminals willing to earn their freedom from incarceration.[1]

In December 1555 21-year-old Francis of Lorraine arrived at Malta with two galleys and a brigantine his personal property as well as with a large group of French knights and adventurers. He was the eleventh of twelve children of Claude de Lorraine, Duke of Guise, and of Antoinette de Bourbon. His eldest sister Mary wed King James V of Scotland and was the mother of and regent for Mary, Queen of Scots (1542–87). Lorraine had not come to satisfy Convent tenure and caravan requirements. Nor as a novitiate, but rather as Grand Prior of France since the age of 11. Recognising his own inexperience, he had selected Pierre de la Fontaine, Hospitaller Bailiff of Lango, as his Lieutenant. Fontaine had selected Hospitaller Giron de Chastaignier to command Lorraine's capitana, while Hospitaller André de Saulcières de Tenance of the Priory of Champagne commanded the padrona. Arriving a few days later was a ship carrying all the things the Grand Prior might need.[1]

A letter arrived from Don Pedro de Montserrat at Greenwich also signed by Don Pedro de Toledo and by Bailiff of Eagle-in-waiting Pedro des Felizes expressing sympathy for the unfortunate storm damage to the galley squadron and observing there were two new galleys in the shipyards of Naples that might be available. Confirmation of the royal gift was received at the year's end, and Don Bernardo de Guimeran was immediately dispatched to Naples to arrange for outfitting and oarsmen.

On 16 January 1556 Prince Philip, son of Emperor Charles V, was crowned Philip II, King of Spain.[2]

Hospitaller Giron de Chastaignier, commanding the Lorraine capitana augmented by a detachment of Hospitallers, proceeded to the coast of Africa, where he took a Turkish vessel of mediocre value. For reasons of winter port closures, absence of sea traffic, and the discomfort of embarked adventurers, the excursion was soon aborted. January is not a good time to be at sea in the Mediterranean, which is why there was an absence of sea traffic.[2]

Following successive French defeats in northern Italy, the Treaty of Vaucelles was signed on 5 February 1556 between Philip II of Spain and Henry II of France. Based on the terms of the treaty, the territory of the Franche-Comté adjacent to Switzerland was relinquished to Philip. While the treaty was soon broken, it was to little effect as treasuries of both countries were bare of funds needed to keep mercenary armies in the field. After Charles V's abdication in 1556 split the Habsburg empire between Philip II and Ferdinand I, the focus of the war shifted to Flanders, where Philip, in conjunction with Emmanuel Philibert of Savoy, defeated the French at St Quentin. England's entry into the war on the side of Spain later in the year led to French capture of Calais, and the end to 211 years of English rule. While French armies were also able to plunder neighbouring Spanish possessions in the Low Countries, Henry was nonetheless forced to accept a peace agreement in which he renounced any further claims to Italy. Franco–Spanish conflict in the Mediterranean soon diminished to insignificance, a development much welcomed at Malta.

Sultan Suleiman, believing Mourad Aga insufficiently active as Sancakbey or Governor of Tripoli and Tagiora, appointed Dragut Beylerbey or Viceroy of all Ottoman-held North Africa between Tunis and Egypt including Tripoli and Tagiora (modern Libya). Tripoli became Dragut's headquarters, while Mourad was returned to Tagiora. At Constantinople, the Ottoman Armada remained under command of Piali Pasha.[3]

April's second deployment to Africa, this time by Francis of Lorraine's entire French flotilla, was more productive. Three Turkish ships were taken, yielding a large number of captives to be employed in construction at Malta. The captured ships also carried cargoes of considerable value, the lot taken to Malta. Meanwhile, Beylerbey of Algiers Salih Reis, having conquered Spain's Peñón de Vélez de la Gomera (presently a Spanish enclave on the Mediterranean coast of Morocco), had late in 1555 requested of the Sultan in Constantinople additional forces with which to continue an offensive in the western Mediterranean. Then came reports of the completion in Ottoman arsenals of large numbers of new galleys and coincident gathering of embarked forces, with an Armada forty galleys strong having 6,000 embarked troops sailing from Constantinople in mid-April 1556 under Piali Pasha, destination unknown. Concerned that Malta might be the next objective on the target list of either Constantinople, Tripoli, or Algiers, Sengle ordered an acceleration of defensive preparations, particularly at Fort Saint Elmo overlooking the otherwise undefended port of Marsamuscietto. In this regard Commander of Orle and Bompas Pedro de Iunient of Aragon, Governor of Fort Saint Elmo, accelerated completion of the new cavalier and spur.

News was received at about this time of the death of Prior of Navarre Francisco Peschier; he was succeeded on 24 April by Commander Juan Ximenez.[2] On the same date the Council appointed Francis of Lorraine General of the Galleys, succeeding Parisot de la Valette. On 1 May seven Ottoman galleys and a galliot in search of drinking water fearlessly anchored in Malta's Marsa Scirocco at the hour of Vespers. Thought to be the vanguard of the Ottoman Armada, their presence caused alarm throughout Malta, particularly inasmuch as the galleys *San Michele Arcangelo* and *Santa Fede* had one day earlier been sent to the Freo Channel to take under tow a Venetian sailing ship laden with timber, iron, and other construction items ordered by Malta. Alerted by the guard-brigantine commanded by Catalan Manel Bosch, the two galleys took course for safety at Sicily, while the Venetian set sail downwind. Forced himself by contrary easterly winds to beach in Mellieha Bay at the north-east of Malta, Bosch was captured by a Turkish reconnaissance party put ashore to alert the main body of trouble, and would die in captivity. But inasmuch as a mass of sails failed to appear on the eastern horizon, the notion of a vanguard was soon dispelled. Shortly after the capture of Bosch the eight oared vessels were forced by Marshal Louis de Lastic with a party including most knights on the island, mounted and foot, to weigh anchor and move up Malta's west coast to Mugiarro (Mgarr) on the south shore of Gozo.[4]

At Mugiarro three Spanish renegades, a part of a galley crew, fled. From them the Maltese eventually learned the eight oared vessels were not the Armada's vanguard but rather the squadron of Dragut. Said by the renegades to be in disfavour with Grand Vizier Rustem Pasha, Dragut consequently no longer had hope of commanding the Ottoman Armada. The three Spaniards also reported that Dragut had hoped to detour the Armada into an assault on Malta, but the Armada was under orders to rendezvous with Beylerbey of Algiers Salih Reis for the conquest of Oran. This news was later confirmed by Francis of Lorraine upon return from a third raid into the Levant, where he had obtained the same information from captives. This news was also confirmed by a ship of Ragusa bound from Constantinople with 'contraband' forced into Malta by a corsair galleon which was the personal property of Parisot de la Valette and Bailiff of Lyon Jean Thomassin. In the event, Dragut, having taken on drinking water, took course for Lampedusa. At Lampedusa the corsair found and seized the laden Venetian that had fled downwind from Freo. Her cargo was exactly what Dragut needed to refortify Tripoli. Among cargo items was an elaborate *fanale* or ship lantern signifying command at sea intended for the Malta capitana. Dragut made it his own. He also made his own a Venetian boy, a scribe of sorts found among the crew who would later be inherited by fellow Italian Uluç Ali, also known as Occhiali. Converted to Islam, this boy, then known as Hassan Veneziano, would three times be appointed Ottoman Beylerbey or Viceroy of Greater Algiers as Hassan III, the first time in 1576.[4]

At Malta preparedness in 1556 was partially delegated to four Council members with orders and authority to procure all things necessary for the defence of Malta as well as of depopulated Gozo while ensuring readiness not just of the principal fortifications in and around Birgu but also at remote bastions on the two islands. These four were Marshal Louis de Lastic, Bailiff of Naples Giorgio Adorno, Bailiff of Lango Pierre de la Fontaine, and Pilier, or senior knight, of Castile Don Luis de Lara. The appointment of Francis of Lorraine meanwhile angered Viceroy of Sicily Juan de Vega, exacerbating his anti-French irritation with the Order of Jerusalem and with Grand Master Claude de la Sengle, and he ordered that any Maltese unit commanded by Lorraine be denied entry into

Sicilian ports as enemies of His Catholic Majesty Philip II of Spain. This was a violation of the Treaty of Vaucelles between France and Spain, and it denied Spain French assistance in combatting the Ottomans, but Pope Paul IV and others were unable to pacify the Viceroy. Senior squadron captain Pierre de Gozon-Mélac was therefore designated lieutenant to the Grand Prior and Regent of the Galleys whenever they must proceed to either Sicily or Naples, leaving the Grand Prior of France at Malta. Aragonese Hospitaller Melchor de Egueras was dispatched to Spain to plead the Order's case before the Spanish King and did so persuasively and successfully. The Viceroy's order was eventually rescinded.[5]

Hospitaller Gil de Andrade was in June sent by fast frigate into the Levant to obtain additional input on the whereabouts of the Ottoman Armada. It was some months before he returned, having been pursued by three galliots and forced to beach on the shore of Apulia (Puglia). Belonging to non-Hospitaller Stefan Sufugnio, the frigate was lost but the crew was saved, fleeing up a wooded mountain. The eye-patched Andrade, it might be noted, was an exceptional seaman. In 1571 he would be personally appointed by King Philip II of Spain as one of seven commissioners to advise Don Juan of Austria concerning conduct of the Battle of Lepanto, still the most costly naval battle in history, and would be at the fleet commander's side throughout the battle.

Antonio Maldonado of Castile was dispatched to Sicily to hire and transport to Malta a company of Spanish infantry; 200 such infantry were located at Messina. Orders and means were sent to Don Bernardo de Guimeran at Naples to hire an additional 400 Spanish infantry in two companies to be commanded by Hospitallers Don Carlo Ruffo of Naples and Giovan Antonio Bisballe of Messina, son of Calabria's Count of Briatico. Also sent to Sicily were the galleys under command of Regent Gozon-Mélac to load provisions for transport to Malta.[5]

It was in June 1556, Bosio wrote of an agent's report, that thirty galleys and ten fustas under Salih Reis of Algiers passed Sicily's Cape Passero bound from Constantinople to Oran, not the forty Ottoman galleys under Piali Pasha cited above. Morgan, in his *Complete History of Algiers* quoting Diego de Haëdo, on the other hand, had Salih with thirty galleys depart Algiers to rendezvous with the Ottoman Armada of forty galleys at Bougie (Béjaïa), Salih dying en route of bubonic plague then raging at Algiers and elsewhere in North Africa. Morgan had it right. The siege of Spanish Oran was subsequently laid ashore and afloat. Unsuccessful, it was lifted in August. As Salih's tombstone outside the Beb-al-Weyd gate to Algiers lends some credence to Morgan–Haedo's version of events, while Mediterranean naval authority R.C. Anderson writes Piali's participation in the siege was the furthest west the regular Ottoman Navy ever operated, Bosio's agent erred in his identification. The foregoing agent's news was nevertheless cause to rescind the Hospitaller recruitment of infantry companies. During the summer months Prior of Messina Signorino delle Gattinara and Hospitallar historian Juan Antonio de Foxá attended ceremonies in Sicily in connection with the transfer of the Kingdom of Sicily from Imperial dominion to the dominion of the Kingdom of Spain.[6]

Seventeen-year-old son of Giannettino Doria and heir-apparent Giovanni (Gian) Andrea Doria, newly appointed by Andrea Doria as General of the Catholic Armada, arrived at Malta on 11 July with nine galleys, the total number departing Malta thirteen including three Maltese and one French together commanded by Francis of Lorraine. The combined flotilla pointed directly to the Barbary Coast. Between Malta and Tripoli the Turkish brigantine of Hassan Ali of Dragut's squadron was captured.[7] From captives the Christians learned Dragut was at Tripoli attending to both the refortification of the city and to the pacification of surrounding Arab and Moorish tribes. He was not pillaging Genovese Liguria as some reports had it, again repaying the Dorias for his four years on rowing benches. While the captors considered the garrison at Tripoli too strong for their meagre force, the two commanders considered avenging Hospitaller losses at Zuara. Zuara, however, was infested with the same plague rampant elsewhere in North Africa. The flotilla therefore headed for Djerba. Spotted at Djerba on 23 July, beached under the abandoned 14th Century castle[8] on the seaward side of the island was a galliot of twenty-one benches and a galley. Captured earlier from Catalan merchants, the latter was easily seized; a short time later the galliot, belonging to Occhiali (Uluç Ali), similarly fell into their hands. Occhiali and the crews, however, escaped safely ashore. Some Christian slaves were freed from the oars; most, however, disappeared with the crews. Two other vessels found on the beach were burned. The combined flotilla returned to Malta on 28 July towing the captured galley and galliot. The galley was assigned to Doria and the galliot to Malta. When re-equipped, the galliot would be commanded by Pierre de la Fontaine's nephew Guillaume and would be employed as a Maltese-flag corsair.[7]

New Pope Paul IV, completely unaware of history but completely at the disposal of *nepotes*, had allied himself with the French in the contest for control of Italy. In July 1556 he declared King Philip II of Spain no longer King of Naples. Philip's new Viceroy of Naples, Duke of Alba Fernando Álvarez de Toledo, promptly marched on Rome at the head of 12,000 Spanish troops.

Paul IV called for a truce while awaiting the arrival of a French force commanded by Francis of Lorraine, Duke of Guise and elder brother of Prior of France Francis of Lorraine. The elder brother failed to arrive. Meanwhile the Pope's pro-French galley squadron included four galleys, the personal property of Pietro Strozzi, then a Marshal of France.

Over the past two years Prior of Saint-Gilles Philippe du Broc had constructed at the arsenal of Villefranche a large galleon funded from his personal estate. In June he donated the completed but unequipped vessel to the Hospital. On Sengle's order she was towed to nearby Nice for outfitting under supervision of Prior of Barletta and Castellan of Nice Paolo Simeoni with assistance of Commander Antoine de Guèvre, Sengle's Secretary. The largest and most versatile ship in Hospitaller history, she was in late July sailed to Malta under the command of Pascal du Broc. At Malta artillery was mounted and she was commissioned for service under command of Catalan Jorge de Sant Joan. En route to Spain in August she encountered Piali Pasha's Ottoman Armada returning from the unsuccessful siege of Oran, and during an inconclusive engagement damaged nineteen of the Ottoman galleys. All forty passed within sight of Malta early in September, several obviously in need of repair.[8]

On 27 August 1556 Emperor Charles V abdicated the Imperial throne and his younger brother became Holy Roman Emperor Ferdinand. Charles's son Philip had earlier in the year acceded to the Kingdoms of Spain, Naples, Sardinia, and Sicily, as well as to Flanders, Milan, and possessions in the Americas.[8]

At Malta Grand Conservator (formerly Draper) Pedro de Montserrat died having recently completed an assignment as the King of Spain's Ambassador to his own Kingdom of Sardinia. Montserrat was succeeded as Grand Conservator by Catalan Nicolás de Aguilón. The three galleys of the Religion under command of Regent Gozon-Mélac were dispatched to Naples to escort the two galleys donated by the King of Spain at the end of 1555. These galleys, completely outfitted including oarsmen under supervision of Bernardo de Guimeran were christened *San Filippo* and *San Iacomo* and were respectively commanded by Neapolitan Giovan Simone Comito and Castilian Pedro de Ligoria. Early in September the five galleys of the Religion came upon three corsair galliots off Stromboli, the largest of which was of twenty-two banks. She was commanded by Succuli Reis, a natural Turk long a prisoner at Malta who the year before had earned his liberty. The three galliots had their masts unstepped in order to keep a low profile less visible to prey and enemy. The oncoming Maltese were sailing in line abreast with the wind astern, the Maltese capitana *Santa Fede* commanded by Gozon-Mélac assisted as Lieutenant by Mathurin d'Aux de Lescout-Romegas at the near end of the Maltese line with *San Michele Arcangelo* commanded by Luis Cortit next in line. Both were readying to board, as were the other three, all eight vessels on the same course. As the enemies closed, Succuli screamed that his oarsmen were Christian, and during the Maltese pause to board by the prow rather than alongside, reversed course and burst through the Maltese line, Succuli between Gozon-Mélac and Cortit, with a fury of arquebus shot and crossbow bolts, sprinting upwind while the Maltese shed their sails. By the time the Maltese also reversed course, it was too late to overhaul the lighter and faster corsair capitana, having less windage. The two smaller galliots, however, each of eighteen banks, were not so lucky getting through the Maltese line and were captured, one by Cortit's *San Michele Arcangelo* and the other beaching on Stromboli, where the crew was hunted down. The Maltese suffered no dead but many wounded, among whom was Don Bernardo de Guimeran with an arquebus round in the arm.[8]

The two French galleys that were the property of Francis of Lorraine returned to Malta early in October 1556 from another excursion to the Levant, bringing 120 captives. Modestly wounded in combat was Hospitaller Giron de Chastaignier, skippering the capitana; he unexpectedly and tragically succumbed to infection of his wound, however, and was succeeded by Hospitaller Antoine d'Aumale de Nancy, a Chastaignier family member.[9]

Of the four galleys that were the personal property of Pietro Strozzi then a part of the Papal Galley Squadron, *Porfiada* captured at Barcelona by Leone Strozzi in August 1551, was commanded by the same Giovanni Moretto (or Jean Moret) who departed Malta in May 1554 commanding one of the same Leone Strozzi's three galleys. Reportedly unhappy with his compensation, Moretto in November 1556 absconded from Civitavecchia with his command, taking her to his native Villefranche in the Duchy of Savoy, an ally of Spain in the latter's contest with France. There Moretto obtained a letter-of-marque authorising his stolen galley to engage in corsair war against both France and the Ottoman Empire while flying the flag of Savoy. From Villefranche the stolen galley deployed to the Levant. Pietro Strozzi was understandably unhappy with these developments, and wished to see Moretto face Church justice; justice for mutineers at the Church the same as justice for mutineers elsewhere.[10]

In December 1556 Francis of Lorraine's two French galleys at Malta were joined by a third French galley flying the flag of the Church with a letter of marque issued by Captain-General of the Church and Papal *nipote* Giovanni Carafa. This latest French galley was the property of a Monsieur de Carcès of Provence and was commanded by Pierre Fouroux. The three French galleys deployed to the Levant in company for corsair raids on targets of opportunity. During their absence, and to the very great sorrow and infinite distress of Grand Master Claude de la Sengle, his Secretary and companion Antoine de Guèvre le Vigneron died at Malta, of exhaustion Bosio reported. Soon afterward Prior of the Church Graciano Gálvez passed to a better life and was succeeded by a Greek of the Latin Church, who in 1523 following evacuation from Rhodes was received into the Langue of Auvergne as Andonis de Bligni-Cressi, later called Antoine Cressin the Burgundian. Prior of Barletta and Castellan of Nice Paolo Simeoni died at Nice. He had been a Hospitaller since before June 1506, when as a lone Hospitaller he turned away an assault by Ottoman Admiral Kemal Reis on the Hospitaller Castle at Leros. A veteran of the Great Siege of Rhodes, he was four years a slave to Kheir-ed-Din Barbarossa, who refused all ransom offers, only to watch helplessly as Simeoni led the breakout of 7,000 Christian slaves to turn the 1535 Siege of Tunis into a rout. He was still a Hospitaller in 1543 when as Castellan he denied the same Barbarossa capture of the Castle at Nice, where he died thirteen years later. His passing was universally mourned by the Convent at Malta and elsewhere. One fifth of the Simeoni estate was, as permitted by Hospitaller statutes, left to the Duchy of Savoy. Finally, news was received at Malta of the death in Provence of Prior of Saint-Gilles Philippe du Broc, who that year donated the new *Grand Galleon*. He was succeeded by Grand Commander Parisot de la Valette, who was in turn succeeded as Grand Commander by François de Toucheboeuf, long-time captain of the Order's Great Carrack *Santa Anna*.[9]

The new year 1557 began as the old year ended, with death in the family, this time of Hospitaller Infante Dom Luis of Portugal at the Hospitaller Priory of Crato in that country. Hospitallers Cristóvão da Cunha and Alonso de Solis were appointed ambassadors to King John III and to Henry, the King's younger brother and Cardinal of Portugal. They were to render the Order's condolences. They were also to ensure the Infante's estate accrued to the Order's Common Treasury.

By Royal decree the Priory of Crato was assigned to the deceased's natural son non-Hospitaller Don António of Portugal. The two ambassadors departed Malta on 3 January 1557 embarked aboard the galley capitana *Santa Fede* commanded by Regent Pierre de Gozon-Mélac, and *San Iacomo* commanded by Pedro de Ligorria. Also embarked were Bailiff of Lyon Jean Thomassin, Receiver-General of the Religion in the Kingdom of France, and Charles d'Urre de Tessieres, bound for Toulon together to recover the estate of Philippe du Broc. By the time the ambassadors to Portugal reached the Court in Lisbon in April, King John III was in the final three months of his life. He died in June and was succeeded by his grandson Sebastien, 3 years of age. The ambassadors were unable to reverse the award of the Priory of Crato to Don António, nor were they able to obtain his father's estate for the Common Treasury. At Malta the Order was beset on the one hand by the broken Treaty of Vaucelles, again leaving the French and Spanish at loggerheads, including French and Spanish at Malta, and on the other hand by the increasing militancy of the Ottoman Porte at Constantinople.[11]

Of the three remaining French galleys in the Papal Galley Squadron, two were the personal property of the aforementioned Monsieur de Carcès, and these were the fastest galleys in the entire squadron. One of these, flying the Standard of Malta and not the Standard of the Church, deployed in December with the mini-squadron of Francis of Lorraine. On sighting the Standard of Malta flying from mini-squadron trucks, Giovanni Moretto took a converging course, exchanged artillery salutes, and hailed the capitana commanded by Antoine d'Aumale of Nancy, seeking to sail in company. Pierre Fouroux of the Carcès galley meanwhile put his skiff in the water, full of armed seamen, and rowed over in a friendly fashion, only to unexpectedly board and seize Moretto's galley. Moretto and his disciples were enchained. Aumale, meanwhile, not only believed himself deceived but was also concerned that Fouroux's action might be inconsistent with the Order's neutrality in the war between France and Spain, not to mention inconsistent with the exchange of friendly salutes. Fouroux agreed to return to Malta and to put the matter before Grand Master and Council. On 2 February the four galleys dropped anchor in Saint George's Cove, 2 nautical miles north of Birgu, as Fouroux refused to come in under the guns of Castle Saint Angelo. The dispute was brought before the Council, which predictably divided along national lines, and Grand Master Sengle was forced to less than a decision. Aware beyond Malta of these proceedings, complaints were lodged against Moretto by Venetian and Florentine merchants, among others, of preying on allied and neutral shipping. The Procurator of the Common Treasury made a case that *Porfiada*, as spoils of the deceased Hospitaller Prior of Capua, should now be the property of the Hospital. Sengle appointed a commission to rule upon the matter composed of Commander of Murello Pietro Vasco of Italy, Castellan of the Religion's Secular Court Antoine de Challemaison of France, and Don Bernardo de Guimeran of Spain. On 9 February the commission ruled that both Moretto and Fouroux be incarcerated, but that Fouroux might remain at liberty on his word not to flee. The commission also ruled that an inventory be taken of everything on board the two galleys. By this time the entire Convent was divided along national lines. On 3 March Hospitaller Giulio Bravo of Verona was dispatched to Rome for Papal guidance, pausing at Naples to obtain a safe-conduct from the Duke of Alba.[12]

Reports of Ottoman Armada activity increased in frequency during April and May, particularly in the latter month as forty galleys exited the Dardanelles, destination unknown. At Malta defensive measures were taken with assignment of Sector Wardens on 5 May, Commanders Bertrand de Vintimille d'Ollières of Provence, Battista Agliata of Palermo, and Don Bernardo de Guimeran of Aragon. Philipp Flach of Germany was dispatched as Captain-at-Arms and Governor of Notabile.

Giovan Antonio Bisballe, Don Carlo Ruffo, and Giovan Vittorio Morello were dispatched to Naples each to return with a company of hired infantry. These last hires were aborted almost before they were initiated on further advice that the Ottoman Armada, increased from forty to sixty-five galleys, did not proceed further west than Preveza, ancient Actium. Dragut's Tripoli corsairs, however, did come up to raid Cariati, north of Crotone on Calabria's Ionian coast, looting and burning the lower town while kidnapping oarsmen and ransomable others. Uluç Ali appeared off the Ligurian coast but did little damage. Altogether, it was a quiet summer in the central Mediterranean. In Italy, Prior of Pisa Francesco Romagnano, a Hospitaller since 1511 and a survivor of the Great Siege of Rhodes, reached the end of his life. He was succeeded as Prior of Pisa by Giovanni di Ventimiglia of Genoa of the aforementioned Provencal family of Vintimille. By virtue of his new position, Ventimiglia was awarded the Grand Cross.[13]

While the foregoing developments were occurring, the Grand Prior of France was recalled to France by King Henry II and by his brother the Duke of Guise. He complained to the Grand Master that he had been at Malta for eighteen months and had yet to deploy to the Levant; his pride and reputation required he see action. Not exactly an appropriate time for an excursion possibly provoking sixty-five Ottoman galleys, the Grand Prior nevertheless threatened to go it alone with his two proprietary galleys. Upon the return to Malta from Toulon of the galleys *Santa Fede* under Regent Gozon-Mélac and *San Iacomo* commanded by Pedro de Ligoria, Sengle was reluctantly persuaded. The crews and oarsmen of two of the Order's five galleys were used to reinforce the other three. The Grand Prior departed Malta on 2 May with five galleys, of which two were his personal property. The five included the new galleys *San Filippo* and *San Iacomo* respectively commanded by Giovan Simone Comito and by Ligoria, the Prior's own capitana commanded by Antoine d'Aumale and padrona commanded by André de Saulcières de Tenance, plus *Santa Fede* commanded by Christophe de Hazeville Vaulchamps. Embarked were full complements of caravan knights as well as additional volunteers plus companies of light infantry experienced in combat at sea, all under command when ashore of Lieutenant-General (and Moretto Commissioner) Pietro Vasco embarked aboard *San Filippo*. Vasco had the additional duty of counselling the young prince. Finally, there were two experienced pilots, Barbaccia and Il Rosso da Piombino.[14]

Flying his personal flag and the Standard of Malta from his own capitana, Lorraine pointed directly for Cape Misurata east of Tripoli and from there across the Gulf of Sirte to eastern Libya's Cape Buonandrea, where fresh water was taken on board. From Cape Buonandrea he proceeded on the wind to the western end of Crete and from there along the north coast of Crete until he learned from a Greek of the presence between Milos and Antimilos of four Ottoman galleys and a galliot of the Rhodes Guard. As guest of the Venetian Duke of Naxos, a vassal of the Turks, he found many friends of the Turks who held the Governor and Captain-General of Rhodes, Deli Giaffer, in high regard, a Corsican renegade of great heart and good judgment. At about this time four galleys of Alexandria arrived at Rhodes to rendezvous with the Rhodes Guard. On 24 May the Grand Prior discovered at Porto Caracolo in Kekova Roads under Lycia a Turkish ship of about 330 gross tons owned and commanded by Recep Chamusa Reis. Bound from Alexandria to Constantinople, her cargo of spices and other precious merchandise was valued at more than 60,000 scudos. In addition to cargo she had eighty good Turkish soldiers embarked. The contest was bloody, leaving many Maltese wounded, particularly aboard *San Iacomo*. The captured ship was placed under command of Aragonese Serving Brother Bartolomeo Cortez. Towed to Kastellorizon, she caught a fresh wind directly to Malta. Two days later, within sight of Rhodes, the Maltese took a Moorish germa of about 160 tons bound from Damietta; fifty-six crew and fourteen wealthy passengers were taken captive. Most passengers were ransomed, others became a cause celebre with the Ottoman Porte. Three of the passengers, two sisters and a brother, returning from Mecca, were among the captives. The mother of the three almost from the moment of capture commenced petitioning the Porte for the return of her children and continued to do so through Francis of Lorraine's death in 1563 and through the Ottoman captivity of Vincenzo Cicala ending a year later. Fati, the elder daughter, was meanwhile converted to Christianity, renamed Catherine after the Queen, and placed in the Queen's household. Similarly, the younger sister, Marguerite, was placed in the household of Catherine's sister Marguerite Duchess of Savoy. The brother was apparently consigned to the oars and disappeared from the pages of history. Having been converted, the girls' patrons and husbands refused their repatriation in spite of an unending series of requests from Sultan Suleiman himself.[15]

Still within sight of Rhodes, the Grand Prior learned from a caique bound from Rhodes to Kastellorizon that, to the great sorrow of the Alexandria squadron, the Maltese were not to be their prey but rather the prey of Deli Giaffer.[16]

Juan de Vega came to the end of his reign as Viceroy of Sicily and was succeeded by Juan de la Cerda, 4th Duke of Medinaceli. In the brief interim between the two, Sicily was governed by Cardinal Pietro Tagliavia d'Aragona, Archbishop of Palermo. Aragona's first order was for the release of Giovanni Moretto, and his galley, as a vassal of King Philip's ally Duke Emmanuel Philibert of Savoy. In addition, Pierre Fouroux was ordered to compensate a number of named merchants of Messina 7,000 scudos in cash and goods, as Fouroux had assertedly confiscated from a merchant urca the property of the named individuals. This order is believed to have hastened the demise of Grand Master Claude de la Sengle. Soon afterward came a letter from 18-year-old Gian Andrea Doria notifying the Grand Master that as General of the Catholic Armada he had approved the letter-of-marque issued to Giovanni Moretto and that Moretto was therefore to be released. Under considerable strain, Sengle replied to these and similar missives to the effect that the Order of Jerusalem was responsible only to the Holy See, from whom a decision on the fate of Moretto and Fouroux was soon expected. On 9 May came a Papal Brief from Pope Paul IV dated the past 15 April lauding the detention of Moretto and ordering that he be remanded in custody with the stolen galley to Civitavecchia. The Brief also ordered that Pierre Fouroux be released from detention and directed to return with his galley to Civitavecchia. The Papal Brief was followed by communications from Pietro Strozzi, the Duke of Guise, and King Henry II of France requesting the same disposition. Within days the Council ordered the release of Pierre Fouroux and his galley pursuant to the Papal Brief. Precipitating the wrath of both third parties, as well as within the Council, the Council ordered Moretto to continue in confinement and his galley to remain at Malta pending further discussion with the Holy See. For the purpose of further discussions, Bailiff of Lango Pierre de la Fontaine of France and Commander Giovan Francesco Langosco della Motta of Vercelli were appointed ambassadors extraordinary to the Holy See. Both ambassadors departed Malta on 14 June on board the galley of Pierre Fouroux with orders to emphasise in discussions with the Pope the Order's neutrality during conflicts between France and Spain. The ambassadors were also to emphasise the Order's almost total dependence on Sicily and the goodwill of the Viceroy for grain supplies.

In part because of reports that the Maltese had suffered heavy losses in taking their two prizes, the first at Kekova Roads and the second off the island of Rhodes, and that survivors were exhausted, and in part because the Rhodes galleys were larger, the bastarda capitana, for example, of thirty banks, Deli Giaffer decided to engage the five Maltese with four galleys, leaving the galliot in port. His three other galleys commanded by Mami Reis, Mustafa Colaxis, and Kara Yusuf, all four were reinforced with skilled arquebusiers, crossbowmen, and janissaries, and left Rhodes on the first day of June so heavily manned that they were difficult to manoeuvre. The Maltese, on the other hand, caught favourable winds and sailed toward Crete, all those embarked at relative ease. Off Turkish Scarpanto (Karpathos) the Turks were sighted somewhat downwind, but the Grand Prior was suspicious of an ambush by shore batteries, and proceeded to the safe harbour of Ierepetra at the eastern end of Crete under a Venetian fortress, where he passed the evening of 3 June. The Grand Prior and many knights went ashore to drink and make merry. An hour into the festivities, however, lookouts sighted the four Rhodes galleys heading on the wind for Ierepetra, though still several miles distant. The Prior was counselled there were but four enemy galleys, they were sailing upwind, and they could not escape, all to shore party exhilaration. The Maltese re-embarked. Thinking the Rhodians had discovered their presence and would soon take flight, they instead saw the bastarda lay on canvas to increase her speed of approach. Deli Giaffer by the same token saw the Maltese approaching; he boarded a caique and under the poops of the other three Rhodians he exhorted the embarked crews, telling them they faced five weakened galleys. He intended taking the Grand Prior's capitana and a second Maltese with his bastarda, while each of the other Rhodians would go one-on-one. Meanwhile, the Grand Prior, with juvenile eagerness, also cracked on more sail without issuing orders either to Saulcieres de Tenance on the padrona, to Pietro Vasco his lieutenant-general aboard *San Filippo*, or to his other captains. Finally, however, he ordered *San Filippo* to join his capitana in investing Deli Giaffer's capitana. So, too, did *San Iacomo* attack the enemy capitana. Rhodian gunfire had meanwhile largely passed harmlessly overhead while Maltese gunfire had been telling with numerous Turkish dead and wounded, particularly the gunfire of Englishman Master John aboard the Grand Prior's capitana. Murderous combat, however, began with boarding. *San Iacomo*, under the enemy capitana's stern, took punishing arquebus fire from on high. Her complement of fighters already decimated in combat with the spice ship, she withdrew to protests from her remaining knights and adventurers, moving on to invest the galley of Memi Reis prow to prow. *San Filippo* put her spur through the Rhodian capitana's port side. Giovan Simone Comito recognised Deli Giaffer, bare-armed with a scimitar in his right hand and a club in his left, rallying his crew, killed by an arquebus round in the middle of his chest. Pietro Vasco aboard *San Filippo* was likewise killed by arquebus fire. The Ottoman galley of Memi Reis exploded, set off by a dying Chevalier of France seeking to take the enemy with him; *San Iacomo* alongside, her skipper Ligoria on the verge of reporting a victory, was disabled and captured. Kara Yusuf's galley was boarded by the quarter from the prow of *Santa Fede* commanded by Hospitaller Christophe Vaulchamps, the latter having skilfully avoided the danger represented by the enemy's own prow. The boarders found damage to galley and crew, not just from artillery but from fire, as well, the crew severely diminished by injuries poorly attended.[17] Because the Ottoman's elevated poop looked down on *Santa Fede*, however, the latter was subjected to withering arquebus and crossbow fire from embarked reinforcements. Eventually all of *Santa Fede*'s exposed gunners were dead and there was no ability to man the artillery and artificial-fire equipment. At this critical juncture Hospitaller Jean de Soubiran-d'Arifat of the Priory of Toulouse, an explosives expert, arrived by skiff from the Hospitaller capitana and with it placed two barrels of gun powder and arquebus shot under Kara Yusuf's stern. When detonated, Ottoman arquebusiers and crossbowmen were forced to vacate their advantageous positions. In the end, the two galleys separated having significantly wasted both complements of embarked personnel, some Hospitallers still aboard the Ottoman taken captive to Rhodes. The Grand Prior's padrona, least well-armed of the Maltese, took on the galley of Mustafa Colaxis but was repulsed.

There was no victor. Francis of Lorraine was wounded in the left arm by an arquebus round as well as by an arrow in the knee. There were many more dead and wounded, including almost fifty dead knights. Some of these were Etienne de Guèvre, Honouré de Glandevez-

Puymichel, Honouré de Glandevez-Peypin, Nicolas de Bermond du Rousset, Guillaume de Montesquieu-Coustaussa, François de Cheylus, Melchior de Simiane, Louis de Pins-Montbrun, mortally wounded novice Nicolas de Nogaret, Georges de Demandolx-Trigance, Bertrand de Pins of the family of Grand Master Odon de Pins (1294–96), Francis de la Douse, François de Montay dit la Prade, and Dominique Alesti, Chaplain aboard *San Iacomo* who would die a slave at Rhodes, all from the Langue of Provence. From the Langue of Auvergne Antoine de Condat and Jean de Clavières de Murat. From the Langue of France Charles de Chambes de Montsoreau,[18] Jacques de la Colonge, Guy d'Aurigny d'Ambleteuse, Jacques de Méaux-Chéry (Boisboudran), Olivier Poverian de Logerie, Antoine de la Touche Marigny, Novice Pierre Agiave, Godart de Géresme de Saint-Blimont,[19] Jean Postel d'Ormoy, Jacques de la Haye, Pierre d'Eltouf de Pradines, and Charles de Montreüil. From Italy Giuliano Aguero of Brescia,[20] Pietro Vasco, Bartolomeo Avogadro, Agostino Amadeo, Sasso Galerati,[21] Ottavio Saccano, and Alberto Ricasoli. From Aragon Don Francisco Enrique de Aragona, grandson of *Hernán Cortés,*[22] Geronimo Tercan, Ernando Diaz de Alfaro, Francisco Ribera, Geronimo Aimar, Don Hernando de Castelui, and Joaquín de Claramunt.[23] Karl von Bernhausen of Germany. From Castile Francisco de Espinola Corvaccio, Alonso de Trujillo, Diego de Carvajal, Miguel de Verdugo, Don Bernardino Sarmiento three years a novitiate, Dom Pedro da Cunha,[24] and Don Luis de Avalos,[25] whose father Francesco Ferdinando de Ávalos de Aquino, VII marchese of Pescara and III marchese of Vasto, later became Viceroy of Sicily. About ninety soldiers and sailors died, plus an uncounted number of oarsmen. Still others were captured and died in captivity. There is no reliable estimate of Ottoman casualties, but later advice from Rhodes indicates that only two of the four Ottoman galleys returned, towing *San Iacomo,* suggesting that both Deli Giaffer's capitana and the galley of Memi Reis went to the bottom. Upon return to Malta on 17 June Francis of Lorraine offered the Order his personal capitana in place of the lost *San Iacomo,* and contributed his fifth share of the value of the two sailing-ship prizes to the Order's treasury. If there can be heroes in a disaster such as this, Bosio[26] anoints Andre de Saulcières de Tenance commanding the Grand Prior's padrona, smallest and least well-equipped of all nine galleys. Tenance's lieutenant Jean d'Aigneville-Marseillan also came in for praise. Nevertheless, this disaster further hastened the demise of Grand Master Claude de la Sengle, who bore ultimate responsibility.[27]

It is interesting that the Abbé de Vertot in his history devotes page after page to the Moretto/Moret theft of a single galley cited above, but does not make the slightest reference to this galley battle and its loss of three galleys, not to mention the tragic loss of hundreds of Hospitaller and Turkish lives to no strategic or tactical purpose.[28]

Having survived the overturned galley in October 1555, Mathurin de Lescout-Romegas had in 1557 been appointed by his former captain Antoine de Thésan-Vénàsque to command of the latter's large corsair galliot and sent into the Levant in company with the fusta of Paolo Micciolo, both flying the colours of the Order of Jerusalem. These suddenly and frighteningly were come upon in an uninhabited bay by two great Turkish sailing vessels each large enough to fight off two or three galleys. Believing they had come upon a part of the Grand Prior's squadron recently in combat with the Rhodes Guard, however, the Turkish crews abandoned ship and took to the forest. Prize crews were embarked and the Turkish ships, full of precious merchandise, were sailed to Malta escorted by galliot and fusta, arriving on 4 July.[29]

Aware that his health was deteriorating, the Grand Master on 17 July appointed Parisot de la Valette his lieutenant with power of attorney. Learning of Dragut's aforementioned raid on Cariati north of Crotone, but attributing it to the Ottoman Armada, Pompeo Soardo of Bergamo was dispatched aboard a fast frigate to obtain more information. He returned a few days later with certain information that the galleys involved had retired to the Levant.[29]

Shortly after Soardo's return and the consequent stand-down at Malta, the Grand Prior renounced the dignity of the General of the Galleys, citing his recall to France. Later in the month, at the Battle of Saint-Quentin, French armies in Picardy commanded by Anne de Montmorency were overwhelmed by Spanish armies commanded by Duke Emmanuel Philibert of Savoy. In consequence of this defeat the Grand Prior's elder brother (also) Francis of Lorraine was also recalled to France, marking an end to French intrigue in Italy until the coming of Bonaparte. The Grand Prior was succeeded as General of the Galleys by Bailiff of Naples Giorgio Adorno and departed Malta on 8 August with his padrona galley. Hoping to end all suspicion of Malta stemming from the presence of the Grand Prior, Claude de la Sengle on 13 August sped Hospitaller Alonso de Escobar with the news to the viceregal court of Juan de la Cerda at Palermo. It was Sengle's final act. He was incapacitated the same day. On 18 August he was carried to Mass at the Chapel in the Garden at Marsa, called for a confessor, who failed to arrive in time, and died that day at the age of 63. A most pious warrior who fought on the walls of Rhodes during the Great Siege, he was interred in the Church of San Lorenzo at Birgu after lying there in state attended by his Seneschal Charles de Hangest du Mesnil Saint-Georges and by the Master of his House Christophe le Bouleur de Montgaudry the Younger. Claude de la Sengle was survived by a niece, Mademoiselle de Mont-Chaner, and with fond regard by perhaps every other Hospitaller.[30]

Chapter XIII

Jean Parisot de la Valette 1557–60

As Lieutenant to deceased Grand Master Claude de la Sengle, Prior of Saint-Gilles Jean Parisot de la Valette on 21 August 1557 convened a General Assembly in the Great Hall of Castle Saint Angelo at Birgu. Attended as four years earlier by approximately 400 knights, chaplains and serving brothers eligible to vote, the purpose of the Assembly was again the election of a new Grand Master. Voting eligibility was restricted by statute to those having five years of residence at the Convent, to those having completed the requisite number of galley caravans, and to those unencumbered by debt to the Common Treasury. Consistent with statutory practice the eight langues retired separately and in camera each selected one of its number to represent it in selection of the President of Elections as well as in selection of the Triumvirate of Elections. These eight initial Electors selected from the Assembly Prior of Pisa Giovanni di Ventimiglia as non-voting President of Elections. For the Triumvirate the eight selected as Knight of Elections Seneschal Charles de Hangest du Mesnil Saint-Georges of the Langue of France, as Chaplain of Elections Jean Pierre Mosquet of Provence, and as Sergeant-at-Arms of Elections Serving Brother Bartolomé Cortès of Aragon. The eight initial Electors having retired, the three Electors of the Triumvirate selected from the Assembly a fourth Elector, and the four Electors in decreasing individual influence selected a fifth Elector, and so on until there were Sixteen Electors at two per langue. The Sixteen Electors were Lieutenant Grand Commander Pierre de Gozon-Mélac and Jean Pierre Mosquet for Provence, Commander of Tortebesse François de Puget and Symphorien de Brandon for Auvergne, Mesnil Saint-Georges and Commander of L'Île-Bouchard Jean d'Aulnis dit Pondevie for France, Serving Brother Bartolomé Cortès and Lieutenant Grand Conservator Luis de Salcedo for Aragon, Lieutenant Admiral Lamberto Doria and Lieutenant Conventual Conservator Giovanni Battista Agliata for Italy, Commander of Torphichen James Sandiland and, because Sandiland was

England's only Hospitaller at Malta, Commander Pedro de Iunient of Aragon for England, Bernhard von Gluck and Peter Baiar for Germany, and Don Pedro de Mendoza and Commander Dom João da Cunha of Portugal for Castile. These Sixteen Electors retired into conclave and for five hours considered their options before the Knight of Elections announced Jean Parisot de la Valette had been elected forty-ninth Grand Master of the Order of Jerusalem.[1]

Jean Parisot de la Valette was born in 1495 at Parisot in Languedoc, 100km north-east of Toulouse, a younger son of Bernard de Valette, Chevalier de France, and of Jeanne de Castres. He was received into the Order of Jerusalem in 1515 at the relatively advanced age of 20, but upon reporting to the Convent never again resided anywhere else, though the Convent itself moved from Rhodes to Italy to Savoy and to Malta during his lifetime. Not yet a commander by 1522's Great Siege of Rhodes, he was assigned to Provence's south-east-facing city wall between the Italian sector on the left and the English sector on the right, and with little doubt participated in the defence of the November breaches in the Italian and Spanish sectors. He was among the survivors permitted an honourable departure from Rhodes on the evening of 1 January 1523, essentially all of them bearing scars. In 1534 Valette was appointed to command the galley *San Giovanni Battista*, moving in 1535 to command of *Santa Maria de la Vittoria* for that year's siege and conquest of Tunis, and remaining in command of *Santa Maria* until end 1536. Two years later, the year of the Battle of Preveza, he was confined at Gozo for four months for having assaulted an unarmed Maltese, his confinement followed by twenty-four months of exile to Tripoli. It is possible the assault and exile grew out of an affair of the heart as he is known to have had at least two such affairs during his life, each begetting a child, the first a son and the second a daughter. Released from exile at Tripoli, Valette purchased a single-masted galliot, acquired a letter-of-marque from the Order of Jerusalem, and became a corsair plundering for profit under the Maltese Cross. This brief period ended with his 1541 capture following combat with two Infidel galliots off the coast of Tunisia, one of his captors Acsac Reis (Zoppo) of Candia seen earlier in this history as a 1504 mentor of Dragut. Wounded, Valette was taken to Djerba and sent to the oars. Exchanged a year later at Tripoli's land-gate for the father of another of his captors, Valette's contributions to Tripoli's defence then and earlier led to his appointment as Governor of Tripoli from April 1546 to June 1549.

In 1552 Valette was appointed Regent of the Galleys for Leone Strozzi's disastrous attempt to kidnap slave labourers at Zuara, and was one of the few to emerge unscathed from an ill-planned undertaking that may have been the greatest disaster in Hospitaller history, certainly greater than the loss of Tripoli a year earlier and by some measures greater even than 1522's noble loss of Rhodes. As Valette's presence at Zuara may have prevented an even greater disaster, he was in April 1554 appointed General of the Galleys for the two years ended in April 1556. Meanwhile, Valette had advanced through the ranks of the Langue of Provence from absentee Commander of Le Bastit to Bailiff of Lango (1555) entitled to wear the Grand Cross, to Grand Commander and senior conventual bailiff (1555–56), to Prior of Saint-Gilles (1556–57) until his 1557 election as Grand Master.

At his first Council meeting as Grand Master, Valette was granted the same compensation as recent predecessors of 7,000 Maltese scudos per year, from which he must fund maintenance of the Magistral Palace. (A silver one Maltese scudo coin, when demonetised in 1886, has been calculated to have had the 2011 buying power of 4.35 euros. Scudo coins of more than one scudo were minted in gold and thus in 2011 would have had a value determined by weight or collector value.) At the same Council meeting, Valette was succeeded as Prior of Saint-Gilles by Grand Commander François de Toucheboeuf, the latter in turn succeeded by Lieutenant Grand Commander Pierre de Gozon-Mélac. Gozon-Mélac continued as Regent of the Galleys pending reappointment of Bailiff of Naples Giorgio Adorno as successor. Days later, on the news of the death of Prior of Champagne Léon de Montalembert, the Priory was conferred on Grand Hospitaller François de Piedefer, who was in turn succeeded as Grand Hospitaller by Jean de la Roche-Andry. Roche-Andry vacated the dignity of Bailiff of the Morea, to which Treasurer Jean de Neuchèze was appointed. Pierre de la Fontaine moved up from Bailiff of Lango to Treasurer. Pending a Brief on the matter expected to be obtained from Pope Paul IV, Gaspard de Vallier was released from confinement since 1551's loss of Tripoli and was reappointed Bailiff of Lango. Cesare Visconti of Milan was appointed Ambassador Extraordinary to inform Pope Paul IV and Italian princes of the death of Claude de la Sengle and of the election of Parisot de la Valette as his successor. Martin de Duero Monroy, received into the Langue of Castile in January 1531, was similarly appointed to inform Emperor Ferdinand and His Catholic Majesty Philip II.

Pierre de Massués-Vercoiran dit le Mas of Provence was appointed to inform His Most Christian Majesty Henry II. To each sovereign the ambassadors were to also describe the failed grain crop and famine in Sicily and to request succour for the people of Malta. Meanwhile, the new Grand Master was already considering the defence of Malta against Ottoman assault, and was at the time focused on the construction of a new walled city to surround Fort Saint Elmo (modern Valletta). He again sent Alonso de Escobar of Castile to pay his respects to Viceroy of Sicily Juan de la Cerda. The Viceroy's nephew Don Manuel de la Cerda soon returned the courtesy. While these new developments occurred at Malta, Ambassadors Pierre de la Fontaine and Giovan Francesco Langosco della Motta remained at Rome seeking a lawful resolution of the Moretto matter which would remove the Hospitaller Order from the peril of vengeful monarchs. The best solution postulated was the return of the stolen galley to its rightful owner while remanding the thief to the custody of the Duke of Savoy. Unfortunately, Pope Paul IV and his Cardinal Protector nephew Don Giovanni di Carafa could not agree to remanding Moretto anywhere other than Civitavecchia.[2]

Shortly after his election, Valette had obtained an agent in Constantinople who proved invaluable throughout Valette's Magistracy. Within four months the agent had placed spies in the household of Grand Vizier Rustem Pasha, in the Secretariat of the Divan or Imperial Council of Ministers, and in the Golden Horn Arsenal. On 20 December 1557 the agent reported that Sultan Suleiman had greatly admired the deceased Deli Giaffer, his Governor and Captain-General at Rhodes, and was determined to take revenge on the Maltese for the incursion into Turkish waters resulting in his death. Neither was the Sultan pleased with the seizure by Romegas of two large cargo ships, also in Turkish waters. In this vein the Sultan was constructing a potent armada able to isolate and destroy Malta. This potent armada was later confirmed by both Ragusa and Venice,[3] and led the Grand Master to expect a siege in the coming spring.

A General Summons was issued calling able Hospitallers to the defence of Malta. Hospitallers Pierre de Châlus and Arduin de Castillon de Beines, each with a galley at Marseille, were individually summoned. Don Francisco de Zanoguerra of Valencia was dispatched to the Holy See to plead for assistance. So, too, was Nicolas de Blanchelayne of Auvergne dispatched to the Courts of Henry II and Philip II. These emissaries departed Malta toward the end of the year. Also toward the end of the year, news was received of the death in France of Prior of Auvergne Imbert de la Morinière. He was succeeded by Marshal Louis de Lastic, who was in turn succeeded as Marshal by Commander Guillaume de Coppier.[4]

In further concern over the Ottoman fleet build-up, Valette dispatched Gil de Andrade to the Levant, Andrade recently appointed captain of the galley *Santa Fede* in succession of Christophe de Hazeville Vaulchamps. He was accompanied by the corsair galliot belonging to Antoine de Thezan Venasque, commanded by Mathurin Romegas. The other three galleys of the Religion, their crews, oarsmen, and embarked soldiery decimated by June combat with the Rhodes Guard, had been sent to Sicily under command of General of the Galleys Giorgio Adorno to load foodstuffs and other provisions for transport back to Malta. And to hire oarsmen and soldiers because it was understood Dragut had been ordered by the Sultan to take the aforementioned armada and by every stratagem and ambush to prevent the reinforcement and resupply of Malta. Adorno nevertheless returned to Malta on 23 January with the galleys in good order, escorting three sailing vessels, two small sailing ships and a Ragusan argosy with cargoes of grain and other foodstuffs. Pilier or senior knight of the Langue of Italy for fifteen years, the strain of the Messina assignment is said to have brought about Adorno's death several days following return to Malta. Adorno was succeeded as Bailiff of Naples by Lamberto Doria and as General of the Galleys by future Grand Master Pietro del Monte who was absent from the Convent. In the interim, until Del Monte's return the squadron was commanded as Regent by senior captain Luis Cortit commanding *San Michele Arcangelo*.[4] Coincidentally, nephew Giorgio Adorno (the Younger), was received in 1558 into the Order of Jerusalem, Langue of Italy, Diocese of Genoa. He would give a good account of himself in defence of the 15 July 1565 general assault on Senglea.[5]

Early in February four French galleys paused in the Freo Channel for drinking water, bound to Constantinople to enlist Ottoman naval support for French operations in the spring against Italian states within the dominion of Philip II. Embarked was Hospitaller Claude de Glandevez-Cuges of the Langue of Provence, who had participated early in January in Francis of Lorraine the Elder's successful siege and repossession of Calais, which had been under English rule since 1347. His report of the current mission was reason for cautious reappraisal of the Ottoman threat to Malta. A bit later still, Andrade and Romegas returned from the Levant confirming the Ottoman fleet build-up if not its destination. At about the same time the Grand Master discovered in his household two agents of the Ottomans who were advising Constantinople of Malta's defensive weaknesses. The agents' middleman was also discovered and the three were hanged. This development further convinced Valette that Malta was the likely Ottoman target, and he summoned from Pesaro in the Duchy of Urbino the monumental architect Bartolomeo Genga, then in service to Duke of Urbino Guidobaldo II della Rovere. Genga had been instrumental in the design of the city walls surrounding Pesaro as well as the design of several churches still standing today. Genga was assigned the task of designing a new city and its walls incorporating Fort Saint Elmo. He was also to recommend improvements to the walls of Senglea. His early recommendations stimulated immediate accumulation of new construction materials.[4]

On 29 March 1558 the Sacred Council received Edmund Eluyn into the Order of Jerusalem, Langue of England, raising hope of a reconstituted Langue of England. Preceptor of Templecomb James Shelley would arrive at Malta on 9 August.[6]

On reports that the Ottoman Armada exited the Dardanelles into the northern Aegean as early as 14 April,[7] Cristóbal Pacheco of Murcia was dispatched to Naples to hire 400 arquebusiers, while Giovan Antonio Bisballe of Messina and Giovan Vittorio Maurello of Cosenza were dispatched to Sicily to hire an additional 200 each. Valette had also written earlier to his friend and familiar Charles d'Urre de Tessières of his appointment as Grand Commander succeeding Pierre de Gozon-Mélac, who had advanced to the dignity of Prior of Saint-Gilles upon the death of François de Toucheboeuf de Clermont. This was a recall for Tessières as the Grand Commander was the senior knight of the Langue of Provence at the Convent. He was to bring with him as much coin and munitions, and as many Hospitallers and soldiers, as available. Transport was to be provided by the two galleons, the large new galleon commanded by Jorge de Sant Joan then at Messina, and the smaller galleon the personal property of the Grand Master commanded by Gaspard de la Motte of Provence then departing Mallorca bound for Marseille and Toulon. She had been detained for several months at Mallorca by Viceroy Gaspar de Marrades on suspicion of being a French corsair vessel, but had been released on order of the King of Spain (this small galleon was one of the two large Turkish sailing ships abandoned by their crews and snared by Romegas and non-Hospitaller Paolo Micciolo ten months earlier). Tessières reached Malta on 26 April 1558 with both galleons, with a large body of Hospitallers from all nations responding to December's General Summons, with a number of individuals arriving to take the Habit, and with soldiery. The galleons also carried a full load of munitions and other supplies, plus Treasury coin.[8]

Soon afterward, Giulio Bravo of Verona was dispatched into the Levant with a fast frigate to ascertain the route of the Ottoman Armada and under order to report back as quickly as possible with certain information. On 3 May Cristóbal Pacheco returned to Malta aboard a chartered urca or flat-bottomed round ship with 400 embarked arquebusiers as well as Spanish knights responding to the General Summons, plus a cargo of wine, salted meat, and biscuit. Pacheco brought news of the death in Spain of Chancellor Lope de Paz. Another veteran of the Great Siege of Rhodes, De Paz had represented Grand Master l'Isle-Adam at the Sultan's pavilion during surrender negotiations. He would be succeeded as Chancellor by the Portuguese Cristóvão de Sarnach.

Not much later there arrived at Malta one Captain Filippo da Vicovara representing Pope Paul IV and his nephew Don Giovanni di Carafa, the latter commanding all Papal military and naval forces. Vicovara carried a Papal Brief dated Rome, the past 8 March 1558, ordering and commanding the Grand Master to release the stolen Strozzi galley to Vicovara and to remand Giovanni Moretto/Jean Moret to his custody. Seeking to comply with the Papal Brief, the Convent 'discovered' that Moretto had successfully fled Malta's 'flooded' prison, but was able to deliver the stolen galley and all of its appurtenances. Prior to departure Vicovara took a series of depositions concerning the escape and then left

Malta on 23 May with the stolen galley in tow bound for Civitavecchia. While Pope Paul was satisfied with this face-saving solution, not so the Duchy of Savoy, which demanded compensation for loss of the 'Savoyard' galley and all of its plunder plus damages and interest. As the Duchy was able to sequester the Order's property in Savoy, this demand could not be ignored. The Grand Master dispatched his nephew Henri de la Valette de Cornusson to treat with the government of Savoy. It was only by the 'grace of God' and Moretto's death, however, that this matter would be amicably resolved in 1564.[9]

Meanwhile, defensive measures continued to be taken at Malta. Don Antonio Bologna of Palermo was assigned as Governor and Captain-at-Arms of Notabile, taking with him Pacheco's 400 arquebusiers. Similarly, Prior of Auvergne Louis de Lastic was posted to Fort Saint Elmo with a substantial number of knights and soldiers. Bastien d'Argilliers of the Langue of France, Don Pedro de Mendoza of Castile, and Iacomo di None of the Piedmont were appointed Sector Wardens of Birgu with near absolute authority in their sectors. On 29 May the galley *Santa Fede*, towing several shallow-water frigates, reached Malta with the infantry companies of Giovan Antonio Bisballe and Giovan Vittorio Maurello. On 1 June the galliots of both Mathurin Romegas and Jacques de Roches returned to Malta, the latter knighted since the fall of Tripoli. Don Bernardo de Guimeran, Resident Ambassador at the Court of Philip II and not subject to the General Summons, appeared at Malta anyway, his departure from the Court licensed by the King of Spain.[9]

News was received from Venetian sources that the Ottoman Armada commanded by Piali Pasha and piloted by Kara Mustafa had reached Castel Tornese on the Moriot coast opposite Venetian Zante on or before 4 June 1558. The Armada's slow speed of advance from the Dardanelles was puzzling to some observers. By 8 June, though, the Armada was sighted off Cape Santa Maria di Leuca at the base of the Italian boot's heel, a lightning move only explained by a proximate rendezvous with Dragut coming up from Tripoli with three galleys and five galliots. Returning to Malta later in the month was Giulio Bravo, who aboard the fast frigate of non-Hospitaller Stefan Sifugno first sighted the Ottoman Armada 120 galleys strong off Crotone's Cape Colonne between Santa Maria di Leuca and Reggio di Calabria on the evening of the same 8 June. Factual totals were 100 galleys and fourteen sailing vessels with an embarked force of 13,000 janissaries, 3,500 sappers, and an indeterminate number of spahis plus Dragut's contribution. With Dragut influencing if not commanding, the Armada one day later sacked and burned Reggio di Calabria with numerous noble women kidnapped for ransom among hundreds of equally innocent men sent to corsair oars.[10]

Departing Reggio, the Armada transited the Strait of Messina northbound and was off the Gulf of Naples on 13 June. The Armada's destination was not Malta but rather rendezvous with the French. That night, 13 June, the Ottomans descended on Massa Lubrense and Sorrento, where not for the first time the damage was done by Dragut with less than eager assistance of Armada commander Piali Pasha. The Monasteries for Nuns of San Giorgio at Cremano and San Giovanni Boccadoro were desecrated, while the nuns were raped and kidnapped. Benedictine sisters of the Monastery of San Paolo were similarly treated. Three thousand men, women, and children were carted away as slaves or for ransom, while the city was plundered and destroyed.[11]

From Sorrento the Armada moved north, passing the territory of France's Papal ally but for San Severino, where it appeared seeking fresh water, then continuing north, where opposite Montecristo and Elba it took a heading to round Corsica's Cape Corse. The Turks thus missed a rendezvous on or before 20 June 1558 with the French Galley Fleet commanded by Hospitaller Prior of France Francis of Lorraine waiting at Ajaccio, on the other end of Corsica. It had been expected by the French that the combined armada would from Ajaccio proceed to assail the Imperial Genovese Armada at Savoyard Villefranche. Lorraine was still waiting at Ajaccio on 27 June when, informed by a lone Turkish galley, that the Turkish Armada had rounded Cape Corse, paused at Calvi, and then taken course for the Spanish Balearics in need of food stores. Lorraine returned to Marseille. There were post-mortems suggesting collusion on the part of Grand Vizier Rustem Pasha and his fellow Croatian Piali Pasha intended to teach French King Henry II to be more attentive to ally Suleiman, whose letters to the French King more often than not went unanswered. There were also reports of rendezvous at sea with Imperial Genovese warships, and payments to Piali to avoid assaults on Genovese territory. The missed rendezvous and delays attending earlier and later sacks, however, were more likely the work of Beylerbey Dragut, who had never profited at Corsica.[12]

Elsewhere Romegas, commanding a galliot that was the personal property of the Grand Master, returned to Malta from a corsair excursion to the African coast having reaped plunder with all of the consequences reaping entails. He brought with him news that Infidel corsairs of North Africa had assembled a mass of galleys and galliots at Monastir, 20-odd miles north of Mehedia, intended for raiding Christian coasts and coastal shipping. Monastir was within Dragut's beylerbeylik. Then of the view that the Ottoman Armada posed little threat to Malta, the Grand Master requested Viceroy of Naples Juan Fernandez Manrique de Lara recall Neapolitan units at Malta. In the interim before Lara acted Valette deployed Regent Cortit and the galleys to North Africa with orders to proceed as far as Cape Misurata looking for prey and to return within fifteen days or on any report of Armada approach.[12]

Cortit and the four galleys departed Birgu on 3 July 1558 bound directly to North Africa, that is, without taking on fresh water at Comino or at another coastal source at Malta or Gozo. Expecting to find water at a juniper grove on the North African coast, they instead found the water source occupied by a band of Moors, some mounted, and were forced to continue along their eastbound route toward Cape Misurata. Near the cape they came upon a large garbo, or small merchant vessel, the crew of which on sighting the Maltese abandoned ship by skiff for the nearby shore. The squadron frigate followed, looking not for the crew but for water. The galleys also beached. They found not water but advice that eight oared vessels of Dragut's squadron had departed Tripoli in pursuit. Given the numbers, his orders, and a fractured mast aboard his capitana *San Michele Arcangelo*, not to mention thirst, Cortit and the squadron returned to Malta. From Cortit's error in proceeding without fresh water came a mandated practice of always filling water barrels before departure.[12]

Having been repulsed at Menorca's Port Mahon, on 1 July an Ottoman ground force of 15,000 descended on Ciutadella, then Menorca's capital city at the western tip of the island defended by a garrison of 700 Spanish soldiers. For eight days the Ottomans battered citadel walls before the citadel magazine was ignited. The remaining defenders attempted a sortie to Port Mahon on 9 July covering women and children in the centre. The sortie failed. When all was said and done, the Ottomans on 10 July sailed away with many of their own dead and wounded.[13] The

Ottomans also sailed away with the city's entire remaining population of 3,099 citizens plus 353 others from outside the city. These mostly disappeared into the slave markets of North Africa together with the 3,000 removed from Sorrento. Most noble ladies from Reggio were ransomed, others removed from that city also disappeared into slave markets. These tragic consequences came nowhere near paying for the Ottoman Armada's deployment to the western Mediterranean, while the Armada's subsequent rendezvous with the French Fleet at Toulon did nothing to advance French ambitions in Corsica.[14]

Reaching Malta on 18 July, Cortit and galley squadron filled their water barrels and proceeded immediately to Messina, where General of the Galleys Pietro del Monte succeeded Regent Cortit in command. Cortit was soon tasked to proceed from Messina to the Vienna Court of Holy Roman Emperor Ferdinand in an attempt to bring rebellious Hospital priors and commanders of Bohemia into line, some of whom had become Lutheran and all of whom had their own Ottoman threat consuming their treasuries.[15]

During an exchange of salutes between Ottoman and French units at Marseille, French Galley Fleet commander Francis of Lorraine was nearly killed by arquebus fire from a galley commanded by the son of former Rhodes Governor Deli Giaffer. In consequence, this unit of the Ottoman Armada commanded by Qasim Pasha was refused hospitality at Marseille and was forced to repair to Genoa for water and provisions, an enemy port where it was royally received. By the end of July the Armada was en route to Constantinople while 73-year-old Dragut was en route to Tripoli.[15] Grand Master Parisot de la Valette, meanwhile, needed to adjust to the death from natural causes of architect Bartolomeo Genga who, fortunately, left him with a scale model of the new city (modern Valletta) to be built on the Sciberras Peninsula opposite Castle Saint Angelo. The estate of former Grand Master Claude de la Sengle was sufficient to fund initial expenditures.[16]

The entire Ottoman Armada transited the Strait of Messina southbound on 6 August 1558 and then turned toward home. Prior of Castile and León Don Diego de Toledo died in Spain. A relative by marriage of the Duke of Alba who had facilitated his appointment, he too left a substantial estate, four fifths of which enriched the Common Treasury. Diego de Toledo was succeeded by Don Fernando de Toledo as

Prior of Castile and by Don Antonio de Toledo as Prior of León. These appointments were entrusted to the care of Don Bernardo de Guimeran returning to his post as Resident Ambassador to the Court of Philip II at Valladolid, and not to a courier because corsairs had been active in the Malta Channel between Sicily and Malta. Dragut, returning to Tripoli from France, had recently hijacked four Maltese grippos with cargoes of grain bound for Malta. The principal reason for the return to Spain of Guimeran, however, was the large number of lords of France taken captive at the Battle of Saint-Quentin in August a year earlier, including Anne Duke of Montmorency, who commanded the losing if numerically inferior force. Guimeran's diplomatic skills and access to ministers as well as to the King himself made him uniquely qualified to plead for their comfort or release. He departed Malta on 20 August along with many another Hospitaller responding to the earlier General Summons. Also departing were the four companies of hired soldiery. All were transported to Syracuse by General del Monte and the four galleys without event. At Syracuse an unplanned rendezvous was made with four galleys belonging to the Genovese Grimaldis also on the lookout for Dragut, reportedly commanding three large galleys and five galliots. Sortieing from Syracuse into the Malta Channel, the two squadrons sighted Dragut but he took to the high seas and was soon over the horizon.[17]

At Mostaganem, 330km west of Algiers, a large Spanish force commanded by Martín Alonso Fernández de Córdoba Montemayor y Velasco, first Count of Alcaudete, was in August 1558 defeated by an equally large force of Turks, Moors, and Arabs commanded by Hassan Pasha, Beylerbey of Algiers and son of Kheir-ed-Din Barbarossa. Alcaudete was among those not surviving. Twelve thousand Spaniards who did survive, including Alcaudete's son, were captured and enslaved at Algiers. The son was ransomed for 23,000 gold escudos. The lot of ordinary soldiers was less satisfactory. One of them, Juan Amador, did not make it back to Spain until 1595.[18]

Former Emperor Charles V died on 21 September at the Monastery of San Jerónimo at Yuste in Extremadura, to which he had retired on abdicating the Imperial throne. He was 58 years of age and a widower. Throughout his reign he had been a forthcoming patron of the Hospitaller Order. His passing was widely mourned throughout the Empire and at Malta.[19]

Five days later Del Monte towed in the absence of wind the galleon the property of the Grand Master from Syracuse to Cape Murro di Porco, 5 miles to the south, where galleys and galleon caught a fair wind for Malta that quickly became a tempest. In gusting wind the capitana's sheet or line controlling the foresail and antenna parted and in the wind whipped back and forth across the prow, very nearly slicing Del Monte in two, while the uncontrolled antenna and sail also threatened anyone nearby. A brave member of the crew rushed to the prow and manhandled the working end of the sheet to a strongpoint where it could do no further damage while a new sheet was attached. All four galleys and galleon safely reached Malta on 26 September.[19]

Arriving with the galleys was Bailiff of Eagle Pedro Fernandez de Felizes della Nucia, who debarked wearing the Grand Cross. In the deed of Philip and Mary restoring the Order of St John in England dated 2 April 1557, Felizes had been confirmed to the English dignity of Bailiff of Eagle, a dignity normally entitled to wear the Grand Cross. On this occasion, however, Grand Master and Council had yet to authorise the Grand Cross partly because Felizes' Langue of Aragon already had the number of Grand Crosses prescribed by statute. There was also the unspoken issue of a Spanish king awarding an English dignity to a Spanish knight. No one at Malta was happy with developments, not the Langue of Aragon, not the budding new Langue of England, and least of all Grand Master and Council, who had had their authority usurped first by award of the dignity and second by assumed entitlement to the Grand Cross. Weighing on the other side of the scales was Felizes' superb record of service to the Order, including participation in defence of the Great Siege of Rhodes. The Grand Master ruled in ordinary Council that only the Pope could confirm assignment to a bailiwick, and that in the interim Felizes was entitled to none of the perquisites of the Bailiff of Eagle. Also arriving with the galleys were English knights George Dudley, Commander of Templecomb James Shelley, and Commander of Quenyngton Oliver Starkey. These joined Lieutenant Turcopolier Henry Gerard and several other English Hospitallers who had arrived earlier at Malta. Between the death of Antoine de Guèvre in December 1556 and the return of Henry Gerard in 1558 James Sandiland of Scotland was the only member of the Langue of England at Malta.[19]

The year of 1558 had been successful for Hospitaller corsairs with armed galliots and other oared vessels preying on Infidels, particularly for Aleramo Parpaglia of Turin, Bidon de Beaulac of the Priory of Acquitaine, Guillaume de la Fontaine of the Langue of France, Antoine de Justas-Châteaufort of Provence, Christophe d'Esselin Goncourt of the Langue of France, Jacques des Roches of Auvergne, and François Jausserand of the Langue of France, all of whom returned to Malta in September and October with rich plunder from the Levant. In addition to plunder and destruction, hundreds of innocents had been carted away as slaves or for ransom. Finally, this group and others like them had introduced to the Order of Jerusalem an ethos of self-enrichment and self-glorification inconsistent with the ideals of a brotherhood. Their activities threatened the very foundations of the Order of Jerusalem.[19]

In preparation for the Chapter General scheduled for 13 November, senior captain Jean l'Evesque de la Cassière assumed command of the galley squadron in place of Pietro del Monte, who as Admiral was required to attend. Cassière took the squadron to Messina but returned during the Chapter General transporting Treasurer Pierre de la Fontaine returning from an embassy to Rome, Procurator for the Priory of Messina Giovan Simone Comito, and Procurator of the Castellany of Amposta Francisco de Zanoguerra.[20]

On Sunday, 13 November 1558 the first Chapter General of the Magistracy of Parisot de la Valette convened in the great room of the Magistral Palace at Birgu, the site also a first. Gathered to left and right in the foreground were knights of the Grand Cross: Bishop of Malta Domenico Cubelles, Prior of the Church Antoine Cressin, Grand Commander Charles d'Urre de Tessières, Marshal Guillaume Coppier, Grand Conservator Nicolau d'Agullon, Admiral Pietro del Monte, Grand Bailiff Adam von Schwalbach, Prior of Saint-Gilles Pierre de Gozon-Mélac, Prior of Toulouse Pierre de Beaulac-Trébons, Prior of Auvergne Louis de Lastic, Prior of Pisa Giovanni di Ventimiglia, Prior of Capua Filippo Pilli, Bailiff of Naples Lamberto Doria, Bailiff of Eagle Pedro de Felizes, Bailiff of Lyon Annet de Varax, Bailiff of Lango Gaspard de Vallier, and Seneschal Charles de Hangest du Mesnil Saint-Georges. Immediately behind the Grand Crosses were acting conventual bailiffs Lieutenant Turcopolier Henry Gerard and Lieutenant Chancellor Pedro de Mendoza. Behind these were the eight

Procurators or Attorneys, one per langue, as well as one per priory, one per bailiwick, and one per commandery, all of the foregoing without arms. And behind the procurators were the twenty-seven most senior knights at the Convent wearing their swords as a badge of their status. And in front of the general congregation was the Grand Master's staff. All were wearing the red mantle with white cross. Following the sermon and ceremonies each langue grouped itself apart from the others and elected two of the Sixteen *Capitolanti* or Legislators who would rule on most matters coming before the Chapter General. The langue of Aragon, because it encompassed Aragon, Catalonia, and Valencia, nominated three negotiators: Grand Conservator Nicolau d'Agullon, Commander Galceran Ros, and Dionisio Coscon. The final Sixteen were: Nicolau d'Agullon and Galceran Ros for Aragon, Francisco de Britto and Pedro de Mendoza for Castile, Tessières and Trébons for Provence, Coppier and Lastic for Auvergne, Pilier or Senior Knight Jean Audebert de l'Aubuge and Charles de Hangest du Mesnil Saint-Georges for France, Del Monte and Giovanni Battista Agliata for Italy, Felizes and Gerard for England, and Schwalbach and Joachim Spar for Germany. These Sixteen retired to the house of Seneschal Hangest, where they were joined by Master of the Grand Master's House Pierre de Gioù as procurator or attorney, Vice Chancellor Martín Rojas de Portalrubio as financial advisor, and Treasury Scribe Augustin de Sainte-Maure to record proceedings. Their decisions were announced on 3 December before the entire Chapter General and included the following: (1) the Order was to maintain five war galleys and two armed galleons; (2) a perpetual annual gift of 100 gold scudos was awarded to the Brothers of the Convent of San Francisco in Jerusalem; and (3) an annual imposition of 50,000 scudos was levied on all commanderies, bailiwicks, and priories as a group payable for three years in addition to ongoing responsions.[20]

In a severe blow to the Order of Jerusalem during the Chapter General, Mary Tudor, the Roman Catholic Queen of England and Ireland, died at St James Palace, Westminster, on 17 November. She was 42 years of age and left Philip II, King of Spain, a widower. With her death the Order of Saint John of Jerusalem in England and Ireland also died. Succeeding to the throne was Mary's half-sister Elizabeth I, who throughout her realm reversed Mary's restoration of Catholicism. Several Hospitallers were dispatched to England to render the Order's condolences, including

Commander of Flanders Michel de Seurre de Lumigny of the Langue of France. At a Council meeting two days following the Chapter General, Jorge de Sant Joan was appointed Conventual Conservator, the Order's de facto Treasurer, while the dignity of Treasurer was at that time simply a title of rank within the Langue of France with little financial responsibility. Sant Joan succeeded the deceased Giovan Battista Agliata of Palermo, an Hospitaller for twenty-eight years who had also served as Treasurer at Tripoli. Because Admiral Pietro del Monte began to suffer from kidney stones and wished to return to Italy for treatment, he was succeeded on the final day of 1558 as General of the Galleys by Charles d'Urre de Tessières.[20]

Recognising that the Order's finances were under strain from the expenses of constructing the new city around Fort Saint Elmo, the Grand Master resolved to repatriate to Malta all funds in France and Spain owed the Common Treasury and to become personally involved in the management of accounts. As several French knights of the Grand Cross and others at Malta for the Chapter General had been licensed to return to France, Tessières was ordered to transport them to Marseille with the four galleys. Upon Tessières' nomination Pierre de Massués-Vercoiran was appointed captain of the squadron capitana *San Iacomo*.[21] Antonio Maldonado commanded *San Giovanni Battista*, Barthélemy Bremont de Rousset *San Filippo*, and Gil de Andrade *Santa Fede*.[22] While in France Tessières was to gather all the funds in the country due to the Common Treasury and to take delivery of convicted felons donated to the Order as oarsmen by King Henry II. Without the latter, the galleys may have found it difficult to navigate in adverse winter weather. Also dispatched was the Great Galleon then commanded by Geronimo de Guete of Aragon in succession to Jorge de Sant Joan. Bound for Mallorca and Cartagena to load items for the Malta Arsenal and foodstuffs for the islands, De Guete was similarly to gather amounts due to the Common Treasury from Aragon and Castile.[23]

Departing Malta for Rome on 13 January 1559 was Giovan Francesco Langosco de Conti della Motta of Vercelli under order of Grand Master and Council to report to Pope Paul IV the failure to respond to the General Summons of Hospitallers by the Diocese of Venice, citing danger to their city rather than to their Order. The recommendation of Grand Master and Council was that these recalcitrants be deprived of

Habits and commanderies as the Venetian Senate evinced no interest whatsoever. On 13 March a Papal Bull was addressed to the Venetian Hospitallers to comply with summonses, not only on pain of defrocking but on pain of excommunication. With the return of the four galleys from Marseille delayed, Valette decided to put the fifth galley in service. Raffaello Salvago was placed in command of *San Michele Arcangelo* and dispatched to Messina to pick up 100 forzati (forced labourers or petty criminals) donated by the King of Spain. With these his galley was fully manned. Following a circumnavigation of Gozo aboard *San Michele* as well as a visit ashore, Valette concluded that the citadel or walled town of Rabat within 270m of weak wall without flanks or terrepleins must be refortified.[24]

The Peace of Cateau-Cambrésis was signed between Henry II of France and Philip II of Spain on 3 April 1559, at Le Cateau-Cambrésis, 20km south-east of Cambrai. Under its terms, France restored Piedmont and Savoy to the Duke of Savoy, and Corsica to the Republic of Genoa, but retained Saluzzo, Calais, and the Three Bishoprics: Metz, Toul, and Verdun. Spain retained Franche-Comté, but, more importantly, the treaty confirmed its direct control of Milan, Naples, Sicily, Sardinia, and the State of the Presidi (an artificial enclave of Tuscan city states) and indirectly through dominance of the rulers of Tuscany, Genoa, and other minor states, of northern Italy. The Pope was also their natural ally. The only truly independent entities on Italian soil were Savoy and the Republic of Venice. Spanish control of Italy lasted until the early eighteenth century. Beyond territorial alterations, the treaty ended sixty years of Habsburg-Valois wars.[25]

With the Peace of Cateau-Cambrésis, Spain and its satellite states found themselves crawling with idle and unpaid soldiery. The Ottoman Empire was meanwhile preoccupied with an armed struggle for succession between sons of Suleiman. Someone somewhere proposed taking advantage of these circumstances by re-capture of Tripoli-in-Africa, seized from the Order of Jerusalem by the Ottomans in August 1551, which had ever since been a haven for Ottoman corsairs and a springboard for their depredations. Any suggestion that Grand Master Valette was the someone is so wildly inconsistent with both the Order's history and Valette's personal history that it is not even debatable. What is also not debatable is that Valette readily, even eagerly, agreed to participate in such an undertaking authorized by King Philip II and commanded by that king's Viceroy of Sicily. Anticipating the advantages of local support, Valette did make some of the initial moves, immediately beginning to cultivate pre-existing relationships developed during his five years at Tripoli, utilizing Jacques des Roches and other Tripoli veterans as emissaries conveying communications and gifts to various African warlords unhappy with Dragut, including the King of Kairouan (70km west of Monastir) and the Sheiks of Djerba and Xercia, and enlisting their support. So began another unhappy and strange chapter in Hospitaller history, strange because of existing strain on the Common Treasury, strange because only five years earlier Valette had been part of an eight-knight commission that declined an offer of Mehedia already in Christian hands. Strange because by all estimation, even that of Dragut, Mehedia was a step up from Tripoli. Strange because Mehedia came with an annual subsidy of 72,000 gold scudos, and strange in terms of Hospitaller failures along the coast of Africa. The Grand Master also committed to the King the full resources of the Order of Jerusalem, to wit, five galleys, one galliot, two galleons, 1,000 hired soldiers, a battery of artillery and its munitions, food supplies for all of its personnel, and a large number of knights. He furthermore warranted to place the Order's contribution to a larger Spanish force under the command of Spanish knights Don Bernardo de Guimeran and Prior of León Don Antonio de Toledo. For his part King Philip assigned command of the expedition to Viceroy of Sicily Juan de la Cerda, 4th Duke of Medinaceli. Medinaceli was a Grandee of Spain, but he had no command experience at sea or anywhere else.

Forty-three years a Hospitaller, Bailiff of Lango Gaspard de Vallier did not live to see a recovery of Tripoli. He died at Malta in May 1559, never quite forgiven for Tripoli's loss. His Bailiwick of Lango would remain vacant until 1561. Suleiman's elder son Selim defeated younger son Bayezid in battle at Konya in central Anatolia. The latter fell back to presumed support at Amasya, where he was Sancakbey or Governor. However, the presumed support failed to materialise and Bayezid fled to Persia, relieving his father's anxiety.[26]

The Great Galleon, under command of Geronimo de Guete, returned from Cartagena on 13 June 1559 with a cargo of munitions but could not clear pratique. Many of her crew were sick and dying of peste, bubonic plague. The sick and dying were transferred to an infirmary at the clearing port in Marsamuscietto while the remainder of the crew were confined on board until the requisite forty days passed with no new cases. Given peace between French and Spanish and the threat such peace represented, Suleiman continued to keep his arsenals humming in order to be ready to defend his empire at sea. Piali Pasha and the Ottoman Armada had meanwhile reached Preveza opposite Santa Maura, where Piali was sufficiently aware of Christian plans that he requested additional embarked soldiery from Sultan Suleiman. Youthful Gian Andrea Doria, General of the Catholic Armada, brought a large squadron of Royal galleys to Naples en route to Sicily for the purpose of embarking Neapolitan soldiery hired for the Tripoli undertaking.[27]

At Paris King Henry II was on 30 June 1559 mortally wounded in a jousting tournament by Gabriel de Lorges, Count of Montgomery and Captain of the King's own Scottish Guard, and soon died at the age of 40. He was succeeded by his sickly 15-year-old son Francis II. The four galleys under General of the Galleys Charles d'Urre de Tessières returned from France early in July with Prior of Bohemia Wenceslaus von Hessenberg and various other commanders and knights of the German Langue who, as a result of Luis Cortit's embassy to Emperor Ferdinand, had come to personally render obedience to Grand Master Valette and to negotiate payment of past-due responsions. In December the Grand Master again dispatched Cortit to the Emperor to render his thanks.[27] Of the squadron, Antonio Maldonado commanded *San Giovanni Battista*, Barthélemy Bremont de Rousset *San Filippo*, Gil de Andrade *Santa Fede*, and Rafaello Salvago *San Michele Arcangelo*. Pierre de Massuez-Vercoiran, known as le Mas, commanded the capitana *San Iacomo* until he was assigned to command embarked soldiery, whereupon he was succeeded in command of the capitana by Antoine du Fay de Saint-Roman. Pierre de Massuez and his brother Louis would both be killed defending Fort Saint Elmo in June 1565 during the Great Siege of Malta.[28]

The Malta galleys were dispatched to a rendezvous with Doria at Naples, and returned on 23 July with four galleys of the Doria squadron under command of Hospitaller Don Bernardo de Guimeran donated for the planned siege of Tripoli. Guimeran, as commander of the marine contingent, carried the King's authorisation to undertake the eradication of Dragut before refortification of Tripoli was completed.

In less than a month since departing Spain he had met with Governor of Milan Gonzalo II Fernández de Córdoba, 3rd duke of Sessa, who had contributed 2,000 Spanish soldiers of the Tercio of Lombardia under command of Don Alvaro de Sande. Guimeran had also met with Andrea Doria at Genoa, who had ordered Gian Andrea Doria to place his entire force at the disposition of Viceroy of Sicily Medinacelli, and he had met with Viceroy of Naples Pedro Afán de Ribera, Duke of Alcalá, who had assigned 2,000 additional Spanish soldiers pending assurance that the Ottoman Armada was indeed not deploying to the western Mediterranean in 1559.

Guimeran had also met with Don Juan Hurtado de Mendoza, Captain-General of the Galleys of Spain, who had been less forthcoming on written orders that he remain in Spanish waters. Guimeran reached Messina on 17 July and met with Medinaceli and Doria. Sultan Suleiman ordered the Sancakbey of the Morea to send to Preveza the soldiery Piali had requested, and ordered Piali to remain at friendly ports unless and until Christians moved against Tripoli.[29]

On 18 August 1559 Pope Paul IV died at Rome in his 84th year. Four months and eight days later he was succeeded by Giovanni Angelo Medici as Pope Pius IV. In September the Ottoman Armada of sixty galleys weighed anchor at Preveza and proceeded to Ottoman Valona on the Adriatic coast of Albania to remind Christians it had not returned to Constantinople. Neapolitan Apulia on the opposite Adriatic shore sought to recall troops committed to the Expeditionary Force.[30]

Friend and foe in North Africa as well as Ottomans at Constantinople and Valona expected the Christian Expeditionary Force to sail for Tripoli in August. At Malta, no one was sure what was happening. Tessières was dispatched to Messina and thence to Palermo seeking information. He was told by Medinaceli that the combined force could not be made ready before October, when wind and weather in the Mediterranean could be unkind and charter-hire of heavier ships would be necessary. The Viceroy had written to Don Alvaro de Sande days earlier directing him to hire another 2,500 Lombard infantry as well as 2,000 German landsknechts recently released by Duke of Sessa Gonzalo Fernández de Córdoba y Fernández de Córdoba. These and earlier hires were drawing pay and drawing down food supplies all the while. Prior to receiving the viceroy's communication, Sande had petitioned the viceroy for the title of

Lieutenant General of the Landing Force, asserting that the initial 4,000 Lombards and Neapolitans would refuse to serve under the Viceroy's designated commander Andrea Gonzaga, unproven 30-year-old son of former Viceroy of Sicily Don Ferrante Gonzaga and brother of Hospitaller Prior of Barletta Giovan Vincenzo Gonzaga. Sande successfully made his point, leaving Andrea Gonzaga commander in name only.[30]

Lieutenant-General Alvaro de Sande arrived at Messina in October with hired Lombard and German soldiery while Viceroy of Naples Pedro Afán de Ribera reacted to Apulian alarm. He recalled 500 Spanish soldiers already transported to Messina by Don Sancho Martínez de Leyva, his Captain-General of Neapolitan Galleys. Unwilling to proceed 500 soldiers short, Medinaceli angrily ordered the raising of twelve companies of Italian infantry in Sicily, normally about 2,400 in strength, and another twelve companies of Italian infantry in Naples. Two of the latter twelve companies were provided by Hospitaller Ippolito Malaspina, younger son of Giuseppe Malaspina, Marchese of Fosdinovo. In Sicily sufficient numbers of scattered Germans were located to form a single company. Spaniard Bernardo de Aldano was appointed General of Artillery, while Luis Osorio of the Spanish Tercio in Sicily was appointed field commander. The College of Cardinals ruling between Popes dispatched three Papal galleys under command of Flaminio Orsini di Anguillara Sabazia, brother-in-law of Piero and Leone Strozzi. Orsini commanded one of the galleys himself, Nicolò Gentile a second, and Pietro Macchiavelli the third. Four other galleys were sent by Duke of Florence Cosimo de' Medici. While these things were occurring at Sicily, Hospitaller André de Saulcières de Tenance, commanding Francis of Lorraine's padrona galley, arrived at Malta on Grand Prior business. The Grand Master used the opportunity to embark his nephew Henri de la Valette de Cornusson for the return voyage to pay the Order's compliments to new King Francis II and to obtain reaffirmation of the Order's privileges in France. Because the Viceroy of Sicily had funded a company of French and Gascon veterans of the War in the Piedmont and appointed Pierre de Massués-Vercoiran to command of the company, Grand Master and Sacred Council appointed Antoine de Fay Saint-Roman his successor as skipper of the galley capitana *San Iacomo*.[31]

The Expeditionary Force that sailed from Messina late in October 1559, sailing vessels towed by oared galleys, consisted of fifty-four galleys and galliots: thirteen of Genoa; three of the Church; six of Malta including the Grand Master's galliot commanded by Romegas; four of Florence; seven of Naples commanded by Sancho de Leyva including two the property of Stefano di Mare; five the property of Antonio Doria commanded by his son Scipione Doria; ten of Sicily commanded by Berenguer de Requesens including two the property of the Marchese di Terranuova, two the property of Vincenzo Cicala, and two belonging to the Lord of Monaco; two galleys of Bendinella Sauli; one galliot the property of Luis Osorio; another galliot the property of Federico Staiti, plus two galliots the property of Medinacelli himself. There were in addition seven brigantines, sixteen frigates, thirty square-rigged sailing ships including two galleons, and twelve smaller ships with various combinations of square and lateen rigs. Embarked were 14,000 combatants flying the colours of Spain, Italy, and Germany. Also embarked was a company of light cavalry. Ministering to the troubled, ill, and wounded was Bishop of Mallorca Don Diego Arnedo. Bernardo de Guimeran returned from a reconnaissance of Tripoli with a report that the garrison had been strengthened to 2,000 Turkish combatants. The end of October marked the eighteenth anniversary almost to the day of Charles V's disastrous 1541 Siege of Algiers when during one of several storms 140 ships were blown onto shoals or beach and destroyed, when every Hospitaller at the 'Tomb of the Knights' was killed or wounded, when up to 17,000 soldiers and seamen lost their lives or were captured, and when the price of a Christian in slave markets fell to that of an onion.[31]

Three days following departure from Messina the Expeditionary Force put into Syracuse, 85 nautical miles to the south, where it remained all of November either because of no wind or too much wind or adverse wind. Waiting there in crowded conditions, people began to fall ill. Tessières informed the Viceroy that in the circumstance his reinforced galleys wished to proceed to Malta, transferring Maltese infantry under Giovan Antonio Bisballe and Giovan Vittorio Maurello from ship to shore while also transporting food stocks from Syracuse to Malta. On 1 December remaining galleys and other oared vessels followed, reaching Malta the next morning. Sailing ships, however, were forced by wind to return to Syracuse.

While galley force commanders and notables were entertained at Malta, the Priory of Aquitaine was vacated by the death of incumbent Jacques

Pelloquin, an Hospitaller for more than a half-century who had been an elector at the 1513 election of Fabrizio del Carretto as forty-third Grand Master. Next in line for the Priory of Aquitaine was Grand Hospitaller Jean de la Roche-Andry, but in that Roche-Andry had ignored his duties as Pilier of the Langue of France, not even reporting to Malta, Jean de Neuchèze was appointed Prior of Aquitaine, vacating the Bailiwick of the Morea. Commander of Flanders Louis de Vallée-Passy was appointed Bailiff of the Morea, while Commander of Chantereine and Treasurer Pierre de la Fontaine succeeded Roche-Andry as Grand Hospitaller. Jean Audebert de l'Aubuge and Seneschal Charles de Hangest du Mesnil Saint-Georges contested for the vacant dignity of Treasurer, with the Council giving the former the nod.

Meanwhile, a company of Maltese and Rhodian pioneers was readied for the Expeditionary Force and placed under the command of Guillaume de la Fontaine, a Malta corsair known as Captain Champagne. Toward the end of December there was a break in the weather, enabling oared vessels under command of Don Bernardo de Guimeran to tow sailing ships to Malta. The galleon of Vincenzo Cicala and a second ship were late reaching the tow rendezvous off Cape Passero, and rebels among embarked soldiery, perhaps impressed soldiery, took the opportunity to flee ashore after first doing as much damage as possible. Most were apprehended, the ringleaders hanged, and others sent to the oars for life. Prior of Bohemia Wenceslaus von Hessenberg, who had arrived Malta in July to profess loyalty to Grand Master and Convent, received license to return to Germany. So, too, did Commander of Meilberg Christoph Sigismund Römer von Maretz and Commander of Striga Heinrich von Ritza, who arrived with the Prior. They were accompanied by Luis Cortit as Ambassador to the Emperor's Court. In December the peste, last seen aboard the Great Galleon in June, reappeared at Malta.[32]

Plague descended on Malta in full force. By early January the infirmary or hospital was full to capacity with seriously ill and dying adventurers and seamen not just filling the great ward but filling every room and corridor. Doria ordered healthy crew to scrub down all ships from mast tops to bilge bottom, from stem to stern. Crew, too. Because it was January, ambient temperatures inhibited flea reproduction, and for this and perhaps other reasons the epidemic was short-lived, though not without a high incidence of death. Incidence was also mostly confined to visiting crews and soldiers and did not immediately strike Hospitallers and native Maltese. Two thousand replacement soldiers were hired in Naples and Sicily to replace the 3,000 dead and fled. The new levies were put under the command of Hospitaller Don Carlo Ruffo, ninth child of Paolo Ruffo, 6th Count of Settimo Sinopoli (Calabria), and Caterina Spinelli. Five hundred more infantry were obtained from the Naples regiment of Hospitaller Colonel Ippolito Malaspina, 300 more from Marcello Doria. On 9 January Guimeran took his towing galleys back to Messina and Calabria for a two-month stock of fresh provisions untainted by the peste, returning to Malta on 29 January.[33]

Four hundred Knights of Malta plus 2,000 infantry under the command of Pierre de Massués-Vercoiran known as le Mas (French infantry) and of Josef Tremark (German infantry)[34] and 200 Maltese pioneers under Cesare Visconte[35] as well as volunteer adventurers were placed by the Grand Master under the joint command of Charles d'Urre de Tessières and Don Bernardo de Guimeran as part of an Expeditionary Force under the overall command of Juan de la Cerda, 4th Duke of Medinaceli and Viceroy of Sicily, with all naval forces under 20-year-old Gian Andrea Doria. There was in addition siege artillery under Chevalier Antoine Flotte de la Roche plus the five galleys of the Hospitaller squadron as well as the Galleon of Malta, the Nave, and three grippos. Beyond the Maltese contribution there were Doria's thirteen Genovese galleys, five from Naples under Sancho de Leyva, four from Sicily under Berenguer de Requesens, three from the Pope under Flaminio Orsini, four from Florence under Duke Francesco da Bibbona, two from Monaco under Jacques de Laurentii,[36] Lieutenant to the Grimaldi Duke of Monaco, five belonging to Antonio Doria under his son Scipione, two under Bendinello Sauli, two under Stefano di Mare, two under the Marquese of Terranuova, and two under Vincenzo Cicala. There were also twenty-nine sailing ships, including those of Malta under Andrea Gonzaga, four galliots absent that of Romegas, and thirty-five smaller vessels, all transporting something on the order of 30,000 soldiers, seamen, and oarsmen. These departed Malta on 9 February 1560.

One hour prior to departure Medinaceli announced the Expeditionary Force's destination was Djerba, and not Tripoli. The Grand Master was taken aback, observing among other things that there was no need for such an Expeditionary Force to take Djerba, that there was no harbour at Djerba able to accommodate sailing ships, even able to accommodate large numbers of galleys such as at present, and that Berber allies were waiting near Tripoli, not Djerba. Medinaceli, however, preferred a less hazardous conquest than Dragut's fortified city. The Expeditionary Force numbering forty-nine galleys, four galliots, twenty-nine sailing ships, thirty-five small craft and 30,000 embarked personnel detoured to Djerba. Arriving the next day, 10 February, Djerba was taken without organised resistance. There Medinaceli proposed to construct a large rectangular *place fort* (Fr) or *castrum* (Lat) at modern Ajim overlooking the narrow entrance to the safe anchorage south of the island. This fortress was to be walled with cannon on the ramparts and living quarters within. From Tripoli Dragut dispatched Uluç Ali (Occhiali) to Constantinople to summon waiting support. [37]

Almost a month later, on 7 March, a violent storm struck the Expeditionary Force, which but for a few galleys was totally exposed at anchor in the open Gulf of Gabès off Valguarnera, modern *Houmt El Souk*. Andrea Gonzaga's warship capitana pulled her anchors and was propelled into the (small) Galleon of Malta. The galleon was undamaged but the Sicilian capitana went to the bottom. Cicala's galleon skiffs were able to rescue some of those on board the Sicilian vessel, including Gonzaga. Several smaller vessels were blown aground in shallow water.[38]

Death from this untoward event, however tragic, was almost insignificant when compared to death from disease during those twenty-six days at Djerba, particularly among galley oarsmen, crew, and others required to remain aboard ship. The incidence of plague aboard Maltese galleys had become a far more serious problem as it had already within the wider fleet. Some 1,500 victims had died before the fleet sailed from Malta, and more had died since. Terminally ill, Tessières took the squadron and all other Maltese vessels including the galleon, and including embarked soldiery and artillery, back to Malta in April, where he was replaced by senior captain Antonio Maldonado. Bremont de Rousset, commanding *San Filippo*, was already dead, as were Jean de Pontau de Barry[39] of Provence, Alessandro Buondelmonte of Florence, Guillermo Podovilla of Valencia, Claude de Rommecourt and Jean de Pons both of the Langue of France, Pedro Garzès de Marcilla of Navarre, Martín de Undiano of Aragon, and Joachim Poussard de l'Homelhère of the Langue of France, as well as a host of Maltese oarsmen and seamen.

There were so many sick and dying that a second infirmary was equipped on the island of Senglea. It was too little too late as a very large number failed to survive.[40]

This withdrawal of Malta's entire besieging force, no longer needed at Djerba, may have been more than fortuitous. It is not clear what Medinaceli expected other than to move on from Djerba to Tripoli before returning triumphant to his Vice-regency. Valette, however, certainly believed that the Ottoman Armada that was at Preveza eight months earlier ready to leap to Tripoli's defence would reappear in 1560, and his agent at Constantinople would long since have confirmed his belief. A sickness-depleted squadron of three (Maldonado's *San Giovanni Battista*, Andrade's *Santa Fede*, and *San Filippo* commanded by Geronimo d'Homedes, nephew of the former Grand Master) even so departed Malta on 24 April to rejoin the Expeditionary Force. The three Malta galleys were no sooner returned to Djerba when came a recall at the end of April of Neapolitan galleys and embarked soldiery by Viceroy of Naples Pedro Afán de Ribera, citing appearance of the Ottoman Armada in Apulian waters. Medinaceli was stunned, having calculated that the Ottomans could arrive no sooner than the end of May and probably later.[40]

While construction of the Djerba fortress had been under way an Ottoman fleet of eighty-three galleys already on standby had assembled at Constantinople under Piali Pasha with Kara Mustafa as pilot. On this news Medinaceli abandoned any thought of Tripoli but could not abandon the fortress, his personal conception. By 7 May, however, the Turkish Armada appeared in the Freo Channel between Malta and Gozo. During the afternoon of 10 May a fishing caique with Uluç Ali, Kara Mustafa, and fellow-corsair Kara Borno sailed among the Christian force anchored off Djerba Island. They found no sign of readiness. That same evening Hospitaller Hugo de Copons the Younger arrived in a fast frigate from Malta conveying the ominous news. Maldonado, Andrade, and Homedes accompanied Viceroy Medinaceli to his newly constructed fort and offered to escort him to safety using the Order's three galleys together with the Sicilian galley *Contessa* moored below the fort. Medinaceli declined the offer.[41] Appearing off Djerba on 11 August, the Ottomans there trapped a yet-unprepared Christian fleet in a cul-de-sac in spite of a second alert arriving that morning. Doria proved unable or unwilling to dispose his forces, drove his galley onto sand banks, and fled in a skiff, as did Requesens. There was no battle.[41]

Fleeing Christian ships were captured one by one. Among them were four Genovese galleys of Gian Andrea Doria, two Papal galleys, all five Neapolitan (refused license to return to Naples), two Sicilian, one of the Monaco Grimaldis, one of the Marquese of Terranuova, two Florentine, two of Vincenzo Cicala, one of Scipione Doria, and one of Stefano di Mare. Another, the personal property of the Marchese of Terranuova, was torched by the marchese himself and run aground. The Ottomans in the same way took possession of fourteen sailing ships. By surrender of the new fort ten weeks later, seven more galleys had been lost: three belonging to Doria, two of Sicily, and one each of Monaco and Bendinello Sauli. Thus twenty-nine of forty-nine galleys were lost. The Malta Squadron reached the high seas by way of the Sfax Channel followed by sixteen other galleys and pursued by Uluç Ali's vanguard. This was where the Papal capitana was lost and where Gil de Andrade's *Santa Fede* was engaged close aboard. All but the Papal capitana made it to the open sea on 12 May and escaped. The Hospitaller squadron reached Malta intact two days later. Charles de Tessières[42] had meanwhile succumbed to his illness and had been succeeded as Grand Commander by Louis du Pont. A number of Hospitallers, however, remained within the new fort. One of these was Charles d'Amanzé, received into the Priory of Champagne in 1543, who had been misidentified as Tessières in the roll of Hospitallers received that year. He died within months of capture, probably of poorly attended wounds. (The two galleys that were the personal property of Vincenzo Cicala were also a part of the Sicilian squadron, as were Terranuova's two and the two from Monaco, and account for reports of six or more Sicilian galleys lost.)[43]

For ten weeks eighteen pieces of artillery battered walls of the otherwise unfinished fort, in which were penned an untold number of soldiers and seamen, Italian, French, and Spanish, under the orders of Alvaro de Sande. There are reports[44] that the older and more elaborate star fort initially constructed *c.*1289 by Aragonese Count of Djerba Roger de Lauria on the north coast at modern Borj El Kebir was also garrisoned and, if so, successfully besieged. It was during this period that Dragut arrived from Tripoli with ten galleys and galliots, not to involve himself with the siege but rather with establishing his dominion. Short of water and following several futile sorties, the defenders surrendered at discretion on 30 July. Dragut would further strengthen the fort and provide it with an adequate source of drinking water, but today only breached walls stand. With the bones of Christians who perished during the siege, Dragut erected near the fort a mausoleum to commemorate the victory; constructing a pyramid 25–30ft in height and 130ft in circumference visible from the sea (the so-called 'Tower of Skulls'). Until 1848 these remained a cemetery. One of those contributing to the Tower was 18-year-old Hospitaller Matteo Caniggiani of Florence, months out of his novitiate.[45] Another not much older was Don Diego de Mendoza from the Basque heartland south of Bilbao. A third was Michele Moleti of Messina, received with brother Francesco only four years earlier. A fourth was Julius Cesar Palavicino of Sicily, who died while commanding a sortie. Yet another was Claude de Rommecourt of a family originally German resettled in Champagne. And still another was Robert de la Tour of Arles in Provence. Allied losses overall totalled 13,000 dead and 5,000 prisoners enslaved. Among the earlier dead was Papal Captain-General Flaminio Orsini, captured during the Papal capitana's engagement in the Sfax Channel and beheaded. Among the ransomable were Don Juan de Cardona; Don Alvaro de Sande; Don Sancho de Leyva; Don Berenguer de Requesens;[46] Don Bernardino de Mendoza, who might have been the brother of Hospitaller Pedro de Mendoza and/or the captain of Requesens' Sicilian capitana;[47] Don Juan de Vargas; Don Gaston de la Cerda, young son of Medinaceli; the two sons of Sancho de Leyva;[48] Bernardo de Aldana;[49] Bishop of Mallorca Don Diego Arnedo;[50] and Antoine de Justas-Châteaufort,[51] who died in captivity having arrived by brigantine before daybreak on 11 May bearing a second letter of warning from the Grand Master to Medinaceli and a second letter to Doria.

Two years later the Cerda son died a prisoner at Constantinople. Juan de Cardona, Bernardino de Mendoza, and Juan de Vargas, among others became captives of Piali's friend and pilot Kara Mustafa, Sancakbey of Mitillini, some say in an attempt to pocket their ransoms. This last, though, seems implausible and inconsistent with Piali's humane treatment of prisoners and with his return on 17 August of Hospitaller Standard Bearer Bidon de Beaulac. A 'gracious response of Piali Pasha to the Grand Master', not to mention the relatively quick release of these captives.[50] All captives in the hands of Kara Mustafa (born a Greek

Christian) were subsequently sold to the Christian Giustiniani lords of nearby Scio (Chios), from where Cardona and others made their way to freedom in 1561. Among the dead Hospitaller defenders of Medinacelli's fort were Alonso de Golfin, Juan de Ovando, and Juan Miguel de Garay. Taken captive were the aforementioned Pierre de Massués-Vercoiran, Cristobal Pacheco, Bernard de le Puget, Giulio Cesare Malvicino, the aforementioned Charles d'Amanzé of Chauffailles and the Priory of Champagne, who died at Constantinople, and Standard-Bearer Beaulac.[52]

Arriving at Malta on 15 May was a frigate that by means of darkness, shallow waters, and a favourable wind had safely transported from Djerba Viceroy Medinacelli, Gian Andrea Doria, Count of Vicari (Sicily) Don Vicenzo Bosco, Hospitaller Don Bernardo de Guimeran, Hospitaller Don Pedro d'Urries, and others.[53] Guimeran and Urries had been requisitioned by Medinaceli to supervise construction of the fort and were largely to be credited with its near completion.[54] Of the four galliots of Sicily gathered under the fort, two were the personal property of Medinaceli, one the personal property of Luis Osorio commanding the Viceregal Spanish tercio assigned to Sicily, and one the personal property of Federico Staiti of Messina. All but the latter were able to escape under cover of darkness early in June.[55]

Not wishing to add to Medinaceli's grief, Grand Master Valette took care to not reproach the Viceroy, who by ignoring the advice of professionals and the orders of his King had brought about this disaster. Rather he concerned himself most about the suffering of the wounded and captured.[53] He also assigned four galleys from the squadron now commanded by Pierre de la Fontaine in succession of Regent Antonio Maldonado, plus two galliots, which together with thirteen galleys under Gian Andrea Doria departed Malta bound for the relief of Alvaro de Sande at Djerba, but were turned back by violently adverse weather. In the event an irate Philip II had directed his naval commanders to confine themselves to defend the Italian coast, while Sande and 5,000 defenders had surrendered on 30 July. Sande, among others, would be taken to Constantinople.[56] Most would disappear into slave markets.

This ill-conceived undertaking, incompetently commanded, culminated in the Ottoman Empire's naval high-water mark and in an equally low-water mark not just for Christian commanders but especially for Christian victims. Imperial Admiral and Prince of Melfi Andrea

Doria died at Genoa on 25 November 1560, five days short of 94 years of age. Predeceased by wife Princess Peretta Uso di Mare and childless, his next-of-kin included his deceased nephew and foster child Giannettino Doria, Giannettino's son and Andrea's presumed heir Gian Andrea Doria, cousin Antonio Doria, deceased nephew Filippino (Filippo) Doria, nephew Erasmo Doria, niece Lazzarina Doria, and nephew Cristoforo (Doria) Pallavicini. He was also survived by Marcantonio del Carretto, Peretta Uso di Mare's child by an earlier marriage, and was interred in Genoa's Church of San Matteo. His memory lives on as Neptune in a painted-to-order portrait by Angelo Bronzino.[57]

Chapter XIV

Jean Parisot de la Valette 1560–64

As if the disaster at Djerba were not enough, there was a disturbing and strange development with the corsair galleys of Hospitaller Arduin de Castillon de Beines, one of which, the capitana, was called *Santa Marta* and the other of which was *Corona* commanded and piloted by a non-Hospitaller brother of said Beines by the name of Honourat de Castillon, Seigneur de Saint-Julien. These galleys had returned from the Levant with good plunder and several Turkish vessels in tow taken in company with the galliot of Grand Master Valette. Prior to unloading, the three ships were sent by the Grand Master to Messina to transfer armaments for his new galley *San Gabriello* under construction. Aboard the capitana was Mathurin de Lescut de Romegas; the galliot was to be disarmed in order to equip the new galley and Romegas was to take command. Galleys and galliot departed Malta on 21 June 1560 and, fighting headwinds, reached Cape Passero a few days later. Proceeding past Syracuse, two large Turkish galliots were sighted off Torre Longina. The Christians exchanged signals concerning strategy, having recognised the galliots as those of Barbarossa Turco and Ionus (Yunus) of Sovrassari (Skyros). The galliots meanwhile did not suspect the Christian presence. The Christian galleys were not those of the Order and they were under no obligation to engage. The Christian corsairs nevertheless resolved to take the galliots; their opportunity came at the Gulf of Vendicari, where the galliots were invested in the dark of night. Hospitaller losses aboard the capitana consisted of Robert de la Tour of Provence and Serving Brother Giles Richard of Auvergne, though many others were wounded, especially Romegas and Beines, the latter mortally so. There were additional losses among the embarked fortune-seekers and soldiery, particularly aboard *Corona*, which engaged the galliot of Ionus Reis, a Turk of Anatolia who in 1542 had escaped captivity at Malta, and had abandoned his ship and fled ashore, where he was captured and killed by militia of Catania. Barbarossa Turco also fled, but successfully with his galliot. A natural Turk, he had adopted his *nom de guerre* and had no relationship to the deceased admiral. Liberated at Syracuse were the oarsmen of Ionus Reis, all Christian. In fear the surviving brother would decamp with the two galleys and embarked plunder plus the captured galliot, which were a part of the Beines estate and thus the property of the Order, Valette dispatched four galleys of the Hospitaller squadron under Regent Antonio Maldonado to Syracuse. Maldonado placed Hospitaller Miguel de Trejo of Castile in command of *Santa Marta* and Gaspare d'Annaia of Bari in command of *Corona*, took the captured galliot in tow, and escorted all three south to Malta, arriving on 27 July. Romegas and the Grand Master's galliot proceeded north to Messina to outfit *San Gabriello*. Honourat de Castillon proceeded to Marseille and sought by legal means to recover his brother's estate. In so doing he was frequently able to deny Maltese use of that port.[1]

Piali Pasha remained at Djerba for eight days following surrender of the fort. While re-embarking siege artillery he also assisted Dragut in repairing relations with Berbers hostile to the corsair's return. Local sheiks sympathetic to the Christian cause, however, were punished or worse. Sande was treated humanely, as were other commanders who were prisoners; with few exceptions non-commanders were sold in the slave markets at Constantinople and Tripoli. From Djerba the Ottoman admiral accompanied Dragut to Tripoli, where he was saluted with a great salvo of artillery. Turkish galleys in addition to normal standards and pennants flew on the stern mast those of Spanish vessels captured in the Battle of Djerba. Grand Master Valette was informed that Bernardo Simon had returned without success from Djerba and Tripoli, where he had been sent by Medinaceli under a safe-conduct to negotiate the ransom for his captured son and for the return of the captured Sword of Saint Louis.[2]

From Tripoli on 16 August the Ottoman Armada once more reached the Freo Channel,[3] where fresh water was always available to those with the strength to take it, this time from Gozo. Valette took the opportunity to attempt ransom of Medinaceli's son and other captives or, short of ransom, to make their captivity more comfortable with bread, blankets, and clean clothing. Piali was invited to relocate from Freo to nearby Maddelena Cove, where Turks were permitted ashore. In ransom discussions between Piali and Rhodiot Iacomo Caloriti, however, there was little progress, Piali asserting that captives were now the property of the Sultan or of individual commanders, and that with one exception his own share of captives had been awarded to his senior commanders including Kara Mustafa. The lone exception was Hospitaller Standard Bearer Bidon de Beaulac, whom he was willing to exchange for 300 gold scudos. This was the same price as paid in 1548 for each Hospitaller captured aboard *Santa Caterina* in the Gulf of Naples. As for Medinaceli's son Don Gaston de la Cerda, Piali asserted he had no knowledge of such a captive. From Malta the Ottomans proceeded to Sicily, pausing at Augusta with some consequent violence before taking the standard route from Sicily across the Strait of Otranto to Corfu or Preveza, then south around the Morea and across the Aegean. Deprived of masts and rudders, captured Christian galleys were on 27 September 1560 towed into the Bosphorus stern first. In a sign of success, the first ship dragged in the sea a standard that earlier belonged to the Spanish on which was depicted Christ's crucifixion, while on her poop clearly visible stood Alvaro de Sande, Sancho de Leyva, and Berenguer d'Oms de Requesens.[4]

Romegas and Gil de Andrade were dispatched to Rhodes with two galleys, the new *San Gabriello*, property of the Grand Master, and *Santa Fede* of the Malta Squadron, aboard which were to be embarked en route several agents intending to foment unrest while at the same time soliciting information on movements of the Turkish fleet. Prior to departure Romegas hoisted the standard of the Grand Master, while Andrade hoisted the standard of the Religion, each presuming command of the expedition; the Grand Master, by reason of Andrade's seniority, ordered Romegas to lower his standard. The two corsairs sailed from Malta on 23 September and reached the Aegean, en route capturing a schierazzo (a small cargo vessel with four sails) off the island of Milos. It was not clear whether they either embarked the agents or, if so, put them ashore at Rhodes. Ultimately they repaired to Otranto, having suffered much cold weather and while at that port the embarked adventurers were put ashore. The attempt by Romegas to take command at the outset was early evidence of his ability to irritate fellow Hospitallers, a habit that would prove his undoing.[5]

French King Francis II died at Orleans on 5 December 1560 only 17 years of age. He was succeeded by younger brother Charles IX, aged 10, and left as widow Mary, Queen of Scots, three days short of 18 years of age. She returned to Scotland the following August.[6]

While the Council of Trent and the Counter-Reformation continued under new Pope Pius IV, at Malta it was finally accepted that the Order's wealth in Britain was lost forever. Other realities were the Lutheran movement in Germany and the Huguenot and Calvin movements in France, all three spilling over borders. These developments threatened the character of the Order of Jerusalem with a drift to dominance by numbers of Italian and Spanish Hospitallers. At Rome Pius IV was conducting a vendetta against Paul IV's pro-French Cardinals, some facing execution. These concerns, however, were outweighed by a new report from Gil de Andrade and Mathurin Romegas. Sent into the Levant in September, they returned in January with relatively confident advice that the Ottoman Armada would in the spring move against Malta itself. An accord between Ottomans and Persians resulted among other things in the strangulation of Suleiman's rebel son Bayezid. The accord, of course, also freed the Sultan to turn his attention to the west and to strategic domination of the Mediterranean. Recent successes at Tripoli, Zuara, and Djerba led the Sultan to believe that the time was approaching to cut out the festering sore of Malta.[7]

Grand Master and Council realised that in the event of a siege of Malta the Order would be entirely dependent on a Spanish Armada still licking its Djerba wounds, and an armada with suspect leadership. Because Rome had lowered its defence subsidy, Spain's Mediterranean Galley Armada was at the time limited to sixty galleys, insufficient on the number, wounds or no wounds, suspect leadership or no suspect leadership, to defeat the Ottomans at sea. There was a need for a capable emissary to and between Pope and King, someone with the diplomatic skills to improve both funding and other support. Count Broccardo Persico of Cremona was so identified. A diplomat par excellence with contacts at both courts, Broccardo was in 1561 received into the Order of Jerusalem as an Hospitaller. He not only represented Hospitaller interests at Rome and Madrid but smoothed relations between Pope and King, most importantly obtaining an increase in the Papal subsidy for Spanish galley construction. There was also a need for a Captain of the local Relief Force, and the name of General of the Galleys and Grand Hospitaller Pierre de la Fontaine came immediately to mind, an individual with the

Grand Master's tenure widely respected within and without the Convent. It was not clear whether in response to his proposed appointment, or whether in response to the Order's circumstances, Fontaine, as a member of the Council, chose that moment to publicly criticise Valette, primarily asserting that funds expended in the disastrous Djerba campaign would have been better utilised to improve Malta's defences. He was appointed Captain of the Reserve Force in spite of his outburst. He was also provided the authority to expend or commit 50,000 scudos on his own recognisance to improve Malta's readiness.[8]

As Capitan di Succourso and Grand Hospitaller Fontaine took course for France with two galleys, his capitana *San Giovanni Battista* under Jean de Cuvyler de Coucy in succession of Antonio Maldonado, and *San Michele Arcangelo* under the Genovese Raffaello Salvago, the latter already a lyric poet and historian intending to write this very same history. Fontaine's purpose was to purchase forest timber in France. He departed Malta on 23 January 1561, sailing past Sicily's Trapani and Favignana en route to Corsica up the east side of Sardinia past Isola Tavolara toward the Strait of Bonifacio. On 2 February the two galleys were hit by a perilous storm with winds of 50 knots and more. While less than hurricane strength, 50-knot winds and the seas they raise can be destructive of long and narrow shallow-draft galleys. One Nasuf Deli Reis, a former corsair galliot captain captured by Regent Pierre de Gozon-Mélac at Stromboli in September 1556 then a slave on Coucy's *San Giovanni Battista*, suggested diverting the two galleys to a nearby Corsican islet called Agugliastro, where he warranted there was good shelter. Eventually weathering the storm at Agugliastro, the two galleys proceeded a short distance further to Porto Figari, a large inlet 3.5nm north-west of Bonifacio. Within a sheltered cove at Porto Figari the two galleys came upon two Turkish galliots and a fusta manned only by chained Christian oarsmen, the crews having fled into the Corsican hinterland. The three vessels were seized and the Christian oarsmen liberated. As 2 February was the anniversary of the Virgin Mary's purification, one galliot and the fusta were sold, with the proceeds going to various churches. The largest and best galliot was sent back to Malta under a prize crew commanded by François Jourdan, a serving brother of the Langue of Provence. Incredulously, Genoa's Bank of Saint George, which administered the island of Corsica, sued unsuccessfully for the return of the liberated Christian slaves. Meanwhile, at Malta Prior of Saint-Gilles Pierre de Gozon-Mélac was elected General of the Galleys in succession of Pierre de la Fontaine. On the former's nomination, Guy de Tianges de Croset of the Langue of Auvergne was appointed flag captain of the squadron capitana *San Iacomo* in succession of Antoine de Fay Saint-Roman.[9]

Bound for Spain, Vincenzo Cicala, with a single galley, joined for mutual defence at Trapani with Don Luis Osorio, commanding a galliot also bound for Spain. Osorio was commander of the Viceregal infantry tercio assigned to Sicily and had embarked aboard his galliot both Hospitaller Don Pedro de Urries and the latter's mother, the Countess of Ayerba. Cicala, famously, had his 16-year old son Scipione embarked. These two ships, both at Viceregal expense replacing galleys lost a year earlier at Djerba, were set upon by three galliots of Uluç Ali (Occhiali) off the Sicilian island of Marettimo. Pedro de Urries was killed in combat. Both Cicalas, Osorio, and the Countess of Ayerba were enslaved.[10] Luis Osorio and the Countess of Ayerba were ransomed from Uluç Ali within months. The two Cicalas were sent in chains to Sultan Suleiman in Constantinople. Vincenzo Cicala would die in captivity in December 1564. His son Scipione, said to have abjured his faith to save his father, much later assumed the name and rank of Cigalazade Yusuf Sinan Pasha and rose from Aga of Janissaries to Provincial Beylerbey and General to Commander of the Ottoman Fleet to, briefly, Grand Vizier of the Ottoman Empire.[11]

Meanwhile, at Malta rumour of war continued to swirl. Marc de la Goutte of Auvergne and Giorgio Vercelli of the Piedmont were directed to ensure all food stocks on the islands were kept ready for immediate delivery to fortresses. Juan de Rojas of Castile and Laurent de Boulieù de Iarnieù of Auvergne were to ensure all private and public cisterns were kept full. Giovan Simone Comito of Naples and Don Francisco Zanoguera of Valencia were to transport women, children, and the aged from the islands to a place of safety. Antonio Peletta of Asti and Lupertio de Poio of Aragon were to move into the fortresses all windmill grindstones and to ensure their safe stowage. Miguel de Pennaroxa of Aragon and Giovanni Vagnone of Turin were to have brought within the walls of Birgu a great quantity of earth for wall repair. Arriving from Naples aboard the ship of Ragusan (Ragusa, Sicily) Vicenzo di Michele were 700 hired infantry commanded by Hospitaller Captains Giovan Vittorio Maurello and Don Carlo Russo. From Rome came 500 more infantry under Hospitaller Captain Cencio Guasconi of Florence arriving on 11 April. On the same date the two galleys dispatched to France under command of Pierre de la Fontaine returned to Malta without Fontaine but with a large sum of coin from French priories and commanderies. Prior of Messina Signorino della Gattinara returned from Spain aboard *San Michele*. A few days later the other three galleys under command of Gozon-Mélac returned to Malta, having first shepherded into port accompanied grain carriers and other supply ships. Embarked aboard the galleys for transport to Malta was 21-year-old Hospitaller Prior of Barletta Don Vincenzo Gonzaga, son of former Viceroy of Sicily Ferrante Gonzaga. He brought with him a large number of Hospitallers returning for the presumed siege as well as a large number of gentlemen adventurers. There were also 300 hired Sicilian infantry under command of Guillaume de la Fontaine, nephew of Pierre called Captain Champagne presumably for a habit of celebrating lucrative corsair outings. Throughout the month of April 1561 cargoes of wine, salted meat, and other provisions had been arriving from Venetian Zante (Zakinthos) and from various locations in the Kingdom of Naples. Insofar as dependence on the Spanish Armada was concerned, the Order's resident ambassador at the Court of Philip II, Don Bernardo de Guimeran, returned to Malta in a show of force by way of Italy aboard the capitana of Don Juan Hurtado de Mendoza's sixteen-galley Royal Squadron. He brought news of his appointment as interim Commander of the Sicilian Galley Squadron pending release from Djerba captivity of Don Berenguer d'Oms de Requesens. The Sicilian Galley Squadron had by then been increased in number to seven first-class galleys. According to Guimeran, the combined total of twenty-three galleys was enough to disturb any Ottoman siege force. These were part of a larger Catholic Armada inclusive of the galleys of Genoa, Naples, and Tuscany that was commanded by Marcantonio del Carretto, 2nd Duke of Melfi and actual heir to the deceased Andrea Doria. Carretto was at the time an unproven 58-year-old with no track record of anything whatsoever. But he was of the blood. Andrea Doria's presumed heir Gian Andrea Doria, who abandoned Alvaro de Sande and 5,000 others to captivity, became Carretto's Lieutenant General.[12]

Hugo de Copons of Aragon, who brought an alert to Djerba one day before arrival of the Ottoman Armada, was in May sent into the Levant for information. This was not the Hugo de Copons, a veteran of the Great Siege of Rhodes and later Galley Squadron Commander, but of the next generation of the same family. He possessed a working fluency in Greek and Turkish. Romegas with *San Gabriello* conveyed Guimeran to Sicily to take command of the Galleys of Sicily while Requesens remained captive at Constantinople. From Sicily Romegas had been ordered to the African coast to prey upon all things Dragut while the Catholic Armada gathered at Messina under Marcantonio del Carretto. On the African coast Romegas invested the Turkish caramussal (elevated-poop merchantman) of Osman Reis, cargo of timber for building galliots, which resisted so forcefully that in the end only nine Turks remained alive and the caramussal was not salvageable. Romegas broke up the timber and sank the ship.[13]

Famine reigned at Messina due to a shortage of grain, while at Malta reserves of food stocks had been accumulated in preparation for siege. Arriving at Malta were three cargoes of grain from Marseilles and greater Provence dispatched by Antoine de Thesan-Venasque, the Order's Receiver at the Priory of Saint-Gilles, on order of the Christian King at the behest of Fontaine and the Order's resident ambassador at the French Court Gilbert de Serpens of Auvergne. To the great relief of the Messina authorities and to the great joy of Messina residents, Valette ordered these cargoes transferred to the small Galleon and Saettia of the Religion and the two vessels towed to Messina by the galley squadron. The towing task, however, delayed the arrival of the Malta Squadron at the rendezvous with Don Bernardo de Guimeran's seven galleys.

Hospitaller Guimeran was under orders of Gian Andrea Doria to transport from Messina to Naples Bishop of Catania Nicola Maria Caracciolo, and departed Messina with his seven galleys one day prior to Gozon-Mélac's arrival. Reaching Milazzo on the north coast of Sicily, Guimeran was informed that two Turkish galliots had been sighted near Lipari, 20 nautical miles to the north. The two galliots were a lure set, according to Bosio, by the astute 76 year-old Dragut while hiding behind Stromboli with his super *bastarda* galley and eight other galleys or galliots 22 nautical miles further north. Guimeran bit on the lure, sighted the two galliots on the morning of 3 July 1561, and went in pursuit to the north. Soon four of his galleys with inexperienced rowing crews were increasingly left behind. Dragut was able to pounce with eleven ships, first on Guimeran's capitana and two others, later on the four laggards. Because as a Hospitaller Guimeran flew the standard of Malta, Dragut believed he had the Maltese capitana in his grasp; his super-galley and another of his galleys grappled Guimeran's capitana port and starboard and corsairs swarmed aboard. There was a bloody if lop-sided contest eventually encompassing all seven Sicilian galleys. As most galley battles were determined by numbers, there was little chance of anything but one outcome. All seven Sicilian galleys were captured, as was Bishop Caracciolo and all other Sicilian survivors. More Christian galleys were lost off Stromboli than Christian ships of all kinds were lost during Barbarossa's celebrated Ottoman victory at 1538's Battle of Preveza. Guimeran, having boarded Dragut's capitana during the battle, was surrounded at Dragut's mainmast and killed before the battle's end. His loss was sincerely mourned by the Knights of Saint John, and his further contribution to the well-being of the Order of Jerusalem would be sorely missed. This was not true at the Spanish Court of King Philip II, where this new disaster so soon after Djerba elicited no expression of sorrow for long-time Ambassador Guimeran but rather an attempt to purge his name from Court conversation.[14]

Dragut took his squadron and seven captures around the western end of Sicily and down to the Freo Channel between Malta and Gozo to water at the latter. At Gozo on or about 5 July his shore parties were fired on and harassed by the cavalry of Antoine du Fay de Saint-Roman, and it was Saint-Roman's sighting of the captured galleys that informed Malta of the Battle of Stromboli.[15] The aforementioned Hugo de Copons returned from the Levant in July with no whisper of Ottoman intent to besiege Malta but with good plunder. He disposed of his galliot at Messina, transferred a share of his plunder to a Guimeran galley for repayment to Gian Andrea Doria of galliot financing, and purchased for himself a large galley. The repayment ended up in Dragut's coffers. Worse, deploying again to the Levant in 1562 in company with Marcello Doria, the two galleys became separated by storm in Rhodean waters. His was captured by the Ottoman Rhodes Guard. In this way the balance of his 1561 plunder was returned. His knowledge of the Turkish language was of no help. Copons and his lieutenant, Hospitaller Fernando de Corbera of Valencia, both died in slavery, perhaps fortunate they were not hanged at the outset.[16]

In Sicily there was widespread shock and concern, not just at loss of the Sicilian squadron but at the capture of Messina resident Vincenzo Cicala and son Scipione together with Tercio commander Luis Osorio, all compounding the despondency of Djerba. In the centre of the island citizens felt insecure, on the coast they were terrified. This terror was not eased by a waning fear of the Ottoman Armada. Corsairs of Tripoli, Algiers, Djerba, Bizerta, and elsewhere were more to be feared than the regular Ottoman Navy. On a report that captives of Kara Mustafa had stolen an idle galley and galliot and made their way to safety at Messina, Dragut, with new captives from new successes, petitioned the Sultan to be made Beylerbey of all North Africa with responsibility for maintaining Ottoman hegemony in the western Mediterranean. While Suleiman apparently remained confident of Dragut's tactical ability, he was not so confident of his strategic and diplomatic credentials. No such assignment was ever forthcoming.

King Philip II meanwhile ordered the remainder of his Catholic Armada to assemble at Messina for the purpose of conveying supplies and a replacement garrison to the fortress of La Goletta commanding the entrance to the Bay of Tunis. His commander, whomever he might have been, was also to belabour Hafsid King of (Greater) Tunis Ahmad III for violations of capitulations between the two kingdoms, principally Tunisian support for the Ottoman Armada.[17]

Pierre de Gozon-Mélac returned to Malta on or about 5 July in possession of Hugo de Copon's assessment of Ottoman intention this year not to deploy more than a handful of galleys necessary to patrol the Greek Archipelago. Gozon-Mélac also brought a letter from Viceroy of Sicily and Duke of Medinaceli Juan de la Cerda setting a one-month time frame for assembly of the Catholic Armada at Messina. Absent the threat of the Ottoman Armada, Valette retained only the large infantry company commanded by Hospitaller Cencio Guasconi, and discharged all other infantry and hired vessels. With a full month free Valette planned a raid on Rachel Amet. A village of 2,000 houses, Rachel Amet was located behind the coast at Cape Misurata (Misrata) in Dragut's beylerbeylik, 115nm east of Tripoli. Coin and items of value were unlikely to be found in a village. Like Zuara in 1552, this was a raid for *non-combatant* slave labourers and oarsmen, at one time an undertaking unheard of among Hospitallers. As Commander of Ground Forces, Valette appointed his Seneschal and Commander of Montchamp Pierre de Gioù. Gioù was able to call upon Gozon-Mélac and the latter's captains, who were Guy de Tianges de Croset, commanding the capitana *San Iacomo*; Jean de Cuvyler de Coucy, commanding *San Giovanni Battista*; Geronimo d'Homedes, commanding *San Filippo*; and Giovan Vittorio Maurello, commanding *San Michele Arcangelo*. The embarked force consisted of 250 hand-picked knights, slightly more than half of the Convent, together with Guasconi's entire company of 500 infantry. Guy de Tianges was to carry the Order's Standard. Ten knights and thirty-five crew were detailed to remain with each galley, while the other 200 knights and 500 soldiers made up the raiding party.[18]

The Hospitaller squadron departed Malta on the morning of 28 July 1561 and proceeded directly to Rachel Amet, 215nm to the south-south-east, arriving the following evening. The transit was most notable for an unseemly spat between Gozon-Mélac and Maurello en route, with Gioù acting as pacifier, and for a disorderly arrival that alerted the Moors of Rachel Amet. Ninety-five women and children were removed from their homes and carted back to Malta on 4 August to no conceivable purpose. To cover this particular failure, the Order responded to all inquiries that the Galleys had returned with more than 2,000 Moors captured in Dragut's domain, deceiving only themselves.[19] The Order of Jerusalem in 1561 was not of the stuff of Pierre d'Aubusson and Philippe Villiers de l'Isle-Adam. From top to bottom it was an Order of opportune corsairs, not even of corsairs of the calibre of Dragut. Nor of Uluç Ali. Not nearly. It had less than four years to get itself back on track.[20]

Bishop of Catania Nicola Maria Caracciolo, captured by Dragut in early July aboard Guimeran's Sicilian capitana, was released six weeks later on a Papal down payment and promise to pay an enormous ransom. Separately ransomed by the Spanish Court were Djerba captive Bishop of Mallorca Don Diego Arnedo, Sicilian Tercio Commander Don Luis Osorio, and the Countess of Ayerba, widowed mother of Don Pedro d'Urries, returned to Malta with others. These were received at Malta aboard the private sailing vessel of Nicolò Petrochino, and on 10 August were transported from Malta to Syracuse aboard two of the Order's galleys. At Malta Luis de Salcedo had been appointed Bailiff of Caspe, succeeding the deceased Don Antonio de Moncada.[21]

Upon return from Syracuse of the two galleys, and given yet more time until a rescheduled rendezvous of the Catholic Armada at Trapani in western Sicily, the five-galley squadron of Gozon-Mélac, together with the Grand Master's corsair galley *San Gabriello* commanded by Romegas, were ordered to Cape Buonandrea on the far side of Libya's Gulf of Sidra seeking opportune captures, all six departing Malta on 29 August. About 200nm east of Malta the expanded squadron sighted a Turkish caramussal under full sail. Only Cuvyler de Coucy's *San Giovanni Battista*, fastest of the six under sail, was able to overhaul the caramussal and board. But Hospitaller dead and wounded, first by enemy artillery, and then by arquebus fire and crossbow bolts, forced the boarders to retire and the two ships separated. Among the mourned was Hospitaller Jean Aleaume de Bouilly of the Langue of France, a Villegagnon through his mother Anne Durand.[22] All that night and the following day pursuit continued toward the west in gradually lessening wind until the sailing vessel was cornered by all six galleys and overcome. Commanded by Hassan Reis, a Greek renegade of Zante, with a crew of eighty Turks, she was bound from the Danube to Tripoli with a cargo of rice and linen. Having removed the crew to the galleys, the caramussal was sent with a crew of liberated Christians commanded by Serving Brother Louis Pagette of Provence to Malta, arriving safely. One day later near Cape Buonandrea the galleys encountered and seized a large Moorish germa bound for Egypt. Fifty crew removed, a prize crew under command of Serving Brother Jean Gottier of France sailed the germa to Malta, also arriving safely. At that point Romegas was licensed to proceed independently while the squadron returned to Malta.[23]

Reaching the mouth of the Nile, Romegas deprived several small prey of their cargo before sighting a supply ship carrying food stuffs to the Alexandria Guard of galleys commanded by Kara Mustafa (another Kara Mustafa, not the Sancakbey of Mitilini). With information obtained from the small prey, Romegas was aware this Kara Mustafa was aboard the supply ship en route to a nearby rendezvous with three of his galleys. With caution the better part of valour, Romegas, with experienced pilot Cicco Pisano of Syracuse, took course for Cyprus and Anatolian Karamania to the north, where he encountered a number of enemy vessels.

Off Cape Antioch (near modern Antakya, Turkey) he boarded and took a Turkish caramussal. He next encroached along the coast of Karamania and between Scandaloro (Alanya) and Alia (Alaiye 20km north-west of Alanya) ran across the large germa merchantman of Dörmus Reis of Antalya far from its accompanying merchant convoy bound from Alexandria to Constantinople. The germa was defended by 150 Turks and by ninety black Africans armed with arquebuses and bows. When the Ottomans realised they were being attacked by a single galley, they decided themselves to board Romegas's ship. The Maltese cannoned the germa, however, before she was able to board, holing her at the waterline. She began to settle. A few Turks climbed into the ship's boat to reach shore and were captured; others sought the safety of night clutching what would float. On board the ship forty men were dead from artillery fire and many others were wounded. Romegas loaded the wounded, the women, and the old on his shore-boat and set them free. The others, together with earlier captures, now totalled 300, among whom were two ambassadors en route to Rustem Pasha at Constantinople. One of these was Mehemet Bey, Lord of the Timar of Seres and Lieutenant to eunuch Governor of Cairo Soliman Pasha. According to Balbi,[24] the other ambassador was the Sancakbey of Alexandria. The cargo of the germa surpassed 100,000 ducats in value; since Romegas did not have space in his ship, however, he sank the germa with her cargo. He permitted one of the ambassadors to send ashore a messenger to collect a ransom of thousands of ducats, but the money failed to arrive. Among the captives there was also a woman said to be 107 years of age by the name Giansever of Cerchies, once a favourite of the Sultan's deceased mother. She was returning from Mecca.[25]

With damage to *San Giovanni Battista* repaired, with the galleys reprovisioned, and with strong caravans of embarked knights, soldiers, and adventurers, the five galleys again departed Malta on 22 September 1561 and two days later rendezvoused at Trapani with the Catholic Armada commanded by Marcantonio del Carretto. Because the Armada was not yet completely assembled, and because the Order had the new galley *San Giovan Battista* ready for sea at Marseille including oarsmen conscripted by the French crown, Gozon-Mélac obtained the permission of Carretto to proceed to Marseille with three galleys, leaving two with the assembling Armada: the deceased Arduin de Castillon de Beines's

Santa Marta, under Geronimo de Homedes, and Gozon-Mélac's former capitana *Corona*, under her first officer. Prior to departing for Marseille, Gozon-Mélac doubled back to Messina and Malta to first embark Bailiff of Eagle Pedro Fernandez de Felizes as ambassador both to the Pope and to the Duke of Savoy to negotiate an end to the Giovanni Moretto–Jean Moret litigation. Embarked at Malta was Commander of Fresno Don Diego Enríquez de Guzmán, Resident Ambassador to the Court of Spain succeeding Don Bernardo de Guimeran.

Gozon-Mélac departed Malta on 16 October with both ambassadors embarked. By way of Syracuse, Messina, and Palermo where Guzmán debarked for conversations with the Viceroy, he again reached Trapani, where he found the Catholic Armada sixty galleys strong plus sailing ships, aboard which were embarked the Spanish Tercio of Flanders and other tercios. The mission, however, had been cancelled and individual units were free to return to their home ports. Gozon-Mélac left the galleys *Santa Marta* and his former capitana *Corona* under the command of Geronimo de Homedes at Trapani with orders that at the first sign of bad weather they should return to Malta. With his flag hoisted aboard *Santa Fede* and with *San Giovanni Battista* and *San Michele Arcangelo*, respectively under Captains Cuvyler de Coucy and Giovan Vittorio Maurello, in company, all three reinforced with personnel from the galleys left behind, he headed without further delay on 28 October for Marseille. Without delay because there was a wind astern pushing them north at high speed. Late the next day they reached the island of Giglio, 10 miles west of Porto Ercole on the Tuscan mainland 265 nautical miles north of Trapani, for an average speed of almost 7.5 knots. At Giglio the three galleys surprised a galliot of Algiers hiding from the wind. She fled on the same wind, but not toward Algiers. This same wind hit Trapani, a port open to the south-west, sinking five sailing ships unable to exit the port against the wind. Many of the sixty galleys were thrown one onto another with a great deal of damage to planking, masts, and rigging, to oars, bow spurs, and rambads, more so than had they emerged from a conventional battle. The two galleys of the Religion, however, neither with a skipper on board, departed as ordered at the first sign of bad weather to take shelter on the north side of the island of Favignana, 10 miles to the south-west. Only *Santa Marta*'s skiff was destroyed while awaiting Geronimo de Homedes' return from a trip ashore. Homedes later, and miraculously, found his charge at the Sicilian port of Mazara still in Trapani Province. Romegas meanwhile exited the Levant and at the end of the month reached the same Mazara to purchase wheat for transport to Malta.[26]

The Bailiwick of Lango left vacant by the May 1559 death of Gaspard de Vallier was at the request of the Court of France awarded to Gilbert de Serpens, the Order's Resident Ambassador. Gozon-Mélac meanwhile reached Marseille with his three reinforced galleys, where he encountered *San Giovan Battista* on sea trials under command of Receiver Antoine de Thésan-Vénàsque. So pleased was he with the new galley's speed both under sail and under oar that he subsequently shifted his flag from *Santa Fede.* He took with him his flag-captain and former skipper of *Corona* Marc de la Goutte, in the event of his incapacity senior by Hospitaller tenure to the other three captains. Following their trial by storm, *Santa Marta* and *Corona* reached Malta safely on 18 November in company with Romegas's *San Gabriello.* Gozon-Mélac arrived soon thereafter, and Goutte returned to *Corona*, where by virtue of tenure he commanded a division of galleys also including Homedes' *Santa Marta* and Romegas's *San Gabriello.* This division was employed during the winter in running provisions from Sicily to Malta.[27]

Grand Master and Council on 29 December appointed three knights as observers to attend the Council of Trent. These were Commander Giuseppi Cambiano of the Piedmont, who was the Order's Receiver and Procurator-General at Rome; Nicolas Durand de Villegagnon, who ably defended Gaspard de Vallier at his trial on charge of responsibility for the 1551 enslavement of 600 Christians and allied Moors, and ever afterward refused to return to the Convent; and Vice Chancellor Martín Rojas de Portalrubio. Paradoxically, of the three observers, only Villegagnon showed up in January.[28] An initial Papal Brief received by the Order in 1562 demanded the missing two observers at the Council of Trent. A second Papal Brief citing the Pope's ultimate authority over the Order of Jerusalem received as an Hospitaller the Pope's 53-year-old cousin and General of the Papal Guard Gabriele Serbellone, better known as Gabrio Serbelloni. By the end of February Serbellone had been appointed Prior of Hungary, entitled to wear the Grand Cross.[29]

Signorino della Gattinara needed to return to Messina from Malta to carry out his responsibilities as the Order's Prior of Messina. Early in

1562 he obtained from the Grand Master and Council the two galleys commanded by Marc de la Goutte and Geronimo de Homedes, and as senior of the three knights he also assumed command, flying his flag from Homedes' *Santa Marta*. Following the Prior's debarkation at Messina, a clash of arms took place between a crowd of Genovese from the galley of Christofino Doria, a part of the squadron of Scipione Doria found in the port, on the one hand, and caravan knights Don Garaù de Cardona, Don Juan de Mompalau, and Don Miguel de Alentorn from *Santa Marta* on the other. The three Hospitallers were severely wounded, the first two soon dying of their wounds and the third losing a hand. Several days later Juan Peres de Baraguan, Navarese lieutenant to Homedes, recognised two of the Genovese culprits, arrested them, and confined them in chains on his galley, where he extracted a confession of guilt. He took the confession of guilt to Scipione Doria and demanded the culprits be charged with murder. Doria did nothing. Seething resentment on the part of Hospitallers exploded into a pitched battle that could only be ended with intercession by the city's Spanish infantry battalion and departure of the two Hospitaller galleys, first for Syracuse and then for home.[30]

Meanwhile, the other four galleys commanded by Gozon-Mélac deployed yet again to Marseille to embark Esteban Calderone bringing Spanish responsions to the Convent, as well as Pascal du Broc de la Baume with responsions of France. Departing Marseille in the heart of winter the four ships were almost immediately hit by a storm lasting twenty days driving them up onto a beach outside of Livorno, unable to enter the port through its narrow entrance. Here Pedro Fernandez de Felizes, ambassador to the Pope and Duke of Savoy, was re-embarked, his mission completed. Many of those on board, however, were ill with more than exhaustion. Some had died, including Charles de Berlaymont of France and Giuseppe Naro of Syracuse. In spite of medical intervention at Livorno, by arrival at Civitavecchia en route to Malta so many oarsmen were incapacitated that the four galleys were unable to clear medical pratique at any port and were able to proceed only under sail.[31]

Reaching Syracuse on 11 March without clearing pratique, the ailing squadron of four galleys lost its commander; Gozon-Mélac fell ill with what may have been peste or may have been malaria. By departure from Syracuse Giovan Vittorio Maurello, commanding *San Michele Arcangelo*, had died of the same disease, as had Luis Britto of Portugal and several young aspirants from Provence who had expected to take the Habit at Malta. Gozon-Mélac died within sight of Syracuse following departure from that port. The squadron in spite of loss of its commander and the overwhelming number of incapacitated combatants and crew seized a Turkish brigantine near Torre Longina south of Syracuse, the capture principally yielding thirty replacement oarsmen. Reaching Malta on 18 March, the squadron was immediately quarantined at the pratique islet (Manoel Island) in Marsamuscietto (Marsamxett) Bay, where the ill were transferred to the islet's infirmary and where everyone and everything else was removed from the galleys for disinfection under the direction of three Medical Commissioners assigned to the infirmary: Catalan Gabriel Gort, Pierre de Loubens of Auvergne, and Giovanni Vagnone of the Piedmont. By 4 April, when there was no longer suspicion of disease, a bit more than 200 individuals had succumbed. These included the Grand Master's cousin Bernard de la Valette, only recently returned from captivity following the 1560 Siege of Djerba. Also succumbing were Francesco Platamone of Palermo and Vincenzio Argentio of Capua, both barely 20 years of age. Grand Master and Council appointed Louis du Pont to succeed the deceased Pierre de Gozon-Mélac as Prior of Saint-Gilles, Commander of Saint-Félix Guiot de Sales to succeed Du Pont as Grand Commander, and Giovanni Vicenzo Gonzaga to succeed Gozon-Mélac as General of the Galleys. Pierre de Gozon-Melac was survived by Hospitaller brother François, within a year to be appointed Bailiff of Manosque.[32]

Giuseppe Cambiano of Turin, a Hospitaller of thirty-four years, was in April 1562 appointed Resident Ambassador and Procurator-General to the Holy See, while non-Hospitaller Vicenzo Campeggio was appointed the Order's first ambassador to the city of Bologna. Given the time of year and habitual excursions to the west of the Ottoman Armada, Hospitaller Giovanni Vagnone was dispatched by frigate into the Levant to gather information on Armada activity. If the time of year were not bad enough, there were reports of a combination of interests between the Corsican revolutionary and French agent Sampiero Corso on the one hand and Dragut Pasha on the other, both seeking Armada assistance for the expulsion of Spanish Genoa from Corsica. At Malta Juan Vasquez de Avilés of Castile and Raffaello Salvago of Genoa were appointed Sector

Wardens to ensure readiness for hostilities, while engineers directing fortification improvements were refocused on the short term.[33]

The Grand Master nevertheless had time in 1562 for his own corsair operations. He exchanged his galley *San Gabriello* for the Order's galley *Santa Marta*, the latter lighter and faster and more appropriate for corsair operations. Valette also completed construction at Malta of a large galliot, the two respectively commanded by Gascons Mathurin Romegas and Pierre de Rocquelaure Saint-Aubin. Putting to sea, Romegas and Saint-Aubin proceeded toward the mouth of the Nile but finished at El Bomba on the modern border between Egypt and Libya, the new galliot not sailing well either under canvas or with oars. Not wishing to return empty-handed to Malta with an experienced Moorish guide on board, the two galleys put a raiding party ashore between Libya's Cape Rizzuto and Talmetta, but the raiding party returned with only thirty-two unfortunate Arab captives. On 17 June, 60 miles from Malta, however, the two corsairs encountered an infidel ship bound from Tripoli to Greece which surrendered without a fight.[34]

The galliot was hauled and lengthened, returning to sea as a galley and as the corsair capitana under command of Romegas, Romegas continuing in overall command of the two ships while Saint-Aubin commanded the mini-squadron's padrona *Santa Marta*.[35] Gaspard de la Motte was appointed to command of the Grand Master's proprietary galleon or Small Galleon of the Religion.[36] The Grand Master's two galleys were united with the five-galley squadron commanded by Vincenzo Gonzaga which in July was sent on a circuit encompassing southern Calabria and the Apulian heel of the Italian boot, but returned to Malta on 16 July having failed to encounter the enemy. Also returning that day was the frigate of Giovanni Vagnone with relatively certain news the Ottoman Armada would not be deploying to the western Mediterranean in 1562. This news came from Avenga, the Grand Master's credible agent in Constantinople.[37] Not many days later Gonzaga's galley squadron was summoned by Gian Andrea Doria to a rendezvous of the Catholic Armada at Sicily with intent to cleanse uninhabited Sicilian islands of corsairs and then to seek out Dragut on the coast of North Africa.

The two Magistral galleys were ordered to Sicily with coin for grain purchases at Licata. Arriving at Pozzallo during the night, they learned from local cavalry that toward nearby Cape Passero a large Algiers corsair galliot of twenty-three banks had been raiding the coast and doing considerable damage. A frigatina was sent ahead to locate and signal the number of enemy if more than one, while the two galleys followed a mile astern ready for combat. Approaching the frigatina as if to take her in tow, the Algerian galliot sighted the two galleys and fled. The pursuit continued through the night but Romegas and his capitana were left behind before dawn; the following evening Saint-Aubin's *Santa Marta* still trailed the Barbary ship 180 miles out of Sicily when the galliot's mainsail antenna suddenly splintered under strain. The enemy commander, renegade Calabrian Küçük Yusuf (Giuseppe Concini), did not lose heart, though, coming alongside *Santa Marta* prow to prow and boarding, Yusuf at the boarders' head, pike in hand. Hospitallers Antoine de Capriol Demandolx and Honouré de Lascaris Castellar of the Langue of Provence were among the first to fall, but when Küçük Yusuf fell mortally wounded the Algerians lost heart. Twenty enemy died in this engagement including Yusuf; another 130 were captured and sent to the oars. About 200 Christian oarsmen were liberated, some in a condition attesting to Yusuf's cruelty. Two days later the two Magistral galleys again reached Sicily to a celebratory welcome before returning to Malta with the galliot in tow.[38]

Two days following the return of the Magistral galleys, Prior of Champagne François Piedefer died at Malta. Fifty-two years a Hospitaller, he was survived by Hospitaller brothers Pierre and Christophe as well as by Hospitaller nephew François de Chaumont, and was succeeded as Prior of Champagne by Pierre de la Fontaine. Fontaine was in turn succeeded as Grand Hospitaller by Bailiff of the Morea Louis de Vallée-Passy, while Vallée-Passy was succeeded by Treasurer Jean Audebert de l'Aubuge. Charles de Hesselin Gascourt was appointed Treasurer.

Released by Gian Andrea Doria at Trapani following a fruitless cleansing of Sicilian islands, the squadron returned to Malta on 22 August with supplies from Sicily. At Malta squadron captains were as follow: Vincenzo Gonzaga himself commanded the capitana *San Giovan Battista*, Marc de la Goutte commanded *Corona*, Olivier d'Aux de Bourneuf of the Priory of Aquitaine *San Giovanni*, Antoine Flotte de la Roche *Santa Fede* renamed *San Iacomo*, and Gil de Andrade *San Gabriello*. Upon his return Gonzaga requested of the Grand Master authority to take his five galleys and the two commanded by Romegas on a voyage of opportunity into the

Levant. Authority was granted but on condition of a loss of one year of seniority for any knight either of complement or caravan failing to wear corselet or cuirass, arm bands, and morion helmet, and to carry either two well-maintained arquebuses or one arquebus and one iron crossbow in addition to sword and dagger.[39]

Vincenzo Gonzaga's expanded squadron departed Malta on 4 September 1562 bound for Cape Lupo (Cape Lucco or Cape Al-Milber) and Port Solimano (a small port on Cape Lupo east of Benghazi, Libya). At Cape Lupo the seven Hospitaller galleys encountered a Florentine squadron of four galleys commanded by Baccio Martelli short of provisions. Resupplied with biscuit from the Maltese, Martelli joined them in counter-pursuit of four galleys and a galliot of the Rhodes Guard, which had earlier seen off the Florentines. Together the eleven galleys pointed north toward Kastellorizon. East of Kastellorizon, at Porto Caracollo (within Kekova Roads), Ottoman-sympathetic Greek sponge fishermen of Lindos informed them that the Rhodes Guard had returned to base. Martelli's four galleys therefore presented themselves off Rhodes to provoke and lure the enemy to a place at which it might be overwhelmed by the allies. Other Greeks, however, informed them they had false information and that the Rhodes Guard was recently seen off Cape Salomone at the eastern end of Crete where a Guard galliot was blown up on shoals and lost. Reaching Karpathos opposite eastern Crete, the weather deteriorated. Assuming the four remaining galleys of the Rhodes Guard were long gone, by common agreement the two captains, Tuscan and Maltese, set course for home, proceeding along the north coast of Crete from Sitia, still without sighting the enemy. Remaining well off the coast in order to not anger non-belligerent Venetians, they made for the Morea and Albania, and on 5 November separated at Venetian Corfu after dividing their modest plunder, a Turkish vessel of sixteen banks, cargo of sultana raisins. Reaching Malta, the enlarged squadron found that on 10 October 1562 Malta suffered a terrible storm that destroyed housing and other structures. Among damaged vessels the storm also destroyed the (small) *Galleon of the Religion* commanded by Gaspard de la Motte of Provence, which had been careened on the beach at Bormola for underwater hull repairs.[40]

Nine days later Juan Hurtado de Mendoza, Captain-General of the Galleys of Spain, was caught by a sudden storm shift and pinned against the coast of Grenada at La Herradura. Twenty-five of twenty-eight galleys were lost (nine Spanish, six Neapolitan, and the rest from Genovese entrepreneurs Antonio Doria, Bendinello Sauli, and Stefano di Mare). Mendoza and some 4,000 others lost their lives.[41]

Grand Master Valette in November dispatched linguist Yiannis Vareles of Constantinople to that city on the pretext of exchanging Turkish captives at Malta. Vareles' real mission was to determine whether if at all this latest Spanish naval disaster had emboldened Ottoman naval planning.[42]

Vice Chancellor Martín Rojas de Portalrubio was assigned as ambassador to the Council of Trent, to join Resident Ambassador to the Holy See Giuseppe Cambiano. Their assignment was to make it known to all participants that the Order of Jerusalem sat on Christianity's eastern frontier, and as a bastion of Christian defence was in need of financial and other support. Portalrubio departed Malta on the last day of the year aboard *Santa Marta*, the Magistral padrona commanded by Gaspard de la Motte in succession of Pierre de Rocquelaure Saint-Aubin. *Santa Marta* transported Portalrubio as far as Syracuse, from where his journey continued to Naples aboard Gil de Andrade's *San Gabriello*. Andrade then joined Gonzaga and the other four galleys of the squadron for winter in Sicily.[43]

Rife with rumour of war, Malta again prepared for siege in 1563, stocking foodstuffs and munitions. On 17 February Admiral and future Grand Master Pietro del Monte arrived in Malta at the head of a contingent of knights and gentlemen adventurers. Del Monte also brought with him a large Neapolitan cargo carrier as interim replacement for the storm-lost *Galleon of the Religion*, the replacement armed with cannon and commanded by non-Hospitaller Francesco Circo. Also on board was a large company of soldiers hired and commanded by Hospitaller Giovanni Vagnone. At Malta it was decided to defer further construction on Fort Saint Elmo's Sciberras Peninsula (modern Valletta) and to concentrate instead on defence works for Birgu abutting Castle Saint Angelo as well as for Fort Saint Michael and the walls of adjacent Senglea. Lieutenant Turcopolier Oliver Starkey of England, Commander of Marseille Bertrand de Vintimille d'Ollioules of Provence, and Commander of La Bamba Antonio Maldonado of Castile were appointed Sector Wardens. In Spain Prior of Catalonia Gaspar de Ferrer died; Don Dimes de Requesens was appointed his successor, while himself succeeded as Bailiff of Negroponte by Juan de Barrientos. At Malta Grand Conservator (Draper) Nicolás de Agulló passed away and was succeeded by Commander Pedro de Iunient. In France Francis of Lorraine, Duke of Guise, was killed on 24 February in combat with Protestant Huguenots. His death was followed ten days later by that of his younger brother and Hospitaller Grand Prior of France of the same name, cause unknown. Coincident with advice of the latter's death came a request from Catherine de Medici, Regent for her son King Charles IX, that Hospitaller courtier and royal ambassador Michel de Seurre de Lumigny be appointed successor Prior of France. It appears the request was finessed as the Priory of France remained in moratorium with Pierre de la Fontaine as heir apparent. Fontaine was meanwhile, with the acquiescence of Grand Hospitaller and senior Louis de Vallée-Passy, succeeded as Prior of Champagne by Bailiff of the Morea Jean Audebert de l'Aubuge, while Charles de Hesselin Gascourt succeeded to the Bailiwick of the Morea and was himself succeeded as Treasurer by Jacques d'Arquinvillier of Picardie. Coincident with these changes, Bailiff of Manosque Jean de Brutin de Poët-Laval died in France. He was succeeded by Commander of Argentens François de Gozon-Mélac.[44]

Gil de Andrade's *San Gabriello* returned to Malta from Naples on 29 April bearing a letter from Pedro Afán de Ribera, 1st Duke of Alcalá and Viceroy of Naples, requesting in the name of King Philip II participation by the Galleys of the Religion in company with those of Gian Andrea Doria in transporting 1,000 Spanish infantry to replace the garrison at La Goleta outside of Tunis. This request furthered the remanufacture of the Order of Jerusalem into an arm of the Spanish Empire, Philippe de Villiers de l'Isle-Adam's greatest fear in accepting Malta from Charles V. It does not appear that Valette hesitated in dispatching on 10 May the five-galley squadron under Vincenzo Gonzaga, even appointing his nephew Henri de la Valette Cornusson to command of *Corona* in succession of Marc de la Goutte. While the foregoing matters developed, the return of Mathurin Romegas and Gaspard de la Motte was anticipated nervously. These two Magistral captains had weeks earlier been sent into the Levant to ascertain the current status of the Ottoman Armada. The two captains returned on 29 May 1563 with certain advice that the Sultan continued to enlarge his armada with new galleys while his foundries were turning out ever larger siege cannon. Even so, beyond an Archipelago Guard, the Armada was not expected to deploy in 1563.[45]

While in the Levant the two Magistral galleys had at the end of April encountered a ship of Lindos carrying various Turks to Rhodes Town with a cargo of wine. The ship was torched. The mini-squadron next headed for the waters of Karpathos, where it came upon a well-armed galleon from Antalya transporting the Sancakbey or Governor of Cairo Ahmad Muhammad Ogli, bound from Alexandria and escorting to Constantinople under command of Suleiman Arnaut a germa with a cargo of rice. The latter vessel was captured without incident as the crew fled ashore; the galleon nevertheless rallied to her defence and fought many hours, killing a number of men aboard Motte's galley. The galleon was overcome only with favour of a dead calm accompanied by a long bombardment, during which the sailing ship was immobile; she ultimately sank with her riches. Captured prior to going under were the Sancakbey, a former Christian married into the royal family, by a different spelling Acmat Mostafa Oghli called Sagher, as well as more than 400 others, of whom 250 were Turks, the rest Moors and black Africans. Arriving at Malta, a ransom of 18,000 ducats was received, part in coin and part in assets carried from Alexandria to Messina. Once liberated, the Sancakbey vociferously and repetitively urged the Sultan to act against the handful of Infidel pirates at Malta raiding Ottoman seas at will.[46]

Prior of Aquitaine Jean de Neuchèze died at the end of May of unreported cause and was succeeded by Bailiff of the Morea Gascourt, the latter in turn succeeded by Jacques d'Arquinvillier who vacated the dignity of Treasurer to which Pierre Pelloquin de la Plesse was assigned. Following these appointments Guillaume de la Fontaine was dispatched to France seeking assistance of his uncle and Grand Prior Pierre de la Fontaine in scheduling a General Assembly of Hospitallers despite turmoil within the Kingdom of France stemming from December's Battle of Dreux. A contest between Catholics and Huguenots, Dreux resulted in the capture of opposing commanders, respectively Anne de Montmorency and Prince of Conde Louis I.[47]

General of the Galleys and Prior of Barletta Vincenzo Gonzaga had in early May arrived at Messina with his five-galley squadron. There he was informed by Viceroy Juan de la Cerda of a letter from King Philip II asserting, according to *Bosio III-462*, that Sala Rais (Salih Reis), Viceroy of Algiers, had taken heart from the storm loss of twenty-five galleys of Spain along with 4,000 embarked personnel at Herradura in October 1562, and was proceeding at the head of 10,000 Turks, Moors, and Arabs to the siege of Oran and Mers-el-Kébir with the assistance of Dragut and thirty oared vessels at sea. The siege had in fact been laid on 3 April, likely without Dragut participation given March sailing conditions and distance from Tripoli, while the besieging Viceroy was Hassan Barbarossa and not Salih Reis, who had succumbed to plague at Algiers in 1556 at age 70 and who had been interred in May of that year outside Algiers' Beb-al-Weyd Gate among other pashas of Algiers.[48] The Viceroy went on to inform Gonzaga that the King had ordered all of 'his' galleys to proceed by way of Italy to Spain for the defence of Oran.

Gonzaga, however, also had orders from the Grand Master to remain within shouting distance of Malta in order to rush to island defence should it become necessary. Gonzaga therefore dispatched Giovan Maria Castrocucco of Naples by frigate to Malta where he arrived on 18 May seeking further orders.

Considering the annual threat to Malta slight at that May date, Valette sent Castrocucco back to the squadron with orders to join in the relief of Oran. While Castrocucco was at Malta the Turkish corsair Ali Reis (Caragiali of Lepanto), commanding a 26-bank galliot, raided Milazzo on the north coast of Sicily 20 nautical miles west of the Strait of Messina. Having sacked the city, he departed with a portion of the population and made rendezvous with eleven other corsairs. The five-galley Malta Squadron joined at Messina the five-galley squadron of Sicily commanded by Luis Osorio and the combined squadrons went in pursuit. On 22 May, 35 miles north of Milazzo at Stromboli, the combined squadrons sighted a single galliot of nineteen banks, which fled north. The chase persisted for 70 miles. The Hospitallers, with cleaner hulls and more practised oarsmen, outdistanced the Sicilians, and among Hospitallers Flotte de la Roche's *San Iacomo* and Olivier d'Aux de Bourneuf's *San Giovanni* cornered and invested the enemy. The numbers were heavily in favour of the Hospitallers and submission of the galliot and her commander Cafsan Reis, a renegade of Corsica, was soon obtained. Eighty enemy were made captive. Galliot oarsmen, all of them Christian, were liberated. So, too, were a large number of captives from Milazzo, mostly women and children who were returned to their homes the following day. Caragiali of Lepanto will reappear in this history, not so renegade Cafsan Reis.[49]

At the end of May Castrocucco delivered the Grand Master's revised instructions to General Gonzaga, the squadron replenished at Messina and Palermo, and the five galleys took course for the Strait of Bonifacio between Sardinia and Corsica. From Bonifacio the squadron on 10 June 1563 reached Palamos on the coast of Catalonia, three days later arriving at Barcelona. The Siege of Oran and Mers El Kébir had been lifted on 6 June upon the arrival of a thirty-five-galley relief fleet commanded by Francisco de Mendoza y Vargas (*el Indio*), Captain-General of the Galleys of Spain, while Hassan Barbarossa's depleted besieging force was back at Algiers by July. Hospitaller galleys nevertheless proceeded to rendezvous with the returning galleys of Spain at Cartagena.[50]

King Philip II of Spain had been convinced by Don Pedro de Vanagas, his Governor of Melilla Fortress on the coast of Africa, that the former Spanish possession of Penon de la Velez Gomera on the same coast could be taken from its Ottoman garrison. According to Vanegas, who had his information from two Ottoman renegades, only a single barque equipped with ladders and a few good soldiers would be sufficient for such an undertaking. Rather than a small force, the same Don Francisco de Mendoza was assigned this additional task. Following the October 1562 storm disaster at La Herradura and the death of his cousin Juan Hurtado de Mendoza, Francisco de Mendoza had been appointed Captain-General of the Galleys of Spain. A former potentate in New Spain, Francisco de Mendoza came down with malaria and died on 26 July 1563 following a brief illness. His commander of ground forces for the undertaking, Don Sancho de Leyva recently ransomed from Djerba captivity at Constantinople, was appointed his successor.

Vincenzo Gonzaga's five-galley Malta Squadron joined a Spanish–Italian fleet of forty-five additional galleys gathering at Malaga, including De Leyva's Naples squadron. The fleet also included the Galley Squadron of Spain, Alvaro de Bazan's Galley Squadron of Seville, three galleys of Savoy under Andrea Provana, and a squadron from Genoa under Galeazzo Giustiniani. During the interlude attending the change of command, Alvaro de Bazan asserted that the Maltese galleys were the slowest of the fleet. Five hundred gold scudos were wagered in rebuttal. Vincenzo Gonzaga selected *San Iacomo*, his heaviest and therefore most handicapped galley, to race against Bazan's capitana. Commanded by Antoine Flotte de la Roche, *San Iacomo* was the victor and the recipient of the wager proceeds.

The fleet sailed on 22 July for the island of Alboran between Mellila and the Penon and a rendezvous with Vanagas and the two renegades. Vanagas appeared aboard a skiff with an elaborate scaling contraption of his own design that the Squadron of Seville took in tow at night to the Penon, leaving the remainder of the fleet in the offing. The renegades were unable to even find a point of approach for the skiff, and on withdrawal Bazan's galleys were taken under fire from the fortress. De Leyva nevertheless put 3,000 troops ashore 6 miles west of the Penon on the last day of July, among whom were 500 hired Maltese infantry interspersed with a large number of knights under the command of the Grand Master's nephew Henri de la Valette commanding *Corona*, his lieutenant Gil de Andrade commanding *San Gabriello*, with Pierre de Montauban de Voguedemar of Provence, Alessandro Ridolfi of Florence, and Esteban de Claramónte of Aragon as sergeants-major. The approach to Penon was harassed by Moorish cavalry and bothered as much by an inability to locate fresh water. These found the city of Velez abandoned but its citizens in number of 10–15,000 visible on the slopes of nearby mountains. Some of these descended to put two companies of Italian infantry to flight, but the Christians even so set up camp in the city. There they remained for three days, and the fortress never stopped firing, killing those who exposed themselves as well as those engaged in resupplying the shore force. There were frequent skirmishes, not only with Moors in increasing numbers but also with Turks sortieing from the Penon. A renegade Spaniard fled the fortress and informed De Leyva that the King of Fez had dispatched 3,000 crossbowmen and arquebusiers to succour the citizens of Velez. De Leyva ordered a Spanish withdrawal.[51]

From Penon de la Velez Gomera most Spanish units proceeded east to reprovision Oran and its port at Mers El Kébir. The Malta Squadron, in company with the three galleys of Savoy and the Genoa Squadron, sailed north to Malaga, arriving on 2 August. Out of curiosity they then took course for Spanish Ceuta on the coast of North Africa opposite Gibraltar, where the governor was the brother of Hospitaller Dom Vasco da Cunha. With all three units under the command of Vincenzo Gonzaga, they then returned to Spain, reaching Cartagena on 21 August. Separating at Cartagena, the Malta Squadron proceeded up the coast of Spain to Barcelona to catch a good wind for home, arriving at the end of the month.

While the Malta Squadron was deployed to Spain and North Africa the two Magistral galleys commanded by Mathurin Romegas and Gaspard de la Motte might as well have been idle. In company with four galleys of Sicily under command of Luis Osorio, the Magistral galleys descended on Favignana Island off the western tip of Sicily, but finding no enemy continued south-west to the coast of Tunisia in search of Infidel thieves who were practically holding western Sicily hostage, again without locating the enemy.[52]

At Barcelona the Malta Squadron was joined by three galleys of the new (October 1561) Order of Santo Stefano under the command of Giulio de' Medici, illegitimate son of Alessandro de' Medici and the first knight to be received into the Order. The three galleys had lost a fourth when her mainmast snapped and she had been taken by two Turkish galliots. All four had come to Barcelona to convey Prince Francesco de' Medici back to Italy following a visit to the Court of Spain, and had been awaiting additional company before returning to Livorno. It was not a happy combination, with the Prince's uncle and Viceroy of Catalonia García de Toledo Osorio dictating the sailing order among other irritants including the detour to Livorno. The Malta Squadron did not return to Malta until 26 October. Transporting Moretti/Moret ambassador Pedro de Felizes aboard the capitana, the latter reported to Grand Master and Council a successful resolution of the six-year dispute and came with reconfirmation of Order privileges in ports of Savoy, Florence, and Ferrara respectively signed by Duke of Savoy Emmanuel Philibert, Duke of Florence Cosimo I de' Medici, and Duke of Ferrera Alfonso II d'Este.[53]

The two Magistral galleys meanwhile returned to Malta to reprovision before continuing on 20 September to the sole of the Italian boot, where off Crotone they sighted two galliots under the command of the corsair Caragiali. These two galliots were a part of the Algiers squadron of Uluç Ali (born Luca Galeni) returning from a summer of raids in Liguria bearing gifts for the latter's Calabrian mother. Signora Galeni was able to alert the two corsairs of the imminent arrival of the Magistral galleys, and when sighted they were speeding toward Ottoman Albania. Caragiali was able to save himself aboard the larger of the two galliots, but the smaller galliot of nineteen banks commanded by Albanian Memi Caragia was overtaken and captured, as were eighty Turkish combatants. The oarsmen, all Christian, took the galliot to Malta with a prize crew. Later, in Morean waters off Navarin (Pilos), the Magistral galleys seized a large Turkish caramussal commanded by Mehedin Reis bound for the Levant with a cargo of black Africans and various other items. Between Africans and crew the two galleys returned to Malta with 150 captives on the same 26 October, as did the Squadron. Unconcerned by the return to Malta of the seven galleys, Dragut Pasha that same day brought eighteen oared vessels down from Cape Passero to the Freo Channel between Malta and Gozo and laid siege to the latter island. During the years since his successful 1551 raid, however, the island's castle had been substantially strengthened. At the time, moreover, Governor Antoine de Fay Saint-Romain of Provence had his presidio reinforced by a strong company of hired soldiers commanded by Giovan Antonio Grugno of Licata. Dragut's assault failed.[54]

A bit after returning to Malta, Prior of Barletta and General of the Galleys Gonzaga was informed of the March death of cousin Ercole Cardinal Gonzaga of Mantua, a principal legate of the Holy See to the Council of Trent, and was persuaded by cousin Duke Guglielmo Gonzaga of Mantua to return to Rome for service to the Church. Giovan Vincenzo Gonzaga would receive the red hat of Cardinal and the deaconry of S. Giorgio in Velabro in 1578.[55]

Seneschal Pierre de Gioù was on 3 November appointed successor General of the Galleys, and was succeeded as Seneschal by the Grand Master's nephew Henri de la Valette de Cornusson. Juan Cerdan de las Cortes, who had aspired to the generalship, was appointed Prior of Navarre, succeeding the deceased Juan Ximenez. Juan de Barrientos, a veteran of 1522's Great Siege of Rhodes, was similarly appointed Bailiff of Lora, succeeding the deceased Pedro Nunnez de Herrera. Juan de Egueras of Aragon succeeded Barrientos as Bailiff of Negroponte. De Gioù meanwhile nominated and the Council appointed Thomas de la Tour de Murât to command of the squadron capitana. Geronimo Zaportello of Catalonia succeeded Henri de la Valette in command of *Corona*. Thereafter the five squadron galleys proceeded to Messina for winter refit or overhaul. Antonio Maldonado was dispatched to Spain in company with the Resident Ambassador to the Court of Spain Don

Diego de Guzmán. Their mission was to resolve financial differences developing with the Regia Camera della Sommaria at Naples and with the Reale Patrimonio at Palermo. The Grand Master's brother, Bishop François de la Valette of Vabres, arrived at Syracuse en route to Malta for a family visit; the two Magistral galleys brought the Bishop to Malta, arriving on 18 November.[56]

With the final adjournment of the Council of Trent in December, Ambassador and Vice Chancellor Martín Rojas de Portalrubio returned to Malta in February 1564 and apprised Grand Master and Council of the final session's fourteen decrees. Meanwhile, the drumbeat of Ottoman readiness for an assault on Malta intensified, and there was again heightened suspicion that 1564 would be the year. Thirteen Christian slaves at Tripoli effected an escape with assistance from Matthias Holland, a Flemish soldier in the pay of Malta, and from a Neapolitan renegade in service to Dragut. They set off from Tripoli in a small boat at night with only perishable vegetables and reached Gozo some days later near starvation, having passed two days without sustenance. These confirmed reports of an extraordinary force assembling at Constantinople, and believed it was destined for an assault on Malta. The thirteen separately reported that, on orders from Constantinople, Dragut was expected to again assail Gozo. Believing an excess of caution better than too little, the Grand Master again issued a recall to priories and commanderies, this time with the risk of crying wolf once too often.[57]

Reflecting his exemplary conduct during the unsuccessful assault on Penon de la Velez Gomera, nephew and Seneschal Henri de la Valette was appointed Captain-General of Rural Malta, commanding the cavalry and any infantry exiting the walls to pursue Dragut or another enemy. Commander of Bordes Louis de Flossat of Auvergne was assigned the same position at Gozo. Pursuant to a request from Marseille, Pierre de Gioù dispatched the galley *San Iacomo* to that city where François de Moreton de Chabrillan (or brother Christophe) was embarked transporting responsions from priories and commanderies in France collected by Grand Prior Pierre de la Fontaine. With these funds several companies of mercenary soldiers could be hired. The galley *Corona* was hauled at Messina for hull modification and her crew and oarsmen were used to reinforce *San Iacomo*. The other three galleys loaded provisions and munitions at Sicily for use during any Ottoman assault and returned to Malta on 13 February 1564.[58]

Not much later the Grand Master received a letter from King Philip II advising that the Galley Armada of Spain was being reinforced by new galleys from arsenals in Spain and Italy, and that the Armada was to be commanded by the aforementioned Viceroy of Catalonia Don García de Toledo as supreme commander and successor to Prince Andrea Doria. The King's letter went on to state that he expected the galleys of Malta to respond to any call from Garcia de Toledo for a fleet gathering to reinforce the presidio at La Goletta or from the Viceroys of Naples or Sicily to defend against raids by Dragut. Finally, the King promised assured assistance in the event of any siege of Malta by the Ottoman Armada. Grand Master and Council were again reminded that their Christian Republic was no more than an extension of the Kingdom of Spain, but reminded too late.[59]

General Pierre de Gioù was ordered back to Messina to abbreviate modification of *Corona* and to be ready with four galleys for any summons from Spain. Gioù and his three galleys departed Malta for this purpose on 5 March 1564. Later, having first transported the Grand Master and staff for an inspection of Gozo's defences, Mathurin Romegas, Gaspard de la Motte, and the two Magistral galleys departed for a reconnaissance mission to the Levant seeking information concerning the Ottoman Armada. Upon entering the Aegean Archipelago through the passage between the Morea and Cerigo (Kythera) a small ship of Barbary was halted and the crew of Turks and Moors seized. On 25 April, Feast Day of Saint Mark the Evangelist, two Turkish caramussals were sighted dead ahead. These turned out to be bound from Constantinople to Tripoli with cargoes of munitions and other items of corsair armament ordered by Dragut. Also on board were many good Turkish soldiers, who put up a stout defence and killed numerous assailing Maltese. The two caramussals were taken, however, with a great loss of life among the shipboard complements. The first of the three captures was leased from a Greek and released absent cargo. The other two, thanks to a propitious wind, were returned quickly to Malta with the Magistral galleys in company. These two captures carried dispatches from Constantinople to Dragut making it clear that 1564 was not the year of an assault on Malta, but suggested the assault would come in 1565. On the same Saint

Mark's Day *San Iacomo*, under Antoine de Flotte de la Roche, returned to Malta from Marseille with François de Moreton de Chabrillan embarked transporting responsions. (This Chabrillan could have been brother Christophe as François was captured at 1552's failed assault on Zuara, and family archives assert he was not ransomed until 1566.) Also returning to Malta was General Gioù and the four other squadron galleys as there had been no summons either from Garcia de Toledo or from the Viceroys of Naples and Sicily.[60]

Chapter XV

Jean Parisot de la Valette 1564–65

During July 1564 seven Maltese galleys cornered a large Turkish sultana (galleon) bound from Constantinople to Venice. Beyond the loss of life and ship, the chief of the black eunuchs of Sultan Suleiman's second seraglio was among the captives. So, too, was a concubine and child, a son of the Grand Turk and the concubine, some opined. (*Bosio III-471*) Whatever the facts, there is no corroborating evidence that the 70-year-old Suleiman lost a child of either sex during this period. This capture, nevertheless, is often cited as cause for 1565's Great Siege of Malta, described in considerable detail in these pages.

The five galleys of the Malta Squadron were in June 1564 combined with the two Magistral galleys for a quick voyage in search of enemy corsairs, all seven under command of Mathurin Romegas, much to the chagrin of those who believed the Order's standard should fly higher than the Grand Master's standard. Senior knight Gil de Andrade commanding *San Gabriello* would have command of any troops put ashore. The seven captains were Thomas de la Tour de Murat, of the squadron capitana; Romegas, of the Magistral capitana; senior captain Gil de Andrade, aboard *San Gabriello*; Olivier de Bourneuf, of *San Giovanni*; Antoine Flotte de la Roche, of *San Iacomo*; Gaspard de la Motte, of the Magistral padrona; and Geronimo Zaportella, of *Corona*. Pierre de Saint-Aubin was lieutenant to Romegas. The seven galleys departed Malta on 14 June bound for Syracuse where information was received that Barbary corsairs were then molesting Monte Sant'Angelo, a part of the Kingdom of Naples well up the Adriatic coast of Italy. The seven galleys accordingly took course for the heel of the Italian boot's Cape Santa Maria de Leuca, from where they turned north through the Strait of Otranto. Reaching the city of Otranto with no sight of the enemy, Romegas reversed course to the south toward the Strofadi Islands, 25 nautical miles west of the Morea, with intent to turn there toward the Aegean. From passing Greek and Venetian vessels, however, the Maltese learned of a large Turkish galleon of about 1,150 gross tons called a sultana mounting twenty pieces of bronze artillery with 200 Turkish janissaries on board bound from Constantinople to Venice, which one day earlier had been sighted exiting Modon headed toward Venetian Corfu and the Adriatic.[1]

The sultana, accompanied by a caramussal, was sighted between the islands of Zante and Kefalonia. The attack was not well organised and in the over-population of galleys was impeded by emulation, which divided Gioù from Romegas, each captain seeking to be credited with the conquest. The flagship of the first suffered grave losses; positioned under the stern castle of the sultana, she was subjected to artificial fire as well as to a storm of arquebus fire from on high. Killed were Pierre de Vigier of Lyon and the Langue of Auvergne, Jeronimo d'Azevedo of Portugal, and Flag Bearer Costantino Castriota of Naples and Rhodes, to mention but a few. Aboard the flagship of the second a single cannon ball killed twenty-two men. The other Maltese galleys, made more cautious by these experiences, circled the sultana and kept in a mode in which their firing interval was continuous. With the withdrawal of the two capitanas, the two patronas prepared to board, Andrade's *San Gabriello* and La Motte's *Santa Marta*. Bairan Ogli, commanding the sultana, with no chance of escape and no hope of relief, surrendered after five hours of punishing combat. Captured with the vessel was Qapu Aga, chief of the black eunuchs of the sultan's second seraglio, while the value of captured cargo was estimated at 80,000 ducats.[1] (*Bosio III-471* also cites a child, a son of the Grand Turk, and the child's concubine mother, but there does not seem to be corroboration for the loss of a Suleiman son.) Among other fatalities were Jean de la Fonde de Funerolx of *San Giovanni,* Jean Bersée de Rochebaron of Auvergne, and Cristobal Pacieco of *San Gabriello*, the latter a veteran of 1560's disaster at Djerba only recently ransomed from captivity at Constantinople. Mortally wounded were Diego d'Inestrosa and Antonio Fernandez Peselin of Castile, who died during the return voyage. Among the severely wounded were padrona Captains Gil de Andrade and Gaspard de la Motte.[2]

The combined squadrons and sultana headed toward Syracuse with the sultana under tow. Her accompanying caramussal, having grabbed a favourable wind, escaped to the north, where upon reaching Valona galliots were dispatched to locate and alert Dragut. Romegas placed Esteban de Claramónte of Huesca in command of the galleon with crew and soldiers. Nearing Syracuse, a favourable wind developed and Romegas ordered a change of course for Malta. Off Cape Passero two beached galliots were sighted; these got under way and fled. Pursued by the galleys, a Greek aboard one of the galliots leaped into the sea and was picked up by *San Iacomo*. The Greek revealed that Dragut was nearby with seventeen oared vessels between galleys and galliots, and was waiting in ambush for the Maltese galleys and sultana. While it was not clear that Dragut was actually in the vicinity or whether this was a desperate ploy, the squadron turned away and the two galliots escaped.[3]

Whatever the fact, Romegas detached a frigate and sent her to Malta to inform the Grand Master that the Barbary squadron might be nearby. The Grand Master ordered the captured galleon sent to Syracuse and his two Magistral galleys returned to Malta with all of the wounded. These included Fernando Ruiz de Corral, who with others stood out in capture of the sultana, and Girolamo Carafa of Naples, who was first on board the captured ship. In the meantime, because of the pursuit and because of contrary wind Claramónte's galleon had been left alone and had a most difficult time laying Syracuse against the wind, reaching safety only at sunset. With the remaining five galleys, Gioù had already put into Messina. He had new orders to proceed to a fleet gathering in Spain intending a second attempt to recapture Penon de Velez de la Gomera, once a Spanish administered rock fortress off the coast of Morocco, lost to Berbers and then to the Ottomans in 1522.

Turning around immediately after debarking the wounded, on 19 July Romegas and his two galleys proceeded back to Syracuse, where Pierre de Rocquelaure-Saint-Aubin and his new lieutenant Giulio Bravo of Verona succeeded Esteban de Claramónte in command of the captured sultana. Claramónte rejoined Gioù for a second tour as sergeant-major together with Beaugeois de Fontaine-la-Neuville of France and Giovanni Vagnone of Turin, all three serving under ground force commander Gil de Andrade. The Magistral galleys towed the sultana to Malta, arriving safely on 30 July. The largest vessel to visit Malta during thirty-four years of Hospitaller occupation, her arrival was an occasion for the citizenry to flock to the harbour. At Messina Gioù had paused for essential repairs to damage sustained during combat with the sultana. Departing after a few days, he put in to Palermo and the island of Favignana, and then on 2 August reached Cagliari at the foot of Sardinia. Meanwhile, news of the capture of the sultana provoked a great outcry at Constantinople, with popular demand for an end to Maltese piracy. Parisot de la Valette's penchant for easy pickings was creating a noose he might not be able to avoid.[3]

With the July 1564 accession of Maximilian II as Emperor of the Holy Roman Empire in succession of his deceased father Ferdinand came plans for a German Diet seeking to align Lutheran and Catholic princes in a united front against Ottoman incursions into the Empire. Grand Master Valette wished to stimulate the youthful and bellicose spirit of the young Emperor for the purpose of diverting Sultan Suleiman's attention from Malta to Empire. Because Grand Prior of Germany Georg Hohenheim von Bombast was aging and feeble, Valette granted authority through a Bull of the Vicariate of Malta for Grand Bailiff of Germany Adam von Schwalbach to represent the Order of Jerusalem at the Diet in company with the Grand Master's nephew Henri de la Valette, and to advocate actions accruing to the relief of the threat to Malta. The Diet of Augsburg did not convene, however, until March 1566.[4]

Grand Hospitaller Louis de Vallée-Passy died in France. One of the last veterans of the Great Siege of Rhodes familiarly termed Monsieur de Flanders, he bequeathed to the Common Treasury the largest single estate in living memory excepting those of certain Grand Masters. He was succeeded as Grand Hospitaller by Bailiff of the Morea Jacques d'Arquinvillier de Tourville, while Arquinvillier was succeeded by Treasurer Pierre Pelloquin de la Plesse. The dignity of Treasurer remained vacant because of the continued insistence of Regent Queen Catherine de Medici that Hospitaller courtier Michel de Seurre de Lumigny be awarded a dignity to which more senior knights were more deserving. Commander Jacques de Vieuxpont was dispatched to the French Court to present the Order's representations respecting seniority.[4]

At Malta a heavy chain arrived from the Order's Receiver at Venice, Cesare Chierigati of Vicenza, which could be used to close either the galley port between Castle Saint Angelo and Senglea or the entire harbour from Castle Saint Angelo to Fort Saint Elmo. At Sardinia, Viceroy Álvaro de Madrigal urged Gioù to pursue with his five galleys a large Algiers galley and five equivalent Algiers galliots of twenty-three banks that had the previous day sacked and destroyed a ship bound for Catalonia. The corsairs had paused at Cape Carbonara, the eastern end of the Gulf of Cagliari, awaiting ransoms for their captives. When they sighted the oncoming Malta galley squadron, however, they took flight. Pursuit began; the galley was overhauled and boarded by Gioù's capitana, by Antoine Flotte's *San Iacomo*, and by Gil de Andrade's *San Gabriello*, all three making short work of the defenders. One hundred and eighty Turks were captured and about 170 Christians were freed from the oars. The captured galley turned out to be *La Pisana* belonging to the Medici Duchy of Florence, lost recently with an accompanying galliot within sight of Livorno. The five galliots, probably[5] of Uluç Ali's squadron returning from Liguria, for reason of this delay had time to escape. A prize crew commanded by Giovan Maria Castrocucco was placed aboard the captive galley and all six vessels returned to Cagliari that same evening of 3 August 1564 to a celebratory welcome. Castrocucco returned to Malta with *La Pisana*, arriving safely on 11 August.[5]

On 28 August Gioù reached Malaga and the Spanish Armada commanded by Viceroy of Sicily García Álvarez de Toledo y Osorio. He was accorded a joyful welcome by Toledo, and his capitana was assigned a place of honour in cruising formations to the left of Toledo's royal galley, the most honoured position to the right of the royal galley occupied by the royal capitana of Portugal. Gioù was immediately joined by Portuguese Admiral Francisco Barreto, wishing company to collect a Lusitanian galleon and caravel blocked by wind in the port of Marbella. The two captains travelled at night, both with lights doused because neither wished to pretend to seniority over the other.[6] Garcia de Toledo's fleet numbered ninety-four galleys and a host of other vessels. Of the galleys, fifteen were Spanish, eight were Portuguese commanded by Berretto, five were Maltese under Gioù, three were Sabaudi commanded by Andrea Provana, and ten were Florentine, some rented to the King, all under the command of Iacomo d'Appiano. There were twelve of Gian Andrea Doria (four under Marcello Doria and eight under Scipione Pallavicino), eight of Seville under Don Alvaro de Bazan, eleven of Naples under Don Sancho de Leyva, eleven of Sicily commanded by Don Federico de Carvajal (four under Don Juan de Cardona and seven belonging to Marcantonio Colonna commanded by Giorgio Grimaldi), four under Giorgio Vaccaro, and four under Marco Centurione. Aboard these and other vessels Toledo had 12,000 infantry commanded by Chiappino Vitelli, Marchese di Cetona, with Don Sancho de Leyva as Colonel of

Spanish infantry. The 12,000 included 500 Maltese infantry, of whom 200 were knights commanded by Andrade with Beaugeois de Fontaine-la-Neuville of the Langue of France, Giovanni Vagnone of Turin, and Esteban Claramónte of Aragon as sergeants-major. The fleet sailed from Malaga on 29 August and two days later appeared beneath Penon de Velez de la Gomera. Toledo put troops ashore 6 miles distant at the Tower of Alcala, where De Leyva made his landing a year earlier. Toledo's galleys and the Portuguese galleon meanwhile cannonaded the Penon from the sea. A weak assault on the part of Moors and Arabs rushed to the rescue was repulsed. Two days later the fortress surrendered; inside the Spanish took possession of eighteen pieces of artillery, one colombine, and two other pieces taken from the Spanish in earlier years. The Spanish also took possession of the island, now a peninsula, and have held it ever since. Leaving in the fortress a garrison of 1,500 men, the fleet withdrew. With the victory Gioù returned to Spain by way of Gibraltar, reaching Malaga on 18 September.[7]

Taking the capture of *La Pisana* as an augury of good fortune but mindful not at all of Emery d'Amboise's 1510 admonition and statute respectively warning of and prohibiting Hospitaller officers from owning or operating corsair vessels, Grand Master Valette ordered Mathurin Romegas to resume corsair warfare soon after repair of his sultana damage as well as of an upgrading of *La Pisana*, which, under the rules of war at sea, was not to be returned to Florence. During the upgrade, however, a *La Pisana* mast fell on deck, killing two workers. Considered a poor augury, *La Pisana*'s participation in the Grand Master's secret undertaking was scratched. Romegas departed Malta on 9 September with the Magistral capitana that he commanded, with Saint-Aubin again his lieutenant, the Magistral padrona *Santa Marta* commanded by Gaspard de la Motte, the galliot taken from Küçük Yusuf two years earlier now commanded by Hospitaller Giovan Maria Castrocucco, two brigantines, and the Magistral frigate, each with embarked combatants including seventy knights and 100 arquebusiers.[8]

The Magistral squadron took course for the waters of Cerigo (Kithera, the island at which Aphrodite, lover of Poseidon, rising from the sea was captured by Praxiteles) not too distant from Ottoman-held Monemvasia on the east coast of the Morea. There Henri de la Valette assumed command as captain-general ashore, commanding a planned assault and capture of Monemvasia conceived by his uncle the Grand Master, their guide an elderly Greek with local origins. Rafaello Salvago was embarked as governor-in-waiting and treasurer. While taking on water at Cerigotto (Antikithera), the squadron was hit by a fierce storm that lasted three and a half days and ended on 19 September; galleys and galliot were damaged, brigantines and frigate were shipwrecked. The mini-squadron nevertheless on 20 September reached a port 12 miles from Monemvasia, where the Maltese corsairs seized two barques the property of Greeks as well as a renegade. The renegade confirmed the small number of Monemvasia defenders. Using ships boats and the seized barques, the guide led the combatants plus a squadron of ships' crew under the steep rise of Monemvasia. Valette found scaling the rock at night to be dangerous, especially because a way might be needed to flee in case of unforeseen developments. For this reason, the mission was aborted with nothing accomplished. Upon their return to Malta on 7 October, Henri de la Valette's uncle was not pleased. At Constantinople this aborted appearance at Monemvasia was said to have nevertheless further infuriated Sultan Suleiman, who immediately replaced and reinforced Monemvasia's garrison, precluding a second attempt.[9]

From Malaga Pierre de Gioù and his five galleys reached Barcelona on 8 October, where responsions from Spanish priories and commanderies were secured on board. From Barcelona the galleys proceeded first to Palamos and thence to Marseille on 7 November, again for the purpose of receiving responsions, this time from French priories and commanderies. While at Marseille the squadron was visited by 14-year-old King Charles IX, his mother Catherine de Medici, and much of the Court. The King embarked on board the squadron capitana for a day-trip to the Pomogue Islands outside of Marseille. Returned to Marseille, all Hospitallers were royally feted by the Court for two weeks. It was not until 22 November that the squadron took course from Toulon to Genoa and Naples and thence to Malta, arriving on 8 February 1565.[10]

At about that time, early February, the Grand Master's agents at Constantinople advised him that Suleiman's maritime war machine was as large as any in Ottoman history, containing 120 galleys in addition to island guard forces and corsair squadrons, also containing heavily armed mahons (maonas), square-rigged galleons and sailing ships with broadside cannon, and transports able to embark a siege force with munitions, provisions, and siege cannon able to destroy the most advanced fortress walls. By all expectation, this was to be the year the pirates of Malta were obliterated. Ambassadors and emissaries at Constantinople similarly warned governments in France, Spain, and Venice; it was Malta or Neapolitan Apulia. But in the seraglio, in the mosques, among Barbary peoples and pilgrims to Mecca, among merchants and people in the street, there was only one word describing the Armada's destination. Malta.[11]

Upon his return from Velez de la Gomera on 8 February, Pierre de Gioù reported to acclamation from Council and public concerning an expedition six days short of eight months. Because four galley captains had completed their tours of duty, Don Francisco de Zanoguera of Valencia was appointed to the command of *San Gabriello*, succeeding Gil de Andrade. Francisco Guiral of Castile was appointed to command of *San Giovanni* succeeding Olivier d'Aux de Bourneuf (during the Siege Guiral and his crew would be assigned to a platform beyond Castle Saint Angelo commanding the entrance to Grand Harbour, a position which Balbi 42 states saved Malta). Jean de la Valette de Cornusson, nephew of the Grand Master, was appointed to command of *San Iacomo* succeeding Antoine Flotte de la Roche, and Don Carlo Ruffo was appointed to command of *Corona* succeeding Geronimo Zaportella. Thomas de la Tour de Murat remained in command of the new flagship *San Giovan Battista*. All of the galley complements, captains, crews, caravan knights, and oarsmen, however, were immediately assigned to labour at defence works, particularly at the completion of walls surrounding the town of Senglea to seaward of Fort Saint Michael. Gaspard de la Motte, commanding the Magistral padrona *Santa Marta*, was reassigned to command the Great Galleon (the *Sultana* captured in July). This ship, armed with her original twenty bronze cannon and re-equipped, was sent from Malta to Licata to load provisions and munitions for the defence of Malta. Pierre de Saint-Aubin moved from Lieutenant to Romegas to command of the Magistral padrona. During this same period Conventual Conservator (Auditor) Jorge de Sant Joan of Mallorca died. An individual of incorruptible faith and saintly life, he left a substantial and liquid estate to the Common Treasury and was succeeded as Conventual Conservator by Catalan Luis Cortit.[12]

Wishing to ascertain the movement of the Ottoman Armada and/or any corsair commander, the Grand Master dispatched Pierre de

Rocquelaure-Saint-Aubin to the Barbary Coast aboard the fast galliot seized from Küçük Yusuf in July 1562, departing Malta on 13 March 1565 bound for Secco di Beit off the east coast of Tunisia. Within a few days Saint-Aubin had taken two Moorish fishing smacks, learning nothing. Days later, however, he encountered a large Levantine merchantman transporting to Tripoli the Sheik of Kairouan accompanied by a large number of Turkish and Moorish arquebusiers. Invested by Saint-Aubin's galliot in a violent clash, there was death on both sides including the German knight Johannes Davit von Angelot. Many of the enemy fled ashore but those captured revealed they had been summoned by Dragut for duty with the Ottoman Armada. This report brought back to Malta led the Grand Master to lean to the opinion that the Spanish fortress of La Goletta outside of Tunis was the Armada's destination, rather than Malta. Giovanni Barelli (Yiannis Vareles of Constantinople), who had been dispatched to Constantinople in November 1562, returned in March 1565. He reported with certainty the numbers and dispositions of the Ottoman Armada. Every Grand Master had authority to receive lay persons into the Order of Jerusalem as Knights of Grace in reward for exemplary conduct, and for this critical information Parisot de la Valette so received Giovanni Barelli into the Langue of Italy. Garcia de Toledo concluded from Barelli's information that the Armada's destination was either Malta or La Goletta, and he resolved to visit them both. But Gil de Andrade was conscripted into Spanish ranks in command of a squadron of four galleys.[13]

At Malta, Commanders Don Diego de Guzman and Antonio Maldonado, both of Castile, were posted to Sicily's Viceregal court as liaison to facilitate the movement of foodstuffs and munitions to Malta. Motte's Great Galleon returned to Malta in March with a full cargo of grain just at a time when a shortage was developing. Not satisfied, the Grand Master sent his two Magistral galleys to Licata for still more grain. He also sent the small galleon captured by Romegas (one of the two large sailing vessels seized by Romegas in June 1557) to Licata for the same purpose. Also concerning Romegas, final payment was received on ransom of the Sancakbey of Cairo captured two years earlier but already released on a promise to pay. With new Viceregency ministers at Sicily, the Grand Master posted Centorio Cagnolo of Vercelli to Sicily as Receiver, succeeding Giovan Francesco Langosco de la Motta, who became Receiver at Malta. On 23 March Geronimo de Guete of Aragon, Baldassar Imperatore of Palermo, and Olivier d'Aux de Bourneuf of Provence were appointed sector wardens with authority to do all things necessary for the sector's defence.[14] Pierre de Massués-Vercoiran (Colonel Mas) was sent to Sicily to hire two companies of infantry; he and others were expected to hire a total of 2,000 infantry at the Order's expense. Pope Pius IV had separately authorised Giuseppe Cambiano of the Piedmont to hire two companies of 500 infantry at Church expense. On 28 March Marshal Guillaume Coppier was appointed Captain-General of the Countryside with responsibility for all forays beyond walled towns. Viceroy Don Garcia de Toledo had meanwhile relayed to King Philip II the information that Yiannis Vareles had brought back from Constantinople. The King had dispatched not only the galleys of Spain to unite with those of Italy, but had also dispatched 25,000 Spanish, German, and northern Italian troops plus 200,000 gold scudos in coin.[15]

Pietro del Monte as Captain and the Langue of Italy were in April assigned responsibility for defending the peninsula of Senglea, including the Fortress of Saint Michael, all of which was separated from mainland Malta by a ditch backed by the wall of the fortress. Senglea's east side was protected from assault by the port called Dockyard Creek, which was enclosed behind a chain stretching from the tip of Senglea to the tip of neighbouring Saint Angelo. This port, also called the Port of Bormola, housed one way or another all of the Christian ships present, and with its docks and moles was the responsibility of the Langue of Aragon under its interim Pilier Catalan Mateo Ferrer. French Creek lies to the west of Senglea, beyond which and within cannon range are the Corradino Heights, which were occupied by the Ottomans soon after their arrival on 20 May. Beyond the tip of Senglea and across Grand Harbour lies Mount Sciberras on a peninsula containing at its tip Fort Saint Elmo. From the 23 June fall of Fort Saint Elmo and even sooner Ottoman cannon on this peninsula were also turned on Senglea. While Senglea was the responsibility of the Italian Langue, the tip of the peninsula, called the Spur, was assigned to Don Francisco de Zanoguera of Aragon and the crew of the galley *San Gabriello.* To the Spur's left facing Corradino was the Post of Sicily commanded by Cola di Naro of Syracuse. To the left of the Post of Sicily was the Post of Don Carlo Ruffo, so called until his death and then termed the post of his successor, manned by the crew of

Corona. His lieutenant was Marcello Mastrillo of Nola. This post also faced the Corradino Heights. To Ruffo's left was Fort Saint Michael facing the ditch, its defenders commanded by Giulio Cesare del Ponte of the Piedmont. Del Ponte remained in command of Fort Saint Michael until succeeded by non-Hospitaller Melchor dc Robles following the arrival at Birgu of the Piccolo Soccorso on 3 July.[16]

On 9 April Viceroy of Sicily Don Garcia de Toledo appeared at Malta with twenty-seven galleys and with his engineers carried out an inspection of the fortifications, properly identifying Fort Saint Elmo as the key to the island's defence and suggesting a ravelin outwork be constructed facing inland. Before continuing on to La Goletta, the Viceroy on 10 April climbed the south coast of Sicily to Trapani in order to catch a favourable wind. Meanwhile, the Ottoman Armada sailed from Constantinople on 22 March under command of Piali Pasha. A Croatian of about 50 years of age, he was 1560's Ottoman victor at Djerba, and was wed to Gevherhan Sultan, daughter of future Sultan Selim II. Fourth Vizier Kizilahmedli Mustafa Pasha, an Anatolian Turk from Sinop, commanded embarked ground forces. More than 70 years of age but still robust and alert, he would in 1566 be Suleiman's commander at the Siege of Hungarian Szigetvár. These two senior officers were together charged with the Siege of Malta. New galleys collected along the way increased the total from 120 to 140, supplemented by twenty towed mahons. These reached the south-western Morea at Modone (Methoni) and Navarin (Pilos) in April, though losing an accompanying sailing vessel with more than 600 spahis and crew on the rocks of Cervi (Elafonisos) under Cape Saint Angelo (Cape Maleo). The balance of the Armada was slowed by the embarkation of a siege force of 28,500 and the vagaries of the wind, which delayed the arrival at Navarin of sailing warships and transports until early May. Among the 28,500 Mustafa had 6,300 janissaries called the Sultan's children commanded by the Lieutenant to the Aga of Janissaries, all veterans and all arquebusiers. There were 6,000 spahis, all Anatolian archers and pikemen commanded by various sancakbeys. There were 5,500 Roumelians and Greeks under the command of their sancakbeys; of these 2,500 were spahis and the balance adventurers seeking fortune, some of whom were accoutred in tiger and leopard skins. There were 500 spahis commanded by the Sancakbey of Karamania, 500 more under Kheder Bey, Sancakbey of Bosnia and friend and confidant of Mustafa

Pasha. There were 500 more adventurers under the Sancakbey of Mitilini and 6,000 Levanti or marines and corsairs. Finally, there were an untold number of dervishes eager to find martyrdom in death. These numbers exclude corsairs of Tripoli and Algiers and points in between.[17]

Prior of Champagne Jean Audibert de l'Aubuge, Bailiff of Negroponte Juan d'Eguaras, and Pilier of the Langue of Germany Konrad von Schwalbach II were made responsible for inventories of food stocks in all parishes, houses, and castles. Women, children, and the aged were shipped to Sicily. Gil de Andrade's command had been increased to eight Royal galleys. On 27 April advice was received from the Order's Receiver at Rome that 500 infantry promised by Pope Pius IV under command of his Hospitaller nephew Camilo dei Medici would be retained at Rome, given a perceived threat to that city. Two hundred infantry separately hired by the Order itself were placed under the command of Hospitaller Asdrubal dei Medici, who would not survive the looming Ottoman Siege. On 28 April Pierre de Gioù returned to Malta with four galleys of the five-galley squadron; he reported that at Messina he was pressed by Viceroy Garcia de Toledo to release his galleys to Sicilian command, but demurred. While at Messina each galley embarked twenty-five to thirty hired arquebusiers in addition to a host of Hospitallers responding to the Grand Master's summons.[15]

On 4 May 1565 the Council ordered the island of Gozo evacuated but for the fortress garrison commanded by Mallorcan Juanito Torreglias, which had been increased by eighty additional personnel. On 6 May there was a muster and inspection of arms and equipment of all knights and serving brothers at Malta and Gozo. The Langue of Provence (sixty-one knights plus fifteen serving brothers) was inspected by Bailiff of Negroponte Juan de Eguaras and Lieutenant Grand Commander commanding the Post of Provence Jean de Montaigu-Fromigières, the Langue of Auvergne (25+14) by Marshal Guillaume Coppier and Prior of Capua Filippo Pilli, the Langue of France (57+24) by Bailiff of Eagle Pedro de Felizes and by Pilier of France François de La Boissière-Carran, the Langue of Italy (159+5) by Admiral Pietro del Monte and Prior of Champagne Jean Audebert de l'Aubuge, the Langue of Aragon (86+2) by Prior of Saint-Gilles Louis du Pont and Lieutenant Grand Conservator Mateu Ferrer, the Langue of Germany (13+1) by Lieutenant Grand Bailiff commanding the Post of Germany Konrad von Schwalbach II and Commander of Marseille Bertrand de Vintimille d'Ollioules, and the Langue of Castile (68+6) was inspected by Bailiff of Caspe Luis Salzedo and Lieutenant Grand Chancellor Luis de Pioz commanding the Post of Castile. The total of knights mustering was 470 including Oliver Starkey, the lone English knight, including as well promotions from serving brother during or immediately after the siege. There were in addition sixty-seven other serving brothers and forty-four chaplains. Most of the latter could be expected to bear arms.[18]

On 8 May 200 infantry of the Spanish Tercio assigned to Sicily arrived at Malta under command of non-Hospitaller Gonzalo de Medrano, transported from Sicily aboard two galleys commanded by Juan de Cardona commanding the Galley Squadron of Sicily. Prior to his return Cardona sounded various bays at the north end of Malta in consideration of any future troop landing. Also arriving on 8 May were Gioù's galleys with an unspecified number of additional infantry. Charles de Grasse Briancon of Provence, Luigi Balbiano of the Piedmont, Catalan Adrien Maimón, Baltasar Payue of Portugal, and Esteban de Claramónte of Aragon were appointed Commissioners responsible for moving all food stocks and farm animals within walled towns, and for poisoning abandoned water sources as they withdrew.

On 11 May the *Great Galleon of the Religion* or *Sultana* commanded by Gaspard de la Motte returned to Malta with 3,500 salme (1,020 metric tons) of grain and with 400 infantry under the command of Colonel Mas. She moored inside the Galley Port. The new chain recently received from Venice was emplaced and closed the Galley Port from the tip of Senglea to Castle Saint Angelo. The Ottoman Armada departed Navarin during the night of 12–13 May on a west-south-west heading, taking it in the direction of both Malta and La Goletta. On 15 May Pierre de Rocquelaure Saint-Aubin was dispatched to the Barbary Coast to ascertain movement on the part of Dragut. On 17 May a private barque dispatched earlier for the same purpose returned with news of Dragut artillery support provided to former Christian ally and King of Tunis Ahmad III. Dragut was otherwise awaiting orders from Mustafa Pasha. The captured galley *La Pisana* as well as the galliot of Küçük Yusuf were recaulked, apparently for service with Toledo's armada.[17] Both, however, were later hauled onto the Arsenal beach.[19]

At the foot of the Strait of Messina the corsair Caragiali had kept a running count of vessels bound from Sicily to Malta and La Goletta, keeping Piali Pasha so informed.[17] On 18 May the Ottoman Armada was within sight of Malta. In succession four warning cannon were fired at Fort Saint Elmo, at Castle Saint Angelo, at the inland capital of Notabile, and at Gozo. That night the Armada ignored Grand Harbour and its fortified towns and passed to the south of Malta before turning up the west coast and anchoring for the night at unpopulated Ġnejna Bay, two kilometers from Mgarr. Uluç Ali, at Navarin with four galliots for the purpose, had reached Tripoli en route to Algiers to respectively summon Beylerbeys Dragut and Hassan, son of Kheir-ed-din Barbarossa. On 20 May the Ottomans made an unopposed landing at Marsa Scirocco, a freshwater source at the south of the island. The next day two of the Grand Master's agents at Constantinople entered Birgu. Arriving with the Ottoman Armada, these two, one an Italian of Salerno and the other an Italian of Kotor, brought to the Grand Master news of recent developments. That same morning Marshal Guillaume Coppier was ordered out with 600-odd arquebusiers under individual commanders Mathurin Romegas, Pierre de Massuez (Colonel Mas), Pierre de Gioù, and others, plus cavalry under Captain Melchor de Eguaras of Aragon. A lopsided harassment ensued over five hours, the Hospitallers emerging victorious but for the loss to capture and slavery of Adrien de la Rivière Sainte-Geneviève, a relative of former Grand Master Claude de la Sengle, as well as the loss in combat of Portuguese knight Bendo Mesquite and the mortal wounding of Olivier de la Tour of the Priory of Aquitaine. Eguaras' cavalry retired to Notabile (Mdina) and not to Birgu with Coppier and the infantry, a positioning that would later work to Maltese advantage. As the Ottomans rolled cannon toward Fort Saint Elmo on 25 May, Colonel Mas and Gaspard de la Motte with 400 and 200 Italian infantry, respectively, plus 100 knights of all nationalities, were sent to reinforce the fort, bringing the garrison from 100 to 800 men. On 27 May the assault on Fort Saint Elmo commenced with persistent fire from up to thirty large cannon. [20]

On 2 June Dragut arrived at Saint George's Bay, 3 miles north of Grand Harbour, bringing thirteen galliots and two galleys of his own as well as about thirty vessels belonging to other corsairs. Embarked were 1,600 combatants aboard his fifteen vessels with at least 900 more on the other thirty. While Dragut believed the assault on Elmo tactically in error, one day later the Turks captured the fort's outer ravelin. Among the dead was Louis de Massués-Vercoiran, arrived at Malta only weeks earlier.[21] On 5 June, reflecting the wounded condition of Bailiff of Negroponte Juan de Eguaras commanding the fort, and the advanced age of Luigi Broglia, Governor of Saint Elmo and veteran of the 1522 Great Siege of Rhodes, the Grand Master elevated older brother Pierre de Massués-Vercoiran (Le Mas) to effective command by appointing him lieutenant to Eguaras.[22] Seventeen days later Le Mas was also killed. Eguaras had been killed days earlier. The enemy soon raised the height of the captured ravelin dangerously above that of the fort's walls. By 10 June the defence of Fort Saint Elmo was nearing impossibility. That night, however, assailing Turks lost 1,000 dead in another unsuccessful attempt at the fort's capture, many of the dead victims of artificial fire set to rolling hoops launched at the assailing force. Such hoops were first used in Germany against the forces of Emperor Charles V,[23] while the local initiative was attributed to Fleming Simone Prevost, later knighted as a member of the Langue of Auvergne. Employing percussion rounds shattering on impact, the guns of Fort Saint Angelo firing across Grand Harbour were another deterrent. One of the Ottoman casualties was the third born and last surviving Kurtoglu corsair brother who had been plaguing Christians for three quarters of a century. An Ottoman commander, he was in the trenches in front of Fort Saint Elmo on 12 June when killed by a Saint Angelo round.[24]

Four days later the same Saint Angelo splintered on his own cannon killed eight fellow Maltese defending Elmo during a seven-hour Ottoman general assault. On this day, 16 June, also killed was Italian knight Giovanni Vagnone of Turin, while the Provencal knight Gaspard de la Motte of La Motte-Saint-Jean was mortally wounded and died three days later. Dead as well was Sicily's Spanish tercio commander Gonzalo de Medrano. Not a Hospitaller, he would nevertheless be interred among Knights of the Grand Cross. Two days later, on 18 June, Turgut Reis, called Dragut and the Drawn Sword of Islam, but born to another name in 1485 on the Bodrum Peninsula to a Carian-Greek mother, was killed by a cannon shard splintered by his own cannon during the continuing assault on Fort Saint Elmo. The same round also killed Soli Aga, Ottoman Camp Master and Sancakbey. On 22 June there was a third

Ottoman general assault, during which the enemy lost 2,000 dead. But not a single officer remained alive within Fort Saint Elmo, while the 100 survivors were all wounded. Relief was impossible.[25]

By the fall of Fort Saint Elmo on 23 June 1,200 defenders had been killed, including upward of eighty-nine knights and six serving brothers. Nine more wounded knights were captured by corsairs.[26] Among the dead was Jean de Durand of Provence, barely a year out of his novitiate, whom *Martyrologe I-274* compares to Jonathan at the Battle of Mount Gilboa heroically defending father Saul among the Israelites besieged by victorious Philistines. Also dead were brothers Jean and Antoine Castelneuf of Provence and brothers Baltasar and Gaspar d'Aoiz (Agoitz in Navarrese). Mourned by his father, mother, three brothers and four sisters was 22-year-old Guillaume de Saint-Bonnet, received four years earlier. Also dead was Alessandro Rusca, whose family fled Transylvania in fear of these same Ottomans under the same sultan. These sacrifices among so many others over twenty-seven days are said to have yielded the time needed for Birgu/Saint Angelo and Senglea/Saint Michael to prepare their defences. Six thousand Ottomans had also lost their lives during the siege to date.[27] It must have occurred to more than one analyst that this Grand Master had eight years to prepare those defences, not twenty-seven days, eight years in which a most formidable redoubt might have been constructed on the Sciberras Peninsula of Fort Saint Elmo, while also improving the Birgu and Senglea defences. On Sunday, 24 June four heads were displayed on lances erected at the Ottoman battery cannonading the Senglea Post of Don Francisco de Zanoguera. These were believed to be the heads of Bailiff of Negroponte Juan de Eguaras of Aragon commanding at Fort Saint Elmo, Commander Melchor de Montserrat y Berga of Valencia, Captain Gonzalo de Medrano commanding the Spanish tercio of Sicily, and of Pierre de Massués-Vercoiran of Provence (Colonel Mas), but they may just as well have been those of any of 1,196 others sacrificed; 129 of them Hospitallers. Montserrat was the younger brother of deceased Grand Conservator Pedro de Montserrat y Berga, who had been wounded forty-three years earlier at 1522's Great Siege of Rhodes. The nine wounded survivors at Elmo who had surrendered to corsairs disposed to hold them for ransom, rather than be mercilessly cut down by janissaries, were spirited off to Algiers. Eight have been identified. These were Francesco Lanfreduci of Pisa; Baccio Carducci and Pietro Guadagni of Florence, the first of whom would die in captivity; Lelio Tana of Chieri in the Piedmont, who would be killed during captivity; Don Juan de Paternoy of Huesca in Aragon; Don Francisco Vique of Valencia; as well as Honorato Fernando de Mesa of Valencia and Don Lorenzo de Guzman of Seville, both of whom would die in slavery.[28]

Last Call at Fort Saint Elmo

Pierre de Massués-Vercoiran (Pr)
Gaspard de la Motte (Pr)
Louis de Maguelone (Pr)
Louis de Puget (Pr)
Jean de Chateauneuf (Pr)
Honourat de Ventimille (Pr)
Emery du Courdurier (Pr)
Olivier d'Aux (Pr)
André du Colombier (Pr)
Louis de Massués-Vercoiran (Pr)
Jean de Gozon (Pr)
Antoine de Chateauneuf (Pr)
Jean de la Gelon (Pr)
Dimitri Sebenauld (Pr)
Pierre Feu (Pr)
Abel de Bridiers (Au)
Laurent de Boulieu (Au)
Jean de Vernon (Au)
Louis d'Argerolles (Au)
Claude de la Roche-Aymon (Au)
Guillaume de Saint-Bonnet (Au)
Pierre de Lonè (Au)
Jean de Vernatel (Au)
Marc Antoine Christian (Au)
Antoine de Monfort (Au)
Guillaume de Corbelle (Au)
Antoine de Noches (Au)
Luigi Raymondo Romano (Au)

Antoine Barbas (Au)
Antoine Lonay (Au)
Edmond de Sancieres (Fr)
Claude de la Bugny (Fr)
Henry de Cressy (Fr)
François du Chilleau (Fr)
François de Bouer (Fr)
Louis de Roggier (Fr)
Jacques de Lubart (Fr)
Artus Bonnet du Breuillac (Fr)
André Robert de Lézardièrre (Fr)
François de Granges Montfermier (Fr)
Audax de Choiseul (Fr)
George Haultoy (Fr)
Simon de Clinchamp (Fr)
Antoine de Moulins (Fr)
Pierre Vignerone (Fr)
Claude Griffon (Fr)
Nicolas Liburnisian (Fr)
Claude Penginet (Fr)
Giovanni Vagnone (It)
Ardicino Grisella (It)
Vincenzo Gabrieli (It)
Ardicino Pescatore (It)
Emilio Scarampo (It)
Francesco Peletta (It)
Iacomo Martelli (It)
Giovanni Vitello Vitelleschi (It)
Decio Mastrillo (It)
Girolamo Galeotto (It)
Alessandro de' Conti di San Giorgio (It)
Paolo Avogadro (It)
Pier Francesco Somaia (It)
Alessandro Rusca (It)
Giovan Antonio Soler (It)
Girolamo Pepe (It)
Pirro Nibbia (It)

Niccolò Strambino (It)
Giovan Battista Gambaloita (It)
Carlo Sassetti (It)
Berardo Capece (It)
Michele de Sis (It)
Paolo Emilio Bozzuto (It)
Giovan Iacomo di Castellamonte (It)
Giovan Girolamo Carrafa (It)
Giovan Battista di Gennaro (It)
Fabritio Valperga (It)
Mario Fagnano (It)
Niccolò Caniggiani (It)
Oratio d'Aquino (It)
Matteo di Corte (It)
Vicenzo d'Afflitto (It)
Bartolomeo Briggia (It)
Carlo Malaspina (It)
Claudio Quirini (It)
Lelio Tana (It)
Giovan Otho Bosio (It)
Girolamo Doria (It)
Paolo Assatati (It)
Pietro Guadagni (It)
Ottaviano Bozzuto (It)
Mario Conti (It)
Giovan Antonio Landolini (It)
Giovan Francesco Gondi (It)
Stefano Fabj (It)
Rosso Strozzi (It)
Giovan Battista Montalto (It)
Vespasiano di Gilestri (It)
Ambrogio Pegullo (It)
Carlo Paladino (It)
Juan de Eguaras (Ar)
Melchor de Monserrat (Ar)
Felix de Queralta (Ar)
Pedro Zacosta (Ar)

Juan Perez Barragan (Ar)
Fortugno Escudera (Ar)
Francisco de Monpalau (Ar)
Antonio de Monferrat (Ar)
Juan de Pamplona (Ar)
Federico Armengol (Ar)
Honourius Fernandez de Mesa (Ar)
Gaspar de Guete (Ar)
Baldassar d'Agny (Ar)
Antonio de Morgute (Ar)
Gaspare d'Aoyz (Ar)
Myguel Bueno (Ar)
Nofre Tallada (Ar)
Juan Sola (Ar)
Wolfgang von Hauneck (Ge)
Johannes von Hassemburg (Ge)
Florian Stezel von Otmut (Ge)
Telmanus von Eyessembach (Ge)
Turç von Dülmen (Ge)
Juan Velasquez de Argote (Ca)
Christobal de Silva (Ca)
Bartolomeu de Pessoa (Ca)
Juan Rodriquez de Villafuerte (Ca)
Francisco de Britto (Ca)
Lorenzo de Guzman (Ca)
Luis de Costilla y Noceda (Ca)
Fernando da Cunha (Ca)
Juan de Espinosa (Ca)
Alonso de Zambrana (Ca)

On Friday 29 June, two Maltese and two Sicilian galleys beached on the shore of Sicily embarked the Piccolo Soccorso of 735 knights, soldiers, and adventurers destined for the relief of Malta. The undertaking was commanded by the Grand Master's nephew Henri de la Valette, while 200 of the embarked force were commanded by Melchor de Robles of Castile, a Knight of Saint James in military service to García Álvarez de Toledo, 4th Marqués of Villafranca and Viceroy of Sicily. Prominent among the others was Hospitaller Vincenzo Carafa, with a party of adventurers; Pierre d'Esparbez de Lussan, Lieutenant to Saint-Aubin, with sixty hired soldiers from the complement of *Santa Marta*; Hospitaller Agostino Ricca, with 230 hired soldiers; Don Diego de Mendoza (brother of Íñigo López de Mendoza, 4th Duke of the Infantado); Dom Vasco da Cunha; and Captain Juan de Funes of Galatia, an adventurer who lost his life within a week of the end of hostilities. Also with the Piccolo Soccorso were Ercole Caraccioli[29] plus forty other Knights Hospitaller.[30] All were soon debarked on the north shore of Malta and made their way to the old city of Mdina (Notabile) in the centre of the island. The four galleys returned to Sicily, the Maltese commanded by Saint-Aubin and Jean de la Valette Cornusson, the Sicilians by Juan de Cardona. During the night of 3 July the 735, including Henri de la Valette, marched 20 miles in a large semicircle around the Ottomans and rendezvoused in Rinella Bay with boats sent by the Grand Master, which took them to Birgu.[31] Most, including the younger Valette, were assigned to the defence of Fort Saint Michael on the peninsula of Senglea.[32]

On 30 June Spahi Memi Çelebi appeared on the shore of the Sciberras (Elmo) Peninsula asking for boat transportation across to Senglea; he was told he must swim. When he did, Christian swimmers met him halfway, assisted him across, and took him to the Grand Master. The name/title Çelebi was a sign of Turkish/Arab rank the Grand Master would have recognised, and Memi Çelebi was privy to Ottoman plans for the Siege of Malta. Born Orthodox Christian as Philippos Laskaris, he was descended from Laskaris Emperors of Nicaea, a breakaway Greek state following the Fourth Crusade's 1204 conquest of Constantinople and dismemberment of the Orthodox Byzantine Empire. The name Lascaris was additionally familiar to the Grand Master. François de Lascaris-la-Brigue mustered in May with Valette's own Langue of Provence. This defecting Laskaris immediately designed the safe route enabling the Piccolo Soccorso to reach Birgu without incident. His other contributions, such as forewarning of a 15 July seaborne assault on Senglea, were equally notable. In 1636 another Laskaris, Jean-Paul de Lascaris of the Langue of Provence, would be elected fifty-seventh Grand Master of the Order of Jerusalem.[33]

Forewarned by Philip Laskaris and forewarned as well by the build-up of Ottoman water craft dragged overland into Grand Harbour from

Marsamuscietto, the Maltese emplaced on 10 July twelve paces offshore of the exposed western side of Senglea heavy pilings twelve to fifteen paces apart connected by chain so strong as to survive impact by a speeding galley. Said by Balbi to be the conception of Valette himself, the purpose was to force attacking Ottomans into the sea, slowing their approach and drenching their powder and long robes.[34] By the morning of the 15 July assault on Senglea there were more than a hundred Ottoman water craft at the inner end of Grand Harbour, some able to accommodate eighty assailants and all together able to accommodate 3,000 of them. The waterborne assault force was commanded by Kandelissù Deli, Mad Kandelissù, a Greek renegade and lieutenant to Hassan Pasha, Beylerbey or Viceroy of Greater Algiers, while the assault force itself was composed of Ottoman janissaries from Algiers, corsair crews, and North Africans, some called 'Teriaki' for the opium they chewed. Among the vanguard of the approaching force was a boatload of imams and other holy men, some reading Islamic scriptures, others shouting imprecations, the lot accompanied by drum beats and trumpet blasts. While the pilings and chain held, some few of the assault force nevertheless made it to the shore, initially assailing the post of Don Francisco de Zanoguera and his nephew Jaime, who with only sixty defenders turned them away. Before the tide was turned, however, Don Francisco was killed by an arquebus round in the groin. The first defender at his post to be killed, he was the same day followed by nephew Jaime and by Fadrique Alvarez de Toledo, illegitimate son of the Viceroy, both of the latter obliterated by the same cannon ball. These commanders were immediately succeeded by Giorgio Adorno the Younger and by a Spanish serving brother. Recognising the failure to penetrate the pilings and chain at Zanoguera's post, ten of the larger Ottoman boats meanwhile attempted to end this barricade and come ashore at the tip of Senglea, where they were exposed to the cannon of Francisco de Guiral at the very end of the neighbouring peninsula containing Castle Saint Angelo. These cannon were packed with grapeshot and small stuff and immediately destroyed nine of the ten boats with the loss of 800 of the initial 3,000 assailants. Overall, some reports suggest 2,500 of the 3,000 assailants were killed, not including Kandelissù Deli.[35]

According to *Balbi 116*, there can be no doubt that Guiral's battery saved the day. Meanwhile, 8,000 additional Ottomans were assailing the landward end of the island/peninsula of Senglea separated from mainland Malta by a ditch. And by walls defended by Melchor Robles, Don Carlo Ruffo, and Mathurin Romegas. Ignoring Biblical strictures some defenders sought vengeance for the 23 June executions of remaining Elmo defenders. Beardless Federico Sangiorgio of Casale Monferrato on the River Po, received into the Order only three years earlier, took vengeance for the loss of elder brother Alessandro by recklessly exposing himself to kill two janissaries and capture two others.[36] Commanded by the aforementioned Hassan Pasha, son of Kheir-ed-Din Barbarossa, not a single Ottoman reached the top of the wall. In five hours the general assault was over. Of the initial 11,000 assailants, 4,000 remained on the field. Christian losses, according to Balbi who was there but who has a tendency to exaggerate enemy losses while minimising Christian losses, were 200 dead and a great number wounded.[37]

Among the Maltese fatalities were four Sicilian knights: Girolamo Balsamo, Bernardino Sortino, Cesare Zavarca, and Alessandro d'Alessi, as well as the Portuguese knight Simão de Souza. Among the gravely wounded was Carlo Ruffo. Luis Cortit lost both legs to a basilica round fired from the Corradino Heights that demolished several parapets of the wall surrounding Birgu. He had time only for a confession. Thirty-six years an Hospitaller, Luis de Godoy of the Langue of Castile would suffer his wounds two more years before succumbing to them.[38] During the remaining siege, Giovan Francesco de la Motta carried out Cortit's duties as Conventual Conservator as well as his own duties as Receiver.[39] Esteban de Claramónte replaced the deceased Francisco de Zanoguera at both his post and commanding *San Gabriello*. Henri de la Valette survived the general assault on Senglea of 15 July, but three days later led a party outside of the fort to destroy an Ottoman bridge over the ditch separating Senglea from Malta-proper, where his prominence was spotted by an Ottoman sniper. Henri de la Valette (Parisot), Commander of La Chapelle, is on Bosio's III-711 list of fatalities, reported as fallen on the Island of Saint Michael (Senglea). On the same list François de la Valette (Parisot) is reported as fallen in defence of Birgu.[40]

Besiegers taken captive on 1 August revealed that a general assault on Fort Saint Michael was scheduled for the following day. Robles and Ruffo were alerted. The alert cost the life of Castile's Esteban Calderón, commanding a party scouting the assault. Bombardment commenced early the next morning and continued until noon, when the enemy immediately attacked. The posts of Robles and Ruffo bore the brunt of the attack, both of them repeatedly assailed by wave upon wave of fresh troops for more than five hours. Defenders emerged victorious but among the fatalities were Pietro Antonio Barrese and Don Carlo Ruffo, both of Naples. In the words of Giacomo Bosio, 'Brother Don Carlo Ruffo, who is so often named in this history, had at his post of combat been wounded. Not yet healed he had nevertheless returned on rumour of this assault to again fight at his post. In company with Brother Pier' Antonio Barrese of the Grand Master's staff, the two fighting back to back with great courage and ardor had with intrepid spirit repulsed the enemy time and again. Near the end of combat they were by the same cannonade blown from their station torn to pieces.' Ruffo was succeeded at his post and in command of *Corona* by Don Ercole Caraccioli, also of Naples. Losing their lives on the same day were Nicolò di Sanmartino of Turin and Alessandro Scarampo of Casale; the latter's cousin Emilio had lost his life a month earlier at Fort Saint Elmo.[41]

On 6 August Francisco Guiral was reassigned from the tip of Birgu's peninsula beyond Castle Saint Angelo to a rapid-response role mustering in the square of Birgu together with Oliver Starkey, Pilier of England, and Konrad von Schwalbach II, Pilier of Germany, each with the men of their respective commands.[42] One day later 8,000 Ottomans assailed Fort Saint Michael and 4,000 others Birgu's Post of Castile. The assault persisted for eight hours, at the end of which 2,200 more Turks had met their maker, as had sixty more Christians.[43] On 7 August during the general assault on Fort Saint Michael and Birgu's Post of Castile, when the outcome still hung in the balance, Vincenzo Anastagi commanding 100 horse and an equal number of infantry from Mdina (Notabile) fell upon the Ottoman rear, making short work of any resisting sick and wounded. The consternation thus aroused, suggesting another relief force had landed, caused assailing Ottomans facing Saint Michael and the Post of Castile to abandon their positions. The Maltese survived to fight another day, and the enemy's morale was sapped.[44] Pedro Fernandez de Felizes succeeded Marshal de Robles in command of the defence of Fort Saint Michael when the latter was mortally wounded on 11 August from an arquebus round to the head.

By the 12 August arrival at Sicily of Alvaro de Bazan commanding the Galley Squadron of Seville, Viceroy of Sicily Garcia Alvarez de Toledo had upward of sixty galleys with substantial numbers of embarked troops available for the relief of Malta; he was constrained, however, by a perceived need for a preponderance vis-à-vis the Ottomans as well as by the dismal record of Spanish fleet action.[45]

On 15 August Bailiff of Eagle Pedro de Felizes was also felled by an arquebus round at the defence of Fort St Michael, and died in early September. He had survived the six-month Great Siege of Rhodes.[46]

Following the death of Robles on 12 August, Pierre de Gioù was assigned to Fort Saint Michael, where, like Dragut, he was wounded in the head by a rock shard.[47] Unlike Dragut he survived.[48] On 17 August Flagbearer Antonio Muñatones of Castile, an individual of signal bravery, took an arquebus round in the hand which became infected and later unreasonably snatched his life.[49]

A relief fleet of sixty galleys with 10,000 embarked combatants was able to sail from Messina on 21 August and from Syracuse on 25 August. The fleet was caught by a gale, though, which blew it to an anchorage at Favignana on 29 August. On the morning of 30 August Mustafa Pasha, the general in command of the Siege of Malta, personally led 6,000 janissaries, spahis, and Levantis (marines) up to if not through the breach in the walls of Fort Saint Michael defended by the Langue of Italy as well as by seamen from ships in the harbour. At the same time 3,000 others assailed a breach at the Post of Castile on the walls of neighbouring Birgu. The first assault was turned back by those of the post still remaining, commanded by Marcello Mastrillo, lieutenant to the deceased Don Carlo Ruffo, and as well by Pierre d'Esparbez de Lussan and those brought with him as part of the Piccolo Soccorso. Earlier in August Lussan's lieutenant Jean-François de Polastron la Hillière was killed by an arquebus round while fighting in the fosse/moat/ditch of Fort Saint Michael.[50]

The next Relief Fleet departure on 2 September from Favignana took it to a rendezvous at the island of Linosa west of Malta, where the fleet was again assailed by bad weather, returning to Sicily on 5 September. Gian Andrea Doria had meanwhile returned to Messina on or before 23 August when he offered[51] to and did that evening depart for Malta to reconnoitre the Ottoman Armada. On 5 September he recommended the Grand Soccorso depart immediately.[52]

On 6 September the fleet again set off for Malta in three squadrons: vanguard, battle, and rear guard. The vanguard consisting of nineteen galleys was commanded by Sancho de Leyva aboard a royal capitana flanked by the capitanas of Genovese entrepreneurs Stefano di Mare and Giorgio Grimaldi. Of the remainder, seven were from the Naples Squadron, four were Florentine, three from the Genovese Piero Battista Lomellino, and two of Alvaro de Bazan. The battle group of twenty galleys was commanded by Garcia de Toledo and consisted of eight royal galleys, three each Florentine and Bazan, two each from Savoy and Genoa, plus Saint-Aubin's *Santa Marta* and Cornusson's *San Iacomo*. Juan de Cardona commanded the rear guard of seventeen galleys, seven of Sicily, seven of Gian Andrea Doria, and three of the Genovese Marco Centurione.[53]

Early the next morning (7 September) these landed on the north shore of Malta 8,000 troops under Alvaro de Sande and 1,600 adventurers under various commanders[54] before returning to Sicily for a second embarkation, first, however, sailing past Grand Harbour to announce their arrival. A list of the more prominent among those put ashore may be found at *Bosio III-659*.[55] Upon sighting reinforcements from Sicily, the Ottoman siege of Malta was lifted beginning that day and ending on 11 September, after which Romegas led a company of soldiers to the remains of Fort Saint Elmo, where he raised the white-cross-on-red-field banner of the Religion.[56] A contemporary source asserts the Turks lost 30,000 dead,[57] Balbi puts the number at 35,000.[58] But as only 30,000 arrived and 10,000 departed, a better estimate is 20,000.

More Hospitaller Last Call During 1565's Great Siege of Malta

Henri de la Valette (Pr)
François de la Valette (Pr)
Antoine de Thesan Pujols (Pr)
Baldassare de Simian-Gordes (Pr)
Jean de Corneillan (Pr)
François de Polastron (Pr)
Gaspard de Ponteves (Pr)

Claude de Lambesc (Pr)
François de la Strade Fleurac (Pr)
Jean de la Tour Reyniers (Pr)
François d'Alons (Pr)
François de Montauban de la Roquette (Pr)
Gaudens d'Hébrail d'Alons (Pr)
Scipione Durre (Pr)
Jacques Pagal (Pr)
Jacques Feyllaire (Pr)
Gaspard Serre (Pr)
François Trenchant de la Barre (Pr)
Antoine de Fay Saint-Roman (Au)
Alain de Montal dit la Prade (Au)
Antoine de Bressoles de Morterolles (Au)
Antoine Bernart (Au)
François de la Beisierre (Fr)
Magdalon de Grossy de Bouilly (Fr)
Adrien de Talmet (Fr)
Olivier de la Tour (Fr)
Nicolas Poitevin de Plessis (Fr)
Guillaume de la Motte (Fr)
Trillen de Montbazon (Fr)
Adrien de la Rivière Sainte-Geneviève (Fr)
Esprit de Brunesay-Quincy (Fr)
Beautrimolet Tremûilere (Fr)
Pierre Barian de la Motte (Pr)
Lorenzo Olivier (Fr)
Baptiste de Mailly (Fr)
Francis de Mellet (Fr)
Fermin Verdure (Fr)
Blaise Ruffin (Fr)
Pierre le Clerc (Fr)
Martin Douay (Fr)
Jean Bernal (Fr)
Pierre le Blanc (Fr)
Nicolò del Bene (It)
Aleramo Parpaglia (It)

Francesco Daniello (It)
Giovan Girolamo Anfora (It)
Vincenzo Perno di Siracusa (It)
Giovan Antonio Landolina (It)
Stefano Faby di Roma (It)
Francesco Saccano (It)
Anniballe Strozzi (It)
Nicolò di Settimo (It)
Cesare Dentici di Napoli (It)
Girolamo Spetiale di Noto (It)
Girolamo Faby di Roma (It)
Scipionne di Patti Messinese (It)
Ottaviano del Fiore (It)
Luigi Balbiano (It)
Giovan Maria Castrocucco (It)
Girolamo Balsamo (It)
Pier Anton Barrese (It)
Asdrubale de' Medici (It)
Don Carlo Ruffo (It)
Giulio Cesare del Ponte (It)
Cesare Zauarca di Sicilia (It)
Giorgio Montiglio (It)
Alessandro d'Alessi (It)
Vespasiano Malaspina (It)
Filippo Doria (It)
Pompilio Savelli da Palombara (It)
Christofano Caloiro (It)
Alessandro Scarampo (It)
Michele de Sis (It)Paolo Emilio Bozzuto (It)
Giovanni Iacomo di Castellamonte (It)
Fabritio Valperga (It)
Mario Fagnano (It)
Oratio d'Aquino (It)
Matteo di Corte (It)
Bartolomeo Briggia (It)
Don Ercole Caracciolo (It)
Giovan Battista Soderini (It)

Alessandro Ridolfi (It)
Tiberio Canfora (It)
Paolo Boniperto (It)
Emiliiano Vialardi (It)
Vicenzo Caroli (It)
Bernardino Sortino (It)
Nicolò di San Martino (It)
Ottavio Capece (It)
Iacomo Raffelli (It)
Bailiff of Eagle Pedro de Felizes (Ar)
Diego Garcia Metelin (Ar)
Luis Cortit (Ar)
Geronimo Zapata (Ar)
Alonso del Frago (Ar)
Francisco Ximenes (Ar)
Bautista de Aoys (Ar)
Miguel de Pennaroxa (Ar)
Francisco Torrellas (Ar)
Don Francisco de Zanoguerre (Ar)
Martín de Sesé (Ar)
Juan de Santa Pau (Ar)
Jaime de Zanoguerra (Ar)
Pedro Zaportella (Ar)
Torcham von Dülmen (Ge)
Georg von Hessenburg (Ge)
Baron Jurgen Bes (Ge)
Hieronymus Rechuch (Ge)
Luis de Paz (Ca)
Bendo Mesquite (Ca)
Luis de Godoy (Ca)
Esteban Calderón (Ca)
Ernando Centeno (Ca)
Don Francisco de Rivera (Ca)
Baltasar Payva (Ca)
Juan Vasquez d'Aviles (Ca)
Bartolomeu de Macedo (Ca)
Francisco Ruiz de Medina (Ca)

Diogo Brandao (Ca)
Simão de Melo (Ca)
Don Enrique de Maulcon (Ca)
Bernabé da Cunha (Ca)
Simão de Melo #2 (Ca)
Simão de Sousa (Ca)
Don Fadrique de Toledo (Ca)
Rodrigo Godinez (Ca)
Antonio de Muñatones (Ca)

Dead combatants other than Hospitallers were primarily hired soldiers and local militia. Of the 470 knights mustering in May joined by forty-seven others of the Piccolo Soccorso, 212 are known to have lost their lives. One of these not mentioned elsewhere was François de Bouliers dit Tour-d'Aigues of the Langue of Provence. One of eleven children of Jean Louis de Bouliers, Baron de la Tour-d'Aigues, only the tragedy of his death earned him a place in history. Others with like status may be found listed above. For three consecutive days last offices were conducted in the Church of San Lorenzo honouring these tragic losses.

Appendix

Glossary of Notable Figures

ACHÉ, ROBERT (Robert d'Aché, Bosio's Roberto d'Axas/d'Ache). French of Fumechon 100km north of Paris. A second son of Jacques d'Aché, Seigneur de Fumichon, and of Jacqueline d'Amfreville. Brother of Jacques II and brother or uncle of Marguerite d'Aché wed to Vice-Amiral of France and Seigneur de Sallenelles Jean Le Brun. Knight of Jerusalem, Langue of France. Received (1502). Great Siege of Rhodes (1522). Commander of Sommereux (1534–42). Bailiff of the Morea (1536–1537), Knight of the Grand Cross. Grand Hospitaller (1537–41). Prior of Champagne (1541–48). (+1548)

ACSAC REIS (Acsac Reis, Acsac Kaptan, Zoppo). Greek of Candia. Sinan Lieutenant at Alexandria (1504). Mamluk Ambassador to Hospitallers (1524). Spanish Siege of Tunis (1535). Captures Parisot de la Valette and corsair galliot (1541). Dragut Lieutenant (1544–c.1560). Battle of Djerba (1560). (+c.1560)

ADORNO, GIORGIO (Giorgio Adorno, Boissat's George Adorne, Bosio's Giorgio Adorno). Italian of the Piedmont. Knight of Jerusalem, Langue of Italy. Received (1513). Knight Commander of Mondovi. Pilier Langue of Italy (1543–58). Admiral (1547–48), Knight of the Grand Cross. Bailiff of Naples (1548–58). General of the Galleys (1547–48, 1548–49, 1557–58). Captain of Arms and Governor of Notabile (1550–51). (+1558)

AIRASCA, BERNARDINO (Bernardino d'Airasca, Bernardino Piossasco d'Airasca, Bosio's Bernardino d'Airasca). Piemontese. Knight of Jerusalem, Langue of Italy. Commander of La Motta. Galley Captain (1500). Knight Commander at Lango (1505). Prior of Messina (1512–21), Knight of the Grand Cross. Admiral (1521–25). Governor of St Peter's

Castle to Evacuation of Rhodes (1522). Captain of Galleys (1523–24). Magistral Lieutenant (1523–31). Prior of Lombardia (1525–31). (+1531)

ANCIENVILLE, CLAUDE (Claude d'Ancienville de Villiers, Roncière's Claude Villiers de Ancienville, Bosio's Claudio d'Anfoiuille Villiers). French of Ancienville in the Hauts-de-France. Son of Claude d'Ancienville, Baron of Réveillon and Lord of Villiers aux Corneilles, and Andrée de Saint-Benoit. Knight of Jerusalem, Langue of France. Received (1510). Commander of Auxerre, and Launoy. Ambassadeur Extraordinaire to the Kings of France and England (1522). Galley Captain (1524). Commander of Troyes (1539–48). Commander of Coulours (1539–48) and of Coulommiers (1547–49). Treasurer (1541–45), Knight of the Grand Cross. Bailiff of the Morea (1545–46). Grand Prior of France (1546–48). Grand Panetier of France and Member of the King's Household. Captain of French Galleys. (+1548)

ANDRADE, GIL (Gil de Andrade, Bosio's Gil d'Andrada). Spanish of San Martiño de Andrade in northern Galicia. One-eyed, according to *Morgan 568*. Younger brother of Hospitaller Fernando de Andrade. Knight of Malta, Langue of Castile. Received (1540). Knight Commander. Malta Galley Captain (1558–64). Sultana Capture (1564). Ground Force Commander at capture of Penon de Velez de la Gomera (1564). In Spanish Service commanding eight galleys (1565). Gran Soccorso (1565). Commodore of Spanish Galleys at Lepanto (1571). (+)

ANDÙJAR, LUIS (Luis de Andújar, Bosio's Luigi d'Andugar). Spanish of Andújar, Andalusia. Knight of Jerusalem, Langue of Castile. Ambassadeur Extraordinaire to Pope Leo X informing the Holy Father of the election as Grand Master of Philippe Villiers de l'Isle-Adam (1521). Ambassadeur Extraordinaire to Christian Princes of the Siege Armada's arrival (1522). Ottoman Siege of Malta (1522). Commander (1522). Pilots ship *Santa Croce* (1522). Magistral Lieutenant dispatched to King John III of Portugal and to various princes of Spain seeking support at Malta (1530). (+)

ARGILLEMONT, MICHEL D' (Michel d'Argillemont, Louis d'Argillemont, Michel de Harzillemont, Bosio's Michele d'Argillemont). One of twenty-two children of ? d'Argillemont, Seigneur de Branges, Loupeigne, Bruys, et al. Knight of the Order of Jerusalem, Langue of

France. Commander of Maupas (1490–1508). Commander of Mont-de-Soissons (1499–1517). Commander of Sommereux (1512–34). Captain of the Galleys (1521–23). Ottoman Siege of Rhodes (1522). Commander of Saint-Etienne-de-Renneville (1524–33). Commander of Sterpigny. Treasurer (1524–26), Knight of the Grand Cross. Bailiff of the Morea (1526–27). Grand Hospitaller (1533–34). Prior of Champagne (1534–36). (+1536)

ARQUINVILLIER, JACQUES (Jacques d'Arquinvillier de Tourville, Jean de Arquinvilliers, Jean de Hargenvillier, Bosio's Iacomo d'Arquembourg). French perhaps of Tourville-sur-Arques, Normandy. A second son of Olivier d'Arquinvillier (died 1520), Chevalier and Seigneur de Saint Rimault, and of Andrée d'Aymeret (died 1519). Brother of Louis d'Arquinvillier (1503–79) wed to Marthe Alleaumé (died 1572). Knight of Malta, Langue of France. Knight Commander. Received (1541). Treasurer (1563). Bailiff of the Morea (1563–64), Knight of the Grand Cross. Grand Hospitaller (1564–71). Gran Soccorso (1565). Prior of Champagne (1571), appointment rescinded by Crown in favour of Michel de Seurre de Lumigny. (+)

ARSAC, ETIENNE (Etienne d'Arsac, Etienne d'Arzac, Bosio's Stefano d'Arzac). French of the Seigneury d'Arsac 270km north-west of Toulouse. Younger son (?) of Thomas d'Arsac, Seigneur d''Arsac, de Castéra, et de Lilhan. Knight of Malta, Langue of Provence. Commander of Marestaing (1541–57). Siege of Zuara (1552). Commander of the Malta Arsenal (1554). Galley Commander (1554–55). Commander of Saint-Felix de Sorgues (1566–78). (+1578)

ASPREMONT, CLAUDE JACQUES (Claude-Jacques d'Aspremont, Jacques d'Aspremont, Jacques d'Aspremont de Nantheuil, Bosio's Iacomo d'Aspremont). French of Sorcy, 60km north-east of Reims. One of three sons and a daughter of Geoffroy d'Aspremont (1445–95), Seigneur de Sorcy (modern Sorcy-Bauthémont) et de Vandy (both due west of Luxembourg), and of Michelle de Suzanne, Dame de Nantheuil (wed 8 November 1476). Younger brother of Guillaume (born near 1480), Isabel (born near 1485), and Jean (born near 1490). Knight of Jerusalem, Langue of France. Commander of Lagny le Sec (Paris), Senlis (1536–41), and Liège. Galley Captain (1535–36), Spanish Siege of Tunis (1535).

Galley Battle of Zuara (1536). Homedes Elector (1536). Treasurer (1537), Knight of the Grand Cross. (*c.*1495–*c.*1575)

AUBE, ROBERT (Robert d'Aube, Robert d'Aube de Rocquemartine, Robert de Roquemartine, Robert d'Aube detto Roquemartine, Bosio's Roberto de Rocca Martin/Roberto di Roccamartina). French of Eyguières, Bouches-du-Rhône, 50km south-south-east of Avignon. A younger son of Jean d'Aube, Seigneur de Roquemartine, and of Alix d'Oraison. Knight of Jerusalem, Langue of Provence. Received Avignon (*c.*1497). Battle of Zonchio (1499). Commander of Avignon (1515–25). Lieutenant Chatelain du Chateau Saint-Pierre (1522). Ottoman Siege of Rhodes (1522). Commander of Trinquetaille (1522–49). Receiver Prior of Saint-Gilles (1523). Grand Commander (1545–46), Knight of the Grand Cross. Prior of Saint-Gilles (1546–49). (1479–1549)

AUBIN, JEAN (Jean d'Aubin, Jean d'Aubin dit Malicorne, Bosio's Jean de Bin). French of Malicorne-sur-Sarthe in north-western France. Second son of Jean Aubin de Malicorne, Councillor and Grand Chamberlain to the Duke of Guyenne, and of Louise de Clermont, Dame de Surgères. Younger brother of Jean d'Aubin Seigneur de Malicorne et de Surgères wed to Jeanne bâtarde d'Angoulême (wed 1501, deceased 1531). Knight of Jerusalem, Langue of France. Commander of La Condrie/Le Pertuis d'Antioche (1512) defending La Rochelle. Ottoman Siege of Rhodes commanding Bastion of England (1522). Treasurer (1529), Knight of the Grand Cross. Bailiff of the Morea (1529–34). Prior of Champagne (January–July 1534). (+1534)

BABINGTON, JOHN (John Babington, John Babington the Elder, Johannis Babington, Bosio's Giouanni Babington). English of Dethick, Derbyshire. Second son of Thomas Babington of Dethick and Editha Fitz-Herbert of Norbury, Derbyshire. Elder brother of Hospitaller Humphrey Babington. Uncle of Hospitaller John Babington the Younger. Knight of Jerusalem, Langue of England. Received (1500). Preceptor of Yeaveley (1510), and of Dalby and Rothely (1523). Common Treasury Receiver in England (1521). Prior of Ireland (1527), Knight of the Grand Cross. Turcopolier (1527–31). Preceptor of Dinsmore (1528). Bailiff of Eagle (1531–35). (+1535)

BARBAROSSA, KHIZR (Khizr Barbarossa, Kheir-ed-Din Barbarossa, Morgan's Heyradin Basha/Barba-Rossa II, Setton's Khaireddin Barbarossa, Boissat's Barberousse, Guglielmotti's Ariadeno, Bosio's Ariadeno Barbaroffa) of Mitilini, Fourth son of Muslim Greek father Yakup and Christian Greek mother Katerina. Brother of Aruj, Isaac, Elias, and two sisters, brother-in-law of Sinan and Salih, father of Hassan and adoptive father of Hassan of Sardinia, uncle of a Sinan son and of a Turgut daughter. Sultan and then Ottoman Beylerbey (Lord) of Algiers and Tlemcen (1518–33). Ottoman Kapudan Pasha (1533–46). Battle of Preveza (1538). Italian Campaign (1543–44). (*c*.1478–1546)

BARRAS, ANTOINE Antoine de Barras, Bosio's Antonio Barras). French of Barras 80km south of Gap-Haute-Alps. Knight of Jerusalem, Langue of Provence. Commander of Gap-Haute-Alps (1528–34). Grand Commander (1546–48), Knight of the Grand Cross. (+1548)

BARRIENTOS, JUAN (Juan de Barrientos, Bosio's Giouanni de Barrientos). Spanish of Barrientos, 50km south-west of León. Knight of Jerusalem, Langue of Castile. Commander of Ciudad Rodrigo (1541). Siege of Algiers (1541). Lieutenant Chancellor (1559). Bailiff of Negroponte (1563), Knight of the Grand Cross. Bailiff of Lora (1563–74). (+1574)

BAZAN, ALVARO (Alvaro de Bazan the Elder. Bosio's Alvaro de Bazan) Marqués del Viso, Admiral of Castile, Captain-General of Spain's Mediterranean Galley Fleet. Son of Pedro de Bazan Viscount de Valduerna, father of Alvaro de Bazan 1st Marqués of Santa Cruz and of Alonso de Bazan Captain-General of Spain's Ocean Armada. Siege of Tunis (1535). (1506–58)

BEAULAC-TRÉBONS, PIERRE (Pierre de Beaulac, Pierre de Beaulac-Trébons, Jean-Pierre de Beaulac-Trébons, Bosio's Pietro de Beaulac detto Trebons). French of Trebons, 160km west-south-west of Toulouse. Knight of Jerusalem, Langue of Provence. Ottoman Siege of Rhodes (1522). Galley Commander (1533). Commander of Montsaunès (1543–44). Commander of La Cavalerie (1546–70). Commander of Vaour (1552–60). Grand Commander (1553–55), Knight of the Grand Cross. Prior of Toulouse (1555–70) (+1570)

BIDOUX, PREGEANT (Pregeant de Bidoux, Pierre Jehan, Pregent de Bidoux, Autun's Bidoulx, Pregianni Provenzale, called by the English John Perry, Bosio's Pierre Iehan or Preianni di Bidoux). Gascon, born near Tarbes, 155km west-south-west of Toulouse. Corsair in Service of France (1494–1514). Knight of Jerusalem, Langue of Provence. Battle of Zonchio (1499). Received (1503), Knight of the Grand Cross. At War With England in La Manche (1512–14). Commander of Gap-Francès (1514–28). Prior of Saint-Gilles (1514–28). Bailiff of Lango (1518–24). Ottoman Siege of Rhodes (1522). (*c*.1468–1528)

BOMBAST, GEORG (Georg Bombast, Georg Bombast von Hohenheim, Georg II Bombastus von Hohenheim, Boissat's George Bombast, Bosio's Giorgio Bombast). German of Swabia. Last of the Hohenheims. Son of Friedrich Bombast von Hohenheim and of Anna Maria Schilling von Canstatt, a sister of Hospitaller Grand Prior of Germany Georg Schilling von Cannstatt. Younger brother of Hospitaller Grand Bailiff Wilhelm Bombast (d 1549). Knight of Malta, Langue of Germany. Knight Commander of Rohrdorf. Commander of Saint-Jean-de-Bassel (1545). Commander of Dorlisheim (1549). Grand Bailiff of Germany (1546-1554), Knight of the Grand Cross. Grand Prior of Germany (1554–66). Prince of Heitersheim (1554–66). Commanded Hospitaller units opposing Suleiman's Final Campaign (1566). (c.1500–66)

BONIFACE, JEAN (Jean Baptiste de Boniface, Jean de Boniface, Bosio's Giouanni de Boniface). French. Knight of Jerusalem, Langue of Provence. Aubusson Pall Bearer (1503). Chapter General (1514). Commander of Condat (1521–23). Warden at Ottoman Siege of Rhodes (1522). Convent Receiver (1527). Bailiff of Manosque (1529–45), Knight of the Grand Cross. Magistral Lieutenant (1533–35). (+1545)

BOSIO, ANTONIO (Antonio Bosio). Italian of Chivasso (Turin). Uncle of brothers Giacomo and Giovan Otto, and brother of Tommasso. Serving Brother then Knight of Jerusalem, Langue of Italy. Ottoman Siege of Rhodes (1522) – Company Commander. Diplomat (1522–30) Ambassador to Kings and Popes. Knighted at Malta (1529). Appointed Bailiff of Santo Stefano (1530) by Pope Clement VII, Knight of the Grand Cross. Killed by carriage overturn (1530). (1495–1530)

BOSIO, GIACOMO (Giacomo Bosio, Iacomo Bosio). Italian of Chivasso (metropolitan Turin). Son of Giovanni Bartolomeo Bosio, Commissioner General for French King Francis, and Anna Bosio. Younger Brother of Gianotto Bosio, Agent at Venice for the Hospitaller Order of Saint John, and of Giovanni Otho Bosio. Historian. (1544–1627)

BOSIO, TOMMASO (Tommaso Bosio, Giacomo Bosio's Tommasso Bosio). Italian. Brother of Antonio Bosio, Uncle of historian Giacomo Bosio. Chaplain of Jerusalem, Langue of Italy. Vice Chancellor (1526–39). Bishop of Malta (1538–39). (+1539)

BOTTIGELLA, AURELIO (Aurelio Bottigella, Boissat's Aurelio Botigelle, Bosio's Aurelio Bottigella). Italian of Pavia. Younger son of Antonio Simone, ducal official at Parma. Knight of Jerusalem, Langue of Italy. Received at Pavia (1507). With French forces opposing the Holy League at Battle of Ravenna (1512). Ottoman Siege of Rhodes (1522). Interim Governor of Malta (1530). Pilier Langue of Italy (1533). Governor of Tripoli (1533). Prior of Pisa (1533–50). Captain of Galleys (1534–36). Spanish Siege of Tunis (1535). Galley Battle of Zuara (1536). (*c.*1490–1550)

BOURBON, JACQUES (Jacques de Bourbon batard de Liège, Bosio's Giacomo di Borbone). Bastard son of Louis de Bourbon, Prince-Bishop of Liège. Grandson of Charles I, Duke of Bourbon, and Agnes of Burgundy, the latter sister of Duke of Bourbon Philip the Good. Historian. Knight of Jerusalem, Langue of France. Received (1503). Commander of St Maulvis, Oisemont, and Fontaine-de-Vaucluse (1508). Ottoman Siege of Rhodes (1522). Lieutenant Grand Hospitaller (1523). Commander of Chantraine (to 1537). Bailiff of Lango (1528–33). Lieutenant Grand Prior of France (1529–35). Treasurer (1533-1534), Knight of the Grand Cross. Bailiff of the Morea (1534). Grand Hospitaller (1534–35). Commander of Troyes (1536–37). Commander of Coulours (1536–37) and of Coulommiers (1537). Grand Prior of France (1535–37). Grand Prior of Jesuits in France (to 1537). (1466-1537)

BOYDELL, ROGER (Roger Boydell, Roger Boydel, Mifsud's Roger Boydell, Bosio's Ruggiero Boidel). English. Knight of Jerusalem, Langue of England. Received at Rhodes (1500). Preceptor of Halston (1506–23).

Preceptor of Ribstone and Wetherby. Preceptor of Baddesley and Mayne (to 1530). Preceptor of Newland (1530–33). Turcopolier (1533). (+1533)

BRACAMONTE, FERNANDO (Fernando de Bracamonte, Bosio's Ernando de Bracamonte). Spanish of Salamanca. Knight of Jerusalem, Langue of Castile. Ottoman Siege of Rhodes (1522). Knight Commander. Knight Commander of Alcolea (1539+). Governor of Tripoli (1539–44). Lieutenant Chancellor and Pilier of Castile (1545). Captain of Galleys (1545–46). Procurator (1548). (+*c*.1553)

BRIANÇON, CHARLES DE GRASSE (Charles de Grasse Briançon, Brianson, Biancon, Bosio's and Pozzo's Carlo de Graffe Brianfon). French of Briançon, 185km north-east of Manosque. Second son of Jean de Grasse Briançon, Seigneur de Briançon, Soleilhas, Gars, Montblanc et autres lieux, and of Catherine de Villemurs. Brother of Hospitaller Jerome killed at Zuara. Knight of Malta, Langue of Provence. Received (1547). Zuara Raid (1552). Commander of Saliers. Ottoman Siege of Malta (1565). Grand Commander (1582–85), Knight of the Grand Cross. General of the Galleys (1584–85). Bailiff of Manosque (1585–1603). Commander of Pézenas (1595). (1526–1603)

BROOKE, RICHARD (Richard Brooke, Mifsud's Richard Broke, Bosio's Riccardo Bruc/Brunè). English of Nantwich, Cheshire. A younger son of Thomas Brooke and Elizabeth Starkey. Nephew of Hosptaller Oliver Starkey. Knight of Jerusalem, Langue of England. Received (1528). Preceptor of Mount Saint Joseph (1534–36+). Pensioned (1540). (+1569)

CAIRADINO (Cairadino, Cairadin, Bosio's Cairadino). Brother of Corsa Reis. Barbarossa Lieutenant. Sheikh or Lord of Tagiora. (1531–36). Captures Paolo Simeoni (1531). Killed in Combat (1536). (+1536)

CAMBIANO, GIUSEPPE (Giuseppe Cambiano, Giuseppe Cambiani, Bosio's Giofeppe Cambiano). Piemontese of Ruffia. Law Studies. Knight of Malta, Langue of Italy. Received (1528). In Service to Holy See (1538). Knight Commander (NLT1551–68) of Fossano. Defense Counsel Loss of Tripoli (1551). Author (1554–56). Ambassadeur Extraordinaire Court of Spain concerning Maduro Matter (1557). Receiver at Rome (NLT 1560). Ambassador to Council of Trent (1562). Ambassador/Procurator-

General Holy See (1562–69). Admiral (1569–70), Knight of the Grand Cross. Bailiff of Venosa (1570–72). (c.1500–72).

CARAFA, VINCENZO (Vincenzo Carafa, Bosio's Vicenzo Carrafa, Pozzo's Don Vincenzo Caraffa). Italian of Terra di Lavoro in the north of the Kingdom of Naples. Brother of Hospitaller Girolamo Carafa. Knight of Malta, Langue of Italy. Received (1513). Commander. Ottoman Siege of Malta/Picolo Soccorso (1565). Prior of Hungary (1574–75, 1581–1600), Knight of the Grand Cross. Prior of Capua (1600–11). (+1611)

CARAGIALI (Caragiali, Karag Ali, Carag Alì, Cargiali, Voguedemar's Cargely, Bicheno's Kara Djaly, perhaps Crowley's Kara Deli, Bosio's Caragiali, Pozzo's Caragiali). Greco-Albanian Renegade of Lepanto. Godfather of Murat of Albania. Corsair of Algiers. Uluç Ali Lieutenant. Raids Milazzo (1563). Romegas and Gaspard de la Motte captures Caragiali lieutenant Memi Caragia and galliot (1563). Ottoman Siege of Malta (1565). Battle of Cape Passero (1570). Battle of Lepanto (1571). Captured at Lampedusa (1599). (+)

CARITAT, FOULQUES (Foulques de Caritat, Bosio's Folchetto de Caritat). French of Orange, 30km north of Avignon. Bastard son (?) of Guy de Caritat, Seigneur de Caritat, Valréas et Camaret, and Viguier (Court Magistrate) d'Orange. Younger brother(?) of Olivier IV de Caritat. Knight of Jerusalem, Langue of Provence. Received (1500). Commander of Douzens (1528–45). Commander of Pézenas (1532–52). Commander of Latronquière (1533–39). Bailiff of Lango (1539–48), Knight of the Grand Cross. Grand Commander (1540–44). Prior of Toulouse (1544–53). (+1553)

CARLEAU, PHILIPPE (Philippe de Carleau, Philippe Carleau, Philippe Karleau, Philippe Kerleau, Bosio's Filippo Carleau, Vertot's Philippes Kerleau). French of Chateau Kerlo (Chateau Kerleau), Basse Bretagne, in extreme north-west of France, 420km north-west of Nouvelle Aquitaine. A second son of Guy Kerleau (Seigneur de Gouazancarrant). Knight of Jerusalem, Langue of France. Ottoman Siege of Rhodes (1522). Commander of La Guerche et de La Nouée en Bretagne (1523–26). Treasurer (1535–36), Knight of the Grand Cross. Commander of Villedieu (1535). Grand Hospitaller (1536–37). Commander of Coulours

(1537–39) and of Chantereine (1537+). Commander of Troyes (1537–39) and of Coulommiers (1542–47). Grand Prior of France (1537–46). (+1546)

CATANEO, FRANCESCO (Francesco Cataneo, Francesco Cattaneo, Bosio's Francesco Cataneo and Giovan Francesco Cateneo.) Italian of Novara. Received (1513). Ottoman Siege of Rhodes (1522). Admiral (1555), Knight of the Grand Cross. Bailiff of Santo Stefano (1555–66). Grand Soccorso (1565). (c1496–1566)

CAVE, AMBROSE (Ambrose Cave, Bosio not cited). English. Son of Richard Cave of Stanford, Northamptonshire, by second wife Margaret Saxby of Northampton. Knight of the Order of Jerusalem, Langue of England. Received (1524). Preceptor of Stydd in Derbyshire (1532). Preceptor of Yeaveley and Barrow in Derbyshire (1531–40). Pensioned (1540). Member of Parliament for Leicestershire and then Warwickshire. Member of Elizabeth I's Privy Council. (*c*.1503–68)

CERVANTES, GONZALO (Gonzalo de Cervantes, Gonzalo Gómez de Cervantes, Bosio's Gonzalo Ceruantes). Spanish of Madrid. Knight of Jerusalem, Langue of Castile. Received (1516). Ottoman Siege of Rhodes (1522). Galley Captain (1531–34). Christian Siege of Modon (1531). Commander of Salamanca (1535–47). Homedes Elector (1536). Master of House and Seneschal (1539–47), Knight of the Grand Cross. (+)

CHÂTEAU-ARNAULD, JEAN (Jean de Château-Arnauld, Bosio's Giovanni de Casteau Arnault de Sarriat). French of Arcins, 40km north of Bordeaux, Knight of Jerusalem, Langue of Auvergne. Knight Commander. Marshal (1531–40), Knight of the Grand Cross. (+1540)

CHIEF, GABRIEL (Gabriel du Chief, Bosio's Gabriello du Chief). French of Auvergne. Brother or cousin of Hospitaller Charles du Chief. Knight of Jerusalem, Langue of Auvergne. Knight Commander (1522). Magistral Master of House (1522). Ottoman Siege of Rhodes (1522–23). Marshal (1527–31), Knight of the Grand Cross. Prior of Auvergne (1531–42). Siege of Coron (1532). (+1542)

CICALA, VINCENZO (Vincenzo Cicala, Vesconte Cicala, Setton's Cigalla, Bosio's Visconte Cicala) of a noble Genovese family related to the Cibo, the Doria, and the Lomellini. Son of Carlo. Uncle of Filippo. Father of Giulio and Scipione (Cigalazade Yusuf Sinan Pasha). Knight of the Portuguese Order of Saint James of the Sword (Ordem Militar de Sant'Iago da Espada). Maritime Condottiero. Corsair. Siege of Castelnuovo (1538). Christian Siege of Mehedia (1550). Battle of Djerba (1560). With Scipione captured by Uluç Ali (1561). Dies a captive at Constantinople (1564). (1504–64)

CLARAMÓNTE, ESTEBAN (Esteban/Estevan de Claramónte, Bosio's Stefano Claramunt, Pozzo's Stefano Claramónte). Spanish of Estadilla, Huesca, 220km north-west of Barcelona. Second son of Jerónimo de Claramunt, Lord of Artasona (Huesca), and of Felipa de Castelblanc. Knight of Malta, Langue of Aragon. Received (1553). Knight Commander (1564). Ottoman Siege of Malta (1565). Succeeds the deceased Francisco Zanoguera at The Spur on the tip of Senglea (1565). Bailiff of Caspe (1593–1605), Knight of the Grand Cross. General of the Galleys (1593–95). (+1605)

CLAVESON, ANTOINE (Antoine de Claveson, Bosio's Antonio de Claveson). French of Claveyson 80km south of Lyon. 3rd son of Geoffroy, Seigneur de Claveson, d'Hostun, et al, and of Jeanne de Bolomier. Knight of Jerusalem, Langue of Auvergne. Commander. Marshal (1523–27), Knight of the Grand Cross. (+1527)

CLUIS, PIERRE (Pierre de Cluis, Pierre de Cluys, Bosio's Pietro di Cluis). French likely of Cluis 300km south of Paris. Brother or cousin of Philippe de Cluis. Knight of Jerusalem, Langue of France, Priory of Aquitaine. Ottoman Siege of Rhodes (1480). Commander of Moissy. Treasurer (1512–1519), Knight of the Grand Cross. Great Siege of Rhodes (1522). Commander of Troyes (1523–36). Commander of Coulommiers (1523–37). Grand Prior of France (1522–35). (c.1450–1536)

COMBAULT, EMERY (Emery de Combault, Merry de Combault de Labouret, Bourbon's Mery Gombault, Bosio's Ammerigo Combaut). French of Labouret, Nouvelle-Aquitaine, 175km east of Bordeaux. Probably studied law. Knight of Jerusalem, Langue of France, Priory of Aquitaine. Commander. Procurator Langue of France (1498). Treasurer (1520), Knight of the Grand Cross. Ottoman Siege of Rhodes (1522) – Commands Grand Master's Bodyguard. Bailiff of the Morea (1522–26). (+1526)

COPONS, HUGO (Hugo de Copons, Hugues de Capons, Ugo Coppons, Bosio's Vgo di Copones). Catalan of Copons, 85km northwest of Barcelona. Knight of Jerusalem, Langue of Aragon. Commander. Galley Captain (1512). Great Siege of Rhodes (1522). Draper (1529–31), Knight of the Grand Cross. Galley Squadron Commander (1529–30). (+1531)

COPPIER, GUILLAUME (Guillaume Coppier de Poisus, Guillaume de Coppier, Gravière's Coupier and Goupier, Boissat's Copier du Daufiné, Bosio's Guglielmo Couppier de Poisus). French of Haute-Savoie. Knight of Malta, Langue of Auvergne. Standard Bearer Spanish Siege of Tunis (1535). Galley Captain (1550). Christian Siege of Mehedia (1550). Lieutenant Governor Tripoli (1551). Lieutenant Marshal and Pilier Langue of Auvergne (1555). Commander of Geneva (to 1563). Marshal (1557–67), Knight of the Grand Cross. Ottoman Siege of Malta (1565). (+1567)

CORTÈZ, GARCIA (Garcia Cortèz, Garcia Cortés, Bosio's Garzia Cortes and Garzia Cortèz). Spanish of Aragon. Knight of Jerusalem, Langue of Aragon. Ottoman Siege of Rhodes (1522). Knight Commander (NLT 1532). Lieutenant Draper (1532–36). Commander of Ascó (1533–46). Governor of Tripoli (1533–35). Procurator of the Treasury (1536). Homedes Elector (1536). Bailiff of Caspe (1536–46), Knight of the Grand Cross. (+1546)

CORTIT, LUIS (Luis Cortit, Balbi's Juan Cortis, Funes's Luys Cortit, Boissat's Louys Courtit, Bosio's Luis Cortit) of Lleida (Lérida), Catalonia. Knight of Malta, Langue of Aragon. Knight Commander. Galley Commander (1555). Regent of the Galleys (1558). Ottoman Siege of Malta (1565). Conventual Conservator (1565), Knight of the Grand Cross. Killed on Wall of Birgu (1565). (+1565)

COSCON, GERÓNIMO (Gerónimo Coscon, Bosio's Girolamo Coscon). Spanish of Aragon. Brother of Hospitaller Vendura Coscun. Knight of Jerusalem, Langue of Aragon. Great Siege of Rhodes (1522). Knight Commander. Grand Conservator (1539–41), Knight of the Grand Cross. Bailiff of Negroponte (1541–47). Bailiff of Caspe (1547). (+1547)

CUNHA, VASCO (Vasco da Cunha in Portuguese, Vasco de Acuña in Castilian, Vasco d'Acugna in Italian). Portuguese of Cunha 50km north-north-east of Porto. Brother of the Governor of Spanish Ceuta. Knight of Malta, Langue of Castile. Knight Commander. Chamberlain to Grand Master Valette (1565). Ottoman Siege of Malta (1665). Spanish Siege of Maastricht (1579). (+1579)

DOCWRA, THOMAS (Thomas Docwra, Bosio's Tommasso d'Ocrai or Tommasso Docraì, Vertot's Docray). English of Yorkshire. Second son of Richard Docwra of Bradsville, County of York. Brother of Hospitaller Launcelot Docwra. Grandson of Hospitaller Thomas Green. Knight of the Order of Jerusalem, Langue of England. Received (*c*.1474). Preceptor of Dynemore. Lieutenant Turcopolier. Prior of Ireland (1494–95), Knight of the Grand Cross. Turcopolier (1495–1501). Prior of England (1501–27). (*c*.1458–1527)

DORIA, ANDREA (Andrea Doria, Andrea d'Oria, Boissat's André Doria, Bosio's Andrea Doria). Italian of Oneglia. Second son of Ceva Doria, co-Lord of Oneglia, and Caracosa Doria. Brother of Davide, Antonio, and Violante, half-brother of Bartolomea Fieschi. Husband of Princess Peretta Uso di Mare (wed 1527), cousin of Antonio Doria (1495–1577), uncle and foster-father of Giannettino Doria (d. 1547), 'uncle' of Filippino (Filippo) Doria, Erasmo Doria, Lazzarino Doria, Bartolomeo (son of Enrichetto) Doria, Cristoforo (Doria) Pallavicini, great uncle of Giovanni Andrea (Gian Andrea) Doria (son of Giannettino), nephew of Domenico Doria. Lord of Genoa. Duke of Melfi. Aragonese Kingdom of Naples (1494–95). Genoa (1512–18). Papal Galley Commander (1526–27). France (1527–28). Spain (1528–60). Siege of Coron (1532). Lepanto Razed (1532). Battle of Anti-Paxos (1537). General of Holy League Armada (1538). Battle of Preveza (1538). Spanish Conquest of Mehedia (1550). (1466–1560)

DORIA, ANTONIO (Antonio Doria, Bosio's Gio. Antonio Doria). Italian of Genoa. Son of Battista Doria and Isotta (Isottina) Doria. Brother of Melchiorre Doria. Wed to Geronima Fieschi. Father of Cesare, Camilla, Giovanni Battista, Scipione, and Lelio Doria. Cousin of Andrea Doria, son-in-law of Brizio Giustiniani. Marquis of Santo Stefano, of Aveto, and of Ginosa. Knight of the Golden Fleece. Commander of

Papal Galleys (1531–33). Spanish Siege of Coron (1532). Spanish Siege of Tunis (1535) commanding thirty sailing vessels. Battle of Anti-Paxos (1537). Battle of Preveza (1538). Spanish Siege of Algiers (1541) with proprietary galleys. (*c.*1495–1577)

DORIA, FILIPPINO (Filippino Doria, Filippo Doria, Filippo d'Oria) of Genoa. Son of Bartolomeo Doria and Lucrezia Del Carretto. Distant relative ('nephew') of Andrea Doria. In service to Duke of Urbino (1508–16). Rescues Andrea Doria by capturing the corsair Godoli (1513). Genovese Admiral (1513–28). Commanding two galleys, he turns the tide of Andrea's looming defeat by Curtogoli off Elba (1517). Battle of Capo d'Oro (1528). *(c.*1475–*c.*1548)

DORIA, GIANNETTINO (Giannettino Doria Patrizio, Giovanni Doria, Boissat's Iannetin Doria, Bosio's Gianettino Doria) Genovese of Oneglia or Genoa. Son of Tomaso and Maria Grillo, Tomaso cousin to Andrea Doria. Adopted son of Andrea Doria. Father of Giovanni (Gian) Andrea Doria. (*c.*1510–47)

DORIA, GIAN ANDREA (Gian Andrea Doria, Giovanni Andrea Doria, Bosio's Giovan' Andrea Doria, Pozzo's Gio: Andrea Doria) Italian of Genoa. Son of Giannettino Doria and great-nephew and adopted son of Andrea Doria. Father of Giovanni Doria called Giannettino. Spain's General of the (Mediterranean) Sea, that is, of Spain's Galleys (1557). Battle of Djerba (1560). Gran Soccorso (1565). (1539–1606)

DORIA, LAMBERTO (Lamberto Doria, Bosio's Lamberto Doria). Italian of Genoa. Son of Luca Doria, Lord of Dolceacqua and Francesca Grimaldi of Monaco. Brother of Bartolomeo II Doria, Lord of Dolceacqua; Lazzaro Doria, Knight of Malta; Giovan Battista Doria; Luca Doria; and Argentina Doria. Knight of Jerusalem, Langue of Italy. Received 1515. Ottoman Siege of Rhodes (1522). Knight Commander. Lieutenant Admiral (1557–58). Bailiff of Naples (1558–69), Knight of the Grand Cross. (c.1495–1569)

DRAGUT (See Turgut)

ENRIQUEZ, DIEGO (Diego Enriquez, Diego Enriquez y Guzmán, Bosio's Don Diego Enriquez). Spanish. Bastard son of Diego Enríquez y Guzmán, 5th Count of Alba de Liste (circa 1530–1604). Knight of

Jerusalem, Langue of Castile. Lieutenant Chancellor (1561–1565), Commander of Fresno (1561+). Resident Ambassador Spain (1563–66). Bailiff of Negroponte (1565–66), Knight of the Grand Cross. (+1566)

FANTONE, CAPTAIN (Captain Fantone, Andrea Magnasco, Giovanni Andrea Magnasco, Captain Fantoni, Bosio's Capitan Fantone or Gio. Andrea Magnafco). Italian of Genoa. Sea Captain owning a merchant sailing vessel. In irregular service to Hospitallers from 1550. Ottoman Siege of Malta (1565) commanding 150 hired soldiers. Knight of Malta, Langue of Italy. Received September 1565. Lieutenant to Guion de Saugniac commanding the Grand Galleon (1565). Magistrale Capitana (1567). Killed in combat at Cerigotto (1567). (+1567)

FELIZES, PEDRO (Pedro Fernandez de Felizes della Nucia, Bosio's Pietro Felizes della Nuzza). Spanish of La Nucia in Valencia. Knight of Jerusalem, Langue of Aragon. Ottoman Siege of Rhodes (1522). Captain of Great Galleon (1540). Galley Captain (1552). Titular Bailiff of Eagle (1557–65), Knight of the Grand Cross. Ottoman Siege of Malta (1565). Commander Fort Saint Michael (1565). (+1565)

FERRER, MIGUEL (Miguel Ferrer, Miquel Ferrera i de Marimon, Bosio's Michele Ferrer). Catalan likely of Ferrera. Brother or Cousin of Hospitallers Francisco, Gaspar, and Geronimo Ferrer. Knight of the Order of Jerusalem, Langue of Aragon. Knight Commander. Bailiff of Mallorca (1529–37), Knight of the Grand Cross. Prior of Catalonia (1537–52). (+1552)

FLACH, PHILIPP (Philipp Flach von Schwarzenberg, Philippus Flach von Schwartzenberg, Bosio and Pozzo's Filippo Flach, not his lieutenant Engelbert Flach). Rhenish of the Saarland. Son of Eberhard Flach von Schwarzenberg and Amalia von Ellenbach. Knight of Malta, Langue of Germany. Received (1546). Galley Commander (1554–55). Lieutenant Grand Bailiff (1555–59). Captain-at-Arms and Governor of Notabile (1557). Knight Commander of Saint-Jean-de-Bassel and of Dorlisheim. Commander HRE Danube Armada (1566). Grand Bailiff of Germany (1571–73), Knight of the Grand Cross. General of the Galleys (1572–73). Commander of Ritterhaus Bubikon (1573–1594). Grand Prior of Germany and Imperial Prince of Heitersheim (1573–94). (c.1525–94)

FLOTTE DE LA ROCHE, ANTOINE (Antoine Flotte, Antoine Flotte de la Roche, Bosio's Antonio Flotta detto la Rocche, Balbi's Antonio Flota de la Rocha). French of Saint-André-de-la-Roche, 8km north of Nice. Third son of Georges de Flotte, Seigneur de la Roche, and Marguerite de la Tour-Sassenage. Knight of Malta, Langue of Provence. Received (1542). Commander of Espalion and Échirolles (*c*.1555). Battle of Djerba (1560). Galley Commander (1562–64). Sultana Capture (1564). Ottoman Siege of Malta (1565). Receiver-General in France (1569). (*c*.1525–Unk)

FONTAINE, GUILLAUME (Guillaume de la Fontaine d'Ognon, Captain Champagne, Bosio's Guglielmo della Fontaine/Fonteine and Capitano Chiampagne). French of Ognon 30km south-south-west of Compiègne. Nephew of Grand Prior of France Pierre de la Fontaine. Knight of Malta, Langue of France. Received (1540). Corsair in Hospitaller Service. Commander of Saint-Jean-de-Latran à Paris. Slave Raid on Zuara, Loses a Hand (1552). Corsair in Hospitaller Service (1556). Battle of Djerba (1560). Grand Soccorso (1565). Commander of Villedieu-Élancourt (1567). Battle of Saint-Denis (1567). (+1567)

FONTAINE, PIERRE (Pierre de la Fontaine, Bosio's Pietro della Fonteine, Pozzo's Pietro de la Fontaine). Third son of Pierre de la Fontaine and Jeanne de Baudry, Dame de Ognon, Malgeneste, and Villiers le Bel. Uncle of Hospitaller Guillaume de la Fontaine. Knight of Jerusalem, Langue of France. Received (1512). Ottoman Siege of Rhodes (1522). Commander of Mont-de-Soissons (1527–33). Commander of La Villedieu–en–Dreugesin (1534–48). Commander of Villedieu-Élancourt (1550–67). Commander of Chantereine (1555–73) and of Hainault-Cambrésis (1562–72). Bailiff of Lango (1555–57), Knight of the Grand Cross. Treasurer (1557–58). Grand Hospitaller (1558–62). General of the Galleys (1560–61). Prior of Champagne (1562–63). Grand Prior of France (1563–73). (1490–1573)

FORTESCUE, ADRIAN (Blessed Adrian Fortescue). English of Hertfordshire. Son of John Fortescue and Cousin of Ann Boleyn's father Thomas Boleyn, 1st Earl of Wiltshire. Knight of the Bath (1503). With Crown forces in France (1513–23). Twice wed. Knight (of Grace) of Malta, Langue of England. Received (1532). Condemned without trial of treason and executed (1539). (1476–1539)

FORTUYN, RAMÓN (Ramón de Fortuyn, Raimundo de Fortuyn, Bosio's Ramóndo Fortuyn, Pozzo's Raimondo Fortuin). Catalan of Mallorca likely the product of a Dutch-Catalan union; child of Empire. Knight of Malta, Langue of Aragon. Wounded in jaw at Zuara where commended for bravery (1552). Ottoman Siege of Malta (1565) where described as born from the womb to be an Hospitaller; at Elmo until gravely wounded. Knight Commander of Aquaviva (1569–99). Senior Commissioner of Valetta Construction (1569). General Assembly Elector (1572). Receiver General (1573). Bailiff of Negroponte (1592–1597), Knight of the Grand Cross. Grand Conservator (1597–99). Chapter General Legislator (1598). (+1599)

GASCOURT, CHARLES (Charles de Gascourt, Charles de Hesselin-Gascourt, Bosio's Carlo d'Hesselim detto Gacourt). French of Gascourt 45km north of Paris. Knight of Jerusalem, Langue of France. Received (1525). Commander. Treasurer (1562-1563), Knight of the Grand Cross. Bailiff of the Morea (1563). Prior of Aquitaine (1563–77). (+1577)

GATTINARA, SIGNORINO DELLA (Signorino della Gattinara, Signorino Arborio di Gattinara, Bosio's Signorino Gattinara). Italian of Vercelli. Son of Carlo Mercurino and of Eleonora Beccaria. Nephew of Mercurino Arborio, Grand Chancellor of Charles V. Younger brother of Filiberto Mercurino Arborio di Gattinara, heir to a vast estate. Resident Ambassador to Holy See for the Order of Saints Maurizio and Lazarus. Knight of Jerusalem, Langue of Italy. Prior of Messina (1528–67), Knight of thee Grand Cross. Captain of the Galleys (1543–45). Captain-General Hospitaller Relief Force (1565).Magistral Lieutenant. (1566–67). (+1567)

GIMEL, CLAUDE (Claude Gimel, Bosio's Claudio Gimel). French of Gimel, Switzerland. Of the family of Hospitaller Pierre Gimel, Aubusson Lieutenant Seneschal. Knight of Jerusalem, Langue of France. Commander of Blodès (Switzerland). Ottoman Siege of Rhodes (1522). Interim Captain of Galleys (1528). (+)

GIOÙ, PIERRE DE (Pierre de Gioù, Pierre de Joux, Bosio's Pietro de Gioù). French of Aveyron. Knight of Malta, Langue of Auvergne. Received (1534). Liaison to Andrea Doria at Siege of Mehedia (1550). Sengle Staff (1553–57). Seneschal (1561–63). Commander of La Marche

(1563+), of Montchamp (1561–68), and of Courtesserre (1563+). General of the Galleys (1563–65). Capture of Sultana (1564). Capture of Penon de Velez de la Gomera (1564). Ottoman Siege of Malta (1565). Bailiff of Lango (1566), Knight of the Grand Cross. Marshal (1567–68), Resident Ambassador Court of France (1568). (*c.*1517–68)

GIRON, FRANCISCO (Francisco Giron, Bosio's Francesco Giron). Spanish likely of Girona. Brother or cousin of Hospitaller Ernando Giron. Knight of Jerusalem, Langue of Castile. Galley Captain (1534–35). In on capture of a galleon, later the Order's Grand Galleon of Alexandria (1534). Spanish Siege of Tunis (1535). Galley Battle of Zuara (1536). Commander of Ciudad Rodrigo (1540+). Commands new Barque of the Religion (1540). Sails new Flanders-built *Barcia of the Religion* unscathed through Barbarossa's Ottoman Armada (1543). (+)

GIUSTINIANI, PIETRO (Pietro Giustiniani, Bosio's Pietro Giuftiniani; Pozzo's Pietro Giuftiniano). Italian of Venice. Son of Paolo Giustiniani of Candia and Rhodes. Knight of Jerusalem, Langue of Italy. Received as a minor (1523). Ottoman Siege of Malta (1565) where he is wounded defending fort Saint Michael. Admiral (1566), Knight of the Grand Cross. Prior of Messina (1567–86). General of the Galleys (1570–72). (+1586)

GLIOR, GASPAR (Gaspar Glior, Bosio's Gafparo/Gafpare Glior). Catalan. Brother or Cousin of Hospitaller Don Garcia Glior. Knight of Jerusalem, Langue of Aragon. Ottoman Siege of Rhodes (1522). Captain of Reserves Tower of Saint Nicholas (1522). Represents Aragon in eight-member team surveying Malta, Gozo, and Tripoli (1524). Commander of Tortosa (1525–29). Draper (1528–29). (+1529)

GONSON, DAVID (David Gonson, David Gunston, Davy Gonson, Blessed David Gonson, Bosio's Dauid Gofm). English of Deptford, Kent. Fourth son of Vice-Admiral William Gonson and Bennet Walter. Knight of Malta, Langue of England. Received (1533). Imprisoned Gozo for duelling (1535). Martyred (1541). Beatified (1929).(1510–41)

GONZAGA, GIOVANNI VINCENZO (Giovanni Vincenzo Gonzaga, Gian Vincenzo Gonzaga, Bosio's Vicenzo Gonzaga). Fourth son of Don Ferrante Gonzaga, Prince of Molsetta and Viceroy of

Sicily, and of Isabella di Capua. Younger brother of Hospitaller Andrea Gonzaga. Knight of Malta, Langue of Italy. Received at age two (1542). Commander. Prior of Barletta (1556–91), Knight of the Grand Cross. General of the Galleys (1562–63). Cardinal of the Roman Catholic Church (1578–91). (1540–91)

GOUTTE, MARC (Marc de la Goutte, Bosio's Marco della Goutte, Pozzo's Marco de la Goutte). French of La Goutte, 210km west-north-west of Lyon. Knight of Malta, Langue of Auvergne. Commander of Les Salles (Auvergne-Rhone-Alps), 100km west of Lyon. Tripoli Garrison (1551). Commander of Selles (1561). Galley Captain (1561–62). Receiver at Lyon (1565). Marshal (1572–74), Knight of the Grand Cross. Bailiff of Lyon (1574–89). Commander of Ormeteau (1576–81). Commander of Montredon (1589). (+ 1589)

GOZON-MÉLAC, FRANÇOIS (François de Gozon-Mélac, François de Gozon, Bosio's Francesco de Gozon detto Melac). French of Chateau de Melac a Saint-Rome-de-Cernon, 165km north-east of Toulouse. Brother of Hospitaller Pierre de Gozon-Mélac. Knight of Jerusalem, Langue of Provence. Siege of Algiers (1541). Galley Captain (1549–50). Commander of Argentens (1550–63). Christian Siege of Mehedia (1550). Commander of Bordeaux (1558–74). Bailiff of Manosque (1563–78), Knight of the Grand Cross. (+1578)

GOZON-MÉLAC, PIERRE (Pierre de Gozon-Mélac, Bosio's Pietro de Gozon detto Melac). French of Rouergue. Directly descended from Dieudonné de Gozon, father of the twenty-seventh Grand Master of the Order of Jerusalem (1346–53) of the same name. Second son of Raymond de Gozon, Sieur de Gozon, de Mélac, et de Saint-Victor, and Béatrix Carmaul. Brother of Hospitaller Jean-Pierre de Gozon-Mélac (Commander of Sainte-Geneviève-sur-Argence) and uncle of Hospitaller Bernard de Gozon-Mélac (Commander of Canabières). Knight of Jerusalem, Langue of Provence. Received (1516). Ottoman Siege of Rhodes (1522). Galley Commander (1544). Lieutenant Grand Commander (1546–57). Captain Barque of the Religion (1547–48). Commander of Canabières (1548–51). Commander of Golfech and Montsaunès (1553–56). Regent-General of the Galleys (1556–57). Grand Commander (1557–58), Knight of the Grand Cross. Commander of

Montsaunès (1558–59). Prior of Saint-Gilles (1558–62). General of the Galleys (1561–62) (+1562)

GROLÉE, ANTOINE (Antoine de Grolée, Antoine de Grolée de Passim, Vertot's Antoine de Colee dit Passim, Setton's Antoine de Grollée, Bosio's Antonio de Grolea detto Paffim or Baglivo Paffim, Antoine de Groslée). French of Groslée in the Haute Savoy, 80km east of Lyon. Knight of Jerusalem, Langue of Auvergne. Commander of Salins (1521–38). Ottoman Siege of Rhodes (1522). Commander of Sainte-Anne (1533–39). Bailiff of Lango (1533–39), Knight of the Grand Cross. Spanish Siege of Tunis (1535). Commander of L'Aumusse (1540–44). Bailiff of (Saint-George de) Lyon (1539–44). (+1544)

GRUEL, CLAUDE (Claude de Gruel, Claude de Gruel de Laborel, Claude de Gruel de la Bourelli, Bosio's Claudio Gruel detto Laborel). French of Laborel, 110km north-east of Avignon. Fifth son of Henri de Laborel de Gruel, Seigneur de Laborel, and of Jeanne Baume de Suze. Knight of Jerusalem, Langue of Provence. Galley Captain (1524). Commander of Marestaing (1531–34). Commander of Lormont (1531–47). Commander of Bourdeaux (1540–47). Commander of Arveyres (1541–49). Grand Commander (1551–53), Knight of the Grand Cross. Magistral Lieutenant to Grand Masters Juan de Homedes and Claude de la Sengle (1536–55). Prior of Toulouse (1553–55). (+1555)

GUETE, GERONIMO (Geronimo de Guete, Geronimo de Huete, Bosio's Girolamo de Guete/Guette, Funes's Ieronimo de Guete, Pozzo's Girolamo de Guette). Navarese of Huete. Knight of Malta, Langue of Aragon. Galley Captain (1545). Captain of Great Galleon (1558–59). Grand Conservator (1570–74), Knight of the Grand Cross. Resident Ambassador to Holy See (1573–74). Castellan of Amposta (1573–75). (+1575)

GUÈVRE, ANTOINE (Antoine de Guèvre, Antoine de Guèvre le Vigneron, Mifsud's Antonio Gaufre nicknamed Vinadiera or Anthony Gaufre, Catalogue's Antoine de Guèvre, Boissat's Antoyne de Geoffroy detto la Vinadiere, Bosio's Antonio Geuffrè detto la Vinadiera). Of mixed French and Scottish parentage. Elder Brother of Hospitaller Etienne de Guèvre of the Langue of Provence. Received as Serving Brother or as Awaiting Proofs of Knighthood, Langue of England

(1546). Scribe. Linguist. Historian. Commander. Secretary to Claude de la Sengle (1549). Interim Ambassador to Rome (1549). Received as a Knight of Grace born in France (1554). Lieutenant Turcopolier (1555–56). (+1556)

GUIMERAN, BERNARDO (Bernardo de Guimeran, Bernat de Guimeran, Bosio's Don Bernardo de Guimeran). Catalan of Guimerà. Knight of the Order of Malta, Langue of Aragon. Gravely wounded Susa assault (1538). Galley Captain (1549–51). Christian Siege of Mehedia (1550). Maltese assault on Zuara (1552). Resident Ambassador to Spain (1557–61). Captain-General Galleys of Sicily (1561). (+1561)

GUIRAL, FRANCISCO (Francisco de Guiral, Bosio's Francesco de Guiral). Spanish. Knight of Malta, Langue of Castile. Received (1535). Knight Commander. Galley Captain (1564–67). Siege of Malta (1565). Castellan of Castile (1570). Bailiff of Negroponte (1580–82), Knight of the Grand Cross. Grand Chancellor (1582–83). (*c.*1517–83)

HANGEST, CHARLES (Charles de Hangest, Charles de Hangest du Mesnil Saint Georges, Bosio's Carlo d'Angest). French of Hangest-sur-Somme, 160km north of Paris. Eldest son of Bon de Hangest (d. 1546), Seigneur du Mesnil-Saint-Georges, du Mesnil-Saint-Firmin, et al, and of Marguerite Marie de Brouilly-Mesvillers. Knight of Jerusalem, Langue of France. Received (1526). Commander of Sommereux (1542–61), of Hainaut-Cambrésis, and of Boncourt (1558+). Seneschal (1554–58+), Knight of the Grand Cross. Lieutenant Treasurer (1558). (+)

HASSAN BARBAROSSA (Hassan/Hasan Pasha). Son of Kheir-ed-Din Barbarossa, son-in-law of Dragut (according to Haedo at *Morgan I-432n* but father-in-law of Dragut daughter according to *Bosio III-624*), son-in-law of the King of Kuku (according to Morgan). Father of Hassan Bey or Mohammad Reis (?). Battle of Preveza (1538). Beylerbey of Algiers (1545–51), (1557–61), and (1562–67). Ottoman Siege of Malta (1565). Battle of Lepanto (1571). (1517–71)

HASSAN OF SARDINIA (Hassan of Sardinia, Hassan Aga/Assan Aga, Bosio's Affan Aga and Sardo). Sardinian of Asinara. Adopted son of Khizr Barbarossa at Djidjelli (1514). Eunuch. Renegade. Barbary Corsair. Barbarossa Siege of Tunis (1534). Spanish Siege of Tunis (1535).

Pasha and later Ottoman Beylerbey of Algiers (1535–43). Spanish Siege of Algiers (1541). Dies of fever at Algiers. (+1543)

HEREDIA, PEDRO FERNÁNDEZ (Pedro Fernández de Heredia the Younger, Bosio's Don Pietro Fernandez d'Eredia). Spanish likely of Zaragoza. All Fernandez de Heredia are descended from either Blasco or younger brother Juan; which brother in this case is unknown. Knight of Jerusalem, Langue of Aragon. Imperial Ambassador to Convent and to Holy See (1525). Flees Convent to Usurp Commandery of Alfambra (1533) as Prior. Defrocked (1533). Reinstated by Pope Paul III as Prior of Alfambra (1535). Paul III reverses himself as Emperor proves mightier than Pope (1536). (+)

HISAR REIS (Hisar Reis, Kizir Reis, Morgan's Aisa Rais, Bosio's Efsè Reis of Anatolia). Nephew of Dragut by Dragut's sister. Barbary Corsair. Governor of Mehedia (1550). Christian Siege of Mehedia (1550). Christian captive (1550–51). Swapped for Dragut captive Giulio Cicala (1552). (+)

HOMEDES, GERONIMO (Geronimo de Homedes, Bosio's Girolamo d'Omedes, Pozzo's Girolamo d'Homedes). Catalan of Zaragoza. Son of leading citizen of Zaragoza Don Miguel de Homedes. Nephew of Grand Master Juan de Homedes y Coscon. Brother of Hospitaller Miguel de Homedes. Knight of Malta, Langue of Aragon. Galley Captain (1560–62). Grand Soccorso (1565). Bailiff of Negroponte (1582–84), Knight of the Grand Cross. Grand Conservator (1584–86). Bailiff of Caspe (1587-1593). General of the Galleys (1589-–91). (+1593)

HOMEDES, JUAN (Juan de Homedes y Coscon, Boissat's Iean d'Omedes, Bosio's Giovanni d'Omedes). Catalan of Zaragoza. Brother of leading citizen of Zaragoza Don Miguel de Homedes, cousin of Francisco de Homedes, uncle of Hospitallers Miguel and Geronimo de Homedes. Knight of Jerusalem, Langue of Aragon. Commander. Ottoman Siege of Rhodes (1522). Draper (1523–27), Knight of the Grand Cross. Bailiff of Caspe (1527–36). Commander of Santa Maria in Trastevere (Rome) and forty-seventh Grand Master of the Order of Jerusalem (1536–53) (1473–Commander of Santa Maria in Trastevere (Rome) and forty-seventh Grand Master of the Order of Jerusalem (1536–53) 1553)

HUSSEY, NICHOLAS (Nicholas Hussey, Nicolao Vsil, Bourbon's Nicolle Hufy, Revue's Huzi, Bosio's Nicolo Husij or Heuffoy). English. Seventh son of Thomas Hussey of Dorset and Christiane Fitzjames of Somerset. Cousin of Edmund and James Hussey. Knight of Jerusalem, Langue of England. Ottoman Siege of Rhodes (1522). Preceptor of Carbrooke (1523–29). Tripoli Feasibilility Inspector (1524). Preceptor of Anstey and Trebigth and of Templebruck. Lieutenant Turcopolier (1529–31). (+1531)

KANDELISSÙ DELI (Kandelissù Deli, Candelizza Deli, Morgan's Candalisa or Candalifa), Bosio's Vlucciali Candelizza). Morgan's old Greek renegade, experienced, cruel, blood-thirsty, but incomparable seaman. "Deli" means "Mad." Barbarossa protégé, Corsair Captain. Vice-Regal Lieutenant at Algiers. Ottoman Siege of Malta (1565). (+1565)

KARA MUSTAFA OF MITILINI (Kara Mustafa, Mustafa Reis, Bosio's Cara Moftafà). Greek of Eski Foça (Greek Phocaia). Ottoman Corsair. Galliot captain (1536–41+). Dragut Lieutenant. Captures Parisot de la Valette (1541). Ottoman Siege of Tripoli (1551). Navigation Pilot (1558–60). Battle of Djerba (1560). Ottoman Sanjakbey (Governor) of Mitilini (1560+). 'Kara' means 'black' in modern Turkish, but alternatively meant 'brave' or 'strong' in old Turkish. The sobriquet 'Kara', a frequent occurrence in Turkish lore, implies the highest degree of manly beauty when applied to a person. (+*c.*1570)

KIZILAHMEDLI MUSTAFA PASHA (Kizilahmedli Mustafa Pasha, Mustafa Pasha, Bosio's Mostafa Bascia) Turkish of Sinop. Son of Mirza Mehmet Bey and Beyazid II's daughter Kamer Sultan. Fourth Vizier (1565). Serdar or Commander of Landed Forces at Siege of Malta (1565). Commander under Suleiman at the Siege of Hungarian Szigetvár (1566). Retired (1566). (+)

LALA MUSTAFA PASHA (Lala Mustafa Pasha, Mustafa Pasha, Lala Kara Mustafa Pasha) Bosniac of Sokolac (Sarajevo). Younger brother of Deli Husrev Pasha. Topkapi Palace Education (Endurun Kolej). Janissary. Sancakbey of Damascus. Serdar or Commander of landed forces at conquest of Venetian Cyprus (1570–71) and in campaign against Georgia and Persia (1578). Fifth Vizier. Grand Vizier (1580). (*c.*1500–80)

LA MOTTE, GASPARD (Gaspard de La Motte, Bosio's Gaspare della Motta). French of La Motte-Saint-Jean. Probably a 2nd son of Renaud-Lourdin de Coligny, Baron of La Motte-Saint-Jean and Jacqueline de Montboissier. Knight of Malta, Langue of Provence. Received (1547). Captain of Magistral Galleon (1562). Captain of Magistral Padrona (1563–65). Captain of Captured Sultana (1565). Ottoman Siege of Malta (1565). (*c.*1526–65)

LANNOY, CHARLES (Charles de Lannoy, Bosio Not Cited). French of Mingoval, Flanders, (now French). Younger Son of Jean IV de Lannoy, Lord of Mingoval, and of Philipotte de Lalaing, who died giving him birth. Wed (1509–27) to Francoise de Montbel with several children. Soldier and statesman in service to the Habsburg Empire. Knight of the Golden Fleece. Prince of Sulmona. Count of Lannoy (1526–27). Commander of Imperial Forces in Italy (1526–27). (*c.*1487–1527)

LASTIC, LOUIS (Louis de Lastic, Bosio's Luis de Laftic). French of Lastic, Puy-de-Dome, Auvergne, 230km west of Lyon. Fourth son and sixth of at least nine children of Louis de Lastic, Baron de Lastic et de Rochegude, and of Anne Motier de La Fayette. Great Nephew of Grand Master Jean de Lastic. Knight of Jerusalem, Langue of Auvergne. Received (1523). Commander of Lavaufranche (1547). Commander of Bourganeuf (1547–76). Marshal (1554–57), Knight of the Grand Cross. Grand Prior of Auvergne (1557–76). (1505–76)

L'ISLE-ADAM, PHILIPPE VILLIERS (Philippe Villiers de l'Isle-Adam, Bosio's Filippo di Villers Lisleadamo). French of Beauvais, Ile de France, 80km north-north-west of Paris. Eighth child and fifth son of Jacques de Villiers, Seigneur de l'Isle-Adam, and Jeanne de Clermont-Nesle. Distant kin of Grand Master Jean de Villiers (1285–93). Uncle of Hospitaller Jacques de Wignacourt. Knight of Jerusalem, Langue of France. Commander of Coulours (1499–1522) and of Troyes (1499–1523). Commander of Croix-en-Brie (1504–15). Captain of Ships (1510). Seneschal to Grand Master Emery d'Amboise (1510), Knight of the Grand Cross. Commander of Saint-Maulvis (1510–34). Bailiff of the Morea (1511–12). Grand Hospitaller (1512–21). Visitor, Corrector, Lieutenant, and Ambassador in France of the Grand Master and Convent (1513–19). Resident Ambassador to France (1519–21). Forty-fourth Grand Master of the Order of Saint John of Jerusalem (1521–34). (1459–1534)

LUSSAN, PIERRE (Pierre d'Esparbez de Lussan, Bosio's Pietro de Sparvier detto Luffan). French of Lussan 55km NW of Avignon. Sixth son of Bertrand d'Esparbez and Louise de Sainte-Felix. Knight of Malta, Langue of Provence. Received (1560). Ottoman Siege of Malta (1565). Captain Magistral Galliot (1567–68). Siege of Zuaga (1567). Commander of Golfech (1583–1617) and Argentens (1583–1617). Resident Ambassador to France (1585–88), Knight of the Grand Cross. Grand Commander (1600–02). Prior of Saint-Gilles (1602–21). Retired (1621). (*c*.1542–*c*.1622)

MAILLOC SACQUENVILLE, LOUIS (Louis de Mailloc Sacquenville, Louis de Mailloc-Sacquenville, Boissat's Commandeur de Sacquenuille, Bosio's Luis de Mailloc detto Sacquenuille/Saquenuille, Balbi's Saquavilla, Pozzo's Lodovico Mailloc Sacquenuille). French of Sacquenville (50km south of Rouen), Normandy. Apparently second son of Jehan de Mailloc, Seigneur de Sacquenville, and Perrine de Pardieu. Knight of Malta, Langue of France. Received (1540). Commander of La Villedieu–en–Dreugesin (1560–61). Commander of Sainte-Vaubourg Normandy (1565–75). Master of House/Seneschal (1565–68). Ottoman Siege of Malta (1565). Receiver in France (1568). Commander of La Croix-en-Brie (1569–92). Commander of Saint-Maulvis (1570). Romegas Disciple (1581). Lieutenant Treasurer (1583). Bailiff of the Morea (1587–92), Knight of the Grand Cross. General of the Galleys (1587–89). (*c*.1523–92)

MAIMÓN, ADRIÀ (Adrià Maimón, Adrián de Maimón, Tuerto (One-Eye), Bosio's Adriano Maimon and Adrian Maymon, Pozzo's Adriano de Maimon). Catalan of Vélez Blanco 140km west of Cartagena. Knight of Malta, Langue of Aragon. Received (c.1540). Loses eye in Combat at Sea (1542). Malta-flag Corsair (1554). Ottoman Siege of Malta (1565). Knight Commander. Bailiff of Negroponte (1584–86), Knight of the Grand Cross. Grand Conservator (1586–97). Prior of Catalonia (1587–1601). (+1601)

MALDONADO, ANTONIO (Antonio Maldonado, Bosio's Antonio Maldonado). Spanish. Knight of Malta, Langue of Castile. Auditor of Accounts (1559). Galley Captain (1559–60). Lieutenant Grand Chancellor (1560). Regent of the Galleys (1560). Ottoman Siege of

Malta (1565). Commander of Fresno (1566–68+). Resident Ambassador Spain (1566–67, 1568–69, 1570–73). Commander of La Bamba (1560–73+). Grand Chancellor (1577–82), Knight of the Grand Cross. General of the Galleys (1577–79). Bailiff of Novaville (1582–84). Bailiff of Lora (1584–92). (+1592)

MARQUET, RAMÓN (Ramón Marquet, Raimon Marquet, Bosio's Raimondo Marquet). Catalan. Brother or cousin of Hospitallers Bernardo and Guerau Marquet. Knight of Jerusalem, Langue of Aragon. Knight Commander. Commander (to 1523). Hospitaller Ambassador to Ottoman Porte (1522). Ottoman Siege of Rhodes (1522), Commands a 150-man Reserve (1522). Bailiff of Negroponte (1523–26), Knight of the Grand Cross. Prior of Catalonia (1526–29). (+ 1529)

MARTINENGO, GABRIEL TADINO (Gabriele Tadino di Martinengo, Gabriele Tadini da Martinengo, Bosio's Gabriello Tadini Martinengo). Italian of Martinengo. Son of Clemente Tadino, brother of Girolamo, cousin of Fabrizio. Military Engineer. Condottiero. Knight of Jerusalem, Langue of Italy. Knight of the Grand Cross (1522). Commander of Santo Stefano a Conversano (1523–24). Prior of Pisa (1523). Bailiff of Santo Stefano (1523–24). Prior of Barletta (1524–43). (1475–1543)

MASSINBERT, OSWALD (Oswald Massinbert, Oswald Massingberd, Porter's Massingbert, Mifsud's Massingberd, Bosio's Vfuardo Mafimbert). English of Sutton, Lincolnshire. Second son of Sir Thomas Massinbert of Sutton (later himself an Hospitaller) and Joan Braytoft of Braytoft, Lincolnshire. Knight of Jerusalem, Langue of England. Defrocked (1534). Preceptor of Yeaveley and Barrow (+1540–43+). Fraternal Charity (1541+). Prior of Ireland w/o Grand Cross/ Preceptor of Kilmainham (1547–58). Lieutenant Turcopolier (1548–53+). (+c1573)

MASSUÉS-VERCOIRAN, PIERRE (Pierre de Massués-Vercoiran, Pierre de Massuez, Colonel Mas, Bosio's Pietro de Masues detto le Mas). French of Vercoiran. Elder brother of Hospitaller Louis. Knight of Malta, Langue of Provence. Knight Commander. Ambassador to the Christian King (1557). Galley Captain (1558–59). Commander of Ground Forces (1559–60). Battle of Djerba (1560). Ottoman captive (1560). Ottoman

Siege of Malta (1565). He and brother Louis killed at Fort Saint Elmo (1565). (+1565)

MELO, TRISTÁN (Tristán de Melo, Tristão de Melo, Tristan de Merle, Tristan de Marle, Bosio's Triftan de Melo). Portuguese of Melo. Knight of Malta, Langue of Castile. Corsair. Galley Captain (1536–38). Battle of Anti-Paxos (1537). Spanish Siege of Susa (1538). (+1538)

MENDOZA, PEDRO GONZALEZ (Pedro de Mendoza, Pedro González de Mendoza the Elder, Bosio's Pietro de Mendozza). Spanish of Guadalajara. Uncle of Hospitallers Don Garcia de Mendoza (received 1559) and Don Bernardino de Mendoza (received 1568). Knight of Jerusalem, Langue of Castile. Received (1519). Commander. Galley Commander (1555–56). Procurator of the Treasury (1557+). Lieutenant Grand Chancellor (ended 1558 and from 1563). Capitulary Bailiff and Pilier (1558), Knight of the Grand Cross. Resident Ambassador Sicily (1559+). Captain Post of Castile at Siege of Malta (1565). General of the Galleys (1566–67). (+1568)

MONCADA, HUGO DE (Hugo de Moncada, Ugo de Moncada, Bosio's Don Vgo di Moncada). Catalan of Chiva, Valencia. Fourth son of Pedro Moncada, Lord of Aitona (Catalonia), and of Beatrice de Cardona. French soldier. Governor of Spanish Calabria (1506). Spanish Admiral and General. Viceroy of Sicily (1509–17). Admiral of Naples (1517+). Failed Siege of Algiers (1519). Viceroy of Naples (1527–28). Knight of Jerusalem, Langue of Aragon. Bailiff of Santa Eufemia (to 1505, 1509–28), Knight of the Grand Cross. Prior of Messina (1507–26). Deprived of Habit (1526). Battle of Capo d'Orso (1528). (*c.*1478–1528)

MONTSERRAT, PEDRO DE (Pedro de Montserrat, Pedro de Montserrat y Berga, Bosio's Pietro de Monserrat). Spanish of Canet, Maestrazgo de Montesa, Valencia. Third son of Pedro de Montserrat Sebastián and of Sibila Berga y Cervera. Elder brother of Hospitaller Melchor de Montserrat. Knight of Jerusalem, Langue of Aragon. Great Siege of Rhodes (1522). Commander of Ambel. Grand Conservator (1552–56), Knight of the Grand Cross. Ambassador to the Imperial and English Courts (1555–56). (+1556)

MONTE, PIETRO DEL (Pietro del Monte, Pierino del Monte, Morgan's Monti, Bosio's Pietro di Monte). Italian of San Savino. First born of Margherita del Monte and of Checco di Cristofano Guidalotti at Monte San Savino, Tuscany. Cousin of Pope Julius III. Nephew of Cardinal Antonio Del Monte. Uncle of Hospitallers Carlo Sforza and Antonio del Monte. Knight of Jerusalem, Langue of Italy. Castellan of Rome's Castel Sant'Angelo (1550–55). Admiral (1555–65), Knight of the Grand Cross. General of the Galleys (1558). Prior of Capua (1565–68). Ambassador to Holy See (1566–68). Forty-ninth Grand Master of the Order of Jerusalem (1568–72). (1495–1572)

MONTGAUDRY, CHRISTOPHE (Christophe le Bouleur de Montgaudry the Younger, Bosio's Chriftofano le Bouleur detto Montgauldri, Pozzo's Christoforo de Montgaudry). French of Normandy and Paris. Knight of Malta, Langue of France. Doria's Siege of Monastir (1550). Doria's Siege of Mehedia (1550). Commander of Saint-Étienne-de-Renneville (1553–79). Sengle's Master of the House (1554). Procurator-General in France (1556). Bailiff of Lango (1569–71), Knight of the Grand Cross. Treasurer (1571–76). General of the Galleys (1573–75). Grand Hospitaller (1576–77), Pilier Langue of France (1576–77). (+c.1577).

MOTTA, GIOVAN FRANCESCO DELLA (Giovan Francesco Langosco de Conti della Motta) of Vercelli. Uncle or Cousin of Hospitaller Girolamo Langosco della Motta. Knight of Malta, Langue of Italy. Received 1541. Receiver for Grand Master Valette (1565). Ottoman Siege of Malta (1565). Conventual Conservator (1565–68), Knight of the Grand Cross. Seneschal to Grand Master Del Monte (1568). Commander of Polizzi Generosa (1568). Resident Ambassador to the Holy See (1568–73). Admiral (1583). Bailiff of Naples (1583–84). (+1584)

MOTTE, GASPARD DE LA (Gaspard de la Motte, Bosio's Gaspare della Motta). French of La Motte-Saint-Jean. Probably a second son of Renaud-Lourdin de Coligny, Baron of Motte-Saint-Jean and Jacqueline de Montboissier. Knight of Malta, Langue of Provence. Received (1547). Captain of Magistral Galleon (1562). Captain of Magistral Padrona (1563–65). Sultana Capture (1564). Captain of captured sultana (1565).

Ottoman Siege of Malta (1565). Mortally wounded Fort Saint Elmo (1565). (*c.*1526–65)

MOURAD AGA (Mourad Aga, Mourat Aga, Murat, Murad, Boissat's Morat Aga, Bosio's Morat Aga). Slav of Ragusa. Eunuch. Endurun Kolej Graduate. Renegade. Barbarossa Kaya. Pasha of Tunis (1534–35). Pasha of Tagiora and of Tripoli (1538–53). Pasha of Tagiora (1553–60). (+*c.*1560)

NIBBIA, FRANCESCO (Francesco Maria Nibbia, Bosio's Francesco Nibbia). Italian of Novara. Son of Giovanni Maria Nibbia and elder brother of Hospitaller Giovan Battista Nibbia. Knight of Jerusalem, Langue of Italy. Received (1502). Ottoman Siege of Rhodes (1522). Commander. Galley Captain (1531). Siege of Modon (1531). Brigantine Scout (1536). Commissioner investigating Gozo population enslavement (1551). Commissioner investigating loss of Tripoli (1551). (+)

NONE, ERCOLE DI (Ercole di None, Heracles di None, Ercole di Piossasch di None, Bosio's Ercole di Non). Savoyard of Turin. Knight of the Order of Jerusalem, Langue of Italy. Received (1502). Commander (*c.*1517–36). Ambassador to Savoy (1528). Admiral (1530–31). Knight of the Grand Cross. Interim Captain of Galleys (1530–31). Prior of Lombardia (1531–35). (+1535)

ORDAS, LOPE DE (Lope de Ordas, Bosio's Lope de Ordas). Spanish likely of Ordes, Galicia, 25km south of A Coruña on the sea. Knight of Jerusalem, Langue of Castile. Brigantine Commander (1533–34). Captain *Galleon of Alexandria* (1534–36). Galley Commander (1539). (+)

ORSINI, GENTILE VIRGINIO (Virginio dell'Anguillara, Bosio's Virginio Orfino). Count of Anguillara (on Lake Bracciano near Rome). Lord of Monterano (includes Montevirginio, also near Rome), Stigliano, Cerveteri, and Ceri. Son of Carlo Orsini and Portia Savelli. Grandson of Gentile Virginio Orsini and Giustiniana Orsini of Salerno. Father of Maddalena and Caterina. Commander and Papal Legate of Papal Naval Forces (1534–48). Spanish Siege of Tunis (1535). Battle of Preveza (1538). Knight of French Order of Saint Michael. (*c.*1497–1548)

PELLOQUIN, JACQUES (Jacques de Pelloquin, Boissat's Iaques Pelloquin, Bosio's Iacomo de Pelloquin). French of Vienne, Nouvelle Aquitaine. Knight of Jerusalem, Langue of France, Priory of Aquitaine.

Carretto Elector (1513). Commander of Roches (1523+). Lieutenant Treasurer (1529). Lieutenant Hospitaller (1533). Treasurer (1534), Knight of the Grand Cross. Bailiff of the Morea (1534–35). Grand Hospitaller (1535–36). Magistral Lieutenant (1535–36). Prior of Aquitaine (1536–59). (*c.*1488–1559)

PIALI PASHA (Piali Pasha, Pyali Paşa, Bosio's Pialì Bascià) Croatian from Viganj. Endurun Kolej (Topkapi Palace) Education. Husband of Sultana Gevher Han, daughter of Suleiman son Selim II. Father of Bey of Alexandria Mahaceret (or Mahomet). Sancakbey of Gallipoli (1554). Bahriye Beylerbeyi or First Lord of Admiralty (1554). Kapudan Pasha (1554–67, 1571). Battle of Djerba (1560). Naval Command Ottoman Siege of Malta (1565). Commands naval force supporting invasion and seizure of Cyprus (1570). Ottoman Armada Command (1572). (*c.*1515–78)

PIÉDEFER, FRANÇOIS (François de Piédefer, Bosio's Francesco de Piedefert). French of Champlost, 170km south-east of Paris. Second of nine sons and two sisters, the offspring of Pierre Piédefer, Seigneur de Champlost, and Charlotte de Neuf-Chastel. Brother of Hospitallers Pierre and Christophe. Uncle of Hospitaller François de Chaumont. Knight of Jerusalem, Langue of France. Received (1510). Commander of La Croix en Brie (1527–45). Chatelain of Malta (1544). Lieutenant Treasurer (1543 and 1546–50). Lieutenant Grand Hospitaller (1544–51). Commander of Boncourt (1551–57). Regent Captain of Galleys (1551–52). Lieutenant Grand Hospitaller (1553). Grand Hospitaller (1553–57), Knight of the Grand Cross. Prior of Aquitaine (1557). Prior of Champagne (1557–62). (*c.*1492–1562)

POLE, ALBAN (Alban Pole, Bosio's Albon Polo). English of Derbyshire. Younger son of Ralph and Elizabeth Pole. Cousin of Hospitaller Henry Pole. Knight of Jerusalem, Langue of England. Received at Rhodes (1500). Preceptor of Mount St John (1520+) and later of Newland, Ossington, and Winklebourne. Bailiff of Eagle (1524–30), Knight of the Grand Cross. (+1530)

POLE, HENRY (Henry Pole, Henry Poole, Harry Poole, Mifsud's Henry Pole, Bosio's Enrico Polo). English of Derbyshire. Eldest son of Henry Pole of Chesterfield, Derbyshire, by Ursula, daughter and heiress of Thomas Twyford of Kirk Langley. Cousin of Alban Pole. Knight of

Jerusalem, Langue of England. Preceptor of Dalby and Rothley (1535–40). Lieutenant Turcopolier (1534+). (1507–59)

PONT, LOUIS DU (Louis du Pont. Louis Dupont, Bosio's Luigi Pont). French of the Haute-Garonne, near Toulouse. Likely an older Brother of Hospitaller Charles du Pont. Knight of Jerusalem, Langue of Provence. Ottoman Siege of Rhodes (1522). Galley Captain (1541). Commander of Latronquière (1544–50). Grand Commander (1560–62). Prior of Saint-Gilles (1562–68). Ottoman Siege of Malta (1565). (+1568)

PONTE, PIERO DEL (Piero del Ponte, Pierino del Ponte, Bosio's Pietrino del Ponte). Italian of Asti in the Piedmont. Younger son of Antonio Giovanni del Ponte, Lord of Castellero and Lombriasco, and Luisa di San Martino di Agliè. Knight of Jerusalem, Langue of Italy. Received at birth (1462). Commander of Pancalieri (1501). Receiver-General Langue of Italy (1501). Governor of the Tower of Saint Nicholas (1503). Governor of Lango (1522). Seneschal (1523–34). Bailiff of Lango (1524–28), Knight of the Grand Cross. Bailiff of Santa Eufemia (1530–34). Forty-fifth Grand Master of the Order of Jerusalem (1534–35). (1462–1535)

POZZO, BARTELOMEO DAL Italian of Verona. Son of Vincenzo and Margherita Moscarda. Brother of Hospitaller Vincenzo dal Pozzo. Uncle of Hospitaller Giacomo dal Pozzo. Knight of Malta, Langue of Italy. Commander/Bailiff of San Giovanni a Mare di Napoli. Knight of the Grand Cross. Historian. (1637–1722)

RAWSON, JOHN (John Rawson the Elder, John Rauson, Mifsud's John Rawson, Bosio's Giouanni Ranfon/Giovanni Ranson). English of Yorkshire. Eldest son of Richard Rawson and Isabella Craford. Brother of Hospitaller Thomas Rawson, Preceptor of Quenington. Father of Hospitaller John Rawson the Younger. Knight of Jerusalem, Langue of England. Received (1497). Prior of Ireland/Preceptor of Kilmainham (1511–27), Knight of the Grand Cross. Turcopolier (1527–28). Preceptor of Dinsmore (1527–28). Prior of Ireland/Preceptor of Kilmainham (1528–47). Preceptor of Ribston and Kilmainham (1529). 1st Viscount Clontarf (1541–47). (*c.*1470–1547)

RAWSON, JOHN (John Rawson the Younger, Mifsud's John Rawson, Bosio's Giovanni Ranfon il giouane). English of Yorkshire. Son of John Rawson Sr. Nephew of Hospitaller Thomas Rawson. Serving Brother, then Knight (1527) as Brother of John Rawson, Sr. With proofs challenged, he was as Son of John Rawson, Sr. again received (1528) as a Knight of the Order of Jerusalem, Langue of England. Ottoman Siege of Rhodes (1522). Preceptor of Quenington (1528). Turcopolier (1533–35), Knight of the Grand Cross. Bailiff of Eagle (1535–40), Pensioned (1543). (+1560)

RAWSON, THOMAS (Thomas Rawson, Mifsud's Thomas Rawson, Bosio's Tommasso Ranfon). English of Yorkshire. A younger son of Richard Rawson and Isabella Craford. Younger brother of Prior of Ireland John Rawson. Knight of the Order of Jerusalem, Langue of England. Preceptor of Quenington (Gloucester). With Order in Italy (1527–30). Chapter General Legislator (1527). (+)

REAULX, EMERY (Emery des Réaulx, Aymery des Réaulx, Bosio's Ammerigo des Reaulx). French of Saint-Pierre-le-Moûtier. Knight of Jerusalem, Langue of Auvergne. Captain of Carracks *Santa Maria* (1521) and *Santa Anna* (1530). Ottoman Siege of Rhodes (1522). Commander of Chazelles-sur-Lyon (1527–29+). Marshal (1540–42). Prior of Auvergne (1542–47). Commander of Chantoin (1544–47). Lieutenant-General to Grand Master Homedes (1546–47). Captain of Galleys (1547). (+1547)

RICARD, RAYMOND (Raymond Ricard, Raymond Ricard the Younger, Raimond Ricard, Bosio's Ramóndetto Riccardi). French of Rivière-sur-Tarn 130 km north of Montpellier. Knight of Jerusalem, Langue of Provence. Received (c.1483). Commander of Vaour (1514-32). Ottoman Siege of Rhodes (1522). Knight of the Grand Cross (1522). Bailiff of Manosque (1523–29). Grand Commander (1529–35). Prior of Toulouse (1535–36). Commander Sainte-Eulalie (1536–41). Prior of Saint-Gilles (1536–41). Commander of Montricoux and Lacapelle (1538–41). (c.1465–1541).

RIVALTA, NICCOLÒ (Niccolò di Rivalta, Niccolò Orsini di Rivalta, Niccolò Orsini of the Lords of Rivalta, Bosio's and Pozzo's Nicolo Orsino di Riualta). Piemontese of Rivalta. Knight of Malta, Langue of Italy.

Received (1528). Corsair. Captain-at-Arms for the Castle of Gozo (1553). Procurator/Attorney, then Receiver in Sicily (1554). Admiral (1567–69), Knight of the Grand Cross. Prior of Naples (1569–84). General of the Galleys (1584). (*c.*1511–84)

ROCHE-ANDRY, JEAN (Jean de La Roche-Andry, Bosio's Giovanni della Roche Chandri) French of Angoulême 150km south east of La Rochelle. Knight of Jerusalem, Langue of France. Commander of Nantes (1523–?). Grand Treasurer (1536–37). Bailiff of the Morea (1537–41). Grand Hospitaller (1541–49), Knight of the Grand Cross. AWOL Bailiff of the Morea (1549–57). Grand Hospitaller (1557–59). (+1559)

ROCHES, JACQUES (Jacques des Roches, Bosio's Iacomo des Roches). French of Roches, 265km west-north-west of Lyon. Servant-at-Arms and then Knight of Malta, Langue of Auvergne. Commander of Villefranche (1550). Harbour Fortress Commander Tripoli (1551). Governor of Fort Saint Michael (1552). Galliot Commander. (1558). (+)

ROCQUEMARTINE, ROBERT (Robert de Rocquemartine, Robert d'Aube, Robert de Roquemartine, Robert d'Aube detto Roquemartine, Bosio's Roberto de Rocca Martin/Roberto di Roccamartina). French of Eyguières, Bouches-du-Rhône, 50km south-south-east of Avignon. Knight of Jerusalem, Langue of Provence. Commander of Trinquetaille (1530+). Lieutenant Chatelain du Chateau Saint-Pierre (1522). Ottoman Siege of Rhodes (1522). Grand Commander (1545), Knight of the Grand Cross. Prior of Saint-Gilles (1546–49). (+1549)

ROMEGAS, MATHURIN (Mathurin d'Aux de Lescout-Romegas, Maturino de Lescut, Bosio's Maturino de Lefcut de Romegasso, Pozzo's Romegasso or Romegas). Gascon of Mansonville, 75km north-west of Toulouse. Knight of Romegas, a cadet branch of the family d'Armagnac. Second son of Jean III d'Aux and Béraude de Beauville. Military Studies at Malta (1542–46). Knight of Malta, Langue of Provence. Received (1547). Survives overturned galley (1555). Seizes two abandoned galleons (1557). Magistral Galliot Captain (1558). Capture of Sultana (1564). Commander of Rouergue. Ottoman Siege of Malta (1565). Defends Fort Saint Michael (1565). Prior of Ireland (1573–82), Knight of the Grand Cross. Grand Commander (1575–76). Commander of La Cavallerie

(1575+). Prior of Toulouse (1576–81). Lieutenant to Grand Master Cassière (1577–81). (1528–81)

RUFFO, CARLO (Carlo Ruffo, Bosio's Carlo Ruffo). Italian of Settimo, Calabria, Kingdom of Naples. Ninth child of Paolo Ruffo, 6th Count of Settimo/Sinopoli (Calabria), and Caterina Spinelli. Knight of Malta, Langue of Italy. Received (1549). Knight Commander. Commissioned Colonel commanding 800 infantry at Battle of Djerba (1560). Galley Captain (1565). Ottoman Siege of Malta (1565). Commanded Defence of Fort Saint Michael (1565). Killed at his post (1565). (*c*.1541–65)

RUSSELL, GILES (Giles Russell, Gyles Russell, Bosio's Giles Rosel, Egidio Roffell, and Egidio Roffelet). English of Strensham, Worcestershire. A younger son of Robert Russell and Elizabeth Baynham. Knight of Jerusalem, Langue of England. Ottoman Siege of Rhodes (1522). Preceptor of Halford (1523+). Preceptor of Dingley and Battisford (1530–34). Preceptor of Mount Saint John (1534). Del Monte Elector (1534). Lieutenant Turcopolier (1534–35). Sainte-Jalle Elector (1535). Preceptor of Temple Bruer (1534–43). Homedes Elector (1536). Turcopolier (1539–43), Knight of the Grand Cross. (+1543)

SAINT-AUBIN, PIERRE (Pierre de Saint-Aubin, Pierre de Roquelaure-Saint-Aubin, Bosio's Pietro de Rocque Laure de Sant'Aubin/Aubino, Pozzo's Pietro de Roque laure S. Aubin vecchio). Gascon of Roquelaure-Saint-Aubin, 45km west of Toulouse. Brother of Hospitaller Bernard de Roquelaure-Saint-Aubin (the Younger). Knight of Malta, Langue of Provence. Magistral Galliot Captain (1562). Magistral Galley Captain, takes Corsair galliot (1562). Lieutenant to Romegas (1564). Sultana capture (1564). Magistral sultana captain (1564). Captain Magistral Padrona (1564). Captain captured galliot (1565). Gran Soccorso (1565). Grand Commander (1596), Knight of the Grand Cross. General of the Galleys (1595–98). Prior of Saint-Gilles (1600–02). (*c*.1538–1602)

SAINT-BLANCARD (Bertrand d'Ornesan, Baron of Saint-Blancard, Bosio's Beltrando Dorvesan Barone di S. Blancars). French of Saint-Blancard. Corsair Admiral. Baron of (Gascon commune) Saint-Blancard in the Pyrenees, Marquis of the Iles d'Or. Lord of Astarac. Eldest brother of Bernard d'Ornesan, Eveque de Lombez, Cistercian Abbot of Nisors and Feuillants (not a brother of Bernardin d'Ornesan, likely a cousin) and of Magdalon d'Ornesan. Four sisters. Father of Bernard d'Ornesan. Companion/partner of Magdelaine de Médicis, La corsaire des Îles d'or. (*c.*1481–1539)

SAINTE-JALLE, DIDIER DE (Didier de Tholon de Sainte-Jalle, Didier de Saint-Jaille, Didier de Tholon de Saint-Jal, Bosio's Defiderio di Tolone detto Santa Ialla). French of Sainte-Jalle. Believed to be the son of Antoine de Tholon de Sainte-Jalle (d. 1479), co-Seigneur de Sainte-Jalle wed 1452 to Geneviève de Gaste de Luppé (born 1427). Brother or half-brother of Pierre, Madeleine, Jeanne, and Louis (born 1465), successor co-Seigneur de Sainte-Jalle. Knight of Jerusalem, Langue of Provence. Commander of Homps (by 1503) and Joucas (by 1503). Pall Bearer for Pierre d'Aubusson (1503). Seneschal (1503), Knight of the Grand Cross. Commander of Montarouch (1521–22). Ottoman Siege of Rhodes (1522). Bailiff of Manosque (1522–23). Prior of Toulouse (1523–35). Commander of Lormont (1528–31). Forty-fifth Grand Master of the Order of Jerusalem (1535–36). (*c.*1470–1536)

SALBAN BERNARDO (Bernardo Salban, Bernat Salvà, Boissat's Bernard Salban, Bosio's Bernardo Salban). Catalan. Knight of Malta, Langue of Aragon. Commander of Tortosa (1538–40). Spanish assault on Susa (1538). Galley Captain (1538–39). Battle of Preveza (1538). Regent of the Galleys (1540). Retires (1541). (+)

SALES, GUIOT (Guiot de Sales, Guiot de Salles, Bosio's Guillot du Sales and Guliot de Sales). Savoyard of Thorenc (60km north-east of Nice). Knight of Jerusalem, Langue of Provence. Ottoman Siege of Rhodes (1522). Commander of Saint-Felix (1543–66). Grand Commander (1562–66), Knight of the Grand Cross. Ottoman Siege of Malta (1565). (+1566)

SALIH REIS (Salih Reis, Salech Reis, Sala Rais, Setton's Sala Beg or Sala Reis, Morgan's Salah Reis, Bosio's Salà Rais/Salec Rais). Greek from the plain of Troy. Father of Mehmet (Morgan's Mahamad). Brother-in-law of Barbarossa brothers by marriage to a Barbarossa sister. Renegade. Corsair. Barbarossa Lieutenant (1512–46). Battle of Formentera (1529). Christian Siege of Tunis (1535). Battle of Preveza (1538). Ottoman

Siege of Tripoli (1551). Lieutenant Pasha of Algiers (1548–52). Ottoman Beylerbey of Algiers (1552–56). (*c*.1486–1556)

SALVAGO, RAFFAELLO (Raffaello Salvago, Bosio's Raffaello Saluago). Italian of Genoa. Lyric poet. Historian. Knight of Jerusalem, Langue of Italy. Knight Commander (1526). Commander of Troia (in Apulia). Bailiff of Genoa. Ottoman Siege of Rhodes (1565). (+)

SALVIATI, BERNARDO (Bernardo Salviati, Bosio's Saluiati) of Florence. Eighth of eleven children of Jacopo Salviati and Lucrezia de' Medici. Brother of Cardinal Giovanni Salviati. Nephew of Popes Leo X and Clement VII. Cousin once-removed of Queen Catherine of France. Cousin of Hospitaller Leone and Marshal of France Pietro Strozzi. Knight of Jerusalem, Langue of Italy. Prior of Rome (1525–61), Knight of the Grand Cross. Resident Ambassador and Procurator-General to Holy See (1528–38). Captain of Galleys (1531–34). Siege of Modon (1531). Siege of Coron (1532). Captain-General of Papal Galley Squadron (1533–34). Roman Catholic Cardinal (1561–68). (1508–68)

SANDE, ÁLVARO (Álvaro de Sande, Álvaro de Sande y Golfín de Paredes, Bosio's Aluaro de Sande) Spanish of Cáceres in western Spain. Son of Don Juan de Sande, Second Señor de Valhondo. Spanish Military Commander. Siege of Tunis (1535). Monastir Garrison Commander (1540). Tercio of Lombardia Commander (1559). Lieutenant-General Commanding Landed Forces Battle of Djerba (1560). Ottoman Captive at Constantinople (1660–62). Ransomed (1662). Commands Grand Soccorso Landing Force at Malta (1565). 1st Marqués de la Piovera (1573). (1489–1573)

SANDILANDS, JAMES (James Sandilands, Bosio's Iacomo de Sandeland). Scot. Second son of James Sandilands, Baron Calder. Knight of Malta, Langue of England. Received (1540). Preceptor of Torphichen (1547–60). Valette Elector (1557). Lord Torphichen (1564–79). Weds Janet Murray (1564). (*c*.1511–79)

SANGORRIN, JUAN (Juan de Sangorrin, Bosio's Giouanni de Sangorrin, Pozzo's Gio: de Sangorin). Spanish of El Sangorrin, 80km east-south-east of Navarre. Knight of Malta, Langue of Aragon, Priory of Navarre. Commander. Galley Captain (1547–48). Dragut Captive (1548).

Galleonetto Captain (1550). Grand Soccorso (1565). Grand Conservator (1574–75), Knight of the Grand Cross. Castellan of Amposta (1575–82). (+*c*.1582)

SANGUESA, GASPAR (Gaspar de Sanguesa, Bosio's Gaspare de Sangueffa). Basque of Sangüesa in Navarre. Knight of Jerusalem, Langue of Aragon, Priory of Navarre. Knight Commander (NLT 1524). Castellan of Trapani (1524–44). Commander of Aliaga (1530+). Governor of Tripoli (1530–31). Ambassador to Emperor Charles V (1532). Knight of the Grand Cross (1544). Grand Conservator (1547–49). (+1549)

SAUGNIAC, GUION (Guion de Saugniac de Belcastel, Guion de Saugniac the Elder, Bosio's Guion de Soniac Belcaftel). French of Belcastel, Aveyron, Rouergue 150km north-east of Toulouse. Knight of Malta, Langue of Provence. Received (1550). Knight Commander. Grand Soccorso (1565). Captain of Great Galleon/Sultana (1565–68). Captain of Galley San Iacomo (1569). Captain of former Capitana San Giovanni (1569). (+)

SCANDER REIS (Scander Reis, Iskender Reis, Alexandros, Alexander.) Probable Ottoman Greek Renegade. Barbarossa lieutenant. Galliot Squadron Commander (1535–36). Galley Battle of Zuara (1536). (+1536)

SCHIATTESI, GIOVAN BATTISTA (Giovan Battista Shiattese, Bosio's Giouan Battifta Schiattefe). Italian of Rome. Knight of Jerusalem, Langue of Italy. Commander of Modica (1522). Ottoman Siege of Rhodes (1522). Small Galleon Commander (1523). Commands Galleon of the Religion (1529). Assault on Modone (1531). Governor of Gozo (1535–36). Lieutenant Admiral (1541). (+1550)

SCHILLING, GEORG (Georg Schilling, Georg Schilling von Cannstatt, Jorge Schilling, Boissat's George Schiling, Bosio's Giorgio Schilingh, Schiling, Schilingh, Gran Bagliuo). German of Neuffen in Baden-Württemberg. Knight of Jerusalem, Langue of Germany. Received (*c*.1504). Commander of Heitersheim. Lieutenant Grand Bailiff (1525). Grand Bailiff (1534–46). Governor of Tripoli (1535–37). Captain of Galleys (1541–43). Grand Prior of Germany and Prince of the Holy Roman Empire (1546–54). (*c*.1490–1554)

SCHILLING, PHILIPP (Philipp Schilling, Philipp Schilling von Canstatt, Bosio's Filippo Schilingh). German of Neuffen in Baden-Württemberg. Presumed younger brother of Georg Schilling. Knight of Jerusalem, Langue of Germany. Commander of Arnheim (1536). Lieutenant Grand Bailiff (1536). Grand Bailiff (1546–48), Knight of the Grand Cross. (+1548)

SCHWALBACH, KONRAD (Konrad von Schwalbach, Conrad von Schwalbach, Bosio's Corrado Scuualbac/Schualbac). Hessian of Schwalbach, Rhine-Hesse. Knight of Jerusalem, Langue of Germany. Seneschal (1495). Commander of St Gallen (1510). Commander of Tobel, Switzerland (1501–28). Grand Bailiff (1512–34), Knight of the Grand Cross. (+1534)

SENGLE, CLAUDE (Claude de la Sengle Montchavel, Claude de la Sangle, Bosio's Claudio della Sengle). French of Beauvais (75km north of Paris). Eldest (?) son of Laurent de la Sangle and Marie de Hangest. Brother of Françoise and Jean. Knight of Jerusalem, Langue of France. Commander of Chanu (1525). Commander of Saint-Étienne-de-Renneville (1533–53). Conventual Conservator and Receiver (1543–47). Lieutenant Grand Hospitaller (1545–46). Bailiff of the Morea (1546–49), Knight of the Grand Cross. Grand Hospitaller (1549–53). Captain of the Galleys (1550). Procurator-General and Ambassador to Holy See (1551–53). Forty-eighth Grand Master of the Order of Jerusalem (1553–57). (1494–1557)

SERBELLONE, GABRIELE (Gabriele Serbellone, Gabrio Serbelloni, Serbelloni, il Grande Gabrio). Italian of Milan. Eldest son of Giovanni Pietro Serbellone and Isabella Rainoldi. Cousin of Pope Pius IV. Condottiero. Captain-General of the Papal Guard, Governor of the Vatican, and Superintendent of Vatican Fortresses (1562). Knight of Malta, Langue of Italy. Received (1562). Knight Commander of Ferrara and Montecchio (1562–80). Prior of Hungary (1562–74, 1575–80), Knight of the Grand Cross. Arms two galleys for corsair employment (1565). Battle of Lepanto (1571). Viceroy of Tunis (1573–74). Imprisoned Constantinople (1574–75). Serves Don Juan in Flanders (1578). (1509–80)

SERPENS, GILBERT (Gilbert des Serpens, Bosio's Giberto/Giliberto de Serpens detto Chestin). French of Bourbonnais en Auvergne. Knight of Jerusalem, Langue of Auvergne. Cited for Valor in Galleon Capture (1534). Knight Commander. Resident Ambassador to Versailles (1549–66). Commander of Ormeteau (1559–76). Bailiff of Lango (1561–66), Knight of the Grand Cross. (+1566)

SEURRE DE LUMIGNY (Michel de Seurre de Lumigny, Michel de Sevre, Bosio's Michel de Seure, Pozzo's Seurè). French of Lumigny en Brie. Son of Antoine de Seurre and of Louise de Verdelot. Knight of Malta, Langue of France. Extraction of Mary Queen of Scots (1548). Captain of French Galliot (1551). Gentilhomme Ordinaire de la Chambre du Roi, Chambellan du Roi, Conseiller (1560). French Ambassador to Court of Saint James (1560–62). Commander of Flanders (1564). Bailiff of Bobigny (1565–71), Knight of the Grand Cross. Prior of Champagne (1571–95). (+1595)

SERVIAN (Servian, Barthélemy Dupuy, Bartolomeo del Pozzo, Bartholomeu del Pos, Serivon, Roncière's Servien). French of Marseille. Called Servian for his Dalmatian roots. Wealthy merchant and ship owner. Corsair. (+1533)

SHEFFIELD, THOMAS (Thomas Sheffield, Thomas Shefelde, Bouhour's Sheffeild, Bourbon's Chifel, Bosio's Tommasso Schefild/Sefild). English of South Cave, Yorkshire. Younger son of Robert Sheffield, MP, and Brother of Elder Son Robert, MP and Speaker, House of Commons. Knight of Jerusalem, Langue of England. Preceptor of Beverley and Shingay (1503). Langue Receiver/Treasurer (1503). Ottoman Siege of Rhodes (1522). Seneschal (1522–23), Knight of the Grand Cross. Bailiff of Eagle/Eccle (1523–24) in Lincolnshire, (+1524)

SIMEONI, PAOLO (Paolo Simeoni, Simone of Cavoretto, Simeone de Balbi, Boissat's Paul Simeon, Bosio's Paolo Simeoni). Piemontese of Chieri. A second son of Alessandro Simeoni and Caterina di Romagnano. Knight of Jerusalem, Langue of Italy. Received (1501). Assigned Leros (1505–06). Galley Captain (1524–26). Barbarossa Pursuit (1526). Commander of Turin (1530). Captive at Algiers and Tunis (1531–35). Siege of Tunis (1535). Prior of Lombardia (1537–45), Knight of the Grand Cross. Captain of Galleys (1538–40). Spanish Siege of Susa (1538). Battle of Preveza (1538). Castellan of Nice (1541–16). Senior Knight of Italy (1545–56). Admiral (1545–51). Prior of Barletta (1551–56). (*c*.1485–1556)

SINAN OF SMYRNA (Sinan, the Jew of Smyrna, Arabs call him Sinan, Turks call him Çıfut, Jews call him Ciphut, and Christians call him Sinan, Bosio's Il Giudeo). Father of unnamed son a captive of Iacopo V Appiano, Prince of Piombino. Brother-in-law (Cognato) of Barbarossa brothers. Uncle of Mehmet Reis son of Salih Reis and of Hassan Barbarossa, son of Khizr. Pirate, Corsair, Barbarossa Lieutenant. Governor of Djerba (1530–36). Ottoman Siege of Tunis (1534). Spanish Siege of Tunis (1535). Ottoman Commander of Suez (1536–44). Battle of Preveza (1538). (*c*.1480–1544)

STARKEY, OLIVER (Oliver Starkey, Bosio's and Pozzo's Oliviero Starquei). Flemish, then English. Member of Parliament. Knight of Malta, Langue of England. Preceptor of Quenyngton (1555). Lieutenant Turcopolier (1560–69). Bailiff of Eagle (1569–88), Knight of the Grand Cross. (1523–88)

STROZZI, LEONE (Leone Strozzi, Boissat's Leon Strozzi, Bosio's Leone Strozzi) of Florence. Nephew of Pope Clement VII (Giulio di Giuliano de' Medici). Brother of Marshal of France Piero Strozzi. Uncle by sister Giulia Strozzi of Hospitaller Lelio Frangipani. Cousin of Hospitaller Bernardo Salviati. Commander of San Iacopo in Campo Corbolini at Florence (1524–54). Prior of Capua (1527–54). Received at Malta (1535). Knight of the Order of Jerusalem, Langue of Italy. Captain of Galleys (1537). Battle of Anti-Paxos (1537). Hospitaller Raid on Zuara (1552). General of Galleys (1553–54). (1515–54)

SULEIMAN (Suleiman bin Selim Khan, Suleyman, Suleiman the Magnificent, Suleiman the Lawgiver). Turkish, born at Trabzon the son of future Sultan Selim and Hafsa Hatun. Father of ten children, four by concubines, one of whom was Gulbahar Hatun and six by wife Roxelana including future Sultan Selim II. Sultan of the Ottoman Empire (1520–66). Siege of Belgrade (1521). Siege of Rhodes (1522). (1494–1566)

TERNO DA CREMA (Francesco Terno da Crema). Italian of Crema in the Lombard, 43km north-west of Cremona. Knight of Malta, Langue of Italy. Received (1526). Corsair. Galleon Captain (1540–45). Galley Captain (1545–46). (+1546)

TESSIÈRES, CHARLES D'URRE (Charles d'Urre de Tessières, Charles d'Urre de Thessières, Vertot's Urre de Tessieres, Bosio's Carlo Durre and Durrè). French. Knight of Malta, Langue of Provence. Tripoli Treasurer (1544). Commander of Jales (1547–54) and Avignon (1554+). Magistral Receiver (1553–57). Grand Commander (1558–60), Pilier Langue of Provence, Knight of the Grand Cross. General of the Galleys (1559–60). Battle of Djerba (1560). (+1560)

THÉZAN-VÉNÀSQUE, ANTOINE (Antoine de Thésan-Vénàsque, Bosio's Antonio de Tezan detto Venafque). French of Saint-Didier, Provence. Son of François de Thézan-Vénàsque, Lord of Saint-Didier, Vénàsque, and Méthamis, and Catherine de Tholon de Sainte-Jalle, daughter of Louis, Lord of Sainte-Jalle. Brother of Pierre, Jean, and Francois. Uncle of Antoine, Claude, Cathelin, and François. Knight of Malta, Langue of Provence. Commander of Garidech (1554–60). Galley Captain (1554–56). Survives Dockyard Creek Tragedy (1555). Corsair Galliot Owner (1557). Receiver Priory of Saint-Gilles (1561–66). Commander of Avignon and Pézenas (1564–72). (+)

THOMASSIN, JEAN (Jean Thomassin, Bosio's Giovanni Tommassin). Knight of Jerusalem, Langue of Auvergne. French of Franche-Comté. Knight of Jerusalem, Langue of Auvergne. Received (1519). Ottoman Siege of Rhodes (1522). Commander of L'Aumusse (1545–53). Bailiff of Lyon (1554–57), Knight of the Grand Cross. (+1557)

TOLEDO, ANTONIO (Antonio de Toledo the Elder, Antonio Enrique de Guzmán, Don Antonio de Guzmán y Toledo, Bosio's Don Antonio de Toledo, Pozzo's Antonio di Toledo). Spanish. Third Son of Don Diego Enríquez de Guzmán (1490–1550), third count of Alba de Liste, and of Doña Leonor Álvarez de Toledo. Nephew of Hospitaller Prior of Castile and León Don Diego de Toledo. Knight of Malta, Langue of Castile. Received (1545). Resident Ambassador to Imperial Court in Flanders (1545–54). Wedding Philip and Mary (1554). Councilor to King Philip (1554–58). Commander Alcazar de San Juan (1558–66). Grand Prior of León (1566–77), Knight of the Grand Cross. (*c.*1527–77).

TOUCHEBOEUF, FRANÇOIS (François de Toucheboeuf de Clermont, Bosio's Francesco Toucheboeuf de Claremont). French of Clermont. Third son of Guy de Toucheboeuf, Lord of Clermont, and Marie de Combarel. Uncle of Hospitaller Guy de Toucheboeuf, Lord of Clermont. Knight of the Order of Jerusalem, Langue of Provence. Corsair. Commander. Captain of Grand Carrack *Santa Anna* (1531–56). Commander of Condat (1543–54). Grand Commander (1556–57), Knight of the Grand Cross. Prior of Saint-Gilles (1557–58). (c.1495–1558)

TURGUT (Turgut, Dragut, Turgut Reis, Dragut Reis, Bosio's Dragut/Draguto). Greek of Karatoprak since renamed Turgut Reis of a peasant family. Father of a daughter, an only child according to Morgan, who weds Mehmet Reis after Turgut's death. Perhaps related to Amurat Dragut. Uncle of Hisar (Khizr) Reis (Bosio's Efse Reis at III-267, Morgan's Aisa Rais), son of his sister. Janissary (1503–05). Pirate (1505+). Ottoman Corsair. Barbarossa Lieutenant (1532–40). Governor of Djerba (1536). Battle of Preveza (1538). Genovese Captive (1540–44). Lord of Mehedia (1545–50). Ottoman Sancakbey of Santa Maura (1550–1553). Lord of Tripoli (1553–65). Ottoman Siege of Malta (1565). (1485–1565)

TYRELL, WILLIAM (William Tyrell, William Terell, William Tirrell, Bosio's Guglielmo Terrell). English of Heron Hall, Essex. Son of Sir Thomas Tirrell and Constance Blount. Brother of eldest son Sir Thomas Tirrell. Knight of Malta, Langue of England. Preceptor of Badisford and Dingley (1534+). Galleon Commander (1535–40). Tower of London (1541). Pardoned and pensioned (1543). (+1557)

ULUÇ ALI (Uluç Ali , Occhiali, Uluch Alì, Giovanni Dionigi Galeni, Ulug'Alì el Fertas, Ali the Apostate, Il Tignoso, Kilic Ali (Ali the Sword), Bosio's Vlucciali, Pozzo's Lucciali, Morgan's Ochali). Italian renegade of Le Castella (Licastella), Calabria, born Giovanni Dionigi. Son of a fisherman. Son-in-law of Chiafer Reis. Corsair. Dragut Lieutenant (1560–65). Battle of Djerba (1560). Ottoman Siege of Malta (1565). Sancakbey or Governor of Tripoli (1565–70). Beylerbey or Viceroy of Algiers (1568–72). Battle of Lepanto (1571). Kapudan Pasha (1572–87). (*c.*1519–87)

UPTON, NICHOLAS (Nicholas Upton, Bosio's Nicolo Octon or Nicolao Vpton). English. Son of John Upton of Northolme, Devon, and

Elizabeth Copledike. Knight of Malta, Langue of England. Preceptor of Ribestone. Lieutenant Turcopolier (1548). Turcopolier (1548–51). (*c*.1511–51)

URRÈ, PONS (Pons d'Urrè, Pons d'Eurre, Poncet d'Urrè, Bosio's Poncet Durrè). French likely of Eurre 30km, south-south-east of Valence. Knight of Jerusalem, Langue of Provence. Commander of Espalion (1519–24). Ottoman Siege of Rhodes (1522). Commander of La Cavalerie (1545–46). Commander of Marseille (1546+). Captain of Great Carrack *Santa Anna* (1523). Grand Commander (1544–45), Knight of the Grand Cross. Bailiff of Manosque (1545–48). (+1548)

VAGNONE, GIORGIO (Giorgio Vagnone, Bosio's Giorgio Vagnone). Italian of the Piedmont. Uncle of Hospitaller Giovanni Vagnone. Knight of Jerusalem, Langue of Italy. Received (1516). Ottoman Siege of Rhodes (1522). Conventual Conservator or Auditor (1535–54). Knight Commander (1548). Sengle Elector (1553). Governor of Fort Saint Elmo (1553–54). Commander of Maruggio (1554) and of Castrovillari (1554). (+1554)

VAGNONE, GIOVANNI (Giovanni Vagnone, Bosio's Giovanni Vagnone). Italian of Turin in the Piedmont. Nephew of Hospitaller Giorgio Vagnone. Knight of Malta, Langue of Italy. Received 1546. Frigate Commander (1562). Ottoman Siege of Malta (1565). Killed Fort Saint-Elmo (1565) (+1565)

VALETTE, HENRI (Henri de la Valetta-Cornusson, Catalogue's Henri de la Valette de Cornusson, Bosio's Enrico di Valletta or Parisotto). French of Chateau Cornusson, Parisot, Occitanie 100km north-east of Touloudr. Nephew of Jean Parisot de la Valette. Older brother of Jean de la Valette-Cornusson. Knight of Malta, Langue of Provence. Received (1550). Commander of La Selve (1560–65), then also of La Chapelle. Seneschal (1563–65), Knight of the Grand Cross. Commander of the Piccolo Soccorso (1565). Ottoman Siege of Malta (1565), Killed by Sniper at Fort Saint-Michael (1565). (+1565)

VALETTE, JEAN PARISOT (Jean Parisot de la Valette, Boissat's Jean de Valette, Catalogue's Jean de la Valette Parisot, Bosio's Giovanni di Valletta detto Parisot). French of Parisot 110km north-north-east of

Toulouse. Son of Guillot de la Valette, Seigneur de Boismenon et de Cornusson, and of Jeanne de Castres. Brother of Bishop Francois de la Valette of Vabres and of Béatrix de La Valette-Parisot, Guillaume de La Valette-Parisot, Baron de Cornusson Guillot de La Valette, and of Antoinette de La Valette-Parisot. Father of Catherine Grecque's child Barthélemy de Valette and of Isabella Buonaccorsi by a Buonaccorsi mother. Knight of Jerusalem, Langue of Provence. Received (1515). Ottoman Siege of Rhodes (1522). Galley Captain (1534–36). Spanish Siege of Tunis (1535). Galliot Corsair (1540–41). Ottoman Galley Slave (1541–42). Exiled Gozo and Tripoli (1544–46). Governor of Tripoli (1546–49). Commander of Cagnac, Reneville, and Pézenas (1554–64). Christian Raid on Zuara (1552). General of the Galleys (1554–55). Bailiff of Lango (1555), Knight of the Grand Cross. Grand Commander (1555–56). Prior of Saint-Gilles (1556–57). Commander of Le (Bastit (1561–63), 48th Grand Master of the Order of Jerusalem (1557–68). (1495–1568)

VALLÉE-PASSY, LOUIS (Louis de Vallée-Passy, Monsieur de Flandres, Bosio's Luis de Vallee Passe). French. Knight of the Order of Jerusalem, Langue of France. Ottoman Siege of Rhodes (1522). Commander (1524). Commander of Flanders (1547–64). Regent of Galleys (1548). Ambassador to France (1548). Grand Hospitaller (1562–64), Knight of the Grand Cross. (+1564)

VALLIER, GASPARD (Gaspard de Vallier de Chambéry, Bosio's Gaspare de Valies/Vallies, Vertot's Valier). French of Isère. Third son of Claude Vallier and Odette Alleman. Brother of Hospitaller Balthazar de Vallier. Knight of Jerusalem, Langue of Auvergne. Commander of Chambéry (1535+) and of Chantoin (1549). Galley Captain (1535–39). Battle of Anti-Paxos (1537). Battle of Anti-Paxos (1537). Spanish Siege of Susa (1538). Battle of Preveza (1538). Bailiff of Lango (1548), Knight of the Grand Cross. Marshal (1548–51). Commander of Chantoin (1549–1551). Governor of Tripoli (1551). Defrocked and imprisoned (1551–57). Bailiff of Lango (1557–59). (*c.*1495–1559)

VILARAGUT, BAUTISTA (Bautista de Vilaragut, Baptista de Vilagut in Catalan, Bosio's Battista di Villaraguto). Catalan of Valencia. Knight of Jerusalem, Langue of Aragon. Knight Commander. Ottoman Siege of Rhodes (1522). One of four commanders assigned post of England (1522). Draper (1531–39), Knight of the Grand Cross. Del Ponte Elector (1534). Castellan of Amposta (1539–60). (+1560)

VILATORTA, JUANITO (Juanito de Vilatorta, Juan de Vilatoro, Joan de Vilatorta, Bosio's Giannotto/Giovanni di Villatorta). Catalan of Sant Julià de Vilatorta, Barcelona, Spain. Likely brother or cousin of Commander of Mas-Deu Jaume de Vilatorta. Knight of Jerusalem, Langue of Aragon. Ottoman Siege of Rhodes (1522). Knight Commander. Commands Galley *San Giovanni* (1526). Captain of Grand Carrack *Santa Maria* (1530). (+)

VILLEGAGNON, NICOLAS DURAND (Nicolas Durand de Villegagnon, Bosio's Nicolo Villegagnon). Of Provins, France. Son of Jeanne de Fresne and Louis Durand, King's Prosecutor in the village of Meaux, ennobled by Francis I in 1516, then taking the name Villegagnon. One of eight (?) brothers to become Hospitallers including Noel, Pierre, and Rene, a ninth, Philippe, succeeding as Sieur de Villegagnon. Knight Commander of the Commanderie at Beauvais, where he dies in January 1571. Vice Admiral of Bretagne. 'The greatest seaman of his time.' Hospitaller Ambassador to Court of France (1568–70). (*c.*1510–71)

VINTIMILLE, BERTRAND (Bertrand de Vintimille des comtes de Marseilles d'Ollioules). French of Ollioules, 60km south-east of Marseille. Tenth of ten children of Gaspard de Vintimille and Anne d'Arcussiak. Nephew of Hospitaller Balthazard de Vintimille. Knight of Malta, Langue of Provence. Received (1547). Commander of Marseille (1563–68+). Ottoman Siege of Malta (1565). Commissioner of Valletta housing (1571). (+)

WEST, CLEMENT (Clement West, Bosio's Clemente Vueft). English. Knight of Jerusalem, Langue of England. Received at Rhodes (1500). Blanchefort Elector (1512). Preceptor of Slebech, Pembrokeshire (1515–38). Assigned a Preceptory (1515). Preceptor of Slebech (Pembrokeshire). Turcopolier (1531–33, 1535–39), Knight of the Grand Cross. Defrocked (1539). Pensioned (1543). (*c.*1482–1547)

WESTON THE YOUNGER, WILLIAM (William Weston the Younger, Bouhour's Watson, Bourbon's Ouafton, Vertot's Ouazon,

Bosio's Guglielmo Veston, Onafcon, Onascon). English. Second son of Edmund Weston of Boston, Lincolnshire, by his wife Catherine. Younger brother of Richard Weston, Gentleman of Edward VIII's Privy Chamber. Nephew of Hospitallers John and William Weston. Knight of the Order of Jerusalem, Langue of England. Commander of Baddesley and Maine. Ottoman Siege of Rhodes (1522) – Commander of English Post. Turcopolier (1523–27), Knight of the Grand Cross. Prior of England (1527–40). (+1540)

ZANOGUERA, FRANCISCO DE (Francisco de Zanoguera, Funes's Francisco de Zanoguera, Balbi's Francisco de Zanoguera, Bosio's Francesco de Sanoguerra). Spanish of Valencia. Knight of Malta, Langue of Aragon. Knight Commander. Procurator at Amposta (1558). Galley Captain (1565). Ottoman Siege of Malta (1565). Commands and is killed at The Spur on the tip of Senglea. (+1565)

Notes

Chapter I

1. Bosio III-1; Boissat 451.
2. Bosio III-2.
3. Bosio III-4.
4. Bosio III-2; Boissat 451 et seq.
5. Bosio III-6; Responsion is an obsolete Anglo-French word meaning a sum required to be paid, especially an annual payment required of a member of a military order of knighthood.
6. Bosio III-7.
7. Bosio III-7 et seq.
8. Bosio III-12; Martyrologe I-163.
9. Bosio III-9 et seq; Sire 151.
10. Bosio III-19.
11. Bosio III-19 et seq; Setton III-214 et seq; Vertot IIBE-275 et seq.
12. Bosio III-21 et seq.
13. Bosio III-25; Bourbon's final unnumbered page; Martyrologe I-32.
14. Bosio III-25.
15. Bosio III-26 et seq.
16. Bosio III-27 et seq.
17. Bosio III-28 et seq.
18. Bosio III-28; Mifsud 141; Guglielmotti's *La Guerra dei Pirati* 22.
19. *Notizie di Paolo Simeoni de'Balbi, da Chieri* by Luigi Cibrario.
20. Bosio III-28 et seq; Martyrologe I-100.
21. Bosio III-32.
22. Bosio III-32.
23. Bosio III-32.
24. Bosio III-27 et seq.
25. Bosio III-33.
26. Bosio III-34.
27. Bosio III-3.
28. Bosio III-35 et seq.
29. Bosio III-36 et seq.
30. Martyrologe I-37.
31. Bosio III-37 et seq.
32. Bosio III-38 et seq; *Life of Marguerite D'Angoulême* I-341 and I-408.
33. Bosio III-40 et seq.

34. Bosio III-40.
35. Bosio III-41; *Life of Marguerite D'Angoulême* I-444.
36. Bosio III-45.
37. *Moriscoes of Spain* 85; Harold Lamb's *Suleiman* 165.
38. Bosio III-44.
39. Bosio III-44; Boissat 480.
40. Bosio III-44 et seq.
41. Bosio III-45 et seq; Merriman III-243.
42. Bosio III-45.
43. Bosio III-47 et seq.
44. Bosio III-46 et seq; Merriman III-244.
45. Bosio III-48 et seq.
46. Merriman III-244.
47. Bosio III-49.
48. Bosio III-49; Merriman III-245.
49. Bosio III-49 et seq; Merriman III-245.
50. Bosio III-51.
51. Bosio III-52 et seq.
52. Bosio III-52 et seq; Merriman III-244.
53. Bosio III-52 et seq.
54. Bosio III-57 et seq.
55. Bosio III-58 et seq.
56. Bosio III-59 et seq.
57. Bosio III-59 et seq.

Chapter II

1. Bosio III-60.
2. Bosio III-60; Setton III-267.
3. Bosio III-60 et seq.
4. Bosio III-62.
5. Bosio III-63.
6. Bosio III-64.
7. Bosio III-64.
8. Bosio III-64 et seq.
9. Bosio III-65; Setton III-296.
10. Treccani.
11. Bosio III-65.
12. Bosio III-65.
13. Bosio III-65 et seq.
14. Bosio III-65; Boissat 495.
15. Bosio III-67.
16. Bosio III-67 et seq.
17. Bosio III-69.
18. Bosio III-69 et seq.

19. Bosio III-70.
20. Anderson 3; Morgan 267; Setton III-234.
21. Morgan 268 et seq.
22. Bosio III-71.
23. Bosio III-71.
24. Bosio III-71 et seq.
25. Bosio III-72; Setton III-328.
26. Bosio III-73 et seq.
27. Bosio III-74 et seq.
28. Merriman III-296; Morgan 264.
29. Bosio III-77 et seq.
30. Bosio III-78.
31. Bosio III-79 et seq.
32. Bosio III-80 et seq.
33. Bosio III-83.
34. Bosio III-82 et seq.
35. Bosio III-84 et seq; Mifsud 201.
36. Bosio III-85 et seq.
37. Bosio III-85 et seq; Riley-Smith *Crusades Vol. 9.*
38. Bosio III-86 et seq.

Chapter III

1. Bosio III-88.
2. Bosio III-89.
3. Bosio III-86 et seq.
4. Bosio III-97.
5. Bosio III-97 et seq.
6. Bosio III-98.
7. Bosio III-99.
8. Bosio III-100.
9.
10. Bosio III-101.
11. Bosio III-103.
12. Bosio III-106.
13. Bosio III-106 et seq; Setton III-352.
14. Bosio III-108.
15. Bosio III-109.
16. Bosio III-111.
17. Bosio III-111; Martyrologe I-367.
18. Bosio III-111 et seq.
19. Bosio III-112.
20. Bosio III-113 et seq.
21. Bosio III-114.
22. Bosio III-113 to 116; Setton III-366; Martyrologe I-195.
23. Bosio III-116 et seq.

24. Bosio III-118.
25. Bosio III-119 et seq; Boissat 536.
26. Setton III-367 et seq.
27. Bosio III-122.
28. Bosio III-123 et seq; Setton III-366 et seq.
29. Bosio III-126.
30. Bosio III-127; Setton III-392.
31. Bosio III-127 et seq.
32. Bosio III-128.
33. Porter II-326.
34. Bosio III-131 et seq.
35. Inalcik 105.
36. Catalogue of Manuscripts in the Cottonian Library 367.
37. Bosio III-132; Setton III-392.
38. Bosio III-133.
39. Bosio III-134.
40. Bosio III-134 et seq.

Chapter IV

1. Bosio III-134 et seq.
2. Bosio III-134; Boissat 548; Norwich 289; Merriman III-305.
3. Bosio III-136 et seq.
4. Bosio III-135.
5. Bosio II-137 et seq.
6. Bosio III-138.
7. Bosio III-139.
8. Bosio III-139 et seq.
9. Bosio III-140.
10. Setton III-396.
11. Bosio III-144.
12. Bosio III-142.
13. Bosio III-142 et seq; Boissat 554 et seq; Merriman 306 et seq; Setton III-396 et seq.
14. Bosio III-145.
15. Bosio III-154 et seq.
16. Bosio III-156 et seq.
17. Bosio III-157.

Chapter V

1. Bosio III-157.
2. Bosio III-158.
3. Bosio III-157 et seq.
4. Bosio III-158.
5. Blackwood's #322 LII-193.

6. Bosio III-159.
7. Bosio II-534; Setton III-400.
8. Bosio III-159 et seq; Bradford 148; Norwich 292.
9. Bosio III-159 et seq; Setton III-399, Wikipedia.
10. Bosio III-160.
11. Bosio III-161.
12. Bosio III-162; Mifsud 206.
13. Bosio III-163.
14. Bosio III-165.
15. Bosio III-162 et seq; Martyrologe I-91.

Chapter VI

1. Bosio III-166 et seq.
2. Bosio III-168.
3. Bosio III-169.
4. Bosio III-170; Merriman III-321; Setton III-425.
5. Bosio III-170.
6. Bosio III-170; Setton III-425.
7. Bosio III-171 et seq; Vertot IIIE-79; Guglielmotti's *Guerra dei Pirati* XV; Martyrologe I-43.
8. Bosio III-172; Norwich 452; Setton III-425 et seq.
9. Bosio III-172; Norwich 452; Setton III-426.
10. Setton III-433.
11. Bosio III-173; Norwich 453.
12. Bosio III-174.
13. Bosio III-173; Setton III-434.
14. Bosio III-177 et seq.
15. Bosio III-177; Merriman III-323; Setton III-446.
16. Bosio III-178.
17. Martyrologe I-7.
18. Bosio III-178 et seq; Guglielmotti *La Guerra dei Pirati* 58 et seq; Merriman III-323 et seq; Bradford 172.
19. Bosio at III-179.
20. Bosio III-182.
21. Bosio III-182; Braudel 187; Merriman III-329n; Setton III-446.
22. Bosio III-183.
23. Bosio III-184 et seq.
24. Bosio III-185.
25. Bosio III-187.
26. Bosio III-188.
27. Bosio III-189.
28. Bosio III-191.
29. Mifsud 203.
30. Wikipedia.

Chapter VII

1. Bosio III-191; Boissat 585; Guglielmotti's *Guerra dei Pirati* 86 et seq.
2. Bosio III-196.
3. Bosio III-192; Merriman III-330; Guglielmotti's *Guerra dei Pirati* 87 et seq.
4. Bosio III-192 et seq.
5. Bosio III-193.
6. Bosio III-195.
7. Bosio III-199.
8. Bosio III-200 et seq; Boissat 593 et seq.
9. Bosio III-201 et seq; Boissat 593 et seq.
10. Bosio III-202; Zimmerman Giovio 179.
11. Bosio III-203.
12. Merriman III-334.
13. Merriman III-336.
14. Bosio III-205.
15. Bosio III-207.
16. Bosio III-208.
17. Bosio III-202 et seq; Merriman III-336 et seq.
18. Bosio III-208.
19. Bosio III-210; Merriman III-339.

Chapter VIII

1. Bosio III-21.
2. Bosio II-213.
3. Bosio III-214; Setton III-461.
4. Bosio III-216; Merriman III-339.
5. Bosio III-217.
6. Bosio III-218.
7. Martyrologe I-242.
8. Martyrologe I-348.
9. Setton III-470.
10. Bosio III-220.
11. Bosio III-221.
12. Setton III-470.
13. Bosio III-223; Morgan 290.
14. Bosio III-222 et seq.
15. Setton III-471.
16. Bosio III-224.
17. Bosio III-228 et seq; Boissat 613.
18. Bosio III-225.
19. Setton III-472.
20. Bosio III-229.
21. Bosio III-226 et seq; Boissat 611.
22. Bosio III-231.

23. Braudel II-908; Morgan 440.
24. Ronciere III-391.
25. Bosio III-232; Morgan 292.
26. Bosio III-233 et seq.
27. Bosio III-233; Maurand.
28. Merriman III-341.
29. Bosio III-235.
30. grippo (a large square-rigged flat-bottomed merchantman preferred for shallow-water destinations).
31. Bosio III-236
32. Setton III-480 et seq.
33. Bosio III-237 et seq.
34. Bosio III-238.
35. Bosio III-239 et seq.
36. Bosio III-240 et seq.
37. Bosio III-242.
38. Bosio III-243.
39. Martyrologe I-15.
40. Bosio III-244.
41. Morgan 293.

Chapter IX

1. Bosio III-244.
2. Bosio III-245 et seq.
3. Bosio III-246.
4. Bosio III-248.
5. Bosio III-248; Setton III-482.
6. Setton III-485 et seq.
7. Bosio III-250 et seq.
8. Bosio III-251.
9. Bosio III-252 et seq.
10. Bosio III-253.
11. Bosio III-257.
12. Funes II-602.
13. Martyrologe II-320.
14. Bosio III-258 et seq; Boissat 635; Anderson 5; Morgan 441.
15. Bosio III-259.
16. Bosio III-261; Mifsud 165.
17. Bosio III-262.
18. Bosio III-263 et seq.
19. Bosio III-265.
20. Bosio III-265, III-344; Dizionario di erudizione storico 244.
21. Bosio III-266 et seq.
22. Bosio III-268; Braudel II-908 et seq.

23. Bosio III-269 to 274.
24. Bosio III-277.
25. Martyrologe I-2.
26. Martyrologe II-222.
27. Martyrologe I-27.
28. Bosio III-277 et seq.
29. Bosio III-278 et seq.
30. Bosio III-279.
31. Bosio III-280; Setton III-536.
32. Bosio III-280; Boissat 654; Setton III-533.
33. Bosio III-283; Boissat 654; Morgan I-464; Anderson 5; Setton III-535.
34. Setton III-537.
35. Bosio III-286 et seq.
36. Setton III-538.
37. Bosio III-287 et seq.
38. Bosio III-287 et seq; Setton III-554.
39. Setton III-55.
40. Bosio III-290 to 299.
41. Bosio III-299 et seq.
42. Bosio III-303 et seq; Boissat 671.

Chapter X

1. Bosio III-305.
2. Bosio III-305 et seq; Boissat 671.
3. Bosio III-309.
4. Bosio III-311.
5. Bosio III-310.
6. Bosio III-314.
7. Bosio III-307 et seq.
8. Bosio III-315 et seq; Boissat 681.
9. Bosio III-317 et seq.
10. Bosio III-321.
11. Bosio III-318.
12. Bosio III-319.
13. Bosio III-321.
14. Bosio III-324 et seq.
15. Bosio III-325; Boissat 691.
16. Bosio III-326 et seq.
17. Bosio III-327.
18. Bosio III-332; Setton IV-582 et seq.
19. Bosio III-328.
20. Bosio III-328 et seq; Setton IV-583; Vertot IVE-14 et seq; Briancon_files.
21. Bosio III-332 et seq; Boissat 699; Setton IV-582 et seq.
22. Bosio III-333 et seq.

23. Bosio III-335; Setton IV-588.
24. Bosio III-336.
25. Bosio III-337.
26. Setton IV-588.
27. *Della cronologia universale della Sicilia* 292.
28. Caird's *History of Corsica* 56.
29. quilicata.it;. Bosio III-338.
30. Bosio III-339.
31. Bosio III-338.
32. Bosio III-339.
33. Bosio III-340.

Chapter XI

1. Bosio III-340 et seq; Boissat 705.
2. Bosio III-340 et seq.
3. Bosio III-344 et seq.
4. Bosio III-347.
5. Bosio III-348.
6. Bosio III-353.
7. Bosio II-616, III-350 et seq.
8. Setton IV-606; Mifsud 122.
9. Bosio III-351 et seq.
10. Bosio III-352.
11. Bosio III-353.
12. Bosio III-354 et seq.
13. Bosio III-355; Setton IV-607.
14. Bosio III-356.
15. Bosio III-356; Morgan 489.
16. Bosio III-357 et seq.
17. Bosio I-v; III-359.
18. Bosio I-v; III-359.
19. Bosio III-361.
20. Bosio III-362.
21. Bosio III-362; Setton IV-623n.
22. Bosio III-364; Setton IV-623 et seq; Città di Calabria 136.
23. Bosio III-364.
24. Bosio III-365.
25. Bosio III-366 et seq.

Chapter XII

1. Bosio III-368.
2. Bosio III-369.
3. Setton IV-758.
4. Bosio III-370 et seq; Morgan 551.

5. Bosio III-372.
6. Bosio III-372 et seq; Morgan 383; Anderson 5.
7. Bosio III-373.
8. Bosio III-374.
9. Bosio III-375; Martyrologe I-116/122.
10. Bosio III-377.
11. Bosio III-376.
12. Bosio III-377 et seq; Guglielmotti's *La Guerra dei Pirati* 330 et seq.
13. Bosio III-378 et seq; Setton IV-695 et seq.
14. Bosio III-380.
15. Setton IV-836 et seq.
16. Bosio III-384 et seq.
17. Bosio III-387.
18. Martyrologe I-39.
19. Martyrologe I-330.
20. Martyrologe I-4.
21. Martyrologe I-348.
22. Martyrologe I-249.
23. Martyrologe I-143.
24. Martyrologe I-3.
25. Martyrologe I-26.
26. Bosio III-387.
27. Bosio III-385 to 389; Boissat 728 et seq.
28. Vertot III-379 et seq, IIIE-170 et seq.
29. Bosio III-389.
30. Bosio III-390; Boissat 736.

Chapter XIII

1. Bosio III-391; Boissat 737.
2. Bosio III-392 et seq.
3. Setton IV-696.
4. Bosio III-394; Boissat 738.
5. Balbi's *Siege of Malta* 113.
6. Bosio III-394; Mifsud 35.
7. Setton IV-700.
8. Bosio III-395 et seq.
9. Bosio III-396 et seq.
10. gutenberg.org/files/7385/7385-h/7385-h.htm.
11. http://michelangelohotel.it/mappe/mappa_it.php?iframe.
12. Bosio III-397.
13. Bosio III-398.
14. Bosio III-397; Anderson 6; Setton IV-700.
15. Bosio III-398.
16. Bosio III-398 et seq.

17. Bosio III-399 et seq.
18. Morgan 400 et seq; Braudel 634.
19. Bosio III-400.
21. Bosio III-412.
22. Bosio III-409.
23. Bosio III-403.
24. Bosio III-404.
25. Bosio III-405.
26. Bosio III-406 et seq; Setton IV-591.
27. Bosio III-407; Setton IV-759n.
28. Bosio III-412, 574.
30. Bosio III-410.
31. Bosio III-411.
32. Bosio III-412 et seq.
33. Bosio III-415.
34. Bosio III-423.
35. Bosio III-417.
36. Setton IV-758.
37. Bosio III-416 et seq; Anderson 9.
38. Bosio III-422.
39. Martyrologe I-47.
40. Bosio III-427.
41. Bosio III-430.
42. Martyrologe I-275.
43.
44. https://guide-voyage-tunisie.com/en/borj-ghazi-mustapha-the-spanish-fort; www.cosmovisions.com/histDjerba.htm). Novitiate
45. Martyrologe I-363.
46. Bosio III-440; Anderson 8.
47. Bosio III-754.
48. Setton IV-762.
49. Spanish Wikipedia.
50. Bosio III-440.
51. Bosio III-431.
52. Bosio III-439.
53. Bosio III-433.
54. Bosio III-417 et seq; Anderson 8 et seq; Crowley 88 et seq; Setton III-758 et seq; Vertot IIIE-176 et seq.
55. Bosio III-427 et seq; III-439.
56. Bosio III-437.
57. Bosio III-442.

Chapter XIV

1. Bosio III-435 et seq; Martyrologe I-58.
2. Bosio III-439 et seq.

3. Bosio III-439 et seq; Setton IV-766.
4. Ibid.
5. Bosio III-441.
6. Bosio III-443.
7. Bosio III-444.
8. Bosio III-444; Treccani-Broccardo.
9. Bosio III-445.
10. Bosio III-446.
11. Bosio III-462.
12. Bosio III-445.
13. Bosio III-446.
14. Bosio III-447 et seq.
15. Ibid.
16. Ibid.
17. Bosio III-448.
18. Bosio III-447 et seq.
19. Ibid.
20. Ibid.
21. Bosio III-449.
22. Martyrologe I-6.
23. Bosio III-451.
24. Balbi 29.
25. Bosio III-451 et seq; Balbi 28.
26. Bosio III-450.
27. Bosio III-451.
28. Ibid.
29. Bosio III-453.
30. Bosio III-454.
31. Ibid.
32. Ibid.
33. Bosio III-455 et seq.
34. Bosio III-456.
35. Ibid.
36. Ibid.
37. Ibid.
38. Bosio III-457 et seq.
39. Ibid.
40. Bosio III-458.
41. Anderson 15; Bicheno 139.
42. Bosio III-458.
43. Ibid.
44. Anderson 15; Bicheno 139.
45. Bosio III-460.
46. Bosio III-461.

47. Bosio III-462.
48. Morgan 422.
49. Bosio III-462.
50. Morgan 422.
51. Bosio III-463 et seq; Boissat 783 et seq; Anderson 16; Morgan 429.
52. Bosio III-467.
53. Ibid.
54. Ibid.
55. Bosio III-468.
56. Ibid.
57. Bosio III-469.
58. Ibid.
59. Ibid.
60. Ibid.

Chapter XV

1. Bosio III-471.
2. Ibid.
3. Bosio III-472 et seq; Martyrologe I-59, 295, 314, 366.
4. Bosio III-473 et seq.
5. Ibid.
6. Bosio III-482.
7. Ibid.
8. Bosio III-478.
9. Bosio III-478 et seq; Anderson 17n; Manfroni I-110.
10. Bosio III-482 et seq; Anderson 16.
11. Bosio III-500.
12. Bosio III-479 et seq.
13. Bosio III-485; Anderson 17.
14. Bosio III-487 et seq; Setton IV-842 et seq.
15. Bosio III-496 et seq.
16. Bosio III-497 et seq; Balbi 28; Anderson 18.
17. Bosio III-498.
18. Bosio III-497 et seq; Anderson 18; Balbi 36.
19. Bosio III-518 et seq; Balbi 107.
20. Bosio III-511.
21. Bosio III-497 et seq; Anderson 18; Balbi 36.
22. Bosio III-504.
23. Bosio III-511.
24. Bosio III-530.
25. Bosio III-511.
26. Bosio III-501 et seq; Balbi 49 et seq.
27. Bosio III-541; Balbi 64.
28. Balbi 71.

29. Bosio III-555.
30. Bosio III-557; Balbi 79.
31. Bosio III-532 et seq; Balbi 63 et seq; Boissat 850 et seq.
32. Bosio III-573.
33. Bosio III-574; Balbi 91.
34. Bosio III-573 et seq; Balbi 91 et seq; Martyrologe I-114.
35. Bosio III-586.
36. Bosio III-585.
37. Bosio III-585; Crowley 133.
38. Bosio III-683; Martyrologe I-310.
39. Bosio III-587; Balbi 100; Pozzo II-7.
40. Balbi 107.
41. Balbi 115; Bosio III-604 and III-712; Crowley 159; Morgan I-433 et seq.
42. Bosio III-605.
43. Balbi 117.
44. Martyrologe I-336.
45. Bosio III-612.
46. Bosio III-603 et seq; Balbi 120.
47. Bosio III-622; Balbi 135.
48. Balbi 141.
49. Balbi 147.
50. Balbi 145.
51. Bosio III-653.
52. Bosio III-646; Balbi 155.
53. Bosio III-634.
54. Bosio III-711.
55. Bosio III-628.
56. Bosio III-610 et seq.
57. Bosio III-667.
58. Anderson 23; Bosio III-685.
59. Bicheno 148.
60. Setton IV-872.
61. Setton IV-870.
62. Bosio III-699.
63. Bosio III-714.
64. Balbi 187.

Bibliography

Anderson, R. (1952) *Naval Wars in the Levant 1559–1853.* Liverpool: University Press

Aprile, F. (1725) *Della cronologia universale della Sicilia*

Balbi, F. (2005) *The Siege of Malta, 1565.* Woodbridge, UK: The Boydell Press

Bicheno, H. (2004) *The Crescent and Cross.* London: Orion Books Ltd

Blackwood's Edinburgh Magazine No. 322 (1842)

Bourbon, J. (1527) *La Grande et merveilleuse et tres cruelle oppugnation de la noble cite de Rhodes.* Wien: KK Hofbibliothek

Boyssat (Boissat), P. (1612) *Histoire des Chevaliers de l'Ordre de l'Hospital de S. Iean de Hiervsalem.* Translated from the Italian by Guillaume Roville at Lyon

Bosio, G. (1601) *Della Terza Parte Dell'istoria della sacra religione ed ill.ma militia di San Giovanni Vol III*

Bradford, E. (1968) *The Sultan's Admiral.* New York: Harcourt, Brace

Braudel, F. (1972) *The Mediterranean in the Age of Philip II.* New York: Harper Collins

Caird, L.H. (1899) *The History of Corsica.* London: Unwin

Cibrario, L. (1826) *Notizie di Paolo Simeoni de'Balbi, da Chieri:* Turin: Stamperia Alliana

Crowley, R. (2008) *Empires of the Sea.* New York: Random House

Currey, H. (1910) *Sea Wolves of the Mediterranean.* London: John Murray

Freer, M. (1737) *The Life of Marguerite D'angoulême, Queen of Navarre. Vols I & II.* Paris: Librairie

Funes, J. (*c.*1650) *Coronica de la milicia y sagrada religion de San Juan Bautista …* Volume 2

Goussancourt, M. (1654) *Le Martyrologe de Chevaliers, Vol I & II.* Paris: Simeon Piget

Guglielmotti, A. (1876) *La guerra dei pirati e la marina pontificia dal 1500 al 1560, vol. 2.* Florence

Inalcik, H. (2000) *The Ottoman Empire.* London: W&N

Lamb, H. (1952) *Suleiman the Magnificent.* London: Robert Hale

Lea, H. (1901) *The Moriscoes of Spain.* Philadelphia: Lea Brothers

Manfroni, C. (1895) *La Marine Militare del Granducato Mediceo Part 1.* Rome: Forzani

Maurand, J. (1544) *Itinéraire d'Antibes à Constantinople*

Merriman, R. (1777) *Rise of the Spanish Empire Vol III.* Toronto: Macmillan

Mifsud, A. (1914) *Knights Hospitallers of the Ven. Tongue of England in Malta.* Malta

Montluc, B. (1592) *Commentaires de Messire Blaise de Montluc.* Bordeaux

Morgan, J. (1731) *A Complete History of Algiers.* London: J Bettenham

Norwich, J. (1982) *History of Venice.* New York: Knopf Publishing

Porter, W. (1858) *History of the Knights of Malta Vols I & II.* London: Longman Brown

Pozzo, B. (1715) *Historia della Sacra Religione Militare di San Giovanni.* Venice: Gerolamo Albrizzi

Riley-Smith, J. (2003) *Crusades.* Milton Park: Routledge

Roncière (La), C. (1906) *Histoire de la marine française.* Paris: Plon-Nourrit

Setton, K. (1976) *The Papacy and the Levant,* Philadelphia: The American Philosophical Society

Sire, H.J.A. (1996) *The Knights Of Malta.* New Haven: Yale University Press

Zimmerman, P. (1995) *Paolo Giovio and the Crisis of 16th Century Italy.* Princeton University Press

Index